Principles and methods
of social psychology

Principles and methods of social psychology

SECOND EDITION

EDWIN P. HOLLANDER
State University of New York at Buffalo

New York

OXFORD UNIVERSITY PRESS

London   Toronto   1971

Copyright © 1967, 1971 by Oxford University Press, Inc.
Library of Congress Catalogue Card Number: 75-146040
Printed in the United States of America

To Pat and Peter

Preface to the second edition

Even with the wide and warming acceptance received by the original edition of this book, it is necessary to keep pace with the times, especially in a field with as much movement as social psychology.

This new edition is thoroughly revised and greatly enlarged, while retaining the essential qualities of the original. Every chapter contains new material, many whole new sections have been added, and other parts of the book considerably altered, to show new emphases in research and theory, as well as in social relevance.

As a book for the first course, the aim continues to be to present a unified view of the field of social psychology organized around the concept of social influence, and with sufficient breadth to accommodate material from psychology, sociology, and cultural anthropology. Further attention has been given also to providing strong links to the world of affairs, with illustrations drawn from newspapers, magazines, books, and other popular sources.

Among the new materials are coverages of "pro-social" or helping behavior, spatial relations in groups, the risky-shift phenomenon, attribution processes, deviancy, social movements, psychological reactance, nativistic approaches to language, and Machiavellianism, to name only a few. More extended treatments are also given to topics which were included in the first edition, such as moral development, adult socialization, exchange processes in interaction, communication effects and attitude change, social change, international conflict and war, and legitimacy of leadership.

The organization of this new edition follows the main lines of the first, beginning with general and historical materials, on through to theory and methodology, and then to the heartland of attitudes, values, and socialization, social interaction, and processes of social, cultural, and group influences. Substantial cross-referencing occurs in this edition, as it did in the first.

Attention to methodology continues to be accorded a prominent place in this revision. Many research studies are described in detail, with accompanying figures and tables to add clarity and robustness to their description. The early chapter on theory and method has been enlarged in the direction of the newer concerns with biasing effects in research, including demand characteristics and experimenter bias, and additional attention to field research.

The extensive chapter on the history of social psychology now incorporates a much expanded consideration of views of human aggressiveness, the contribution of Freudian psychology, the early research on social facilitation, and the naturalistic study of groups in the sociological tradition, among other points of elaboration.

Once again, I have not felt compelled to put each and every topic in a single slot. Broad topics, such as attitudes, social interaction, and group processes, are variously treated in different relationships throughout the book, though they are given a primary focus in their respective chapters. More than half of the book is devoted to those chapters.

Topics appear, and reappear, in new combinations at various points, to show the field's organic character. The reference group concept, for example, is mentioned at many points, since it has such a distinctively social psychological tack. Similarly, ideas of social exchange, and of interpersonal perception and attribution, are used as tools at many junctures, quite apart from specific treatments in various places.

As before, a good deal of attention has been directed to preparation of carefully focused chapter summaries, which are accompanied by selective references for additional reading. These materials should provide an expansion of points, for the student interested in further reading. Special care has been directed to identifying those books which are available in paperback editions. The master bibliography at the end runs to about 1200 references and should constitute a worthwhile resource for further study.

Although a textbook inevitably is a personal endeavor, by one or a few people, it draws on wider inputs from many people. Once again, I would like to record my intellectual debt to a host of colleagues and friends, as well as my teachers and students, who have contributed to my thinking. Prominent among these are three of my closest co-workers, Raymond G. Hunt, James W. Julian, and Richard H. Willis, who have had a gentle but persistent effect in shaping many aspects of my approach.

Still others whom I wish to thank for having given me, at various times, the benefit of their ideas and comments about one or more issues treated here are: Michael Argyle, Freed Bales, Kenneth Berrien, Leonard Berkowitz, Rob Farr, Claude Faucheux, Gordon Haaland, George Homans, Irving Janis, Herbert Kelman, George Levinger, James Lubalin, Leon Mann, Joseph Masling, Robert Pages, Luigi Petrullo, Dean Pruitt, Milton Rokeach, Robert Rosenthal, Irwin Segal, Marvin Shaw, Richard Sorrentino, Ervin Staub, Fred Strodtbeck, Edgar Vinacke, David Wiesenthal, and Sheldon Zalkind, among many unnamed others. The usual disclaimer is in order to free them of any liability whatever for transformations their contributions might have undergone; I alone take responsibility for the result.

Much of this revision was undertaken during 1969-70 while I had the benefit of a sabbatical leave in the Department of Social Relations at Harvard. I wish to record my gratitude to the Department for the pleasant surroundings and good fellowship I found there. In addition, I especially wish to thank Rona Cline and Sue Hoffman of the Social Relations Library who were exceedingly helpful in facilitating my access to material and keeping me on the right track.

The labor associated with bringing the completed manuscript into reasonable shape was accomplished this past summer at Buffalo, largely through Linda Hereth's competent and diligent secretarial aid, for which I am delighted to extend my great thanks. Once again, I wish to acknowledge my appreciation to Frederick Schneider and Frank Romano, respectively, for the admirable design and illustrations, and my thanks this time to Patricia Cristol for her fine copy editing, to Barry Fallon for his great aid in proofreading, to Phil Kennedy for doing additional illustrations, and to Mervyn Goldstein for preparing the subject index.

My wife, Pat, was enormously helpful throughout and contributed substantially to this revision, not least in her initial reading and criticism of nev and revised materials. I am deeply grateful to her, and to my son, Peter, who also assisted wherever possible with enthusiasm, and who with my wife put up gracefully with the pressures and inconveniences of my writing schedule.

Buffalo, New York   E. P. H.
January 1971

Preface to the first edition

This is a textbook for students in the first course in social psychology. It takes for granted very little prior preparation, though in most instances students will have had an introduction to psychology, sociology, or perhaps cultural anthropology. Where necessary, I have recalled and reviewed basic points from these fields in building toward an understanding of social psychology's distinctive approach.

My aims in writing this book are twofold: first, to show in a balanced way as much as possible of the totality of the field; second, to do so within the framework of a systematic treatment. As I see it, a textbook should convey the major trends of study, their theoretical origins, and the principles they sustain, without the need for an exhaustive catalogue of findings. My intent is to provide the student with what he needs to know concerning the range and shadings of research on a particular topic, and to discuss research studies with specific regard to some explicit point in the body of the text at a given juncture.

The prime concept in my treatment of the field is social influence. I see this as a central process common to many phenomena which are often treated quite separately in social psychology, among them attitude change, socialization, role behavior, conformity, and leadership. As a significant element in understanding this central process, time—and the human capacity to live in and react to a time dimension—is stressed throughout. The book's approach is therefore very much person-centered within a systematic scheme that looks at social influence in transactional terms. In this sense, it brings together the contemporary emphases on cognition, the perceptual features of social interaction, and concepts of social reward and social exchange.

Social psychology has substantial relevance to the world of affairs. To show some points of contact, I have drawn freely on findings from sociological, political, and economic sources, as well as newspapers and other popular publications, in dealing with such topics as social class differences, the language of advertising, voting behavior, and international relations. In so doing I have tried to enliven interest for relevancy and infuse a sense of the exciting and vital nature of the field and its subject matter. I have also employed examples of a light nature from daily life. These examples do not, of course, illustrate a point in the same way as a research finding, nor are they treated as such.

The organization of this book proceeds from the general and the historical through to the special place of attitudes, and of social interaction, and then on to the nature of particular social, cultural, and group influences and phenomena. In order, the first three chapters present a broad set of definitions and terms of reference, an historical perspective on the field, and a detailing of methods within the context of their relationship to theory. These chapters should provide a solid foundation for a better grasp of the import of issues and findings covered in the topical chapters which follow.

Because of the organic character of the field, I have made frequent cross-references between these topical chapters to show the kind of interrelationships that prevail over topical boundaries. I have not felt compelled, in this regard, to pigeonhole each and every topic in a single place. Broad topics, such as attitudes and social interaction, are variously treated in different juxtapositions though they are given a primary focus in their respective chapters. Prejudice is considered in the attitude chapters, then in further detail in Chapter Ten regarding personality, and again in connection with inter-group relations in Chapter Thirteen.

Suggested readings, with selected references, appear at the end of each chapter and are meant to be read after digesting the chapter itself. These materials should provide an expansion of points, as well as a useful continuity to and preparation for the chapters which follow; they are listed where they are most applicable, though they may be quite suitable for later chapters as well. Special care has also been given to identifying those books which are available in paperback editions.

My intellectual debts to colleagues and friends, in and out of the field, are considerable and I could not hope to repay them here. What I have put into this book also benefits from my own students and teachers, in whom I have been most fortunate. For their special help in reading and commenting on various portions of the manuscript, I am pleased to thank F. Kenneth Berrien, Stephen C. Jones, James W. Julian, Joseph M. Masling, and Marvin E. Shaw. While I take the usual responsibility for the result, I very much appreciate their useful criticisms.

Particular thanks are owed to Leonore Ganschow who helped enormously in seeing me through the typing of the several versions of the manuscript. I also greatly appreciate the work of Alison M. Bond in editing the manuscript and carrying it through production, the fine design of Frederick Schneider, and Frank Romano's illustrations. My wife, Pat, was my most diligent reader and greatest source of aid, especially in the final phases of work. I am delighted to note her invaluable contribution, as well as the supportive efforts of my son, Peter.

London, England   E. P. H.
January 1967

Acknowledgments

The following copyright holders are gratefully thanked for giving their permission to reproduce the material indicated:

Academic Press, Inc. for the figure on p. 267 from the *Journal of Experimental Social Psychology*, 1969, 5, 195; and the table on p. 297, ibid., 1965, 1, 163.

The American Psychological Association for the figure on p. 109 from the *Journal of Abnormal and Social Psychology*, 1962, 64, 139; the figures on pp. 255 and 256, ibid., 1960, 61, 183 and 185; the figure on p. 234, ibid., 1964, 69, 293; the table on p. 576 and the figure on p. 577, ibid., 1961, 63, 248 and 249; the figure on p. 232, ibid., 1957, 55, 247; the figure on p. 335, ibid., 1961, 62, 653; the figure on p. 103, ibid., 1951, 46, 42; the figure on p. 560, ibid., 1954, 49, 68; and the figure on p. 141, ibid., 1955, 51, 673; for the figure on p. 263 from the *Journal of Comparative and Physiological Psychology*, 1955, 48, 394; for the figure on p. 221 from the *Journal of Personality and Social Psychology*, 1966, 4, 9; the figure on p. 565, ibid., 1970, 14, 371; the table on p. 414, ibid., 1969, 11, 40; the figure on p. 408, ibid., 1965, 2, 828; the figure on p. 235, ibid., 1968, 8, 340; the table on p. 95, ibid., 1969, 12, 99; the figure on p. 581, ibid., 1965, 1, 131; the figure on p. 17, ibid., 1969, 13, 80; the figure on p. 175, ibid., 1970, 14, 134; and the figure on p. 416, ibid., 1970, 15, 14; for the figure on p. 163 from the *Psychological Bulletin*, 1968, 69, 321; and the tables on pp. 567 and 593, ibid., 1959, 56, 247 and 260.

The American Sociological Association for the figure on p. 93 from the *American Sociological Review*, 1950, *15*, 258; for the figure on p. 610 from *Sociometry*, 1964, *27*, 496; the figure on p. 611, ibid., 1958, *21*, 330; the figure on p. 584, ibid., 1963, *26*, 501; the figure on p. 278, ibid., 1965, *28*, 300; and the figure on p. 487, ibid., 1961, *24*, 400.

Appleton-Century-Crofts for the figure on p. 519 from R. Radloff and R. Helmreich, *Groups Under Stress: Psychological Research in SEALAB II*, 1968.

Chappell & Co., Inc. for the portion of a song on p. 11, "Never Say No," from *The Fantasticks* by Tom Jones and Harvey Schmidt.

Columbia University Press for the figure on p. 97 from P. F. Lazarsfeld, B. Berelson, and Hazel Gaudet, *The People's Choice*, 2nd edition, 1948.

Harper & Row, Publishers, Inc., for the table on p. 91 from R. G. Barker and H. F. Wright, *Midwest and Its Children: The Psychological Ecology of an American Town*, 1954; for the table on p. 615 from D. C. Cartwright and A. Zander (Eds.), *Group Dynamics: Research and Theory*, 2nd edition, 1960; and for the figure on p. 66 from M. Sherif, *The Psychology of Social Norms*, 1936.

Holt, Rinehart and Winston, Inc. for the figure on p. 99 from T. M. Newcomb and E. L. Hartley (Eds.), *Readings in Social Psychology*, 1947; the figure on p. 446 from E. E. Maccoby, T. M. Newcomb, and E. L. Hartley (Eds.), *Readings in Social Psychology*, 3rd Edition, 1958; and for the figure on p. 31 from R. Rosenthal and L. Jacobson, *Pygmalion in the Classroom: Teacher Expectation and Pupils' Intellectual Development*, 1968.

Houghton Mifflin Company for the table on p. 169 from T. Sizer (Ed.), *Religion and Public Education*, 1967.

Human Relations for the figure on p. 100 in their issue of 1948, *1*, 522.

The Journal Press for the figure on p. 92 from the *Journal of Social Psychology*, 1934, *5*, fig. 1.

The *Journal of Conflict Resolution* for the table on p. 530 from their issue of 1961, *5*, 85; and for the figure on p. 543 in their issue of 1963, *7*, 588.

Alfred A. Knopf, Inc. for the excerpt on p. 480 from A. Harrington, *Life in the Crystal Palace*, Avon Books, 1967.

The Linguistic Circle of New York, Inc. and the Johnson Reprint Corporation for the figure on p. 367 from *Word*, 1958, *14*, 154.

McGraw-Hill Company, Inc. for the figure on p. 208 from S. Koch (Ed.), *Psychology: A Study of a Science*, Volume 6, 1963; and the figure on p. 137 from C. T. Morgan, *Introduction to Psychology*, 2nd edition, 1961.

The Macmillan Company for the figure on p. 365 from R. Brown, *Psycholinguistics*, 1970.

Personnel Psychology for the figure on p. 617 in their issue of 1962, 15, 50.

Princeton University Press for the figure on p. 200 from S. A. Stouffer, L. Guttman, E. A. Suchman, P. F. Lazarsfeld, S. A. Star, and J. A. Gardner (Eds.), *Measurement and Prediction*, 1949.

Random House, Inc. for the passage on pp. 552-553 from R. W. Mack, *Transforming America: Patterns of Social Change*, 1967.

Russell Sage Foundation for the figure on p. 172 from H. L. Hoffman and L. W. Hoffman (Eds.), *Review of Child Development Research*. Volume 1, 1964.

Rutgers University Press for the figure on p. 320 and table on p. 321 from H. Cantril, *The Pattern of Human Concerns*, 1965.

The University of Chicago Press for the figure on p. 499 from W. F. Whyte, *Street Corner Society*, 1943.

World Publishing Company, Inc. for the passage on pp. 479-480 from G. Talese, *The Kingdom and the Power*, 1969.

Contents

Figures

Tables

Principles and methods
of social psychology

1

The contemporary field of social psychology

Humanity's agenda brims over with social psychological issues. The onrush of events has made Man's relationships with his fellows more complicated than ever, and the consequences are more evident through the cascade of mass communications. Clearly, we are astride massive problems involving dislocation, conflict, inequity, and survival itself, which do not yield to ready solutions.

In the face of these realities, the social sciences offer the potentiality for providing a fuller awareness of the human dimension in various social phenomena. By pursuing research and generating conceptions about processes underlying these phenomena, it is possible to see them more objectively and even to give direction to remedial actions where needed. But in any case, the basic approach of developing a body of scientific information about human social behavior can readily be seen as an advance in Man's quest for self-knowledge.

Some features of social psychology

Social psychology is one of the scientific fields concerned with the objective study of human behavior. In particular, social psychology directs its attention to *understanding* the influences producing regularities and diversities in human *social* behavior. It approaches its study

3

through the analysis of data obtained by objective, scientific methods.

The distinctiveness of social psychology stems from two major factors: first, its interest in the *individual* as a participant in social relationships; and, second, its emphasis on *understanding* the social influence process underlying these relationships. The term "understanding" includes several levels, from simple descriptions, through analysis and accuracy of prediction, to explanation of phenomena. In achieving a systematic understanding of social behavior, social psychologists increasingly have conducted experiments to test the validity of their predictions.

At the same time, greater interest is evident in the applications of social psychological knowledge to public policies and programs. The viewpoint and approach of social psychology have achieved wider attention, and its utility for helping to deal with lively contemporary concerns seems promising.

DISTINCTIVE ASPECTS OF THE FIELD

All scientific fields have four major aspects: a set of phenomena, a body of theory, research methods, and accumulated findings. In social psychology, these aspects may be characterized more fully as follows:

> • First, *a set of phenomena of concern,* in this case, those involving *social influence.* This covers person-to-person interactions, as well as those relationships prevailing between groups or total societies, or those of an individual with these broader social entitities. Some examples of influence phenomena are seen in attitude change, socialization, conformity, and leadership (see Figure 1.1).
> • Second, *a body of theory* concerning influence phenomena, that is, concepts which help to explain them in part or in larger wholes. Basically, a theory consists of one or more functional statements about the relationships which produce phenomena. These might involve, for instance, concepts such as "group cohesiveness," as in the functional statement: "Other things being equal, conformity to a group's standards is positively related to that group's cohesiveness."
> • Third, *a set of research methods* for obtaining evidence

about these phenomena by recognized, objectively based procedures for gathering data systematically. Some of these are laboratory and field experiments, questionnaire surveys, and observational methods.

• Fourth, *accumulated findings* in the form of recognized knowledge about these phenomena. This is expressed in terms of research data and the principles they support, and is represented, for example, in scientific findings gathered together and summarized in textbooks.

These aspects of social psychology necessarily depend upon one another, and are almost inseparable. Thus, findings test theory, but theory serves to direct research by providing one or more guiding hypotheses. Moreover, the methodology employed in social psychological research is often dictated by the theoretical basis for the research and what has been found previously by others applying a given method.

Several advantages are gained by the kind of systematic approach to human behavior represented in social psychology. The primary one is the fundamental value of any scientific enterprise—the rewards of broadening and deepening our knowledge. Once achieved, though, this knowledge can be applied in many ways: in organizing our efforts as humans more constructively; in developing individual potentialities with greater effectiveness; in reducing the social stresses under which men often live out their lives; and in providing thereby a larger degree of mastery by Man over his environment.

It is important to recognize that each of us *is capable* of making basically valid inferences about social psychological relationships. But whether valid or not, we do make inferences a good part of the time, as recent work on "attribution processes" by Jones and Davis (1965) and Kelley (1967) suggests. However, it would be hard to develop sound generalizations about these relationships if we simply relied on individual observations; indeed, that was the case for the millennia before systematic social science came on the scene. Consider, for instance, the simple fact that attributions are typically made about the characteristics of individuals from their behavior, without much attention to the situation in which they are encountered. Tourists, as an example, very often operate with cultural blinders. They make inferences about the characteristics of the "people" of a city from the flimsy encounters they have with taxi-drivers, hotel porters, and waiters. The role setting in which these individuals are encountered, and the distinctive social conditions under which they must operate, rarely enter into the attributions.

Even astute observations are not usually brought to explicit awareness, nor are they formulated in such a way as to be testable by others. Here is an excerpt from a student's account of the effect on passengers of a bomb threat to an airplane they were about to board:

> During times of external stress, such as during the Northeast power blackout, people commonly band together in a close-knit fraternity until the threat eases. This bomb scare was a similar situation. There was an immediate threat to the lives of the passengers and crew and this common danger unified the group; there was a sense of solidarity through shared experience (*Harvard Crimson*, February 6, 1970, p. 2).

The important relationship drawn here, between a shared threat and the cohesiveness of a group, is basically sound; and the example is a very apt one. But it can be altered by other factors which were not directly present in this situation, such as competition for scarce resources. When that happens the sense of a common plight may change to panic in the face of a self-protective impulse on the part of some group members.

There is therefore more complexity in social behavior than meets the eye. A single functional relationship, interesting as it is, does not by itself provide a view of the *system* of relationships at work. Indeed, it can be misleading by creating the impression that a straight-line function exists between two variables, when in fact a curve better describes it—a "good thing" is good up to a point, after which more of it is less good. The idea of a multi-causal network, as a system of relationships, is more difficult to grasp, but far closer to the basis for many social phenomena we observe.

Nevertheless, there are manipulators of behavior who have evolved successful techniques of influence for their own purposes; propagandists and politicians come readily to mind as illustrations of these. They often will have found certain regularities of behavior that they can induce for their own profit. In one sense, they have hit upon predictable relationships in human affairs; in another sense, however, such practices, whatever their successes, are limited by the superficiality inherent in knowing only that some appeal evidently worked, but not *why* it worked.

All in all, astute observations and successful manipulations are not an adequate substitute for scientific study on a more systematic basis. The essential reasons can be summarized briefly. First, there is the obvious limitation imposed on any one person's unique observations and attributions. Then, too, each of us carries expectancies, often culturally based, which can distort our view. Finally, we all succumb at times to subjective feelings which shade our judgments, without our realizing it. Language usage frequently reveals our tinted perceptions. One person sees another as being "vivacious," but someone else refers to the same other person as "boisterous," and it is not hard to tell which likes the other person more and which less. In the same vein, none of us is entirely free of such self-serving, though sometimes unspoken, observations as "You are obstinate and stubborn; I am firm and resolute." "You are unprincipled; I am merely flexible." "You are acting out of sheer prejudice; I am acting out of reason."

THE INDIVIDUAL AS A FOCUS

A distinctive feature of social psychology lies in its study of the *psychology of the individual in society*. This interest carries with it a probing of the many features of the social environment which have an impact upon him. Social psychology therefore draws upon the storehouse of materials available from sociology and cultural anthropology, among other behavioral sciences. It also employs some concepts and terms from these older disciplines. On the whole, however, social psychology retains a primary emphasis on the *psychological* level of analysis.

Social psychology is often represented as a halfway house between psychology on one side and sociology and cultural anthropology on the other. But this metaphor ought not to be stretched too far. Increasingly, the field of social psychology carries its own distinctive approach to the analysis of social processes, based in concepts requiring extensions from the level of individual psychology to that of wider social behavior. This does not mean, however, that social psychology merely accepts generalizations from work in the experimental psychology laboratory. Rather, it employs psychological concepts, and the insights provided by an understanding of psychological processes, to account for the dynamics of social phenomena. To take one example, we know that people are capable of modifications of behavior through learning; therefore, principles of learning have direct utility in understanding the processes which go to make up the socialization of children into society. The question of why we learn *some* things from others in our social environment, and *not* other things, is a reasonable issue challenging the social psychologist's interest.

Another example is represented by perception. Knowing how an individual perceives the social environment and is motivated to take action within it, affords an important insight into his behavior. A person's own interpretation of his world—his "psychological field"—provides a better basis for understanding than would a strictly literal description of the things or events in his environment. Still, a great deal of the content of each person's psychological field from birth onward is determined by what he encounters in his society, and shares with others there.

A major reason why the study of human behavior differs from the study of inanimate matter is Man's highly developed reflective capacity. In the memorable words of Teilhard de Chardin (1961), Man not only knows but *knows that he knows*. It is this quality which allows a fusing of experiences and perceptions into the distinctiveness of a human life. Past, present, and future, each contributes to a continuity which serves as a premise for action.

Acting in the present, individuals draw on past experiences and expect future outcomes, whether as gains or otherwise. Homans (1967b) has called this process of *relationships over time* "historicity," by which he means that behavior grows out of a "past history combined with present circumstances" (p. 90). Historicity applies to individuals, but it also shapes the life of groups and of whole societies through the imprint of a shared past and some sense of a mutual future among their members.

SOCIAL EXPECTANCIES

The continuity of life is illustrated by the development of social expectancies. These are the anticipations, which grow out of experience, about one's own and others' behavior. The structure of everyday social relations depends upon a shared awareness of these regularities. They are infused in the various social *roles* we fulfill, and the *norms* and *values* which serve as guides for conduct, whether in small groups or in the broader society, such as a nation.

Expectancies about the behavior of others have essentially two components: one is an anticipation and the other a demand. Parsons (1951) has referred to these as *prediction* and *prescription*, respectively. While we may anticipate something about another's behavior, we may not necessarily require it of him. But if we are linked in an interdependent relationship, we may expect and demand a high degree of predictability. The substance of many "role relationships"—between friends, parents and their children, or bridge partners—requires a considerable adherence to expectancies, though it need not be total. The main thing is that, in these interdependent relationships, appropriate behavior by the other person is a necessary condition for acting appropriately one's self.

Some expectancies are quite sweeping in character. An exemplification of this is the "norm of reciprocity" which appears to prevail widely (Gouldner, 1960). Essentially, this norm dictates that a favor should be returned, and that, correspondingly, the individual who is the source of a favor should not be hurt in return. Though widely applied, the norm is not unconditional. As we shall see with many relationships in the realm of social behavior, other factors will affect its interpretation and shade its application. The key point, however, is that the norm of reciprocity serves as a foundation for the process of *social exchange* which pervades many of the interactions between people. Various writers, such as Homans (1958, 1962), Thibaut and Kelley (1959), Blau (1964), and Adams (1965), have extended and elaborated the exchange concept as a major viewpoint for analysis in social psychology. The common feature in these formulations is that humans expect to exchange rewards, and to have an equitable balance of rewards as against costs in ongoing interactions with others.

But what of the expectancies an individual has about his own actions? Several *cognitive consistency* theories have been especially important as a basis for study in contemporary social psychology. They all operate under the broad proposition that inconsistent "cognitive elements"—thoughts, perceptions, attitudes—create an unpleasant state that serves to produce a change in cognition, or behavior, or both. The most far-reaching of these formulations is Festinger's (1957) theory of *cognitive dissonance*. In brief, this theory postulates that when an individual holds "non-fitting" cognitions about himself and his behavior, as well as the environment, he will bring these into line, sometimes by behavioral shifts, as when a heavy smoker finds it cognitively dissonant to continue smoking while valuing long life and health. There is, in short, the expectancy of consistency, and this is especially strong regarding attitudes about one's self. As a general rule, when an individual becomes aware that he is acting in a fashion discrepant with an attitude of importance, either the attitude or the behavior will change. Other interesting ramifications flow from these notions of consistency, including effects on interpersonal attraction and rejection.

Another kind of expectancy, associated with those just considered above, has to do with the "free behaviors" over which an individual believes he has control. This is the primary focus of Brehm's (1966) theory of *psychological reactance*. In this formulation, a free behavior is defined broadly as covering those activities over which the indi-

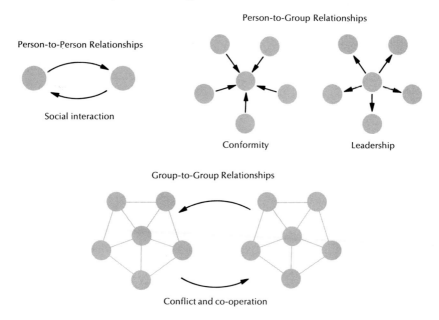

Figure 1.1: Some influence relationships studied in social psychology.

vidual believes he has a latitude for choice. When an external force, in the form of other persons or social norms, appears to be restricting a person's freedom, he experiences reactance. Moreover, a threat to a free behavior tends to enhance its attractiveness and the choice it represents.

One more case of a threat to freedom is a request which implies some undesired interdependence. The offer of assistance, or a request for assistance, may constitute such a threat. This relates back to the expectancy of social exchange, insofar as accepting a favor commits one to a reciprocal reward.

The phenomenon of reactance is frequently observable, in an acute form, in parent-child relationships. With apologies to Brehm, here is the way the fathers in *The Fantasticks* put it in song, while plotting the romance between their respective son and daughter, whom they had deliberately appeared to be keeping apart.

> Dogs got to bark, A mule's got to bray
> Soldiers must fight, And preachers must pray
> And children, I guess, must get their own way
> The minute that you say "no."*

In these pages, only a brief suggestion has been given of the character of expectancies and their significance. But treated even in this limited fashion, hopefully they have provided a link to several key aspects of social psychology to be considered now.

The study of social influence

The central concern of social psychology is with processes of social influence. Humans by necessity are oriented toward other humans in their environment and social influence occurs whenever one individual responds to the *actual* or *implied* presence of one or more others. This definition refers to several different kinds of events, some less obvious than others. It also covers a broad spectrum from subtle directives for action in an evenly balanced relationship to conditions of great control by one entity over the other.

* Copyright © 1960 by Tom Jones and Harvey Schmidt. Reprinted by permission of Chappell & Co., Inc., New York.

In the simplest case, social influence has to do with the reciprocal effect of one person upon another in *social interaction*. It is a process basic to human experience, beginning with earliest childhood, and constitutes a model or "paradigm" of other social relationships. Most of the characteristics we possess are in one way or another affected by social interaction, including our personality and related values and attitudes.

Social psychology is also concerned with the wider play of influence relationships that prevail between a *group and an individual*—conformity, leadership, prejudice, morale, and other group phenomena. Several of these are pictorialized in Figure 1.1. In the *conformity* instance, more than one individual exerts influence on another in terms of a prevailing pattern of social behaviors or attitudes—what we will call a norm. A counterpart to this exists where an individual affects a group or larger social entity, such as an organization, political party, or nation, as in the case of *leadership*. Here the source or agent of influence is an individual who is able to direct and alter the behaviors and attitudes of others. *Prejudice* is an inter-group phenomenon that has origins in strongly held group identifications. Similarly, *morale* provides a convenient summation of a shared group attitude which affects other outcomes for individuals.

Social influence also takes place in the relationship that exists between *two or more groups*, which could be defined in the narrower sense of cliques in a dormitory, or in the wider sense of inter-group or international relations. The tendency to make a show of determination in conflicts between contending groups or nations is a frank expression of an attempt to influence the adversary. Phrases like "deterrence," "saving face," and "standing firm" illustrate the point.

A pivotal matter in any consideration of social influence is the recognition that behavior more probably will remain unchanged so long as alternative modes of action are not available. This is not just force of habit. For change to occur it is essential that avenues be perceived for achieving desired outcomes. When we speak of social influence, then, we should add: where there are *alternative* modes of response which are perceived by the individual to be available to him. Furthermore, these modes of response must be relevant to anticipated returns in the future.

Persons may be influenced not only by the existence of present pressures, but by past experience with others in society and the learning that this has produced. Accordingly, there may be alternative sources of influence, and these may operate in an intentional or unintentional fashion. Furthermore, the influence source may not actually be present, in which case identification with the source takes its place; or, even though present, the source may have an unintended effect by serving as a model, as in the case of vicarious learning.

Humans have a vast capacity to learn from new experiences, to indulge in higher forms of symbolic processes, and to identify with others not immediately at hand. Therefore, they have resources with which to *resist influence* and to *exert counter-influence*.

For purposes of clarification, it is useful to distinguish a particular set of events which involve assertions of influence that are observable and have distinguishable components which can be studied. These can be called "influence events." They do not exhaust the category of influence phenomena for reasons just noted above, but they help to explain many of their dynamics.

Viewed at a general level, all influence events involve four essential elements which are not fixed but are alterable in time. Though these may be variously labeled, and can be treated at different levels of abstraction, they fundamentally come down to:

- An *influence source* which, at a given moment, might be another person, a friend, a father, a leader; a group of others; or a communicator, such as a public figure appearing on TV. Influence sources can be perceived by the recipients of their communications to have attributes arising from actual interaction with them, or from what has been learned from other sources about them.
- A *communication* or *message*, that can be in the form of behavior, in terms of actions seen to have certain properties, or in the usual form of a verbal message, either of which embody an assertion of influence.
- A *recipient of the communication*, the target of influence at the moment, possessing personal motivations and associated

perceptions, which include group identifications and attitudes guiding response.

     • A *social context*, the setting in which the influence assertion occurs. Accuracy in predicting an influence effect often depends upon knowing the structure of the situation which defines the nature of the relationship between the recipient of the assertion and the source.

Influence events differ across many situations, but the four elements noted can usually be found. In the case of face-to-face interaction, both persons have the characteristics of influence source and recipient insofar as they have a reciprocating effect upon one another. Generally speaking, in conformity the group is the influence source. In leadership, the influence source is a person and the "recipients" of the communication are the followers in the group. But direct interaction is not a requisite for social influence effects to be evident. It does serve though as a basic process linked to the others just mentioned. We will now consider some instances of influence in social interaction.

SOCIAL INTERACTION AND INFLUENCE

To what degree can individuals affect one another through social interaction? There are of course limits set by biological factors. Men cannot fly like birds, however much they may be persuaded to do so. But the physiology of the individual can be affected by social factors. Most members of our society, even though hungry, will not readily eat socially disapproved foods—e.g. grasshoppers, whale blubber, or octopus—though other people consider them delicacies within their cultures. Indeed, the discomfort from eating them may result in illness and vomiting. The writer witnessed a graphic instance of this effect when several people at a party became ill after learning that the "delicious hors d'oeuvres" the hostess had just served were made of rattlesnake meat.

     Many of the disorders we think of as being "psychosomatic" derive from social interaction. The actions of other people can make us laugh or cry, and feel pains of anguish. The person who is unhappy with his relationships, at work or at home, can develop quite real physical symptoms, such as a stomach ulcer or even a heart attack. In good part, this is evidence of Man's capacity to symbolize and to react internally to anticipated threats by unseen, but nonetheless significant, physiological changes.

In a provocative experiment on physiological arousal, Schachter and Singer (1962) have shown that when subjects were injected with the drug epinephrine, to create a non-specific state of emotional arousal, they were strongly inclined to display emotional reactions paralleling those of another person—a confederate of the experimenters'—who had been instructed to behave in a giddy way with half the subjects and angrily with the others. In the first instance, the confederate threw paper airplanes, initiated a mock game of basketball, and hopped about, at times singing; in the second, he made unpleasant remarks to the subject, and generally gave signs of being angry. In both conditions, subjects showed a high degree of matching behavior and tended to label their "feelings" in line with the confederate's performance. In a related experiment, Schachter and Wheeler (1962) found comparable results with the arousal of humor.

The main point of this work is that subjective feelings, when sufficiently aroused, necessitate interpretation by the individual from cues in his immediate social setting. Schachter (1964) contends this interpretive process involves cognitive labeling. In other words, strong subjective feelings require explanation, probably because the lack of an explanation is essentially negative. There are some complications in the Schachter and Singer findings, especially in the interesting but unexpected fact that subjects in the control groups, given injections of a placebo (a substance without the drug), also expressed emotions matching the performance of the confederate (cf. Shapiro and Crider, 1969). Substantially, this reveals an influence effect in that, with or without the actual drug, the sense of excitation can be communicated and yield the label of "joy" or "anger" or "fear" as a function of how another person seems to be reacting.

In connection with placebo effects, there is a considerable volume of research which suggests that the physician-patient interaction is characterized by a strong expectancy that the medical ministrations will help. Summarizing nearly one hundred studies of more than forty-five hundred patients, Haas, Fink, and Hartfelder (1963) found that pain reduction was reported from placebos in an average of 27 per cent of the cases. What is notable about these studies is that they included the gamut of diseases, from colds and rheumatism to multiple sclerosis and cancer. For some disorders, it has been found that the rate of relief from taking placebos can run to 75 per cent of the cases.

"Contagion effects" represent a striking phenomenon of social inter- action and influence. In a recent book, *The June Bug*, Kerckhoff and Back (1968) report on their study of an "hysterical epidemic" which occurred in a dress factory in the South, predominantly employing women. Several workers had complained of insect bites in the weeks preceding the major outbreak, and the plant had been sprayed three times with a powerful disinfectant. Nonetheless, complaints continued to occur. Then the rumor began to spread that insects had arrived in a batch of cloth from England. In the ensuing days, sixty-two em- ployees reported symptoms of the bug bite—dizziness, nausea, aches and pains. Public health experts who had been called in concluded that some individuals had been bitten by some bug, but that the bulk of the complaints were due to the ballooning of anxiety.

As social psychologists, Kerckhoff and Back were not satisfied to merely leave it at that. They raised a number of questions, such as: Why at this time and place? Why were only *some* of the people af- fected? If social contagion, what was the medium of transmission, and from whom to whom? By a careful study of affected persons, and a sample of unaffected ones, they found that situational factors of strain on the job, combined with personal factors, such as family circum- stances, produced the initial cases of onset, mainly among workers who were less popular. Thereafter, the contagion spread to more so- cially central workers who, in turn, influenced their acquaintances. We then see the full-blown epidemic.

> . . . as larger and larger numbers of persons exhibit the behavior, the sheer size of the affected category makes the credibility of the phenomenon greater. Ultimately almost everyone believes in "the bug," and cases begin to occur throughout the population. At that point, the pattern becomes a kind of "crowd response" (Kerckhoff and Back, 1968, p. 115).

Panic situations such as this provide a picture of social influence processes running out of control. The most anxious individuals gain visibility and ascendancy; their influence becomes disproportionate and the situation is made to seem worse than it is (Kelley, Condry,

Dahlke, and Hill, 1965). Then more and more individuals are pulled along and the panic multiplies itself much as with affected cells in cancer.

Evidently numbers matter in influence, at least to a point. A novel experiment by Milgram, Bickman, and Berkowitz (1969) examined this question in connection with the drawing power of crowds of different size. On a street in midtown Manhattan, in the midst of the busiest part of New York City, passersby encountered one or more people staring up at a sixth-floor window of a building and maintaining their upward gaze for a minute. The number of gazers in the center of a previously designated fifty-foot strip of sidewalk was contrived to be 1, 2, 3, 5, 10, or 15 persons.

For the minute during which the upward gazing was occurring, motion pictures were taken of the fifty-foot sidewalk observation area. It was possible, therefore, to determine, by counting, just how much effect on the actions of passersby these "stimulus crowds" of varying size produced. The passersby could look up at the building, without breaking stride, or make a more imitative response by stopping and standing with the crowd. In all, 1424 pedestrians entered the observation area during the five experimental runs, with all six of the numbers of gazers, in a random sequence, over two afternoons. The results of this experiment are shown in Figure 1.2, in terms of the percentage of passersby who only looked up, or who stopped while looking up, for the varying crowd sizes.

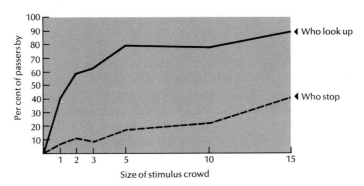

Fig. 1.2: Mean percentage of passersby who look up and who stop, as a function of the size of the stimulus crowd. (From Milgram, Bickman, and Berkowitz, 1969, p. 80.)

Comparing those who just look up with those who actually stop, it is clear that the latter percentage is consistently smaller than the former, though both behaviors increased with the size of the crowd. Where a response is more demanding, in time or effort, its occurrence is reduced. The major findings support the notion of a contagion effect, seen in the influence on the behavior of passersby. The expectancy that larger numbers means attention to something of greater importance or greater interest is one probable justification for this effect, though there are still other variables to be contemplated.

VARIABLES OF STUDY

A variable is an attribute or condition which can vary in one or more ways and which can be systematically shown to *affect* or *be affected by* other attributes or conditions. In theories, relationships are postulated between variables which can then be tested by research, as a basis for their verification. Also, in the very act of testing theories, we gain by the necessity to specify variables clearly and measure them with care. This in itself contributes to understanding.

A number of variables are given distinctive attention in social psychology. They serve to both define the interests of the field and provide explanatory propositions when linked together in functional statements.

Perhaps the most widely studied variable in social psychology is the concept of *attitude*. A long history of work has been directed toward the investigation of attitudes, their sources and their effects on social behavior. Essentially, attitudes are perceptions about persons, things, or events in the environment. They also have motivational qualities insofar as they direct behavior. The most vital consideration in defining attitudes is the way in which they "set" the individual to view and respond to the world in certain ways. In large measure, they conveniently sum up the past history of the individual's experience to allow differential predictions of social behavior. The internal consistency of atttitudes with each other, and with behavior, is another aspect of study. They are, therefore, an important part of our personal orientation to the world, the "psychological field" which shapes distinctive reactions to social stimulation.

Associated with the concept of attitude is the variable termed *val-*

ues. Fundamentally, values represent persisting motives which lead the individual to choose certain goals over others. Values have substantial directive force in human experience. Men die for values such as "duty," "freedom," and "honor." Not all values are as potent, in a long-range sense, as these; others have a more immediate, instrumental quality, such as tidiness or punctuality. As with most variables dealt with in social psychology, they are learned through a process of exposure to others who hold these values. Furthermore, they provide an underlying structure for attitudes.

Another variable is *group cohesiveness*, which essentially refers to the degree to which members of a group find it attractive. In terms of the specifics of deeper psychological analysis, attraction can be thought of as reflecting individual motivation to belong. In turn, such motivation can be separated into several components, regarding those rewards expected through affiliation. These will be considered shortly. Another point here, however, is the possibility that variables may be either independent or dependent, as a function of the sequence within which they are viewed. They are not necessarily fixed permanently as one or the other, with regard to direction of effect. Thus, cohesiveness in a group may be an outcome of certain other processes, or it may be looked at as a factor producing certain outcomes.

A different kind of variable in social psychology is represented in *roles*, which refer mainly to a variation of quality rather than quantity. In essence, roles are the different behaviors which we display in connection with a given social position we occupy; accordingly, there are behaviors associated with the role of mother, with the role of teacher, or with the role of employer. All of us have a multiplicity of roles which we must fill in the course of our daily lives. Indeed, in any one day we may be obliged to fit into a wide range of roles including several in the family circle alone. Roles are behaviors. Yet they have considerable *psychological* significance as is revealed by the social expectancy in the girl's response to her boyfriend—"Let me be a sister to you." On the psychological level, then, roles can be defined as a function of social expectancies.

As was pointed out earlier, expectancies play a part in another variable in social psychology that varies qualitatively—*norms*. Where there are general behaviors, including approved attitudes, which are socially prescribed in a given situation, we may speak of a norm, or sometimes a "social norm" or a "group norm." This mainly means a standard of conduct, but it also conveys the sense of matching behaviors to the expectations of others in that situation. Notice that both roles and norms necessarily involve a process of person perception. A study of that particular psychological process, therefore, gives us a good deal of leverage in understanding influence relationships producing social behavior.

A particularly important variable of study today is embodied in the concept of *reference groups*. This too has properties of a qualitative variable in terms of the different "psychological affiliations" a person may have with groups even apart from actual membership. It may also vary quantitatively in terms of the strength of affiliation or motivation to belong. While it was common in the past to consider individuals to be directly affected by groups to which they belonged, it was found that this did not account for many variations of effect. People might apparently be members of a group, in some descriptive sense. Yet a more analytic probing of the psychological significance of group membership revealed that they might or might not be motivated, in a psychological sense, to accept this group's standard of conduct or outlook. Furthermore, it became evident that even where an individual did *not* literally belong to a group he might be affected by it. In a socially mobile society, aspirations for achievement tend to encourage this identification process, and reference groups therefore represent those aspirations which may have high value.

Simply noting group membership is therefore not enough; we must also know whether the individual actually "refers" himself to a group, for example, by using it as a source of attitudes, standard of conduct, or as a basis for judgment. For the social psychologist, this raises the question of why the person is motivated to retain identification with a group, or instead accepts a standard held by another group to which he aspires. Herein lies one of the crucial points of study regarding social behavior, the *psychological rewards in group affiliation* and, relatedly, in the acceptance of influence.

PSYCHOLOGICAL REWARDS IN THE ACCEPTANCE OF INFLUENCE

When an individual is influenced by others, he gives up something but he also obtains one or more rewards in exchange. At the most general level, there are three categories of psychological reward which account for a great deal of such specific content as feeling close to someone or developing a greater sense of understanding, and which sustain coherence in life. Individuals do not simply *get* these rewards; they also *give* them to others, in line with the process of social exchange discussed earlier. These rewards are social identity, social support, and social reality.

> • *Social identity* refers to the attachment a person feels toward others, individually or collectively, which gives him a sense of having a place in society. It is related to the idea of having status, both as a literal position and as a standing in the eyes of relevant others. Accordingly, social identity provides a significant social anchorage for the person in terms of "belonging."
>
> • *Social support* refers to the favorable response a person secures from others which sustains his behavioral sequences. In this sense, support may be thought of as arising from signs of recognition and approval in terms of the "social reinforcement" received for valued actions and attitudes.
>
> • *Social reality* refers to the shared outlook which a person acquires from others. It provides him with a way of viewing the world that helps to simplify complexity and clarify ambiguity.

Whether we speak of conformity to group norms, attitude change as a result of persuasive communication, interaction between friends, or leader-follower relationships, these rewards are all implicated as features of influence. They each take on special significance as a consequence of time and setting and interdependence. In many short-run, impersonal events involving a degree of compliance—such as the reactions of passersby on a city street, in the Milgram *et al.* (1969) experiment—the most salient reward is probably social reality. The implicit puzzle posed by seeing people gazing upward creates a desire for information, or at least some clarification. On the other hand, in the study by Kerckhoff and Back (1968) on the response to "the bug" by women in the dress factory, strong elements of social identity and of social support were present, in addition to the definition of the situation through social reality. These rewards may cluster, as in this last instance, or take on separate significance.

Where there is continuity in the relationship between an individual and one or more others, it is quite likely that more than just one of these rewards is being served. There is, of course, a limiting condition involved in any consideration of influence events as well as ongoing relationships, and that is the premise that the individual has available alternatives. If he does not, especially under coercive circumstances, then we are dealing with total social control which gives rise to other processes (cf. Gamson, 1968), with a different order of psychological arousal, including self-protective impulses. The situation in which individuals are forced together is treated a bit more in Chapter 7 on social interaction.

The context of society and culture: a larger perspective

Social influence phenomena occur within a societal context and draw upon that context. The extent to which social behavior is comprehensible frequently depends upon knowing the relationship between the parties involved, and their shared expectancies as defined by a given society. What might, for example, seem to be an inequitable exchange from the standpoint of one society might be entirely equitable in another due to the values and symbolic rewards prevailing there.

All of us are to some extent captives of the society in which we were reared. In the process of growing up within this social environment we learn to adopt the manner and ways of others. The content of this process varies enormously depending upon the people and circumstances we contact during these years of development and after. It is not surprising, then, that the person brought up in the city necessarily learns modes of adaptation and acquires behaviors and outlooks which are different from those of the person brought up, let us say, on a farm or in a fishing village, even though in the same country.

The other people with whom we have contact are part of a *society*. Their *culture*, represented in the patterns of life which they lead, consists of the ongoing practices and institutions passed on, though perhaps modified, from generation to generation. In our own society, some illustrative cultural patterns are represented in our language, the monogamous family, private ownership, and the four-year baccalaureate degree.

CULTURE AS AN OUTLOOK

There is another significant thing about a culture: it gives us an *outlook on the world*. The social psychologist, aware of culture as a context of experience, is interested in *how* the individual's perceptions, as well as his motivations, are affected by it. To expand our understanding of social behavior, we must not only recognize that other people are important social stimuli to which we react, but also that collectively people *create* other socially significant stimuli that have symbolic value —words, preferred foods, money, flags, and so on. These bring about significant social responses, too. Accordingly, the social psychologist focuses attention not only on the relationship of persons but also on the individual's interpretation of and reaction to things which exert influence through their socially symbolic meaning. This is a vital feature of the perceptual quality of culture considered in greater detail in Chapter 8.

THE "HUMAN NATURE" FALLACY

On the whole, people are inclined to think of the characteristics of those in their *own* region or country as "human nature." Their personal observation of how others behave leads them to conclude that somehow this has applicability to men or women in general, even though this behavior depends upon learning in society. Not uncommonly, therefore, we may hear statements such as these:

> "It's only human nature for people to want to get ahead."
> "It's only human nature for people to want to take advantage of others."
> "What do you expect of a man?"
> "Isn't that just like a woman?"

The fallacy in this thinking lies in extending observations in one society to generalizations about the tendencies of people living elsewhere, under different social and cultural influences. We can see this in better focus if we imagine someone from the Orient contending that eating with chopsticks is "human nature" since after all it characterizes those he observes in a large share of the earth's population. The widespread belief in the essential similarity of other humans is an example too of the workings of the psychological phenomenon of perceptual constancy.

On the matter of overreaching from a limited perspective, the extensive field work of cultural anthropologists demolishes these simple notions. It reveals, for instance, that a concern with getting ahead, or achieving higher status, is not typical of all societies in the world, even though it may seem to be true of people in our own society. As a matter of fact, it is not even true of everyone in our own society, as we can recognize by recalling individual exceptions we have known. Nor is it true, as some would have it, that women universally are kitchen-bound, or that they must traditionally occupy a passive position. The well known field studies of Margaret Mead and many other cultural anthropologists indicate that male roles and female roles are culturally determined (Mead, 1949). Not only are there cultures in which cooking is "man's work," but indeed the outstanding "cooks" in our own society are male chefs. In some modern nations of the world, a very high proportion of physicians are women. Why should our culture have defined it as man's work when, alternatively, nursing is considered woman's work? There are even more profound questions which are now being asked, by the "Women's Liberation Movement" among others, about the assumptions of an almost mythological kind which have restricted opportunities for women.

"YOU CAN'T CHANGE HUMAN NATURE"?

Perhaps *most* misleading of cultural myths is the commonplace that "you can't change human nature." This contention, that mankind possesses unyielding inborn characteristics, denies the evidence of Man's greatest capacity, that of adaptability through learning. Imagine, for example, the reaction from adults if children were to use the argument that "you can't change human nature" in opposing their parents' guidance. Plainly, whatever Man's nature, it varies considerably as a result of the infusion of cultural experience through learning.

There are those who accept a more traditional view of human nature as a "closed system" in which there are conceived to be a relatively stable, unchanging set of characteristics that are Man's endowment. The contrasting view considers Man to be in an "open system" relationship with his social environment, a relationship that is crucial as a process which may yield greater perfectibility in human nature and human affairs. Two points of reference worth noting again are: the great diversity of human adaptations to varying social environments, and the vast capacity of humans to communicate and to partake of the features of organized societies with a continuity of patterned life through culture.

RACE, CULTURE, AND BEHAVIOR

Another widespread misconception is founded in the belief that observed differences in behavior between the peoples of various societies are the result of inborn racial characteristics. Sometimes this is captured succinctly but erroneously in the phrase "It's in the blood." Reproduction, however, involves only the germ cells, and since only these and these alone carry genes from both parents, randomized through the process of reduction-division, genes don't depend upon blood, nor does race. Any racial classification constructed will almost certainly contain persons who possess the usual blood types of man—O, A, B, and AB, though in different proportions. Speaking to the issue of genetics and race, Dunn and Dobzhansky (1952) said:

> People differ in the color of skin, eyes, hair, in stature, bodily proportions, and in many other traits. Each trait is determined by several, often by many, genes. How many variable genes there are in man is unknown; certainly hundreds, possibly thousands. Because of this, some of us have blue and others brown eyes, some have prominent and others flat noses, some are tall and others short. Such differences are, of course, common among people of the same country, state, town, members of a family, and even brothers and sisters. We do not suppose that every person with blue eyes belongs to a different race from everybody with brown eyes. It would be absurd to do so because blue- and brown-eyed children are frequently born to the same parents (p. 117).

Nevertheless, because physical factors are more readily observed, it is frequently assumed that they must necessarily be associated with genetically determined dispositions toward some common behavior. Therefore, it is important in the first place to distinguish between physical characteristics and the cultural patterns we observe in a society such as a nation. Also, it is essential to recognize that neither societies nor nations nor religions need be made up of people with common physical qualities. No less than Americans, Frenchmen, for example, are widely variable in physical "type."

A nation after all is a political unit; one is a "national" of a country by virtue of living within a political boundary. A religion is comprised of people who share a common faith and may live in various societies or nations, just as a society or a nation may be made up of people of differing religions or even different languages. Switzerland has three official languages, and Canada, not uniquely, has two. Many nations of the world have a diversity of religions. Buddhism and Mohammedanism are among the major religions, in addition to Christianity, having widespread adherents.

Yet races, religions, nations, and languages are often confused with one another—as when people speak of a "French race" or a "Jewish race" or a "Slavic people" or a "Catholic nation." Such usage in the first place presents an oversimplified, pigeon-holed picture of the great diversity of human life; more particularly, it totally disregards the wide range of *individual differences* that exist within any human grouping.

Anthropologists have increasingly spoken of "breeding populations" rather than all-encompassing racial categories based on skin color. Essentially, a breeding population is made up of a grouping of people who usually breed with each other more often than they do with outsiders. Thus, certain genetic characteristics tend to be enhanced in the population, on a probability basis. However, many of the identifiable features that distinguish recognizable groupings actually cut across breeding populations since the process of natural selection is not confined to the boundaries. Hence, there are great variations possible even within breeding populations; in the case of skin color, the label "white" encompasses an enormous range of actual color that includes large populations from Scandinavians with light pigmentation to people in the Indian subcontinent with dark pigmentation.

Fox (1968) points out that rather than ignore genetic diversity, we should examine and appreciate it as an evolutionary asset to our species. It is also helpful to recognize, he says, that any kind of ranking of genetic attributes is not given in nature but depends on the values assigned by the rankers in a society.

When we focus on those distinctively "human" things, like speaking a language, we find them the most highly subject to the wide-ranging influences of diverse societies. This appears to be quite clearly an environmental effect and not a matter of genetic factors. The illogic of this latter view is illustrated by the fact that nobody would adopt, let us say, a French baby in the naïve expectation that when he grew up they could learn French from him. Common sense as well as the best scientific evidence indicates that all normal human infants are capable of learning any language spoken by humans, given sufficient exposure to it; they are not born with a tendency toward any particular language. Let us also be clear that, just as with language, a multitude of other patterns of behavior and outlook are available to be learned from the particular humans we encounter in the formative years. How these effects are produced requires some probing of heredity and environment.

Heredity and environment as a social issue

Since the terms "heredity" and "environment" are still pitted against one another in everyday discussion, it should be emphasized that they are *not* opposing forces. Any behavior depends in some degree upon the mutual effects of heredity within environment.

By definition, heredity is that which is biologically based, usually in the sense of genetic determinants. Though heredity is sometimes bleakly viewed as though it were destiny, this is unnecessarily defeatist; it fails to take account of the environmental sources which can shape alternative outcomes. We may not literally change the genes with which we are born, but we can encounter or even seek environmental factors to which they will respond more favorably. Recent work on DNA, which provides an understanding of genetics in terms of biochemical coding, lends emphasis to Montagu's (1956) point that genes are

> . . . chemical packages which vary chemically under different conditions and tend to accelerate the chemical reactions of other chemical packages. Genes do not act as such in a vacuum, but they interact with the environment in which they occur. . . . Development is the resultant of the interaction between the inherited pattern of genes, the genotype, and the environment in which those genes undergo development (p. 72).

Environment has to do with all of those experiences from the time of conception, including possible intra-uterine involvements, which can bring about physical or behavioral effects. One widespread misconception, which slights the environment, is to consider that shared behaviors within a family are the result of heredity. The fact that you can "see them with your own eyes" is supposed to be proof enough. Thus, the child, who is overweight and whose parents are also overweight, is obviously a victim of his genes—or is he? Since eating is a matter of family social patterns, which might include routine second helpings, the environment clearly pleads a strong case. If a father imbibes excessively and his son follows in this pattern, is that heredity? Or might it not actually be environment? Plainly, "like father like son" can be equally apt as a reference to environmental learning. Just as children, in growing up, learn to speak the language of those around them, they learn the eating habits, as well as the many other features of behaving which are characteristic of those others. Parents, often blind to this implicit learning process, are too readily inclined to see the mannerisms their children share with them to be hereditary in a genetic sense. Visiting relatives are not excused from making the same error of observation.

PSYCHOLOGICAL ATTRIBUTES

Another error in understanding heredity is the assumption that if a given physical characteristic which is genetically based is associated with a behavior, then the behavior too is genetic. It is still common to hear, for example, that redheads have very inflammatory personalities and tend to be easily excited. There is no scientific basis for this contention, yet, given the belief, the effect could follow. This is an example of the "self-fulfilling prophecy" (Merton, 1948), a wide-reaching phenomenon about which more will be said later. Where the members of a society among whom we live share certain expectancies about us as redheads, then act toward us in distinct ways, in turn leading us to defensive action, is that heredity?

The very condition which is alleged to be genetic—a personality trait—can be environmentally produced by a social psychological process originating in expectancies. This process fits the circumstance of the so-called "minority group" in many human societies. Indeed, the same condition is true with respect to the differentiation of males and females. If young girls and boys are encouraged toward sex-typed behaviors, these are environmentally determined and hardly outcroppings of biological sex determinants, as many believe. In fact, in our society the social distinctions between little girls and little boys begin quite early, as the color-coding of pink and blue outer-garments reveals. Accordingly, the doll-play of a boy past the nursery stage is viewed as inappropriate and the girl in the sandlot ball game may be tolerated but is a "tom-boy" to the gang, to her parents, and in the view of broader society.

In producing social behaviors, heredity provides a capacity for a *wide range* of behavior that may then be encouraged and sustained by stimulation from the environment. Learning is, of course, central in affecting this outcome. Furthermore, in a society where doing well on some things is more important than doing well on others, the reinforcement provided by social approval, and the availability of relevant resources, make it more likely that those kinds of performance of the first, or valued, sort will out-run those of the latter, or less valued sort. As Gardner (1961) has put it:

> The virtues which flower in any society are the virtues that the society nourishes. The qualities of mind and character which stamp a people are the qualities that people honor, the qualities they celebrate, the qualities they recognize instantly and respect profoundly (p. 151).

Table 1.1: IQ differences of identical twins reared apart under conditions of different educational advantage. (After Newman, Freeman, and Holzinger, 1937.)

NUMBER OF PAIRS	AVERAGE AGE AT SEPARATION	AVERAGE DIFFERENCE IN EDUCATIONAL ADVANTAGES ON 10-POINT RATING SCALE	AVERAGE SUPERIORITY IN IQ POINTS OF TWIN WITH GREATER ADVANTAGE
6	15 months	Very unequal (5.1 average difference)	15.2
7	9 months	Somewhat unequal (2.4 average difference)	4.6
6	24 months	Relatively similar (1.6 average difference)	1.0

In the matter of intelligence, as measured by the IQ, psychological research has supported the concept of an interdependence between hereditary capacities and environmental opportunities and enrichment. For example, nineteen pairs of identical twins who had been reared apart were studied by Newman, Freeman, and Holzinger (1937). Since hereditary factors are constant for identical twins, any variations in intelligence can be attributed to environmental opportunities. As shown in Table 1.1, the greater the educational advantage, the greater the IQ of the twin with that advantage.

While an IQ test score is sometimes taken to be indicative of a genetic capacity, it may readily be biased by cultural elements, for example by the nature of the test questions asked. There is yet to be developed an authentically "culture-free" IQ test, though attempts in this direction are being made. Differences in IQ scores therefore reveal environmental influences as well as hereditary ones.

The effects of social expectancies in the performance of children on IQ tests, and in class work, has been intriguingly revealed in a recent experiment by Rosenthal and Jacobson (1968), reported in their book *Pygmalion in the Classroom.* The basis for their work is the notion that social expectancies act as self-fulfilling prophecies in interpersonal relations, and that their effect can be discerned in the educational process.

Rosenthal and Jacobson conducted their experiment in a public elementary school in California. All of the children there, in grades one through six, were given a standard non-verbal intelligence test which their teachers were told was a measure of "intellectual blooming." The impression was created that the test would identify children who were likely to experience marked intellectual growth. About 20 per cent of the children, supposedly on the basis of test scores—*but actually picked at random*—were labeled potential "bloomers." The same IQ test was then administered again to all the children after one semester and after a full school year. The results revealed differential gains in IQ for the supposed bloomers, as against the other youngsters, and most markedly and significantly for grades one and two. As is shown in Figure 1.3, the effects of teachers' expectancies, after a full school year, yielded sharp differences in average gain in IQ between the experimental and control groups for those grades, but not the later ones.

Rosenthal and Jacobson interpret these results as indicating that the teachers were more encouraging and friendly to the children from

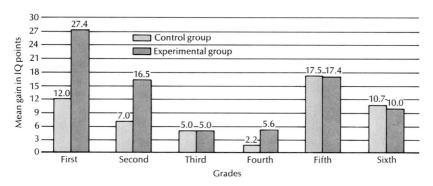

Figure 1.3: Mean gains in IQ, after a school year, for control and experimental groups in six grades. (From *Pygmalion in the Classroom* by Robert Rosenthal and Lenore Jacobson. Copyright © 1968 by Holt, Rinehart and Winston, Inc. Reprinted by permission of the publishers.)

whom they expected better intellectual performance, and that this motivated those children to higher achievement. This effect was most pronounced with the younger children, which is not surprising in terms of a developmental sequence. However, questions have been raised about the reliability of the IQ test employed in this experiment, the mode of administration, and the maximizing effect of the repeated use of the same test, in terms of raising scores. Each of these criticisms is important, but answerable, and the basic comparison between the experimental and control groups in the two early grades is still a striking one. Moreover, the data suggest how much IQ test scores can be affected by social factors. Beez (1970) reports a comparable finding.

INTELLIGENCE AND HERITABILITY: A RECENT CONTROVERSY

The most notable recent instance of controversy about the effects of heredity on IQ was occasioned by an article Arthur Jensen (1969) wrote for the *Harvard Educational Review*. After assessing a great volume of research, he declared that much of an IQ score can be credited to genetic factors. He also suggested that while children from lower socio-economic backgrounds were capable of learning through trial and error, or by rote, middle-class children outdistance them in their ability to deal with abstract ideas and in problem solving. One target of the article was compensatory education, exemplified by Project

Headstart, a pre-school program of "enrichment" especially for children from poor families. The argument raised was that such programs were futile because they were up against hereditary handicaps in these children.

Rebuttals to the Jensen article have been directed toward both the evidence presented and the conclusions drawn (e.g. Deutsch, 1969; J. McV. Hunt, 1969; Kagan, 1969). Among the most controversial aspects of Jensen's position is his interpretation of intelligence in terms of the concept of "heritability," by which he means ". . . the proportion of phenotypic variance due to variance in genotypes" (1969, p. 42). From an examination of data on the correlation of intelligence measures for unrelated and variously related persons, including identical twins raised separately or together, he concludes that the heritability of intelligence is quite high. Others, viewing the same data, have a different interpretation. Hunt (1969), pointing to several findings on the relationship of learning to human abilities, and to intelligence tests and tests of academic achievement, says that intelligence is best seen as a dynamic product of the ongoing interaction of children with their environment, and not as a static, predetermined quality.

Another line of argument concerns Jensen's acceptance of the IQ as a measure of a genetic characteristic; he takes average IQ differences between racial and social class populations as evidence of genetic differences when these same data can be interpreted as well to reveal environmental differences (Kagan, 1969). What is essential in all this is to recognize that the concept of "race differences" deals broadly with populations, rather than with specific individuals. Indeed, on this crucial issue, Jensen (1969) himself forcefully asserts:

> The important distinction between the *individual* and the *population* must always be kept clearly in mind in any discussion of racial differences in mental abilities or any other behavioral characteristics. Whenever we select a person for some special educational purpose, whether for special instruction in a grade-school class for children with learning problems, or for a "gifted" class with an advanced curriculum, or for college attendance, or for admission to graduate training or a professional school, we are selecting an *individual,* and we are selecting him and dealing with him as an individual for reasons of his individuality. Similarly, when we employ someone, or promote someone in his occupation, or give some special award or honor to someone for his accomplishments, we are doing this to an

individual. The variables of social class, race, and national origin are correlated so imperfectly with any of the valid criteria on which the above decisions should depend, or, for that matter, with any behavioral characteristic, that these background factors are irrelevant as a basis for dealing with individuals—as students, as employees, as neighbors. Furthermore, since, as far as we know, the full range of human talents is represented in all the major races of man and in all socioeconomic levels, it is unjust to allow the mere fact of an individual's racial or social background to affect the treatment accorded to him. All persons rightfully must be regarded on the basis of their individual qualities and merits, and all social, educational, and economic institutions must have built into them the mechanisms for insuring and maximizing the treatment of persons according to their individual behavior (p. 78).

Yet, there remains a sense in which even the vague imputation of a distinction in intelligence between races, or breeding populations, can exert a social toll. Clark (1965), for one, says that negative attitudes held by white teachers are an important factor in determining deficiencies in the performance of black pupils. Certainly the findings of Rosenthal and Jacobson (1968) discussed above suggest that such a process could operate as a self-fulfilling prophecy. Indeed, the operation of categorical thinking in interpersonal relationships is bound to be unfair and even stigmatizing to some individuals. Arguments pro and con on issues of heritability therefore come back ultimately to what it is that society values and that its members accept as social reality.

We return then to the starting point, Man's relationship to Man, which has produced a long history of controversy. In the next chapter, we will review some of that history by examining the tradition of thought about human social behavior, its sources and effects, and potential for change. Thereafter, we move on to the contemporary period of social psychological study.

SUMMARY

Social psychology is one of a number of fields concerned with the objective study of human behavior. Its particular focus is upon understanding *social behavior* exemplified in the effect of one individual, or a group, upon another individual, whether in an actual or implied sense. Based on *social influence process*, these effects produce phenomena such as conformity, leadership, prejudice, morale, and inter-group conflict.

While people are generally interested in social behavior, social psychology seeks to achieve an understanding of its underlying processes through objective study and the use of scientific methods. One distinctive quality of social psychology rests in its emphasis on the *individual* in society. It employs psychological concepts and psychological processes, in terms of individual perceptions, motivations, and learning, to account for social influence. The major rewards associated with the acceptance of influence are *social identity*, *social support*, and *social reality*.

Social psychology views *social interaction* as a basic feature in many social influence events. These events involve four elements: an *influence source*, a *communication*, a *recipient*, and a *social context*. Social interaction is essential to survival in early life, and to the development of characteristics which are distinctively "human" such as the learning of language. It can affect not only the overt behavior of the individual but his physiological states as well. Thus, we often find the cause of "psychosomatic" disorders in the stresses of social interaction.

In studying social influence, social psychology attends to variables such as attitudes, values, group cohesiveness, roles, norms, and reference groups. Its research is also aimed at the effects of *expectancies* on behavior. These include *reciprocity* and *social exchange*, as well as such self-expectancies as *consistency* and *freedom of choice*.

Social psychology is also aware of the context of society and culture, in the sense of the other people in the social environment and their way of life. It goes beyond the confined view of any one culture regarding "human nature," to a broader conception of Man's capacities for adaptation to the diversity of cultural demands. It also recognizes the faultiness of generalizations regarding genetics and race, especially when applied to social behavior.

Social psychology emphasizes neither hereditary nor environmental determinants of social behavior but rather looks upon them as interdependent influences. Though many behaviors and other psychological attributes, such as intelligence, are assumed to be hereditary, especially when seen as a family characteristic, this inference slights environmental effects. The operation of the *self-fulfilling prophecy* in bringing about behavioral outcomes, due to the expectancy that certain ones and not others should occur, also accounts for many of the observed differences in performance between individuals.

SUGGESTED READINGS

From E. P. Hollander and R. G. Hunt (Eds.) *Current perspectives in social psychology.* (3rd ed.) New York: Oxford University Press, 1971.

Introduction to Section I: *Basic orientations and processes*
1. Robert B. Zajonc: *Social facilitation*
5. Jack W. Brehm: *A theory of psychological reactance*
6. Hadley Cantril: *The human design*
67. Stanley Milgram: *The experience of living in cities*

SELECTED REFERENCES

*Benedict, R. *Patterns of culture.* New York: Penguin Books, 1946.

Brehm, J. W. *A theory of psychological reactance.* New York: Academic Press, 1966.

*Dunn, L. C., & Dobzhansky, T. *Heredity, race and society.* (Rev. ed.) New York: New American Library, 1952.

*Homans, G. C. *The nature of social science.* New York: Harcourt, Brace & World, 1967.

*Kerckhoff, A. C., & Back, K. W. *The June bug: a study of hysterical contagion.* New York: Appleton-Century-Crofts, 1968.

Lindzey, G., & Aronson, E. (Eds.) *Handbook of social psychology.* (Rev. ed.) Cambridge: Addison-Wesley, 1968.

*Mead, M. *Male and female.* New York: Morrow, 1949.

*Montagu, A. *Human heredity.* New York: New American Library, Mentor Book, 1960.

*Rosenthal, R., & Jacobson, L. *Pygmalion in the classroom.* New York: Holt, Rinehart, & Winston, 1968.

* All books thus indicated, here and in subsequent chapters, are available in paperback editions.

2

Historical and modern approaches to social behavior

Any study of human affairs carries a guiding image of Man. The assumptions underlying this image are often "tinged with the coloring of some secret, imaginative background," as Whitehead put it.

Though philosophers and other thinkers have been preoccupied with the sources of social behavior since ancient times, they have all too frequently been handicapped by their own assumptions. In approaching the modern field of social psychology, it is useful to examine the backdrop of these ideas to be aware of the legacy they have left.

Three stages in the study of social behavior

There have been three distinct stages in achieving knowledge about social behavior (see Figure 2.1). Each has added to the succeeding one so that today all are embodied in contemporary work. The oldest is *social philosophy,* which has its origins in antiquity. It is characterized by conjecture and speculation, usually in the absence of any systematic gathering of factual information, since it is most often based on authority or reason alone. The method of "rationalism" in earlier scientific efforts exemplifies one characteristic of the traditional philosophical approach, that is, reliance on the power of thought apart from testable data.

36

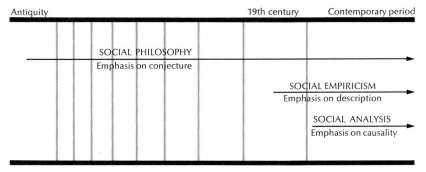

Figure 2.1: Stages in the emergence of three approaches to the study of social behavior represented in the contemporary period.

The next stage, beginning in the nineteenth century, is termed *social empiricism*. It represents the advance toward a fuller description of human attributes and the conditions of human society. In general, it is characterized by systematic data-gathering which goes beyond conjecture, though of course it may be and often is guided by it. Any raw tabulation of social statistics, such as public health figures, represents social empiricism. Another example is seen in simple polling procedures, such as a "straw poll" to indicate *how many* people intend to vote one way or another, without probing the "why" of that intent.

Social empiricism provides the basis for the next stage, *social analysis*, which is a twentieth-century development and the dominant emphasis in contemporary social psychology. It signifies a more penetrating study of underlying relationships aimed at testing and establishing theory. While the word "analysis" can mean several things, including some which apply to philosophy, we specifically intend to signify the search for causal relationships through the study of data gathered by systematic empirical research. The major feature of this approach is to go beyond simple descriptive data to the level of verifying relationships between variables; this quest frequently involves experimentation aimed at determining the validity of relationships postulated by theories.

Latter-day forms of social philosophy and social empiricism are still with us offering contending views usually devoid of procedures for verification. We see this in many reaches of life where a simple finding is generalized out of proportion to its validity. Such claims to being scientific must necessarily be viewed in the context of standards embodied in modern social analysis.

The backdrop of social philosophy

A central theme in social thought, as we noted in Chapter 1, is seen in the critical and long-standing heredity-environment controversy, sometimes stated in terms of "nature-nurture." Two kinds of questions flow from this dichotomy. The first rests fundamentally on the issue of what mankind in general brings into the world as distinctive human characteristics. This represents the vital core of the "human nature" issue. The second question concerns the expansion of this issue to whether these characteristics are "good" or "bad."

Classic responses to the question of the qualities of human nature, and of the necessary conditions of human society, tended to share several failings in common. First, readily generalizing about observed behaviors in one society they applied the "human nature" fallacy to mankind in general; second, they distilled out of the richness of human relationships an all-embracing explanation for every facet of life, rooted in some one factor, e.g. power, self-interest, imitation, and pleasure; third, they emphasized a static view of Man devoid of any adequate accounting of his great potential for *learning* and for *changing* in the face of new experience. The tradition of "instinct" theories, the major thrust of which lies in imputing an inborn tendency to all humans, illustrates all of these failings. In this section we propose to consider five such viewpoints, each within its own social context.

INSTINCTUAL VIEWS IN GENERAL

Regarding the primary issue of "nature or nurture," the Greek philosophers Aristotle and Plato are often compared for their different though not entirely opposite responses. They were not, however, the first to consider this fundamental issue which is a feature within the Babylonian Code of Hammurabi dating from before 2000 B.C. Aristotle was nonetheless a leading exponent of the view that Man's behavior was the result of an instinctual nature, while in Plato's view Man was seen to be more subject to the effects of organized society. In this respect, Plato suggested various social innovations, including the reign of "philosopher kings," in order to render changes in human behavior in his idealized society. He also considered Man's relationship to society to be a "contract" in which Man received certain benefits by behaving within the regularities of an organized society. Plato thus signified his reliance on the social effects of learning, though he was interested as well in individual differences in capacity.

As to the "goodness" or "badness" of Man's inherent nature, many controversies have raged over the centuries. Perhaps best known as a spokesman for a dour view of Man, though by no means alone in his stand, was Thomas Hobbes, who lived in the seventeenth century and is renowned for his social commentary, *The Leviathan* (1651). Man, devoid of a regulated society, in Hobbes's memorable words, was given to a life that was "solitary, poor, nasty, brutish, and short." Among his other views which made a persisting impression was his advocacy of the pleasure-pain principle which held that Man would inherently seek pleasure and avoid pain. This idea, later elaborated by Jeremy Bentham and the utilitarians, also found its way into twentieth-century thought in the theories of Sigmund Freud.

In the eighteenth-century Age of Reason, Hobbes's views, which had gained wide adherence, came under assault from Jean-Jacques Rousseau, and such thinkers as Kant, Diderot, Goethe, and Condorcet. Man was innately good, they said; but society spoiled this "noble savage" and developed malevolent characteristics in him; there was no innate "badness" to Man's nature.

Followers of Hobbes and his later disciples scorned the "noble savage" concept, referred to its proponents as "the Romantics," and provided a resounding theme still echoed in political debates. The Hobbesians asserted that theirs was the "realistic" view of Man and in this they were abetted by the prevailing philosophy that accompanied the approaching Industrial Revolution. The nineteenth century produced an atmosphere that heavily favored the doctrine of justifiable dominance by some humans over others and fitted the insistent trends of "Darwinian" thought to which we shall be turning shortly.

There is of course no one answer to the complex question of whether Man is "good" or "bad." The terms themselves can be relative and often depend upon cultural standards. However, with broad regard to life-sustaining or life-denying tendencies, the history of mankind, including recent times, affords evidence of both extremes. Given human susceptibility to the forces in the social environment, the best response seems to be that Man has the capacity for extremes of high morality and conscience as well as for the basest forms of degradation in his treatment of fellow Man. It is hardly an exaggeration at all to say that human affairs are balanced quite precariously between these two extremes.

On the positive side, the mere existence of organized societies indicates the presence of widespread co-operation and of trust in the essential good will to be expected and received from others. Moreover, individual men often show limitless efforts of a humanitarian and altruistic kind. It is no cliché but a fact of daily existence that people usually trust others and think that most other people are decent. In 1964 a survey conducted by the National Opinion Research Center found that 77 per cent of a nationwide sample responded affirmatively to the question, "Do you think that most people can be trusted?" In 1948 the figure had been 66 per cent (*Trans-action*, 1966).

On the negative side, however, the human species is the only one known to maintain organized efforts to kill and otherwise harm its members. Erik Erikson has used the term "pseudospeciation" to name the process of perceptual differentiation of other human groups which transforms them into virtually a different species, as in warfare. It is then *not* another human being one is killing, the child of a human mother and father, but "the enemy," under various labels. We often speak of "bestial behavior," though the beasts in nature are far less inclined to assault, kill, or maim their kind. Of course they engage in combat and predatory activity against other species, as in the hunt, though the ethologist Konrad Lorenz (1966) contends that other aggressive behavior is largely reactive to provocations and is not organized.

Human history is written with the bloody pen of calamitous wars, including the relatively recent spectacle of the organized brutalities and agonies of death camps for civilians. Conquests, repressions, slavery, and other atrocities and iniquitous social practices are still woven into the fabric of human life. Indeed, Lorenz, who subscribes to the view that Man is given to "spontaneous aggression," has bleakly observed in a recent interview that characteristics which are highly prized in members of a supposedly civilized society can readily be turned to dreadful ends. Lorenz says:

> Loyalty to an ideal, the somewhat belligerent enthusiasm for a cause, nationalism—if all this is exaggerated somewhat, you very quickly end up with a dangerous barbarian capable of splitting your skull with the clearest possible conscience (1970, p. 5).

Others see Man's aggressiveness, in the sense of hostile behavior, as an outgrowth of social circumstances and learned response patterns. This issue is extremely complicated, and not an either-or matter. There are abundant signs of both extremes in Man's behavior, but let us consider the matter of aggressiveness somewhat more.

HUMAN AGGRESSIVENESS

With the backdrop of violence in two world wars and many lesser wars, directed not only against combatants but ever more widely against civilians, a large arena has existed for the playing out of aggressive acts. Now, with the increasing volume of crime, and of violence as a form of social protest, there has been a distinctly heightened interest in the sources of human aggressiveness.

Some commentators and social critics take it for granted that humans are aggressive by nature and that, given the least opportunity, will do some of the "skull-splitting" referred to in the quote above from Lorenz. He himself is prominent among those who adopt an innate conception of aggression, especially from his extensive observation of animals. But he considers that Man has not developed the controls over spontaneous aggression which many other species possess.

The author with perhaps the most potent message about Man's aggressive instinct is Robert Ardrey whose two major books (1961, 1966) have achieved a very wide readership. A writer and reporter of considerable skill, Ardrey has dramatized the view that Man has "an aggressive imperative," which propels him toward war and the weapons of war. Furthermore, he asserts that "Man is a predator whose natural instinct is to kill with a weapon" (1961, p. 316). In his second book, he elaborates the view that humans have an instinctual drive to gain and defend exclusive territory, the "territorial imperative" which Ardrey says grows out of an animal nature.

Given the bewilderment and concern about these issues, the writings of Lorenz and of Ardrey, along with other popular books by Morris (1968) and Storr (1968), have attracted a great deal of attention, not least from vocal critics in the scientific community. Among their criticisms is the skepticism expressed regarding simplistic assumptions and conclusions derived about the nature of Man from animal studies. Berkowitz (1969b), for instance, argues that Lorenz and Ardrey draw gross analogies between human behaviors ". . . and supposedly similar response patterns exhibited by other animal species. Attaching the same label to these human and animal behaviors, the writers then maintain that they have explained the actions" (p. 374). The stress in Berkowitz's own extensive writings on aggression is on its reactive quality, with particular reference to frustration as a source.

Montagu (1968) is critical of Lorenz for speaking in the name of ethology when presenting his own views, and for disregarding the views of others in the field. As Montagu puts it:

> He neglects, for example, to discuss the possibility that a considerable proportion of aggressive behavior represents a reaction to frustration. Nor does he pay the least attention to the view that in many instances aggressive behavior is situational, provoked by situations and conditions which have nothing whatever to do with anything "phylogenetically" or otherwise "programmed" in the individual. . . . The roles of learning and experience in influencing the development and expression of aggression are largely ignored by Lorenz. Yet the evidence is abundant and clear, both for animals and man, that learning and experience play substantive roles in the history of the individual or of the group in relation to the development of aggression. Where aggressive behavior is unrewarded and unrewarding, as among the Hopi and Zuni indians, it is minimally if at all evident (1968, p. 14).

Some of the criticism of the views of Lorenz, Ardrey, and kindred others, probably stems also from the challenge they present to the belief in the perfectibility of Man. Stripping away a good part of their overstatement, they appear to be saying that aggression, along with violence and other socially destructive acts, is due to bad "human nature" that exists as a closed system, rather than to an imperfect social environment. But even Lorenz, with his biocentric orientation, is by no means oblivious to social and political forces that may put Man in an aggressive stance—as witness again his statement quoted earlier here (p. 41). At least on the face of it, he appears to be speaking out against those social influences which might trigger so-called "spontaneous aggression." That takes care of one side of it, i.e. avoiding negative influences. Here, the critics of an innate view of aggression can essentially agree that aggression is *available* as a response if it is appropriately aroused, whether by frustration or nationalism or whatever. The implications of this process in war were summed up by a group of psychiatrists as follows:

> In the course of human history, deep-seated stereotypes have evolved around war that not only play a role in serving human needs, but also constitute an important psychological barrier to its elimination. The educational systems of all nations teach that war is right and proper under certain circumstances. War's destructiveness and violence are sanctioned in the name of a greater good for the group, and thus what the individual might view as wrong or immoral becomes, by group sanction, not only right but supremely right. . . . War is glorified as brave, just, righteous, and honorable. . . . However, such a conversion from the "peacetime ethic" of "love thy neighbor" to a "war ethic" that sanctions mass killing requires special training, indoctrination, and propaganda (Group for the Advancement of Psychiatry, 1964, pp. 233-234).

HEDONISM AND "ECONOMIC MAN"

Associated with the pleasure-pain principle was the doctrine of "psychological hedonism" or self-gratification, whose major proponent in the nineteenth century was Jeremy Bentham. In his view, Man searched for gain at the expense of others. Taking this viewpoint literally there would be no room for altruism, since the advocates of this doctrine looked upon altruism as another form of self-satisfying activity. Indeed, though Bentham did not see Man as an irresponsible member of society, but rather as one who practiced what he called "ethical hedonism" too, his viewpoint could make *any* act seem self-serving, as can be easily pointed out.

Put in simple logical terms, the prime failing of hedonism rests in the consideration that it provides for no alternative predictions about human behavior since it is predicated on the dual assumption that whether a person does a thing, or does *not* do the thing, the motivation is the same, i.e. self-gratification. This amounts to an "if A, then B: if not A, then B" proposition. It tells us nothing about how we might differentiate the two opposite situations. It fails on two other grounds, by neglecting to take account of the "mixed motive" character of many actions, and by confusing explanation with mere labeling. To say that the captain of industry who hoards his money is motivated in the identical way as the one who gives large sums to philanthropy, is to reach a logical absurdity and to provide no basis whatever for the differential prediction of behavior or an understanding of why it occurs.

Like the pleasure-pain principle with which it is linked, the doctrine of hedonism omits the range of social psychological relationships which may act on an individual to direct his behavior in one as opposed to another channel. Furthermore, it operates on one shaky premise which was fondly cherished as the basis for Adam Smith's eighteenth-century economic theory; that is, that individuals are continually alert to what is in their best interest regarding the return of gain or profit. Whatever the promise of a thoroughly rational view of Man's relationships, this was an untenable premise. Utter rationality in the marketplace, as a useful basis for explaining economic behavior, remains a dubious concept. In a comparable sense, the general utility of a simple hedonistic explanation for predicting and understanding social behavior is doubtful.

"SURVIVAL OF THE FITTEST": SOCIAL DARWINISM

Among the landmarks in the development of contemporary social science is the pronounced influence of the work of Charles Darwin. His theory of evolution, published in *Origin of Species* in 1859, altered the course of thinking and stimulated others such as Herbert Spencer and Karl Marx to apply his laws of natural selection to the development and course of society. His evolutionary viewpoint played a decisive part in shaping social theory. The "class struggle" element in Marxian ideology owes its origin in some measure to the "Social Darwinism" to which Marx was favorably disposed.

Laying overwhelming stress on the competitive rather than the cooperative aspects of life, Darwin attributed a natural aggressiveness to Man, hence the so-called "struggle." Yet he did recognize that apart from just natural selection there were social effects on Man's moral qualities. The concept of social transmission of cultural influences was therefore not foreign to his thinking. Darwin's popularized doctrine of natural selection had been construed largely in terms of physical evolution, despite the fact that he himself, in *The Descent of Man* (1871), emphasized his belief in moral and social evolution through social and cultural factors. Nevertheless, Social Darwinism, as developed by his disciples, led to an emphasis on "struggle for existence" in terms of conflict between individuals and groups rather than with the environment.

It is clear that Darwin himself did not intend to suggest that this "struggle" necessarily meant a conflict between individuals. Indeed, he saw the "survival value" inherent in social practices such as co-operation and interdependence. In *Origin of Species* he had said: ". . . I use this term [struggle for existence] in a large and metaphorical sense including dependence of one being upon another, and including (which is more important) not only the life of the individual, but success in leaving progeny" (Ch. 3, p. 62).

Followers of Darwin, such as Herbert Spencer, who had advanced his own evolutionary ideas in an 1852 paper anticipating Darwin's viewpoint, employed the "Darwinian" view to argue for the superiority of some groups and the inferiority of others, and thus justified war, colonialism, business ethics, and other social practices featuring implicit competition or conflict. Many nineteenth-century thinkers, concluding that human nature itself differed racially, ethnically, nationally, and between social classes, saw this as a function of biological factors determined by the evolutionary processes of natural selection. Montagu (1956) says that the concepts of "struggle for existence" and "survival of the fittest" led many distinguished intellectual leaders of the time to the persuasion that the bondage of "the lower classes" and the exploitation of the lands of "inferior" people were not only biologically justifiable but the clear judgment of Nature (p. 27). Though unsubstantiated, the consequences of such views linger today in many forms, especially in terms of an alleged "competitiveness" as a universal feature of human relationships.

FREUDIAN PSYCHOLOGY

Sigmund Freud grew up in the intellectual atmosphere of the Darwinian age, and his approach was unquestionably touched by its dominant features. But his own towering conceptions, notably surrounding the effects of early experience and the processes of the unconscious mind, place Freud with Darwin as an authentic pioneer in the history of thought. His contributions to the understanding of the psychology of the individual are evident not only among his followers but also in the writings of those who today would resist being called "Freudians." His ideas have widely permeated the social sciences, not just psychology alone.

Perhaps less understood are the explicit and implicit conceptions of social psychology embodied in Freud's writings. He is known for his view of society as a mainly hostile force, imposed upon Man's instinctual impulses and leading to frustration and the mechanism of repression, much of which is encompassed in his work *Civilization and its Discontents* (1930). Though acknowledging there that civilization serves to protect people against natural dangers and regulate their relations so that they do not destroy one another, he contended that its restriction of aggressive and sexual impulses, which he saw as innate, produced undesirable "character traits."

Freud also contended that the ideal of a society ought not to be one of "liberty," which he saw as illusory anyway, but equality of treatment, in terms of justice for all its members. Reflecting on the hostility toward civilization which expressed itself in an envy of primitive people, he concluded that this was merely a phantasy because these people were not happier or better off than civilized men, much as some might wish to regress to their level.

In his *Group Psychology and the Analysis of the Ego* (1921), Freud addressed himself to the nature of group phenomena and presented a theory of groups which draws heavily on his concept of the libido as the basis for the emotional bond among members. In these terms, group members share in an identification with the group leader who serves as an ideal, and these bonds are of singular importance in the maintenance of the group's stability, more so than are the bonds members have with one another. The linkage between followers and their leaders is an important one, though as with Max Weber's (1947) concept of the leader's charisma, it lacks precision. Under the sway of the group, Freud felt that individuals were inclined toward emotionality rather than rationality. It is interesting to note, however, that the two major examples of groups he chose were the church and the army. In any event, his viewpoint was consistent with concepts of imitation and the group mind that Freud had been exposed to earlier in his career, and which will be considered shortly.

Freud's view of Man's relationship to society, and to group life, was tightly bounded by his own subjective observations in a given culture. He readily accepted observed aggressiveness in Man as proof of its innateness rather than as a response to social forces. Indeed, embittered by the barbarity of the First World War, he postulated a "death instinct" in *Beyond the Pleasure Principle* (1920) which has since found no substantive support in contemporary social science. Finally, in emphasizing the impulsive and irrational elements of behavior, notably through the concepts of the *id* and the unconscious mind, Freud underrated man's rationality and potentialities for communication and co-operation.

Essentially, then, Freud was quite pessimistic regarding society and its institutions, though he rarely is found dull in expressing his ideas. Indeed, it is because he is such a brilliantly stimulating and compelling thinker that it is important to see his contributions in the appropriate light. In this respect, Hall and Lindzey (1968) contend:

> Freud, of course, was not a social scientist, and when he turned his attention to social phenomena, it seems to have been with the intention of indicting society for its deliterious influences on personality. The view of society that one gets from neurotic patients is not likely to be a favorable one, and it was probably difficult for Freud, as a practicing psychiatrist, to maintain a dispassionate attitude toward society. Moreover, "society" did not treat Freud well in the early years of psychoanalysis, nor later when the Nazis came to power (p. 273).

All in all, the legacy of Freud's thought regarding society is a mixture of idealism and despair which he himself would have found intriguing.

IMITATION AND THE "GROUP MIND"

A century ago Auguste Comte posed the paradox of how Man could at one and the same time *shape* society and yet *be shaped* by it. Often called the father of modern social science, Comte revealed in his statement a critical question surrounding the interrelation of Man and society: how to reconcile the individual and social qualities of Man's life and experience. One answer to it was developed as a quite distinctive French school of thought during the latter part of the nineteenth century. Its explanation was simple: in groups or crowds, persons were influenced by a "group mind" which reduced their individual autonomy; with this went the notion of *imitation* as the essential vehicle by which Man was influenced by others in his society.

The most significant figure in this movement was Gustave LeBon, best known for his work *The Crowd* (1896) in which he presented this formulation:

> The most striking peculiarity presented by a psychological crowd is the following: Whoever be the individuals that comprise it, however like or unlike be their mode of life, their occupations, their character, or their intelligence, the fact that they have been transformed into a crowd puts them in possession of a sort of collective mind which makes them feel, think, and act in a manner quite different from that in which each individual of them would deal, think, and act were he in a state of isolation (p. 27).

Earlier LeBon had postulated that Man has a natural tendency to imitate. Imitation, he said, was a social necessity which could be observed in the powerful influence of fashion. This viewpoint was elaborated by the other notable figure of the French school, Tarde, in his book *The Laws of Imitation* (1890). Historically, both Tarde and LeBon were influenced by the "principle of suggestion" which grew out of Charcot's then current work on hypnosis. To their view, crowd behavior, which they often used interchangeably with the term "group behavior," was a reflection of the suggestibility found in persons who had been hypnotized.

In his critique of Le Bon's thesis of suggestibility in crowds, Floyd Allport (1924) asserted that this interpretation places a premium on the significance of aggregation while underplaying the role of individual psychological states in "crowd actions." To Allport's view, the only new elements added to those states by the crowd situation were "an intensification of the feeling already present, and the possibility of concerted action. The individual in the crowd behaves just as he would behave alone, *only more so*" (p. 295).

Neither of the two key propositions in the views of the LeBon-Tarde school of thought—that Man had a natural propensity toward imitation, and that this operated through the presence of a group mind when individuals were together collectively—has any scientific standing today. However, their consequences remain, in that there are still those who mistakenly think of social psychology mainly as the study of crowds and the group mind. While there is an active interest in crowd behavior, as witness the experiment by Milgram *et al.* (1969) presented in the previous chapter, it is by no means a central focus of attention. An interesting presentation of some aspects of crowd behavior appears in Milgram and Toch (1968).

But why was the group-mind thesis put forward by men of acknowledged intellectual stature? Answering this in his discussion of the emergence of social psychology, Asch (1959) says that the conception of a group mind was a way of taking account of Man's social nature, and adds:

> It started with a serious problem—with the clarification of group characteristics and group membership. It had its roots in a formulation by no means strange today, namely, that one cannot understand an individual by studying him solely as an individual; one must see him in his group relations (p. 369).

Newcomb (1951) has pointed out that what the group-mind concept was intended to cover is better understood in terms of self-other perceptions as shared norms. In this respect, he says that a great shortcoming of this older viewpoint was that it "had nothing to say about the conditions under which such sharing took place" (p. 40). Where the individual gets caught up in a group or crowd, what happens, according to Newcomb, is that "what the individual wants to do and what he perceives as demanded by his role come to be identical . . . for once in his life others expect him to be exactly what he wants to be. His world of social reality perceives him precisely as he perceives himself" (p. 44). This view provides a way of putting aside the mysticism which for so long surrounded the conceptions of group and crowd behavior.

And now what of the related matter of imitation? It too has proceeded through a line of continuity to the present day. In one of the first two major textbooks in social psychology, E. A. Ross (1908) used the imitation-suggestion tradition as a key principle for his work. In the other text of that same year, William McDougall presented a social psychology built on the concept of instinct, adding a forerunner of the attitude construct of today, his conception of "sentiments."

Though Ross, a sociologist by orientation, considered imitation to be a widespread social phenomenon, McDougall from a psychological vantage point rejected any such reliance on imitation. Indeed, even within his commitment to an instinct orientation, McDougall plainly stated that an instinct of imitation does *not* exist because, as he put it:

> Imitative actions are extremely varied, for every kind of action may be imitated; there is therefore nothing specific in the nature of the imitative movements and in the nature of the sense-impressions by which the movements are excited or guided . . . most important is the fact that underlying the varieties of imitative action, there is no common affective state and no impulse-seeking satisfaction in some particular change of state . . . further, if we consider the principal varieties of imitative action, we find that all are explicable without the assumption of a special instinct of imitation (1908, pp. 106-107).

Nonetheless, in one of his later works entitled *The Group Mind* (1920), McDougall asserted that an important effect of groups is the "exaltation or intensification of emotion" which they produce in their members. He went on to say that those of lower intelligence bring members of higher intelligence down to their own level. This view has found little support from subsequent study, although it is interesting to note that it is a direct precursor of a similar position expressed by Freud in *Group Psychology and the Analysis of the Ego* (1921).

So far as is presently known, there is no generalized tendency toward imitation as a social influence process. To the contrary, the evidence suggests that imitation is selective in terms of whom we imitate and what we imitate (see Bandura and Walters, 1963; Flanders, 1968). In his critique of the doctrine of imitation, Newcomb (1950) has pointed out that no child imitates indiscriminately and that many a parent laments the fact that his child utterly fails to imitate the "correct" models set before him. Furthermore, he goes on, no individual acquires a completely conforming response to all of the "standard" behaviors of his society. Moreover, fads and fashions may appear to be good illustrations of widespread imitation, yet many fads simply fail to catch on or are short-lived, and only a few become incorporated in the culture. Finally, Newcomb concludes:

There is a considerable body of experimental evidence indicating that imitation presupposes a process of learning . . . imitation, in fact, is subject to the same range of conditions which are known to determine the many variations of learned behavior. People imitate or do not imitate, depending upon what they have learned, are capable of learning and are motivated to learn. It is this fact, probably, which accounts for the highly variable conditions under which imitation occurs (p. 11).

The concept of general imitation fails because it is overly broad and neglects the important features of learning that arise from individual motivation and perception. In a recent exhaustive review of research on imitative behavior, Flanders (1968) indicates the vast amount of complexity associated with processes underlying imitation. Among the numerous variables affecting imitative behavior are the characteristics of a "model," that is the person or persons imitated. Some of these are: the ability to control resources which are valued by the imitator, as in the case of parents vis-à-vis the child; greater status, as in prestige; and nurturance, in terms of affection.

It is factors such as these which provide a necessary foundation for an understanding of Man's social relationships. Because it, too, neglected these considerations, the doctrine of instinct proved equally unsatisfactory and eventually gave way to a more penetrating view of Man's propensities for learning within a social environment, to be considered further in Chapters 4 and 5 especially.

Social empiricism

Until the nineteenth century it was quite unusual to find systematic efforts to obtain information concerning the conditions of human life and Man's experience. The Darwinian revolution, among other forces, did however instigate several developments in this vein.

GALTON AND THE GENETICS OF MENTAL DIFFERENCES

Francis Galton, who was much taken by Darwin's views of natural selection, conducted an investigation directed especially at the genetic transmission of genius by tracing the genealogy of families whose members gained great prominence. His *Hereditary Genius,* originally published in 1869, is among his best known efforts. In some sense, Galton may be credited with the development of the study of individual mental differences, although he was inclined to a narrow focus which omitted the favorable environmental factors in the lives of his subjects. Nonetheless, Gardner Murphy (1949) has stressed that "Francis Galton grasped the implications of the evolutionary outlook for psychology and made his ingenious experimental contributions to this area of research" (p. 353).

BINET AND INTELLIGENCE TESTING

In France, during the 1890's, Alfred Binet began his attempts to develop measures of human intelligence. Working with Simon, he took as his immediate task the matter of detecting and measuring mental defects. While their eventual test of 1905 had failings, particularly in terms of standardization and the fact that some of the sub-tests were harder and others easier than they supposed, this opened the intelligence test movement and provided the forerunner of the modern IQ test. Terman's 1916 "Stanford revision," an American version, is with us even today in still more refined form known as the Stanford-Binet test. While this work said little about social effects on intelligence and could not specify the processes which produced it, it stands as a landmark in social empiricism. It provided a descriptive measure of a human characteristic and led to a fuller understanding of differentials and similarities among men.

Other works reported in 1903 and 1905 by two Americans, Kelly and Norsworthy, paralleled the Binet-Simon work. They gave sensory and motor tasks to feeble-minded children and normal children to measure ranges of performance. Though the feeble-minded youngsters tended to do distinctively less well than normal children, there was a fairly even transition from the lowest to the highest scores across both groups. "In Norsworthy's language, the feeble-minded were not a 'species'; the most intelligent of the feeble-minded could not be sharply distinguished from the least intelligent of the normal" (Murphy, 1949, p. 354). The significance of this early empirical work was of inestimable importance in terms of what it revealed about the faultiness of assumptions concerning "superior" versus "inferior" levels within the human species. Furthermore, as Gardner (1961) has observed, broad-scale use of objective intelligence tests made it clear that rich resources of intellectual capacity existed at every level of the socio-economic ladder.

COMTE AND DURKHEIM: SOCIOLOGICAL BEGINNINGS

Auguste Comte is perhaps best known for his comprehensive philosophy of the sciences, *Positive Philosophy* (1830). Among his important conceptions was the recognition that the individual develops his mental processes only through society and that he must always be considered in terms of his social setting. In contrast to other thinkers of his time, Comte also furthered a view of Man as a reasoning being. He urged a positivist approach in the scientific study of Man which represented a significant underpinning for the empirical movement.

Emile Durkheim gave an added impetus to the interrelated developments of theory and research on social behavior. His general aim was to make sociology an empirical study, and his contributions to the methodology of the social sciences were of seminal importance. True to the positivist position, Durkheim insisted that for an empirical treatment of social data it is necessary to have "social facts." He rebelled against the rationalistic approach which had characterized so much of the work of other social thinkers.

In his doctoral thesis, *Division of Labor* (1893), Durkeim had cited the increased suicide rate in the nineteenth century as an argument against the rational emphasis of the utilitarians. Following up with his famous study *Suicide* (1897), he combined statistical description and theoretical constructs to isolate factors operating to produce suicide. Durkheim cited statistics from political, religious, and family life to support his analysis, and demonstrated, for example, that the suicide rate bore a significant relationship to marital and parental status. Married persons had a lower rate than single persons and parents had a lower rate than childless couples, with the parents in large families having the lowest rate of all. He interpreted these results as demonstrating the strong preservative power of group attachments. Apart from the empirical features of this work, Durkheim employed the concept of a "collective mind" to further his view that the individual has no existence except as a member of society. While he openly rejected the psychological level of analysis as a basis for understanding social phenomena, Durkheim nonetheless created an avenue for the study of how social influences produced effects on "individual" features of human existence. His contribution to modern sociology is of redounding significance.

Two other trends reflecting social empiricism are represented by the tradition of "demography" and in the field work of anthropologists describing pre-literate cultures. Both of these involve descriptions of human attributes and the conditions of life.

Demography is the study of population characteristics including numbers of people and their distribution geographically. Its recognized areas of concern have been birth rate, death rate, and migration. Today demography constitutes a distinctive area within sociology, and is perhaps best known to the public in terms of the population census. The first national census in the United States was conducted in 1790, and since then it has been continued on a total population basis every ten years. The modern census reflects the highly diversified quality of demography today by its wider concern with many facets of human society, beyond population size and movement, such as marriage and divorce, education, employment, income, and standard of living. These and many other characteristics of the population by area and locale provide a rich pool of descriptive data about significant aspects of the human condition.

The tradition of field expeditions in anthropology, coming down from Edward Tylor in the last century, and of Bronislaw Malinowski and Franz Boas in this, also reveals a great deal about the diversity of human life. Under the guidance of George P. Murdock, the massive array of data accumulated on the cultures of the world, and on their patterns, has been codified in the form of the Yale Human Relations Area Files. Use of these materials affords a significant link to social analysis by strengthening our understanding of general patterns of life and by revealing the weakness of glib assumptions about human nature.

Social analysis

If the tradition of social empiricism can be said to provide a description of human characteristics and attributes, then social analysis represents its extension toward establishing a scientifically valid foundation for what is described. In probing beneath the descriptive data to understand the nature of causal relationships, social analysis gets closer to social processes, including those of change, by taking account of the factors which interrelate to produce social behavior.

THE BEHAVIORAL SCIENCES

In the contemporary scene, the use of social analysis is characteristic of what have come to be called the "behavioral sciences." These are psychology, sociology, cultural anthropology, and to some extent political science and economics. The term "behavioral science" is a relatively new one in our vocabulary. We can describe it in one sense as a body of knowledge regarding certain describable conditions in the human being and/or his environment which lead to certain describable consequences in his actions, and in another sense as techniques or methodologies which typify the study of conditions leading to these consequences. A very comprehensive coverage of work in the behavioral sciences is provided in the helpful book by Berelson and Steiner (1964) entitled *Human Behavior: An Inventory of Scientific Findings.*

LEVELS OF ANALYSIS

All of the behavioral sciences are to some degree concerned with social behavior, though they approach it at different levels and in terms of the specifics of varying social institutions. By levels, we mean the essential units of study. In the case of psychology, it is clear that the individual is the prime focus of attention. The psychologist is concerned with the differences as well as with the commonality in human behavior. The fact that some psychologists may also study animal behavior reflects a comparative approach which ultimately can have implications for humans. Sociology tends to be interested in behavior at the level of groups and organizations or social institutions; though these are comprised of individuals, the major thrust of study tends to be on the nature of social-structural features as they affect social behavior, for example, in terms of social class or the structure of organizations. Cultural anthropologists, sometimes called ethnologists, direct their attention to the cultural or societal level of analysis as do some sociologists. In the case of political science and economics, the study of social behavior is conducted within the context of political and economic social institutions. In fact, however, there is currently less separation between these disciplines because of an increasing adoption of a social psychological framework for analysis.

A SOCIAL PSYCHOLOGICAL FRAMEWORK

Among the more distinctive trends in the behavioral sciences today is the degree to which they reflect a coming together for purposes of empirical study, very often within a social psychological framework. By this we mean that they employ the variables and techniques which have been found useful in studying the relationship of the individual to his social environment. For example, roles represent describable social practices, in the form of appropriate behaviors; but in terms of underlying individual processes, they also have meaning as psychological expectations. Similarly, organizations may be established according to the structure of a formal organization chart, yet be far more affected by interpersonal relationships determined as well by the personalities of those involved.

Today we can find a good deal of research cutting across disciplinary lines and employing this framework. In the case of voter behavior, for instance, Angus Campbell and a research team composed of social psychologists, sociologists, and political scientists study such matters as the psychological basis of party identification through survey research on presidential elections (*The American Voter*, 1960). S. M. Lipset, by training a sociologist, has been involved in studies of political loyalty and participation (*Political Man*, 1960). A number of political scientists have made major contributions to an understanding of political attitudes and personality, among them Fred Greenstein *(Personality and Politics*, 1969) and Robert E. Lane (*Political Thinking and Consciousness*, 1969). Hadley Cantril, a social psychologist, had conducted research on the psychological sub-structure of political affiliation (*The Politics of Despair*, 1958 and Free and Cantril, *The Political Beliefs of Americans*, 1967). A psychologist, George Katona, is well known for his extensive research on consumer attitudes of optimism and pessimism as these relate to buying practices (*The Powerful Consumer*, 1960, and

The Mass Consumption Society, 1964). Furthermore, the physiological correlates of social behavior are being increasingly studied, as is exemplified by the volume *Psychobiological Approaches to Social Behavior* edited by Leiderman and Shapiro (1964).

Social analysis in the twentieth century has been shaped by a number of distinctive theoretical contributions which go beyond the tradition of social philosophy to lend themselves more readily to scientific test through research. Accompanying these was a technological advance in measurement procedures and in statistical analysis. Even more dramatic is the computer revolution. Thus, the interrelationship of theory and empirical efforts was established early as a characteristic feature in the evolution of social psychology, and its potential remains considerable. To better understand this trend, we will briefly review several major approaches to social behavior which have had a significant impact on social psychology today.

Forerunners of modern social psychology

In the more than half-century since 1908, when the first two social psychology textbooks in English appeared, profound changes have occurred to displace the central theoretical views they presented. As noted earlier, E. A. Ross, writing in a sociological tradition, afforded considerable weight to the imitation-suggestion conception in accounting for social behavior; William McDougall, within a psychological tradition, presented a view heavily flavored with the concept of instincts. Both of these views proved unsatisfactory in themselves, at least partly because of their quality of overstatement. But neither man was so committed to a singular view as to reject other modes of accounting for social behavior. Thus, in association with his thinking, Ross was interested in the interpersonal effects of one person on another, and McDougall—whose book influenced more than a generation of thought through many successive revisions—helped to further the concept of attitude.

The instinct idea had been so overblown, it would have fallen in any case of its own weight. But in 1926, a devastating critique by L. L. Bernard, the eminent sociologist, helped to expose its weaknesses. It received a further push from the burgeoning of "behaviorism" in psy-

chology, beginning in the 1920's. The leader of the behaviorist movement was John B. Watson who renounced both the doctrine of mind
and of instincts as a valid basis for psychological research. He asserted
(Watson, 1919, 1925) that the proper study of psychology was behavior
and that the task of the psychologist was to determine the relationship
between stimuli and responses, the so-called S-R link. His viewpoint
was heavily environmentalist insofar as he felt that *all* behaviors, including social behavior, were learned through experience.

Within the framework of behaviorism, Floyd Allport in 1924 published a text in social psychology in which he emphatically stated that
group concepts were unnecessary for explaining individual behavior in
groups. To his view, there was no psychology of groups, but only a
psychology of individuals. He contended that individuals reacted to
group pressures in terms of their own motivations or perceptions and
not because of a "group mind" (see p. 48 above). Yet, he felt that
the context of the group, and in general the social situation, had an effect in shaping the motivations and perceptions of individuals and, in
this regard, he acknowledged the importance of attitudes. His viewpoint had a profound effect on social psychology at the time and led to
a line of systematic experimentation in social psychology.

SOCIAL FACILITATION

Though the first laboratory of experimental psychology was established
at Leipzig in 1879 by Wilhelm Wundt, the research conducted there
for several decades was almost entirely in the broad area of psychophysics, e.g. optical perception, discrimination of weights, and other
aspects of sensory functioning. What makes this at all remarkable is
that in the late 1800's the necessary techniques were available to study
social components of these and other phenomena, but they were not
employed. Ironically, Wundt himself had long been interested in culture's affect on behavior, culminating in his ten-volume work, *Völkerpsychologie,* published between 1910 and 1920. Also noteworthy is the
link he had with modern anthropology through one of his students,
Franz Boas, who became an eminent cultural anthropologist and the
major professor for Ruth Benedict and Margaret Mead when they were
graduate students at Columbia in the 1920's (Clausen, 1968a, p. 41).
Though Wundt's stature as a scientist was very great, he evidently did

not infuse his work in the laboratory with his other more "social" interest in culture.

It was not until 1920 that Moede, in his *Experimentelle Massenpsychologie,* reported on a series of demonstrations which he had conducted at Leipzig on the presence of other subjects as a factor in individual performance on a standard psychological task. Earlier, Triplett (1897) published what is widely considered to have been the first self-consciously social-psychological experiment. Briefly, it involved the effects of competition on the average time it took children to complete 150 winds of a fishing reel. Working alone, and then competing in pairs against each other, Triplett found that performance was improved under the competition condition. Subsequently, Münsterberg (1914) reported results which showed that knowing the judgments of stimuli others made affected the individual's own judgments of them, and this provided an additional impetus to further experimental work in social psychology.

Floyd Allport is credited with having developed the concept of "social facilitation" in his 1924 textbook, though the research just noted provided a backdrop for that development. Earlier, in 1920, he published the results of a set of experiments on "coaction." He had his subjects work separately, in cubicles, or around a table, on various tasks. Comparing the performance of the same subjects on these tasks, he found that working in groups facilitated performance on some, but inhibited it on others. The most notable exception to improved performance under group conditions was in a problem-solving task which involved refuting incorrect syllogisms. Unlike the routine tasks of multiplication or vowel cancellation, here subjects were asked to provide relatively unique solutions which could be miscued by the wrong solutions of other subjects. Subsequent work by Goodwin Watson (1928) and Marjorie Shaw (1932) followed up on the question of whether individuals or groups did better on a task. Their findings indicated that performance varied with the task and situational conditions enough so that the primary issue was unresolved, though the way was open for more specific research questions.

In a review of some of this work, Zajonc (1965) concludes that the presence of others constitutes a source of arousal, but that the effects of this aroused state will depend on the nature of the persons' interaction. A distinction is required, he says, between audience effects and coacting effects, which influence performance and learning differently. The generalization which Zajonc feels lends meaning to these results is that the presence of others as spectators or as coacting partners increases the probability of *dominant responses*. Thus, in learning new material, the presence of an audience serves as a handicap, since the dominant response is not yet correct; in performing something already well learned, the audience facilitates a dominant response, which is more likely to be the correct one.

ATTITUDE MEASUREMENT

In this period, the measurement of attitudes also gained a footing through the work on "social distance" by the sociologist, E. S. Bogardus (1925), and the attitude-scaling technique developed by the psychologist, L. L. Thurstone. This topic is considered more fully in Chapter 6.

By "social distance" Bogardus meant the degree to which a person would be willing to admit a person of another group to more immediate contact with him, e.g. from "admit to my country" to "admit to marriage in my family." Today this work finds its extension in scaling procedures which determine a person's position on a continuum, usually of approval or disapproval, as in the Guttman scale. Thurstone's work encouraged the development of attitude scales which involved "weighting" attitudinal items on favorability. Illustrating this, Thurstone and Chave (1929) constructed a scale of attitudes toward religion which included items ranging from "high" to "low" favorability.

In the early 1930's attitude research was further facilitated through the development by Rensis Likert of a simpler form of attitude scaling which is still widely utilized today. All of these procedures relied on the advances in statistical methods which were becoming available at the time. These gave greater impetus to the use of subtler research designs and to the testing of hypotheses through refined statistical inference.

From these beginnings, an incalculable amount of research on attitudes has made this area a very lively one in the contemporary field. One landmark of sorts was attained with the publication two decades ago of *The Authoritarian Personality* (Adorno, Frenkel-Brunswik, Levinson, and Sanford, 1950). Among other things, it brought attitude research into the study of ideology as a component of personality. The "F Scale," a Likert-type measure of authoritarianism (the "F" is for Fascism), was found to be correlated with other psychodynamic qualities, such as mental rigidity, anxiety, and denial, apart from its essential measurement of ethnic prejudice. In the few years following the book's arrival on the scene, and continuing for many years since, a great volume of research with the F Scale has been reported (see Titus and Hollander, 1957; Christie and Cook, 1958). Though there are deficiencies in the original scale, the importance of this line of work, especially for understanding personality factors in social behavior, has been considerable. Several items from the F Scale are presented as part of the discussion of attitude scales in the next chapter (see pp. 107-108).

INTERACTIONISM

During the same era, others were concerning themselves with the social interaction of individuals. George Herbert Mead (1934; Strauss, 1964), a leading social psychologist, gave expression to a set of conceptions which led to what has come to be called "interactionism." His essential idea was that social interaction was not a literal matter of behavior alone but was enhanced by the capacity to "take the role of the other." The day-to-day relationships between people, he said, were based on their understanding of each other's role. Thus, he considered that we could go beyond awareness of our own behavior to a sense of what is dictated for a person in a role with which we are interrelated, a "reciprocal role." To take one illustration, if a person applies to a bank for a loan and is refused that loan by a bank official, he does not necessarily think of that official as unkind. The behavior usually is *not* seen as a consequence of the other's personal inclinations but as a *result of role*. Hence, in some symbolic sense his position is understood in terms of other demands made on his behavior, beyond personal inclination.

The fact that individuals are able to imagine themselves in the place of another, and to even see themselves as others might see them, was Mead's way of dealing with Man's capacity to transcend his own self and have experiences from a broader vantage point. This quality of human relationships was also very congenial to the thinking of another prominent sociologist of the time, Charles Cooley (1909, 1922). He contended that individuals were able to experience social influences from various group sources in an imaginative way. This has its counterpart today in the "reference group" affiliation concept mentioned earlier. Cooley developed the concept of the "looking-glass self," conveying the idea of how we believe others see us. This was an early forerunner of the considerable emphasis today on the self-concept. It is also related somewhat to the importance McDougall attached to the "sentiment of self-regard" in human affairs (see Chapter 10).

Both Mead and Cooley gave prominent weight to the individual's reactions to symbolically realized phenomena, quite apart from actual external stimuli of the moment, and thus their position was distinct from that of the "behaviorists." There was a further difference which had its effect on the development of social psychology. The behaviorists tended to encourage the experimental method and this gave further impetus to the expansion of experimentation on social behavior in the 1920's. The "interaction" movement of that time did not have an experimental tradition but emphasized the refinement of theory; research in this framework was to come later. There was, however, one line of research on groups which had some of the quality of "interactionism." This was in the work of J. L. Moreno on "sociometry" beginning in the 1930's.

SOCIOMETRY

Moreno's most important conception was the idea that person-to-person relations, especially *choice and rejection,* were central features of life. An important element in sociometry, as the name suggests, is a measurement technique for graphically revealing the attraction patterns in a group. These diagrams are called "sociograms," exemplified by the one shown in Figure 2.2 which illustrates a sociometric "star," "isolate," and "clique."

As a psychiatrist on the staff of a school for delinquent girls, Moreno (1934) diagrammed their friendship patterns with his procedure. He found, as one instance, that the choice of friends within a given group remained fairly stable, with over 90 per cent of the choices the same after three months, thus indicating a considerable reliability to his method. His sociometric procedure also provided interesting confirmation of the widening gulf between children of the opposite sex during the primary school years. While he found that 25 per cent of the

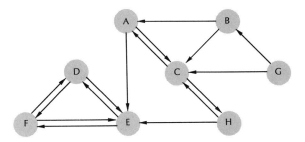

Figure 2.2: Sociogram illustrating patterns of attraction in a group of eight persons where each chooses two whom he most likes. Person *C* is a sociometric "star" chosen by four persons. Person *G* is an "isolate" who is unchosen by the others. Reciprocated choices occur where arrows are parallel in opposite directions. Persons *D*, *E*, and *F* are a "clique" who all reciprocate each other's choices.

choices for a companion among kindergarten children cut across sex, by the fourth grade that figure was only 3 per cent, and even by the eighth grade it had only risen to 8 per cent. Others have used sociometric techniques in a wide variety of settings, including a study of the attraction patterns among residents of an entire New England village by Lundberg and Stule (1938). They interviewed 256 persons there, and found only three cases, all older people, who were isolates, without friends. Twenty-nine respondents mentioned no friends in the village, but had friends in the adjoining area; thirteen of these respondents actually were chosen as friends by other villagers. A great many people had just one or two friends, when reciprocal choices (mentioning and being mentioned by the same person) were studied. The sociometric "star" of the village was a wealthy widow, of an old family, who had been generous in her donations to village undertakings. She was mentioned as a friend by seventeen villagers, but she herself named only one person, a local physician, as her friend.

Other extensions of sociometry (see Moreno, 1960) have become incorporated in "peer rating" and "peer nomination" measurement procedures for assessing an individual's standing in a group, in terms of how others rate him as a co-worker or a leader, for example. Furthermore, Moreno is responsible for the development of "psychodrama," a technique for the treatment of mental disorders through the reconstruction and acting out in a group of particularly significant events in one's life, with others including patients and clinical staff members taking various roles in the dramatization. Another facet of his prodigious work with groups is the "sociodrama," a technique involving a comparable procedure of role-enactment with nondisturbed persons interested in developing greater awareness of their social interactions. Moreno also founded a journal, *Sociometry*, now published under the auspices of the American Sociological Association as "A Journal of Research in Social Psychology."

NATURALISTIC STUDIES OF GROUPS

A number of other notable developments were occurring in the study of groups in the first half of this century. Though they did not share in a single system or employ a given procedure, as in the case of sociometry, these efforts yielded a number of rich leads. Prominent among this early work was the landmark study by Thomas and Znaniecki (1920) entitled *The Polish Peasant in Europe and America*. This enormous enterprise was no less than a multiple case history of the adjustment to migration of large numbers of Poles coming to America. These investigators provided data which revealed the potent influence of the social group on the behavior and attitudes of the individuals comprising it. The concept of "definition of the situation" which they advanced was shown to be of considerable importance in separating the observer's view of a situation from the way that the *persons actively participating in that situation defined it*. Moreover, the work of Thomas and Znaniecki was directly relevant to the growing interest in values and attitudes, which they treated as intertwined, with values both undergirding and giving direction to the expression of attitudes.

Thrasher's study entitled *The Gang* (1927) was another groundbreaking effort which exemplified what has been called the "Chicago School" of field research. His work demonstrated the attractiveness of the peer group as a source for norms and roles, and also how much adolescents depended on peer group approval. The size of the gang was also important; if it grew too large, Thrasher found that, when the gang met, experiences were more difficult to share and cohesiveness was reduced. As a general rule, the smaller gangs were more tightly knit and had a greater impact as reference groups.

One more example of a significant early study of groups in a natural environment is research begun in the late 1920's and early 1930's at the Hawthorne plant of the Western Electric Company in New Jersey. At the outset, in 1927, six girls who assembled relays were separated from the large shop and placed in a test room divided from the main department by a partition eight feet high. The intent was to investigate the effect on their output of variations in lighting, rest pauses, hours of work, and methods of payment.

The results were perplexing. Every change that was introduced brought an increase in productivity, even if it represented a reversion to an earlier condition of work. What ultimately appeared to account for this enhancement effect was the sense of social cohesion that developed among these workers, *not* the conditions that were being studied. A brief but thorough account of this work is reported by Homans (1965), and a critique by Carey (1967).

It was then that the investigators, under the direction of Elton Mayo, turned their attention to the "human relations" aspect of this phenomenon. Most importantly, they found how little management knew about the attitudes of employees toward work conditions, and especially how unaware management was of the work group's standards, particularly concerning what was felt to be a proper day's work. The longer-range consequences of the Hawthorne studies lie in the opening wedge they represented for the human relations movement in industry. The term "Hawthorne Effect" is still widely used to mean the alterations in behavior and in attitudes which may occur in research subjects when they are self-consciously aware of having been selected and separated from others to be studied. This phenomenon is a forerunner of "demand characteristics" and other biasing effects considered in Chapter 3.

EXPERIMENTATION ON THE PRODUCTION OF SOCIAL NORMS

Following Floyd Allport's (1920, 1924) earlier experimentation on social facilitation, a major endeavor in the 1930's was Muzafer Sherif's (1935) research on the production of social norms. Arthur Jenness (1932), a student of Allport's, had conducted an experiment which derived from the Münsterberg research, already noted, on the effects of shared judgments. Jenness had students judge the number of beans in a bottle, then discuss this with others to arrive at a single judgment, after which they made a second judgment alone which indicated a shift toward the group's standard.

The distinctive element in Sherif's work was his attempt to study the creation of a group norm under controlled laboratory conditions. His experiment was planned to allow measures of judgments by subjects before, during, and after the group phase. Moreover, he deliberately chose a task that was "ambiguous" insofar as it lacked the element of objective verification. In short, it increased the subjects' need for "social reality," in the sense of a reliance on others.

Sherif approached "social norms" as both: (1) products of social interaction; and (2) stimuli which are represented to any person who is a member of a group with those norms. In his experiment, Sherif made use of the so-called "autokinetic effect." A spot of light projected in a totally darkened room will be seen to move, and this phenomenon is subject to wide individual differences. Such apparent movement

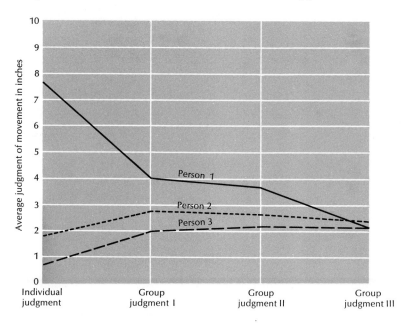

Figure 2.3: Illustration of convergence in average judgment of light's movement for three persons in the autokinetic situation, beginning with individual judgments alone. (From Figure 6, p. 103, in *The Psychology of Social Norms* by M. Sherif. Harper & Row, 1936.)

is brought about by the fact that our eyes are never completely still; they make small, but continuous shifts. Sherif puts subjects in a darkened room alone in the first phase of his experiment. Over many trials, each was asked to look at the spot of light and report the direction and degree of movement. Then each subject was taken back to the room again, but this time in the company of others. Reporting their judgments aloud as they watched the spot of light, they soon converged toward a group standard of apparent movement. This "convergence effect" is shown in Figure 2.3 for three individuals making judgments alone and then at three intervals in the presence of others.

After they had had this experience with the group, Sherif studied subjects again alone and found that they now retained the group norm rather than their own private standard as a basis for judging movement, thus demonstrating both aspects of norms. This work did much to encourage further experimentation on the psychological aspects of group phenomena. It also showed the harmonious way in which group concepts, like social norms, could be subjected to psychological analysis.

GROUP INFLUENCES ON ATTITUDES

In the late 1930's Theodore Newcomb conducted a study which further substantiated group influences on normative attitudes. He pursued his research among students in the real-life environment at Bennington College, a small women's college with a heavy emphasis on the humanities. Bennington was among those colleges in the forefront of a liberal political trend, and, because so many of its students came from politically conservative homes, Newcomb sought to assess the effects of Bennington's campus community on their attitudes. With attitude measures taken at the beginning of college, Newcomb studied these students over a four-year period, while simultaneously obtaining similar data from students at other colleges for use as a comparison. He found that there were significant shifts toward more liberal political views over the four years at Bennington. Employing sociometric techniques, he showed that social acceptance within the campus community was linked with approved attitudes. The most popular girls tended to be at the upper end of the distribution on the liberal political attitudes. Of particular interest was the conflict this posed for some students between parental attitudes and those of the college-group. The long-range consequences of this have been interestingly revealed in recent follow-up research (Newcomb, 1963), in which the women from the original study were contacted more than two decades later. Newcomb found that the liberally inclined women had been selective in marrying men who were also liberal politically, even though they tended to be drawn from the same upper-class, conservative backgrounds. One way to maintain attitudes, Newcomb concludes, is to select as a mate someone who shares those attitudes.

LEWINIAN "FIELD THEORY"

Perhaps the single most important theoretical contribution in the more immediate history of social psychology comes from the thinking of Kurt Lewin. It was Lewin in the 1930's who established a whole new school of social-psychological thought embedded in his concept of the "psychological field." An excellent recent source on Lewin's life and work is the book by Alfred Marrow (1969).

Lewin held that social situations, including conditions in a group, represented themselves in individual psychological states. Interaction theory, broadly speaking, had encompassed *past* social interaction as it produced symbolic relationships. Lewin's "field theory," on the other hand, was more concerned as a starting point with the individual's *present* psychological states, particularly perceptions of the moment, as they affected his responses. He was, in short, less interested in how these states came about. While behaviorism had largely disposed of any necessity for the attitude concept, attitudes were vital in Lewin's theory as "perceptual sets." Thus the content of mind was supremely relevant in Lewin's approach. He said: "Every psychological event depends upon the state of the person and at the same time on the environment, although their relative importance is different in different cases" (1936, p. 12).

An exemplification of Lewin's work is provided in the influential experiment he did with Lippitt and White (1939) on social "climates." Briefly, in a natural setting they created a number of boys' clubs, involving ten- and eleven-year-olds, which met periodically over a several week period. Adult leaders were experimentally introduced in these groups to create climates of "authoritarian," "democratic," and "laissez-faire" leadership by their behavior. Using techniques of observation and sociometry, they studied the effects on the groups produced by these styles of leadership. The results of this experiment indicated clear differences in the effects of the psychological climate induced by these styles. Authoritarian leadership, for example, produced passive acceptance of the leader, but it was accompanied by a great deal of aggressiveness toward the other group members, especially in the absence of the leader. In general, a major consquence of

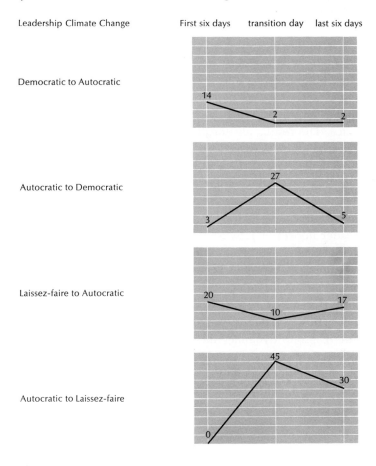

Figure 2.4: Index of average amount of "horseplay" observed in groups changing from one leadership climate to another. (Based on data from Lippitt and White, 1947.)

authoritarian leadership was to place a tight lid on spontaneous reactions among the boys, such as "horseplay."

An interesting illustration of the release of this kind of activity as a result of shifts in leadership style, is shown in Figure 2.4. The data in this figure reveal the average amount of horseplay among the boys during the first six days, under one kind of leadership style, and then for a transition day and the last six days, all under a different style. On the whole, horseplay in the initial period is lowest under authoritarian leadership and highest under laissez-faire leadership, but this "lowness" is purchased at a price. When the lid is off, a dramatic upsurge in activity occurs. Going from a climate that is autocratic to one that is either democratic or laissez-faire produces this effect, though it is highest and stays highest in the autocratic to laissez-faire change. This research demonstrates Lewin's point that individual and group behavior depend upon the properties of the situation and the "field" conditions they produce. The results also neatly reveal how past experience conditions expectations and actions in new situations—as seen in the effects of shifts in leadership. But there is a "cultural effect" in these findings. When Meade (1967) did a similar experiment in India, he found that the grade-school boys he studied reacted less well to the democratic leadership pattern.

The broader impact of Lewin's work was especially felt in opening the potentialities for experimentation on small-scale "social systems" in the laboratory. Its consequences were of immeasurable importance to the coming of age of social psychology. One important outgrowth was the development of research on "group dynamics." Lewin felt it was entirely within reason to study the properties of groups; an important feature of group dynamics therefore was the groundwork it provided for the introduction of methods for inducing group-based effects upon individuals. Experimentation today in social psychology derives a good deal from Lewin's work, though a concern with elements of interaction is increasingly in evidence in such research as well.

Current trends in social psychology

Each of the traditions we have been considering has had an important though varying impact on the current field of social psychology. There have been continuing advances in both the theoretical conceptions begun in social philosophy and the research approaches growing out of social empiricism. Today there are many trends in social psychology, at the level of social analysis, which allow for the testing and refining of hypotheses concerned with the underpinnings of social influence.

One trend of continuing consequence is what Klineberg (1954) has called the "interpenetration of general psychology and social psychology" in terms of an examination of the manner in which social factors enter into the psychological processes of motivation, perception, and learning, and correspondingly, how older concepts from social psychology such as imitation and suggestion can be understood in terms of these processes.

The use of experimental procedures in highly controlled "laboratory" settings is another trend which has continued. Influence phenomena exemplified by conformity and leadership have been increasingly subjected to study under these conditions. This has provided further insight into an understanding of such phenomena in terms of social motivation and the processes occurring in social interaction.

In a related way, there has been an increasing trend toward the study of aspects of this social learning process that bear upon "socialization" in childhood. How the youngster comes to have his psychological attributes shaped by his social milieu is a central focus of this work; this also has important implications for features of personality development. Such work has been extended as well to cross-cultural studies emphasizing the diversity of social demands as well as their commonality.

Among the other lines of new work in the field is the innovative experimentation on factors influencing pro-social or "helping" behavior in emergencies. This research is related as well to interest in the moral development of children.

The analysis of cognitive processes, including perceptual and attitudinal correlates of behavior, occupies a considerable amount of attention in the contemporary scene. It is exemplified by continuing work on the formation and interrelationship of attitudes, and the influence effects of mass communications in terms of attitude change. There also is considerable attention being given to interpersonal attitudes, in terms of attributions of motives and attitudes to others, and to one's self, from observed behavior. Studies of the psychological features of language, represented in work on "psycholinguistics," constitute another lively area within the cognitive sphere.

A persisting feature of the field has been the interest in applications of social-psychological knowledge to social problems. Such research is being done in the areas of prejudice, morale, inter-group and international relations, urban life, and social movements, among others.

SUMMARY

There have been three distinct stages in achieving knowledge about social behavior. Each leads to the next and all are embodied somehow in contemporary study. They are: *social philosophy*, dating from antiquity and characterized by speculation without factual verification; *social empiricism*, originating in the nineteenth century and involving the gathering of facts largely of a descriptive form; and *social analysis*, a twentieth-century development aimed at understanding the relationships underlying social phenomena.

Social philosophy was concerned for a long time with the issue of what is "human nature" and whether its characteristics were "good" or "bad." As posed, these questions were difficult to resolve since the evidence was conflicting and support could be mustered for either view of Man. Moreover, philosophical viewpoints tended to offer a static conception of human conduct with instincts such as power, imitation, and pleasure each invoked as the single, all-embracing explanation of behavior. These instinctual views proved faulty on several grounds, but especially because of their disregard of the dynamic quality of human learning within the experiences provided by the social environment. The failings in this kind of excessive generality apply as well to the contentions of Social Darwinism, which emphasizes conflict and competition as implicit features of life, and to Freud's assertions regarding "innate aggressiveness" and the "death instinct." Other unsupported conjectures in the more immediate background of social psychology were those regarding imitation and the "group mind" advanced by Gustave LeBon and Gabriel Tarde.

Social empiricism came about in part as a response to the Darwinian era and its focus on the evolution of Man and his qualities. Galton, with his work on genetic transmission, and Binet, who developed the first standardized test of human intelligence, were in the vanguard of this movement. Others who provided a foundation for empirical study of the qualities and conditions of human life were the sociologists Comte and Durkheim and the cultural anthropologists Tylor, Malinowski, and Boas.

Social analysis, as a way of probing beneath the surface of description alone, is a distinctive feature of the twentieth-century "behavioral sciences." These may be considered to be psychology, sociology, cultural anthropology, and to some extent political science and economics. While these fields differ in their level of analysis, each may employ a social psychological framework of analysis within or across disciplines.

Modern social psychology grows out of traditions which are founded in psychology and sociology, the first emphasizing attributes of the individual and the other, qualities of the social environment. The experimental emphasis of John Watson and his behavioristic movement in psychology had a profound effect on the development of experimentation in social psychology, particularly through the pioneering work of Floyd Allport. The measurement of attitudes, the development of concepts regarding social interaction, and the study of groups through techniques of sociometry and by experimentation were other important historical landmarks. Bogardus, Cooley, Mead, Moreno, and Sherif were among the great contributors in these efforts. Lewin's Field Theory, which underscored the individual's perception of his world, was an especially significant departure for much current research. Today, social psychology stands as an empirical field encompassing studies of group processes and learning through interaction, the socialization of the young including social effects on personality, attitudinal and perceptual elements in language and communication, attitude change and mass communications, and inter-group as well as international relations, among other problems.

SUGGESTED READINGS

From E. P. Hollander and R. G. Hunt (Eds.) *Current perspectives in social psychology*. (3rd ed.) New York: Oxford University Press, 1971.

2. Solomon E. Asch: *The data of social psychology*
4. Robert W. White: *Motivation reconsidered: the concept of competence*
10. John W. Gardner: *Individuality, commitment, and meaning*

SELECTED REFERENCES

*Berelson, B. R., & Steiner, G. *Human behavior: an inventory of scientific findings*. New York: Harcourt, Brace & World, 1964.

*Freud, S. *Group psychology and the analysis of the ego*. New York: Bantam Books, 1960. (Originally published in German, 1921.)

*Heilbroner, R. L. *The worldly philosophers*. (Rev. ed.) New York: Simon & Schuster, 1961.

*Kardiner, A., & Preble, E. *They studied man*. New York: New American Library, Mentor Book, 1963.

Marrow, A. J. *The practical theorist: the life and work of Kurt Lewin*. New York: Basic Books, 1969.

*Montagu, A. (Ed.) *Man and aggression*. New York: Oxford Univ. Press, 1968.

3

Theory and method in social psychology

The heart of any scientific activity rests in the important relationship between theories and the methods used to verify them. A theory provides several functions in science. A major one is explanation, achieved primarily by organizing information into coherent relationships. However interesting it may be, a "fact" by itself must be related to other facts before it has scientific meaning. Another function of a theory is to point the way toward the kind of questions to ask about facts and phenomena.

Opinions do not help to settle questions of fact, nor do they help us to understand the "why" of events. Furthermore, people will sometimes disagree about what constitutes fact. An inevitable problem surrounds what set of facts, from what source, will be acceptable as *evidence*. A cardinal task in science accordingly is to provide objective evidence through established methods of research. In this chapter we will be considering ideas which guide research—theories—and the methods used in social psychology to test them.

The essence of theory

Theories are quite purposeful and practical. For one thing, they direct our thinking by indicating relationships, explanations, and significant questions. They also lead to effective technology by suggesting what

75

results should follow from some process. Furthermore, in *testing the hypotheses* growing out of a theory, we are able to refine it through the study of research findings, thus achieving a theory which is more explanatory.

Basically, a theory consists of one or more functional statements or propositions that treat the relationship of variables so as to account for a phenomenon or set of phenomena. The implicit selection of some variables as relevant to these phenomena, and the exclusion of others, also points up the usefulness of theory in refining some distinctions and eliminating others. For example, in the social psychology of leadership it has become apparent that a distinction is required between competence in handling a group task, on the one hand, and popularity on the other. In thus making a new distinction, a theory can yield further understanding of a social process. This refinement, however, calls for an additional procedure for measurement which necessarily poses a methodological requirement.

As we shall see, a simple analogy can serve as a theory, just as a complex mathematical formulation can. A theory may also vary in its degree of comprehensiveness in representing the phenomenon with which it deals. Thus, it may be too inclusive, insofar as it includes unnecessary details, as in the outmoded phlogiston theory of combustion. Or it may be incomplete in the sense of leaving out variables of relevance. One case of this latter failure to account for social behavior was the long absence of concern for the degree of an individual's motivation to identify personally with a group; this is now rectified by the more recent conception of reference-group affiliation. The measurement of this variable has aided considerably our understanding of otherwise confusing findings regarding the effects of group membership.

While not usually thought of as theories, proverbs growing out of simple "folk wisdom" provide us with statements of a functional sort which can be used to illustrate the qualities of theory. For example, note the proposition in "out of sight, out of mind" and in its opposite number, "absence makes the heart grow fonder." Both of these proverbs make assertions about personal contact as a variable affecting interpersonal attraction. In the first case, the assertion is essentially that as contact decreases, individuals develop weaker attraction; the other is essentially an opposite proposition. As with many other pairs of proverbs one could cite, these are in direct conflict. Moreover, neither statement by itself is complete in accounting for outcomes. To construct a more adequate theory explaining the phenomenon requires the introduction of still other variables, including some about the relevant relationship and attributes of the individuals involved and the alternatives available to them. This essential inadequacy of proverbs points up the larger problem of any theory which suffers from incompleteness.

Since it is also possible for a theory to be loaded with excess baggage, unneeded for an adequate explanation, there is value attached to simplicity of explanation. This quality is what is referred to by the term "parsimonious" when discussing a theory's merit. But given the complexities of social behavior, the too ready tendency toward simple analogy can be a treacherous pitfall. Analogies by themselves, however parsimonious, often prove as misleading as proverbs. Society is *not* one enormous "organism"; nor is a government a "ship of state," in the literal sense of a captain and crew; and in actuality increased supply does not push up consumption like a "hydraulic pump."

Because theories make assertions about the relationship between certain variables only, they often lead, as we have said, to a selective emphasis. Though selectivity can be a limitation when, for example, we overlook some important factor, it is indispensable in guiding research and the interpretation of evidence. There are several such emphases in theories of social behavior to which we now turn our attention.

SOME THEORETICAL DISTINCTIONS IN SOCIAL PSYCHOLOGY

Generally speaking, theories of social behavior may emphasize the *characteristics of a person growing out of his past experience* or the *characteristics of his immediate social situation.* The first emphasis is clearly in keeping with a psychological tradition, while the second is somewhat more indicative of a sociological one. We have already noted how each emphasis contributed to early formulations of social psychology. Apart from their origins, though, each is useful in giving direction to research; nevertheless, we should be aware that at the extreme either one is an oversimplification. Their main characteristics can be briefly summed up as follows:

> • Research emphasizing the *individual* views social behavior as being intimately tied to such personal charac-

teristics as achievement motivation, self-esteem, rigidity, or authoritarianism, to name just a few. These are essentially *qualities of personality* which vary from person to person. *They are measured to study the typical responses of a person across various social situations and relationships.*

• Research emphasizing the *situation* looks upon individuals as being influenced by pressures emanating from the demands of the present social structure including the expectations of others. A good deal of research on conformity exemplifies this view of social behavior as being readily altered by *operative factors* in a situation, such as a group's cohesiveness or its social structure. *These situational factors are measured to study their effect in producing typical responses across persons in the same situation.*

These two emphases are no longer quite as important in producing distinctive research as they once were, since it is quite possible to embody both within a given study. Today, there are clear evidences of precisely this closure of approach. A particularly apt illustration is to be seen in work relating the individual's perception of his world to behavior. While Lewin conceived of the "psychological field" with particular regard to the perception of the present situation, others have looked at it in the more historic sense of how the individual *comes* to see his situation as he does. But in either case, subjective perception appears to provide one key to social behavior. Its implications are conveniently summed up in W. I. Thomas's classic dictum that "situations defined as real are real in their consequences." This means that since people "define" a situation, their perception of it represents a source of "reality" on which to base action. Elements of a person's situation thus take on significance for him in line with his past experience as well as his anticipated gains. Hence, both personality characteristics and properties of the situation are mutually involved in social behavior.

PERSONALITY AND THE SITUATION

Human behavior is highly dependent upon learning from interaction with others. Therefore, people come to any situation with a history of interactions in other situations. This past contributes to those characteristics of behavior, a personality, which gives each person uniqueness. Accordingly, past experience affects present action through the impact it has had on characteristic ways of responding.

Consider this as an example. The situational emphasis, illustrated in Sherif (1935), looks upon conformity as a feature of the uncertainty or ambiguity of stimuli presented to individuals. It is a common finding that an ambiguous social situation increases reliance on the judgments of others because individuals are less sure of their own perceptions. This encourages the need for "social reality," i.e. reality as other individuals see it or corroborate it. Though this need is instigated by a property of the situation, there are nevertheless individual differences in "tolerance of ambiguity," which may become relevant, too.

There are three ways in which the nature of "the situation" may be defined, and these are often used interchangeably. It is usful to consider their differing qualities, if only briefly. One usage is oriented toward *social structure*, with regard to status and formal role demands. Another usage emphasizes a dominant *psychological condition,* as in "ambiguous situation," or "competitive situation," though obviously the condition may exist as a consequence of structure in the first place; however, it is the emphasis on the psychological components of a social situation which makes for distinctive social psychological study. A third use of the situational term is in connection with a literal time-space locus, what Barker (1968) calls a *behavior setting*. He is interested in the ecological, person-to-situation relationships which may be structural as well as psychological.

Going beyond structure to the *psychological conditions* which it may induce, consider "situations" where fairly uniform effects are produced by a factor such as threat. An illustration would be in an organization which is in for a major reshuffle. Great uncertainty prevails about who and what will be affected. The stake people have in getting the facts is likely to be high. Indeed, an uncertain situation with intense motivation to obtain information is exactly what has been found to foster the production and spread of rumors (Allport and Postman, 1943). Even here, however, there could be individual differences in susceptibility to rumors, depending upon individual experiences and personal expectancies.

In connection with *behavior settings,* Barker (1968), the leading proponent of "ecological psychology"—essentially, the study of the context of behavior—says "it is one of the great achievements of psychology that in spite of the variation of every individual's behavior, methods have been devised for identifying and measuring individual behavior constants" (p. 5). But, he asserts, as much attention needs to be given to the regularities of behavior individuals may be called upon to display in the same behavior setting. The recent book by Jackson (1968), on his study of school classrooms, illustrates this approach. Here there are literal physical variables, such as crowding, which clearly affect psychological states and induce highly regularized behaviors. He reports:

> . . . in several different ways students in elementary classrooms are required to wait their turn and to delay their actions. . . . Furthermore, delay is only one of the consequences of living in a crowd and perhaps not even the most important one from the standpoint of constraining the individual. . . . The denial of desire is the ultimate outcome of many of the delays occurring in the classroom. The raised hand is sometimes ignored, the question to the teacher is sometimes brushed aside, the permission that is sought is sometimes refused. . . . (P)art of learning how to live in school involves learning how to give up desire as well as how to wait for its fulfillment (p. 15).

BEHAVIOR AND COGNITION

Cutting across the personality-situation relationship is another distinction, presented in terms of a primary concern with behavior or cognition. For the latter word, the term "perception" is sometimes used; and, to add an historical distinction, the contrast is sometimes stated as one between "behavioral and phenomenological" approaches (Hitt, 1969). These come down, at bottom, to actions on the one hand and thoughts and feelings on the other.

A behavioral theory, as the term implies, is concerned with behaviors, usually alterations in behavior which can be systematically shown to vary with environmental stimuli. In the strictest sense, such theories would not concern themselves with what occurs within the individual in eliciting behavior. Some concepts of learning, which can be adapted to social behavior, such as the "reinforcement" views of Skinner, fall within this category. The term cognitive conveys the idea of "knowing." A cognitive theory therefore would be concerned with the inner experiences of the individual in inducing action. Lewin's Field Theory, which we have already encountered in terms of the "psychological field" concept, is a theory of this kind. It emphasizes in particular the individual's perception of events he experiences. Thus, any theory which involves attitudes as relevant variables is cognitive. This does not mean that a cognitive emphasis disregards behavior but rather that it looks upon cognitive factors as "mediators" of behavior, i.e. variables which intervene between the stimulus and response.

There are impelling philosophical issues imbedded in this distinction which are not necessarily bridged through research. When Asch (1959) says that the inner experiences of the individual have a place as data in social psychology, he means an *important* place because of his image of Man. Skinner (1957), as a strict behaviorist, views Man as reactive to external stimuli and not to self-awareness. Those who are phe-nomenologically oriented grant the importance of behavior, but they see Man more as the source of his actions, and less under the control of outside forces.

Still another distinction is made between conscious and unconscious processes. For the most part, unconscious elements affect behavior without direct self-awareness, so that they might readily be seen as "external forces," much as are the behaviorist's stimuli, in controlling behavior. To say that a theory emphasizes consciousness means that it is more concerned with the individual's awareness of the experiences on which he acts. One example is Bem's (1965) theory of self-percep-tion which asserts that individuals infer things about their own psycho-logical states by perceiving their own behavior. Another example is seen in the theory of cognitive dissonance (Festinger, 1957). Here the individual is viewed as perceiving and avoiding conflicts between his store of cognitive elements—attitudes, perceived actions, and the like. Alternatively, theories of the *unconscious* owe their existence to the concepts of Freud and his followers, and especially to the importance they attach to unrecognized motives affecting behavior. Several the-ories regarding the development and functioning of attitudes treat them as sources for affecting behavior through unconscious processes of this kind.

There are *not*, of course, four or six or eight *kinds* of theories in social psychology as these bi-polarities might suggest. Their emphases overlap, and many theoretical views represent a mixture of them. This can be exemplified in a number of ways. Theories emphasizing the situation are frequently behavioral and unconcerned about consciousness-unconsciousness; and theories emphasizing cognition usually convey as well an implicit concern with the personalistic qualities of the individual, whether at a conscious or unconscious level. Thus, studies of the effects of culture on individual psychological states, such as perception, employ measures to get at conscious as well as unconscious factors, for example through various kinds of standard psychological tests. In sum, the mainstream of social psychology today reveals a considerable admixture of these viewpoints. It tends toward a cognitive approach, with an emphasis on attitudes and values, including self-perceptions, and other conscious states associated with behavior. On a practical level, the relevant variables to be measured in a study depend upon the problem under investigation.

The nature of variables in social psychology

Though social psychology is quite wide-ranging and interdisciplinary in its scope, any single social psychologist defines a research problem in terms of the particular variables which suit his special interests. This makes for what may seem to be research on some narrow issues, when it is a case of the research question being brought down to manageable scale. Fitted together, the findings of tightly defined studies can provide a broader view of influence phenomena. Regarding the selection of a promising question for research, Weick (1969a) observes:

> When you select a specific question you lay aside much of the complexity you have registered. . . . The question is a fragment of all that you initially thought about, but the fragment may also contain some of the more important properties of that representation. Fragments, in other words, can be consequential (p. 992).

As we have seen, theories in social psychology can offer many polarities. Arguments arise whenever these matters are treated strictly in either-or terms. It would therefore be decidedly paralyzing to attempt to consider these whenever framing a researchable question. It is also worth recalling that two important characteristics of social behavior rest in its *multi-causal nature* and in its *historicity*. We have already noted that more than one variable may, and often does, produce social behavior. Also, we have said that the history of past relationships affect responses in the present. For example, the precise sequence of past events holds an important key to causality, as in the everyday query of "Who said what first?" Since the variables studied in social psychology are not easily categorized as "dependent" or "independent," their relationships are not best seen in simple stimulus-response terms. Furthermore, the fact that there are *ongoing processes* at work means that we must take account of time relationships to specify what is altered and what alters others things in turn.

A convenient way to give further body to these points is to discriminate between the several different kinds of variables that may be involved in any social psychological study. In the first place, we have *elements*, usually people or groups of people. Second, we have the *states* of these elements, as in the case of individual attitudes or group cohesiveness respectively. Third, we have the *processes* themselves, into which these elements enter, the best example of which is social interaction. And, finally, we have the *outcomes* of these processes.

Theories usually make assertions about elements and their relationships, often in terms of the states that they possess. Outcomes tend to be those phenomena of interest, like conformity and social attraction, which *depend* upon the states of elements and processes. Sometimes, though, states may themselves be outcomes of a prior process. Indeed, a state usually arises from some causal sequence which can be tied back to earlier processes whether or not there is direct concern with these processes. When we refer to cohesiveness, for example, we may be referring to it as a state possessed by a group which presently enters into some process, or as an outcome of a process, perhaps just completed. There are, then, some arbitrary distinctions concerning elements, states, processes, and outcomes, which are mainly a matter of the focus of the scholar. Therefore, it is well to bear in mind that in social psychology a term such as "conformity" may refer to something produced, or to something producing other outcomes—that is, to a *consequence* of prior processes or to a *cause* of subsequent effects, and that this difference is essentially a function of time-reference.

The research strategy of the social psychologist is inevitably shaped by the juxtaposition of variables in his guiding ideas or theory. In addition, he must make some choices in regard to how he will measure his major variables and decide on a research procedure within the diversity of empirical methods available for social psychological research. Before reviewing these, it is useful to consider several characteristics of empirical research.

Some characteristics of research in social psychology

The term research itself is many-faceted. To some it means consulting past findings in the library; to others, it may mean gathering facts selectively to make an argument, as in a debate. Empirical research, however, relies upon data obtained systematically, through observations and measurements, under natural or experimental conditions.

AN EMPIRICAL APPROACH

Studies of any kind in social psychology do not, strictly speaking, test theories directly. More properly, we say that they obtain data "empirically" to support or refute hypotheses. An hypothesis is a direct statement or indirect deduction from a theory which provides the guiding orientation for conducting a study, in terms of the treatments and measurements employed.

In general, empiricism refers to that stage of science which stresses the objective gathering of data. For social psychology today, as in many other fields of scientific activity, empirical evidence offers a basis for testing and discovering relationships. It is not an "end-point" in itself, but rather an aid to *social analysis* insofar as it contributes to understanding some phenomenon of social influence. This is especially important in developing and evaluating theory, as we have pointed out.

The essence of empiricism resides in making observations and measurements according to rules which allow *replication* by others. It also involves applying logic rather than accepting the untested assertions of past authority. In modern science certain standards are demanded for the acceptance of a piece of evidence, that is, a "finding." Some of the key considerations in establishing acceptability are these:

objectivity of observation including measurement
verifiability by repeated observation
use of standard methods
recognition and control of extraneous or chance factors
relationship to what has gone before
soundness of logical inference.

Social psychology has benefited from the empirical methods developed in the related and older behavioral science disciplines of psychology, sociology, and anthropology. Psychology in particular has a century-long tradition of experimentation, the most controlled of empirical methods. Drawing on this tradition, social psychology has inclined toward an insistence on rigorous data-gathering and refined analysis, whether by experimentation or by studying association.

EXPERIMENTAL AND CORRELATIONAL STRATEGIES IN GENERAL

In experiments, measurement provides for a comparison between two or more treatments or, in "before-after" designs, between measurements taken in advance of and following some intervening treatment. As a means of comparison a "control" group is also instituted to which *no* treatment is applied; thus the effect of the actual treatment represented in the independent variable may be seen. In this sense, we control for the effect of extraneous factors in order to see whether the independent variable and not something else yields an effect on the dependent variable.

A good deal of research in social psychology involves comparisons. Oftentimes these comparisons are made between *two or more groups* of people measured at approximately the *same* time. Other comparisons frequently involve measurements taken *two or more times* on at least *one* group, and often more. For the process of comparison to be internally sound, the researcher seeks to eliminate error factors such as artifacts in the particular sample drawn or in the measurement technique itself. Thus, random selection is usually employed to reduce the probability that initial differences exist between the experimental and control groups prior to the introduction of some experimental treatment. A broader question relates to interpreting the differences found and generalizing the conclusions drawn.

Another kind of research employs indices of association, such as correlation. This is the usual strategy embodied in studying the results of questionnaire surveys. Whereas experiments involve some treatment in the environment to see the effect on the dependent variable, correlational analysis involves the relating of measurements with one another —age with attitudes, education with child-rearing practices, popularity with productivity.

Both approaches allow for the testing of hypotheses, though the latter method usually allows *less* generalization about the direction of causality than the former. Still, in doing correlational analysis, it is possible to institute "controls" by studying one relationship at a time, holding others constant by statistical procedures. The difference of strategy lies in the fact that in the experiment the control is instituted by a treatment provided in the environment itself, while in computing a correlation it may be applied only within the data once collected.

As is the case with many other facets of research in social psychology, this distinction is not so sharply drawn as once appeared (Cronbach, 1957). A melding may occur as a result of the nature of the research problem. An experiment may, for example, involve correlational analysis to ascertain variations in the *relationship* between two dependent variables as a result of the effects of an independent variable; such an instance would be seen in an experiment to test the relationship between the amount of communication with a person and liking for that person as a function of his status relative to the subjects. Different levels of relative status would be introduced as the major treatment to ascertain the effects on communication or liking in themselves. But their association might even be more interesting.

BIASING EFFECTS

In the past decade, a considerable volume of interest has been generated about the psychology of research, and the effects of research procedures on persons who are subjected to them. The work of Orne (1962) on the "demand characteristics" of an experiment, and of Rosenthal (1963, 1969) and his colleagues on "experimenter bias," has created a healthy concern about the biasing effects which arise from the subject, the researcher, and their interaction. There are also testing biases, such as practice effects and response set, which have long been of interest, but since these have negligible "interpersonal" components, they need not be directly considered here.

Orne's (1962) initial observation of *demand characteristics* came out of some pilot work he was doing as a psychiatrist interested in hypnosis. He devised a number of extremely monotonous and meaningless tasks which he thought waking subjects would refuse to do, or at least give up after a short time. To his amazement, he found that his subjects continued to perform a repetitive task, such as serial additions of each adjacent two numbers on sheets filled with rows of random digits, hour upon hour until, after more than five hours, Orne gave up. His subjects had persisted in a futile task even when they were instructed to complete a sheet, tear it into thirty-two pieces, and then go on to the next sheet. From this experience, and those of a similar kind, Orne concluded that persons who agree to serve as subjects, particularly in experiments, have agreed implicitly to comply with those "demands" which are part of the experimental situation. In short, they are inclined to play the role of the "good subject." People in that role may be eager to comply to implicit cues, in a desire to fulfill expectancies in line with their perception of the experimental hypotheses. Orne calls the totality of these cues the "demand characteristics" of the experiment.

Given the propensity of humans to attempt to understand the elements in new situations, it is not so surprising that they should try to fit the appropriate role. The problem of course is that this creates an unintentional bias which can alter the results of research. But this apt comment from Back, Hood, and Brehm (1965) is useful in placing this matter in perspective:

> The experimental subjects are humans who assent to devote some time to being studied. To do so they accept some experimental procedures which represent situations of little similarity to any life situation. They do not, however, give up for the time being all the possibilities for human functioning, which may include other capacities and motives than those measured in the specific experiment. . . . The experiment is not a one-way street in which the experimenter does something to the subject and expects an outcome, but a whole system in which subjects, observers, and experimenters are involved (p. 181).

The Orne work suggests that the high degree of receptivity of subjects can produce bias, in the sense of compliance to the experimenter's perceived demands. However, it can also produce a negative effect, as Masling (1966) has discussed, especially if the subject has become more aware of what is happening. A recent study by Silverman, Shulman, and Wiesenthal (1970) lends some support to Masling's contention. Male and female students from an introductory psychology class, who had not taken part in any experiments before, were assigned either as subjects in an experiment involving deception with "debriefing," to inform them of what occurred, *or* as subjects in an experiment without deception. Thereafter, all subjects completed standard psychological tests, which had been used in the deception tasks. These investigators found that subjects who had been deceived in the earlier experiment showed decreased compliance, coupled with an increased tendency for favorable self-presentation, compared to subjects in the non-deception condition.

The other major source of concern regarding experiments with humans is the effect of "experimenter bias" (Rosenthal, 1963), which refers mainly to the way in which the experimenter's handling of the subject, including the instructions, may produce effects in line with his expectancies. This is an extension of the self-fulfilling prophecy phenomenon discussed earlier in connection with the Rosenthal and Jacobson (1968) study on the school children labeled as intellectual "bloomers." Numerous findings also indicate the influence of the characteristics of the experimenter, or of the interviewer in a survey, including sex and race differences vis-à-vis the subject (Rosenthal, 1969). Furthermore, deception in experimentation, mentioned earlier, though often vital in creating experimental conditions, has unwanted effects, not the least among which is the ethical problem it poses (Kelman, 1967).

Taking stock, we have considered biasing factors in experiments under the headings of demand characteristics and experimenter bias. Research with human subjects, when viewed broadly, appears to have three main sources of bias, which are in one way or another implicated in the two characterizations just noted. They are: *role-enactment,* in the sense of being a "good subject;" *reactions to the researcher,* especially in terms of perceived cues; and *self-consciousness* at being "evaluated." We have already suggested some of the features of the first and second of these. Concerning self-consciousness, the subject in a research study, whether an experiment or an interview survey, may be responding to a concern that his adequacy is being investigated. Rosenberg (1965) has called this effect "evaluation apprehension." He contends that subjects, particularly in experiments, are desirous of winning a positive evaluation from the experimenter, and accordingly develop subjective hypotheses about what it is that will produce that result as against a negative one. Even the promise of anonymity is not enough to dispel this kind of concern for some people.

Webb, Campbell, Schwartz, and Sechrest (1966) suggest that whenever there is awareness of being part of a research study, some contamination of responses is possible, especially in terms of the heightened and altered reactivity of the subjects. To reduce such effects, they urge the greater use of *non-reactive* measures, such as those of an observational kind. A motion picture record, employed in the Milgram *et al.* (1969) experiment on a crowd effect, illustrates one approach to avoiding unintented reactions. Some fascinating examples of another kind, from Webb *et al.* (1966, p. 2), are these:

> The floor tiles around the hatching-chick exhibit at Chicago's Museum of Science and Industry must be replaced every six weeks. Tiles in other parts of the museum need not be replaced for years. The selective erosion of tiles, indexed by the replacement rate, is a measure of the relative popularity of exhibits.
>
> The degree of fear induced by a ghost-story-telling session can be measured by noting the shrinking diameter of a circle of seated children.
>
> Library withdrawals were used to demonstrate the effect of the introduction of television into a community. Fiction titles dropped, nonfiction titles were unaffected.
>
> The role of rate of interaction in managerial recruitment is shown by the overrepresentation of baseball managers who were infielders or catchers (high-interaction positions) during their playing days.
>
> Racial attitudes in two colleges were compared by noting the degree of clustering of Negroes and whites in lecture halls.

Before closing this section, it is worth noting that the considerable attention to biasing effects in social psychological research today is an encouraging sign of maturity. Studying the sources of bias and of error lends strength to any scientific enterprise. The real weakness lies in blithe ignorance of them. Some years ago, in commenting on the study of factors leading to error in survey methodology, Hyman (1954)

said that, "The lack of demonstration of error in certain fields of inquiry often derives from the nonexistence of methodological research
into the problem and merely denotes a less advanced stage of that
profession" (p. 4).

In the section to follow, we will consider a variety of research methods employed in social psychology with examples from research literature for each. We begin with four major methods of study and then
review several specialized techniques. These are not entirely separate
from one another, since any one study can involve their application in
various combinations, but they are best seen in a separate state for
clarification and illustration.

Major methods of study in social psychology

The major methods of study are: observation, field studies, questionnaire surveys, and experimentation of two varieties, i.e. in the "field"
or the "laboratory." The key features which vary in these approaches
are the *naturalness of the environment for the subjects of the study*
and the degree to which the experimenter is able to *exercise control
over their environment* in the sense of altering some things and holding others constant. These features are related in that maximum control by the investigator tends to be found in experiments conducted
under conditions created in a laboratory.

It should be made clear that there are no hard and fast lines separating these methods since they can be employed in concert with one another. Furthermore, of necessity, some become part of the others. This
is most notably true regarding "observation," which we treat alone first,
but in the recognition that behavior may be observed under a diversity
of research conditions.

OBSERVATION

In general, observation is the oldest technique for studying behavior.
By our use of the term "observation," however, we especially mean
looking on in a *systematic* way for certain categories of response, and
for factors which appear to be associated with those responses. In
social psychology and other behavioral science fields today, research in

many situations involves the method of "field observation." The term "field" refers to a *natural situation* in which people carry on normal pursuits, usually without being aware they are being studied. The investigator does not apply treatments but does seek to focus his attention on certain behaviors to ascertain their sources and their effects.

For example, in observing a group meeting interest might be directed to the response of individuals to particular kinds of statements made by other individuals, or to those kinds of statements to which an individual reacts. We will return to this shortly. As another illustration, the field investigator might be interested in observing children under different conditions. One notable exemplification of this is found in the work of Barker and Wright (1954) who observed the different "behavior settings" in a small town in Kansas they called "Midwest." After extensive categorizing of these settings as features of the cultural milieu of the entire community, they determined what characteristic patterns of behavior occurred in each milieu. In Table 3.1 their results from the observation of children in the second grade are shown. The

Table 3.1: Patterns of behavior of the same children in different behavior settings (Table on p. 54, *Midwest and Its Children* by R. G. Barker and H. F. Wright. Harper & Row, 1954).

	BEHAVIOR SETTING			
	CLASSROOM, BEFORE SCHOOL	ACADEMIC ACTIVITIES	PLAYGROUND	MUSIC CLASS
Milieu	Second-grade classroom, 8.30-8.50 a.m. Monday through Friday	Scheduled periods for work; books, paper, pencils, etc.	School playground at recess; swings, teeter, balls, etc.	Scheduled period in music room; piano, music books, etc.
Behavior pattern	Unorganized activity; free locomotion; medium tempo, noise, and energy; cheerful mood; large variety of behavior	Organized activity; little change in positions; slow tempo, noise and energy; serious mood; limited variety of behavior	Unorganized or partly organized activities; fast tempo, loudness, and vitality; exuberant mood; large variety of behavior	Organized activities; variation in tempo, noise, and energy; medium cheerfulness; little variety of behavior, singing predominant

striking feature is not only that these same children show these different behavior patterns in different milieu day after day, but that in succeeding years other second-graders show similar patterns of behavior in these same milieu. This dramatically underscores the effect of culture in eliciting regularities of behavior.

An essential feature of effective observation in the field is not to allow the investigator's presence to intrude on the activity of the people under observation. In most cases this is facilitated by remaining at a distance while noting behaviors in one or more prescribed categories. An example of this which tests an hypothesis about the common quality of conforming behavior across situations is provided in the work of Floyd Allport (1934). He gathered observational data on the behavior of different persons in several kinds of situations and then plotted the

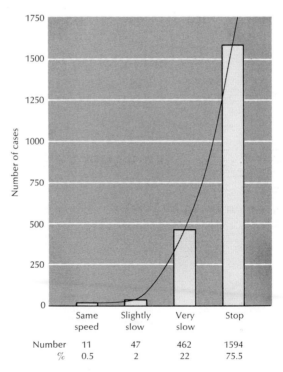

	Same speed	Slightly slow	Very slow	Stop
Number	11	47	462	1594
%	0.5	2	22	75.5

Figure 3.1: Motorists' behavior at stop sign and cross traffic corners; 2114 cases observed by M. Dickens. (Based upon data from F. H. Allport, 1934.)

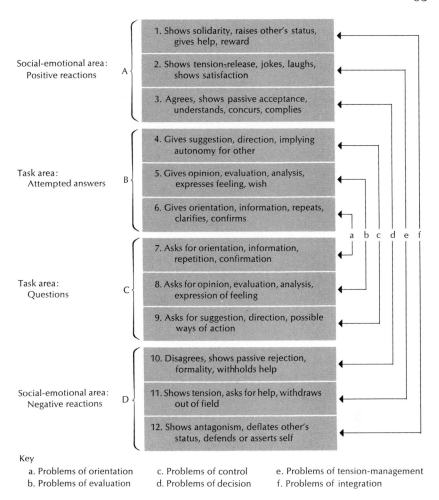

Figure 3.2: The original system of categories used in observation and their relation to major frames of reference. (From Bales, 1950a.). For a revised version see Bales (1970), p. 92.

distribution of frequencies of such responses, relative to a social standard. With persons observed in such situations as bringing a car to a halt at a stop sign, coming to work at a definite time, and practicing religious forms on entering a church, he found a distinctive pattern of response which he called a "J-curve." The horizontal axis in Figure 3.1 shows the degree of conformity with the expectancy for stopping at a stop sign, and the vertical axis the frequency with which it occurred. While it is of course true that a finding such as Allport's is evidently of a descriptive nature, its particular importance at the time was in pointing up the similarity of the curves obtained across the various situations studied. Here again, then, we see a regularity of response.

Observation is especially appropriate as a first stage in field studies. It should be emphasized once more, however, that the method of observation is almost always implicitly involved as a source of useful data even in other methods of study. Thus, research on groups—whether in the field or laboratory—often requires a measure of the qualities of social interaction. In laboratory experiments, for example, behaviors can be tallied within the categories developed by Robert F. Bales in his technique of "interaction process analysis" (1950a, b), thus permitting the test of hypotheses about the effects upon, or effects of, interaction. Figure 3.2 indicates the twelve kinds of distinctive behavior within which the interactions of the group members can be coded. Each behavior is connected with its opposite number by a line with arrows.

FIELD STUDY

A field study differs from observation alone in that it requires contact with the persons studied to obtain information from them. Thus, they are necessarily made aware of and involved in the study. In his research on the "cash posters," as an instance, George Homans (1954) was interested in testing certain conceptions about social interaction among women working as clerks in the billing department of a utility firm. He spent many weeks unobtrusively observing the pattern of social relationships in the office as the women moved about. He ascertained which workers took the initiative in seeking out and talking to which others, and this provided him with his major observational data on the attraction of persons to one another in this group. Then, as with many field studies that begin with observation, Homans interviewed these women to obtain additional data regarding their attitudes. Among other findings, his results supported the hypothesis that popularity, as measured by the number of choices received from others on a sociometric rating, was directly related to the frequency of interaction with others. A similar set of measures was obtained in another field study, *The June Bug* (Kerckhoff and Back, 1968), discussed in Chapter 1.

The essence of a field study then is the requirement of direct contact with individuals in a natural life setting. It is appropriate for use whenever investigations of behavior, and of attitudes, are carried out by studying people in such settings as their home or school. The Homans study illustrates the point that the investigator makes observations of behavior, but also requires direct contact with people to get information from them through an interview and sociometric ratings. His purpose is to obtain data that would otherwise be unavailable without such contact.

Mann and Taylor (1969) conducted a number of field studies to examine the relationship between estimated and actual position in waiting lines. In one of these, they studied children in several lines at a Melbourne theater, on three consecutive mornings. A special children's program was being shown during a vacation period, and to attract a large audience the management announced that Batman T-shirts would be given away to the first twenty-five arrivals at each morning showing. The location of a precise critical point near the front of the line offered an opportunity for these investigators to determine whether systematic distortions occurred in judgment about the length of the line, even where the shortness of the line made the possibility of accuracy quite high.

Starting with the first youngster in line, every second or third one, up to the fiftieth position, was asked to estimate the number of children ahead of him, and the chance of getting a shirt. Other questions were also asked about reactions to others trying to "jump" the line and to keeping one's place in line. In all, sixty-six children, mainly twelve- to thirteen-year-old boys, were interviewed. The results on the question of estimation are shown in Table 3.2. They indicate a significant tendency, in the direction predicted by Mann and Taylor, for

Table 3.2: Children's estimates of position in line as a function of actual position in line for Batman T-shirts. (After Mann and Taylor, 1969, p. 99.)

ACTUAL POSITION IN LINE	ESTIMATES OF NUMBER AHEAD IN LINE		
	Over-estimate	Under-estimate	Correct
1-25	14	9	17
26-50	6	20	0

those in the front of the line to overestimate or correctly estimate the number in front, while those past the twenty-fifth position underestimated it. The perceptual judgment of position was therefore distinctly associated with the heightened desire, in the nature of a "wish-fulfillment," to get the shirt after all. This phenomenon has previously been observed in research by Bruner and Goodman (1947) on value and need as factors affecting children's perceptions of the size of coins.

QUESTIONNAIRE SURVEY

Another device for gathering information, usually on a wider population, is the questionnaire survey in the field. In a questionnaire survey, or "sample survey" as it is sometimes called, the central interest is in how a population, falling into certain descriptive classes, e.g. age, sex, level of education, birth order, responds to certain questions. There is of course also considerable interest in the relations between responses. Unlike a field study, the focus of attention is usually *not* on a particular group in a natural setting, but on a collection of respondents. It is the interrelationship of respondent attributes and responses which is being sought primarily. This is normally achieved by correlational methods. Though questionnaires may be employed in a field study, usually the field study is distinguished more by its focus on behaviors, or reports of behaviors, quite apart from questionnaire data.

Sometimes a natural event can be employed as the independent variable in a questionnaire survey, and it takes on the quality of a scientific experiment. For example, in studying attitude change as a result of a political campaign, measures can be taken before and after the event, and the effects of the campaign assessed, particularly as it influences persons with varying shades and intensities of commitment. Some studies of attitude change use a procedure called the "panel survey," which involves interviewing the same people repeatedly. For instance, as part of a study of elections, a panel of respondents might be interviewed one or more times to see how their initial position with regard to the candidates and the parties was modified by, or affected their reaction to, the campaign. Lazarsfeld and his coworkers (1948) have conducted a number of such surveys, the first in the 1940 presidential election. In that survey, they were able to demonstrate, for example, that the greater the number of cross-pressures an individual is subjected to—by

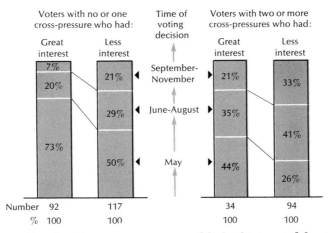

Voters with no or one cross-pressure who had:		Time of voting decision	Voters with two or more cross-pressures who had:	
Great interest	Less interest		Great interest	Less interest
7%	21%	September-November	21%	33%
20%				
	29%	June-August	35%	41%
73%	50%	May	44%	26%
Number 92	117		34	94
% 100	100		100	100

Figure 3.3: Showing that cross-pressures and lack of interest delay the time of final voting decision. Their joint effect is especially strong. Separately, they show about equal strength. (After Lazarsfeld, *et al.*, 1948.)

conflicting political attitudes, social positions, or group affiliations—the less interest he has in the election and the later he decides his vote (see Figure 3.3). This kind of relationship has been found repeatedly since. The Bennington study by Newcomb (1943), on the effects of a college environment, was essentially a field study in a different context, though it tested a similar hypothesis regarding the consequences of conflicting affiliations.

As Figure 3.3 reveals, there is a relationship between the number of cross-pressures to which an individual is exposed and his interest in the election, seen by the relative proportions for the numbers in the columns. As the numbers at the base of each column reveal, fewer cross-pressures also yield greater interest, proportional to that for more cross-pressures. Almost three-fourths of those in the first column knew in May how they would vote in November, while only one-fourth of those in the last column did, which demonstrates the major relationship regarding delay of voting decision.

Another example of a questionnaire survey is the research conducted by Albert Hastorf and Hadley Cantril (1954) following a particularly rough football game between Princeton and Dartmouth in which Dick Kazmaier, a Princeton All-American, was severely injured in his last appearance with the team in a home game. Passions were high that day and following the game there were many accusations concerning which team started the rough play on the field. In a survey conducted a week later among a sample of those in attendance, these researchers were able to test an implicit hypothesis regarding the relationship of school loyalty, essentially a "reference group" conception, to perceptions about a commonly observed event, the football game. They found that 86 per cent of the respondents at Princeton felt the Dartmouth team to be at fault, while 55 per cent of the Dartmouth respondents mainly felt it to be a matter of more equal blame. They had witnessed the same game.

Clearly, students at these institutions saw and interpreted the happenings on the gridiron in line with school loyalty. This underscores the profound psychological effect of group affiliation on perception. It also was further evidenced when a sample of Princeton and Dartmouth students were shown an identical movie of the game. Thus,

> When Princeton students looked at the movie of the game, they saw the Dartmouth team make over twice as many infractions as their own team made. And they saw the Dartmouth team make over twice as many infractions as were seen by Dartmouth students. . . . When Dartmouth students looked at the movie of the game they saw both teams make about the same number of infractions (Hastorf & Cantril, 1954, pp. 131-132).

FIELD EXPERIMENTATION

In general, the experimental method in social psychology involves the alteration of conditions in the situation to determine the differential effect upon the responses of subjects. It may also proceed by studying the effect of the same experimental conditions upon persons who differ on some characteristic. Experiments may be done in natural-life settings, in which case we call them "field experiments," or in highly controlled, artificial settings, which we refer to by the term "laboratory experiments." We begin with the first of these.

The method called "field experimentation" is considerably more complex and difficult than would be the usual field study or questionnaire survey. Here the investigator actually arranges to create situations in a natural environment to study the consequences produced. To control for the effects of extraneous factors requires a "control group" matched on all other possible variables. Thus, some individuals might be exposed to a unique treatment to which other similar individuals are not. Illustrating this, Kurt Lewin instigated a number of studies on the effect of different social practices in producing changes in behavior, with the aim of testing hypotheses in particular about more pronounced changes occurring from commitments made in a group discussion. In one of these experiments (1947) some mothers of infants, as a control, were given individual instruction encouraging them to use orange juice, among other foods, in baby feeding. Other mothers were given the treatment of being allowed to take part in a discussion, in groups of six, to consider the advantages of different foods in a baby's diet and reach a common decision. In this experiment, groups reached decisions favoring orange juice in about 25 minutes. As will be seen in Figure 3.4, those mothers who took part in the decision, and were more publicly committed, had a significantly higher rate than the control condition for giving orange juice. Furthermore, this difference persisted after four weeks, and probably far longer.

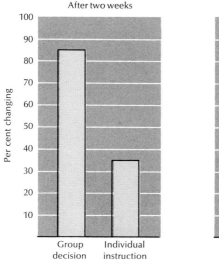 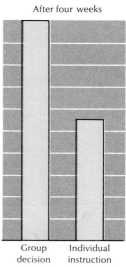

Figure 3.4: Percentage of mothers following completely group decision or individual instruction in giving orange juice. (Adapted from "Group Decision and Social Change" by Kurt Lewin, from *Readings in Social Psychology*. Copyright © 1947 by Holt, Rinehart and Winston, Inc.) Reprinted by permission of the publishers.

92186

An experiment by Bennett (1955) has served to refine the implications of this earlier work. She found that the major effect of group discussion was traceable mainly to the process of making a decision in a group, involving especially the degree to which *group consensus* is obtained *and* perceived by individual participants.

A classic illustration of field experimentation is represented in the work of Coch and French (1948) who conducted an experiment in a factory where pajamas were manufactured. The fundamental independent variable was the degree to which workers were permitted to participate in planning a needed production change. Some workers were allowed total participation, and others were allowed only indirect participation or no participation. The results showed that participation in any degree yielded significantly higher production than did no participation. The findings for the three kinds of conditions are indicated in Figure 3.5 and graphically affirm the implicit hypothesis that participation in decision-making induces attudinal differences which affect subsequent performance.

The field experiment often takes the form of creating certain conditions which induce a "psychological set," that is, a pre-formed perception, to see its later effects. This can be done with simple written instructions given in a classroom. Thus, in one such experiment, Kelley

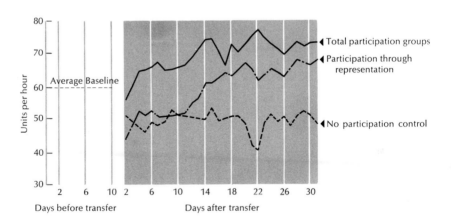

Figure 3.5: Smoothed production curves for total participation groups, and for participation through representation and no participation control groups, after transfer to new production procedure. (Adapted from Coch and French, 1948.)

(1950) was able to test an hypothesis about the way different sets, once created, can lead to divergent perceptions of the identical stimulus person. He gave students in a college classroom brief written descriptions of a guest lecturer prior to his actual appearance. Two kinds of descriptions were used. These were the same in every way, except that in one case the person was described as a "rather cold" person and in the other as "very warm." Students received one or the other description without knowing that different terms were being used. After hearing the same lecture, the students who had received the "set" for warmness rated the lecturer as more considerate, more informal, more sociable, and in general more favorably on other factors of personality, than did those students who had received the "set" for coldness. This finding supports the hypothesis that first impressions can be markedly affected by prior information. Concerning impressions, it should be noted that the Rosenthal and Jacobson (1968) research, inducing expectancies in teachers regarding some children's potential for rapid intellectual development, was a field experiment. Another discussed in Chapter 1, was the research on gathering a crowd by Milgram *et al.* (1969).

LABORATORY EXPERIMENTATION

The most controlled method employed in modern-day social psychology, and the one increasing most in use, is "laboratory experimentation." It involves the introduction of conditions, in a controlled environment (hence the term "laboratory"), which will simulate certain features of a natural environment. This permits the creation of a situation with closely supervised manipulation of one or more variables at a time to observe effects produced, something that would be quite difficult to achieve in a natural setting.

A classic example of laboratory experimentation is provided in the Sherif (1935) research with the autokinetic effect (see pp. 65-67). That work is significant in pointing up the effects on perception of the judgments of others, especially where the stimulus to be judged is highly ambiguous. An extension of Sherif's work is represented in the experimentation done by Solomon Asch (1951). In his research, a group of people, usually eight in number, are seated side by side. On a screen before them they each see a line which they are asked to match by size with one of three unequal lines. These are labeled and group members are asked to give their response aloud. Except for one person, the "critical subject," the group had actually met before and received instructions to respond unanimously with wrong judgments on certain trials. Thus, the critical subject faced a unanimous contradiction of his own perception on these trials. Asch found a distinct movement toward the majority estimates in the direction of the group's distortion of accuracy. There was, however, marked variability from one subject to another. About one-quarter of the subjects remained completely independent. Overall, 32 per cent of the judgments of critical subjects were in the pro-majority, or incorrect, direction. When a person reporting in advance of the critical subject was instructed to give a response contrary to the group's erroneous judgment, the effect was considerably altered. Under conditions of such support from even *one* other person, the critical subject gave a more accurate response indicative of what he actually saw. Asch says: "The results clearly demonstrate that a disturbance of the unanimity of the majority markedly increased the independence of the critical subjects. The frequency of pro-majority errors dropped . . . to 5.5 percent" (1951, p. 185). Laboratory experimentation of this kind supports the hypothesis that our reports of what we perceive are susceptible to the influence of others and are highly sensitive to the degree of support from others.

Leavitt (1951) conducted an experiment whose results dramatize the consequences of the group's communication structure on performance and satisfaction. He arranged different communication patterns or "nets" for groups (see Figure 3.6) which had the effect of restricting in varying degrees the channels for passing messages between members. Thus, in the circle, subjects could communicate only with those persons on either side of them; in a wheel the central person could communicate with any of the others, but they could only communicate with him, and so on. The task was to solve a problem involving the discovery of the symbol group members shared in common on the cards given them. Leavitt found that the communication nets were significant determiners of behavior, accuracy, and satisfaction of group members. This demonstrated the extent to which a feature of the social situation can be influential in affecting such outcomes. In general, the wheel was found to be most efficient, in terms of the single fastest correct solution. However, the circle tended to be more satisfying to the group members. Other relationships found indicated that the "centrality" of a

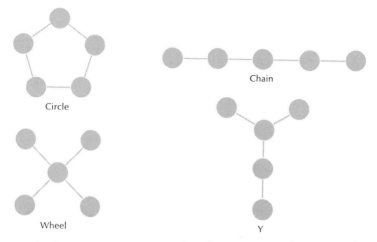

Figure 3.6: Communication nets used in the experiment by Leavitt (1951).

group member's position in a net had a great deal to do with his satisfaction.

One element sometimes embodied in laboratory experimentation is a "confederate" or "stimulus person," instructed to behave in a certain way so as to determine the effects of such behavior on the subjects, as in the Asch experiment already described. An experiment by Schachter (1951) illustrates the utility of this procedure. He had college students indicate in advance what kinds of clubs they would like to join. Two kinds of clubs were then comprised: one kind with students who indicated moderate to extreme interest in them, and the other kind made up of students who had favored being in other clubs. These were defined as being "high cohesive" or "low cohesive" groups, respectively. In one-half of each of these two kinds of groups, members discussed material relevant or non-relevant to the group.

In every group there were three participants who served as confederates of the experimenter. In each meeting one played the role of a "deviate" who rejected the group's main viewpoint, another played the role of a "slider" who shifted toward the group's main viewpoint during the meeting, and the third, a "non-deviate," championed that main viewpoint throughout. The latter two confederates were controls to establish evidence of the differential reaction of the group to the "deviate." This permitted a test of several postulates from Festinger's influential theory of social communication (1950). The two most relevant postulates can be paraphrased briefly as follows: the force to communicate to a particular group member will increase as the discrepancy in opinion between that member and the communicator increases; and, that force will decrease to the extent that he is no longer wanted as a member of the group. One dependent variable in this study, therefore, was the amount of communication directed to each of these participants over the time of a group meeting.

In Figure 3.7 curves for this variable are given for the three confederates for the groups studied under the condition of *high* cohesiveness and *relevant* discussion. The "deviate" was found to receive the highest number of communications from the other group members with a rise and then clear drop-off, toward the end of the session. For the "slider" this was much less so. This reflects a rejection of the deviate, which was also noted in the responses to a "post-interaction" questionnaire which measured other dependent variables, i.e. nominations for a steering committee and a measure of willingness to eliminate someone from the group. These measures were mutually supportive in indicating a will-

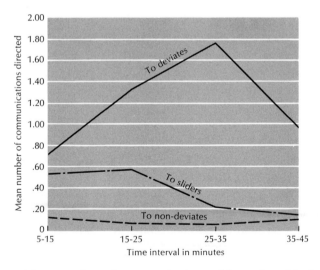

Figure 3.7: Mean number of communications addressed to "deviates" who reject group views, and to "sliders" and "non-deviates" during meeting under conditions of high cohesiveness and relevant attitudes. (Based on data from Schachter, 1951.)

ingness to reject the "deviate" significantly more than the "slider" or "non-deviate" by not having him on the steering committee and indeed by dropping him entirely from group membership. Thus, group pressures toward conformity were brought to bear, and operated to produce the rejection of members who failed to conform to group expectancies regarding relevant attitudes.

Specialized techniques of research

The methods of study we have been considering represent the major approaches to investigations of social behavior and the factors associated with influence upon it. As we have pointed out, each may involve some features of the others. There are, in addition, a number of specialized procedures which cut across any or all of the methods. These are techniques of gathering or organizing data which provide answers to questions concerning the processes involved in influence relationships. There are essentially four of these which have a justifiable place in our consideration of the research methods of social psychology. They are: depth interviews, projective techniques, attitude scales, and content analysis. Since these are not mutually exclusive of one another, they may be and are used in combination. Thus, depth interviews are frequently supplemented by the administration of projective techniques. These may be scored in turn by content analysis procedure. Similarly, attitude scales may be administered in connection with an interview.

DEPTH INTERVIEWS

An interview is a way of studying individuals intensively. It provides for a degree of freedom in getting at information that otherwise would be unavailable in the more structured questionnaire format. Putting it another way, a questionnaire is a highly structured interview. With the more conversational approach usually permitted in an interview, a good deal of latitude is provided for the spontaneous probing of certain attitudes held by the respondent. This is especially true in depth interviewing which is designed to be penetrating and demands considerable skill on the part of the interviewer, who must retain throughout a sense of what particular kinds of information are to be obtained. With the feature of personal contact, he is also able to observe the behavior of the interviewee while responding.

One example of the contrast between a broad questionnaire survey and a depth-interview approach is found in the work on attitudes by Smith, Bruner, and White (1956). Rather than survey a large population, they devoted considerable attention to only ten persons, who were interviewed intensively over an extended period of time. The aim of the research was to understand better the relationship between political attitudes, particularly regarding the Soviet Union, and personality. Formal questioning was supplemented by tests and an opportunity was also afforded for spontaneous and penetrating discussion. Their major conclusion was that the relationship between personality and these particular attitudes did not fit a consistent pattern.

Lane (1969) has extended this line of work asking college students to write autobiographical essays, which he calls "ideological self-analyses." They are oriented around two basic questions: "Of what use to me are my political ideas?" and "How did I come to have these political ideas?" He thereby provides his subjects with considerable latitude for response, several steps beyond a formal interview. His specific results are not easily summarized, but what is most relevant is the role he finds for "political consciousness" in personality. This is related to the functional features of attitudes, discussed in Chapters 5 and 6.

PROJECTIVE TECHNIQUES

A way of extending an interview to further probing beneath the surface of verbal expressions is provided by projective techniques, which represent one kind of personality test. The term "projective" refers to the fact that the individual respondent "projects" his impressions of relatively ambiguous and standardized stimulus materials, thus giving a view of his underlying attitudes or perceptions. Probably the best known of the projective techniques is the Rorschach Ink-Blot Test. This test involves standard inkblots, which have been used for several decades with a range of adults; these are presented one at a time to a person in order to get reactions from him which are then scored by an established system.

In social psychology, the projective techniques which tend to be most often used are those involving sentence completion, and to some extent word association and storytelling about standard pictures. The latter approach is exemplified in the so-called Thematic Apperception Test (TAT), which is used for a variety of purposes. The social psychologist's main interest in projective techniques is not so much personality as such, but the person's psychological field, that is, his interpretation of the world and his attitudes toward its features. David McClelland and his colleagues, for example, have made extensive use of projective devices in measuring achievement motivation, usually by analyzing the content of the specific stories told in connection with TAT pictures (1953). On balance, projective tests are a useful technique for getting at what McClelland has called the "content of mind," since the person usually is not fully conscious of precisely what his responses may convey and accordingly is less guarded.

ATTITUDE SCALES

For several decades there has been a good deal of interest in attitude scaling. This method provides a way of systematically measuring one part of a person's psychological field. We shall be further considering procedures for attitude scaling in Chapter 6. Our interest here is in presenting a particular kind of attitude scale used as a measure of personality, i.e. the "attitude-trait" scale.

In general, an attitude scale is composed of a set of "items," usually statements, with which a person indicates degrees of agreement or disagreement. In the attitude-trait scale, these responses usually have to do with others in the person's social world. This is taken to be indicative of a characteristic mode of reacting to others and is exemplified in the scale of authoritarianism, called the "F Scale," developed at the University of California during the 1940's (Adorno, et al., 1950) and discussed in the last chapter. Items from that scale are designed to assess various kinds of conventional attitudes found to cohere in the "authoritarian personality." Here are some examples from that scale:

> Obedience and respect for authority are the most important virtues children should learn.
> What this country needs most, more than laws and political programs, is a few courageous, tireless, devoted leaders in whom the people can put their faith.

There is hardly anything lower than a person who does not feel a great love, gratitude, and respect for his parents.

If people would talk less and work more everybody would be better off.

People can be divided into two distinct classes: the weak and the strong.

Human nature being what it is, there will always be war and conflict.

A sum of the responses of agreement or disagreement for about 30 of these items represents a measure of authoritarianism. Other scales of this sort, which are taken to be insightful of personality are those for dogmatism, rigidity, empathy, and so forth. What distinguishes this approach from earlier measures of personality is that previously persons were asked to describe their own behavior by agreeing or disagreeing with a set of statements such as "I find it difficult to get up in the morning." This represents the classic approach of personality inventories, such as the Bernreuter and the Minnesota Multiphasic Personality Inventory (MMPI). More recently, as a development within social psychological study oriented toward individual differences, measurement of *other-perception* through these scales is applied to assess personality features.

CONTENT ANALYSIS

The technique known as "content analysis" is a procedure that covers a variety of different tasks. Mainly, however, this technique refers to the coding and categorizing of qualitative materials so as to permit their quantification. One way of seeing the problem is to recognize that any verbal communication, e.g. a statement, a letter, a newspaper editorial, carries various elements within it which might be studied quantitatively in terms of the frequency with which they occur. One such study was conducted by Sargent (1939). He compiled a representative list of twelve terms regularly encountered in the editorials appearing in each of two major metropolitan newspapers when referring to the same events or people. Without revealing their source, he had sixty college students indicate if they liked, disliked, or were indifferent to these terms. Some illustrative pairs of terms were: "progressive" vs. "radical," "crop control" vs. "farm dictatorship," "investigator" vs. "inquisitor." He found a consistent tendency for the responses to indicate less favorability for those terms used by one of the papers; in the pairs given here that paper's terms are given last. Sargent concluded that the "loaded" terms used in this paper's editorials were reacted to in a direction consistent with the political and economic policies of the paper.

Another intriguing use of content analysis is shown by a study conducted by deCharms and Moeller (1962) on the values expressed in American children's readers. They had two people independently score every third page from representative children's readers drawn on the basis of at least four from each 20-year period beginning in 1800. These were mainly from the fourth-grade level. The aim of this content analysis procedure was to quantify several kinds of values, or imagery, including achievement motivation. This variable has been found to be a rather stable feature of personality which relates to the individual's entrepreneurial activity (McClelland, et al., 1953).

This particular study was prompted by McClelland's extension of his theory to include cultural development. Through the analysis of literary materials, he found confirmation of his hypothesis that achievement motivation preceded economic and technological growth in the Athe-

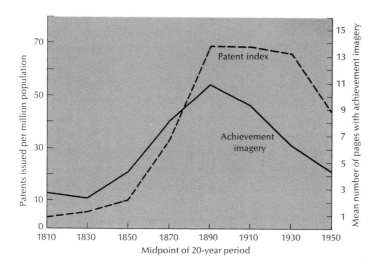

Figure 3.8: Mean number of pages out of 25 containing achievement imagery, and patent index per million population, both plotted against time. (From deCharms and Moeller, 1962.)

nian civilization of classic Greece (1958). In his book, *The Achieving Society* (1961), he further illustrated this pattern by citing the content of children's readers in various cultures. Accordingly, one of the key hypotheses that deCharms and Moeller tested in their study was that the incidence of achievement imagery found in these books would be positively related to the number of patents issued, corrected for population growth. Clear affirmation of this hypothesis is shown by the high statistically significant correspondence between the two curves plotted in Figure 3.8, one for the incidence of achievement imagery and the other for patents issued. Both reveal a peak close to the turn of the century and a steady decline since. Apart from any precise interpretation of what these curves reveal, the notable quality of this study lies in the way it demonstrates the use of content analysis to get at the psychological correlates of cultural trends.

The generalizability of findings: some conclusions

All of the methods and techniques of social psychology we have covered in this chapter are designed to provide data to evaluate theories. This is necessarily a dynamic function which involves constant re-evaluation. No finding by itself is sacrosanct since there is never absolute certainty in science; and a theory is potentially subject to alterations when new data come in.

But what is the purpose in all this if our generalizations must be limited? As we have tried to suggest by the illustrations, the essence of the dialogue between theories and findings is to broaden our understanding and increase the range of applicability of our conclusions. In short, the purpose is to improve our generalizations about processes of social influence, and the behavior to which it gives rise. This is only possible to the extent that we employ methods that provide a good test of our theories, and good theories for guiding our pursuit of new data.

SUMMARY

Theories and the methods employed to verify them are essential features of any scientific pursuit. Theories are practical too for they select and refine variables for emphasis, and provide hypotheses for testing against data.

In social psychology, theories may emphasize characteristics of the individual or of his immediate social situation. A situation may be treated in terms of *social structure, psychological components,* or time-space relationships, as a *behavior setting.* Either the individual or situational emphasis taken to the extreme is likely to produce an oversimplification in view of the multi-causal nature of social influence and the behaviors to which it gives rise. Increasingly, both emphases are accounted for in research on these processes. An especially important point of closure between them resides in the concept of the "psychological field" which gives attention to the way the individual is "set" to define situations in which he finds himself.

Another pair of theoretical distinctions in social psychology, which determine the variables studied in research, are "behavioral" vs. "cognitive" theories and those theories embodying "conscious" vs. "unconscious" determinants of behavior. These distinctions cut across individual and situational orientations to produce a variety of combinations. Accordingly most theoretical views providing research on social influence are a combination of these leading to the measurement of some variables and the exclusion of others.

Variables in social psychology are not easily categorized as "dependent" or "independent" in any persisting sense. The element of time-relationship must be taken into account in determining whether a variable is altered by, or alters, other variables, or combines both processes in sequence. The several kinds of variables studied in social psychology may be *elements,* such as people or groups; *states,* such as attitudes; *processes,* such as social interaction; or *outcomes* of these processes, represented in social phenomena. The treatment of a variable as one or another of these depends upon the aim of the researcher.

We obtain data "empirically" in social psychology to test hypotheses which may be direct statements from a theory or deductions from it. Empiricism refers to gathering data objectively and according to rules that allow for replication by others. Two distinctive empirical methods are experimentation, which involves the introduction of an experimental treatment matched with a control, and studies of association through a procedure employing some mode of correlational analysis.

The four major methods of study in social psychology are: *observa-*

tion, field studies, questionnaire surveys, and *experimentation* in the "*field*" or the "*laboratory.*" These methods are not exclusive of one another and observation, in particular, is frequently employed as part of the others. Reference to research in the field means carrying on a study in a natural situation such as an office, home, or school; research in the laboratory refers to conducting a study in a highly controlled, artificial situation.

Observation usually takes the form of looking on systematically for behavior falling into various categories. A field study may employ observation but also requires *contact* with the persons being studied to gather data from them. A questionnaire survey may also be conducted in the field, but with a greater emphasis on studying a population in terms of the relationship between certain descriptive categories, such as the age, sex, and education of respondents and their responses to certain questions, usually of an attitudinal nature. A natural event may also be exploited to study its effect on persons with different attributes, as in a survey of political attitudes during an election campaign.

Field experimentation is very demanding in that it involves the creation of situations, in what is otherwise a natural environment, to measure their consequences in contrast to an untreated control. Laboratory experimentation permits the selective manipulation of one or a few variables under artificially arranged conditions which are highly controlled by the experimenter.

In addition to these major methods of research in social psychology, there are a number of specialized techniques which may be used separately, or in concert with them, to obtain relevant data. These are *depth interviews, projective techniques, attitude scales,* and *content analysis.* Depth interviews study individuals intensively and usually go beyond the scope of a questionnaire alone. Projective techniques also are utilized to get beneath the surface of verbal expression to a view of the person's unconscious processes. Attitude scales provide an avenue for the systematic measurement of one or more dimensions of the person's outlook on the world, his "psychological field"; the "attitude-trait" scale is especially geared to measuring attitudes toward others. Content analysis in the main refers to the coding and categorizing of qualitative material, usually in verbal form, in terms of measuring certain variables that may lie within it.

Findings in science never hold absolute certainty, nor are theories forever fixed. One purpose of research in social psychology is to verify theories and to refine them so as to increase the understanding of social influence and the range of generalizability of conclusions about it.

SUGGESTED READINGS

From E. P. Hollander and R. G. Hunt (Eds.) *Current perspectives in social psychology.* (3rd ed.) New York: Oxford University Press, 1971.

7. George C. Homans: *Discovery and explanation in social science*
15. Gordon W. Allport: *The open system in personality theory*
18. David C. McClelland: *The achievement motive*
27. Robert Freed Bales: *Interaction process analysis*

SELECTED REFERENCES

Blalock, H. M., & Blalock, A. B. *Methodology in social research.* McGraw-Hill, 1968.

Deutsch, M., & Krauss, R. M. *Theories in social psychology.* New York: Basic Books, 1965.

Festinger, L., & Katz, D. (Eds.) *Research methods in the behavioral sciences.* New York: Dryden, 1953.

Hyman, H. H. *Survey design and analysis.* Glencoe, Ill.: Free Press, 1955.

*Lana, R. E. *Assumptions of social psychology.* New York: Appleton-Century-Crofts, 1969.

*Lazarsfeld, P. F., & Rosenberg, M. (Eds.) *The language of social research.* Glencoe, Ill.: Free Press, 1955.

Proshansky, H. & Seidenberg, B. (Eds.) *Basic studies in social psychology.* New York: Holt, Rinehart & Winston, 1965.

Selltiz, Claire, Jahoda, Marie, Deutsch, M., & Cook S. W. *Research methods in social relations.* (Rev. ed.) New York: Holt, Rinehart & Winston, 1959.

Shaw, M. E., & Costanzo, P. R. *Theories of social psychology.* New York: McGraw-Hill, 1970.

Steiner, I., & Fishbein, M. (Eds.) *Current studies in social psychology.* New York: Holt, Rinehart & Winston, 1965.

*Webb, E. J., Campbell, D. T., Schwartz, R. D., & Sechrest, L. *Unobtrusive measures: nonreactive research in the social sciences.* Chicago: Rand McNally, 1966.

4

Adjustment and the psychological dynamics of social influence

Man influences and is influenced by others. Man's many distinguishing attributes—language, social organization and symbols, a sense of values and of continuity—can only be acquired from contact with other humans. This vital relationship arises from social interaction and involves the interplay of psychological processes such as motivation, perception, and learning. Our interest in this chapter will be directed toward how these processes are involved in the ever-present necessity for adjustment, especially in terms of the social forces affecting the individual.

The concept of adjustment refers to the quality of adaptive change basic to human experience over time. It involves the *present* necessities of the individual, the way these have been shaped by *past* experience, and their relationship to *future* satisfactions. Beginning with earliest life, adjustment therefore depends upon *a process of learning*, within social influence relationships.

Adjustment in broad perspective

While it may be glibly said that all human beings must adjust to their environment, this tells us little by itself. The very term adjustment can be viewed in various ways. Furthermore, every individual "adjusts," however disruptive or bad that may be in terms of socially disapproved actions. Apart from the obvious fact that one had to contend with

114

physical factors in the environment to sustain life, adjustment also grows out of the many demands of the "social environment." Individuals encounter these demands directly in social interaction, and also through the societal practices and group expectancies in their surroundings.

SOME DEFINITIONS OF ADJUSTMENT

Basically, there are two great traditions in the conception of adjustment. The first is the classic socio-cultural emphasis on the individual's adaptation to social demands. Juxtaposed to it is the emphasis which gives primary attention to the individual as a standard for assessing adjustment. The latter view can be subdivided into a concern with the individual's satisfactions in his relationships with the social environment or, even further in a humanistic direction, his growth and "actualization." Hence, we arrive at what are three relatively distinctive, but by no means fully separate, approaches to individual adjustment:

> • Adjustment can mean the process of adapting certain individual tendencies or desires—e.g. motives, attitudes, values—to social requirements. This view emphasizes a conception of *society as a force* requiring an individual's compliance through socialization. Some views of "mental illness" implicitly see it as a problem of "bad conduct" rather than of "disease" (e.g. Szasz, 1961).
> • Adjustment can be viewed in "ego-centric" terms as the satisfactions achieved by the individual through a more or less pleasing relationship with his environment. This view focuses upon *individual needs* and satisfactions in certain relationships, or transactions, with other people, within the social constraints of a culture. Social exchange concepts exemplify this orientation (e.g. Homans, 1967a).
> • Finally, adjustment is sometimes presented in terms of an *unfolding of the individual's potentialities* through maturation and experience. This is a view growing out of those theories of personality which emphasize self-actualization (e.g. Maslow, 1970). It is also encountered somewhat in the literature of existentialism.

In a sense, all of these have a place in social psychology, since they involve individual psychological factors which are influenced by the social setting. Furthermore, though differing in emphasis, these views relate to the key theme of individuals functioning within the framework of social demands and the requirements for social acceptance.

Whatever the approach to adjustment, its essential quality is one of dynamism, that is, the prospect for change. From an external viewpoint, adjustment occurs whenever the individual encounters new experiences that require a response. But there are also internal motivations of the individual, which arising from past learning may operate to move the individual toward the achievement of social goals in the environment such as status, recognition, or power. Yet even those internal motives construed to be physiologically based, such as hunger, are fulfilled in socially prescribed ways: what we eat, when we eat, and how we eat are learned in the context of a society and its pattern of culture.

Indeed, the first and most pervasive of the social influences of early life is the highly selective quality of the experiences a society provides for us. Asch (1959) puts it in these terms:

> Each social order confronts its members with a selected portion of physical and social data. The most decisive feature of this selectivity is that it presents conditions lacking in perceptual alternatives. There is no alternative to the language of one's group, to the kinship relations it practices, to the diet that nourishes it, to the art it supports. The field of the individual is, especially in a relatively closed society, in large measure circumscribed by what is included in the given cultural setting (p. 380).

The group-based quality of human society is an inescapable fact of life. Social relationships pervade human experience and carry demands in the form of the expectations of others. These are especially important where those others are significant to an individual's identities. The flow of social interaction progresses within the context of group norms and role demands. In psychological terms, the perception an individual holds of what others expect of him is a vital determinant of his social behavior; and the degree to which an individual perceives others as rewarding him enhances his motivation to be identified with them; this motivation also serves to heighten the individual's perception of expectancies.

There are then purposive, motivational features of ongoing experience which are future-oriented in terms of goals to be achieved or desires to be fulfilled. These play an important part in understanding the alterations of behavior occasioned by social interaction. They are intimately involved in the demands made for adjustment, as we shall observe in further detail shortly. While humans may seek the familiar and the comfortable ways of the past, these habitual patterns are modifiable through new experience and learning in contact with others, in terms of influence events.

ADJUSTMENT AS A RESPONSE TO INTERNALIZED FRUSTRATION AND CONFLICT

Because individual motives cannot always be satisfied, we often find ourselves in a state of "frustration." This factor accounts for many theories of adjustment based in the ego-centric definition offered as the first above. Furthermore, the satisfaction of one motive is sometimes inconsistent with the satisfaction of another equally impelling motive; this leads to a state of internal "conflict." In many contemporary views, frustration and conflict are conditions which represent the essential psychological bases for adjustment. They can lead to *expressive* behavior, as a relief from the tension produced by frustration, or to behaviors which can be *instrumental* in achieving the goal.

Several kinds of "mechanisms" or "techniques" of adjustment, which derive from Freud's views, can be seen as responses to frustration and conflict. Though we may generally react so as to indulge some of these more than others, all of us employ these techniques at some time in dealing with frustration. They are shown graphically in Figure 4.1 where the individual is seen to be aroused to move toward a goal which is blocked by a barrier that could be of a literal physical nature. More significantly, however, it might be of a social-psychological nature, as exemplified by a conflict of values represented in wanting to do something of questionable morality.

One obvious way to deal with the barrier is to find an alternative goal, which can be called *compromise*. Should you wish to see a par-

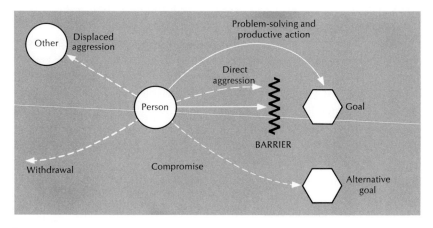

Figure 4.1: Diagrammatic representation of major adjustive responses to frustration.

ticular new movie, you might settle for seeing another one if the crowd is too large at the theater. Another technique of adjustment is *withdrawal,* in which case you would "deny" the desire and, in the instance here, decide not to see any movie at all. Two other techniques of adjustment which appear to resemble each other, but which are quite different, are *direct aggression* and *displaced aggression.* Neither is likely to be productive of securing the goal since both are essentially expressive behavior that has little instrumental value.

Direct aggression is usually thought of as an assault on the barrier, or what appears to be the barrier. The clearest exemplification of this is found where the individual strikes out, verbally or otherwise, toward the evident source of frustration. Thus, the crowd might occasion some negative remarks, loudly stated, possibly directed at the theater management's poor policies in keeping people waiting without their knowing whether enough seats will be available for them.

Displaced aggression is seen in the classic instance of kicking the dog, that is, a hostile reaction toward a bystander or other innocent party as a way of dealing with frustration. Interpersonal relationships are affected by such displaced aggression as indeed are inter-group and international relations as well. A recent book, edited by Berkowitz (1969), especially his introductory chapter reassessing the "frustration-aggression" hypothesis, provides a good source on this matter.

The adjustive technique of surmounting the barrier through *problem-solving* and *productive action* is usually thought of as the highest order of adjustment. It illustrates instrumental behavior, which can also occur through a process of thought. This ability to indulge in higher level symbolic activity through thought represents Man's great potential for mastery over his environment and the forces of circumstance. What is more, human adjustment has a future-oriented quality which transcends the present and implicates complex relationships between motivation, perception, and learning. They are highlighted by the concept of psychological reactance.

ADJUSTMENT AND PSYCHOLOGICAL REACTANCE

Reactance is a distinctively social psychological concept, applicable to an aspect of adjustment. It deals with the outcome of a threat to an individual's freedom of choice, especially in matters over which he believes he has mastery. Brehm (1966) defines it as "a motivational state directed toward the re-establishment of the free behaviors which have been eliminated or threatened with elimination" (p. 9). As was noted in Chapter 1, a person experiences reactance when other persons, or social norms, are seen to be restricting these behaviors, and this tends to make them more attractive. In other words, a freedom we see slipping from our grasp takes on greater value than one which is not immediately vulnerable to loss.

This concept has a good deal of plausibility, though it raises a number of interesting particulars regarding alternative conceptions of adjustment. The matter of "rationalization," which can take the form of withdrawal as well as compromise, suggests that the value of an unattainable goal will be *lowered,* as in the "sour grapes" phenomenon. Reactance suggests the opposite. The distinction here appears to be in the salience and implication attached to the expected freedom of choice. The disconfirmation of such an expectancy is *not* simply an unpleasant tension in the wake of an accomplished fact but is, as Brehm (1966) puts it,

. . . a motivational state with a specific direction, namely, the re-
covery of a freedom. Indeed, the only reasonable expectation about
the effect of reactance on the importance of a lost free behavior is
that importance may increase (p. 11).

Some of the so-called "boomerang" effects in research are explicable
in reactance terms. A number of recent experiments indicate that unfavorable reactions can be attributed to the impression of a loss of
freedom (e.g. Brehm and Cole, 1966), or to the extent of coercion
perceived to be operating on another subject (e.g. Goranson and
Berkowitz, 1966). More will be said about reactance effects in Chapter 7, in connection with social interaction.

The psychological underpinning of social behavior

Man as we observe him is not in a *natural* state. Human behaviors are
constituted within and conditioned by the envelope of influence relationships in a society. That we are directly affected by this process,
though the specific content of experience may vary, is due to social
interaction. As infants we depend upon other humans for survival and
are influenced by them. We are all capable of thus becoming initiated
into human society if, as Newcomb (1950, p. 50) suggests, we have
these three capacities:

> • A capacity for *irritability*, in the sense of being sensi-
> tive to the absence of those environmental conditions
> upon which survival depends. If we are not irritated by
> excessive heat or cold, or by hunger, we will not respond
> to the environment in such a way as to sustain life.
> • A capacity for *response* when irritated. If as infants
> we cannot suck or swallow or breathe, we will not be
> able to survive.
> • A capacity for *learning*, that is, profiting by experi-
> ence. While we could survive without the capacity for
> learning, it is of the greatest importance to adjustment
> and the acquisition of distinctively human behavior.

Given the availability of these three capacities, new members of a
society may take part in social interaction and, in so doing, be influ-

enced to acquire appropriate social behaviors. The task of the social psychologist is to provide understanding of how this process proceeds. Thus we can distinguish two levels of influence: one of high dependency having to do with the *initial* shaping of approved behavior in childhood as part of the "socialization process," that is, the upbringing of the child in the ways of the culture where *no* apparent alternatives are offered; and the other of less dependence where influence operates *after* early upbringing as part of adjustment to *new* social demands where there *are* alternatives for response that can be learned.

Individuals are brought within the framework of acceptable attitudes, values, and behaviors of the society in which they live through a process involving a great deal of *implicit* learning. By this we mean the acquisition of many of these attributes in the absence of any deliberate design to learn them or to teach them. This is in contrast to *explicit* learning, where either or both of these conditions of deliberateness are present. What is even more striking, however, is that what is learned in this implicit way is readily found congenial. Few of us, for example, resist the norms of our society in matters of monogamy, private ownership, and the use of the mother tongue. This is the essence of the point quoted above from Asch (1959). It is also true, as Erich Fromm (1949) has put it, that society shapes experience in such a way that ". . . *people want to act as they have to act* and [therefore] find gratification in acting according to the requirements of culture" (p. 5).

When instinct theories were in vogue, the problem of defining the motivational attributes of humans was relatively simple. There was, however, in the instinct idea a dubious logic, which largely led to its abandonment as applied to human affairs. It was simply *not* sufficient to make assertions of a circular sort such as "people strive for social acceptance because they have an innate tendency to seek social acceptance." As we noted earlier, the concept of instinct was especially misleading because it slighted the effect of Man's profound capacity for learning, in the broadest sense of adaptation. However, with the demise of instinct as a principle governing human conduct, it quickly became evident that other explanatory schemes would be necessary. This led to several kinds of distinctions which are still important points of reference today.

The first of these essentially distinguishes between *primary motives* which are physiologically based and necessary for the maintenance of life—such as hunger, thirst, the need for oxygen—and those learned or *acquired motives* which arise as a consequence of experience in society. The other kind of distinction has to do with the nature of human motivations that make Man distinctively different from other species. As we will see, however, the concept of motivation is itself undergoing considerable revision. Before turning to that, there is some merit in considering how the sources of human behavior have been looked at by social scientists, if only for an historical perspective on the complexity of the problem.

GENERAL CLASSIFICATIONS OF HUMAN MOTIVATION

The rich diversity of human motivation is widely acknowledged. But because the classification of motives was for so long identified with the imputation of different instincts to account for each and every observable behavior, the pendulum swung toward behaviorism with its minimal interest in motivation as such. In contemporary social psychology, it is fair to say that the global classifications of motives affecting social behavior are viewed with growing interest particularly in terms of the clustering of *social motives*. The question of Man's basic motivations remains an open and intriguing one.

For the last several decades, there has been a distinct flight away from the heavily deterministic viewpoints characterizing traditional behaviorist and psychoanalytic images of Man. The writings of Gordon Allport, Abraham Maslow, and Carl Rogers have been among the more influential sources of this change. A quest for growth, becoming, choice, and self-actualization are seen to move Man, not so much through reaction as by what Allport called "proaction"—acting *on* the environment. In this context, Rokeach (1968) observes, "Perhaps the major way in which contemporary psychology differs from the psychology of twenty years ago is that Man is now seen to be not only a *rationalizing* but also a *rational* creature—curious, exploratory, and receptive to new ideas" (p. 186).

This trend away from determinism is evident in Maslow's (1954) "hierarchy of motives." His essential idea is that motives may be arrayed from the strongest and most dominant through those that lead to actualization as the former are satisfied. In order, his hierarchy is as follows:

Physiological needs, such as hunger, thirst, sex, physical activity.

Safety needs, including security from physical and psychological deprivation.

Belongingness and love needs covering relationships of a responsive, affectionate, and affiliative nature.

Esteem needs seen in the desire of all people for a stable and high evaluation of themselves summed up in self-respect and the esteem of others.

Actualization representing the fusion or culmination of the other needs in a desire for self-realization or fulfillment of one's total capacities.

Some years ago, from his work across many cultures, the anthropologist Ralph Linton proposed three "psychic needs" which he found ". . . to be the most general and most significant for the understanding of human behavior" (1945, p. 7). Though their origins are not necessarily innate, he said they appeared to have great generality in observed behavior. They are:

The *need for emotional response from others,* which could arise from the early dependency relationships in infancy.

The *need for security of a long-term sort,* which takes account of the ever-present fact that humans have the ability to perceive time beyond the present and into the future. Hence, humans have a need for reassurance and hope but can live with the prospect of later gratification.

The *need for novelty of experience,* which comes into play when the other needs are satisfied. It finds its counterpart in boredom and the need for experimentation.

Robert White (1959) has extended the latter idea of a desire for experimentation, and an avoidance of boredom, to the concept of *effectance.* He sees as characteristic of Man a seeking for competence in handling the environment. Rather than be inborn in an instinctive sense, he contends that effectance motivation is part of Man's *need for exploratory and playful activity aimed at achieving competence* in an adjustive way. He says: "Putting it picturesquely, we might say that the effectance urge represents what the neuromuscular system wants to do when it is otherwise unoccupied or is gently stimulated by the environment. . . . The motive need not be conceived as intense and powerful in the sense that hunger, pain, or fear can be . . . [though] there are plenty of instances in which children refuse to leave their absorbed play in order to eat or visit the toilet" (p. 321).

The several viewpoints regarding social motivation reviewed here have certain common elements. Essentially they suggest the following commonalities regarding the human condition:

> Man requires social relationships and identifications but also a sense of his own personal identity and fulfillment.
>
> Man requires regularity, predictability, and order in his experience, but also the opportunity for activity and for experimenting with his own capacities in meeting the environment and having new experiences.

Summing up these points, we find what appears to be a set of paradoxes. How can Man want what seem to be contradictory satisfactions? One answer of course lies in the primary consideration that they are *not contradictory but complementary*. It is also noteworthy that we have been talking about "Man" in general, not a given person. Pursuing that point, though any one person may embody tendencies toward these satisfactions, they do not all operate for him simultaneously. A time-space factor is implicitly involved. In Maslow's conception, for example, he places motives in a hierarchy such that those at one level do not have a pronounced effect on an individual in a situation where those at a more basic level are as yet unsatisfied for him; hence Maslow's appropriate comment that ". . . Man lives by bread alone—when there is no bread."

MOTIVATION: A BRIEF REVIEW

Thus far we have been treating motives as if they somehow "pushed" individuals toward goals. However, the idea of motivation as a drive state is much too confining. In a more up-to-date vein, Cofer and Appley (1964), for example, have placed considerable weight on generalized "arousal" as a pervasive feature of action. In line with the concept of expectancy, they see such arousal as having a future-oriented quality, which they term the *anticipation-invigoration mechanism*. For an amplification of the "new look," see Dember (1965).

A "motive" may not be a single push, or pull, but an arousal of a sequence of behavior in an anticipatory, even playful, way. Furthermore, that sequence may serve multiple purposes. As Krech and Crutchfield (1948) point out, the regular church-going behavior of people who seem largely disinterested in religion can be revealed to be ". . . a meaningful, motivated action, fulfilling present needs and goals of gregariousness, social approval, wealth display, rest, or something else" (p. 32).

The traditional idea of motivation is concerned with behavior in terms of the goals toward which it appears directed. The problem, however, is that people often do the same thing for different reasons, and these reasons are never directly observed but are usually inferred from behavior. Furthermore, the actions implied by the same motive—or state of arousal—may differ widely depending upon the other people who are influential in supporting such action. Thus, a desire for "social acceptance" can lead one person to drive fast cars in a drag race and another to produce poetry.

The special relationship between motives and the goals they imply is of singular importance. Despite the fact that many social behaviors appear to be entirely dependent upon social practice, they nonetheless rely on the intertwining of motives and goals. Customs and institutions, and the appearance of imitation and suggestion, do not reduce the importance of the individual as an aroused actor. Granting the social basis of our attitudes and prejudices, it is not correct to understand them as being simply a result of some process of social habituation. Rather they should be seen as actions or reactions which anticipate desired outcomes, even though these may be obscured to immediate view. For example, the fact that individuals dislike those disliked by other members of their community does not stem just from exposure to social attitudes. This merely describes a circumstance that can better be explained by the motivation to participate with and be identified and accepted by important others.

Lewin treated these mechanisms as tension states. He considered that objects, persons, and activities have *positive valence* for the individual if they attract him and *negative valence* if they repel him. A main determinant of valence rests in the person's past experience with the particular stimulus in question. Hence, a hungry individual in our society is likely to have a positive valence for beefsteak, but a negative valence for whale blubber; for a hungry eskimo, we should not be surprised to find these valences reversed.

The valence of goals varies depending upon the individual's particular state of arousal. Having eaten heartily of our steak, we are less likely to have a high valence for the same fare very soon after. This highlights the intimate association of perception in understanding arousal as a motivational-perceptual state. It also points up the necessity to view behavior as a sequence of activities involving anticipations that may or may not be met, particularly in terms of adjustment to frustration.

The most comprehensive treatment of motivation and learning in terms of *generalized arousal* is presented in the extensive work of Berlyne (e.g. 1960, 1966, 1967). The essential point of his concept is that there is an optimal range of arousal; given a low state of arousal, anything which moves the individual to greater arousal will be reinforcing, but only up to a point. Here he introduces the concept of "optimal arousal," and postulates a curvilinear relationship between arousal and performance such that either low or high arousal will produce poorer performance than in the middle, optimal range. As a person continues to work at something, his optimal level of arousal regarding it may shift. Tasks which involve the element of novelty, surprise, and complexity, are in general more likely to be arousing and to maintain interest. However, this too depends upon the individual's state of general arousal at the time.

> Human beings in everyday life tend to welcome novel or complex experiences when they are in a normal, healthy, alert mood. But they seem likely to prefer familiar stimuli that are easy to deal with when they are either tense or drowsy. The problems and challenges presented by novel and complex stimulation are apparently gratifying when a person is equal to coping with them but not when his capabilities are below par (Berlyne, 1967, p. 92).

This is the "I'm-too-tired-to-care" phenomenon with which we all have had some experience. Yet, it does not quite explain how, at a low ebb though we may be, a novel thing can spur us to action. An un-expected telephone call, a sudden invitation to go out, the awakening delight in understanding something—any might do the trick. Berlyne deals with this issue by considering that arousal is not a unitary variable, but rather one which may differ in quality and consequences. It tells us something about general psychophysiological states, though as an intervening variable which requires further definition in terms of antecedent and consequent variables (1967, p. 12). From a social psychological standpoint, this means the necessity to know more about the individual, including his expectancies.

In this regard, an additional point of interest is that the disconfirma-tion of an expectancy may serve as the source of an arousal (Watts, 1968). The strength of arousal will, however, depend upon the sub-jective probability associated with the expectancy and the *importance* to the individual of achieving the anticipated outcome. This is the more general basis for "reactance" effects, considered earlier. Accord-ingly, where both the probability and the importance are extremely high, the state of arousal ensuing from a disappointment may be be-yond the optimal level, thus leading to dysfunctional actions, often re-flecting an inability to act appropriately, due to overwhelming arousal —which is another way of saying "acting very mad."

PERCEPTION: A BRIEF REVIEW

The process of perception is basic to the organization of the indi-vidual's psychological field. As Allport (1954) and Bruner (1957) have pointed out, perception begins as an act of *categorization*. We define "reality" in terms of the categories into which we place experience. In the absence of appropriate categories, we may use old ones to account for new experience or develop new categories. Perception, therefore, relies heavily upon past experience. However, perception is also *selec-tive* in its processing of new experience. To paraphrase Gibson (1966), information is extracted from stimulation depending upon what mat-ters at the moment.

The categorical quality of perception is illustrated when primitive tribesmen see an airplane in flight for the first time. For them, the best category growing out of past experience would be "bird," and it is often the case that the airplane is first categorized by them under the label of "big bird." If they also have reason to be fearful, which implies present motivation to avoid harm, they might further perceive the bird in the more selective sense of a "big *angry* bird." In sum, perception employs categorization in the purposive sense of finding meaning. It is therefore *aimed at interpretation.*

In psychology, perception is said to depend upon sensation, and a distinction is usually made between those terms. Essentially, sensation is the awareness of a stimulus—e.g. hearing a loud noise—while perception is the interpretation of that stimulus as a result of further processing by the individual. The loud noise could be disregarded. Or, if perceived under essentially tranquil conditions, it might be interpreted as a car backfiring; and, under tense conditions of high threat, it might be interpreted as a bomb exploding.

The intimate commerce between perception and motivation operates reciprocally. Individuals are likely to perceive events as a function of anticipated outcomes, but the reverse is also true: *they are likely to be aroused by what they freshly perceive.* The phenomenon of motivational effects on perception has been documented by a considerable volume of research over several decades. Levine, Chein, and Murphy (1942), for example, found in a classic experiment that hungry persons who had not eaten for many hours tended to perceive many more "food items" on an ambiguous ground-glass screen than did non-hungry persons.

Value and need can also directly affect perception, as Bruner and Goodman (1947) showed in a well known experiment. They asked ten-year-old children to try to match the actual size of several different coins by turning a knob to alter the magnitude of a disc of light. Cardboard discs were used as a control. On the average, perceptions of the size of real coins were found to be overestimates. However, children from poorer families differed significantly from children from wealthier families in overestimating size, especially of the quarter and half-dollar. The greater need associated with the value of money for the poorer children was the basis for explaining this perceptual discrepancy. Some questions have been raised about the generalizability of these results in light of nonconfirming studies (e.g. Carter and Schooler, 1949). However, the phenomenon of perceptual distortion has often been demonstrated to apply to valued stimulus materials of different kinds such as tokens which could be exchanged for candy (Lambert, Solo-

mon, and Watson, 1949). Tajfel (1957) has pointed out that contradictory findings can be explained largely in terms of the *relevance* of
size to value. Thus, where size is not important as a feature of value,
then the phenomenon is usually not found.

A circumstance in which size is prized occurs in estimates of the
number of people in a political crowd. Boasting about which candidate
or public figure attracted the larger crowd is a vital part of politics,
and crowd estimates reflect that consideration. The sponsors of a meeting typically give inflated estimates of the number of people who turn
out, especially for open-air gatherings where a "count of the house" is
less easily achieved. The police, who frequently give the "official"
estimate, are not likely to be able to do anything approaching an
actual count of large crowds.

In an article about counting political crowds, Jacobs (1967), a
journalist, provides some striking instances in which the size of a crowd
was variously estimated by different participants on the scene. An
example he gives, with actual figures, is from the 1960 presidential campaign when one of the candidates, the then Vice President, Richard
Nixon, stopped at the Milwaukee Airport to address a gathering. As
will be seen in Figure 4.2, the party officials estimated the welcoming
crowd there at 12,000, while the police put it at 8,000. A reporter said
there were 5,000. As it turned out, the *Milwaukee Journal* had a crowd
picture which showed about 2,300 heads and, counting those along the

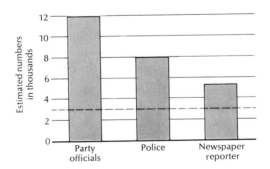

Figure 4.2: Three estimates of the size of an open-air political gathering.
(Based on data from Jacobs, 1967, p. 38.) The dash line at 3000 indicates
the number published by a newspaper, based upon a count from a photograph.

fringes, the paper concluded that the actual crowd could not have been more than 3000.

This kind of puffery is not, of course, confined to a single party nor to political events alone. Civic pride often causes an inflation of the number making up the "official count" for an event, such as the traditional ticker-tape parade through midtown New York, routinely said to bring out "millions." As Jacobs (1967) notes, however, this is a gross overestimate.

> In 1960 *The New York Times* used official city maps, measured sidewalk widths, and calculated that the traditional ticker-tape parade route from Battery Park to City Hall could hold no more than 141,436 spectators. Even allowing generously for those hanging out of office windows and watching from side streets, the total could not be more than 500,000 the *Times* concluded (p. 38).

It might be said that these examples are atypical of the phenomenon under consideration. But are they? Do the officials that report inflated figures operate only in a calculated way with a full awareness of the process of inflation, or do they want to believe that more people turned out and accordingly perceive it that way? Does the fisherman who tells the story of "the big one that got away" perceive that it actually was not so big after all? There is no one answer to the essential question posed here, but self-deception is an aspect of cognitive functioning that can be understood within the concept of expectancies in a dissonance theory framework; it is dissonant to believe that efforts aimed at a desired outcome have failed. Cognitive dissonance is considered at greater length in Chapter 6.

Everyday experience reveals the selective effect of motivation on perception each time we are tuned to some qualities or things and neglect to notice others that are also present. The effect of perception on motivation is another readily observable phenomenon seen when individuals encounter experiences which are novel for them—such as trying a new food—and thus develop a "taste" which takes on the properties of a motive. This restructuring effect of new information is also humorously revealed in the heavy smoker's statement: "I've been reading so much lately about the evils of smoking that I've decided to give up reading."

Changes in our psychological field resulting from the input of new information are a source of influence of considerable importance. There are, however, underlying reasons for the tendency to resist such restructuring, as we shall see.

Perception "sets" the individual to expect to encounter the world in a characteristic way. One reason that the statement just quoted is funny is that it prepares the listener for one thing and confronts him with another. This is true of a good deal of humor, which often operates by playfully disturbing a "set."

A fundamental principle of perception which grows out of the phenomenon of set is that individuals *tend to perceive experiences in the way they expect to perceive them.* This is sometimes summed up in the principle of perceptual *constancy,* that is, the tendency to perceive things in the same way as before. The importance of this point in social psychology rests in the significant association between expectation and outcome. Recall, too, the concept of "definition of the situation" in terms of the way this leads to anticipations in advance of experience. Since people frequently act in accordance with their expectation or anticipation of what will occur, they effectively increase the prospect that it will occur. This is the essence of the "self-fulfilling prophecy" concept mentioned in Chapter 1.

The specific content of our perception, in the sense of our categories for defining experience, and the sets we may be operating under, as well as the motives instigating them, are referred to as "functional" features of perception. It is this in particular that we have been emphasizing to this point. There are also "structural" features of perception which have great generalizability since they arise from the nature of physical stimuli as they relate to the neurological characteristics of humans.

One such structural principle is that of *wholeness,* a tendency to see stimuli as fitting together. Related to this is the principle of *closure* referring to the adding in of absent elements so as to achieve wholeness. Another ramification of this is the *imputation of causality* when stimuli are encountered in certain proximal or sequential relationships. Thus, individuals tend to perceive events which occur in sequence to be related causally. If a given event is followed by an observed outcome, that event takes on the quality of a "causal factor." This is the basis for the notion of luck and many other magical beliefs seen in the use of such "charms" as a rabbit's foot.

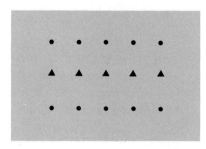

Figure 4.3: An illustration of "grouping" in perception.

An additional quality of structural perception is the principle of *grouping*. Grouping is illustrated whenever things which have a common attribute are perceived as related. In Figure 4.3, for example, we are likely to see three lines rather than a rectangle or isolated dots and triangles.

The Gestalt psychologists have devoted a great deal of attention to the way in which perception is affected by patterned relationships; indeed, the German word *"Gestalt"* means a pattern or configuration. An essential quality of any pattern resides in a *contrast* effect between a figure and its background. A "figure-ground" relationship refers to which part of the pattern stands out as a figure and which serves as background. This is essentially a matter of "imbeddedness," pointing up the consideration that a stimulus is perceived within the context in which it is placed. When a shade of gray is viewed against a black background, it is seen as lighter than when it is seen against a white background.

Structural properties of perception are by no means separable from the functional features arising from past experience and present motivational states. Patterns may be learned, as is revealed when we acquire the sense of "squareness," shown, for example, in Figure 4.4. The nine dots are not seen separately but are perceived to form together a dominant pattern. Hence, motivational-perceptual processes depend to a considerable degree on learning.

We also learn things about persons *through* these processes. "Person perception" is quite central to social influence phenomena. Heider (1958), a leading figure in the study of perception, is noted for his concept of "phenomenal causality." Individuals, he asserts, make at-

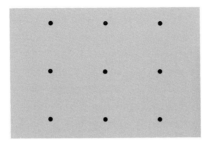

Figure 4.4: An illustration of "wholeness" in perception.

tributions about the causes, dispositions, and inherent properties of others they encounter. These perceptual processes are involved in information-seeking, the interpretation of motives, and influence events as seen in persuasion, conformity, and leadership.

Kelley (1967) has extended this analysis in what is called "attribution theory," discussed further with Heider's views, and the work of Jones and Davis (1965), in Chapter 7. For Kelley, a fundamental issue is the *perceptual basis for subjective validity*. In other words, when a person has an impression, let us say, of someone else, how does he determine that his impression reflects the "inherent properties" of that person and not his own characteristics or some unique interaction with that person? Paraphrasing Kelley (1967, p. 197), there appear to be four factors involved:

> *Distinctiveness:* the impression is attributed to the other person if it uniquely occurs when the other is present and does not occur when the other is absent.
> *Consistency over time:* each time the other person is present, the individual's reaction must be the same or nearly so.
> *Consistency over modality:* his reaction must be consistent even though his mode of interaction with the other person may vary.
> *Consensus:* attributes of the other person are experienced the same way by additional observers.

When these criteria are fulfilled, or mainly so, the individual feels more secure in his attributions. If not, he feels uncertain and is likely to be hesitant in his actions. Furthermore, he is inclined to be more susceptible to the influence of those who can provide more stability to his attributions. In that circumstance, social reality becomes highly salient as a reward. Kelley (1967) contends that these concepts are useful in organizing a great deal of the social psychological literature on the conditions governing: the susceptibility to persuasion; the immediate success of persuasion; and the persistence of its effects. These points are pursued later, notably in Chapters 6 and 7.

Adjustment and learning

Learning is the major process of study in psychology. There is good reason for this emphasis in view of Man's great capacity to adapt his behavior. Basically, learning refers to *actual* or *potential* alterations of behavior which may be more or less permanent. This definition takes account of the fact that the effects of learning need not be observed directly to be ready for later elicitation, and that they need not take hold in a lasting sense. Thus, the psychologist is interested in responses, but he also takes account of the internal restructuring of the psychological field, which is closer to what occurs when, in the conventional sense of that term, we "learn" in school.

The study of learning in terms of observable responses has been approached in two distinctive ways: the *conditioning of involuntary reflexes*, and *instrumental conditioning*. Both approaches have yielded concepts which are useful in social psychology. In the first case, learning is studied in terms of involuntary acts which grow out of the association of a new stimulus with a response such as salivation, eye-blinking, or any other reflexive act. In the other case, learning is studied in terms of voluntary or "emitted" behaviors which can have instrumental value in achieving a goal. The former approach, often referred to as "classical conditioning," is identified most with the work of Ivan Pavlov; the latter, sometimes called "operant learning," is associated most with the work of B. F. Skinner. These approaches are not as different as would appear since they each rely on associative learning under motivating conditions. Furthermore, neither depends upon conscious processes for elicitation.

Both approaches to learning look upon motivation as an energizer of action or reaction. Perception is also involved in both in terms of the cues which elicit behavior in line with the satisfaction of motives. The fundamental principle which underlies any learning and which therefore applies to both approaches can be summed up briefly: whenever an action or reaction satisfies a motive, this increases the probability of that action or reaction occurring subsequently when the motive is again aroused.

REINFORCEMENT

In any learning, adaptive behavior is not literally created so much as its probability is increased. Skinner says that he "reinforces" an already emitted behavior and by an appropriate sequence of "reinforcement" increases its probability of emission. But reinforcement need not be thought of only as something outside the person, such as an attractive goal-object. Berlyne (1967), for example, considers the best definition of reinforcement to be "whatever has to be added to contiguity to obtain learning" (p. 3). Mowrer (1960) contends that reinforcement can be conceived as a positive feeling—of anticipation or hope—experienced internally by the individual. His current theory of learning is built on the emotional states of hope and fear as counterparts to what Skinner calls positive and negative reinforcement.

Stotland (1969) has recently published a book, *The Psychology of Hope,* in which he treats hope as a function of the perceived probability and importance of attaining a goal. When both are high, the person will experience a greater positive affect, which can be described as joy, euphoria, pleasure, or satisfaction. The lower the probability of achieving an *important* goal, the more likely will the person experience anxiety. Stotland maintains that individuals are motivated to escape and avoid anxiety, which means its threat in itself can serve as a state of arousal that is motivating.

In a related way, Atkinson (1957) has proposed a theory of achievement motivation in which he sees it as a function of the tendency to approach success and the tendency to avoid failure. The first tendency is assumed to be a consequence of a combined function of a relatively stable personality characteristic of approaching success, the subjective probability of achieving that success, and the positive valence attached to success. An outgrowth of this work has been the incorporation of the proposition that, once aroused, motivation will persist until it is reduced (Atkinson, 1964). Failure to reduce the tendency to achieve success results in the tendency persisting so that, when the motivation to succeed exceeds the motivation to avoid failure, individuals are more likely to persist longer at that task, *even when failing*, than if they were continually succeeding at a relatively easy task (Atkinson and Cartwright, 1964).

Adjustment can be looked upon as a progressive process of learning, mainly of appropriate instrumental acts, but also of motivational-perceptual processes which guide integrated response sequences. Two important and interrelated features of learning that affect these sequences are summed up by the terms "generalization" and "discrimination." Given positive outcomes, responses become *generalized* to other similar stimulus patterns; and, alternatively, selective perception can occur between stimulus patterns so as to yield a *discriminated* response depending on their different qualities.

It has been found that learning not only is instigated by motivation but that it also persists where motives continue to be served. This need not be on a constant basis, however. Reinforcers have been found to be especially necessary at the *start* of learning to produce appropriate and consistent responses. Furthermore, their absence after learning leads to comparatively rapid "extinction" of responses. Yet, responses do persist in the absence of reinforcers if learning has taken place with a schedule of *partial* rather than *continuous* reinforcement.

In Figure 4.5, cumulative response curves are shown for these two conditions of learning in the extinction phase. They indicate that under "extinction," i.e. when all reinforcement has ceased, responses learned under 100 per cent reinforcement fall off more rapidly than do responses learned under partial reinforcement. One striking finding is that the most persisting learned responses are usually those associated with a kind of partial schedule—the condition of "variable reinforcement" in which the respondent does not know on which response-trials he will be reinforced. This is said to account for the appeal of gambling with its unpredictable hence variable, pay-off sequence.

The implications from studies of learning can now be briefly summarized. Whether learning is construed within the framework of classical conditioning or instrumental conditioning, motivational-perceptual processes are involved, including generalization and discrimination of

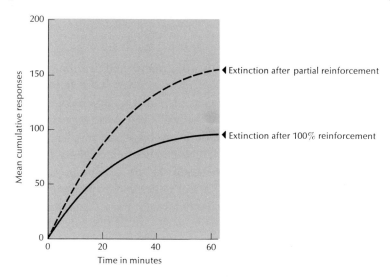

Figure 4.5: Cumulative response curves over time illustrating extinction effects following partial reinforcement and constant reinforcement. Responses have ceased when the curves become horizontal. (From *Introduction to Psychology* by C. T. Morgan. Copyright © 1961 by McGraw-Hill Inc. Used by permission of McGraw-Hill Book Company.)

stimulus patterns, as a basis for response. Associations are thereby developed which increase the probability of a similar response being occasioned again under comparable circumstances. The individual may experience a "good" feeling when his actual or implied response is the same as that he gave before under pleasant-feeling circumstances. The tenacity of a response is affected by the initial conditions of learning. Thus, extinction of a response is less likely if "partial" reinforcement was provided rather than "continuous" reinforcement, though continuous reinforcement is useful in the initial sequence of learning. Learning does not necessarily involve conscious processes but can affect thought in the sense of reconstituting the psychological field. Furthermore, learning need not involve observable behavior. As Mowrer (1960) has suggested, "Given the right circumstances, behavior can be facilitated, extinguished, or inhibited *without occurring*" (p. 64). A distinction exists between training and performance which is particularly seen in imitative learning, discussed in the next chapter in connection with socialization.

A further matter associated with adjustment and learning is represented by Helson's (1959) concept of *adaptation level*. It has numerous applications in social psychology. Defined in psychological terms, it is the stimulus value which is "neutral" and with regard to which other stimuli are judged, for example, as larger or smaller, better or worse, easier or harder. In social judgments, adaptations frequently take the form of perceiving one's self as the person in the center. Someone says he is a "moderate" about government spending. He then considers anyone who is more moderate to be a "spendthrift" and anyone who is less moderate to be a "tightwad." Similarly, he may say that he is "friendly," but that you are "familiar" and I am "aloof."

Adaptation level phenomena operate whenever we become "used" to something. If we have come to expect relatively positive statements from another person, say a friend, then a negative statement may loom far larger than if we had not had the prior, positive experience. The alternative case is also true: positive evaluations from someone who has tended to be negative are seen in a more positive light than if positive evaluations had come to be expected from that person (Aronson and Linder, 1965).

A whole society can adapt, in the sense of becoming blasé about things which once were electrifying—whether casualty figures in war, traffic fatalities, or space spectaculars. A number of commentators noted, for example, how much less interest was evidenced in the second "Moon walk" than in the first. It would be hard to retain that same peak of excitement, since much of the sheer "phantasy" of it all seemed gone.

The concept of adaptation level is particularly useful in social psychology for understanding reactions to new information. As a general rule, communications are judged within the scale of attitudes currently held by the individual recipient. Thus, the communicator who appears to advocate a moderate position on an issue such as civil rights would be perceived as a "raving radical" by a recipient positioned more negatively on this issue, and as a "go slow conservative" by a recipient positioned more affirmatively on it. This phenomenon is considered further in Chapter 6, regarding attitude change.

LEARNING-TO-LIKE THROUGH EXPOSURE

In connection with adaptation effects, some recent experimental work by Zajonc (1968) has suggested that mere exposure to certain stimuli serves to increase the favorability of a person's perception of it. In one experiment, he presented subjects with pictures of men's faces either once, twice, five, ten, or twenty-five times. They then rated these men in terms of how much they might like each one of them personally. He found that a positive logarithmic relationship prevailed between the number of exposures of the pictures of a person and the ratings of like-ability received from the subjects. This seems to be at odds with the old belief that "familiarity breeds contempt." Maddi (1968) suggests that there are three limiting factors which could affect the positive relationship of familiarity and liking, i.e. meaningfulness (a plus), monotony (a minus), and individual differences (either, depending upon personal preferences). He says that the true relationship between these variables is probably curvilinear, with familiarity shading into boredom so that very high as well as very low prior exposure could produce a negative feeling (see Maddi, 1961).

In this vein, Harrison (1969) conducted an experiment in which his subjects rated 200 "public figures," politicians, actors, scientists, industrialists, and murderers, plus a group of forty fictional characters, for familiarity and liking. All of these stimulus persons were Americans who had appeared on the cover of either *Time* or *Newsweek* in one or more of five years, the latest of which was 1966. In general, his results support Zajonc's findings, in that a strong relationship prevailed between the familiarity of these stimulus persons and liking for them. However, he found that persons who were unknown had virtually no chance of being liked, which is thoroughly predictable, while those who were quite familiar might be disliked. In particular, politicians from the recent past were among those who had *high* familiarity and *low* liking-ratings. Many of those were still active and therefore vulnerable to controversy.

Harrison (1968) suggests, as an explanation for the link between familiarity and liking, that novel stimuli pose a problem in terms of response tendencies. Though Berlyne (1960, 1966) proposes that such stimuli will be explored more, they can lead to antagonistic and competing response tendencies because they represent unknown elements. However, after the initial hurdle is passed, the once novel stimuli become familiar enough to elicit a positive response, especially when compared to other, authentically novel stimuli. This applies to places, as well as to people. The first time you visit a place, it is novel and unfamiliar; so long as the experience there was not negative, its familiarity may make it more appealing than an alternative, strange place, when the choice presents itself later.

Learning and social influence

A convenient way to approach social influence is to see it in terms of learning. As it is presently understood, learning is a process of adaptation occasioned by new experience. It therefore directly involves the input of information to the individual as a basis for his response. Whenever one person or some persons collectively provide information to another person, the elements of an influence relationship are produced. While all learning is *not* indicative of social influence, all influence relationships have the essential features of learning in these terms.

In recent years a good deal of research has been done leading to the conclusion that individuals are affected, often unknowingly, by the reinforcement others provide. For example, in summarizing the results of thirty-one studies of this phenomenon, Krasner (1958) reports that there is considerable regularity in the effect of verbal and non-verbal acts of one person on the behavior of another. These reinforcements may be such things as saying "good" or nodding affirmatively. Verplanck (1955) conducted an experiment which illustrates this effect quite conclusively. He had experimenters systematically agree to opinions offered unknowingly by other people in conversation. His results are shown in Figure 4.6 in the form of cumulative response curves. They may be interpreted as revealing that a considerable increase in the *proportion* of opinion statements occurred during the conditioning trials, even though the cumulative total of all statements there remained stable, at about the same level as in the pre-conditioning trials. In the extinction trials, the pattern of response returned to something quite like the pre-conditioning phase. Bachrach, Candland, and Gibson (1961) have demonstrated a comparable effect using a group of

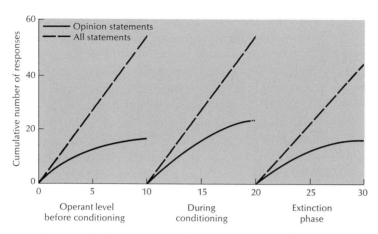

Figure 4.6: Smoothed cumulative frequency curves of opinion statements and of all statements for ten-minute segments of the experiment. (From Verplanck, 1955.)

others to reinforce the verbal responses of individuals by such positive reinforcers as saying "Yes," "Good," or "Mmm," and such negative ones as saying "No" and giving horizontal head motions.

The influence effects of reinforcement have also been studied with regard to leadership. Thus, in a laboratory experiment conducted by Pepinsky, Hemphill, and Shevitz (1958), it was found that those subjects who had been low on leader activity could be encouraged, without awareness, to increase that kind of behavior by the group's support of their statements; on the other hand, those who had been high on leader activity were affected in the opposite way by the group's evident discouragement of their statements.

The procedure was first to construct four-man production groups with two true subjects and two of the experimenter's confederates. Their task was to assemble parts into various shapes. For the positive "feedback" condition, the confederates showed highly favorable re-actions to any attempts to lead by either subject; for the negative feedback condition, they indicated resentment of "bossy" people when such attempts at leadership occurred. Two twenty-minute periods constituted the "work session." The results demonstrated a marked and highly significant effect of positive and negative feedback on the frequency of attempts to lead. In the former instance, subjects who had been reluctant to take an initiative, soon were giving direct orders, while those in the negative condition became silent. The other independent variables were personality measures of need for achievement and need for affiliation, which did not yield significant effects.

Experimentation with the phenomenon of conformity has also revealed the consequences of reinforcement by others upon an individual's willingness to accept the erroneous judgment of the group, as in the Asch experiment described in the last chapter. One tack in such work is to have the experimenter reinforce the "independence" of the subject by introducing the experimental treatment of telling him in advance that he is more accurate or correct than his co-workers. This characterizes one aspect of the work of Kelman (1950), Mausner (1954a), and Luchins and Luchins (1961). Another tack that such research may take is to have the group serve as a source of reinforcement of one's sense of accuracy, in advance of presenting erroneous group judgments. This is illustrated in an experiment by Hollander, Julian, and Haaland (1965) where "dependence" upon the group was variously contrived by having true subjects report first among five group members in a situation requiring the judgment about a simple unambiguous task over twenty trials. Some subjects found everyone agreeing with them on all twenty trials, some on fourteen randomized trials, and others on ten randomized trials. A control condition provided no feedback of others' judgments. Then, in all conditions, the true subjects were placed in the *last* response position for the twenty additional trials. This time all of the other group members appeared to be giving totally erroneous responses, and in *advance* of the subject. Conformity was measured by trials on which subjects gave this same incorrect response.

As is seen in Figure 4.7, those subjects who had the prior experience of agreement from others on all twenty earlier trials (100 per cent condition) gave the highest initial conformity, in the first block of the five later trials, but with a great drop over time, associated with extinction. Support in the form of partial reinforcement (70 per cent and 50 per cent conditions) yielded lower initial conformity to the group's erroneous judgments but greater persistence of response.

In two subsequent experiments (Julian, Regula, and Hollander, 1968; Julian, Ryckman, and Hollander, 1969), subjects received initial support in their judgments from none, 1, 2, 3, or 4 of their peers on each

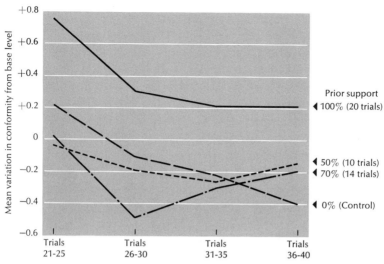

Figure 4.7: Subsequent conformity responses by blocks of five trials each for subjects exposed to different levels of prior group support in the first twenty trials. Scores are given as average difference from base level, combining sexes. (Based on data from Hollander, Julian, and Haaland, 1965.)

of the initial twenty trials. A comparable effect was obtained as a function of the number of others showing support. In the Julian *et al.* 1968 experiment, using same-sex groups, sex differences were observed in the effect of very limited support, i.e. from just *one* other person. Women showed far higher conformity in that condition than did men who, in fact, appeared to reject the group because three others had disagreed with them.

This kind of research provides a link between social influence and learning as a function of new experiences which can have observable sequential effects. Summarizing this point, it seems apparent that what is learned in any influence situation is a greater or lesser dependence upon the agent or source of influence as a basis for judgment and related action. There is considerable virtue, therefore, in looking at social influence in terms of a sequential learning process.

It is also worth noting again that partial reinforcement tends to produce a more persisting response. In their review of thirty-five studies covering subjects in a wide variety of training situations, Jenkins and Stanley (1950) conclude that "the most striking effects of partial reinforcement are apparent in response strength as measured by resistance to extinction" (p. 231). This has particular importance to social psychology in view of the discontinuous quality of reinforcement provided in social interaction. In the upbringing of a child, for example, it is rarely possible to provide constant reinforcement. This may make the learning of appropriate behaviors slower, but it has the effect of heightening the persistence of that behavior when reinforcement is no longer provided regularly, or not at all, as in conditions of extinction.

Throughout this chapter we have emphasized the continuing thread of Man's capacity for learning. While individuals adjust in terms of the experiences of the past, they also encounter new experience and the demands it makes for adjustment. Accordingly, the exposure to change and to novel experience or information is a central feature of social influence. In that regard, an influence relationship can be thought of as inducing a process which functions to change behavior and associated attitudes by an informational input. That humans are also capable of a high level of information-processing, in the form of thought, lends further weight to this point.

SUMMARY

Man's distinctive characteristics depend upon learning from contact with other humans. Social interaction is a vital feature of social adjustment, in terms of the relationships the individual has with the other people in his environment. Adjustment can be viewed as comprising processes of motivation, perception, and learning which interrelate to produce integrated behavior. Studies of these processes in individual psychology have been useful in helping to understand social influence.

Adjustment can be viewed in at least three ways: first, in terms of *social forces* requiring compliance and the striking of a *balance* between these and individual psychological states; second, in the *egocentric* terms of the satisfactions obtained by the individual from the environment; third, as an *unfolding* of individual potentialities. All of these views implicitly convey the idea of change and dynamism, but also of habituation.

Adjustment to society is a pervasive requirement of life. For the most part, however, individuals readily accept the selective quality of experience and related demands of society. Because an individual's motives cannot always be satisfied, a state of *frustration* occurs which represents an essential psychological basis for adjustment. Adjustive techniques include compromise, withdrawal, direct aggression, displaced aggression, problem-solving and productive action.

Motivation instigates behavior sequences aimed at goal-achievement. In psychology, a distinction is usually made between *primary motives,* such as the "hunger drive," which are physiologically based and necessary for the maintenance of life, and *acquired motives,* which are learned, e.g. achievement of social acceptance. Both imply goals which are incorporated in the psychological field. Moreover, the primary motives are subject to social influence, insofar as their satisfaction is regulated by society.

Attempts to codify Man's basic motivation have produced various systems. These point to the complementary quality of Man's requirement for: social relationships as well as personal identity; regularity and predictability but also new experience.

For the individual to adjust, he must modify his responses as well as reconstitute his psychological field. This involves motivational-perceptual processes which operate together to affect learning, through such mechanisms as "discrimination" and "generalization" of response to stimuli.

Perception is a process of categorization that is selective as a function of past experience, present motives, and anticipated future gains. It also directs the interpretation of stimulus patterns toward constancy and wholeness, in terms of the context in which they are imbedded. For social psychology, a key feature of perception is the phenomenon of "set" which leads individuals to perceive stimuli the way they expect to perceive them.

The study of learning of responses has been approached in terms of *classical conditioning* and *operant learning.* Both have yielded useful concepts for the understanding of social behavior. In either case learning depends upon motivation as an energizer of action or reaction. Where a motive is satisfied, this tends to increase the probability of the same response when the motive is again aroused. Where satisfaction of the motive is no longer provided, learning under conditions of constant reinforcement is not as effective in producing later consistency of response as is partial reinforcement. Perception is also affected by the process of learning, in the sense of restructuring the psychological field. Thus, *adaptation level,* which refers mainly to perceptions of the intensity of stimuli, grows out of what an individual has become used to from past experience.

Social influence can be looked upon as a phenomenon involving learning through the input of new experience. Experimentation has revealed that individuals are affected by the "reinforcement" others provide through verbal and non-verbal acts. This has been shown to affect statements of opinion, leadership, and conformity. Any influence relationship induces a process which functions to change behavior and related attitudes. It usually involves the essential elements of information transmission and implicates features of learning.

SUGGESTED READINGS

From E. P. Hollander and R. G. Hunt (Eds.) *Current perspectives in social psychology.* (3rd ed.) New York: Oxford University Press, 1971.

  3. Roger G. Barker: *The ecological environment*
Introduction to Section II: *Culture, learning, and group identification*
32. Fritz Heider: *Perceiving the other person*
42. Herbert C. Kelman: *Three processes of social influence*

SELECTED REFERENCES

Bandura, A., & Walters, R. H. *Social learning and personality development.* New York: Holt, Rinehart & Winston, 1963.
*Berkowitz, L. (Ed.) *Roots of aggression.* New York: Atherton, 1969.
Cofer, C. N., & Appley, M. H. *Motivation: theory and research.* New York: Wiley, 1964.
Crowne, D. P., & Marlowe, D. *The approval motive: studies in evaluative dependence.* New York: Wiley, 1964.
*Lazarus, R. S. *Personality and adjustment.* Englewood Cliffs, N. J.: Prentice-Hall, 1963.
*Levine, D. (Ed.) *Nebraska symposium on motivation.* Lincoln: Univer. of Nebraska Press, 1967. (Contains chapters by D. E. Berlyne—Arousal and reinforcement; I. Katz—The socialization of academic motivation in minority group children; H. H. Kelley—Attribution theory in social psychology; J. P. Scott—The development of social motivation; T. F. Pettigrew—Social evaluation theory.)

5

Socialization and the acquisition
of attitudes and values

The myriad effects of attitudes are evident all around us. For attitudes carry expectancies about our own behavior and the behavior of others, and they touch on all aspects of social life. Our tastes, manners, and morals reflect our attitudes and, relatedly, the social values which underlie them. How an individual views his world and acts toward it can be understood in great measure through a study of his attitudes.

Attitudes, as well as values, are acquired through socialization. As Elkin (1960) puts it, socialization is ". . . the process by which someone learns the ways of a given society or social group well enough so that he can function within it" (p. 4). This process applies not only to childhood but to adult life as well.

In the broadest sense, therefore, attitudes and values can be considered to be psychological representations in the individual of the influence of society and culture. They are very largely inseparable from the social context which produces, sustains, and elicits them under appropriate circumstances. Yet, attitudes retain the flavor of unique individual experiences as well. They are learned and tend to persist as a consequence of past social interaction. These experiences are conveniently summed up in the individual's present attitudes which, in turn, have directive effects on his ongoing, future-oriented activity.

The study of attitudes and values has occupied a major share of attention in social psychology for many decades. They are the result of social influence and help to account for individual differences in reactions to similar circumstances. Though in some way attitudes bear on each of the topics covered in this book, this chapter and the next will be directed especially to presenting the various characterizations of attitudes, their acquisition, measurement, and processes affecting their change. It is useful to set the stage by considering first some general matters concerning socialization, before proceeding to further specifics regarding attitudes and values.

The nature of socialization

An infant is born with potentialities for a wide variety of behaviors. But, as Irvin Child (1954) has noted, he is "led to develop actual behavior which is confined within a much narrower range—the range of what is customary and acceptable for him according to the standards of his group" (p. 655).

The complex process of being "led" into the ways of a society is conventionally called *socialization*. More than behavior alone, however, this process involves the acquisition of dispositions to view the world in distinctive ways and be attuned to certain satisfactions in it. A child in our society, for example, learns that monogamy, private ownership, and cleanliness are approved. These are social "values." He also acquires a host of "attitudes," in terms of beliefs about objects, including persons and situations, which then guide his actions.

Any society relies upon its members' adherence, broadly speaking, to certain regularities in *attitudes* and *conduct;* essentially, these form the expectancies which smooth the activities of society, especially in interpersonal relations. But expectancies are not uniform, they vary from setting to setting. What is appropriate at home may not be at the office, and the attitudes expressed among friends may not be the same as those voiced among strangers. As we noted before, learning these discriminations is necessary as a function of *role behavior*, which depends upon the setting, activity, and the others with whom we are interacting. However, the *values* of a society, and the *goals* they imply, provide support for many regularities in society by giving widespread sanction to some kinds of conduct and not to others. Notions of privacy, of honor, or of equity, are examples of those kinds of values which help to structure many social relationships.

While societies have organized means for "socializing" in formal ways, most obviously through the institution of schooling, the process proceeds largely in unorganized, informal ways via contact with family members, other people, and mass media outlets, notably television. Such contact provides the vehicle for taking on many attitudes and values, often through implicit learning.

In general, attitudes toward objects or entities may be acquired through: *exposure* to the object of the attitude; *interaction* with others holding the attitude; and deep-seated personality *dispositions*, including one's values, arising out of upbringing practices and family structure. These acquisition patterns are not firmly segregated, but may operate in combination, especially when viewed over time. Indeed, whatever the mode by which they are acquired, attitudes appear to be reinforced from childhood onward by association with others, in varying group identifications and social realities, beginning with the family.

Socialization as an area of social psychological study

In one sense, socialization is a vital part of developmental psychology, a lively field in its own right. In another sense, socialization is implicated in virtually everything social psychologists study. Indeed, Clausen (1968) says,

> If one takes a developmental perspective, socialization may be regarded as the core of social psychology. As a process, socialization entails a continuing interaction between the individual and those who seek to influence him, an interaction that undergoes many phases and changes (p. 3).

A total view of socialization is therefore not possible within the confines of this chapter. Elsewhere here, in the chapters and sections dealing with adjustment, social interaction, culture, personality functioning, peer group influences, prejudice, and conformity, among a host of other headings, matters which involve socialization are covered. What is of particular importance now is to suggest and illustrate the ways in which society and its agents bring about the acquisition of attitudes and values, so as to provide a framework for understanding the processes which underlie such learning.

Another point to be aware of is that the study of socialization does not signify approval of a society's practices. Social demands made upon individuals can be excessive, conflicting, or unjust—enough so that many members of a society or group within it might be vulnerable to mental disorder or great discontent. Fromm (1955), Henry (1963), and Laing (1960), are among those who have commented pointedly on these effects. Therefore, though the *process* of socialization serves as the principal focus of study, let it be clear that its *content* can also be looked at critically, with a view toward effecting change. Indeed, as an instance, several social psychologists have been leading proponents of compensatory education programs, such as Project Head Start, aimed at remedying deficiencies in the content of pre-school socialization (see Martin Deutsch and associates, 1967).

Before continuing with a detailing of various features of socialization, it will be helpful to characterize more explicitly the nature of attitudes and values and their relationship to one another, viewed in a cultural context.

The relationship of attitudes and values

Both attitudes and values have properties which define what is *expected* and what is *desired*. They can both therefore be thought of as motivational-perceptual states which direct action. Despite this common quality, it has been traditional to treat attitudes and values as distinctive. The major reason for this is as much a matter of stress as of function. For one thing, individuals hold many more attitudes than values. As Rokeach (1968) has put it:

> An adult probably has tens or hundreds of thousands of beliefs, thousands of attitudes, but only dozens of values. A *value system* is a hierarchical organization—a rank ordering—of ideals or values in terms of importance. To one person truth, beauty, and freedom may be at the top of the list, and thrift, order, and cleanliness at the bottom: to another person, the order may be reversed (p. 124).

Another distinction between attitudes and values has to do with their cultural linkage. A culture is usually seen to have certain values, rather than attitudes. As was pointed out in connection with the work of McClelland on the "achieving society" (1961) in Chapter 3, achievement motivation may be a cultural value. In simple terms, it represents the culture's emphasis on achievement as a significant social goal. The greater stability of values is usually accounted for in part, therefore, by their existence as guiding influences within the culture.

SOME POINTS OF DEFINITION

An *attitude* may be defined as a learned and relatively enduring organization of beliefs about an object or situation disposing a person toward some preferred response (Rokeach, 1968, p. 112). The term "enduring" emphasizes the perceptual constancy of attitudes as *sets*. In this regard, Asch among others considers that attitudes are "enduring sets formed by past experience" (1952, p. 585). The term "organization of beliefs" stresses the consideration that attitudes do not simply stand alone so much as they *cluster together*. The reference to "response" reveals the *motivational* force attitudes exert on action. People typically hold attitudes toward a wide range of social entities including, for example, the institutions and organizations of society, racial and religious minorities, and political and social issues. Thus, to take one illustration, they believe an interrelated cluster of things about political affairs, may accordingly reject other views, and are disposed toward certain behaviors, as exemplified in voting, writing letters to congressmen, or their political activities.

Values may be considered to be the core component of a clustering of attitudes which direct behavior on a long-range basis toward some goals in preference to others. In a motivational sense, therefore, values have a more central quality (see Figure 5.1). Furthermore, they have been found to be less subject to the effects of a situational change. Within a culture, a fair degree of congruence is usually found in the ordering of values. In one illustration of this, Morris (1956) had a sample of American college students rate thirteen "ways of life"— "preserve the best that man has attained," "cultivate independence of persons and things," and so on—and then analyzed these for major factors. In order, five factors emerged which may be paraphrased as follows:

> Participation and involvement with others
> Activity rather than receptivity

Enjoyment in progress and achievement
Social restraint and self-control
Self-indulgency.

More than five factors would undoubtedly better describe a person's total value system. However, when Morris compared the relative "loadings" of these factors with those secured in other cultures, he found several differences despite this shortcoming. In India and Norway, for example, the highest loading among these value factors was found to be "social restraint and self-control." Furthermore, "self-indulgency" which had been rated lowest but nonetheless positively among American students, was rated negatively in India, Norway, China, and Japan.

There is a question, however, about the breadth and stability of these values across a total society. This is a point to which we return in Chapter 11, in connection with sub-cultural variations. Nonetheless, a degree of consistency is frequently found in the value systems of members of the same society who have been exposed to a dominant cultural pattern. Osgood, Ware, and Morris (1961), for example, found a considerable parallel between the values from Morris's study using rankings and those obtained from a "semantic differential" procedure used with another group of American college students at a later time. Bearing in mind that there may still be a fair degree of individual difference in values, we now will consider the broader influences of cultural factors in attitudes and values.

CULTURAL FACTORS IN ATTITUDES AND VALUES

Taking on the appropriate attitudes toward other people, toward groups, toward food and other objects in the environment is basic to being human. Attitudes about culturally significant objects carry an implicit valence in a positive or negative sense. Foods serve as one apt illustration. Among the earliest experiences in any culture are those which have to do with approved or disapproved foods, as well as the scheduling of meals.

In American society, for example, the culture dictates a breakfast which typically could consist of fruit juice, cereal or eggs. Other societies have cultural patterns emphasizing a breakfast of rice, or yoghurt, or kippers. We eat three meals a day and accept that pattern much as the air we breathe. We also expect to eat them "on time," which in itself is culturally relative. Thus, it comes as a jolt to find a different pattern when, for instance, Americans traveling in Spain discover that restaurants customarily open in the vicinity of 9 p.m. for the evening meal. Even the sense of time, and the significance attached to it, is dependent upon the learned patterns of a culture, as the work of such anthropologists as Hallowell (1937) and Hall (1959) reveals (see Chapter 8).

The characteristic values of a culture have a quite pervasive effect as orientations for individual judgments, often in an adaptation level sense. As a case in point, in our society we are inclined to value height. In other societies, our own culturally based view of the merit of tallness may be eyed differently, especially if people tend to be considerably shorter. A story illustrating this comes from an American visitor to Hong Kong who was ordering a suit from a tailor there. The visitor, ranging a bit over six feet in height, was asked by the tailor whether he would prefer a two- or three-button model. The man disclaimed a preference so the tailor apologetically urged him to take a two-button suit, explaining "It will make you look shorter."

What any society dictates by way of cultural patterns materially influences its members' expectations about events and things in the environment. When people encounter contradictions of their expectations, especially when the issue has immediate importance to them, as in the matter of eating, they are likely to experience some distress. This quality of shaping experience makes attitudes and values very consequential as systems affecting human life. In speaking of this effect, Ralph Linton (1945) says:

> Behavior which is not in accord with the individual's system elicits responses of fear, anger, or, at the very least, disapproval. . . . Thus an individual who performs an act contrary to one of his own value-attitude systems will experience considerable emotional disturbance both before and after (p. 112).

ATTITUDES AND VALUES AS MOTIVATIONAL-PERCEPTUAL STATES

In the last chapter we spoke of learning in terms of motivational-perceptual processes. Attitudes and values can be thought of and will be dealt with here as motivational-perceptual *states* (F. H. Allport, 1955). An individual's attitudes set him to respond through the perceptual quality of selecting, categorizing, and interpreting experience in line with expectation; an individual's values are associated with the central tendency of a cluster of his attitudes in a long-range motivational sense. Attitudes and values are both learned in terms of a restructuring of the psychological field. This process is a dynamic one insofar as attitudes and values are subject to change through the acquisition of new information. However, attitudes appear to be more susceptible to apparent change while the basic value underlying them may persist.

As we have already observed, attitudes and values are important in social psychology because they sum up the past experience of the individual in terms of *directive* motivational-perceptual states, growing out of learning. It is also possible that learning in turn will bring about a restructuring of these states. Thus, a directive motivational-perceptual state can be thought of as an outcome of a process of learning which fashions further learning. This process therefore has consequences not only in terms of observable behaviors but also with respect to potentials for the individual's action.

Though there is a commonality between attitudes and values, they are not necessarily in harmony. Indeed, a given value can lead to different and even opposite attitudes in the same person. For example, the need for achievement may yield a belief in one's right to individual betterment through competition, as well as a belief in the necessity to work with others co-operatively. In addition, a given attitude held by one person can arise from a different value than that underlying the same attitude held by someone else. One person might believe in helping the poor out of a sense of social obligation for the improvement of society, while another might believe the same thing out of a sense of superiority. Furthermore, the quality and texture of their actions toward the poor would vary accordingly.

A schematic representation of the probable relationship between an individual's attitudes and values is shown in Figure 5.1. As indicated there, the same value may give rise to conflicting attitudes, as might be the case for attitudes 8 and 10, for example. Different values may sustain one attitude, though with variable intensity, as noted for 3 (A and C), 4 (A and B), 7 (A, B, and C) as instances.

Even given the refined measuring techniques presently available, it

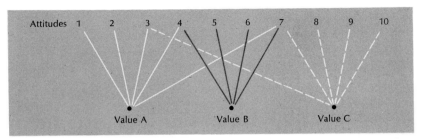

Figure 5.1: Diagram showing schematic relationship between three values with varying clusters of attitudes. Note that each value has several attitudes organized about it to indicate what is merely a sampling of those attitudes.

is difficult to separate attitudes and values entirely since there are so many points of interrelation between them. One thing appears to be generally agreed; attitudes are inclined to be more susceptible to change—at least in their outward expression—as a consequence of real or contrived circumstances. In this connection, Hovland (1959) points out that experimentation on attitude change routinely shows a more pronounced effect in shifting attitudes than is evidenced from questionnaire surveys. He also indicates that this is probably due in part to the fact that experiments often deal with attitudes which are more trivial to individuals than those studied in surveys. Thus, political attitudes can be highly significant as a feature of the individual's value system and hence be less subject to change.

The systematic measurement of values has usually been based on a limited number of values which may represent the central core for many attitudes. Allport, Vernon, and Lindzey (1951), for example, have developed a widely used, standardized scale for measuring the relative importance individuals attach to six values:

> *Theoretical:* being oriented toward a quest for truth through empiricism, criticism, or rationality.
> *Practical:* stressing utility and adherence to prevailing economic views.
> *Aesthetic:* giving prominence to form, harmony, and symmetry as sources of enjoyment.
> *Social:* emphasizing humanistic orientations such as altruism and philanthropy.

Power: weighting personal power and influence, including those aspects of politics.

Religious: seeking transcendent or mystical experiences through which to understand the unity and meaning of life.

An individual's value system is established by means of a "profile" derived from his indicated preference among alternatives on many items in the scale. Employing this measure, Allport, Vernon, and Lindzey have demonstrated that a group of medical students was high on the theoretical scale but low on the religious scale; the opposite was the case for theology students. Generally speaking, vocational preferences have been found to be part of a clustering of attitudes, related to basic value systems, and not the result of a single attitude toward a given field.

Among the most interesting recent developments in the study of values is Rokeach's (1968) research on the relationship of *instrumental* and *terminal* values to attitudes and behavior. He constructed two alphabetized lists, the first with instrumental values, such as *broad-minded, clean, forgiving, responsible,* and the second with terminal values, such as a *comfortable life, equality, freedom,* and *salvation.* He asked subjects to simply rank-order each list in terms of the values' importance. Subsequent research and refinement indicated that these rankings, initially with eighteen and later with twelve values on each list, had considerable stability over time. Their test-retest reliabilities after seven weeks were above 70 per cent. Data were also obtained on similarities and differences in the instrumental and terminal values of various groups, varying in age, sex, education, occupation, religion, and politics. Rokeach found that there was a systematic relationship between the reported *behavior* of subjects and whether they had ranked a given terminal value very high or very low. For example, college students who reported that they went to church "once a week or more" typically ranked *salvation* first among the terminal values; other college students, who reported attending church "once a month," "once a year," or "never," typically ranked salvation last among these values (1968, p. 169).

Regarding the relationship between values and attitudes, Rokeach obtained some unusual data on the association between rankings of *equality* and *freedom*, two political terminal values, and attitudes toward civil rights demonstrations. Subjects who reported that they were sympathetic, and had even participated in these demonstrations, on the average ranked *freedom* first and *equality* third, among the twelve terminal values. Those responding that they were sympathetic, but had not participated ranked *freedom* first and *equality* sixth, while those who indicated they were "unsympathetic" ranked *freedom* second and *equality* eleventh.

The entrenched nature of values has been studied in an experiment by Vaughan and Mangan (1963) who employed a variant of Asch's (1951) group pressure situation. In this work, subjects were selected whose profiles on the Allport-Vernon-Lindzey scale revealed a high and low score in two value areas. Each subject was placed in a group with three other apparent subjects, all seated in a semi-circle, facing a screen. The experimenter flashed statements on the screen, each for no more than two seconds, and the subject's task was to report, in his turn, what the statement said. The experimental procedure was contrived so that these statements represented a value which had previously been ranked either very high or very low by the subject. The three other apparent subjects were instructed to report incorrect recognitions of these sentences. Thus, half the time these incorrect responses were in opposition to the subject's high value, and the other half of the time in contradiction to the low value. An actual sentence, involving an *economic* value was "Production efficiency is a matter of *vital* concern." It was incorrectly reported by the other subjects as: "Production efficiency is a matter of *minor* concern." Another sentence, regarding a *religious* value was: "Theology must be considered a *fruitful* study." It was incorrectly reported as: "Theology must be considered a *fruitless* study."

After two non-crucial trials, in which the subject responded first and the apparent subjects agreed without comment, the response position of each subject was then randomly determined so that he had an equal number of trials in the second, third, or fourth position. This permitted a test of the effects of the amount of group pressure, in accordance with Asch's (1951) work on the size of the majority.

In line with their major guiding hypothesis, Vaughan and Mangan (1963) found when the task content represented a "high" value there was significantly less yielding to group pressure than when it repre-

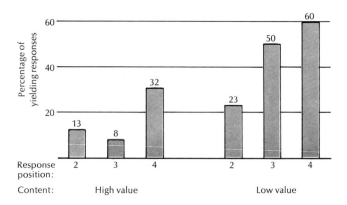

Figure 5.2: Percentage of yielding responses on high and low value statements by subjects in three response positions. (Based on data from Vaughan and Mangan, 1963.)

sented a "low" value. Their results are shown graphically in Figure 5.2. As the figure reveals, there is a striking difference in the amount of yielding under these two major conditions. Moreover, there is an expected position effect seen in the greater susceptibility to influence when a larger number of respondents give erroneous reports before the true subject. For "high" value material, the leap upward in yielding is resisted until the subject is in the fourth position; for "low" value material, it occurs from the second to the third position. Thus incorrect recognitions were more strongly resisted when an important value was involved, and this was only overcome, and at that only somewhat, by pressure from the entire group of respondents.

An important aspect of values, then, is that they are resistant to influence. That hardly means that they are unchanging. But, if socialization in childhood has done its job effectively, they are at the very least resilient. We now turn to a consideration of that process.

Some features of socialization in childhood

In considering the socialization of the child, two guidelines are especially important here: first, we are primarily interested in changes which occur through learning, rather than just as a function of growth and maturation; and second, we are emphasizing changes based in a social influence relationship, involving direct interaction, or other symbolic communications.

The socialization of the young can be seen as a model for many other influence events in life. The child is dependent, and a state of dependency in later life is a decidedly important variable in accepting influence from others. The child is often confused and unsure about some things, and that too is a variable, often characterized as uncertainty or ambiguity, which bears on this effect at a later time. The child desires affection and approval, and such rewards also play a part in shaping influence more broadly.

DEPENDENCY AND IDENTIFICATION

There are, however, some unique relationships in childhood which intensify these factors and make them crucial to social development. These are centered in the family with its unique role in socialization. The pre-eminence of the family in this process has several bases. Not the least of them is the repeated finding that prolonged separation from the security of the home environment, and especially early in life from the mother, leads to serious psychological effects including intellectual retardation. Moreover, much that we associate with male and female behavior in a society is developed out of early identifications in the family circle (Kagan and Moss, 1961). The family also provides the youngster with his first and most significant "reference group." Indeed, one might well look upon the family as the child's first "culture," and Henry (1963) has said that each family represents a unique subculture. There are of course many consequences of this kind of affiliation that can be seen in the later orientations and conduct of the child.

Beginning in earliest infancy, the parent, or a parent-figure, provides satisfaction for the child's primary needs. As a consequence, a motive for social approval can be seen to grow out of a process of associative learning. This process ultimately leads to the acquisition of attitudes and values through what Mowrer (1950) calls "secondary reinforcement." Examples of this process are shown graphically in Figure 5.3.

The parent is the agent for providing food and thus becomes linked, as the arrows reveal, with the reinforcement given by it (A). Thereby, a positive association with the parent leads to parental approval becoming a goal which is itself reinforcing. To secure that goal, the child

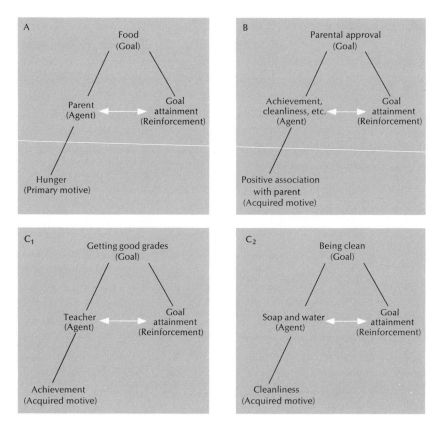

Figure 5.3: Schematic representation of associative learning of attitudes and values as acquired motives. In each case the agent intervenes between the motive and goal, thus becoming identified with the reinforcement produced by goal attainment. In A, a primary motive leads to the agent becoming valued as a goal in itself. In B, the attitudes associated with the agent are acquired under conditions of dependency. In C_1 and C_2, two examples of these values as goals in themselves are shown as indications of how the sequence proceeds.

behaves in line with values, such as achievement and cleanliness, which become agents for securing parental approval (B). Now each of these agents becomes a secondary motive, implying goals, such as "getting good grades" or "being clean," and, in turn, the teacher (C_1) and soap and water (C_2) come to be agents associated with reinforcement. And so the process goes, taking on more complexity through childhood.

It is possible, therefore, to view the acquisition of attitudes, values, and behaviors as a phenomenon of generalization to associated stimuli. In a related way, the process can be seen as a social exchange in which the parent provides a reward and is rewarded, first by the great sense of joy usually accompanying the arrival of a new baby, then by the baby's signs of recognition in smiling and cooing. There are also "cognitive restructuring" explanations that place less weight on specific behaviors and more weight on the perceptual differentiation which underlies them. This cognitive-developmental viewpoint is exemplified in work on imitative learning, and moral development, to which we will be giving attention shortly.

The dependent child very much requires supportive contact from adults. This is of course a matter of the critical demands for physical survival, but there are also potent psychological rewards associated with securing social identity, social support, and social reality. The family is the first group to provide these. It therefore initiates orien-

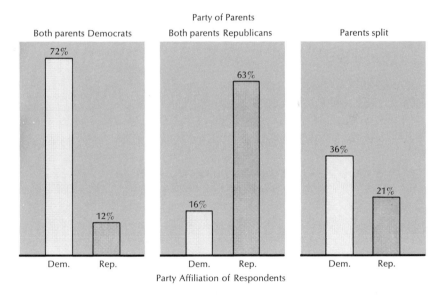

Figure 5.4: Relation of parents' party affiliation to that of offspring. Based on 1489 respondents. Those indicating no party affiliation and minor party affiliation are the absent cases which would yield a 100 per cent total for each of the three major headings. (Based on data from Campbell, Gurin, and Miller, 1954.)

tations which persist through the child's later relationships in society. This is exemplified by a good deal of research on the transmission of political attitudes from parents to their children. In summarizing this work, Hyman (1959) reports that attitudes toward public affairs and political party affiliation are consistently found to approximate closely those of the parents, or at least the father (p. 31). Campbell, Gurin, and Miller (1954) find from their survey of a national sample of voters that, given the same political preference by both parents, there is approximately a two-third probability over-all that children will hold that same party identification in adulthood (p. 99). This pattern of association is shown in Figure 5.4. Later work by Campbell, Converse, Miller, and Stokes (1960) suggests that this effect may be offset and diminished by the growing number of Americans who characterize themselves as only "leaning" toward one of the major political parties, or who are now "independents." But, in any case, the prospect exists for there to be an initial influence from the parents which can then be altered by later exposures. This bears on adult socialization, regarding which more will be said in due course.

IMITATIVE LEARNING

Oftentimes, especially in childhood, learning occurs by imitation without obvious reinforcement, or an intention to teach. Hence, children are observed to have taken on characteristics of behavior and speech which parents would hardly have wished to have them learn. How does this occur?

Flanders (1968) has presented an analysis of four kinds of "training conditions" in imitative learning. Figure 5.5 shows a classification of these, as well as the incentive conditions which might prevail during subsequent performance testing. Each of the four training conditions represent a combination of contingent reinforcement (reinforcement which depends upon a correct response) from M, the "model," and O, the "other" person, observing the model. In the non-reinforcement cell, neither M nor O receive reinforcement; in the direct reinforcement cell, only O receives reinforcement; in the vicarious reinforcement cell, O observes M receiving reinforcement; and in the double reinforcement cell, both M and O are reinforced.

Of particular interest is the *vicarious* reinforcement condition, which typifies many imitation situations. There, it has been found that the imitation of M by O increases, if M is successful in obtaining rewards, and is a function of the percentage of M's responses which are rewarded. On the other hand, O's imitative behavior does *not* become increasingly resistant to extinction by observing partial reinforcement to M. Thus, the greater tenacity of response associated with partial reinforcement holds for direct reinforcement but evidently not for vicarious reinforcement (Flanders, 1968, p. 321).

As Campbell (1961, 1963) notes, the tendency of O to imitate M is a "behavioral disposition." Its subsequent performance requires the additional step of incentives, that is, later reinforcement, during the performance phase.

As shown in Figure 5.5, the reinforcement there may be considered at three levels of intensity, that is, minimal, moderate, or maximal. Flanders (1968) holds that the strength of the behavioral disposition to imitate may not be revealed unless the incentive condition is *sufficient* to elicit it in performance. In short, imitative behavior will only be manifested if the conditions under which it is to be performed are sufficiently reinforcing; a corollary to this is that training can occur, without evidencing itself, due to an insufficiency of reward in the performance setting.

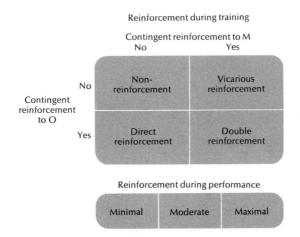

Figure 5.5: Reinforcement conditions for training and performance in imitative learning. (Adapted from Flanders, 1968, p. 321.)

A particularly significant line of experimental work in this area is research on the imitative learning of aggressive responses (e.g. Bandura and Walters, 1963; Bandura, 1965a, b, c). In a typical experiment, a young child enters a familiar playroom and finds a person, sometimes a teacher and other times another child, playing there. That person serves as a model for the child by behaving very aggressively toward a large Bobo doll (an inflatable plastic clown of small adult size), and by attacking other dolls and animals. This is the "training phase." Later, in the performance phase, the child who observed this behavior is placed in the playroom again, this time alone with the toys, including the Bobo doll, previously attacked by the model. Bandura and his colleagues find that evidently well-adjusted children will imitate the aggressive actions they have observed the model display. Furthermore, this imitative behavior can be acquired with no contingent reinforcement to either the model or the observer in the training phase (see Figure 5.5, upper left cell). There are factors which will contribute to this acquisition including identification with the model, a matter that will be of concern in the next chapter.

What distinguishes the Bandura approach is his contention that the "matched-dependent" concept (Miller and Dollard, 1941), regarding variables affecting the acquisition of novel responses, relies too much on a motivated subject being positively reinforced for matching the correct responses of the model through trial-and-error. Bandura (1965a) argues that imitative learning of that kind is actually a case in which ". . . the behavior of others provides discriminative stimuli for responses that already exist in the subject's behavior repertoire" (p. 5).

The essential distinction here is that Bandura sees the acquisition of behavioral dispositions (Campbell, 1961, 1963) toward imitation in cognitive terms, as a consequence of an observer noting the association of stimuli. There is not a response in the usual behaviorist sense, but a symbolic process which occurs. Bandura also considers, however, that reinforcement of the model or of the observer during the performance phase, will affect responses then.

In an experiment demonstrating some of these effects, Bandura (1965c) had children about five years of age individually observe a five-minute motion picture on a television set. In the film, they saw a man twice carry on a sequence of novel assaults on the long-suffering

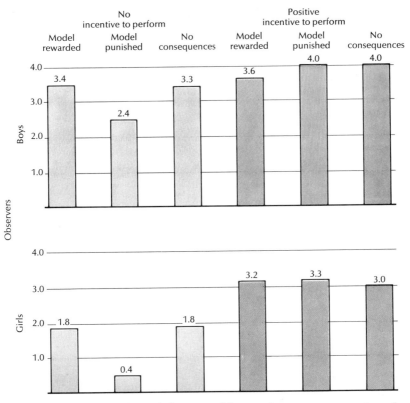

Figure 5.6: Mean number of four possible matching responses given by children in the performance phase who had observed aggressive behavior by a model receiving one of three reinforcement treatments, and who themselves did or did not receive incentives to reproduce the model's behavior. (Adapted from Bandura, 1965c, p. 592.)

Bobo doll, including three distinctive behaviors—striking the doll with a mallet, sitting on it, and punching it in the nose—each of which was accompanied by distinctive comments such as "Sockeroo . . . stay down" and "Pow, right in the nose, boom, boom." One of three treatment conditions followed: In the first, the adult model was generously rewarded by another man who entered the room referring to him as a "strong champion" and providing him with all kinds of candies, Cracker Jack popcorn, and the like; in the punishment condition, the man entered referring to the model as a "big bully" and shaking his finger at him; in the no consequences condition, neither of these end-ings were shown.

Immediately following, the children were taken to a playroom in which they found the same toys and other objects they had seen in the film, plus many other toys of a different sort. Children spent ten minutes in the playroom and were observed for imitative responses by two raters. This provided a measure of performance with *no direct incentives*. Subsequently, the children were brought to a room with an assortment of fruit juices in a colorful dispensing fountain, and were told that for each of the physical and verbal responses of the model that they could recall, they would receive a pretty sticker-pic-ture. This was the measure of acquisition, with a *positive incentive*. Figure 5.6 shows the mean number of matching responses of four which children reproduced as a function of each of the three treatment condi-tions, during the no incentive and the positive incentive phases.

The results presented in that figure indicate that the children ex-posed to the "model-rewarded" and the "no consequences" conditions performed about the same number of matching responses in the *ab-sence* of an incentive; and boys imitated more of the model's behavior than did girls. Whether the model had been rewarded or not made no difference, though when the model had been punished it had the effect of diminishing the matching responses considerably. When positive in-centives were introduced, however, they completely eradicated the observed performance differences in imitation, thus revealing an equiv-alent amount of learning, in the sense of acquisition, among children in the three major conditions. Bandura's conclusion is that "reinforce-ments administered to the model influenced the observers' performance but not the acquisition of matching responses" (p. 593). In line with Flanders's (1968) formulation, given sufficient incentive in the per-formance condition, the imitative behavior is available.

Moral values

Any consideration of socialization, even of a general nature, must take account of the compelling reality that society depends upon the indi-vidual internalizing a sense of those things in human relationships which are "right" or "just" or "proper." This is often considered to be embodied in *conscience*. The development of moral values is therefore a quite crucial aspect of socialization. Indeed, in his 1908 text in social psychology, McDougall observed:

> If we would understand the life of societies, we must first learn to understand the way in which individuals become moulded by the society into which they are born and in which they grow up, how by this moulding they become fitted to play their part in it as social beings and how, in short, they become capable of moral conduct (p. 174).

However unwittingly, parents provide models for a child's behavior, and this has a determining influence upon the development in the child of moral values. Identification with parents is a central feature in this process. Aronfreed (1968) contends that affective ties with a model, such as a parent, are important mediators in learning moral values. Kagan and Moss (1961) report that "many researchers agree that one of the major signs of a strong identification was the child's adoption of the behaviors, motives, attitudes, and self-conceptions of a model" (p. 469). There is, however, considerable complexity in the identification process. In another paper, Kagan (1958) defines identification as an "acquired cognitive response" which has the property of making a person react to events occurring to a model as if they were happening to him. Rather than be directly taught, it appears to involve "imitative learning," as discussed earlier. Among the most important outcomes of identification is the acquisition of conscience.

CONSCIENCE

One measure of conscience is the ability to resist temptation. Sears (1960) has conducted a series of experiments with nursery school children to study the strength of conscience. In one of these, a five-year-old child is left alone in a room filled with toys that can be played with. On the table is a bowl of candy that the child has been specifically told *not* to touch. A younger child then enters the room. He or she has been told that it is all right to take the candy. The central interest of this experiment is in how the older child handles the younger child. Some children try to distract the younger one with the toys. Others are found to threaten physical punishment. Sometimes the older one shares in taking the candy. Following observation of the child confronted with this conflict, Sears interviews the mother to get at determinants of the observed behavior. He finds that the child's ability to exercise self-control is a function of a greater or lesser degree of *identification* with the parents. Thus, a boy who immediately helps himself to the candy is often found to have a weak identification with his father.

In general, Sears concludes that identification results in the first place from *dependency* upon the parents. If they provide adequate models of moral conduct, the child is likely to incorporate this value and will learn to behave morally. This depends upon a balance of discipline and affection. Identification originally arises from a desire to keep the parents close by and approving but later takes on the properties of a personal conscience. This work reveals, as have other findings, that many children at the age of five are quite capable of having developed a conscience.

STAGES IN MORAL DEVELOPMENT

An approach to moral development, in terms of stages, has been a significant outgrowth of the work of Piaget (e.g. 1932, 1947, 1948). His cognitive-developmental orientation stresses the unfolding of capacities as a function of maturation. From his extensive work on thought in young children (Piaget, 1932), he contends that moral values are not taught in a step-wise way; they are learned by a restructuring of the child's psychological field spontaneously, as a consequence of development and exposure to new experience. The work of Piaget has been of redounding importance in studying human development in terms of psychological states.

Piaget maintains that the unique pattern of a child's thinking, at various stages of cognitive development, is the key to the child's understanding of social relationships. Two patterns which are of paramount importance are *logic* and *justice*. He sees logic as covering the equilibrium between ideas, rather than between persons, and justice as governing *interpersonal relations* (Piaget, 1948). *Reciprocity* and *equality* are basic features of justice. In a number of Piaget's (1947) studies, he finds that the awareness of reciprocity develops at about six or seven. Recent research by Kohlberg (1969) also confirms the appearance of reciprocity as a moral justification of actions at about the same age level.

While Piaget (1948) defines three essential levels of moral development—the pre-moral, the heteronomous, and the autonomous—Kohlberg (1964, 1967, 1969) has elaborated this mode of analysis to differentiate six stages of moral judgment, at three levels, as shown in Table 5.1. These stages take account of Piaget's views, as well as those of

Table 5.1: Classification of moral judgment by levels and stages of development. (From Kohlberg, 1967, p. 171.)

LEVELS	BASIS OF MORAL JUDGMENT	STAGES OF DEVELOPMENT
I	Moral value resides in external, quasi-physical happenings, in bad acts, or in quasi-physical needs rather than in persons and standards.	Stage 1: Obedience and punishment orientation. Egocentric deference to superior power or prestige, or a trouble-avoiding set. Objective responsibility. Stage 2: Naïvely egoistic orientation. Right action is that instrumentally satisfying the self's needs and occasionally others'. Awareness of relativism of value to each actor's needs and perspective. Naïve egalitarianism and orientation to exchange and reciprocity.
II	Moral value resides in performing good or right roles, in maintaining the conventional order and the expectancies of others.	Stage 3: Good-boy orientation. Orientation to approval and to pleasing and helping others. Conformity to stereotypical images of majority or natural role behavior, and judgment by intentions. Stage 4: Authority and social-order maintaining orientation. Orientation to "doing duty" and to showing respect for authority and maintaining the given social order for its own sake. Regard for earned expectations of others.
III	Moral value resides in conformity by the self to shared or shareable standards, rights, or duties.	Stage 5: Contractual legalistic orientation. Recognition of an arbitrary element or starting point in rules or expectations for the sake of agreement. Duty defined in terms of contract, general avoidance of violation of the will or rights of others, and majority will and welfare. Stage 6: Conscience or principle orientation. Orientation not only to actually ordained social rules but to principles of choice involving appeal to logical universality and consistency. Orientation to conscience as a directing agent and to mutual respect and trust.

other writers who have pursued analyses of moral development. The Kohlberg stages form a sequence representing a progressive advance from one to the next, with children's concepts oriented toward their present stage, or one above it, rather than those below it (Rest, Turiel, and Kohlberg, 1969).

In ascertaining the stage of moral judgment at which a child is functioning, Kohlberg employs ten hypothetical cases which pose moral dilemmas. A typical one is the following case:

> In Europe, a woman was near death from cancer. One drug might save her, a form of radium that a druggist in the same town had recently discovered. The druggist was charging $2,000, ten times what the drug cost him to make. The sick woman's husband, Heinz, went to everyone he knew to borrow the money, but he could only get together about half of what it cost. He told the druggist that his wife was dying and asked him to sell it cheaper or let him pay later. But the druggist said, "No." The husband got desperate and broke into the man's store to steal the drug for his wife. Should the husband have done that? Why?

The "pro" and "con" arguments children give in this case have been summarized by Rest (1968). They illustrate the attributions made in rendering a moral judgment about the same action at each stage, with a differentiation not offered at the preceding stage.

Stage 1:   Pro—He should steal the drug. It isn't really bad to take it. It isn't like he didn't ask to pay for it first. The drug he'd take is only worth $200, he's not really taking a $2,000 drug.

Con—He shouldn't steal the drug, it's a big crime. He didn't get permission, he used force and broke and entered. He did a lot of damage, stealing a very expensive drug and breaking up the store, too.

Stage 2:   Pro—It's all right to steal the drug because she needs it and he wants her to live. It isn't that he wants to steal, but it's the way he has to use to get the drug to save her.

Con—He shouldn't steal it. The druggist isn't wrong or bad, he just wants to make a profit. That's what you're in business for, to make money.

Stage 3:   Pro—He should steal the drug. He was only doing something that was natural for a good husband to do. You can't blame him for doing something out of love for his wife, you'd blame him if he didn't love his wife enough to save her.

Con—He shouldn't steal. If his wife dies, he can't be blamed. It isn't because he's heartless or that he doesn't love her enough to do everything that he legally can. The druggist is the selfish or heartless one.

Stage 4:   Pro—You should steal it. If you did nothing you'd be letting your wife die; it's your responsibility if she dies. You have to take it with the idea of paying the druggist.

Con—It is a natural thing for Heinz to want to save his wife but it's still always wrong to steal. He still knows he's stealing and taking a valuable drug from the man who made it.

Stage 5:   Pro—The law wasn't set up for these circumstances. Taking the drug in this situation isn't really right, but it's justified to do it.

Con—You can't completely blame someone for stealing but extreme circumstances don't really justify taking the law in your own hands. You can't have everyone stealing whenever they get desperate. The end may be good, but the ends don't justify the means.

Stage 6:   Pro—This is a situation which forces him to choose between stealing and letting his wife die. In a situation where the choice must be made, it is morally right to steal. He has to act in terms of the principle of preserving and respecting life.

Con—Heinz is faced with the decision of whether to consider the other people who need the drug just as badly as his wife. Heinz ought to act not according to his particular feelings toward his wife, but considering the value of all the lives involved. (After Rest, 1968.)

From a content analysis of the free responses that children give in dealing with these dilemmas, it is possible to place them at a particular stage. It is also possible to view the total responses of children at various ages to observe the developmental sequence in the stages of moral judgments employed by them. Kohlberg (1964) has done this with children who were 7, 10, 13, and 16 years of age, and the

trends for the six stages, by these four ages, are shown in Figure 5.7.
Regarding these findings, Kohlberg (1964) says:

> It is evident that the first two types decrease with age, the next two
> increase until age thirteen and then stabilize, and the last two con-
> tinue to increase from age thirteen to age sixteen. These age trends
> indicate that large groups of moral concepts and attitudes acquire
> meaning only in late childhood and adolescence, and require the
> extensive background of cognitive growth and social experience
> associated with the age factor (p. 402).

It should be emphasized that there are individual differences in the
progress of children through these stages. Furthermore, there is a
heavy infusion of social and cultural influences which enhance or even
diminish the development of more advanced moral judgments. Some
cross-cultural research by Kohlberg (1969) indicates a degree of generality to the stages of development, but with variations strongly sug-

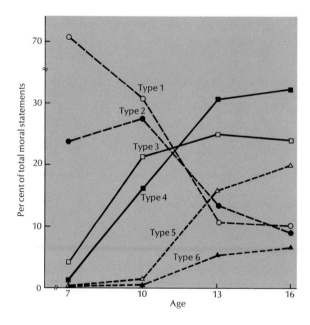

Figure 5.7: Mean per cent of statements, indicating each of six types of
moral judgment stages, given by children at four ages. (From Kohlberg,
1964, p. 403.)

gesting the operation of these influences. It appears that the opportunity to develop the more advanced judgments represented at Stages 5 and 6 is occasioned by culture.

While Kohlberg contends that his stages form an "invariant sequence" in terms of developmental progress, individuals who are capable of thinking at advanced stages can at times operate at lower stages, given the appropriate inciting circumstances, such as interpersonal conflict, undue stress, or deprivation. Alternatively, an individual who still is at the earlier stages, can rarely understand or behave in terms of the advanced stages.

PRO-SOCIAL AND HELPING BEHAVIOR

A recurrent interest in social psychology is the way in which moral values get translated into moral actions. Berkowitz (e.g. Berkowitz and Connor, 1966; Berkowitz and Daniels, 1963, 1964; Berkowitz and Friedman, 1967) is among those who have contributed considerably to research in this area, notably with regard to responsibility in dependency relationships. Latané and Darley (1968, 1969) and Latané and Rodin (1969) have conducted experiments on "bystander intervention," which are discussed in Chapter 7. The propelling thrust of this work is a concern with what makes for "pro-social" as against "anti-social" behavior.

Staub (1969, 1970) has been doing experiments with children, aimed at understanding the processes associated with their helping another child in distress. From this work, he has uncovered what appears to be an inconsistency in the development of this kind of moral action. In one experiment (Staub, 1970), he had boys and girls, alone or in same-sex pairs from the same classroom, hear sounds of a child's severe distress from an adjoining room. They were drawn from kindergarten, first, second, fourth, and sixth grade classes. While helping may be expected to increase with age, in terms of moral development, and the growth of empathy (Aronfreed, 1968), actually taking action may be inhibited by various factors, especially the child's growing self-consciousness and awareness of social constraints. Staub reasoned, however, that the presence of another child might reduce fear and inhibition of action, so that pairs of young children would help more than would children who heard the distress sounds alone.

The procedure followed in the Staub study was for the experimenter to give the subjects drawing paper, supposedly to find out what kinds of pictures children of different ages like to draw. Apparently discovering that she had forgotten to bring crayons, she said she would go to get them and then gave the children a game to play while she was away, and added, "Before I go, I'd better check on the girl who is in the other room." The experimenter then entered the adjoining room, turned on a tape recorder and returned in about a minute to say, "She is all right, she is playing now. I hope she won't stand on that chair again."

About a minute and a half after the experimenter left, the tape-recorded sequence began, consisting of a noise made by a falling chair, followed by a minute of severe crying, sobbing, moaning, and related distress sounds. The experimenter observed the response of the subjects from behind a one-way mirror. If the child went into the adjoining room, presumably in an attempt to help, the experimenter came back immediately; if the child left through the other door, very possibly to find the experimenter, she met the child in the corridor; if neither of these happened, the experimenter returned to the room a minute and a half after the distress sounds had ceased and awaited a report from the child. If there was no report of the crying, the experimenter then asked questions to elicit a report. All children were thoroughly debriefed to assure them that no one was actually suffering, that nothing was amiss, and the session was continued with pleasant activities designed to show that nothing was wrong.

Staub's response measures were divided into three categories: *active help*, which included either going into the room from which the distress sounds came or looking for the experimenter; *volunteering* unsolicited information to the experimenter about the distress sounds when she returned to the room; and *no help*, that is, neither of the other two responses. The results showed, altogether, that 31.8 per cent of individual children and 61.3 per cent of pairs either actively helped or volunteered information. The smallest percentages of help were found among the youngest children and the oldest, those from the sixth grade.

Figure 5.8 shows a comparison of helping behavior across grades for children in the "alone" and in the "pair" conditions of the Staub experiment. A probability index, called "hypothetical pairs," is also in-

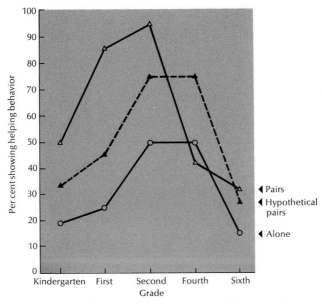

Figure 5.8: Per cent of helping behavior, from children at five grade levels, when alone or in pairs. "Hypothetical pairs" is a probability index derived from individual scores. (From Staub, 1970, p. 134.)

cluded. It was derived from individual subjects' helping scores as a predictor of how a pair of them might have done. The results indicated that actual pairs did help more than individuals alone or the "hypothetical pairs." However, the differences between these conditions varied greatly by grade.

Helping behavior first increased and then decreased with grade, which suggested the operation of greater inhibitions on the older children. The conversations recorded between children, while they listened to the distress sounds, and subsequent responses to questions asked by the experimenter, indicated that one reason for the low frequency of help in the sixth grade was fear of disapproval and criticism by the experimenter for taking action. The older children tended to report that they were afraid that they would "get yelled at," or that the experimenter "would get mad." In this connection, Maccoby (1968) has commented that formal socialization, such as occurs in the classroom, may overemphasize prohibitions of the "Thou shall not" variety without providing children with sufficient awareness that under certain circumstances these behavioral restrictions do not apply.

To test the idea of permissibility, Staub (1969) conducted another experiment with seventh grade pupils. In one condition, the subjects received indirect permission to engage in behavior subsequently required to help the distressed child in the other room by being told that they could get more drawing pencils there if they should need them. In the other condition, such permissibility was not extended. The effect of opening up this channel of action was to significantly increase helping behavior. Two other points bear mention, before leaving this set of investigations. One is that the children who heard the distress sounds in pairs were known to each other, since they were from the same classroom. Their greater helping behavior is in consonance with the finding of Latané and Rodin (1969) that pairs of adult friends helped a woman in distress significantly *more* than pairs of strangers. The presumption is that fear of disapproval for inappropriate action is reduced in the company of friends. The other point of interest is an alternative explanation of the *decrease* in helping with age, namely that it is a consequence of attribution of blame. Older children, being aware that the supposed victim had previously climbed on a chair might have decided that she herself was responsible for the consequences (Staub, 1970, p. 137).

Further light on the nature of environmental supports or inhibitions on pro-social behavior comes from the comparative research on Soviet and American child-rearing practices reported by Bronfenbrenner (1970) in his new book, *Two Worlds of Childhood*. In the Soviet Union, he finds that the formal socialization of youngsters is organized early, in nursery school. It emphasizes strong peer group ties in the classroom, along with the use of older children and adults as models. By contrast, Bronfenbrenner says American children are increasingly deprived of close contact with appropriate adult models, and are exposed to a relatively disorganized bombardment of conflicting social pressures. As a result, Soviet upbringing appears to lead to greater pro-social rather than anti-social behavior. In answer to the question, "Why?", Bronfenbrenner responds:

> The answer is obvious enough. The Soviet peer group is given explicit training for exerting desired influence on its members, whereas the American peer group is not. Putting it another way, the Soviet

peer group is heavily—perhaps too heavily—influenced by the adult society. In contrast, the American peer group is relatively autonomous, cut off from the adult world—a particularly salient example of segregation by age (1970, p. 115).

The influence of the peer group, in the context of relationships in the family, is considered further in Chapter 11. It is worth observing now, however, that the growing influence of peers in socialization, which has been widely commented upon, may be a function of a greater parental willingness to have the peers serve this function.

Attitudes and values in personality development

All in all, there is a great deal of significance associated with early experience if only because things which are learned first give direction to subsequent learning. Indeed, later learning may be handicapped by the necessity to "unlearn" some things before learning others. In psychological terms, this is called "pro-active inhibition" or "negative transfer." Its consequences are seen whenever the familiar or habitual must be discarded in favor of new behaviors. This phenomenon appears to be a general factor in resistance to change.

THE IMPACT OF SOCIAL INTERACTION

To say that attitudes and values grow out of early experience does not mean that hereditary factors are excluded in the process. They obviously inter-relate with experience in various ways. Thus, a good deal of work indicates that glandular functioning, which is hereditarily based in the physiology of the individual, can affect the way the individual is reacted to by others. A child with a high activity level, for example, will necessarily collide with many more social restraints than will one with a relatively placid disposition. The former child therefore has a set of experiences which are likely to yield a quite different sequence of learning than is the case for the latter.

Physical attributes can similarly produce differential outcomes. Whether these are valued by a society or not is of substantial significance to the way the person is reacted to by others. Kagan (1966), for instance, reports that boys who are shorter and broader than their classmates, in the early grades, are more likely to behave impulsively rather than reflectively because of anxiety in interpersonal relations.

The recent interest among psychologists in reconciling motivational and cognitive processes has led to further research on the reflection-impulsivity dimension. In a series of studies (Kagan, 1965a, b; 1966, a, b; Kagan and Kogan, 1969) the impulsive child has been found to answer more quickly and therefore to make more errors than does the reflective child. In a typical task, called the Matching Familiar Figures, the child is asked to select one among several alternatives that will exactly match a standard. This test has considerable utility in distinguishing between tendencies toward impulsivity as against reflection, and reveals a high correlation with other cognitive tasks including inductive reasoning, reading ability, and serial learning. The bulk of the evidence suggests that there is a cognitive style involved in the child's approach to various kinds of problem solving, and that this may have correlates in interpersonal relations and the child's self-concept. The distinctions society usually makes between the sexes is another determinant of the actions of others which may yield certain characteristic directive states in the individual. Being blind, being fat, or physically attractive—all of these in some respect affect the experience of the individual. In each instance, a physical attribute conditions social interaction.

THE SELF-CONCEPT AS A CENTRAL ATTITUDE

Related to the individual's physical attributes, and the way in which these mold interaction with others, are the attitudes an individual holds toward himself. It is common to find that these attitudes, summed up in the term "self-concept," are among the most vital for the individual's relationship and adjustment. Recalling our example in Chapter 1 of the red-headed child who repeatedly encounters the notion that he or she has a "bad temper," we can see how beliefs about one's own selfhood can be occasioned by impressions transmitted from others, however faulty in fact. In Chapter 10 it will be further noted how crucial these self-oriented attitudes are in the functioning of an individual's personality. Attitudes of self-esteem also shape the course of social interaction.

Acquiring attitudes and values is more than merely a matter of exposure to them. Other variables such as motivation must be operative to facilitate their successful acquisition. One facilitator is the identification with the parent or other model through social interaction. Another has to do with the structure of the family pattern. Clearly, then, it is a mistaken conception to think of socialization as involving a shaping of personalities in just one given mold. Because of the unique qualities of experience, socialization produces varying effects between persons. Birth order exemplifies such a factor. Thus, the work of Schachter (1959) indicates that first-born children tend to be more dependent and more easily made anxious than are later-born children. A common explanation for this finding is that parents are more likely to be concerned about their first-born and to transmit that feeling in their attentive treatment of the child.

Apart from underlying psychological states, socialization involves many kinds of learning, such as how to throw a ball. However, it is not so much behaviors which directly concern us at the moment. Rather it is the orientations conveyed to the child about his world.

FAMILY STRUCTURE

The pattern of family relationships, especially regarding the exercise of parental power over the child, has also been found to be a significant source of attitudes and values. Where the father is a strong, punishing figure, this frequently gives rise to a persisting orientation to the world called "authoritarianism." Its dominant value is *power*, whether in terms of aggressive display or submissive yielding.

Erich Fromm was among the early delineators of the behavioral and ideological properties of authoritarianism. The rise of the Nazis in Germany prompted him to write *Escape from Freedom* (1941). This monumental work describes the ambivalent power orientation of the authoritarian person and accounts for the historic cultural patterns which produce it and sustain it.

In a related vein, Maslow (1943) soon afterwards produced a definitive paper on the authoritarian character structure. Fundamentally, said Maslow, it embodies an ideology that views the world in terms of a jungle ". . . in which every man's hand is necessarily against every other man's, in which the whole world is conceived of as dangerous, threatening, or at best challenging, and in which human beings are conceived of as primarily selfish or evil or stupid" (p. 403).

During the 1940's at the University of California, extensive interviewing was done to ascertain the personal histories of individuals who held authoritarian attitudes. This necessitated a measure of authoritarianism now called the California F Scale (Adorno, Frenkel-Brunswik, Levinson and Sanford, 1950). The essential thrust of this extensive work was that a variety of attitudes toward other people arise not from contact with the object or even another attitude, but from an authoritarian *family structure*. Among these attitudes are ethnocentrism and prejudice, categorical and conventional thought, superstition and suggestibility, and tendencies opposed to self-examination. Some items from the F Scale were presented earlier in Chapter 3 (see pp. 107-108).

Another line of work on family structure as a source of attitudes is seen in research by Bronfenbrenner (1961a). He has conducted classroom surveys and interviews on the distribution of power in the home, in terms of mother- or father-oriented patterns. Such patterns evidence differential effects on the attitudes and behaviors of adolescents, with the role of the father having special importance. Bronfenbrenner also finds differential effects associated with the sex of the child. Thus, leadership and responsibility are affected by interaction with the parent of the same sex. He finds highest leadership ratings are obtained by *boys* from families in which the *father* is often present and gives affection; the most independent *girls* come from homes where the *mother* is present and gives affection. In terms of distribution of power, boys tend to be the most responsible when the father is the principal agent of discipline and girls when the mother has relatively greater power. Where the parents exercise equal power in the family, children of both sexes tend to be less responsible (Bronfenbrenner, 1961a, pp. 267-269).

The importance of this kind of research lies in specifying the structural features of learning experiences in the family which can have a long-range consequence in terms of attitudes and values. It also points up the persisting consequences of early social interaction.

Socialization is therefore very much a matter of taking on appropriate attitudes and values. This begins in the family where the child encounters the first representation of the culture but broadens to continue on through life. It involves, as we shall see, several kinds of processes, all of which are subject to the effects of ongoing experience through adulthood.

Socialization in adulthood

Even in relatively stable societies, socialization is not completed in childhood. Though children may learn to imitate adult roles, through a continuing process which Merton (1957) calls "anticipatory socialization," much of what is required of adults is learned later. Many of the complexities, conflicting demands, and subtle discriminations in modern society necessitate adult socialization.

BEHAVIOR AND VALUES

In his treatment of socialization in later life, Brim (1966) indicates that for a person to perform satisfactorily in a role he must know what is expected of him in *behavior* and in *values*. This distinction parallels Merton's (1957) analysis of the institutionalized *means* by which cultural *goals* are achieved. For socialization to proceed, it is essential, says Brim, that individuals have knowledge about the behavior and values required, and that they also have both the ability and the motivation to fulfill these demands. This leads to a descriptive cross-classification with knowledge, ability, and motivation each intersecting behavior and values, yielding the six cells shown in Table 5.2.

The highest priority in childhood socialization is represented in the combination of motivation and values (F). Children learn to transform their own desires into a greater sense of social identity and approval from others, which eventually leads to the acceptance of basic cultural values (see Figure 5.3).

On the other end of the scale, Brim considers that the usual concern of adult socialization lies in the combination of knowledge and behav-

Table 5.2: Cross-classification of content in six modes of socialization. (Adapted from Brim, 1966, p. 25.)

	BEHAVIOR	VALUES
Knowledge	A: Routine training	B: Orientation courses
Ability	C: Remedial training	D: Counseling
Motivation	E: Total-institution training	F: Child socialization (Adult resocialization)

ior (A). Society assumes that the adult knows the values to be pursued in different roles, and that all that remains to be done is to teach him how to behave. Routine training programs are set up along these lines. But sometimes the reasons why various things are done needs explanation; in the broadest sense, this leads to "orientation" programs which are designed to inculcate values (B). Professional training usually combines the two. If there are things an individual is unable to do, even after routine training, it may be that remedial training will be necessary (C). Where the individual has problems which interfere with his ability to carry on his activities, then a form of "counseling" may be prescribed (D). Finally, "total-institutions," such as the military establishment, jails, and hospitals, socialize the behavior of those in their confines by the use of special rewards and punishments (E). These are typically social in nature, as illustrated by the extension of status and privileges, at one end, and by the withholding of liberties and social contact, at the other (Goffman, 1961).

Even with its diversity, Brim contends that the primary concern of adult socialization is to affect behavior. Society spends much less time redirecting the values of adults, unless they are entering what is a wholly new society, as in the case of immigrants, where they may be exposed for a time to something akin to childhood socialization (F).

This scheme is useful for thinking about the various things which go on within the larger scope of socialization. However, it is descriptive and, as Brim points out, it is based on *what society does* to the individual to bring him into line. An alternative perspective, which Brim considers, is the *individual's selection of settings and orientations* in adulthood. This is seen in the operation of "reference group" perspectives.

REFERENCE GROUPS

There is a great potential for shifting to new norms and new roles in new settings, as part of adult socialization. The new affiliations encountered, and the values implied by the "shared perspectives" of different groups, create considerable cross-currents for the individual (e.g. Shibutani, 1955; Sherif and Sherif, 1964). As Hyman and Singer (1968) observe

> The reference group concept reminds us that individuals may orient themselves to groups other than their own, not merely to their

membership groups, and thereby explains why the attitudes and behavior of individuals may deviate from what would be predicted on
the basis of their group membership. Thus a theory of the group
determination of attitude has been properly enlarged by the concept
of reference group. . . . The point to be stressed is that the links in
the interpersonal chain do not have to be forged exclusively via direct social relations (p. 9).

Smith, Bruner, and White (1956) have advanced the idea that reference groups have sway over the attitudes an individual *holds,* but
that membership groups are more likely to have sway over the attitudes he *expresses.* The latter groups have greater power to withhold
support in the face of apparent deviation. Where these groups happen
to be melded into one, the individual is likely to be highly disposed
to take on and maintain attitudes which are shared in it. Newcomb's
(1943) Bennington College study demonstrated the impact of socialization to a new membership group which had reference group features. In an extension of this work, looking at the value-orientations
of college students, Brickman (1964) studied the question of what
happens when students go home from the college environment and
then back again. His general conception was that where a person was
a member of one reference group at college, and then moved for a
short period into another reference group at home, those in the latter
group would perceive and react to him primarily in terms of the college reference group and thus would behave toward him as if he held
the views which they believed to prevail at college. He would thereby
be called upon to defend the college norms and, in a sense, play the
role of the "typical student" at his college, thus producing an even
greater commitment to the values he felt to be normative there.

Several weeks prior to Christmas vacation, Brickman had 72 Harvard undergraduates fill out two "values questionnaires." The first
dealt with the students' *own feelings* about such value-orientations as
those toward authority, sensuality, equality, and the manipulation of
other people. The second tapped the students' *perceptions* of how
these same value-orientations prevailed at Harvard and at home. After
the students had spent three weeks away over Christmas vacation,
they once again filled out the questionnaire dealing with their own
value-orientations. The major focus of study was on whether these
subsequent ratings would move toward the perceived Harvard norm

or the perceived home norm. Brickman confined his analysis to those items, from the initial testing period, where the student's perception of the Harvard norm was on one side of his own values, and the perceived value norm at home was on the other.

Brickman's findings are instructive for what they revealed, even though his major conception requires qualification. Though he found, in general, that the students' value-orientations did undergo a statistically significant shift in the direction of the perceived norm at college, those students who spent the *greatest* amount of time at home during the vacation were *least* likely to shift toward the Harvard norm. Clearly, there were other variables involved, such as the desire to spend time at home, and with whom—questions which Brickman did not deal with directly. But his findings are nevertheless suggestive of the impact of multiple reference groups, as influence sources, which must in time be somehow reconciled. As Shibutani (1955) observes,

> The inconsistencies and contradictions which characterize modern mass societies are products of the multitude of communication channels and the ease of participation in them. . . . Even in common parlance there is an intuitive recognition of the diversity of perspectives, and we speak meaningfully of people living in different social worlds—the academic world, the world of children, the world of fashion.
>
> Modern mass societies, indeed, are made up of a bewildering variety of social worlds. Each is an organized outlook, built up by people in their interaction with one another; hence, each communication channel gives rise to a separate world (p. 566).

How, then, do individuals maintain a degree of coherence in their attitudes and values? From his research, following-up the Bennington girls after almost a quarter of a century, Newcomb (1963) suggests that this is accomplished by selecting favorable social interactions, of a more sustaining sort, as in marriage. He raised the question of the conditions under which the girls who had become less politically conservative during their Bennington years would remain relatively liberal women decades later, as against the conditions which would propel them back toward relatively conservative positions. The most striking single variable in Newcomb's result was the choice of a spouse who tended to be similarly oriented. Though his Bennington graduates found their husbands in their own "set," which tended to be quite high on socio-economic indicators and typically conservative, they chose husbands who were generally inclined in a liberal direction and who helped them to maintain an environment that was supportive of their political orientations. The general implication of this process is that, despite the demands of adult socialization, including those imbedded in marital roles, people may act to select and even create environments that are favorable to the maintenance of those values and attitudes which they find most congenial.

An important way in which people accomplish this is by their deliberate choice, where possible, of a vocation or profession with the kind of desired associations that would thereby be encountered. Professional socialization is an intriguing area in its own right, having to do with the procedures by which people are initiated into the traditions and norms of their field, whether it is the military services or medicine. Each of these exemplifies a sub-culture into which neophytes become socialized, and each has been studied in those terms (e.g. Becker, Geer, Hughes, and Strauss, 1961; Janowitz and Little, 1965) as a process of adult socialization.

SUMMARY

Attitudes and values are acquired as a vital part of being introduced into the ways of a society. They both may be considered to be the psychological representations of social influences retained by the individual. The concept of attitude is important in social psychology in that it conveniently sums up the *past* experience of the individual to account for present actions. As such attitudes help to explain the different responses of people to what is apparently the same situation.

An *attitude* is essentially an organization of beliefs which sets the individual toward a preferred response. A *value* can be viewed as the core of a clustering of attitudes. Both attitudes and values reside in the psychological field and define what is *expected* and *desired*. Both can be conceived of as motivational-perceptual states which direct behavior.

An individual holds many more attitudes than values. Values tend to be sustained and shared in common within a culture. Around these there may be considerable variations in individual attitudes. Attitudes and values have an important effect in *organizing experience* and *directing action*. In their outward expression, attitudes generally appear to be more susceptible to change than are values. Attitudes and values are not necessarily in harmony. A given value may give rise to inconsistent attitudes.

The acquisition of attitudes and values is part of the process of being led into the ways of the society called *socialization*. Attitudes are acquired in three ways: *direct contact* with the object, *interaction* with those holding the attitude, and *upbringing* experiences within the family's structure. Attitudes are held in line with reference-group affiliations and may change as new reference groups are taken on. The early socialization of the child, called *primary socialization*, mainly occurs in the family. The dependence of the child on the family, especially at a time when few alternatives are available to him, leads to a persisting impact on attitudes and values, including political ideology. In general, the acquisition of attitudes and values is heavily affected by a process of learning through social interaction. This process may shape the child's crucial development of attitudes toward himself in terms of his *self-concept*. Physical attributes can be significant in determining the character of this interaction.

An important consequence of childhood experience is *identification* with parents as models for action. It has an effect, too, upon the development of a conscience and of moral values. Identification is determined by dependence upon the parents in the context of a balance of discipline and affection. *Family structure* is another feature of early life which may lead to a persisting set of attitudes, such as authoritarianism, which carries over into later life.

Socialization does not end in childhood, but continues to have importance in adulthood as social demands are encountered in *new roles* and *group identifications*. Typically, adult socialization depends upon *acquiring knowledge* and *suitable behaviors* in accord with these demands. Professional training exemplifies a mode of adult socialization which also involves the *inculcation of values*. Taking on the shared perspectives of *reference groups* is another means by which individuals may alter their outlooks and pattern of behavior. Rather than being entirely vulnerable to pressures from their membership groups, adults are able to some extent to select or even create relationships which they find congenial, in friendships, vocations, and marriage.

SUGGESTED READINGS

From E. P. Hollander and R. G. Hunt (Eds.) *Current perspectives in social psychology*. (3rd ed.) New York: Oxford University Press, 1971.

8. Herbert H. Hyman and Eleanor Singer: *An introduction to reference group theory and research*
9. Philip W. Jackson: *Life in classrooms*
13. Orville G. Brim, Jr.: *Socialization in later life*
38. Theodore M. Newcomb: *Persistence and regression of changed attitudes: long-range studies*

SELECTED REFERENCES

*Adorno, T. W., Frenkel-Brunswik, E., Levinson, D. J., & Sanford, R. N. *The authoritarian personality*. New York: Harper, 1950.

Brim, O. G., & Wheeler, S. *Socialization after childhood*. New York: Wiley, 1966.

Bronfenbrenner, U. *Two worlds of childhood*. New York: Russell Sage Foundation, 1970.

*Campbell, A., Converse, P. E., Miller, W. E., & Stokes, D. E. *The American voter*. New York: Wiley, 1960.

Clausen, J. A. (Ed.) *Socialization and society*. Boston: Little, Brown, 1968.

Hyman, H. H. *Political socialization: a study in the psychology of political behavior*. Glencoe, Ill.: Free Press, 1959.

Kohlberg, L. *Stages in the development of moral thought and action*. New York: Holt, Rinehart & Winston, 1969.

Sears, R. R., Maccoby, E., & Levin, H. *Patterns of child-rearing*. Evanston, Ill.: Row, Peterson, 1957.

*Smith, M. B., Bruner, J. S., & White, R. W. *Opinions and personality*. New York: Wiley, 1956.

6

The nature and measurement of attitudes and the dynamics of attitude change

Attitudes play a major part in both capturing and shaping experience. They have accordingly been a major focal point for study, as we observed in the last chapter. The structure, function, and measurement of attitudes, and the factors affecting their change, are interrelated aspects of study that are basic to this effort. In this chapter, we will consider these aspects, as well as the relationship of attitudes and actions.

The structure and functions of attitudes

In the early study of attitudes, it was quite common to rely largely on the description of an individual's attitudes, their direction in terms of valence, and the belief systems that they constituted. More recently, attitudes have been viewed with considerably greater stress on what can be called their *structural relationships* and *functional features*. The first of these newer emphases has been called "cognitive interaction," which conveys the idea of a relationship between attitudes within the psychological field. It also encompasses the processes by which new experiences become absorbed as added information. Within this approach a great deal of contemporary research has been directed toward attitudinal consistency and congruity, about which we shall say more shortly. The second emphasis, on functional features, concerns especially the motivations which attitudes serve.

COMPONENTS AND ASPECTS OF ATTITUDES

There are a great many ways to approach the organization of attitudes, but for convenience, we can consider them with reference to three major components and three aspects of study. Regarding the components, Katz (1960) observes that attitudes have been treated with respect to a *cognitive component*, which refers to belief-disbelief, an *affective component*, which deals with like-dislike, and an *action component*, which embodies a readiness to respond. The relationship of these components continues to be a lively interest in contemporary social psychology (e.g. Rosenberg, 1956, 1960a, b; Campbell, 1963; Festinger, 1964a). Thus, believing or not believing something, and liking one or the other alternative, are by no means simple distinctions to make. As Rokeach (1968) has pointed out, a firmly entrenched belief, especially when challenged, is usually found to have considerable positive affect. There may be little apparent liking—in the sense of positive valence— associated with one's belief that the earth is round, yet a contradiction of it would generate strong feeling. This point bears on consistency which will be considered below.

The four major aspects in the study of attitudes are: the *relationships* of their components, especially in terms of cognitive interaction and individual adjustment; the *rewards* associated with them; their *source*, that is, the patterns by which attitudes are acquired through learning; and attitude *change*, with reference to the influences on the individual which result in the incorporation of new experience and the modification of attitudes. In this chapter we shall be dealing with each of these and also with techniques of measurement which are important in their study. Moreover, since they are highly interrelated, a good deal that can be said about one aspect bears upon the others. The source of attitudes, for example, has direct implications for their change. Knowledge of how individuals "acquire" attitudes and "retain" attitudes can have implications for understanding why individuals "act" on some and not others.

Table 6.1 shows these three components as they bear on four broad aspects of study in the sphere of attitude research. This table is de-

Table 6.1: Some components and aspects of the study of attitudes.

	ASPECTS			
	Relationships	Rewards	Sources	Change processes
COMPONENTS				
Cognitive (Believing)	Consistency	Social reality	Internalization (Credibility)	Balance, congruity, and dissonance reduction
Affective (Liking)	Feelings	Social identity	Identification (Attraction)	Interpersonal balance
Action (Responding)	Situations	Social support	Compliance (Control)	Social expectancies and conformity

signed to be illustrative of the general tendencies which prevail and, as with most such "pigeon-hole" schemes, it does not do full justice to the richness of some phenomena. However, it may be read across, as well as down, to give the sense of which elements typically go together in research. For instance, the "affective" component is related to *feelings*, to the reward of *social identity*, to sources in *identification* based on attraction, and to attitude changes occurring through shifts in *interpersonal balance*, other things being equal. Looking at the column marked "relationships," the arrows are to signify that the three components of attitudes, while emphasizing respectively *consistency*, *feelings*, and *situations*, are often studied in combination, e.g. consistency across situations.

Viewed broadly, there are several qualities of attitudes which we may now generalize as follows: they are beliefs and feelings about an object or set of objects in the social environment; they are learned; they tend to persist, though subject to the effects of experience; and they are psychological states which affect action, as a function of varying situations.

THE CONSISTENCY OF ATTITUDES

Individuals are not fully aware of their attitudes, and this accounts partly for their possible inconsistency with one another. Indeed, to a considerable degree attitudes exist at a low level of consciousness. Unless circumstances force the individual to face conflicts between them and perhaps resolve them, they may remain unnoticed. At the broadest level, Rokeach (1968) has suggested that there may be many inconsistent relationships—between attitudes and values, attitudes and attitudes, values and values, and either of them with cognitions regarding one's own behavior or that of others. In his view, becoming aware of inconsistency has productive features, though it may be initially upsetting. He sees the potentiality for making people aware of inconsistencies, particularly in their terminal values, as useful in re-education, for instance regarding prejudice:

> What I am proposing here is somewhat analogous to the effects that may be generated by showing a person undergoing a medical examination an X-ray of himself that reveals previously unsuspected and unwelcome medical information. It may be assumed that in every person's value-attitude system there already exist inherent contradictions of which he is unaware for one reason or another— compartmentalization due to ego-defense, conformity, intellectual limitations, or an uncritical internalization of the contradictory values and attitudes of his reference groups (p. 167).

A major situational determinant of manifest inconsistency in expressed attitudes occurs in connection with the roles an individual must take requiring him to say one thing in one circumstance and something else in another. Depending upon the nature of his role, a person expresses attitudes within the framework of the social expectancies of others, as well as his own motivations.

It may also be the case that an individual will say one thing but do another. This variance between attitudes and actions is a kind of inconsistency which can be tied to the variable nature of social circumstance, as we shall note again later in this chapter. In addition, such apparent inconsistency suggests the importance of distinguishing between *private attitudes* and *public commitment*, that is, between internalized states and externalized *compliance*. "My tongue hath sworn," wrote Euripides in *Hippolytus*, "but not my mind." The relationship between the private and the public is by no means direct as Kelman (1961), among others, has observed, in his distinction between internalization, identification, and compliance (see Table 6.1). In short, an individual may or may not change his underlying attitude due to the force of circumstance, and what occasions the difference is a matter of vital interest.

Another kind of inconsistency, that between the cognitive and affective components of an attitude, has gained particular attention in the

work of Milton Rosenberg. In one of his studies (1956) he found substantial evidence that these components tended to be highly correlated
with one another. Thereafter he set forth the proposition that "When
the affective and cognitive components of an attitude are mutually consistent, the attitude is in a stable state" (1960a, p. 322). Thus, if an individual undergoes a change of belief, his feelings about the object
of the attitude should change accordingly; the reverse proposition is
harder to test, but should be equally true. In another experiment
(1960c), Rosenberg employed hypnosis to induce shifts in the direction of negative feelings toward foreign aid. He then found that his
subjects' beliefs altered in the same negative direction to be consistent
with the negative affect. Apart from the question of the stability of
these changes, it is difficult to maintain a fine separation between cognitive and affective components as dependent and independent variables (Rokeach, 1968).

Undoubtedly the most prominent program of work directed at an
understanding of the consistency of attitudes, and of attitudes and actions, has been the one growing out of Festinger's (1957, 1964b) "cognitive dissonance" theory. The main assumption of this work is that
psychological structure is made up of an organized set of cognitions.
In maintaining this structure, individuals avoid dissonance and seek
consonance among their cognitions, including attitudes. A dissonant
relationship exists between two attitudes, or cognitive elements, when
one implies the opposite of the other, e.g. "I feel rain, but there are
no clouds in the sky."

Dissonance theory is considered more extensively later in this chapter. It shares with other consistency theories the assumption that people are disinclined to accept new cognitive elements—e.g. information
—which violates a belief system they already hold. The idea is summed
up in the half-comic, half-serious quip: "Don't bother me with the
facts; my mind's made up." This may be seen as an instance of "selective exposure" (Klapper, 1960), but it involves other elements, too.
Consider as an example the *post-decisional* feature of dissonance reduction. Before making a commitment, there typically exists more
openness to alternatives. Afterward, the choice made is strengthened
because it is cognitively inconsistent to believe that one has chosen
the less desirable alternative. Therefore, within the dissonance framework, commitment to action has been found to be a key feature in

determining the stability and change of attitudes. Studies by Festinger and his associates (e.g. Festinger, 1957, 1964b; Festinger and Carlsmith, 1959; Brehm and Cohen, 1962) are among those lending support to the adaptation of attitudes to a change of behavior, or circumstance.

Two recent reports of research, conducted in very different settings, also sustain this formulation. In the first of these, Knox and Inkster (1968) carried out two essentially identical field studies at different race tracks. They asked some bettors to indicate on a judgment scale how confident they were that the horse they had chosen would win, *before* they placed a bet, and other bettors to respond to the same question right *after* they had bet. Both of these studies revealed identical findings, that is, significantly higher confidence among the respondents in the post-bet condition. Their results, from both betting studies, are shown in Figure 6.1. The percentages there indicate the proportion of respondents in a condition who gave a confidence rating above the median for those in the study. After checking and then rejecting the possibility that there could have been switches in choice which might have accounted for this finding, these investigators concluded that the explanation lay in commitment to choice, in keeping with dissonance theory.

In another experiment of a similar nature, but with additional refinements, Mann and Abeles (1970) studied two samples of voters in the 1968 presidential election. They were interviewed either before entering or upon leaving the voting station. Both groups were asked about

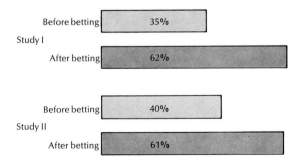

Figure 6.1: Per cent of above average confidence ratings given in two studies by bettors who were contacted just before or just after placing a bet. (Based on data from Knox and Inkster, 1968.)

their confidence that the presidential candidate for whom they had voted would win, and also whether they had made their decision early in the campaign, in the middle of it, or late in it. The findings of this study indicated a trend in the predicted direction, the same as in the study just noted, that is, greater expressed confidence in the victory of a candidate just after voting for him than just before. However, even more meaningful, an analysis of respondents by time of decision showed that those who had decided early in the campaign, were significantly more confident than the others before *and* after, but with their highest average confidence rating in the after condition. Thus, a long-standing commitment tended to enhance the effect of dissonance reduction still more.

This cognitive "shift" as a consequence of commitment—a kind of *fait accompli* effect—is nicely illustrated in *Life* magazine (June 17, 1966, p. 44) in an interview with the highly successful dress designer Mollie Parnis. She speaks of the threat and doubts that she experiences when her "reputation is at the scaffold" four times a year, and continues:

> When I look at the collection seconds before I present it to the buyers and press, I think, "God, I am mad—I should have stopped last year when I was good." I think of dozens of points that I should change, but it is too late. Yet after the collection is shown my panic disappears and my whole attitude switches. Then I won't alter anything and if anyone suggests a change, I resent it.

This statement also exemplifies the interrelated functioning of the cognitive and affective components of attitudes. With the presentation of her collection an acknowledged fact, Miss Parnis experiences strong positive feelings about it which serve to resist any dissonant elements, such as suggestions for changes in the collection.

We have dealt here only with some facets of consistency concepts applicable to attitudes; a bit later we will consider others in connection with cognitive balance in attitude change. At this juncture, it is useful to widen our focus to the other features of attitudes.

ATTITUDES AS ATTRIBUTIONS

A fascinating feature of many attitudes is how little they are seen as part of ourselves compared with how much they are accepted as properties of the objects of these attitudes. The essence of this process is aptly captured in Heider's (1958) observation that, "Attributions may not be experienced as interpretations at all, but rather as intrinsic to the original stimuli" (p. 256). This phenomenon is dramatically evident in prejudice and discriminatory practices where the *results* of prejudice are often attributed to the target group as the *reasons* for "their problem." Newsmen of late have been contending, perhaps just more openly, that the reporting of unpleasant news is often the basis for attributing intentions to them: "If you'd only stop giving so much unnecessary coverage to bad events. . . ."

Attitudes are attributions, often about the intentions and attitudes of others. Kelley (1967) considers this process to be determined by cause and effect linkages; the primary criterion for attribution, he says, is whether the effect or consequence appears to vary with the presence or absence of the entity or object. In a general way, this provides a basis for understanding what goes on psychologically in instances of the kind just cited.

Attitudes are also inferred from the perceived behavior of the entity. In their "correspondent inference theory," Jones and Davis (1965) suggest that attributions are essentially explanations for observed behavior. An attitude may thus be inferred from such observations. A *correspondent inference* is one in which the attitude explains the action, at least to the perceiver's satisfaction, as exemplified in an inference such as: "The legislator voted for higher taxes because he favors a balanced budget." Correspondence is highest, in these terms, when the person observed is seen to have a choice. In other words, if he did *not*, but appeared to be coerced in his behavior ("He voted as he did because it was made a matter of party loyalty"), then the inference about his own attitude would be less correspondent (see Chapter 7). In general, however, behavior rather than the situational context in which it occurs is the basis for attribution (Jones and Harris, 1967).

Individuals may also make attributions about themselves from what they do and say. In his self-perception theory, Bem (1965, 1967) considers that when individuals have "weak" internal signals they must rely on what they say and do as a basis for knowing their attitudes. It may not be so outrageous after all to have someone assert: "I don't know what I think until I hear what I say." Bem and McConnell (1970) have demonstrated recently that subjects in an attitude change experiment could not readily recall their "before" attitudes in the "after" condition, and that they often attributed the latter attitudes to their earlier position. The self-perception concept will be dealt with further, in connection with forced compliance, later in this chapter.

FUNCTIONAL FEATURES OF ATTITUDES

The functions that attitudes serve fall into several categories. In keeping with our earlier discussion, it should be borne in mind that the complexity of human motivation is such as to involve various kinds of social goals which may be served at one time. Thus, holding and expressing certain attitudes fulfill the individual's needs to achieve social identity, social reality, and social support. By believing those things which our associates believe we achieve all of these goals in some ways.

The most prominent exponent of the study of the different kinds of functions served by attitudes is Daniel Katz. His emphasis lays stress on the psychodynamic factors, especially of a motivational sort, with which attitudes are involved. In his definitive presentation of this approach (1960), he says:

> Stated simply, the functional approach is the attempt to understand the reasons people hold the attitudes they do. The reasons, however, are at the level of psychological motivations and not of the accidents of external events and circumstances. Unless we know the psychological need which is met by the holding of an attitude we are in a poor position to predict when and how it will change (p. 170).

The four kinds of functions which according to Katz form the motivational basis for attitudes are:

1. the instrumental, adjustive, or utilitarian function
2. the ego-defensive function
3. the value-expressive function
4. the knowledge function

Essentially, the *adjustive function* refers to the favorable responses the individual achieves from his associates by evidencing acceptable attitudes. This conveys the idea of reward or goal-attainment in terms of some socially valued object. Katz and Stotland (1959) have indicated that attitudes which serve the adjustive function may be the means for reaching the desired goal or be identified with experiences that have previously led to the satisfaction of such goals. In general, then, attitudes may be rewarding because they yield social rewards, including approval from others or because they are somehow related to those rewards.

With regard to underlying processes, the *ego-defensive function* allows the individual to protect himself from acknowledging his deficiencies. The mechanism of denial, which is a form of avoidance, permits the individual to defend his self-concept. To a considerable degree, for example, attitudes of prejudice help to sustain the individual's self-concept by maintaining a sense of superiority over others, as we note further in Chapter 10.

Through the *value-expressive function* of attitudes, the individual achieves self-expression in terms of those values which are most cherished by him. While the ego-defensive function may mean the individual holds back self-knowledge, in the case of the value-expressive function he seeks openly to express and acknowledge his commitments. In this instance, the reward to the person may not be so much a matter of gaining social support as it is one of confirming the more positive aspects of his self-concept.

In regard to the *knowledge function,* Katz says that people seek a degree of predictability, consistency, and stability in their perception of the world. Knowledge represents the cognitive component of attitudes which gives coherence and direction to experience. This emphasis is very much in line with the trend toward an understanding of cognitive interaction and the stability of cognitive structures dealt with above.

The motivational functions which Katz presents must be understood to be interrelated rather than highly segmented, as might appear. Accordingly several motives may be simultaneously served by holding a given attitude. Consider, for example, the worker who has a set of social and political attitudes concerning management and the role of government in society. These attitudes may implicate all four functions. In utilitarian terms, they may advance the worker's lot economically through his union activity, his voting preferences, as well as gaining for him the approval of his co-workers. In terms of the ego-defensive function, the worker can continue to see himself on the side of right, and management more on the side of wrong, even when his union makes economic demands which reflect the same emphasis on economic gain which is ascribed to management in negative terms. The value-expressive function may be served by avowals of liberal social measures. These, in turn, are sustained by the social reality of his co-workers' construction of their world, which becomes a part of the knowledge he readily accepts. Incidentally, had we reversed the example and used an executive instead of a worker the same implications would hold though the content would be substantially the opposite.

Despite the fact that these functions may be interrelated, Katz nonetheless notes that arousing and changing attitudes require different kinds of appeals in terms of the primary functions served by an attitude. Thus, in changing attitudes which are mainly utilitarian, whatever their other functions, he says that it is necessary that the attitude and its associated activities be seen as no longer providing its former satisfactions. In a comparable way, arousing attitudes which have a major ego-defensive function, in order to change them, often poses threats to the individual's self-concept. In that case, the consequences may be unexpected and in the reverse of the intended direction (see Katz, Sarnoff, and McClintock, 1956).

Where attitudes have a pronounced value-expressive element, a change demands the individual's recognition that his former attitudes no longer serve to adequately express his newly acquired values of significance. Changing attitudes which serve the knowledge function is most readily achieved in a condition of high ambiguity which increases the need for cognitive clarity analogous to perceptual closure. This phenomenon often is seen in circumstances where rumors become rife. It also applies to conditions which favor the acceptance of influence in terms of conformity (see Chapter 14).

In general, the functional approach to attitudes focuses primary attention on the individual and his underlying psychological states. We will consider the processes involved more fully in Chapter 10 in connection with personality. By implication, this approach is also oriented to the motivational circumstances that are implicated in the acquisition of attitudes, which we will now consider.

Problems and procedures in the measurement of attitudes

There are several problems involved in the measurement of attitudes, perhaps the most important of which is to define a cluster in "attitudinal space" and obtain an index of how individuals differ within it. Associated with this is the necessity to assess those attitudes that are related meaningfully to behavior. There are also technical questions in attitude measurement which concern, for example, the way that measurement procedures themselves may affect the responses of individuals.

Regarding the first issue, the very term "attitude" is multi-faceted in its meaning. In breadth, it may cover many attitudes or a very narrow issue. Thus, a person may be generally favorable to "desegregation," but within that complex can be opposed to bussing white children to predominantly Negro schools. In terms of action, that person might take part in civil rights activities, perhaps through financial contributions to appropriate organizations, and yet argue against bussing on other grounds. As we shall point out, this is not necessarily an inconsistency but a matter of the "situational hurdles" that the action component of an attitude can surmount (Campbell, 1963).

Another consideration is the *centrality* or *peripherality* of an attitude. In his analysis of attitudes, Rokeach (1963) indicates that they exist on a continuum from "primitive beliefs," which are very central to a person's psychological field, through to "peripheral beliefs," which are relatively inconsequential. In studying attitudes, therefore, some attention is required to place a given attitude in the totality of an individual's attitudinal space. Highly central attitudes are likely to be more stable and considerably more important as bases for action than are peripheral attitudes. One implication of this, as we shall see, is that appeals which are effective in changing some attitudes may be less effective in changing others that are more firmly entrenched in personality—for example, in terms of the ego-defensive function.

TRADITIONAL APPROACHES TO ATTITUDE MEASUREMENT

Attitudes have usually been measured through attitude scales, questionnaires, interviews, projective tests, and observations of behavior. These have been treated previously in Chapter 3. Our aim here is to focus major attention on some of the dimensions and problems which underlie traditional attitude measurement, especially through attitude scales.

The preoccupation with a single issue rather than with the clustering of attitudes, has been a major feature in the tradition of attitude measurement. This tradition has mainly emphasized dimensions dealing with single issues in terms of the direction, degree, and intensity of an attitude toward a given object. These components are incorporated in questionnaire studies and interviews, as well as in attitude scales. Thus, individuals may be asked *how* (pro or con) they "feel about" something, and then "how strongly" they feel.

The *direction* of an attitude is essentially the cognitive component of belief-disbelief, often stated in terms of agree-disagree. The *degree* of agreement or disagreement extends this concern to how much plus or minus valence is associated with the attitude. The *intensity* of an attitude is essentially the same as degree since it, too, measures the affective component, usually in terms of "strength of feeling." Indeed, when degree and intensity were plotted against one another, it became apparent that they were highly interrelated; holding a more extreme position was accompanied by more intensity of feeling. Cantril (1946) noted this relationship over two decades ago and, as is shown in Figure 6.2, Suchman (1949) reported it from his work among soldiers. The figure shows that attitudes of a highly negative or positive valence are

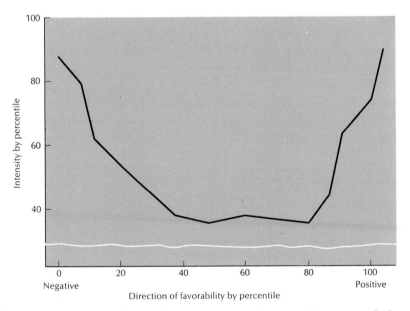

Figure 6.2: Relationship of direction of attitudes of soldiers toward their jobs and the intensity of those attitudes. (From Suchman, 1949.)

held with greater intensity. Thus, both degree and intensity appear to measure the affective component of an attitude, while direction is more an indication of the cognitive component. Based upon our earlier discussion of the consistency of these components, it is understandable that they are found to be highly related.

ATTITUDE SCALES

The most widespread approach to measuring attitudes has been the attitude scale. In general, such scales consist of a number of statements with which a person may agree or disagree along a dimension with several points, usually ranging from "highly agree" to "highly disagree." In this way both the direction and the degree are indicated by the response to each statement or "item." Typically these items all relate to some common social entity, person, issue, or activity. Responses are then summed to provide a score indicating the person's overall attitude. This is the essential procedure in the Likert-type scale, as is noted further below.

The development of an attitude scale requires the selection of a number of statements that will discriminate between people having different attitudinal positions. Thus, to be adequate, an attitude scale should represent a range of different positions that an individual might hold and it should avoid confounding two distinct issues in one item. This problem is illustrated in "double-barreled" items, such as: "If social class distinctions are to be reduced, the graduated income tax should be eliminated." A person might agree with the first part and disagree with the second, or the reverse. In either case, two separable issues are confounded with one another.

One of the earliest attitude scales was that developed by Thurstone with Chave (1929). They had people judge items, not in terms of their own attitude, but regarding their judgment of the position the statement represented on a scale of favorability or unfavorability toward the object of the attitude. Where there is high agreement about the position of the item among the judges, the item is considered to have a scale score for that position. Thus, the score for an item is determined by the agreement of judges prior to the actual use of the scale. When respondents agree with items later, they receive these scores toward their total. Thurstone adapted this procedure from psychophysics and it is called the method of "equal appearing intervals."

Thurstone's major contribution was in approaching the measurement of attitudes on an affective dimension. His scaling method itself, however, is no longer in wide use. Apart from the relative ease of other methods, research by Hovland and Sherif (1952) raised some serious questions about the basis for its procedures. They found that individuals tend to judge items with reference to their own position as an anchor point. Though Upshaw (1965) has challenged the inference from these findings, and offered support for Thurstone's methodology, contrary evidence continues to be reported. Waly and Cook (1965) have established that ratings of the "plausibility" of statements about a social issue—segregation—are affected substantially by whether or not the rater agrees or disagrees with the statement.

Undoubtedly the most common attitude scale in use grows out of the work of Likert (1932). It is sometimes referred to as a summated scale and is simple to construct. In this case, prior judgments of the items are not obtained, but statements are collected which represent apparently positive or negative views of the attitudinal object. The California F Scale, discussed here and in Chapter 3 (p. 107), is built on the Likert procedure. The subject indicates his degree of agreement or disagreement with each item, usually on a scale ranging from one to five or one to seven. Then, a score is obtained by summing the values for each of these separate responses.

Another basic approach to scaling a person's position on an issue was developed by Bogardus (1925). His social distance scale, which we discussed in Chapter 2 (p. 60), measures attitudes toward various ethnic groups, including nationalities, by a series of statements ranging from the most favorable to the least favorable, i.e. greatest social distance. Subjects are asked to indicate for each of these groups how willing they would be to admit them to the following relationships:

1. to close kinship by marriage
2. to my club as personal chums
3. to my street as neighbors
4. to employment in my occupation
5. to citizenship in my country
6. as visitors in my country.

The important feature of this scale is that it is constructed so that accepting the first alternative should imply the acceptance of all the others. Thus, if an individual says yes to the first statement, he should accept the subsequent statements in the series as well.

A modern counterpart of this scale, which *positions people* in terms of favorability or unfavorability toward some attitudinal object, is the Guttman Scale (1950). It seeks the underlying order within a series of questions that can be responded to by a simple "yes" or "no." This procedure is called "cumulative scaling." It often involves the mathematical treatment of a matrix of responses and has been applied particularly to data obtained from questionnaire surveys. In simplest form, a cumulative scale would be illustrated by a set of questions about age, as follows:

1. I am 31 years of age or older
2. I am 26 years of age or older
3. I am 21 years of age or older
4. I am 16 years of age or older.

A person responding "yes" to question 1 would have to respond "yes" to the subsequent items. Hence a "yes" on 1 implies all of the others. A "no" to question 1, but a "yes" on question 2 would imply "yes" to 3 and 4. A "no" to all four questions would place a person below 16 years of age. Notice that age is a perfectly linear dimension and that it is easily graduated. This is not as assured in attitudes.

An attitudinal scale of the Guttman type is shown in Figure 6.3. It concerns the issue of how much authority local government agencies should have in dealing with organizations found to be polluting the environment. In keeping with Guttman's intention, if the responses work out in a totally consistent way, and they rarely do (a 90 per cent "fit" is considered excellent), then respondents would fall into only one of five "positions" relative to the essential issue of governmental authority in these matters. The ideal of total "reproducability" is *not* necessary, practically speaking, for this scaling procedure to be useful in identifying position differences which might not be indicated by single items or total item scores.

Because an attitude scale is essentially a one-dimensional measure, it cannot represent all of the complexity of attitudinal systems. To

Q: In dealing with organizations found to be sources of pollution, local government agencies should
   have the authority to:

A. Order an immediate halt and, unless there
   is rapid compliance, close them down until
   there is compliance.

B. Levy stiff daily fines once they are warned
   and until there is compliance.

C. Use publicity and moral suasion to secure
   compliance.

D. Deal privately with their officials to
   request compliance.

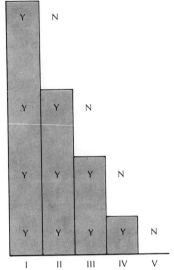

Figure 6.3: Illustration of four-item Guttman Scale. A respondent answers
"yes" or "no" to each item. A "yes" response to the first item suggests that the
respondent is willing to grant all of these kinds of "authority" to government
and would *not* say "no" to the ones following. The "no" respondent on the
first item might say "yes" or "no" to the second, with the "yes" suggesting
"yes" to the subsequent items, and so on. If the respondents "scaled" in a
perfectly consistent fashion, there would be *five types* of "position" into which
each could fall, i.e. grant *all* of the kinds of authority to government, grant
none of them, or grant B-C-D, C-D, or just D. These position types are indicated by the Roman numerals.

get around this limitation requires the use of multi-dimensional ratings
or the application of factor analysis to responses given over several
scales. One approach to such multi-dimensional scaling is represented
in the *semantic differential* (Osgood, Suci, and Tannenbaum, 1957)
which is discussed more fully in Chapter 9. In this procedure, an
attitudinal object is presented to the subject for rating along many
dimensions, e.g. "good-bad," "strong-weak," "active-passive." From
these ratings, with several dimensions for each, the three major factors
of *evaluation, potency,* and *activity* can be extracted. An individual's
"attitude" toward the object can then be represented as a point in
attitudinal space where his ratings for these factors coincide. Thus,

"government" might be rated by a person as favorable on the evaluative factor, very powerful in terms of potency, but relatively inactive. In general, evaluation along a negative to positive scale appears to account for the greatest part of the cognitive interaction of attitudes and associated behavior.

RELIABILITY AND VALIDITY

As with all psychological measures, attitude measurement in any form involves considerations of adequacy in terms of both *reliability* and *validity*. These issues have to do respectively with the degree to which a measure is consistent, and whether it measures what it is supposed to measure. Further problems arise, too, in avoiding bias from the framing of the question, the sequencing of items within the format of the attitude scale or questionnaire, and the effect of the interviewer.

Up to a point, the reliability of an attitude measure is increased by more items. A one-item attitude scale would be a highly wavering measure at best since even a minor shift in response could show up as a wider inconsistency. Consider, for instance, a "one-item" test that an executive once boasted he used when screening new junior executives. He took them to lunch and watched to see if they salted their food before tasting it, or after. Accordingly, many items are used in constructing scales and questionnaires. Ideally these items should be correlated positively with one another in terms of the internal consistency of measurement. For example, in the semantic differential procedure just noted, several dimensions make up each of the factors thus increasing the reliability of these factors.

The problem of gauging reliability over time is complicated by the practical consideration that when an attitude measure is repeated for the same subjects, they may remember their earlier responses and strive to be consistent. On the other hand, it is recognized that since attitudes change, their measurement over time can never be totally reliable. In a longitudinal study by E. L. Kelly (1955), he retested married couples with several attitude scales and other psychological measures that he had administered to them as engaged couples sixteen to eighteen years before. He found that attitudes had the lowest repeat reliability, that is, had changed the most over the years. The measures of values and of vocational interests had the highest consistency.

The extent to which a measure is valid necessarily depends in part on its reliability. In these terms, the internal consistency of an attitude measure usually is a sufficient basis for permitting adequate validity. However, there is a larger question of validity which concerns the relationship of what a person says at one time to how he acts at another. The next section considers this behavioral aspect of the validity of attitude measurement.

Attitudes and situational hurdles to action

Broadly speaking, expressed attitudes bear a rather consistent relationship to behavior. But again this depends upon the kind of attitudes and the kind of circumstances that prevail for action. There is, for example, sufficient correspondence between political attitudes revealed in a preelection survey, and the actual outcome of an election, to permit relatively accurate forecasting. Where there are misreadings from such surveys, they can be accounted for by faulty sampling procedures or by a large bloc of "don't know" respondents who could move either way. In our national elections, in particular, outcomes often hinge on a few percentage points, making advance predictions a delicate task indeed.

When attempts have been made to study the correspondence of attitudes and behavior in concrete situations, the results have often revealed apparent inconsistencies (e.g. Festinger, 1964a). An early investigation in this vein by LaPiere (1934) found that the observed behavior of persons in a face-to-face situation was not in line with their expressed attitudes. In this study, LaPiere was accompanied on a trip by a young Chinese couple. Together as companions they visited many hotels and restaurants and were regularly given service that reflected no negative attitude toward Orientals. Yet, when LaPiere sent questionnaires to these same establishments several months afterward, he found that the vast preponderance of their replies indicated that they would not accept Orientals as their guests. A comparable study by Kutner, Wilkins, and Yarrow (1952) found that many restaurant owners who failed to answer a request for reservations for a group including some Negroes did serve a group composed of two white women and one Negro woman when they actually appeared in person.

The substance of these findings is that people in a situation involving face-to-face contact are likely to respond differently from the manner indicated by their answer to a letter or a questionnaire or, in the case of the latter study, by the absence of a response to a request. One resolution of this apparent anomaly is offered in Rokeach's (1968) contention that behavior is always a function of at least two attitudes, that is, an attitude toward the object and an attitude toward the situation. Regarding the two studies we have just noted, he says that one reasonable explanation of their apparent inconsistencies is that:

> . . . the investigators did not obtain all the relevant attitudinal information needed to make accurate predictions. The subjects not only had attitudes toward Chinese and Negroes but, being managers of an ongoing business, also had attitudes about how properly to conduct such a business. The investigator's methods, however, are typically focused on obtaining data relevant to attitude-toward-object and are generally insensitive toward attitude-toward-situation (p. 126).

Experiments also have been conducted on the relationship of attitudes and overt activity. In one of these, DeFleur and Westie (1958) requested white girl students to permit themselves to be photographed sitting with a Negro male. The subjects were free not to permit the photograph to be taken at all, or, if they signed an authorization, to allow the photograph to be used in various ways ranging from display in the laboratory to use in a national campaign for integration. It was found that about a third of the subjects behaved differently from their expressed attitudes—mostly in a less tolerant direction—when it actually came to signing a document indicating their willingness to be photographed with the Negro. Linn (1965) conducted a similar experiment and found that fully half of the subjects did not conform to their verbalized attitude regarding the criterion of being photographed, but that these differences operated in both directions. Some subjects who had expressed a generally intolerant attitude were willing to be photographed, and some who had expressed a tolerant attitude were unwilling to be photographed when confronted with the necessity to sign an authorization.

Campbell (1963) has also emphasized the necessity to consider different situations in explaining what is an apparent inconsistency between attitudes and behavior, or between one behavior and another. In Campbell's view, there are *situational hurdles,* which present higher levels of difficulty for an adequate response. Thus, the restaurant manager may not be inconsistent when he actually accommodates people but says in a mail questionnaire that he would be unwilling to serve them. The face-to-face situation, as we have already observed in Rokeach's comment above, presents a circumstance which is of a different order. Indeed, Campbell indicates that to be truly inconsistent would mean to *agree* to accept people on a questionnaire, and then *refuse* to serve them when they actually appear (p. 160).

The implication of Campbell's "hurdle" approach is made still more concrete in his discussion of the work of Minard (1952) who conducted research on ethnic relations in a West Virginia coal-mining community. His data indicated that the pattern of integration was different in town and in the mines. The mines were integrated but the town substantially was not. Thus, 20 per cent of the miners had favorable attitudes toward Negroes and acted in accordance with their attitudes both in the mine and in town, while 20 per cent had negative attitudes toward Negroes and acted accordingly all the time. Minard found that the great majority, or 60 per cent, altered their behavior

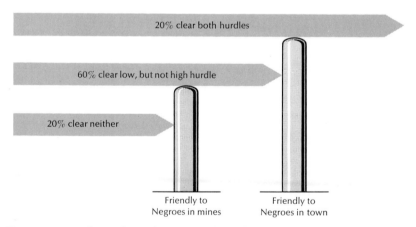

Figure 6.4: Relationship of situational hurdles to attitudes, from Minard's study (1952) of coal miners. (Adapted from Campbell, in *Psychology: A Study of a Science,* v. 6, edited by S. Koch. Copyright © 1963 by McGraw-Hill, Inc. Used by permission of McGraw-Hill Book Company.)

toward Negroes from the mine setting to the town setting, treating them more as equals in one and inferiors in the other. Campbell says that the miners' behavior and attitudes are consistent with respect to the higher hurdle in going from one situation to the other. Indeed, these two situations represent a Guttman-type cumulative scale.

As will be seen in Figure 6.4 there are no instances of miners who say they are friendly in town but not in the mine. This means that there are none who are truly inconsistent. Twenty per cent clear both hurdles; another 20 per cent fail to clear either of the hurdles. It should be plain therefore that the validity of attitude measurement in terms of action rests in some degree on the kind of situation, and attendant social pressures, which are likely to encourage the expression of an attitude. Insofar as attitudes predispose behavior, they do so in relationship to the immediate situation.

Processes of attitude change

A major theme of the previous section is that underlying attitudes predispose behavior in terms of a situation which serves as a frame for that behavior. Relatedly the very expression of attitudes depends upon the social setting. Thus, apparent changes of attitude occur by shifts that an individual perceives in his situation, in terms of what will be appropriate or approved. These may or may not reflect underlying changes. Kelman (1961) distinguishes between *compliance,* which merely reveals an overt expression of an attitude as a social convenience, and two other processes, *identification* and *internalization.* The former involves greater changes in the person's psychological field on the basis of modeling, while the latter presents a basic change in a value.

In general, when an individual acquires new information his attitudes may be altered by a reorganization of his psychological field. The potential of new experience is always in the direction of such change. Yet, the structure of attitudes tends toward stability. As we have repeatedly noted, an individual's attitudes are usually anchored in one or more groups to which he belongs or, in any case, accepts as a standard. To the extent that he is motivated to be identified with a group, his attitudes are unlikely to change if they derive support from that group (Kelley, 1955). This bolstering effect is a major source of resistance to change. On the other hand, as illustrated by Lewin's work earlier (p. 99), a group can also serve as a vehicle for producing change.

In considering the dynamics of attitude change, the significance of two kinds of factors accordingly must be recognized. The first of these is the processing of new information through cognitive interaction; the second is the impelling quality of social identifications in maintaining an attitudinal structure. Both are involved in persuasive communication.

PERSUASIVE COMMUNICATION

The attempt to influence people to change their attitudes and related behavior is widely practiced through persuasive communication. The advertiser who seeks to have people use his toothpaste, the politician who wishes to have their vote, as well as the numerous social and civic agencies that desire to affect social change, are all engaging in persuasive communication. Implicit in these activities is the intent to exert social influence.

As Bauer (1964) points out, much of the early work on attitude change was based on an asymmetric model of the influence process. Communication was viewed as a one-way influence process, usually for exploitative purposes, and the recipients of the communication were considered to accept passively messages directed to them. A noteworthy break with the tradition came from the work of Katz and Lazarsfeld (1955), who found that individuals were not as directly affected by communications from the mass media, so much as they were influenced by a process of transmission through their relevant reference groups. Katz and Lazarsfeld referred to this as the "two-step flow" of communication, meaning a flow from the mass media, through opinion leadership in relevant groups, to the individual. Thus, they emphasized the necessity to view the individual in terms of his total social involvements, including especially reference group affiliations.

Increasingly, the recipient of the communication has been studied in terms of his active selection and processing of the messages which come to him. In this regard, both the relevance of these communications, as well as their source, have been given greater attention. This particular approach has come to be called the "transactional" view of communication (Bauer, 1964). Two major themes pervade this view. One is that the recipient of the communication is not passive but may be actively resistant to it. The second is the idea that acceptance of the communication as a basis for change involves a transaction between the communicator and the recipient, producing influence effects where there is an equitable exchange. As Bauer (1964) puts it:

> The process of social communication and of the flow of influence in general must be regarded as a transaction . . . in the sense of an exchange of values between two or more parties; each gives in order to get. The argument for using the transactional model . . . is that it opens the door more fully to exploring the intention and behavior of members of the audience and encourages inquiry into the influence of the audience on the communicator by specifically treating the process as a two-way passage (p. 327).

Persuasive communications, especially from the mass media, are therefore limited in their effect partly due to selective perception by the audience. There is a strong tendency to accommodate new information within already existing attitudinal systems, and as Klapper (1960) observes, ". . . persuasive mass communication functions far more frequently as an agent of reinforcement than as an agent of change. Within a given audience exposed to particular communications, reinforcement, or at least constancy of opinion, is typically found to be the dominant effect" (p. 15).

The transactional model of persuasive communication follows the format already discussed (pp. 13-14) regarding social influence processes in general. There we dealt with four elements in influence processes— an influence source, a communication, a recipient of the communication, and a social context. In the case of attitude change, the influence source is more usually called a communicator, and the recipient the audience.

Figure 6.5 presents diagrammatic representations of three prominent models of communication and attitude change. The first of these is the traditional advertising-propaganda model with its one-directional quality. The communicator actively seeks to manipulate the recipient by the content of the communication, in terms of its appeal and the information it presents. By contrast, the audience is seen in relatively in-

A. Traditional advertising-propaganda model

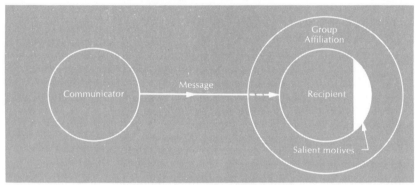

B. Two-step flow of communication model

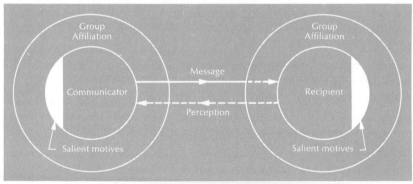

C. Transactional model of communication

Figure 6.5: Three models of persuasive communication. In *A* the expectation is that the recipient acts on the message when his salient motives are aroused. In *B* the message is initially screened by the recipient's group affiliation before it affects the salient motives. In *C* the message is interpreted by the recipient within the context of his own group affiliations and motives and his perception of those of the communicator.

active terms, except for salient motives on which the communicator plays. The second kind of model, represented in the Katz and Lazarsfeld (1955) "two-step flow" concept, gives somewhat more emphasis to the social characteristics of the audience, in terms of reference-group affiliations acting as a filter for the message. Finally, the transactional model gives greater weight to the interaction of the motives and social identities of communicator and recipient. Here the audience is considered to perceive these qualities of the communicator as a critical feature in accepting his influence, in line with the concept of attribution.

Cognitive consistency, which we considered earlier as a feature of attitudinal structure, is a state of the recipient which has great relevance to the transactional view of an exchange. The implicit question is what the communicator offers the audience which justifies an alteration in an already formed attitudinal structure and one which is likely to be sustained by important social identities. Rosenberg and Abelson (1960), for example, contend that persuasive communications will generate attitude change to the extent that they are seen by the recipient as helpful in resolving cognitive imbalances, particularly in the affective and cognitive components. There may also be a benefit received in terms of new knowledge. However, it is important to stress the general point that the cognitive component of an attitude, regarding what an individual believes, is knowledge for him even if it is not objectively verifiable. Indeed, the absence of correct information is no barrier to the individual's persistence in holding an intense attitude, in the affective sense. In the case of an attitude which serves an ego-defensive function, new knowledge may therefore be resisted tenaciously. In a study by Katz, Sarnoff, and McClintock (1956), for example, it was found that a factual appeal to those holding negative attitudes toward Negroes had little appreciable effect. As these investigators point out, such appeals assume that the recipient is interested in more accurate, complete information, but this assumption is questionable. They found that a somewhat more effective approach, among those persons who were not too high on ego-defensiveness, was to present case material about the personality dynamics of prejudice.

Since cognitive interaction has broad implications for attitude change, we will now examine it in greater detail beginning with a review of its essential features.

ESSENTIAL PRINCIPLES OF COGNITIVE INTERACTION

While there are differences in the various theories of cognitive interaction, they all rely on certain essential points of convergence. These
principles, summarized by Osgood (1960), may be paraphrased as
follows:

1. Modification of cognitive structures, i.e. attitude
   change, results from the psychological stress produced
   by cognitive inconsistency.
2. The interaction of cognitive elements depends upon
   their being brought into some kind of confrontation
   with one another. In this regard, Osgood points out
   that the psychological awareness of inconsistency or
   incongruity does not so much follow the rules of logic
   as it follows the rules of what is called "psycho-logic"
   (Abelson and Rosenberg, 1958).
3. The magnitude of stress toward attitude change increases with the degree of cognitive inconsistency.
   Thus, in Festinger's theory, the magnitude of dissonance is the motivational factor producing changes of
   attitude or of behavior.
4. The dynamics of cognitive interaction under stress
   operate to reduce total cognitive inconsistency. This
   idea, that disturbances in a system set in motion processes to restore balance in that system, grows out of
   the work of Cannon in connection with his study of
   the physiology of emotion (1932). It is now well
   known as the principle of "homeostasis." It also has
   roots in Freud's concept of repression which operates
   to force out of consciousness elements of experience
   that threaten the ego.

BALANCE APPROACHES TO ATTITUDE CHANGE

The earliest formulation of the consistency idea, in terms of attitude
change, came from Heider's (1946, 1958) *balance theory*. He con-

sidered attitudes toward objects, as well as persons, to have positive or negative valences, which might or might not coincide with one another. Hence, there would be balance or imbalance in the attitudinal system. Heider contended that there is always movement toward a balanced state, that is, "a situation in which the relations among the entities fit together harmoniously; there is no stress toward change" (1958, p. 201). Therefore, the basic concept of balance is that a tendency exists for individuals to resolve attitudes which are not similarly signed.

Heider was essentially concerned with situations in which there were two persons, a Perceiver and an Other, each of whom may have an attitude toward a given object X. If P likes O, the assumption is that the latter's attitude should be the same as his own. Two friends, for example, might share a common positive attitude toward a presidential candidate. Thus, a balanced state would be P positive toward O, P positive toward X, and O seen as positive toward X as well. If they differed on that issue, then an imbalanced state would exist. In that event, they might try to persuade each other or else avoid the topic until the election was over, in order to retain actual or apparent balance.

In Heider's P-O-X model, then, balance occurs when there are no negative signs, or two negative signs, in the relation between P, O, and X. The assumption that an unbalanced relation produces tension and generates forces to restore balance has direct implications for social interaction, and these are discussed at greater length in the next chapter. An extension of Heider's work by Newcomb (1953) takes account of the two-way relation between people. Newcomb postulates a "strain toward symmetry" which causes two people, A and B, who like each other, to be similarly oriented toward an object X. Thus, interpersonal attraction is facilitated by the perception that a relevant attitude is shared in common, a basic point in the next chapter as well.

Also related to the Heider balance concept is the *congruity theory* put forth by Osgood and Tannenbaum (1955). They deal with two cognitive elements which are paired with one another in terms of a positive or negative relationship. The major feature of this approach is that it allows for more exact prediction of the direction and degree of attitude change. Thus, Osgood and Tannenbaum assert the proposition that the more extreme the valence of an attitude, the less likely it is to change when paired with something of opposite valence. Suppose we like a public figure at the highest scale value of $+3$ and then learn that he is in favor of a policy which we dislike at the relatively moderate level of -1. The prediction then is that our attitude toward the policy will be considerably more likely to "give" in a more favorable direction, rather than our attitude toward the political figure shifting in an unfavorable direction. Another technique for determining the degree of change, in terms of "belief congruence," has also been proposed by Rokeach and Rothman (1965).

One important implication of such congruity relationships is that a communication source with a high positive valence can be more persuasive in advocating a less favored course of action. Alternatively, when a communication source that is viewed very negatively urges a policy which is relatively favored, the policy may itself be seen in more negative terms. Osgood (1960) gives the example of a Soviet representative making proposals for world disarmament, and says, "A large segment of the American press editorializes about the deceptive nature of these proposals. . . . It is cognitively inconsistent for us to think of people we dislike and distrust making honest, conciliatory moves . . ." (p. 341).

Abelson and Rosenberg (1958) have coined the term "psycho-logic" to indicate the contrast between actual processes of cognitive interaction and logic. Among their *rules of psycho-logic*, they give the following: 1) A likes B and B likes C implies that A likes C; 2) A likes B and B dislikes C implies that A dislikes C; 3) A dislikes B and B dislikes C implies that A likes C. The latter relationship, for example, is made explicit in the proverb, "The enemy of my enemy is my friend." While these rules are not strictly speaking logical, they appear to operate in many realms of human conduct.

COGNITIVE DISSONANCE

Earlier, the most prominent theory for dealing with the effects of communication on attitude change was identified as the dissonance model developed by Festinger (1957, 1964b) An up-dating of its features has recently been provided by Aronson (1968). Essentially, this theory contends that individuals are motivated to seek consonance of their attitudes. Thus, attitude change operates in terms of movement toward such consonance and away from dissonance. When individuals experience dissonance, they also actively avoid situations which would increase that dissonance. Festinger (1957) gives the example of a survey conducted on smoking habits and attitudes. It was found that 29 per cent of non-smokers, 20 per cent of light smokers, but only 7 per cent of heavy smokers believed that a relationship had been established between smoking and lung cancer (p. 155). To continue smoking in the face of the belief that it is dangerous increases dissonance.

Action which is contradictory to a person's attitudes has been studied in a number of experiments generated by the dissonance theory. In a study by Festinger and Carlsmith (1959), they induced subjects who had just taken part in a very boring task to tell another person that the task was quite interesting in order to help the experimenter get subjects to participate in the study. They found that subjects given $20 for providing this false information changed their attitudes less, in the direction of believing that they liked the task, than subjects given only $1. The results are diagrammed in Figure 6.6.

Festinger explains the results of this experiment in terms of dissonance created by "insufficient rewards" (1961). Subjects who received only $1 found it necessary to rationalize a falsehood for such a small sum by believing that they had really liked this dull task. On the

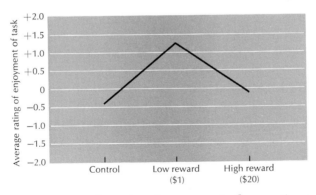

Figure 6.6: Average ratings given in response to the question on enjoyment of the task following compliance by two experimental groups. Control group represents no compliance and no monetary reward. (Based on data from Festinger and Carlsmith, 1959.)

other hand, those who received the high reward of $20 experienced very little dissonance in telling others that this was an interesting task since they had received enough money to amply justify their actions to themselves without changing attitudes. In a repeat experiment with Belgian university students, Nuttin (1966) replicated the Festinger and Carlsmith study but added a condition of "consonant compliance" where these students were to report that the task was boring and dull. Here again, the low reward led to a significant attitude change. The results for the "dissonant compliance" condition were in the same direction as those in the Festinger and Carlsmith experiment, but were not statistically significant.

In a related study, Brehm and Cohen (1962, pp. 74-78) assigned students to conditions with different financial inducements, in terms of four levels, i.e. 50¢, $1, $5, or $10 for writing an essay which was against their own attitudinal position. They found that the lower the financial reward, the greater the reported opinion change toward the position of the essay. Similarly, Lependorf (1964) has reported, from an experiment with children, that there was less change of attitude with a 50¢ reward than with a 5¢ reward. Chapanis and Chapanis (1964) have argued in the case of the Festinger and Carlsmith study that subjects given $20 had their suspicion aroused, and thus did not change their attitudes. However, this criticism should not hold for the smaller sums in the latter experiments.

Bem (1967) presents a critique of the Festinger and Carlsmith experiment in terms of his self-perception theory, noted earlier. He interprets the attitude change as an attribution by subjects of what *caused* them to tell others that a boring task was interesting. In an "interpersonal replication," he had subjects listen to a tape recording which described the circumstances of a subject, in one of the conditions, and his actions. Then, Bem had the "listening" subjects estimate the attitude of the subject toward the boring task. His findings were in line with the original experiment. Listeners judged the subject receiving the $1 reward as having a more favorable attitude. Bem says that the reason for this is that the larger reward was attributed to be the greater cause for telling the falsehood, and that postulating a state of dissonance is not needed to explain this. Kelley (1967) contends that a resolution to this difference of interpretation rests in whether or not the subject in such an experiment feels he has a choice to freely express his attitudes. In a related vein, Aronson (1965) asserts that unless subjects are caught up and involved in the importance of the task, rather than considering it trivial, there will be no dissonance effect.

INDUCEMENTS, FORCED COMPLIANCE, AND REACTANCE

Festinger adopts the general position that the less inducement or force used to elicit overt compliance, the greater will be the underlying opinion change toward that position. This was demonstrated in an experiment by Freedman (1965). Boys from second, third, and fourth grade classes were brought to a playroom individually and were told *not* to play with a very desirable toy, while the experimenter was out of the room. In the condition of mild threat, the child was only told: "Do not play with the robot. It is wrong to play with the robot." In the high threat condition, the same statement was used with this addition: "If you play with the robot, I'll be *very angry.*" Those children who had not played with the toy were placed in the same situation several weeks later, with no threat. Freedman found that the ones who had resisted temptation under mild threat were less likely to play with the toy in this second session than those who had resisted under severe threat. Thus, Festinger's concept of the stronger effects of a less forceful persuasive communication was confirmed for subsequent behavior.

Considerable interest has been generated in the controversy about the greater effect on attitude change of smaller inducements. Janis and Gilmore (1965) conducted an experiment in which college students were paid $1 or $20 to present good arguments in favor of adding a year of physics and a year of mathematics to the college curriculum. As a "high incentive," some were told that this enterprise was being conducted under "public welfare" auspices on behalf of a number of leading universities in the United States. For the "low incentive" condition, others were told that the information was being gathered for a new publishing company that was trying to build up its market for science textbooks. Their results showed that subsequent attitudes changed most favorably for subjects receiving the greater monetary reward, rather than the lesser reward, and significantly so under the "high incentive" condition. It should be clear, however, that apart from just the degree of reward, there was also an issue of "value" here, in the sense of the end being served by compliance to the request.

There are a number of additional leads flowing from the earlier "forced compliance" research, and a variety of experiments have been performed since to delineate these further. What, for instance, are some other circumstances under which a negative rather than a positive relationship would exist between incentives and attitude change? Carlsmith, Collins, and Helmreich (1966) created two conditions: in the first, male high school students were offered payments ranging from fifty cents to five dollars to make a counter-attitudinal statement in a face-to-face, "role-playing" contact with a peer; in the second, similar students were offered identical amounts to write an anonymous essay, again against their own attitude. Subjects then indicated "how interesting" and "how much fun" the experiment had been on a post-experimental questionnaire. As Figure 6.7 reveals, the results support the traditional dissonance effect of a negative relationship between the magnitude of the reward and the attitude change, in the face-to-face contact condition, but the opposite, a positive relationship, is found in the essay-writing condition. Students in the face-to-face condition were treated essentially as in the Festinger and Carlsmith experiment, noted above, whereas those in the essay-writing condition were behaving anonymously. Among other implications, this finding points to the importance of a *public-anonymous* variable as an element in the induction of dissonance, though other considerations are also involved.

In another experiment, by Linder, Cooper, and Jones (1967), the feature of *freedom* was introduced. Subjects were given an opportunity to refuse the experimenter's request to engage in counter-attitudinal behavior. This was the "volition" condition. It produced the dissonance effect when the situation called for the subject to behave in a way that was counter-attitudinal; alternatively, those *subjects not given a free choice* to refuse to take part, did not show the dissonance effect. Other experimentation, by Holmes and Strickland (1970), has yielded parallel findings. Subjects who were given a free choice of continuing in the study, which required counter-attitudinal essay-writing, showed the greatest attitude change for the least rewards. This lends support to Kelley's (1967) contention about the pivotal importance of the variable of choice in swinging outcomes one way or the other.

At least several antecedant conditions have been pointed to here as

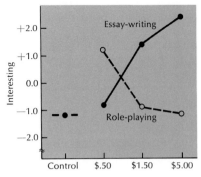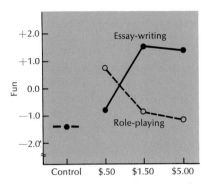

Figure 6.7: Responses to two post-experimental questions by subjects in the essay-writing and role-playing treatments, under three conditions of compensation. The value drawn for the "control" is the average value for the control groups. (Adapted from Carlsmith, Collins, and Helmreich, 1966, p. 9.)

variables in dissonance arousal, that is, the value being served, the degree of public commitment, and the sense of volition in taking part.

Another interesting tack revealed in recent studies of dissonance is the effect of counter-attitudinal statements upon the individual's self-concept. Aronson (1969a, b), among others, contends that lying is dissonance-producing only where it has negative consequences to the individual's self-concept. When an individual lies, it is an immoral act only insofar as he judges it himself to be so: "white lies" may be justified as part of smoothing social interaction, and are not indicative of outright deceit. Lies told in the course of ongoing interaction *might* be seen as deceit, however, and could jeopardize the relationship of the individual with those whom he has misled (Collins, 1969; Bramel, 1969). Heslin and Rotton (1969) have recently found that praise for telling a counter-attitudinal "lie" yielded greater attitude change in that direction than did praise for taking a counter-attitudinal position as part of a "debate," with the conclusion that the reward was more meaningful when the individual felt a greater personal commitment.

A general point of criticism about such experiments has been raised by Rosenberg (1965). He contends that the degree of reward for advocating a position opposite to one's own is contaminated by the presence of *evaluation apprehension* in the experimental setting. By this he means that the subjects, apprehensive from a desire to present themselves favorably to a critical experimenter, may resist appearing to be easily swayed by inordinately high monetary rewards. Rosenberg says, subjects

> . . . will develop *hypotheses* about how to win positive evaluation or to avoid negative evaluation . . . It seems quite conceivable that in certain dissonance experiments, the use of surprisingly large monetary rewards for eliciting counterattitudinal arguments may seem quite strange to the subject, may suggest that he is being treated disingenuously . . . and, guided by the figural fact that an excessive reward has been offered, he may be led to hypothesize that the experimental situation is one in which his autonomy, his honesty, his resoluteness in resisting a special kind of bribe, are being tested. . . . The subject who has formulated such a subjective hypothesis about the real purpose of the experimental situation will be prone to resist giving evidence of attitude change . . . (p. 29).

In a replication of the essay-writing experiment by Brehm and Cohen (1962, pp. 74-78) noted above, Rosenberg had the experimenter who determined the subjects' final attitudes dissociated from the experimenter who presented the essay-writing task. Using this procedure, he found that the greatest amount of change occurred for the subjects paid the largest sum of money. These nonconfirming findings add further weight to the prospect that the prediction from dissonance theory regarding the effects of small inducements may be limited by other conditions.

Worchel and Brehm (1970) tested a reactance prediction that fits

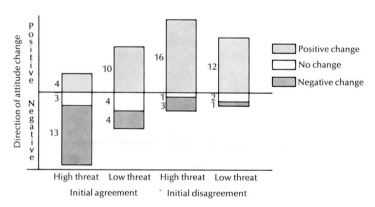

Figure 6.8: Number of subjects showing indicated change in attitudes by initial position and threat to freedom present in communication. (Based upon data from Worchel and Brehm, 1970.)

many of the findings reported in this section, namely, that a strong threat to a person's freedom to decide something for himself will produce a "boomerang effect." As an additional feature, they took account of their subjects' initial agreement or disagreement with the position advocated in the persuasive speech to be read. Subjects on both sides of the issue were exposed to speeches either for or against their own position, and these either had a freedom-threatening component or did not.

The results shown in Figure 6.8 indicate that subjects who read a speech advocating a position they had agreed to initially, but with a freedom-threatening component, moved significantly away from that position while the subjects in the three other conditions moved significantly toward the advocated position. Indeed, of the three conditions, the highest proportion of subjects shifted in the *positive* direction when the high threat accompanied a communication representing an *opposite* position from the subjects' initial one. The investigators explain this apparent anomaly by the suggestion that this case represents less threat since the individual already holds an opposite view and has demonstrated his freedom. But where he holds the same view as the communication, he may feel obliged to demonstrate he has the freedom to move in the other direction. Accordingly, there is a complex relationship between the content of the communication relative to the individual's own position and his freedom to shift away from it. Which now brings us more directly to a consideration of the communicator and the content of communication.

THE COMMUNICATOR AND THE CONTENT OF THE COMMUNICATION

Much of the research on the role of the communicator as a source of influence has centered on his *credibility*. This general characteristic embodies several features which the recipient may perceive to give the source validity, including expertise and trustworthiness. There are also such factors as background, appearance, and other identifiable features of the person which might determine his acceptability. Part of the content of his communication, therefore, is the impression he conveys to the audience in terms of these characteristics.

In an experiment by Hovland and Weiss (1951), college students were given material to read presented as articles drawn from newspapers and magazines. These dealt with various technical topics including the feasibility of an atomic submarine, the use of antihistamine drugs, and so forth. In half of the communications, attribution was made to sources considered to be trustworthy, and in the other half to sources considered to be untrustworthy. As might be expected, immediately after the messages had been read, the material attributed to trust-worthy sources generated significantly greater amounts of attitude change than that attributed to untrustworthy sources. Furthermore, regardless of which situation they had been in, subjects had acquired about the same level of information. Four weeks later, subjects were tested again for longer-range attitude change. Now it was found that attitudes originally influenced by the trustworthy source showed a decrease in the amount of agreement with the message, while those influenced by the untrustworthy source showed an increase in the amount of agreement with the message. Hovland and Weiss dubbed this the "sleeper effect" and concluded that it might have arisen as a result of the subjects' recalling the content of a communication but forgetting its source after a time.

In another experiment, Weiss (1957) tested the hypothesis that a communicator who agrees with the views of an audience on a given issue of importance will be more effective in changing attitudes on an-other issue, though unrelated. His results indicated that this effect did occur and suggests that in it there is an element of increased trust-worthiness as well as a sense that the communicator shares some important characteristics with the members of his audience. In this respect, an experiment by Zimbardo (1960) indicates that if the com-municator is the best friend of the recipient the greatest attitude change occurs, even if the communication is highly discrepant.

In general, the work of Hovland and his associates (Hovland, Janis, and Kelley, 1953) demonstrates the force exerted by the communica-tor in determining the effectiveness of the content of his message. Two of the specific kinds of things that they have investigated are the *order of presentation* of material and the presentation of *one or both sides* of an issue. From many studies by the Yale group, it appears that the order, in terms of the primacy or recency of a message, is complexly related to attitude change (Hovland, 1957).

Primacy refers to the advantage of the initial position presented, and recency to the advantage of the last position presented. In Cohen's

(1964) coverage of research dealing with the communicator's message, he points out that research on primacy-recency yields highly differential results as a consequence of other factors such as awareness of intent to influence, complexity of the message, and the attempt to measure the communicator's effects.

Overall, the primacy effect operates best to reinforce an attitude already held. However, it can be reduced by a long delay between the first and second presentations. Miller and Campbell (1959) suggest that because of a high degree of forgetting, time differentials may be decisive in determining the effects of persuasive communications. In short, primacy may lose its impact if there is a sufficient delay before hearing an alternative viewpoint.

If, after hearing one side of an issue, the audience is obliged to take a public stand before hearing the alternative view, there is a strong primacy effect. Hovland, Campbell, and Brock (1957) presented one side of a controversial issue to a group of students and then asked them to write their opinion on it for publication in a magazine read by their peers. Other students, in a control group, heard the same presentation but wrote out their opinions anonymously, with no mention of any publication. Without prior announcement, both groups then heard the other side, and their attitudes were again measured. The results revealed that public expression tended to make subjects more resistant to influence by the second presentation than were those giving less public, anonymous expression.

On the whole, the findings regarding primacy indicate that it is affected by a number of other factors. This is equally true with regard to the presentation of one side vs. both sides of an argument. Presenting just one side is more effective in reinforcing an audience's attitude already in the desired direction, while presenting both sides is more effective with an audience whose attitudes are not in that direction (Hovland, Lumsdaine, and Sheffield, 1949). Motivational factors are also involved. Thus, order of presentation is a more important determiner of attitude change for subjects with a low degree of interest than for those with high interest (Cohen, Stotland, and Wolfe, 1955). McGuire (1957) found that when communications highly consonant with audience attitudes were presented first by a communicator, followed by those that were not consonant, more attitude change resulted than when the order was reversed.

EFFECTS OF FEAR AROUSAL

Appeals which arouse fear motivation have been found variously to affect attitude change. In a study by Janis and Feshbach (1953), college students were divided into three experimental groups and given communications, varying in intensity, concerning the importance of dental hygiene. Data were gathered before and after on the students' dental practices. Those who had received the most fear-arousing communication, involving the presentation of pictures of diseased gums, changed least toward the recommended preventative practices for dental care. Those who had received the more moderate messages changed significantly more in the intended direction. Janis and Feshbach concluded that a result of fear arousal was to reduce compliance, due to the inhibiting effects of anxiety.

Similar results were also obtained by Janis and Terwilliger (1962) using appeals to smokers, ranging from high to low threat, concerning the health hazards of smoking. Alternatively, Leventhal and Niles (1964) found that smokers who reported more fear on the issue of smoking and cancer showed greater agreement with the recommendations of a persuasive communication. Berkowitz and Cottingham (1960) found that a higher fear appeal produced greater attitude change than a lower fear appeal on the issue of the safety features of auto seat belts. In another experiment by Leventhal and Niles (1965), a group of automobile drivers were shown color movies of gory accidents to induce emotional arousal aimed at gaining agreement with appeals such as "Never drive after drinking." While the results showed high immediate agreement from those who had seen these films, the effect was sharply reduced a week later.

McGuire (1966, p. 485) reconciles these apparently disparate findings by emphasizing the necessity to take account of the recipient's initial concern with an issue as a determinant of the effect of a fear appeal. His essential point is that given a high initial concern, a fear-arousing communication may overwhelm the recipient with anxiety and accordingly reduce the effectiveness of the communication. Optimally, the high fear arousal would be most effective with those people having a low level of initial concern. His two-factor theory considers that the "drive" function of fear facilitates attitude change while the "cue function" interferes with the reception of a fear-arousing communication. McGuire observes that studies by Niles (1964) and Millman (1965) support this interpretation.

In considering McGuire's (1966, 1967) position, Janis (1967) maintains that it is quite arbitrary to assume that all interference effects result from the cue function and all facilitation effects from the drive function. With somewhat different assumptions, Janis argues that fear may cue greater vigilance and a heightened reliance on authoritative recommendations. The traditional question of "the effectiveness" of fear-arousing appeals in inducing attitude change should be replaced, he says, by the more appropriate query: "What are the determinants of the optimal level of emotional arousal for inducing acceptance of a given type of persuasive message, or of persuasive communications in general?" (1967, p. 210).

Among the more important consequences of arousal is the individual's increased interest in knowing what is happening to himself in his surroundings. This is a central feature of Schachter's (1964) theory of emotional arousal, discussed in Chapter 1, i.e. that environmental cues which stimulate arousal bring into play cognitive factors to help the individual explain his feelings. Lazarus (1966) also finds that among the effects of fear arousal is an upsurge in interest in relevant information, whether from internal or external cues. In such instances as disaster, Janis (1962) reports that the availability of authoritative information at the time when ambiguity is greatest can make a critical difference between panic and productive activity.

Summarizing the effects of fear, Janis (1967) delineates the major behaviors which follow from what he terms "reflective fear," that is, fear which is based in thoughtful reflection, and which can vary in intensity as a result of additional information. This distinguishes it from a neurotic type of panic state where emotional arousal persists at a high level and the individual is essentially impervious to new information. Janis contends that,

> . . . a person's level of reflective fear is roughly proportional both to the perceived probability of the dangerous event materializing and to the anticipated magnitude of the damage, if it does materialize, that could be inflicted on himself, his family, and other significant persons or groups with whom he is identified (1967, p. 170).

Janis says the three behavioral consequences of reflective fear are: *heightened vigilance,* which takes the form of greater attention to threatening events, and thinking about alternative actions for dealing with them; a *strong need to seek reassurance* to reduce emotional arousal; and the development of a *compromise attitude,* which combines the elements of vigilance and reassurance. From his extensive research on hospitalized patients, Janis (1962) gives as an example the victim of heart disease who, realizing he might be vulnerable to another heart attack, makes plans for protective action if another attack should occur, while remaining vigilant to any signs of worsening of his condition, with related worries about collapse or even death.

Concerning the efficacy of persuasive communications with a strong threat appeal, the experimental findings suggest that beyond an "optimal range" it can arouse psychological resistance which impairs its effectiveness. On the other hand, when the threat, in terms of a warning, is quite mild, it may be dismissed as inconsequential. However, even this small level of arousal can be facilitating, as is indicated in a study by Leventhal, Singer, and Jones (1965). They secured a measure of the behavioral response of different versions of a communication to students regarding the effectiveness of anti-tetanus immunization. With the co-operation of the university health center, it was possible to determine whether students in the sample actually obtained these shots. A mild fear appeal was found to be about as effective in producing this outcome as was a strong fear appeal. Compared with the control condition, in which a communication made the same recommendations but without the element of threat, both fear-appeal conditions were more effective, especially when accompanied by information about how to get the shots. Interestingly, none of the students who received the recommendation and this information, *without* the fear-producing appeal, actually appeared at the health center for the shots. In many areas of protective action, such as health care, it therefore appears to be necessary to induce a mild threat which creates sufficient arousal to instigate action.

RESISTANCE TO PERSUASION: INOCULATION EFFECTS

Hovland, Janis, and Kelley (1953) advanced the hypothesis that "when a person is perceived as having a definite *intention* to persuade others, the likelihood is increased that he will be perceived as having something to gain and, hence, as less worthy of trust" (p. 23). The idea that communicators have "an axe to grind" is a commonplace. Yet, resistance to persuasion has been found to depend upon various factors. Walster and Festinger (1962) conducted an experiment which lent general support to the resistance hypothesis. An appeal from communicators who were allegedly unaware of being "overheard" by an audience had a greater effect than when they made a "direct" appeal to a comparable audience, provided the audience had strong feelings on the issue initially. In another study involving the "incidental" character of the communication, Festinger and Maccoby (1964) obtained comparable findings. They predicted that if a person is exposed to a counter-attitudinal communication, when his attention is distracted, then the effect of that communication would be greater because the individual's defenses are down. They found confirmation of this, but other interpretations have been suggested. McGuire (1966) contends that, if anything, distraction should inhibit the acquisition of the message, and therefore lead to less effectiveness.

Some recent data from an experiment by Haaland and Venkatesan (1968), in which they introduced visual and behavioral distractions, indicates support for McGuire's contention. They found that distracted subjects were less able to recall the arguments from the persuasive communication, and showed less attitude change, as well. The issue is by no means a closed one, however, since it bears directly on one of the most central processes underlying influence, that is, the perception and integration of new informational inputs.

It is not enough to say, therefore, that open attempts to influence are rejected. Thus, Mills and Aronson (1965) found that an overt, frankly stated desire to influence can enhance persuasiveness, if the communicator is "attractive" to the audience. Similarly, Mills (1966) reports that a communicator who indicates a liking for the audience, as part of a persuasive appeal, is more effective in gaining agreement from that audience than one who does not indicate a liking. In terms of our earlier discussion of the transactional model, actions of the communicator which establish a favorable perception of him by the audience materially increase his prospect for both overcoming resistance to persuasion and becoming influential. Zimbardo's finding (1960), considered above, indicates that close friends are acceptable communication sources, even when their communications are discrepant. This appears to be a function of trust, especially regarding the perception of the motives of the communicator (Allyn and Festinger, 1961).

Various studies (McGuire and Papageorgis, 1962; McGuire, 1964; McGuire and Millman, 1965; Freedman and Sears, 1965) indicate that the forewarning of a desire to persuade tends to bolster the audience's defenses by a rehearsal of their supportive arguments. There are, however, individual factors, such as self-esteem, also involved. In general, resistance to persuasion is associated with high self-esteem (Hovland and Janis, 1959, p. 230), a point to which greater attention is given in Chapter 10 with regard to the functioning of personality.

McGuire (1964) has proposed an *inoculation theory* which raises a serious question about the notion that supportive communications tend to bolster resistance to persuasion. He asserts that messages which are in line with existing attitudes merely reiterate the obvious and, if anything, occasion overconfidence. Therefore, he concludes, pre-exposure to a weakened dose of the opposition material actually provides the individual with stronger defenses against the counter-attitudinal attack. McGuire and his co-workers, as well as others (Tannenbaum, 1967; Tannebaum, Macaulay, and Norris, 1966), have investigated inoculation effects in a belief area *not* likely to have been exposed previously to powerful attacks, i.e. cultural truisms regarding health care. The issues used in these studies were various health practices, including frequent tooth brushing to prevent dental decay, regular medical check-ups, and the use of X-rays to detect tuberculosis. The main attack on such beliefs came from a favorable source, such as a professor of medicine.

The results of this research indicate substantial support for the inoculation theory. They demonstrate that prior exposure to essentially diluted counter-arguments, which are mentioned and then refuted, is more effective in producing resistance to strong attacks, even from a favorable source, than is the mere presentation of supportive arguments in advance. There remains an open question regarding how widely the findings on cultural truisms about health care generalize to more controversial and ideologically loaded issues. However, Tannenbaum (1967, p. 293) considers that the study by Papageorgis and McGuire (1961), demonstrating that the refutation of one set of arguments appears to generalize to create resistance to another set of arguments, is impressive evidence for the inoculation theory. Indeed, in that study, the warning of an impending attack enhanced the effectiveness of both refutation and supportive defenses, but particularly the latter, which Tannenbaum (1967) points out did not have the necessary threat component to begin with.

ASSIMILATION AND CONTRAST EFFECTS

Our next concern here focuses on the way in which the recipient of the communication perceives it in terms of his own position. The importance of this consideration is evident through much of the material that we have been surveying. In the final analysis, it is the individual who categorizes and interprets the message in light of his past experience.

For a long time, attitude studies operated with the assumption that the position advocated by a communication would be seen in about the same way by different people. This was the basis for the judging procedure in Thurstone's development of the equal-appearing intervals attitude scale. However, as we noted above, Hovland and Sherif (1952) found that there were variable judgments associated with attitudes, because individuals use their own position in evaluating other positions in terms of assimilation or contrast. In this context, *assimilation* means the acceptance of material from a communication source as tolerable within one's own view of things. *Contrast* means a rejection of such material as beyond that range. Exemplifying this, Hovland, Janis, and Kelley (1953) indicate that individuals who are in favor of the position advocated will consider a communication to be fair and unbiased; those who are opposed will see it as unfair and propagandistic.

Subsequent work by Hovland, Harvey, and Sherif (1957) demonstrated that individuals who hold extreme positions tend to see other positions in sharp contrast with their own. In this experiment the issue of the desirability of a prohibition on drinking was studied in two states, Oklahoma and Texas, where the so-called "wet-dry" issue has been hotly contested. Three kinds of communications were directed at subjects through a taped presentation. One was strongly "wet," one strongly "dry," and one "moderately wet." Figure 6.9 shows the results in terms of the three kinds of communications and the recipients' positions ranging from A (very dry) through H (very wet). As is seen

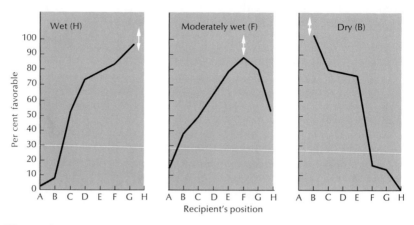

Figure 6.9: Percentage of favorable evaluations ("fair," "unbiased," etc.) of wet (H), moderately wet (F), and dry (B) communications for subjects holding various positions on prohibition. Recipients' positions range from A (very dry) to H (very wet). Position of communications indicated by arrow. (From Hovland, Harvey, and Sherif, 1957.)

there, the degree of distance between the recipient and the communication greatly influences the acceptance of the communication.

This research illustrates the judgmental quality of an attitude. In their book *Social Judgment,* Sherif and Hovland (1961) extend this view as follows:

> . . . an attitude toward an object, person, group, or social issue is not directly observable but is inferred from a persistent and *characteristic* mode of reaction to that stimulus or stimulus class. This characteristic mode of reaction signifies differential treatment of the object of attitude. It is inferred that the object of attitude is placed in a category or class favorable or unfavorable in some degree, high or low in some degree, acceptable or unacceptable in some degree in the individual's scheme of things. In short one essential aspect of the attitudinal reaction is a categorization process, whether or not the individual is aware that he is passing a judgment (p. 5).

We may say, then, that attitudes operate as categories for defining an individual's experience, rather than single points on a scale. These are inferred through a pattern of approval or disapproval of items on attitude scales, or in terms of other behaviors. Accordingly, Sherif and Hovland (1961) contend that every individual has a range of positions which constitute his latitudes of acceptance, rejection, and non-commitment for the topic area represented by an attitude. The *latitude of acceptance* is represented by the person's own position on a topic as well as those positions which are most acceptable to him; the *latitude of rejection* constitutes the positions that the individual would find most objectionable to his own; the *latitude of non-commitment* is indicated by the "don't know" and "no opinion" categories in questionnaire surveys, which usually reveal issues respondents view with disinterest.

The idea of latitudes is especially important for its emphasis on the individual's construction of his world, within a set of ranges rather than in terms of a fixed scale point. This approach has been greatly elaborated by Sherif, Sherif, and Nebergall in their book, *Attitude and Attitude Change: The Social Judgment-Involvement Approach* (1965). If a communication is extremely discrepant from an individual's own position, they find that it produces resistance to the advocated change, and even a boomerang effect, particularly if the individual is highly involved in the issue. Sherif, Sherif, and Nebergall have demonstrated that, as the individual's involvement increases, the latitude of non-commitment becomes absorbed within the latitude of rejection. The latitude of acceptance is not directly affected so much as is the rejection of almost any other viewpoints.

A readiness to accept influence toward attitude change is therefore likely to be greatest where the communication is not extremely discrepant and the issue is not vitally important to the individual. This effect is shown in Figure 6.10 from research by Freedman (1964). As predicted, with low involvement, attitude change is directly related to the degree the communication is discrepant from the individual's own position. Under high involvement, however, the greatest change occurs with a moderately discrepant communication, and a sharp drop-off in effect occurs for a highly discrepant communication.

In the Zimbardo study (1960) he obtained a different finding. There greater involvement on the part of the individual produced greater dissonance and hence more attitude change from a discrepant communication. This may be a function of how the range of discrepancy is defined. A further consideration, quite obviously, is the credibility of the communicator. Zimbardo used a close friend as the communicator.

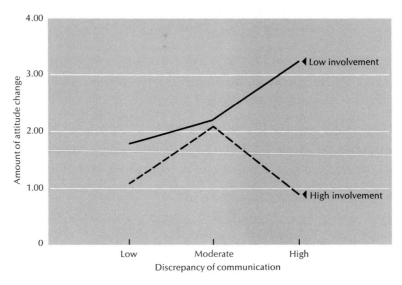

Figure 6.10: Mean amount of attitude change from initial to final response for two levels of involvement and three levels of communication discrepancy. (From Freedman, 1964.)

Relatedly, Aronson, Turner, and Carlsmith (1963) have found that with greater prestige the communicator's message was harder to reject even if it was highly discrepant. Once again, therefore, the perception by the recipient of the characteristics of the *complex* represented by the communicator *and* his message is vitally important.

ROLE-PLAYING EFFECTS

Several of the experiments reported in this chapter involved the use of "role-playing," wherein subjects pretend to be in a given setting which requires them to act, and perhaps feel, as a participant there would. If the intensity of this experience generates sufficient arousal, it can produce attitude changes that extend well beyond the time-space confines of the experimental situation. One provocative illustration of this comes from recent research on role-playing as a device for changing smoking habits.

In this study by Janis and Mann (1965), fourteen women who were known to be smokers were asked to play the role of patient as part of an experiment. Each was received in what appeared to be a physician's office and heard an experimenter, acting the role of the physician, telling her that he had some "bad news." The news consisted of the fact that a supposed X-ray examination had revealed that they had lung cancer and therefore, allegedly, they would be obliged immediately to undergo surgery. They could ask questions, and they did. From this relatively spontaneous interchange, they learned that the surgery would be painful, that there was some risk of its not being successful, that they would find it necessary to be in a state of recuperation for many weeks, and so on.

While the role-playing group showed markedly greater changes in attitudes and in smoking behavior, a control group of twelve subjects (the "exposed controls"), who had received comparable information by listening to a tape recording of one of these interview sessions, were also affected. Figure 6.11 shows the results of subsequent follow-ups, the first after two weeks, with regard to the mean number of cigarettes these subjects smoked daily. As Mann and Janis (1968) report, there was a substantial decrease in the number of cigarettes smoked by both groups.

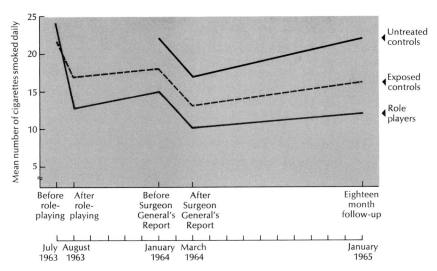

Figure 6.11: Long-term effects of emotional role-playing, and passive exposure to comparable information, on cigarette smoking. (After Mann and Janis, 1968.)

The next follow-up interview was conducted in March 1964, after the appearance of the Surgeon General's Report on Smoking and Health. An interviewer phoned the subjects and revealed no connection with the original experiment, merely explaining that people were being contacted as part of a survey on smoking. All but one of the original role-playing subjects were contacted. Retrospective data also were obtained concerning their own estimates of cigarette consumption for January 1964, just before the report was issued. At the same time an additional sample of 31 female volunteers, smokers who had not previously participated in the role-playing research, were drawn from the same college attended by experimental subjects. This group constituted the "untreated controls," who were almost identical on relevant background characteristics—age, educational level, and the amount of cigarette consumption reported for the year prior to the experiment (1968, p. 340). The last follow-up interview was carried out in January 1965, approximately eighteen months after the original role-playing experiment. This time, to minimize any possible association, subjects were contacted by a female interviewer who introduced herself as coming from an opinion survey organization.

The essential findings of the Mann and Janis (1968) follow-up are shown in Figure 6.11. They indicate that the significant difference in average daily cigarette consumption between the experimental and exposed control groups persisted until January 1965.

> Thus, eighteen months after the experimental sessions the effectiveness of the emotional role-playing procedure, as compared with passive exposure to the same information about lung cancer could still be observed. . . . The additional group of untreated controls reported a decrease in cigarette consumption immediately following the appearance of the Surgeon General's Report. But by January 1965, their smoking intake was identical with their pre-report level. This short-lived effect corresponds to the trend data reported by large scale surveys on smoking among the American public. . . . The large majority of smokers who were influenced by the Report evidently quickly reverted to their normal smoking habits. In contrast, the emotional role-players and the passively exposed controls showed a relatively sustained decrease following exposure to the Surgeon General's Report. These findings suggest that passively listening to the recording of a dramatic emotional role-playing session had a sustained effect on smoking behavior, although actively participating in the role-playing procedure was even more effective (Mann and Janis, 1968, p. 341).

In a further study, Mann (1968) extended and replicated the earlier research by comparing three matched groups of men and women who were exposed to various types of role-playing. The first group enacted the role of a cancer victim, as in the earlier experiment; in the second group, each person took the role of a debater presenting a case against smoking; in the third group, a shame-arousing procedure was employed which required each person to play the role of a helpless smoking addict. In terms of attitude change, Mann's results indicated that the fear-arousing procedure was far more effective than either of the other two. Neither a "cognitive" treatment, as in the debating role, nor the "shame" condition, as in the addict role, produced as much effect. An inescapable conclusion, therefore, is that emotional role-playing, exemplified in taking the role of a patient who is a likely candidate for surgery, induces a sense of personal vulnerability that may lead to a marked reconstruction of the person's psychological field.

While it would be a mistake to generalize this effect to any and all situations of threat, it suggests how a set of potent factors may profoundly alter attitudes and their associated behaviors. In general, profound experiences may have a dramatic effect on attitude change. When an individual is confronted with a major change in his life habits, or in his awareness about an issue central to his existence, changes in attitude may be very rapid indeed, and their effects quite perceptible (Rokeach, 1968, p. 167).

The operative factors in the Janis and Mann situation were its real-life immediacy, the importance of the issue to the individuals involved, and the presumptive "credibility" of the experimenter as a prestige source (Elms, 1966). Since we noted earlier that extreme fear arousal can operate to immobilize people, it should be added that a clear alternative for action should be readily perceived by the subjects if a desired effect is to be produced. An apt illustration of this is seen in Cohen's research (1957) which supported the generalization that attitude change is more likely to occur if information relevant to motive satisfaction is presented *after* these motives have been aroused, rather than before. Given the high salience of the motivation induced in the kind of role-playing situation just described, it should follow that especially those subjects who beforehand had been relatively unconcerned were sufficiently aroused to take action. Others, who did not change as dramatically, may have been overwhelmed by this fear-inducing experience.

Social influence and attitudes: a final word

In this chapter we have considered the ways in which attitudes developing out of influence relationships are altered in the course of ongoing interaction and the input of new experience. Our emphasis, in terms of attitude change, has been on a transactional model of communication. This model has ramifications which apply to a broad sphere of social relationships. Moreover, concepts of balance and dissonance, of interpersonal perception and social exchange, have wide relevance.

The effects of direct interaction on attitude change are attended to further in the next chapter. It should be apparent that interpersonal contact produces such effects in a wide-range of life situations. In the case of prejudice, for example, extensive literature sustains the proposition that such contact, particularly on an equal status basis, undermines the attitudes which nourish prejudice and its manifestations (Allport, 1958).

In subsequent chapters we will consider a number of relationships which draw upon concepts examined here. We will observe that leadership and conformity, as examples, have common elements paralleling those we considered with regard to communication and attitude change as a process of influence. Thus, leaders are communication sources who transmit messages and are perceived and reacted to as such. In the instance of conformity, the communication source may be a broader social entity, in the form of a group, and its messages may be represented in the normative practices which it encourages. All of these partake of the characteristics and processes embedded in influence relationships.

SUMMARY

In the study of attitudes, recent trends have inclined toward a greater stress on their *structural relationships* and *functional features*. The relationship between attitudes, in this newer emphasis, is called *cognitive interaction*.

There are three major components of attitudes, the *cognitive* component of belief-disbelief, the *affective* component of like-dislike, and the *action* component of readiness to respond. These are not sharply distinct from one another but share a common relationship. Four interrelated aspects in the study of attitudes are the *relationships* of their components, the *rewards* they provide, their *source,* in terms of the patterns by which they are learned, and attitude *change,* referring to the social influences affecting them, including new information.

An individual's attitudes may be inconsistent. Social pressures often produce the necessity for an individual to act in a way contrary to his attitudes. Therefore, there may be disparity between an individual's *private attitudes* and *public commitments.* It may also be the case that there is an inconsistency between the cognitive and affective components of an individual's attitudes, in terms of his beliefs and feelings. Festinger's *theory of cognitive dissonance* deals with inconsistency in terms of the individual's avoidance of open conflicts between attitudes as well as other cognitive elements. Thus, individuals are disinclined to accept new information which violates an attitude which they hold. This theory also postulates that attitudes change to accommodate changes in behavior or circumstance.

Attitudes may serve several motivational functions. Katz considers these to fall into four categories: the *instrumental,* the *ego-defensive,* the *value expressive,* and the *knowledge* functions. Arousing and changing attitudes require different appeals in terms of the primary function an attitude serves. Rather than be entirely distinct from one another, these functions are interrelated in various combinations.

There are numerous problems associated with the measurement of attitudes, including the very breadth of the concept attitude itself. Attitudes may also vary with regard to their *centrality* or *peripherality* within the person's psychological field. The most widespread approach to measuring attitudes continues to be the *attitude scale.* In general, such scales consist of a number of statements with which a person may agree or disagree on a dimension with several points often ranging from "highly agree" to "highly disagree." Through this procedure the cognitive component of an attitude is measured by its *direction,* and its affective component by the *degree* of agreement or disagreement as well as by *intensity* of feeling. A score revealing the person's overall attitude can be obtained by summing the responses made to the scale items. A more recent procedure, involving a number of scales, is represented today in the technique called the *semantic differential* which constitutes a multi-dimensional scale. It measures the three major factors of *evaluation, potency,* and *activity.*

Attitude measurement involves considerations of accuracy with regard to *reliability* and *validity.* These issues have to do respectively with the consistency of measurement and the degree to which a measurement actually assesses what it is supposed to measure. Reliability is usually gauged by the internal consistency of an attitude scale as well as by its "repeat reliability" when administered more than once over time. Validity is sometimes determined by checking the relationship between attitudes and behavior.

The validity of attitudes when checked against behaviors in a given situation often appears low. However, this occurs as a result of situational factors which may elicit or inhibit behaviors. These factors can be considered *situational hurdles* which intervene between attitudes and action.

Two kinds of factors are involved in the dynamics of attitude change. One is the *processing* of new information through cognitive interaction, and the other is the function of *social identifications* in maintaining attitudes. The effect of persuasive communication in changing attitudes has been studied as an influence process in terms of the *communicator,* the content of the *message,* and the characteristics of the *recipient.* The *transactional model* of persuasive communication takes account of these elements and the process of exchange which occurs between the communicator and the recipient leading the latter to alter his attitudes. Cognitive consistency dictates that an individual may reject or selectively perceive new information to retain his attitudinal structure. The consistency approach to attitude change gives considerable attention to *dissonance, cognitive balance,* and *congruity.* These approaches all rely on the idea that disturbances in a system of attitudes induce processes to restore balance or consistency in that system. Research on cognitive dissonance has emphasized the effect on attitudes of actions which are contradictory to them.

The effectiveness of a communicator in changing attitudes depends upon his credibility to the recipient as well as upon his message. He may also strive to present the content of his message in such a way as to make it more acceptable with respect to the already prevailing attitudes and group affiliations of the recipient. The effects of *primacy* and *recency* of information are complexly related to attitude change. Primacy, in terms of the advantage of the initial position presented, appears to operate best to reinforce an already held attitude. The *balance of presentation* is also important. Presenting just one side is more effective in reinforcing an audience's already held attitude, and presenting both sides is more effective with an audience whose attitudes are not already in the direction of the communication. Fear-arousing appeals have been found variously to affect attitude change; those who are already concerned appear to be made more anxious by such appeals. Resistance to persuasion is complexly related to the perception of the communicator, and the personality of the recipient, in terms of factors such as self-esteem.

Attitudes have a judgmental quality which operates in terms of *contrast* and *assimilation* effects. Contrast occurs when the recipient perceives the communication as discrepant from his own *latitude of acceptance* and places it within his *latitude of rejection*. Individuals are more likely to reject a discrepant communication if they are highly involved in an issue, since such involvement increases their latitude of rejection. However, even a highly discrepant communication from a communication source which is very positively favored will be assimilated as a basis for attitude change. Intense experiences, including those induced in role-playing may change attitudes through a combination of factors which operate in common to arouse the recipient.

SUGGESTED READINGS

34. Daniel Katz: *The functional approach to the study of attitudes*
35. Charles E. Osgood: *Cognitive dynamics in the conduct of human affairs*
36. Elliot Aronson: *Dissonance theory: progess and problems*
37. Milton Rokeach: *The organization and modification of beliefs*
39. Muzafer Sherif and Carl I. Hovland: *Judgmental processes and problems of attitude*
40. Raymond A. Bauer: *The obstinate audience: the influence process from the point of view of social communication*
41. Robert P. Abelson: *When the polls go wrong and why*

From E. P. Hollander and R. G. Hunt (Eds.) *Current perspectives in social psychology.* (3rd ed.) New York: Oxford University Press, 1971. Introduction to Section VI: *Attitudes and cognition*

SELECTED REFERENCES

Abelson, R., *et al.* (Eds.) *Theories of cognitive consistency: a sourcebook.* Chicago: Rand-McNally, 1968.

Brehm, J. W., & Cohen, A. R. *Explorations in cognitive dissonance.* New York: Wiley, 1962.

Cohen, A. R. *Attitude change and social influence.* New York: Basic Books, 1964.

Edwards, A. L. *Techniques of attitude scale construction.* New York: Appleton-Century-Crofts, 1957.

Festinger, L. *A theory of cognitive dissonance.* Evanston, Ill.: Row, Peterson, 1957.

Festinger, L. (Ed.) *Conflict, decision, and dissonance.* Stanford, Calif.: Stanford Univer. Press, 1964.

*Hovland, C. I., & Janis, I. L. (Eds.) *Personality and persuasibility.* New Haven: Yale Univer. Press, 1959.

*Hovland, C. I., & Rosenberg, M. J. (Eds.) *Attitude organization and change.* New Haven: Yale Univer. Press, 1960.

Insko, C. A. *Theories of attitude change.* New York: Appleton-Century-Crofts, 1967.

Rokeach, M. *Beliefs, attitudes, and values.* San Francisco: Jossey-Bass, 1968.

Shaw, M. E., & Wright, J. M. *Scales for the measurement of attitudes.* New York: McGraw-Hill, 1967.

Sherif, C. W., Sherif, M., & Nebergall, R. E. *Attitude and attitude change: the social judgment-involvement approach.* Philadelphia: Saunders, 1965.

*Sherif, M., & Hovland, C. I. *Social judgment.* New Haven: Yale Univer. Press, 1961.

7

Social interaction, interpersonal perception, and social exchange

Social interaction is a pervasive feature of life. Much of the substance of our experience is shaped by social relationships involving interaction. All of our individual characteristics, concerns, and aspirations are somehow affected by it. It is no wonder then that the study of social interaction occupies a central place in social psychology.

Regarding the importance of interaction, Hare, Borgatta, and Bales (1955) have said that ". . . our very ability to experience, to decide, and to control our own behavior through our decisions is dependent in many subtle and involuntary ways on our relationship and interaction with our fellows" (p. 192). By understanding processes of interaction, therefore, we can clarify many broader features of social influence including cultural, organizational, and group effects upon the individual.

Some features of interaction

Social interaction refers essentially to a *reciprocal relationship* between two or more individuals whose behavior is *mutually dependent*. It may also be thought of as a communication process that leads to influence upon the actions and outlooks of individuals.

The widespread nature of interaction exists not only among humans but also in related species. In the monkey family, for example, interaction serves as communicative behavior which signalizes certain rela-

243

tionships. From his extensive studies of primate societies, Carpenter (1963) observes:

> When two primates approach each other, the quality of the conditioned social interaction is indicated by each to the other, by the pattern and rate of behavior and by *mutual recognition* of species and individual characteristics. For example, two gibbons of the same group, when coming together after even a short period of separation, express friendly predispositions by a stereotyped pattern involving facial expression, a momentary embrace and a special little cry (p. 49).

Broadly speaking, social interaction encompasses what Schutz (1958) calls an interpersonal situation, that is, one in which two or more persons interact for some purpose. Such interpersonal situations need not involve face-to-face relationships, but may be in the nature of "implicit" interaction. Family members separated by many miles may still have a forceful interpersonal effect upon one another through shared expectancies. More often, however, social interaction, as it is conventionally considered, implies contact, though not necessarily face-to-face.

Interactions may be of a sustained kind, or only episodic, and at times very short-lived. These have different expectancies associated with them, and the latter especially may hold greater ambiguity and the prospect for greater self-revelation (Thibaut and Kelley, 1959). This is exemplified when people encounter one another while traveling.

Interaction of a more enduring sort has several features which can be studied in psychological terms. One is the *interdependence of behavior* between the interacting parties; this involves the way in which one person's behavior serves as the stimulus for the other's behavior. A second feature is the mutual *expectancy of behavior,* in the sense of interpersonal perceptions of one another. Underpinning these is the third feature of an implicit *evaluation* in terms of the value attached to others, their actions and motives, as well as the satisfactions they provide. Before considering these further, it is useful to review the essential nature of interaction.

BASES FOR SOCIAL INTERACTION

The need for social interaction can be accounted for in several ways. In the first place, it serves the function of inculcating those general characteristics shared with others within one's own society. In more specific terms, as we have noted earlier, it affects the development of the individual's distinctive personality (e.g. Sears, 1951a; Secord and Backman, 1961). A repeated finding, for example, is to the general effect that the self-concept of the individual depends upon interactions with others. As Cottrell (1950) has noted, a vital interest in social psychology concerns the way in which types of interaction act to pattern the self-concept. This patterning appears to follow the line that the expectations of important others, especially in childhood, will condition the individual's own view of himself.

There are many other effects of social interaction upon the perception, motivation, and especially the learning and adjustment of the individual. These begin early in life as a neophyte in a particular society develops relationships with others. It is clear that in infancy there is the necessity to obtain satisfaction from others for fundamental biological needs required to maintain life. But it is also true that the nature of Man's condition is essentially an interdependent one within a human society. Therefore, it is not only that physical survival depends upon others but that others stimulate in us those qualities regarded as "human." Because the kinds of distinctly human behaviors learned may differ with varying cultures in terms of language, marriage, economic practices, art, religion, the use of techniques, tools, and other social artifacts, we are all subject to insistent social influences to learn some things very well and others not at all. The profound effect of culture, transmitted through social interaction, will be considered in the next chapter.

There are grounds, too, for believing that social interaction reduces the effect of stress. Bovard (1959) and Zajonc (1965) have reviewed studies which indicate that the presence of members of the same species provides an arousal effect for individuals. Schachter's research (1959) yields the finding that under stressful conditions of fear or hunger college students show an increasing desire to have contact with others. Earlier findings have sustained a similar conclusion. Thus, Titmuss (1950) reports that children separated from the close interactions of their family, by evacuation from London during the intensive bombings of that city during World War II, experienced more stress than those who endured the bombings with their family. Other wartime research has indicated the importance of social interaction among soldiers in resisting the stress of battle (e.g. Mandelbaum, 1952; Marshall, 1951). Social interaction, therefore, has a vital preservative role for the individual, as its effects are felt through certain physiological mechanisms. Moreover, as we shall be noting further, the development of personality can be seen as a function of ongoing interaction which leads to patterned dispositions.

THE STRUCTURE OF INTERACTION

The characteristics of the situation in which interaction occurs is of considerable importance in determining which features of behavior individuals are likely to present to one another. Though this seems obvious enough, it is all too easy to see someone as "competitive," for example, rather than to recognize the competitive elements in the situation in which he is encountered. Such elements exemplify the *structure of interaction.* Two people might be involved in a situation mainly structured as a competition for a mutually desired goal that only one may obtain: consider as one instance the plight of two close friends who wish to marry the same girl. Alternatively, people may be involved in an essentially co-operative enterprise where the goal is only available if the individuals assist one another in its achievement, as in the case of the cast working on a dramatic production. Other kinds of relationships which grow out of the structure of the situation include dominance, as represented in the exertion of power, and conflict of interests. Strikes exemplify this latter phenomenon at the extreme. In his field study, entitled *Wildcat Strike,* Gouldner (1954) reports a graphic illustration of conflict's effect on the perception of motivation:

> The great majority of workers viewed their strike as a justified and legitimate action. Workers usually defined the strike in ethical terms, holding it to be morally justified. As many of them said, "We're out to get our rights." The strike was not interpreted by them, as management was inclined to define it, in the amoral concepts of power. Their hostility toward the "swearing" supervisor, and against supervisors who overstepped their bounds, expressed *moral* indignation (p. 59).

FORMAL AND INFORMAL INTERACTION

In the most general terms, interaction may be divided into two large categories of structure. First, interaction proceeds with reference to a *formal* structure in terms of patterned relationships which society requires; second, it operates within an *informal* structure generated and sustained by individual perceptions and motivations. What is called the formal level of interaction is exemplified mainly in social roles, while the informal level consists of such factors as interpersonal attraction, loyalty, and a sense of equity. The biggest differentiation between formal and informal interaction rests in the consideration that the latter depends more upon individual *dispositions* and *satisfactions*. It should also be noted that interactions in a formal setting can take on the quality of informal interaction. If sustained, such a relationship would then be highly dependent upon personal inclinations. The formalized ritual of a wedding ceremony might lead the best man and a bridesmaid, unacquainted before, to develop a sustained interest in one another.

The essence of formal social interaction is its highly *prescribed* character. This is usually embodied in the concept of *role*. Oftentimes what we do and say is "programmed," virtually to the last cliché, by a confining role. The stilted quality of some formal, ceremonial roles is seen, for example, in acceptance speeches at the "Oscar" motion picture awards. With lavish displays of dubious humility, the recipient accepts the honor, "not for myself but for all the *little people,* including my hairdresser, to whom I owe so much." Sometimes the spell is broken by unintended humor, as in the case of a sports figure who accepted a trophy at an award dinner by blurting, "I don't appreciate this honor, but I deserve it from the bottom of my heart."

The more serious side of formal roles is seen in the stable responsibilities they entail. Mothers, in any society, are expected to behave toward their children in ways which conform broadly to the role which is referred to as "mother." *Role behavior* may therefore be defined essentially as the expected behaviors for an individual in terms of a particular position which she or he occupies at a particular time. Given the specification of a time-space referent, *role* describes the suitable behaviors for a social position, or *status*. Linton (1945) presents a definitive statement of this relationship in these terms:

> The place in a particular system which a certain individual occupies at a particular time will be referred to as his *status* with respect to that system. . . . The second term, *role* will be used to designate the sum total of the cultural patterns associated with a particular status. It thus includes the attitudes, values and be-

havior ascribed by the society to any and all persons occupying this status. . . . Every status is linked with a particular role, but the two things are by no means the same from the point of view of the individual. His statuses are ascribed to him on the basis of his age and sex, his birth or marriage into a particular family unit, and so forth. His roles are learned on the basis of his statuses, either current or anticipated (pp. 76-77).

Formal features of interaction are more usually learned without explicit intent. Newcomb (1950) has pointed out that this proceeds via "reciprocal role relationships." The child, for example, interacts with his parents and thereby acquires a sense of the appropriate behavior for a parent, just as the pupil in school learns and often can readily imitate the behavior expected of the teacher. Berne (1964) contends that all adults retain the vestiges of the role of child and of a same-sex parent. These roles come into play, often unwittingly, in interaction. It is not unlikely to find, as most parents do, that at times they are behaving toward their children as their own parents behaved toward them, and often with a sense of distaste and no better response from the children.

Interaction of a formal variety is highly vulnerable to the effects of varying settings. Jeanne Watson (1958) has distinguished three of these as the *familial, sociable,* and *work* settings. Each distinctively directs interaction in a patterned way. Thus, a familial setting is one in which the individual is accepted by the others and can be at ease in the sense of not having to "prove" himself. A work setting is much more focused on a task; the individual's value may therefore be judged according to his contribution to the achievement of group goals. A sociable setting is one in which individuals can satisfy their inclinations for social relationships, but nonetheless must display themselves favorably. Accordingly, each setting occasions particular patterns of interaction.

An essential ingredient of interaction is the challenge it presents to understanding the outlook of the other individual involved. This is particularly so in informal interaction. In formal interaction, relationships run off without the penetrating kind of perception of the other individual's motives or attitudes or values that we encounter, for example, in friendship. However even in formal interaction, we are alert to the behavior and intent of the other person.

In this regard George Kelly has highlighted the necessity to view social interaction as involving "interpersonal understandings" which arise from each person's effective construing of the other person's outlook. He gives a compelling example of one kind of formal interaction—largely dictated by traffic laws—which we encounter in driving down a highway. He says:

> . . . we stake our lives hundreds of times a day on our accuracy in predicting what the drivers of the oncoming cars will do. The orderly, extremely complex, and precise weaving of traffic is really an amazing example of people predicting each other's behavior through subsuming each other's perception of a situation. Yet actually each of us knows very little about the higher motives and the complex aspirations of the oncoming drivers, upon whose behavior our own lives depend. It is enough, for the purpose of avoiding collisions, that we understand or subsume only certain specific aspects of their construction systems (1963, p. 95).

Deviations from these "construction systems" vary from city to city, and from country to country, so that the traffic metaphor fits the wider fact that local customs produce their own expectancies (Hall, 1959). A "stop-sign" in some places is no more than an invitation to reduce speed while gliding through an intersection, and when there it is hazardous to be unaware of that practice. Car horns sometimes take the place of brakes, and the application of the idea of "right of way" is unbelievably stretched by local driving patterns.

Interdependence, co-operation, and competition

One element of significance in social interaction has reference to how much the parties are functionally interdependent. Interdependence usually means the degree to which individuals require one another to achieve rewards which would be unavailable to them otherwise. This is co-operative interdependence. Another kind of interdependence occurs in competition where the goal of winning may be available only to one person, as in a game of chess. This distinction is an oversimplification, however, since there are many competitive situations where both parties gain by co-operative actions. Such situations are sometimes in the nature of "non-zero-sum" games—meaning that *the win-*

nings by one side need not be balanced by losses from the other. Diplomacy is an interdependent relationship that involves competitive but also co-operative elements.

In a recent analysis of competition, Julian (1968) stresses such co-operative elements and also emphasizes the importance of seeing it as providing rewards other than "winning." He maintains that another salient source of reward is self-evaluation by comparing one's self to others, in keeping with Festinger's (1954) "theory of social comparison processes" which postulates the need to evaluate the "self." Julian points out that competition in games and other activities make self-evaluative comparisons easier because rules force a higher degree of comparability than is found in other less well-defined interactions, and this necessitates co-ordination.

> We have probably all experienced the frustration of waiting for an "opponent" to make his next play in a game of chess or cards. . . . Some tasks such as these may have negative, frustrating effects because of the demands which they make for close coordination, and this frustration may be particularly high if you are competing with your fellow participants (Julian, 1968, p. 293).

Several factors appear to be vital in maintaining interdependent relationships. One of these is the availability of joint rewards. Another is the matter of trust, which is often said to arise from "communication." Scheff (1967) proposes that *attribution* is a central feature in developing the necessary "consensus" for co-ordinate activity. Though consensus depends upon communication, communication is less a variable which acts alone and more one that facilitates the operation of other variables. This effect is seen, for instance, in research on "games."

GAMES AND GAME THEORY

The study of co-operation and competition, as well as other processes such as conflict, has been facilitated by work on "game theory." Vinacke (1969) says, "A game may be defined as a contest conducted under specified rules, in which the outcome is not known in advance, but depends upon the actions of the participants" (p. 293). This definition is rather broad, but it serves to place gaming within the general framework of social interaction.

What makes the study of games particularly interesting are the aspects of decision and conflict which it implies. Basically, a decision problem involves choosing among a number of alternatives and, in the purest case, with each alternative having a specifiable consequence. Moreover, a decision to make a given choice can only be meaningful where the chooser has ordered preferences among choices. As Rapoport (1966) points out, however, most decision problems are not so simple. He observes, "As a rule, an action may lead to a number of different outcomes, and which one will actually obtain in a given instance is not known to the chooser" (p. 17).

The other term, *conflict*, suggests more than a two-person competition that characterizes many games. It also implies the important element of conflicting motives within each participant, in terms of the desired alternatives. This is what gives many games their "mixed-motive" character. Rapoport and Chammah (1965) point out that the non-zero-sum game is more interesting psychologically than a zero-sum game, such as tic-tac-toe, because of this mixed-motive quality. Conflict conducted in a perfectly rational manner, in zero-sum games, is more confining, and less subject to "irrational" considerations. It is for this reason that the "prisoner's dilemma," played as a non-zero-sum game, has special research interest (Rapoport and Chammah, 1965),

	Player II	
	Choice A (Trust)	Choice B (Mistrust)
Choice A (Trust)	(I) +1 (II) +1	(I) −2 (II) +2
Choice B (Mistrust)	(I) +2 (II) −2	(I) −1 (II) −1

Player I

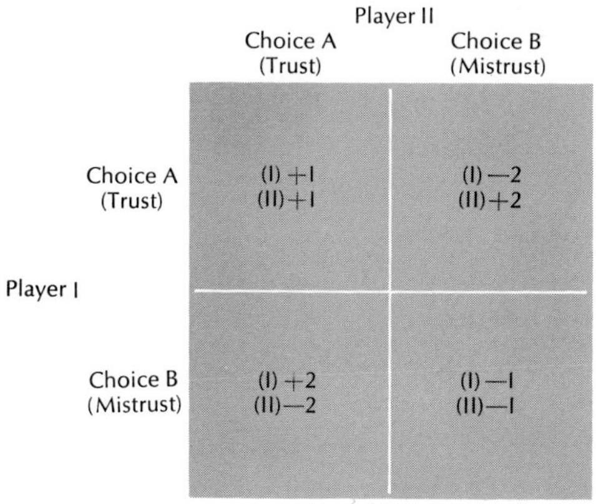

Figure 7.1: Illustration of "prisoner's dilemma" matrix. Outcomes for Players I and II are determined by the cells in which their choices intersect. (After Rapoport and Chammah, 1965.)

pp. 10-11). A basic "pay-off matrix" for this game is shown in Figure 7.1. In it the values received by Player I always precede those received by Player II in each cell. On any trial the task requires an independent choice of A or B by each player. Only after both have made their choices is the outcome revealed. The task is therefore competitive but it also makes demands of a co-operative nature, if the participants are not to hurt one another.

The name of the matrix comes from the analogue to a situation where two persons are apprehended for and charged with the same crime. They are questioned separately by the police without an opportunity for discussion between them. Both are told that if they give evidence to convict the other person they will be freed. Looking at the matrix, —1 represents the payoff associated with conviction as a result of confessions by both prisoners and +1 the payoff associated with acquittal. Should only one confess, he is set free for having given "state's evidence," and may be presented with a reward as well; this payoff is +2. The prisoner who holds out and is convicted on the basis of the other's evidence has a payoff of —2, since he bears the burden of the full charge.

If A is the choice *not* to give evidence, and B is the choice to give it, then it is apparent that the AA outcome is preferable as a positive payoff to both persons. However, in the absence of knowledge about the other person's intentions, the choice of B is the sounder alternative for either person as a *strategic move*, without considering the moral issues. But since the B choice appeals to both players, they may end up in the BB cell, with a loss to both, which is the basis for the dilemma. If the players trust one another, they will respond A and both gain. If they distrust one another, they will respond B and both lose. Where either one is trusting and the other is not, the trusting one stands to lose and the other to gain.

Using this kind of matrix with money gains or losses in the cells, Loomis (1959) conducted an experiment in what appeared to be a two-person situation. Among his interests was the effect of perceived trust and of varying degrees of communication in producing a more trusting response. The task presented to the participants was to earn as much money as they could by judicious choices in the matrix. No special point was made in the instructions regarding co-operation or competition. Subjects gave their choices in separate cubicles and received back

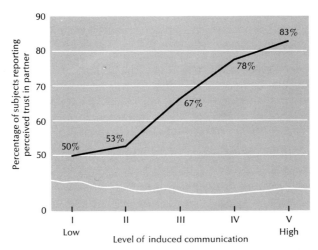

Figure 7.2: Perceived trust of partner in matrix choice by increasing levels of communication induced experimentally. (Based on data from Loomis, 1959.)

results contrived by the experimenter. Apparent communications from the "partner" were also arranged in terms of five levels from the least information about how to make mutually beneficial choices to the greatest information. These communication levels were labeled from I through V. In advance of each trial each subject was also asked to report his anticipation of his partner's choice, thus revealing his perceived trust.

Loomis found that 87 per cent of the subjects who perceived trust were trustworthy themselves. Furthermore, the amount of communication permitted produced a direct relationship with perceived trust. As will be seen in Figure 7.2, greater degrees of trust are evidenced as one proceeds from level I to level V in communication.

Though the Loomis (1959) study clearly indicates that increased communication does facilitate co-operation, and other findings are in accord with it (e.g. Deutsch, 1958; Daniels, 1967; and Terhune, 1968), players who are suspicious of one another show less co-operation as a consequence of communication. Pilisuk and Skolnick (1968), for example, found that allowing players to indicate their intentions before they chose often gave the impression of their being more co-operative than they actually turned out to be. This seemed to be a sign of deceit and, as a result, there was a reduction of trust. Harking back to Scheff's (1967) analysis, noted earlier, it appears that communication in such games is a vehicle which allows other variables to come into play from past history, present expectations, and anticipated payoffs.

In regard to payoffs, the work of Pruitt (1967) on the "decomposed prisoner's dilemma" is instructive. He presented what was essentially the identical matrix to subjects, but from each of three different standpoints of what each player would gain or lose on each play. He found that the variations from one matrix to the other led to increases or decreases in the level of co-operation. Hence, the conjecture seems reasonable that subjects defined these situations differently, held different expectations, and therefore interacted differently with their partners.

Another aspect of the prisoner's dilemma has been emphasized by Vinacke (1969), who maintains that it is the *consistency* or the *shifts* in strategy, in sequence, which provide the basis for understandings between players. He notes:

> A particular choice can represent an individualistic strategy, a mere response to the other's previous choice, an invitation to adopt a certain strategy, a punishment, etc. When choices represent a sequence of steps by which the subject can signal his willingness to risk loss and his response to the other's acceptance of his choice, a commitment process can be instituted. In consequence, trust is greatly enhanced (p. 300).

CONFLICT AND THREAT

Deutsch (1949a, 1949b) has contributed a number of productive concepts and findings useful to an understanding of co-operation. Among these is the proposition that co-operation increases as persons recognize their mutual interdependence and trust one another. He has done extensive experimentation on these phenomena, more recently with regard to the effects of conflict and threat on bargaining.

In a major program of research with these variables, Deutsch and Krauss (1960, 1962) have employed the "Acme-Bolt trucking game." Each player "operates" a trucking firm, Acme or Bolt, through a control box and visual display panel, with lights showing the movement of the trucks. A constant sum of money, *minus* a cost for the trip's elapsed

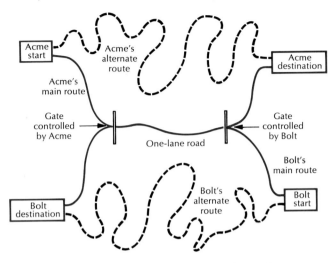

Figure 7.3: Subjects' road map in the Acme-Bolt trucking game. (From Deutsch and Krauss, 1960, p. 183.)

time, is paid each player for carrying a load from a starting point to a destination. As shown in Figure 7.3, each player has two routes to his destination, a short main route, and a long alternate route.

The characteristics of the Acme-Bolt game are such that if a player takes the alternate route, he loses at least ten cents on the trip, and if both take the main route, they will meet on its one-lane section and be deadlocked unless one of them backs up. The conflict lies in the consideration that it is to each player's interest to go through the one-lane section before the other, but some agreement on insuring access to the main route is mutually beneficial. As with most bargaining and conflict situations, this problem contains a mixture of co-operative and competitive elements which provide the basis for understanding the variables affecting the ease or difficulty with which bargainers can conclude an agreement.

In the initial work of Deutsch and Krauss (1960) they investigated the effect of a threat, in the form of "gates" that a player could close to indicate that the other player would be prevented from completing his trip on the main route. In this experiment, the three basic conditions were such that both players, only one player, or neither player possessed a gate. The investigators hypothesized that strengthening

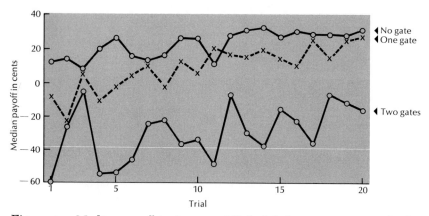

Figure 7.4: Median payoff to Acme and Bolt, jointly over twenty trials, for no gate, one gate, or two gates conditions. (After Deutsch and Krauss, 1960, p. 185.)

the competitive interest by providing gates would introduce elements of self-esteem which would make co-operation most difficult in the two-gate situation, and least difficult in the no-gate situation.

Figure 7.4 shows the results of this experiment. These support the assumption that the joint outcomes, that is, the Acme plus Bolt payoffs, were highest in the no-gate and lowest in the two-gate condition. As will be seen in the same figure, the one-gate condition produced fairly high joint payoffs, but the player with the gate did far better, at least initially, than did the one without it. However, this competitive advantage gradually diminished as the player with the gate used it less often and an equilibrium was reached near to an optimal level.

Since these findings, and others of its kind, have been generalized to international affairs, especially regarding the qualities of mutual threat as a "deterrent," they have been widely discussed and evaluated. Without venturing too deeply into the complexities of the issues raised, notably by Kelley (1965), it is worthwhile to consider several points for the sake of clarification. One salient criticism is that the gates act to structure the situation so that players are forced to take the alternate route; however, if they are involved in conflict, but without the gate, they would be obliged to deal with one another in a more direct fashion to work out an agreement. Another consideration is that threats of using the gate are not always actuated, but may merely be signaling devices to communicate intent. In this respect, a related point concerns the difference between the use of the gate as a threatening device and as an actual punishment. In a probing review of his work, Deutsch (1969) considers some of these points and contends that:

> . . . in a cooperative context, weapons can be used to facilitate coordination; but, of course, they are rarely used this way except to start horse races. To avoid misinterpretation, I would stress that a credible, appropriate threat *can* induce compliance rather than counter threat and open resistance if the threatened party perceives itself to have considerably weaker punitive power and/or if the threat is perceived to be a legitimate response to inappropriate behavior. Again, let me note that I would not be "caught dead" in the non-contingent statement that threat is *never* useful; it should, however, be used with full awareness of its dangers (p. 1086).

Another extension of this work, which Deutsch (1969) reports, has to do with research on the basic idea that a bargainer is supposed to gain an advantage if he can commit himself irrevocably to a course of action. In this experiment, the Acme-Bolt game was altered to resemble the game of "chicken" by indicating to the subjects that if their trucks were to meet at any point along the one-way section of the main route, this would constitute a "collision," and the trial would be terminated with financial penalties to both players. Furthermore, instead of the gates, a commitment device, called the "lock," allowed each subject to have his truck move irreversibly forward. Should a player use the lock, the other knew immediately of his action by a clear signal.

In general, the results of this research on an irrevocable commitment indicate that when both players were able to use the lock, they did worse than when neither could do so. When only one player had this device, it proved to be a relative advantage, as against the other player, but not an advantage when compared with players in the no-lock condition. The essential pattern was repeated with subjects who played a longer game, a trial at a time, without knowing how many there would be until they were finished; there were, in fact, twenty trials in all. The outcome of the longer game essentially paralleled the findings already noted, but with signs of greater co-operation, especially in the no-lock condition.

JOINT REWARDS

A number of investigations have looked specifically at the effects of joint or shared rewards on co-operative behavior. In one of these, Azrin and Lindsley (1956) asked pairs of children to play a "game," in the course of which they were reinforced with candy when they made a co-operative response. The children faced one another across a table with a glass partition between them. Each had a metal stylus and a metal plate with three holes. The children received instructions which said they could play the game any way they wanted to by placing the styli in the holes. They were then told: "While you are in this room some of these [jelly beans] will drop into this cup. You can eat them here if you want to or you can take them home with you." The children were then left alone.

The apparatus was so wired that, if the styli were placed in opposite holes within .04 seconds of each other, a red light flashed on the table and a single jelly bean fell into a cup that was accessible to both children. This was considered to be a co-operative response and the candy served as the reinforcement.

All pairs learned to co-operate within ten minutes. Azrin and Lindsley (1956) report further:

> Observation through a one-way vision screen disclosed that leader-follower relationships were developed and maintained in most cases. Almost immediately eight teams divided the candy in some manner. With two teams, one member at first took all the candy until the other member refused to cooperate. When verbal agreement was reached in these two teams, the members then cooperated and divided the candy (p. 101).

The perceived equitability of rewards is therefore quite relevant in interdependent relationships. An experiment conducted by Miller and Hamblin (1963) illustrates this point. They created conditions of high interdependence and low interdependence among students formed into three-person groups. Their task was to choose accurately which of a variety of numbers had been selected by the experimenter. On any one trial the problem was considered solved only when *each* group member knew the answer. Across the interdependence conditions, they arranged

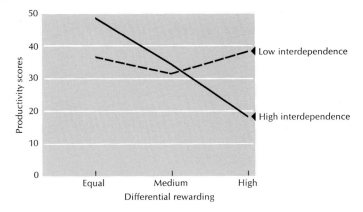

Figure 7.5: Mean productivity scores for differential rewarding under conditions of high and low interdependence. (Based on data from Miller and Hamblin, 1963.)

differential rewarding such that members of one-third of the groups in each of these conditions received equal rewards, one-third received rewards based on their order of completion (the medium reward condition), and the last third provided high reward to just *one* subject who solved the problem first in a group. For each group, productivity scores were computed based upon the average time to complete the task. Figure 7.5 presents the results of this experiment. The major guiding hypothesis, that high interdependence would have a significant inverse relationship to productivity as a result of the differential rewards, was confirmed. Equal rewarding yielded the greatest productivity where interdependence was high. With low interdependence no systematic effect on productivity was found. It is clear, then, that interdependence is a major determinant of whether equitable rewards are related to productivity in groups.

In general, where members of a group earn a common score based on the group's performance, there tends to be a greater degree of cooperation. In one earlier demonstration of this, Mintz (1951) used a situation in which several individuals had to pull cones out of a large glass jar with a narrow neck. When rewards were provided to each individual on the basis of his own time score, traffic jams usually developed at the neck so that participants had greater difficulty getting their cones out. Where group scores were provided, the groups developed a strategy for taking turns in withdrawing the cones. This result is in keeping with the concept of co-operative interdependence discussed above.

Research findings have generally tended to support the positive consequences of interdependent interaction in groups (e.g. Deutsch, 1949b; Gottheil, 1955; Grossack, 1954; Hammond and Goldman, 1961; Raven and Eachus, 1963). There are, nonetheless, some ambiguities about the work on co-operation and competition which arise from varying definitions. For example, co-operation might occur in a situation where the individuals were in groups that were competing with one another for high scores. In that case, co-operation within the group might be directly affected by the needs for competition between groups. Also, Shaw (1958) has found that a higher level of motivation produced by competition may lead to a decrease in the *quality* of performance. Since performance is often measured by a simple index of quantity, this might be obscured. There is also the issue of the difference between performance and member satisfaction to be considered.

An experiment dealing with a number of these considerations was conducted by Julian and Perry (1967). They placed students together in teams of four, each to work out a laboratory exercise in experimental psychology. Co-operative or competitive relations were varied both *between* groups and *within* groups by the instructions given. In the "pure co-operation" condition, students believed that grades would be assigned on the basis of the number of team points; each member of those teams which got 90 per cent of the possible points would get an A, 80 per cent B, and so forth. In the "group competition" condition, the instructions indicated that grades would be assigned on a curve such that each member of the team turning in the best exercise would get an A, the next best team a B, and so on. This involved individual members co-operating, but groups competing. In the "individual competition" condition, with no group competition, grades were to be assigned on an individual basis with the best paper receiving an A, the next best a B, and so forth.

The quantity of output was measured by the number of words used in specifying a research design and in presenting the exploratory material. Without awareness of the treatments groups received, quality was judged in terms of the orderliness and logic of the hypotheses and of the research design. It was found that individual and group competition both produced a high quantity and a high quality of performance. The purely co-operative condition yielded the lowest level of group performance. On the other hand, it is noteworthy that pure co-operation did yield the greatest satisfaction with their relations among the group members. Performance and satisfaction are by no means the same, as we will point out more fully in Chapter 13.

DOMINANCE AND POWER

In general, the dependence of one person on another is likely to increase the possibility of influence. One kind of interdependent relationship which enhances the acceptance of influence is represented in the case of dominance. In other terms, this can be referred to as a relationship involving power. Bierstedt (1950) has distinguished between influence and power mainly on the grounds of persuasiveness versus coercion. He says that "Influence does not require power, and power may dispense with influence. Influence may convert a friend, but power coerces friend and foe alike" (p. 731). At the extreme, then, the presence of usable power presents a situation of coercive dominance. Influence, as we have previously discussed it, consists of the transmission of information designed to alter the response pattern of one or more individuals who have more than one perceived alternative for response. With power at the disposal of the agent of transmission, however, there is usually no perceived alternative but to comply, at least in observable actions.

A further point concerning power is represented in the work of Thibaut and Kelley (1959). They distinguish between power of two kinds—*behavior control* and *fate control*. In the first instance, by varying his behavior, A can make it desirable for B to vary his behavior too; in the second case, A can affect B's behavior regardless of what B does. Thus, power can be looked at in terms of the degree to which the less powerful person can affect certain outcomes in his own behalf. In most relationships, however, even where usable power is of the fate control variety, its exploitation may lead to unwanted effects in the form of covert resistance and outright hostility which could jeopardize the function to be fulfilled. More often it is behavior control that is in operation, and it necessarily implies a two-way influence process.

A clearer pattern of dominance, where one individual exerts behavior control over another, is found in most organizational structures. There is usually a boss, or supervisor, or manager, or president, or chairman, who holds access to certain rewards which can be bestowed by him on others, or withheld. Such things as promotions, salary increases, public praise, recommendations, and other openings to opportunity are examples of these rewards. When individuals are involved in this kind of relationship, it is commonly the case that the one of less power expends some effort to construe the relevant features of the more powerful person's psychological field so as to gain rewards by his own actions and statements. This reciprocal influence has been considered by Jones (1964) in terms of *ingratiation*.

In an asymmetrical power relationship of this kind, one person is heavily dependent upon the other. To offset this, says Jones, ingratiation is employed through compliments, signs of agreement, and a generally favorable presentation of oneself to the more powerful person. As the dependent person becomes more attractive, the more powerful individual may be more inclined to provide rewards rather than withholding them. The idea of ingratiation then is essentially one of strategic interaction. As we shall be pointing out later, strategies are very much a part of controlling social interaction toward favorable ends.

The effectiveness of influence, or power, requires the perception of the direction of dominance by the parties in interaction. A neat demonstration of this is found in the results of research done by Miller, Murphy, and Mirsky (1955) manipulating the dominance hierarchy in a colony of ten monkeys. Relative dominance was measured by various observations over many months when monkeys were paired with one another and competing. As is generally found in such colonies, there was a considerable amount of consistency to the dominance hierarchy. An experiment was then performed which involved conditioning members of the colony to be fearful of one low in the hierarchy. The essential hypothesis was to the effect that this would raise the placement of the "stimulus monkey" within the hierarchy.

In Figure 7.6 the actual dominance hierarchy for the ten monkeys is given before the experimental phase and then after three conditioning periods. In these, monkeys *D* and *E*, from the middle of the hierarchy, were each placed in an apparatus where they could see but not be seen by Monkey *I* who was in the adjoining compartment. In the original

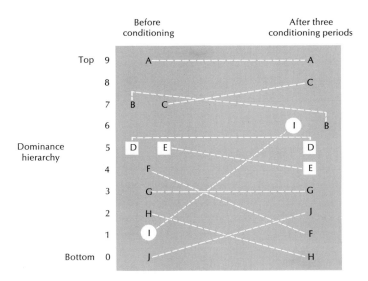

Figure 7.6: Shifts in dominance hierarchy in a colony of ten monkeys following three periods each of avoidance conditioning of Monkey *I* ("stimulus monkey," in circle) for Monkeys *D* and *E* ("conditioned monkeys," in boxes). (Adapted from Miller, Murphy, and Mirsky, 1955.)

hierarchy, Monkey *I* was next to the bottom in dominance and was accordingly selected to be the "stimulus monkey." The procedure followed the lines of simple conditioning. As Monkey *I* became visible to the monkey being conditioned, that monkey was given an electric shock which continued until he pressed a lever which removed the "stimulus monkey" from view and terminated the shock. When Monkeys *D* and *E* had learned to press the lever in the apparatus each time Monkey *I* was visible, each was considered to have been conditioned.

Recall that the results of this experiment were mainly of interest with regard to changes in the hierarchy of the monkey colony. In Figure 7.6 the most marked change in standing is found for Monkey *I* who went up from the ninth place to a tie for third place, after the three conditioning periods for *D* and *E*. These two "conditioned monkeys" in turn dropped to places below that of Monkey *I* whom they had been conditioned to fear. Many other shifts in the standing of monkeys in the hierarchy were also evidenced. For example, Monkey

F, who had previously been next in dominance to *D* and *E,* fell to the ninth position, occupied before by *I.*

There are probably three kinds of perceptions at work here: first, the perception by the conditioned monkeys of the hitherto low-dominance monkey as one to be avoided for reasons of fear; then, the corresponding perception by the low-dominance monkey of the fearful reaction to his presence in the colony by the conditioned monkeys; and finally, the perception by the other members of the monkey colony of this new and different pattern of behavior being evidenced by formerly dominant monkeys toward one who was perceived to be of low dominance. The point of all this is clearly and succinctly summed up in the notion that dominance must be perceived to have its effects. When one monkey behaves as if he were less dominant than another, whether out of fear or whatever motive, this lowers his perceived standing in the hierarchy.

Another kind of situation involving dominance occurs in the interaction of husband and wife within the family. Strodtbeck has been among those interested in this feature of family interactions. In one of his experiments (1951), he asked husbands and wives to think about three families they knew well and to discuss such questions as which of the three had the happiest children, or was the most religious. Basically, Strodtbeck was interested in whether the husband or wife would be most often influential in these discussions. With white Protestant American couples he found that men and women were influential in about the same number of decisions. He compared this with results he obtained from couples coming from the Mormon and Navaho sub-cultures. Mormons generally emphasize the male role as more dominant while the Navahos emphasize the female role. With ten additional couples from each of these two sub-cultural groups, he found distinct confirmation that the most powerful partners in these discussions were in line with the sex role expectations noted. His results are shown graphically in Figure 7.7. The essential conclusion here is that a cultural pattern emphasizing certain role demands for dominance determines the direction of interaction.

Across all couples, Strodtbeck found, too, that the most talkative member of the pair was significantly more likely to be the one whose opinions were decisive. Interestingly, such persons were also found to be willing at times to reciprocate by showing agreement with their partners. This kind of "trading" phenomenon is associated with certain

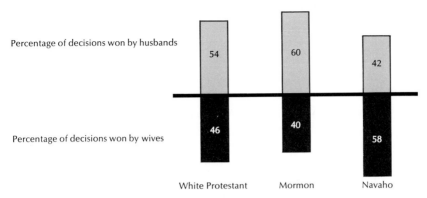

Percentage of decisions won by husbands

54   60   42

Percentage of decisions won by wives

46   40   58

White Protestant   Mormon   Navaho

Figure 7.7: Percentage of decisions won by husbands and wives, with ten couples from each of three subcultural groupings. (Based on data from Strodtbeck, 1951.)

features of social exchange which we will consider shortly. An additional point is that this study illustrates interaction as a communication process. The more dominant person strives to influence the other person to alter his or her attitudes. As a general rule, persons are more likely in the first place to enter into interactions with those who already share some relevant attitudes with them. But they also develop attitudes which are in line with those of another person or group they find attractive.

Communication from others, in any case, is more likely to be rewarding, and this appears to be a rather stable attribute of interaction, as Newcomb (1956) points out. It provides information about one's self and conveys "social reality." The trend toward consensus through social interaction, in terms of the development of common attitudes, produces a situation in which those with common attitudes interact more, and those who interact develop common attitudes. This is illustrated by the perplexity expressed when someone's candidate has lost an election after it had seemed "just everyone" that person knew had voted for him.

EFFECTS ON HELPING BEHAVIOR: BYSTANDER INTERVENTION

Among the most important effects of interaction is the inhibition or facilitation of responses, a matter with a long history in the field of social psychology, discussed in Chapter 2. A modern-day derivative of this phenomenon is "helping behavior" to which considerable attention is being directed (see Chapter 5, p. 173).

The research of Latané and Darley (e.g. 1968, 1969) has been in the forefront of the endeavor to discern the processes underlying "bystander intervention," which refers specifically to taking action to help someone in need. One variable which appears to make a difference in such a response is the presence of other people, and the nature of their relationship to the bystander.

A recent experiment by Latané and Rodin (1969) illustrates the degree to which these associations can operate to reduce or enhance the prospect of helping. Following the pattern of other research on helping behavior (e.g. Latané and Darley, 1968, 1969; Staub, 1969, 1970), male subjects heard someone fall and apparently injure herself in the room next door. Whether subjects tried to help, and how long they took to do so, were the main dependent variables in the experiment. Subjects were placed in one of four conditions: alone, with a friend, with another subject who was a stranger, and with another person who was actually a confederate of the experimenter's instructed to behave in a passive manner when the sounds of injury were heard.

In each instance, subjects were recruited to take part in a market research study and were asked to bring a friend. The friend was paired with the subject only in that experiment condition; otherwise, he was run in one of the other conditions. The subjects, alone or in appropriate pairs, were met at the door by a "market research representative." She took them to the testing room, past an office where they were able to see a desk and bookcases piled high with papers and files. After entering the testing room adjacent to it, the representative said that she would be working next door in her office for about ten minutes while they completed their questionnaires. She then went to the office, shuffled papers, and made noise to remind the subjects of her presence. Four minutes after leaving the testing room, she turned on a tape recording of a loud crash and a scream as her chair evidently collapsed and she fell to the floor moaning and saying such things as "I can't get this thing off me." The entire incident took just 130 seconds.

The results of this experiment showed marked differences among the four conditions. Briefly, 70 per cent of the subjects who heard the fall while *alone* in the waiting room went to help the victim before the

130 seconds had elapsed. In contrast to that condition, the presence of the non-responsive confederate inhibited helping so that only 7 per cent of the subjects in this condition intervened. They were not, however, unaware of the emergency since they frequently glanced at the confederate who continued working on his questionnaire during the entire time.

With pairs of stranger, it was found that in only *40 per cent of the pairs* did at least one person offer help, which means that only 8 subjects of the 40 in this condition intervened. In making a comparison with the alone condition, therefore, it was necessary to compute a hypothetical base line combining all possible "groups" of two scores obtained from subjects in the alone condition. This base line is shown with the results in Figure 7.8. At every point, fewer subjects in the two-strangers condition had intervened than would be expected on the basis of this alone response rate. Finally, in the two-friends condition, at least one person intervened in 70 per cent of the pairs. Yet, this is not as high as the alone condition, when a correction is made for the fact that there are two people free to act. Thus, as compared

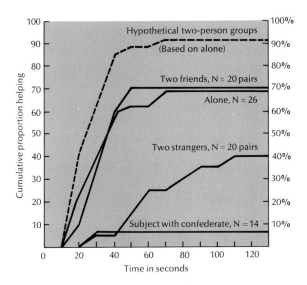

Figure 7.8: Cumulative proportion of subjects helping during 130 seconds in "alone" and various "together" conditions. (Adapted from Latané and Rodin, 1969.)

with the 91 per cent hypothetical base rate for two-person groups, even friends inhibit each other from intervening, though much less so than do strangers and, markedly less so in contrast to subjects paired with a non-responsive confederate.

These results replicate earlier findings by Latané and Darley (1968) with an emergency created by smoke trickling into a waiting room. In both of these experiments, the findings substantially indicate that the presence of passive confederates clearly inhibited subjects from taking action. The explanation of this finding can be considered in two directions, social influence and diffusion of responsibility. The former suggests that people are susceptible to the apparent reactions of the others present; if other bystanders indicate by inaction that they feel the emergency is not serious, this influences whether the observer will take action. However, the possibility exists that a state of "pluralistic ignorance" may develop, in which each bystander is influenced by the *apparent* lack of concern of the others, when in fact they may be highly concerned but uncertain and confused. The other explanation regarding diffusion of responsibility suggests that where an individual is alone he feels total responsibility for dealing with the emergency and will bear a good part of the blame if he fails to act. When others are present, the responsibility is diffused, as well as the potential blame, and therefore the individual might be less inclined to intervene, since it is less "his business." In summarizing the pros and cons of these explanations, Latané and Rodin (1969) say:

> Both the "social influence" and "diffusion of responsibility" explanations seem valid, and there is no reason why both should not be jointly operative. . . . Although . . . they may not do so at the same time. To the extent that social influence leads an individual to define the situation as nonserious and not requiring action, his responsibility is eliminated, making diffusion unnecessary (pp. 199-200).

There are implications from this research which ramify more widely in social psychology. Diffusion of responsibility, for example, is an explanation which has been put forth regarding various phenomena, including the behavior of crowds, and the "risky-shift" in group decision-making (see Chapter 13, pp. 515-517). It is also associated with the concept of "pluralistic ignorance" which refers essentially to a circumstance where group members *privately* hold a common doubt or skepticism regarding a value or norm, but publicly espouse acceptance of it without realizing others actually feel as they do. The classic illustration of this is embodied in the tale of "The Emperor's New Clothes." We shall have more to say about this process at a later point.

THREATS TO FREEDOM: REACTANCE EFFECTS

As previously noted, a threat to a "free behavior" tends to enhance its attractiveness and to produce *reactance*. In interpersonal relations, the offer of assistance, or the request for assistance, can imply an interdependence which constitutes a threat to freedom.

An experiment by Brehm and Cole (1966) tested the hypothesis that a favor arouses reactance in direct proportion to how important it is for the person receiving the favor to be free of any pressures it might create. Accordingly, such reactance should tend to result in the refusal to perform a favor subsequently for the favor-giver. Male students were told that they were taking part in an experiment on first-impression rating of another person, who actually was a confederate of the experimenter. Half the subjects were run under a "low importance" condition and the other half under a "high importance" condition. In the first instance, the experimenter stated that the ratings were being obtained for an undergraduate student as part of a class project and that there was no need to be too concerned about the accuracy of the first-impression ratings. In the latter instance, high importance was created by having the experimenter state that the ratings were being gathered for a professor, under a major research grant from a prestigious foundation, and that the accuracy of the ratings was very important.

While the true subject was sitting alone, the experimenter's confederate arrived in the room and, in the "favor" situation, provided a soft drink for him, refusing any money offered in payment. The other half of the subjects received no such favor. Thereafter, the subject and confederate were seated at a table, separated by a removable shield, and asked to answer three questions aloud which would serve as the basis for the first-impression ratings. In all conditions, the confederate's answers to the three questions were always exactly the same and were designed to be relatively non-committal, though plausible. After the first-impression ratings had been completed, the experimenter removed the shield from between the subject and confederate and then picked up a stack of typing paper, placed it in front of the confederate and said, "Will one of you stack these papers into ten piles of five for me, please?" The confederate then began stacking them and the experimenter, from a distance, recorded the number of piles of paper stacked by the confederate before the true subject began to help, if he helped at all.

In the low importance condition, 14 of the 15 subjects who had received a favor helped stack papers, but in the high importance condition only 2 of the 15 subjects who had received a favor provided this assistance. The investigators concluded that the low importance condition made it less significant to be free in the evaluation of the confederate, and the favor was accordingly reciprocated. But, in the high importance condition, the significance of this freedom was increased, and the operation of reactance reduced the reciprocation of a favor. For the "no favor" treatment, on the other hand, a more equal division of subjects was found, with 7 out of 15 helping in the high importance and 9 out of 15 in the low importance condition.

Other reactance studies have demonstrated the importance of the perceived motivation of the favor-giver. Goranson and Berkowitz (1966), for example, studied the relationship between the norms of reciprocity and of social responsibility. Their results indicated that female subjects would only reciprocate the prior aid from another person if that aid had been given voluntarily rather than by apparent coercion. Where it appeared that the other person had been forced to be a benefactor, reciprocation of aid was sharply diminished.

In a further extension of the work on interpersonal dependence as a threat to freedom, Jones (1970) conducted an experiment in which college students were or were not given a choice about helping another person—a graduate student doing dissertation research—presented as either greatly in need of help or only slightly so. Hence, there was choice versus no choice on the part of the subjects, and apparent high need or low need on the part of the other person. Also, half of the students were led to believe that this other person would seek their aid in the future; to create this impression of long-duration assistance, these subjects were told that the research involved a series of five experiments and that many subjects would need to be recruited to take part in all of them.

The main dependent variable in the Jones experiment was the amount of time the subjects volunteered to stay after their regular session to help out by participating in a muscular tremor test, without additional research credits in their course. As predicted, he found a statistical interaction effect such that subjects with no choice were more likely to give help to the "high dependence" person, whereas high choice subjects gave more help to the person of "low dependence." Furthermore, in the *no* long-duration condition, no choice subjects volunteered for significantly more time with the person of high dependence. Consistent with the concept of reactance, these findings indicate that when one is *not free to refuse* a request from a dependent person, more help is offered to that person, if the need seems greater. However, where one is free to refuse, there is an increasing tendency to reject requests from a high dependence person, especially if it involves a long-duration commitment.

Interpersonal attraction

A basic aspect of social interaction is the attraction-repulsion dimension of liking versus disliking. Clearly, whether or not we like someone affects the initiation as well as the continuance of social interaction. Social psychology has traditionally viewed attraction mainly as an interplay of individual dispositions which can be affected by situational factors, such as social structure and physical proximity. But attraction is more than a single state or process. For instance, a distinction can be made between how a person feels toward another, how he believes the other person feels toward him, and how that person makes him feel. Still another consideration is that attraction may be based in feeling a sense of liking or love for another person *intrinsically*, as against being attracted to another person *extrinsically*, with regard to benefits the association may bring, such as advice or prestige (Blau, 1964, p. 20).

Attraction in the first sense is closer to the word's literal meaning. When we find someone "attractive" we are drawn to them, even if only temporarily, as in an "emotional crush." Znaniecki (1965) has dealt with the particulars of attraction concretely. He says, concerning courtship, that men are supposed to initiate social interaction with women:

Consequently, it is at first more important for a woman than for a man to appear beautiful, sexually attractive, in order to induce men to court her. But, inasmuch as she also has a choice, her response to a man's initiative will depend upon her aesthetic valuation of him. . . . After preliminary social interaction has started, other standards of personal evaluation are introduced. . . . Positive response of one to the other's attempt to initiate symbolic communication; manifestations of recognition by one of the other's self as valuable; and agreement with one's verbally expressed attitudes: all contribute to raise the personal evaluation of the other (p. 163).

In his work on sociometry (see Chapter 2, pp. 62-64), Moreno (1941, 1953, 1960) emphasizes the importance of interpersonal attraction and repulsion as central features of interaction. Summing up their effects, Tagiuri (1958) says:

No characteristic of others seems so ego-involving as their positive and negative attitudes toward us. . . . Indeed, other things being equal, when the role differentiation in a group is not too great, the category of like and dislike "packages" most of the determinants of interaction. . . . It is as if like and dislike were summaries of a great number of diverse components (p. 317).

The precise character and source of feelings of attraction are not revealed by sociometric devices alone, however. Therefore it is useful to ask additional questions in this regard. One noteworthy extension of sociometry is in so-called "relational analysis" (Tagiuri, 1952) which also takes account of a person's perception of who will choose him. Furthermore, dimensions other than liking *per se* have been extensively studied, too, by sociometric devices, as we will have occasion to consider further especially in connection with leadership.

Newcomb (1956, 1961) has delineated four criteria as bases for interpersonal attraction. Each is a kind of hurdle which must be surmounted in developing a friendship with another. These criteria can be broadly paraphrased as: *propinquity*, in terms of physical closeness; *similarity of individual characteristics*, including group memberships and other social identities such as educational background or social class; *common attitudes and values*, especially about matters of mutual relevance; and *personality and need compatibility*.

PROPINQUITY AND ATTRACTION

A factor which is routinely found to produce a greater prospect for attraction is propinquity. This refers to the physical closeness or contact between individuals. Its function, quite obviously, is to make possible the operation of other factors which can increase attraction. A repeated finding concerning mate selection, for example, is that individuals find mates who live close by. One of the indirect justifications for going off to college, in another locale, is to increase the range of contact with possible mates.

Homans (1950) has formulated the general proposition that, all other things being equal, the degree of liking between persons increases as a function of their interaction. However, in a later statement of his position (1961), he points out that these "other things" may be crucial. He sums up the case in these terms:

> If two men interact and at least one of them finds the activity of the other not rewarding or even positively punishing, he will sooner or later, if he is free to do so . . . decrease interaction with the other man. . . . What makes the difference is whether or not a man is free to break off interaction with another whose behavior he finds punishing. If he is not free, our proposition about the relation between interaction and liking no longer holds good. . . . When the costs of avoiding interaction are great enough, a man will go on interacting with another even though he finds the other's activity punishing. Thus the members of some families and the neighbors in some villages keep on interacting, though they fight like leopards whenever they meet (pp. 186-187).

In an elaborate study of attraction, Newcomb (1961) invited 34 students transferring to the University of Michigan—17 in each of two years—to live together in a house near campus. None of the 17 men in each of the groups had known one another before. All had agreed to take part in a program of research. Over the course of a semester of living together, each of these two separate groups filled out attitude scales and value measures and also estimated the attitudes of the others in the house. The intent of the research was to determine the bases for attraction. Initial attraction was found to be highly related to propinquity, in terms of the proximity of the room assignments of these stu-

dents. Later attraction grew out of greater similarity in perceived attitudes. Generally, the students increased their accuracy in perceiving
the others' attitudes, regardless of attraction.

All in all, says Newcomb, propinquity is still the most convincing primary influence on positive attraction (1956). He goes on to say:

> Everyday illustrations readily leap to mind. Adults generally have
> strongest attraction toward those children, and children toward
> those adults, with whom they are in most immediate contact—
> which is to say, their own children and their own parents. And this
> commonly occurs, let me remind you, in spite of the fact that nei-
> ther parents nor children choose each other. Or, if we are willing
> to accept the fact that selection of marriage partners is an index of
> positive attraction, then the available data are strongly in support
> of a theory of propinquity (p. 575).

But after propinquity other variables come into play. In his extensive
writings (e.g. 1950, 1953, 1956, 1959, 1961) Newcomb has stressed the
importance of *attitudinal* similarity as a determinant of interpersonal
attraction. It is not merely the *actual* similarity of attitude that he considers to determine attraction, but the *perception of similarity*. There
are, however, a number of complexities associated with this concept, as
we shall see.

In a field experiment recently reported by Curry and Emerson
(1970), they did a replication of Newcomb's work. In this research,
there were nine groups of eight persons, in each of which the members
were initially strangers. Six of the groups were composed of males and
three were composed of females. The duration of study was eight
weeks. As in Newcomb's experiment, the subjects were transfer students from other institutions and fell in the age range from 19 to 25.
Unlike Newcomb's sample, which was made up exclusively of undergraduate males, the Curry and Emerson study included both sexes, and
some graduate students.

The key questions to be answered by the replication were whether
Newcomb's results held for both males and females, whether repeated
administration of the same measures might affect the results, and
whether variations between clusters might call into question Newcomb's balance theory interpretation of his results.

For the most part, the findings of this replication experiment revealed
considerable variation between groups. There were no systematic sex

differences other than a higher degree of actual agreement on value-rankings among the females. The repeated use of instruments apparently did not alter the basic relationships observed, aside from greater perceived agreement in value-rankings. Accordingly, Curry and Emerson conclude that attraction more likely operates as an independent variable which influences perceptions, but that this does not need to be explained by the A-B-X formulation. They suggest that social exchange theory, in terms of reciprocity in ongoing social relationships, may fit their findings more parsimoniously.

SIMILARITY AND COMPLEMENTARITY

An issue which has commanded great attention in research on attraction can be summed up in the two aphorisms: "Birds of a feather flock together" and "Opposites attract." In more technical terms, the first of these is referred to as the *similarity* hypothesis and the second as the *complementarity* hypothesis.

Though these appear to be antithetical notions, the current view is that they need not be (Levinger, 1964). As Wright (1965) has also noted, the similarity hypothesis has greater support, but there are circumstances where complementarity of need is relevant to attraction. In matters of friendship it is usually found that those attracted to one another do tend to have similar patterns of attitudes, values, and interests (Lindzey and Borgatta, 1954). Other work has sustained the general conclusion that mutual attraction is enhanced by a similarity of interests and values which facilitates social communication. Jones and Daugherty (1959) conducted an experiment designed to investigate how persons would perceive others in interaction as a function of their respective standing on the political and aesthetic values of the Allport-Vernon-Lindzey scale. They found that whether the similarity or complementarity hypotheses held depended on the particular value being considered as well as the particular context of interaction. In short, similarity of values may be of varying importance depending upon the kind of interaction, its locus, and its function.

The view of interaction that says people will be attracted to those who have personalities complementary to their own, has been detailed by Winch, Ktsanas, and Ktsanas (1954) in their theory of mate selection. Two studies to test the theory (Winch, 1955; Winch, Ktsanas, and

Ktsanas, 1955) yielded results indicating that people with dominant needs tend to be married to people with submissive needs. In the latter study especially, they report that:

> . . . an important dimension of marital choice in the group sampled (25 university-trained married couples) is the assertive-receptive dimension. More specifically, high "assertives" tend not to marry persons who are like themselves in this respect but rather persons who are high "receptives" (p. 513).

Altrocchi (1959) has explained this by the contention that "marital partners may have developed complementary need patterns as a *result* of their process of establishing a reciprocal role relationship" (p. 306). However, in a study by Bowerman and Day (1956) no support was found for either the similarity or complementarity hypotheses with couples who were dating. On the other hand, Kerckhoff and Davis (1962) found selective support for both. They conducted a longitudinal study of need complementarity and similarity on family values over a seven-month period with dating couples; it indicated need complementarity was a major facilitator of long-range progress toward marriage.

Kerckhoff and Davis took account of how long these couples had been dating prior to the study; those who had gone together for eighteen months or more were classified as "long-term" couples and the others as "short-term." Value similarity was found to be significantly related to progress toward marriage for the short-term couples, while need complementarity was significantly related to progress for the long-term couples. These findings were interpreted to indicate that in the early phases of a relationship agreement on values serves as a filter determining whether it will continue at all, but that after some point the "meshing" of needs takes on greater importance in determining its persistence on a more permanent basis. This interpretation has been altered somewhat by a recent replication of this study by Levinger, Senn, and Jorgensen (1971). They suggest that two processes are involved here, the first a matter of *discovering* relevant things about each other's "individual orientations" and the second a sense of *developing* "pair communality." Thus, measures of the partners' similarities could fail to get at their investment in the relationship itself.

If this picture presents some confusion, one source lies in the welter of different kinds of measures of personality, values, and attitudes used. But cutting through a bit of that confusion, it seems clear that similarity is important for some kinds of relationships and complementarity for others. In most studies where similarity is found to hold as a factor producing a mutual bond, attitudes and values are those elements which are being measured. Complementarity, on the other hand, may be more relevant to need satisfaction in an enduring interaction. As Jones and Daugherty (1959) note, however, it is necessary to analyze the most likely behavioral consequences of a particular personal attribute in different interaction settings (p. 34). For example, the need to dominate is important where social control and influence are encouraged. In such a setting, ascendant people may respond more positively to submissive people, while elsewhere the "dominator" may seek association with other dominators. Thus, the subordinate with dominance tendencies who works for a dominant superior, may comment that he dislikes working for the latter because they "are too much alike." Furthermore, Rosow (1957) says that being different on an attribute like "compulsivity" may not be a harmonious arrangement either. It seems clear, then, that depending upon the context of interaction, complementarity can be a source of either friction or harmony. Additional work is required to specify further what particulars of similarity or complementarity are crucial to attraction, and in what kinds of relationship, in which settings.

EYE-CONTACT AS A MEASURE OF ATTRACTION

In social interaction, the eyes perform a number of important functions. Argyle (1967) reports that two people engaged in conversation look each other in the eye intermittently with glances varying in length from about one to seven seconds. Though the proportion of time each person may make eye-contact with the other may vary from zero to 100 per cent, the proportion of time of eye-contact typically runs in the range from 30 to 60 per cent (Argyle, 1967, p. 106). Much of this activity can be considered as information seeking, that is, finding out about the other person's reactions. However, eye-contact may also be indicative of attraction, as a signal preparatory to increased interaction. It may also be perceived as an indicator of social approval, as Weisbrod (1965) found in studying patterns of eye-contact in a seven-

member seminar. Individuals in the group who looked most at others
when they were speaking were rated by speakers as valuing them
more. Furthermore, speakers felt more powerful in the group the more
looks they received while speaking.

Regarding attraction, the extent of eye-contact may reveal the level
of mutual involvement between two persons. There are, however, constraints on the amount of such involvement which might be tolerable,
and Argyle and Dean (1965) have suggested that physical proximity
is a variable which affects eye-contact inversely. They performed an
experiment with males and females, paired with members of the same
or opposite sex instructed to maintain a steady gaze during the course
of a three-minute conversation. The main independent variable was
the distance between subjects, with pairs holding conversations at
distances of two feet, six feet, and ten feet, and the main dependent
variable was the amount of return eye-contact. In this experiment, the

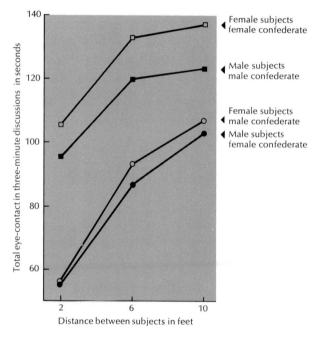

Figure 7.9: Relation between eye-contact and distance for different combinations of subjects and confederates. (From Argyle and Dean, 1965, p.
300.)

true subject was seated across from the confederate, behind whose back were observers looking at the subject through a one-way vision screen to record his eye-contact.

The main Argyle and Dean prediction was that if physical proximity were increased, compensatory changes downward would occur in the amount of eye-contact, and that this effect would be most marked in opposite-sex pairs. Their results are shown in Figure 7.9. In general, eye-contact increased with greater distance in feet. For the opposite-sex pairs, there was much less eye-contact over-all, and a distinctly low level at the two-foot distance.

Eye-contact, therefore, has some intriguing potentialities for revealing the degree of attraction between persons. Not surprisingly, it is more emotionally toned in male-female relations. This feature is capitalized on in some new research on romantic love by Rubin (1970). He undertook the development of an attitudinal scale of love, which involved several steps for refinement to have it measure something other than liking. The scale was then administered to 182 dating couples who were college students. The scale's content fell into three major components, each of which is illustrated by an item given below:

> *Affiliative and dependent need*—e.g. "If I could never be with _____ (the girl friend's or boy friend's name), I would feel miserable."
> *Predisposition to help*—e.g. "If _____ were feeling badly, my first duty would be to cheer him (her) up."
> *Exclusiveness and absorption*—e.g. "When I am with _____, I spend a good deal of time just looking at him (her)."

In the next phase of the research, Rubin conducted an experiment to test the notion that couples scoring high on his scale would spend more time gazing into one another's eyes than would couples who scored low. His main prediction was confirmed: couples who were strongly in love based on the love scale spent more time in eye-contact than couples who were only weakly in love.

Some other revealing highlights from Rubin's study of love are these: women spent more time making eye-contact with the men than the men spent making eye-contact with the women; apart from love scores, women tended to *like* their boy friends more than their boy friends liked them; for both sexes, scores on the love scale were highly correlated with the respondents' estimates of the likelihood that they would marry their partners, with women's estimates of this prospect higher than men's.

As a check on the predictive validity of the love scale, Rubin found that the initial scores were positively related to questionnaire reports six months later regarding the progress these relationships had made toward marriage. This pattern of results fits the premise that love is an interpersonal attitude which can be measured, and that one of love's manifestations is an exclusive absorption with the other person, revealed in heightened eye-contact. It is now appropriate to move from the eyes to interpersonal perception, more generally, and processes of social exchange.

Interpersonal perception

In our consideration of the attractiveness of individuals to one another, an inevitable feature of concern is the perception of a person. The term "interpersonal perception" is preferred, however, when we mean the way individuals view and evaluate one another in direct interaction, and we shall use it here in that sense. As Tagiuri (1958) points out, this is a process of considerable complexity which encompasses the interrelationship of the perceiver, the person perceived, and the situation which serves as a backdrop for this perception.

Many of the principles of perception which we considered before, in Chapter 4, have applicability to interpersonal perception. Tendencies toward *perceptual constancy, wholeness, imbeddedness, closure,* and especially *causality* all play a part in this process. There are, however, two major ways in which person perception differs from object perception. First, unlike objects persons are perceived to have motives which determine their actions. Second, the person perceived is himself capable of perceiving and may accordingly react to his own perception of the perceiver.

The most noteworthy contribution to the area of interpersonal perception has grown out of the work of Heider (1944, 1946, 1958). His contention is that the perception of attributes of other (O) controls the way the person (P) behaves toward him as well as what he expects from him. For Heider, interpersonal perception is vitally affected by several kinds of perceptual factors, including *constancy*, *balance*, and *phenomenal causality*. All affect the flow of interaction.

CONSTANCY

A central function in interpersonal perception is to give constancy to P's view of O. A certain psychological economy results from constancy in that an individual is not obliged to alter his view of O each and every instant. Typically, he retains a relatively cohering, consistent view of O, but this can lead of course to a biasing effect in perceiving O's behavior. Past interaction or prior knowledge of any sort can weigh heavily since primacy of experience is important. New experience may not be so quickly absorbed in altering perceptions (Ichheiser, 1949), after initial impressions create expectancies. Of this process, Gergen (1968) says:

> As a person is exposed to facts about another, such facts are ordered and assimilated. Noting a person's abrasive speech or brusk treatment of others, for example, may lead one to conceptualize this person as "aggressive." The concept is thus used to encapsulate a series of observations, and the conceptualization of a body of observations forms the cornerstone for what we know as "understanding" of the other. Once such judgments are formed they tend to remain intact and unchanging. On the one hand, new information about a person may simply be assimilated into the already existing conceptual structure. . . . On the other hand, if later information grossly violates the once crystallized judgment of the other, it may be either distorted or misperceived (p. 299).

Other factors are associated with constancy. As in all perception, interpersonal perception involves an act of categorization. Thus, others are seen in terms of consistent attributes including affiliations and positions which may be assumed to determine their action. Quite commonly, the situational determinants of action are given little weight and P will persist in perceiving O as the master of his own actions. At the extreme, this is exemplified in the case of the "self-made man," whose success is largely seen to reside in his own initiative, aggressiveness or other attributes, without reference to the sustenance along the way from others, as well as fortuitous circumstances.

BALANCE AND IMBALANCE

Also prominent in the Heider approach to interpersonal perception is the notion of cognitive balance. What this means in terms of social influence process may be simply stated. To the extent that O is seen by P as identified with things valued by P, and having other attributes P perceives favorably, P is more likely to accept communications from O directed at changes in his behavior or attitudes. Heider (1946, 1958) has provided a convenient summary of such interrelationships in terms of concepts involving positive and negative valence which he treats in terms of *balance* and *imbalance,* as discussed in the last chapter (see pp. 214-216).

If person P likes another person O and desires a certain object X, a balanced state results if he strives to be with the other person and to achieve the object; it is also part of balance to assume that the other person likes him too, and so forth. Imbalance would result, if for example P were to discover that O, whom he admires, does *not* like X the way he does, or that O does not like him. Heider's statements are essentially qualitative insofar as they deal with valences of either a plus or minus sort. They lead to some rather simple predictions concerning balanced and imbalanced states, as will be seen in Figure 7.10. Where

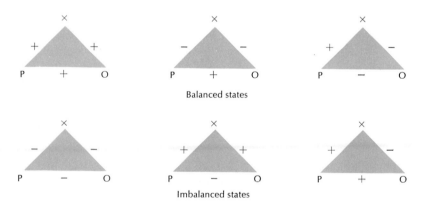

Figure 7.10: Diagrams indicating three balanced states and three imbalanced states. P is the Person; O is the Other; X is a factor they can each perceive. (After Heider, 1958.)

all the signs are positive in these diagrams, a state of balance exists. If there is one negative sign or three negative signs, then there is an imbalanced state. This follows from the mathematical rule that multiplication of two minuses yields a plus.

The Heider balance approach has led to similar analyses extending these ideas by Newcomb, Osgood and Tannenbaum, and Festinger, among others. These are treated in specific detail elsewhere. An essential point here concerns the facts that social interaction can be viewed as having a basic underpinning in what can be called an evaluative or affective dimension based on positive or negative valence, both in perceiving O as well as in the common objects or persons that P and O mutually perceive.

There have been a number of attempts to study the balance concept in terms of interpersonal evaluation behavior. Deutsch and Solomon (1959), for example, conducted an experiment in a two-person situation where the object X was an attribute of P's. They hypothesized that if P and O shared the *same* evalution of X then P would be more positive toward O than if their evaluations were different. This experiment generally supported the balance concept, though other motivational factors were found to be involved also.

In the Deutsch and Solomon experiment, P's evaluations of O were transmitted to the experimenter with no process of reciprocal interaction over time. Jones (1966) conducted a comparable experiment where subjects actually exchanged evaluations of one another's performance in an ongoing process. In this circumstance, he found a tendency for subjects to respond more in terms of reciprocity by exchanging social approval as a reward. Thus, a positive evaluation by O of what P perceived as his own poor performance yielded a more positive response to O by P than did a negative evaluation. Where there is continuing interaction, therefore, an exchange concept appears to fit interpersonal evaluation behavior better than a simple balance concept. This is also the conclusion of the experiment, reported earlier in this chapter, by Curry and Emerson (1970).

Another refinement of Heider's balance conceptions is suggestion by research which indicates that it is less applicable when the P-O relationship is negative (Jordan, 1953). Rodrigues (1968), for example, found that subjects in certain conditions worked toward creating agreement between P and O, even when the P-O bond was negative. In short, the alteration of the negative relationship took precedence because of what Zajonc (1968) sees as an "agreement" bias, that is, a preference for a positive P-O bond. In earlier work, by DeSoto and Kuethe (1959), subjects were asked to estimate the likelihood that one imaginary person would like another. In the absence of any other information about these persons, they found that there was a general inclination to perceive them as liking each other.

Price, Harburg, and Newcomb (1966) have contended that the usual dichotomy in Heider's system of balanced versus imbalanced states should be altered to take account of three possibilities, i.e. balanced, imbalanced, and *non*-balanced states. The last (*non*-balanced) takes account of those structures in which P does not like O, and, therefore, is not actively engaged since O's attitudes are not consequential to P. What this amounts to is to say that imbalanced states are found to be unpleasant, if P is positively disposed toward O. Then, he is more actively engaged toward the rectification of imbalance. In Figure 7.10, two "*non*-balanced states" would be represented in the two diagrams at the lower left. The first of these would be characterized by P not favorable to O, and finding that he and O are both negatively disposed toward X. In effect, this is a basis for agreement which would tend to be put in balance, if P cared enough, by becoming positive toward O. As Rubin and Zajonc (1969) note, however, a "generalization" bias can account for this effect. They used a paired-associates learning approach to study the effects of balance and generalization biases with eight P-O-X triads that had men's names for the P and O terms and with three possible third terms as X—i.e. "me," "Larry," and "integration." They found a general tendency for the subjects to be biased toward greater agreement, with the balance effect holding for structures which included a positive P-O bond. Generalization biases were found in terms of "friendliness" (if A likes B then A likes C)—and "popularity" (if B likes A then C likes A). These extensions are helpful in fleshing out the alternative biases which may operate in interpersonal perception.

PHENOMENAL CAUSALITY

As we have already suggested, the causality of action is usually perceived to rest in O rather than in the situation in which he finds himself. However, various kinds of discriminations are made in terms of other perceived attributes of O, such as his status, as well as certain of his other characteristics.

In extending Heider's views, for example, Pepitone (1958) says that for analytic purposes, "It is useful to assume that interpersonal relations consist of valued acts, valued positively or negatively depending on whether they are tension reducing or inducing, and the context of such acts. Of particular significance in the latter category are the causal conditions which surround given acts" (p. 259). He then distinguishes these three dimensions of causality:

> *Responsibility* for the social act, in the sense of the causal agent (O).
> *Intentionality* of the agent, in regard to what he (O) seeks to achieve in motivational terms.
> *Justifiability* of the action, in the sense of what P thinks of O's action.

Thus, of the various features of person perception one that seems to be of extreme importance is the perceived cause for action. In general, it is found that persons of higher status are seen to be more the locus or cause for their own action than those of lower status. Furthermore, a benevolent action that appears to be motivated by an individual's desire rather than a social demand is usually viewed more positively. Similarly, if O is in a role obliging him to perform a disliked action toward P, then O is usually excused if, as in the case of a role, the external cause of his behavior is apparent.

Some research of interest on this point grows out of the work of deCharms, Carpenter, and Cuperman (1965) on the "origin-pawn" variable in person perception. They had subjects read stories in which a person was being persuaded to do something, some by attractive persons and others by unattractive ones. The subjects were to judge the *source* of the person's action. The investigators found that the person was seen to be more an *origin* of action when the persuasive agent was attractive than when the agent was unattractive. The epitomy of origin was a person perceived to be motivated by his own intrinsic interests.

When a person appears self-motivated, he is said to be "internally" directed, in contrast to the person who is "externally" directed. This contrast forms the basis for Rotter's (1966) internal-external personality measure, which he views as a matter of where the individual sees the major determinants of his reinforcements. This is discussed further in Chapter 10.

Heider's (1958) view of interpersonal perception makes an important distinction between personal and impersonal causality, which essentially distinguishes between the actor and the context of action. The observer looks for a sufficient reason to account for why the person acted, and once having fixed on an intention, the action is likely to be considered "explained." Thus, personal causality is often inferred from the behavior rather than the situational context in which it occurs. Heider says that behavior ". . . has such salient properties it tends to engulf the total field rather than be confined to its proper position as a local stimulus whose interpretation requires the additional data of a surrounding field . . ." (1958, p. 54).

Jones and Davis (1965) have elaborated this mode of analysis in their *correspondent inference* theory (see Chapter 6, p. 195). Their focus is centered on the bases on which observers infer the *personal attributes* of the actor from his actions. If the assumption is made that the actor was aware his action would have the observed effects, and that he has the ability to bring about these effects, then they are *intentional*. From the effects of the action, the perceiver may then make a correspondent inference about the actor's intentions. Jones and Davis employ the idea of "correspondence" to refer to ". . . the extent that the act and the underlying characteristic or attribute are similarly described by the inference. . . . [Thus] correspondence of inference declines as the action to be accounted for appears to be constrained by the setting in which it occurs" (p. 223). Suppose a person is perceived to be acting in a domineering way; then, the most correspondent inference is that this reveals the person's intention to be dominant, which in turn grows out of a disposition toward dominance. However, given the additional information that he has been assigned to a directive role as group leader, this inference is far less correspondent.

The Jones and Davis (1965) approach to intentionality also takes account of cases where the actor *fails* to evidence certain behaviors. Though not cast in precisely these terms, they are dealing essentially with a disconfirmation of expectancy, when a given behavior anticipated by the perceiver is not forthcoming. Under such conditions, there may be ambiguity as to whether or not the actor wanted to produce the effect, or wanted to but was not able to do so. The experiment by Jones and deCharms (1957) exemplifies a feature of the resulting pattern, in indicating that a group member who does not perform adequately is perceived more favorably when the failing is seen to lie in his own incompetence, rather than in a lack of motivation where he is competent. The larger issue raised by Jones and Davis is characterized by their central asumption that ". . . actions are informative to the extent that they have emerged out of a context of choice and reflect a selection of one among plural alternatives" (1965, p. 264).

In an experiment by Walster (1966), some additional light was shed on the way consequences affect attributions. She hypothesized that the tendency to try to assign responsibility to someone when an accident is reported increases as the consequences of the accident become more serious. Indeed, an analysis by Bucher (1957) corroborates a tendency for disaster reports to reveal a great number of attempts to assign responsibility to someone. Typically a prime question raised is "Who is to blame?"

Walster's procedure was to tell men and women students that they would have a chance to actually help select materials and procedures to be used in testing an hypothesis about interpersonal judgments. They were to evaluate a tape recording to ascertain if there was any trouble understanding what the people were talking about, and then fill out a questionnnaire said to be of the kind to be used later in the research. To induce the different experimental treatments, each subject was given one of the four different tape recordings used, which they listened to alone in a cubicle.

All four of the tapes began identically with a "neighbor" telling about a young man who had a car accident. The car was bought second-hand and was about six years old. He had parked it on a street near the top of a hill, and though he had set the hand brake, the car started rolling. The descriptions on the four tapes then separated with different information provided about whether the car was stopped in time or not; and whether the damage to the car was severe or slight, and the possibility that someone else might have been hurt. The students then answered several questions beginning with the degree of responsibility that should be assigned to the young man for the automobile accident.

Walster found significantly more responsibility was assigned to him for the severe accidents than for the mild ones. Though he had been described on all of the tape recordings as having taken identical safety precautions, the data indicated that the subjects *perceived* him as having taken fewer safety precautions depending upon whether the car failed to stop in time and the severity of the consequences. This process of perceived causality probably holds more generally in attributing responsibility.

ACCURACY OF INTERPERSONAL PERCEPTION

It is widely found that individuals assume a similarity between their own perception and the perception of others, particularly where the others are positively valued. This is related as well to the broader question of accuracy of social perception.

Steiner (1955) reports conflicting evidence regarding the relationship between accuracy of perception and the nature of interaction. In specific terms, he concludes that accuracy in perceiving the other person will have consequences in social interaction only to the degree that such accuracy is relevant. The fundamental point, however, continues to be that persons behave largely in terms of how they perceive the attributes of others. For the most part, accuracy of such perception can be facilitating, though in conflict situations, for example, it may have the opposite effect. There are, however, additional methodological as well as conceptual difficulties associated with any discussion of the matter of accuracy of person perception (Cline, 1964).

Bronfenbrenner, Harding, and Gallwey (1958) have found, for example, that it is necessary to distinguish between two kinds of person perception which are not highly correlated one with the other. The first of these can be thought of as "interpersonal sensitivity" which has special regard to the ability to perceive a given individual uniquely in terms of a specfic situation of interaction. This can be thought of as having features of empathy or understanding. The second kind of process they note is a "sensitivity to the generalized other" which broadly means accuracy in perceiving major trends in the social environment, including such things as the kind of music which people are more likely to prefer, food preferences, and the like.

Social psychologists must of necessity be concerned with both kinds of processes. The perception of persons, whether it comes about from the direct experience of the individual, or through the channels of communication from other individuals, has considerable relevance for understanding social interaction. But there does not yet appear to be any consistency of evidence regarding a general characteristic of "interpersonal sensitivity," in the specific sense of repeated accuracy of interpersonal perception (Shrauger and Altrocchi, 1964).

On the other hand, a fruitful line of work has emerged from research on the relationship between attributes of the perceiver and his perceptions of others' attributes. Dornbusch, Hastorf, Richardson, Muzzy, and Vreeland (1965), for example, have found that children who are more dependent tend to describe other children in terms of generosity, giving aid, or needing aid. Girls who are more aggressive describe other girls with more emphasis on aggressive behavior than do non-aggressive girls. With boys who are non-aggressive, however, they found more attribution of aggression to others than with aggressive boys. In either case, they conclude that where their respondents gave more accounts of behavior relevant to some dimension of personality, that indicated a probable adjustment problem for the child in that dimension. Sex differences in interpersonal perception are also quite commonly found in studies of accuracy (Shrauger and Altrocchi, 1964), though these are not indicative of a systematic superiority of either sex.

CREATING EFFECTS IN INTERPERSONAL PERCEPTION

Just as the perception of O by P affects the interaction between them, so it is possible for O to deliberately arrange his behavior in such a way as to affect P's perception and actions toward him. We have already touched upon this in connection with Jones's (1964) concept of "ingratiation," which involves performing acts likely to put one in a more favorable light in relationship to another person, particularly one of more power.

A wide-ranging approach to the creation of such effects is to be found in the work of Goffman (1959), who is concerned with "impression management." Goffman employs dramaturgical concepts in treating this phenomenon. Thus, persons may be thought of as being "out front" or "back stage" in their relationship with one another. A couple entertaining their guests for dinner, says Goffman, present an enactment designed to coincide with certain of the prevailing expectancies regarding host and hostess. In the kitchen together they may behave otherwise. Sometimes, he says, the individual acts in a calculating manner, to "stage" things in a way designed to produce certain specific responses from the others. At other times, however, the individual may employ such techniques without awareness.

Since P may recognize that he is being confronted with a performance designed to make an impression on him, he may carefully assess the communications from O, in terms of verbal assertions and behaviors; moreover, P may check these two channels for consistency, as when O says the dinner is marvelous but eats very little. This is in keeping with the general idea that people compare what an individual says with how he acts. In other terms, we might say that there are two major inputs to interpersonal perception, the behavioral and the verbal.

Embedded in social interaction, therefore, is the prospect for persons to structure relationships toward the end of bringing about positive outcomes. In this respect, social interaction involves what Weinstein and Deutschberger (1964) call an *interpersonal task*. They say that P attempts to organize the various factors in his interaction with O so that O is forced into a position that fits P's preferences. They refer to this process as *alter-casting*, which comes from "casting" the other individual (*alter*) in a role.

While Goffman is concerned with the way that the identity of the participants leads to a playing out of their interaction, Weinstein and Deutschberger contend that this encounter is a bargaining process in which tactics are employed to place the other individual in a position which will be more personally advantageous. The task, then, is more than one of self-presentation, it is rather the management of the interaction aimed at influencing O's definition of the situation to P's advantage. The quest for certain rewards in interaction is a matter to which we will be returning in due course.

PERCEPTIONS OF EQUITY AND JUSTICE

In many social interactions there is the possibility that one or more of the participants will perceive an inequity or injustice in the distribution of rewards. An early recognition of the potency of this factor came out of research done during World War II by Stouffer and his col-

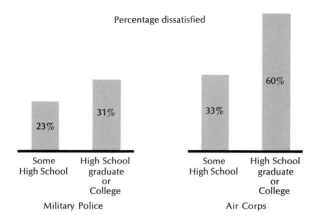

Figure 7.11: Dissatisfaction expressed with promotion policy by privates and privates first class, with two levels of educational background, in the Military Police and Air Corps. (Based on data from Stouffer, *et al.,* 1949.)

leagues (1949) regarding the concept of "relative deprivation." This concept refers to the way actuality may be matched against expectation to induce an attitude of satisfaction or dissatisfaction in individuals. In the Stouffer study, the paradoxical finding was that army air corps men were less satisfied with promotion opportunities than were those in the military police. This was despite the objective reality that opportunities for promotion were vastly greater in the air corps where, at the time, 47 per cent of all enlisted men were non-commissioned officers, while the rate in the military police was 24 per cent.

The relative deprivation concept explains this by suggesting that the men compared themselves with those "in the same boat." Thus, the high promotion prospects in the air corps induced high expectations, while in the military police far lower expectations for promotion prevailed. As will be seen in Figure 7.11, comparing lower ranking men from both groups, greater dissatisfaction is found among the air corps men than the military policemen, and among the better educated than the less educated. In both instances a greater discrepancy exists between expectation and actual achievement.

This finding has since been generalized as a basic comparison process related to the reference group as a standard. In an experiment involving the manipulation of relative deprivation, Spector (1956) varied the perceived probability of promotion and found that among those subjects *not* promoted, those who held high expectations for promotion were far more dissatisfied with the "system" than those with low expectations.

In general, an injustice can be thought of, therefore, as the reaction to an imbalance or disparity between what an individual perceives to be the actuality and what he believes should be the case, especially insofar as his own situation is concerned. This is the fundamental point in Homans's (1961) concept of "distributive justice," which refers to a condition where an individual's investments are balanced by his rewards. In connection with social exchange, he considers that a "profit" can refer to "rewards" minus "costs" incurred. A cost, briefly, can be anything that is given up or forgone in the process of interaction. Among these costs may be the investments of the individual, which would include his standing, his background of education, experience, and the like. The idea that this is merely a matter of economic gain is therefore not appropriate because of the diversity of values represented in "investments" and "rewards."

While individuals may therefore compare their rewards with another and perceive them to be smaller, they may not feel dissatisfied since there is a proportionality between the rewards received by each as against the investments of each. Thus, Patchen (1961) has found that the satisfaction with their wages of workers in an oil refinery was primarily based on the total equity they perceived in wage comparisons, rather than on the actual pay differences alone. Workers were satisfied with their wages if they felt that they were making sufficiently more money than other workers with whom they compared themselves in terms of job responsibility and seniority.

That is far from the whole story, however. In the concrete work situation, Adams (1965) maintains that equity is a function of the *balance* effected between a person's inputs and outcomes on the job. Inputs include his qualifications for the job and how hard he works at it, while outcomes include pay, fringe benefits, status, and the intrinsic interest he finds in the job. From the point of view of his equity theory, Adams contends that the major expectancy is that an equitable input-outcome balance will prevail. On the other hand,

> Inequity exists for Person whenever he perceives that the ratio of his outcomes to inputs and the ratio of Other's outcomes to

> Other's inputs are unequal. This may happen either (a) when he and Other are in a direct exchange relationship or (b) when both are in an exchange relationship with a third party and Person compares himself to Other (Adams, 1965, p. 280).

An alternative expectancy theory regarding positively valued outcomes has been suggested by Vroom (1964). He argues that the quantity and quality of work is directly determined by the perceived value of the rewards offered and the perceived probability that appropriate behavior will lead to these rewards. Hence, there is reward value, with its own valence, and the expectancy of attaining the reward, both of which vary and combine to determine motivation. This bears a distinct similarity to Atkinson's (1957, 1964) theory of achievement motivation and Stotland's (1969) concept of hope, both discussed in Chapter 4. The higher the reward value and the greater the expectancy, the stronger the motivation to engage in the rewarded behavior.

In any concept of justice versus injustice, or equity versus inequity, it must be realized, of course, that O's perception of his own investments, costs, and rewards do not always coincide with P's perceptions of them. With two persons in any interaction, therefore, it is not the actuality, nor is it the other person's perception that matters most. It is the individual's own perception of his situation which continues to have overriding significance in determining his response pattern. Accordingly, inequities may be perceived by individuals despite the fact that there is no inequity seen in the "social reality" of others.

Social exchange

As we have seen, face-to-face interaction leads to reciprocal behavior. Each person creates products for the other, in the form of rewards which can be reinforcing. The value of the reward will, however, depend upon the requirements of the participants. These rewards are also balanced by the costs of the interaction in terms of the values given in return or forgone. The general character of this process is referred to as "social exchange." Blau (1964) captures its basic features as follows:

> Mutual attraction prompts people to establish an association, and the rewards they provide each other in the course of their social

interaction, unless their expectations are disappointed, maintain their mutual attraction and the continuing association.

Processes of social attraction, therefore, lead to processes of social exchange. The nature of the exchange in an association experienced as intrinsically rewarding, such as a love relationship, differs from that between associates primarily concerned with extrinsic benefits, such as neighbors who help one another with various chores, but exchanges do occur in either case. A person who furnishes needed assistance to associates, often at some cost to himself, obligates them to reciprocate his kindness. Whether reference is to instrumental services or to such intangibles as social approval, the benefits each supplies to the others are rewards that serve as inducements to continue to supply benefits, and the integrative bonds created in the process fortify the social relationship (p. 21).

Though they are stated in terms of economic transactions, social exchange concepts embody a considerable range of different motivations and comparisons, beyond the simple notion of profit in a straight hedonistic sense. Thus, satisfactions in interaction may lie in many directions, including challenges to one's competence in handling the environment, and playful activities.

Two major contributions to an understanding of social exchange, apart from those of Blau (1964) and Adams (1965), come from the work of Homans (1958, 1961) and Thibaut and Kelley (1959). Both involve certain concepts associated with a rewards-costs relationship. Homans sees social exchange as the underlying factor accounting for certain features of face-to-face interaction. He contends that the rules governing social interaction apply in various settings and can be understood primarily in terms of reinforcement. Homans says that persons give off *activity,* which is essentially behavior, as well as *sentiments,* which can be thought of as indicators of attitudes and feelings. Both activity and sentiments can operate to *reinforce* or *punish* the behavior of others in interaction.

An illustration of exchange grows out of a study by Calvin (1962). He was primarily interested in the effects of social reinforcement among college girls. He had some girls show systematic approval of others who happened to be wearing blue. Over time such approval yielded a significant increase in the wearing of blue. Of particular importance here, as a derivative result, he found that the girls who gave the approval experienced an upsurge in their own popularity. Much as Homans would predict, this demonstrated an exchange relationship in terms of giving appreciation and being liked in return.

Homans proposes that both the *quantity* and *value* of the activity or sentiment can affect the behavior of another individual. His propositions concerning the effects of activity are these:

> (I) The more often a person's activity is rewarded, the more likely he is to perform the activity.
>
> (II) If in the past the occurrence of a particular stimulus, or set of stimuli, has been the occasion in which a person's activity has been rewarded, then the more similar the present stimuli are to the past ones, the more likely the person is to perform the activity, or some similar activity, now.
>
> (III) The more valuable the reward of an activity is to a person, the more likely he is to perform the activity.
>
> (IV) The more often in the recent past a person has received a particular reward, the less valuable any further unit of that reward becomes to him.
>
> (V) When a person's activity does not receive the reward he expected, or receives punishment he did not expect, he will be angry, and in anger, the results of aggressive behavior are rewarding (Homans, 1967a, pp. 33-40).

He considers these propositions to be the minimal essentials in explaining the simpler features of social behavior. They each limit, modify, or enhance such behavior, not in isolation but in combination with one another. Thus, the first proposition states that the more often a person's behavior is rewarded, the more often he is likely to perform it; yet, the fourth proposition indicates that the more often an activity is rewarded, the less valuable further units of that reward become. As Homans says, no reward leads to apathy, but too much reward reduces its value and leads to satiation.

As noted previously, Homans defines profit as total reward minus total cost. In ongoing interaction, both parties are mindful of their respective profits. If these exchange activities yield no profit, the interaction is unlikely to continue. The important consideration of the cost of any activity is defined by Homans in terms of the value of the reward that would be obtainable through alternative activity which has to be given up.

For Thibaut and Kelley, similarly, interaction should be rewarding for the parties to continue. They recognize, also, the necessity for a trading-off in terms of rewards and costs for both parties. Specifically *rewards* are defined by Thibaut and Kelley as ". . . the pleasures, satisfactions, and gratifications the person enjoys. The provision of a means whereby a drive is reduced or a need fulfilled constitutes a reward. We assume that the amount of reward provided by any such experience can be measured and that the reward values of different modalities of gratification are reducible to a single psychological scale" (1959, p. 12). Alternatively, they define *costs* as ". . . any factors that operate to inhibit or deter the performance of a sequence of behavior. The greater the deterrence to performing a given act—the greater the inhibition the individual has to overcome—the greater the cost of the act. Thus cost is high when great physical or mental effort is required, when embarrassment or anxiety accompany the action, or when there are conflicting forces or competing response tendencies of any sort" (1959, pp. 12-13).

As with the Homans idea of cost as value forgone, Thibaut and Kelley employ the concept of *comparison level*. This is a standard against which the person evaluates the attractiveness of the relationship in terms of whether he receives what he thinks he deserves relative to his costs. Associated with this concept is the *comparison level for alternatives*, which represents the reference point employed in deciding whether or not to remain in the interaction. In one sense, it can be looked at as the lowest level of reward which the individual will accept in order to continue in the relationship. In another sense, it relates to Helson's (1948) adaptation level concept of what one has come to expect.

Aronson and Linder (1965) conducted an experiment to test the proposition that the feeling of gain or loss of esteem is rewarding or not as a function of past adaptation. They predicted ". . . that a gain in esteem is a more potent reward than invariant esteem, and similarly the loss of esteem is a more potent 'punishment' than invariant negative esteem" (p. 156). In their experiment, the subjects were female college students who, though led to believe they were assisting in an experiment, actually interacted with a confederate pretending to be a subject, over a series of meetings. The confederate expressed either a uniformly positive attitude toward the true subject, a uniformly negative attitude, a negative attitude which turned to a more positive one, or a positive attitude which turned toward one that was more negative. Thus, there were four treatment conditions. In each condition, the confederate was instructed to carry on relatively uniform conversations with the subject, consistent with the need for some spontaneity. Though the subject and confederate met in the same room, they were separated by a screen which prevented visual contact. After each brief meeting, the subject heard the experimenter in the other room questioning the confederate, who was allegedly a naïve subject, about her impressions of the subject. The major dependent variable was a measure of the subject's liking for the confederate, which was contrived to be part of a necessary procedure related to the cover story that this was an experiment on conditioned verbal responses. A separate interviewer conducted the closing interview in which the first question was to give a frank impression of the other girl.

The main findings of the Aronson and Linder experiment are shown in Table 7.1. These indicate that the confederate was liked significantly more in the negative-positive condition than in the positive-positive condition, and that there was also a strong trend in the predicted direction of less liking in the positive-negative condition than in the negative-negative condition. The implications of this research for social exchange directly fit Homans's concept of the reduced value of a reward which has come to be expected from another. Thus, the person who is a continuing source of good will and esteem—a parent, a friend, or a spouse—may become *less* potent as a source of reward than a stranger. Alternatively, such a source of relatively consistent reward can also be a greater source of potential punishment when withdrawing such reward (p. 169).

There are some intriguing features about the association of comparison level and the comparison level for alternatives. In general, a person

Table 7.1: Mean liking of confederate by subjects in each of four conditions of condeferate's sequential evaluation of them. (From Aronson and Linder, 1965,

CONFEDERATE'S SEQUENCE OF EVALUATION OF SUBJECT	MEAN LIKING OF CONFEDERATE
Negative-Positive	7.67
Positive-Positive	6.42
Negative-Negative	2.52
Positive-Negative	.87

will be highly satisfied with his outcomes if his comparison level and the comparison level for alternatives are both exceeded by actual outcomes, and the converse holds as well. Kelley (1967) indicates that information may also be rewarding if it aids in making attributions. He suggests that the comparison level for alternatives may therefore be applied in choosing among sources of information.

While there are similarities between the two exchange concepts we have been considering, there are also some differences. Thibaut and Kelley, for example, are more concerned with the idea of a norm and its development. Homans tends to accept the fact that norms of conduct exist. In this respect, Gouldner's (1960) discussion of a "norm of reciprocity" is closer to the matrix notion of Thibaut and Kelley. Essentially, reciprocity represents a widespread social norm which dictates that good acts are reciprocally rewarded, as in the return of a favor.

Exchange concepts in general fit a framework which is distinctively social-psychological in that they are concerned with motivations and in varying degrees with perceptions. Blau (1964) has extended some of these ideas in harmony with Goffman's work on "impression management," and pointed up the problem of social acceptance in the human condition.

In Blau's view it is not enough for a person to be attracted to a group or to a relationship because of the possible rewards the group has to offer him. He must achieve acceptance and intergration into the group. This in turn rests on his impressing others that he would be an asset in the group or relationship by providing rewards for them as well. Blau (1964) says:

> A person who is attracted to others is interested in proving himself attractive to them, for his ability to associate with them and reap the benefits expected from the association is contingent on their finding him an attractive associate and thus wanting to interact with him. Their attraction to him, just as his to them, depends on the anticipation that the association will be rewarding. To arouse this anticipation, a person tries to impress others. Attempts to appear impressive are pervasive in the early stages of acquaintance and group formation. Impressive qualities make a person attractive and promise that associating with him will be rewarding (p. 20).

This demand in new relationships appears to be bound into the social fabric. Inescapably, acceptance is conditional on showing some qualities which others in a group, or in a more limited association of two, perceive as valuable. The corollary is that unattractive qualities in the view of others offer no reward as a basis for association.

Social exchange is thus a ubiquitous feature of social interaction, whether we wish it to be or not. It should be emphasized, however, that the rewards received are *not* to be understood as being *precisely* equal since their value is determined by the needs of the recipient. This realization goes a long way in helping to understand what might otherwise appear to be an "unfair" exchange in a continuing social interaction.

SUMMARY

Social interaction holds a central place in social psychology as an influence process. It refers, in particular, to the *reciprocal relationship* that exists between two or more individuals whose behavior is *mutually dependent*. Most of the behavior we observe is in some way affected by present or past social interactions.

Face-to-face interaction is built upon social expectancies which reside in the psychological field and have to do in large part with past experiences. Expectancies direct individuals to be set for and to evaluate certain outcomes of interdependent behavior.

The essential need for social interaction arises from several functions it fulfills: inculcation in the ways of the society, the development of personality, and the reduction of the effects of stress.

The *structure of interaction* refers to the nature of the interdependent relationship, such as co-operation or competition, dominance and conflict. Mainly, structure can be approached in two ways. In the first place, it can be viewed on a *formal* level, which has to do with regularities dictated by the society and its culture. This approach is best exemplified in the concept of *roles*, usually defined as behaviors expected of individuals in terms of the positions or *status* they occupy in a given situation. The essential quality of this emphasis is to describe the pattern of regularized social practices. Many features of social interaction are governed by such formal social demands. These are usually learned through "reciprocal role relationships," such as child with parent.

Another way of viewing social interaction is in terms of an *informal* structure. It can be looked at as an ongoing stimulus-response sequence of behavior which is sustained by various definable rewards to the parties involved. The primary interest here rests in *individual dispositions and satisfactions* in the interaction, including attraction and interpersonal perception.

Co-operation and competition are not necessarily antithetical. Competition often involves co-operative elements. Moreover, a desire to compete may be based on an interest in *self-evaluation* under a set of rules. *Games* are of this order, and they are studied in social psychology with regard to processes of decision and conflict between participants. The Prisoner's Dilemma is illustrative of one such game utilized in research, especially under *non-zero-sum* conditions where the winnings of one player need *not* be balanced by losses to the other. The availability of threats tends to bring about their use by players and accordingly reduces co-operation and intensifies conflict.

Research on "bystander intervention" indicates that individuals are more likely to help those in distress when they are alone rather than when with other bystanders. The greatest inhibition to helping occurs when a bystander is with strangers. Involvement with others may also constitute a threat of freedom, and produce *psychological reactance,* because of the prospect of interdependence.

In looking at the underlying process of social interaction, a basic dimension is valence, that is, liking versus disliking. This has special relevance to *interpersonal attraction* which grows out of propinquity, similarity of individual characteristics including attitudes, and personality and need compatibility. Interpersonal attraction has been found to depend a great deal upon the perception of similarity of attitudes by the persons involved. Usually, social interaction itself enhances personal attraction through a process of social communication. In general, such communication is likely to give rise to favorable rather than to unfavorable outcomes. Studies of *eye-contact* reveal that it provides a measure of attraction, particularly in male-female pairs.

Interpersonal attraction depends upon a process of *interpersonal perception* which refers to the evaluations of persons through direct interaction. Principles of perception have applications to interpersonal perception, but the perception of persons differs from object perception in two major ways. First, persons are perceived to have motives deter-

mining their actions; second, the person perceived is himself a perceiver who may react to his perception of the other. Heider stresses
constancy, balance, and *phenomenal causality* in interpersonal perception. Accuracy of person perception is a factor which can also greatly
affect social interaction depending upon its relevance. Such accuracy is
shaped by the nature of the situation in which interaction occurs and
does not appear to be a consistent interpersonal characteristic. Persons
may also try to make certain impressions on others by various strategies, including the way they define the interaction situation.

Social interaction is also a transaction involving a process of *social
exchange.* In general, interaction operates in terms of reciprocity, that
is, the expectation that a benefit given will be returned. The nature of
interaction is such that one person shows certain behaviors in the presence of another. Each therefore can do things and say things that will
be rewarding for the other. The value of the reward will, however, depend upon the unique requirements of the individual participants.
These rewards are also balanced by the costs of the interaction in
terms of values given in return or forgone.

SUGGESTED READINGS

From E. P. Hollander and R. G. Hunt (Eds.) *Current perspectives in social
psychology.* (3rd ed.) New York: Oxford University Press, 1971.

Introduction to Section V: *Social interaction and role*
28. W. Edgar Vinacke: *Variables in experimental games*
30. Raymond G. Hunt: *Role and role conflict*
31. Alvin W. Gouldner: *The norm of reciprocity: a preliminary statement*
33. Erving Goffman: *The presentation of self in everyday life*
45. George C. Homans: *Fundamental processes of social exchange*
48. Bibb Latané and John M. Darley: *Bystander "apathy"*

SELECTED REFERENCES

*Argyle, M. *The psychology of interpersonal behaviour.* Baltimore: Pen-
guin Books, 1967.
*Berscheid, E., & Walster, E. *Interpersonal attraction.* Reading, Mass.:
Addison-Wesley, 1969.
Blau, P. M. *Exchange and power in social life.* New York: Wiley, 1964.
*Gergen, K. *The psychology of behavior exchange.* Reading, Mass.: Addi-
son-Wesley, 1969.

*Goffman, E. *The presentation of self in everyday life.* Garden City, N. Y.: Doubleday Anchor, 1959.

Gordon, C., & Gergen, K. J. (Eds.) *The self in social interaction.* Vol. 1. New York: Wiley, 1968.

*Heider, F. *The psychology of interpersonal relations.* New York: Wiley, 1958.

Homans, G. C. *Social behavior: its elementary forms.* New York: Harcourt Brace, 1961.

Jones, E. E. *Ingratiation.* New York: Appleton-Century-Crofts, 1964.

Moreno, J. L. (Ed.) *The sociometry reader.* Glencoe, Ill.: The Free Press, 1960.

Newcomb, T. M. *The acquaintance process.* New York: Holt, Rinehart & Winston, 1961.

Thibaut, J. W., & Kelley, H. H. *The social psychology of groups.* New York: Wiley, 1959.

*Znaniecki, F. *Social relations and social roles.* San Francisco: Chandler, 1965.

8

Culture as a source of social influence

Culture is a form of nonbiological, social heritage that flows from the past, generation by generation. Mumford (1951) has captured this dominant theme in these terms: "Every human group, every human being, lives within a cultural matrix that is both immediate and remote, visible and invisible: and one of the most important statements one can make about Man's present is how much of the past or future it contains" (p. 38).

In the preceding chapters we have referred to the all-embracing influence of culture on our actions, interactions, attitudes, and values. Now we will turn attention to its own unique features. We begin with the fundamental point that in any human society individuals are bound to culture for a coherent outlook and approach toward life. These essential aspects of culture are also the very things which most differentiate segments of humanity from one another.

In highlighting this contrast in the ways of life among different societies, Linton (1945) has said: "The first man who wandered into a strange camp and found that he could not talk to the people there nor understand everything that he saw, must have had the fact of cultural difference brought home to him. Also . . . his observations must have provided him with material for numerous fireside talks. . . . The meat of any really good traveller's tale is not the strange places that it tells about but the queer people" (p. 27).

The basis for culture

In simplest terms, Man depends upon his culture for the development of his human qualities. Among the most important of these are *social organization for the control of the environment* and *communication across time and space.* A culture provides people with a number of ready-made answers for crucial life problems. It dictates the routine relationships and social arrangements which help to handle survival needs, the protection and education of the young, and many other necessary social functions. A culture, then, is an adaptation, a means for coping with the world.

ORGANIZATION AND ADAPTATION

Only in the last 10,000 years has Man begun the adaptation to agriculture and technology. In the larger time-scale of something near two million years of human existence, Man's dominant adaptation was as a hunter-gatherer (Lee and DeVore, 1968). Only a scant few per cent of humans who have *ever* lived now live in the culture of industrial societies, and it is debatable whether this transformation will prove to be a successful adaptation. Though it is a rather apocalyptic view, these two anthropologists say:

> It is still an open question whether man will be able to survive the exceedingly complex and unstable ecological conditions he has created for himself. If he fails in this task, interplanetary archeologists of the future will classify our planet as one in which a very long and stable period of small-scale hunting and gathering was followed by an apparently instantaneous efflorescence of technology and society leading rapidly to extinction (Lee and DeVore, 1968, p. 3).

If Man does survive, his enormous capacity for higher level mental activity and learning will play a pivotal role. Their potential for bringing about change in the human condition, through discussion, the exercise of influence, and problem-solving, are a source of hope. But they are also inhibited in some ways by the "crust of custom" that a culture represents. The very thing which gives cultures their continuity and stability—a shared outlook on what is right and proper, the expectancies and traditions which make up a prevailing social reality—may act as a check on necessary adaptations. In his new book, *Future Shock*, Toffler (1970) paints a grim picture of widespread dislocation as people find themselves increasingly disoriented by adaptive crises in a time of ever-faster and unanticipated change. Yet, culture is a human product that can be directed by humans rather than being seen only as a source of control. Later in this chapter we will consider aspects of cultural change and the planning of alternative futures.

COGNITION AND COMMUNICATION

From a social psychological standpoint, culture is among other things a shared perspective or outlook. A significant part of a culture's influence lies in the pervasive psychological effects on the perceptions, including the attitudes and values, of a society's members. Through processes of communication, individuals acquire a sense of common meaning and purpose without which they would be lost. In this chapter we will especially emphasize this form of cultural influence.

In his analysis of culture's affect on cognition, Triandis (1964) places particular emphasis on those constructs which people use to *categorize* their social environment. He refers to this as "subjective culture," in the sense that it affects the individual's reaction to stimuli as well as the assumptions held about the relationships of categories. This position is associated with conceptions of language as a meaning system which affects perception (Whorf, 1956), discussed in the chapter to follow.

The "mazeway" theory put forth by Wallace (1961, 1962) illustrates another approach to the cognitive elements of culture. In any given culture, he contends, there are *mazeways* of thought whose content need not be identical across all members of the culture, but which is predictable enough to be relatively similar. These are guides to construing relationships much as was said in the last chapter about interpersonal construction systems affecting interaction (Kelly, 1963). Thus, the person newly introduced into a largely foreign culture must be able to put himself in the distinct cognitive system of the culture so that he is better able to predict its constructions of reality, and modes of interaction. An example of this is provided in the extensive research by Triandis, Vassiliou, and Nassiakou (1968) on the "role perceptions" of Americans and Greeks. Their work bolsters the point expressed by Wallace, and by Hall (1959, 1966)among others, that misunderstandings may be generated between members of different cultures due to divergent expectancies. In the studies by Triandis and his co-workers, American and Greek respondents judged many roles, on descriptive scales, to ascertain the commonality of perception of what was appropriate behavior for these roles. The cultural differences revealed are informative. For instance:

> The implication of such differences is that an American interacting with a Greek might behave inappropriately for the level of intimacy that is appropriate at a particular time, because he may not realize that more intimacy is required before the particular behavior is permissible. Thus, for example, he may try to *kiss*, to *quarrel with*, to *ask for advice of*, to *advise*, to *laugh at jokes of*, to *correct*, etc., before the Greek sees that the relationship is ripe for such intimacies. On the other hand, he may wait too long before he *invites to dinner*, *congratulates*, *mourns for*, etc., than would be appropriate from the Greek's point of view since, for instance, a dinner invitation does not require as much intimacy in Greece as it requires in the United States (Triandis *et al.*, 1968, p. 38).

Cultural patterns are not static, of course. Communication across time and space affects their development and character. Culture contact is doubtless the most pervasive source of influence, particularly where a dominant culture serves as a model for a less dominant one. But differences in culture also originate quite obviously in geographic and historic factors unique to a society. The kind of climate and weather it experiences, its natural resources, its relationship with neighboring societies—including, for example, threat along a frontier— may account for many cultural differences. These, however, are overlaid with adaptations and change that come about from circumstances including communication as well as contact between cultures.

Throughout the modern world, the impact of the mass media, especially motion pictures with their vivid quality of real presence, has markedly enhanced cultural movement toward "Westernization," even in such ephemeral forms as an attachment to cowboy garb. Nevertheless, as Hall (1959, p. 33) says, "culture is more than mere custom that can be shed or changed like a suit of clothes." These external matters of form should not be confused too much with content for reasons we shall make evident shortly.

The nature of culture

As employed in the anthropological sense, culture has a broad meaning that includes but does not refer only to those particular enrichments of life identified with literature, music, and art, as in a Molière play, a Mozart symphony, or a Mondrian painting. Rather, it encompasses a society's shared practices and products which are sustained by tradition. These could be endlessly catalogued but can be briefly exemplified by monogamy, money, manufacturing and the distinctive tools it requires.

The relationship between culture and society has also been commented upon in a variety of ways. There are several fine points that are still matters of contention. However, we can paraphrase Kroeber and Parsons (1958) and say that *culture* constitutes those meaningful symbolic systems which are transmitted over time and shape social behavior and its artifacts; *society* can be considered to be comprised of individuals who share these systems and accordingly live within a set of specific interpersonal and collective relationships. A culture, therefore, is a way of life while a society is made up of people who live by its directives. When we speak of a "member of a culture," then, we actually mean a "member of the society of culture X" (p. 583).

The anthropologist E. B. Tylor, is credited with providing the first formal definition of culture almost a century ago: "that complex whole which includes knowledge, belief, art, law, morals, custom, and any other capabilities and habits acquired by man as a member of society" (1877, p. 1). This definition provides a kind of "sum total" of the different content categories which go to make up culture. As such it suffers from the weakness of omitting the important element of *integration,* in terms of the meshing of the components of culture as they exist in a society's social institutions, status systems, and the like. This is one feature of "functionalism" which has a significant place in sociology and will occupy our attention shortly. While Tylor's definition represented a landmark, it therefore tended to be highly descriptive and quite open-ended in its content. Tylor was also given to a reliance on applying Darwinian concepts of "selection" as an explanation of cultural evolution.

A more contemporary view of culture is represented by Ralph Linton's definition which places stress on integration and learning. He defines a culture as ". . . the configuration of learned behavior and results of behavior whose component elements are shared and transmitted by the members of a particular society" (1945, p. 32). This emphasis on transmission gives due attention to the *communicative* aspect of culture over time. In this vein, culture can be viewed as a passing on of the ancestral adjustments that have been made to the environment. Thus, culture in effect represents the accretion of experience in contending with prevailing life conditions (e.g. Sumner and Keller, 1927). Others have seen humans as even more actively creating symbols, defining experience, and transmitting meanings through culture, particularly via language (e.g. Goldschmidt, 1959). In this vein, Jaeger and Selznick have offered a definition of culture as ". . . everything that is produced by, and is capable of sustaining, shared symbolic experience" (1964, p. 663).

TRADITION, SYMBOLIZATION, AND INTEGRATION

These ways of conceiving culture recurringly emphasize the interrelated features of tradition, symbolization, and integration. *Tradition* especially means the continuity of culture in providing directives for routinely coping with the major imperatives of life, such as birth, death, kinship, and the passing on of worldly goods. Any culture therefore dictates a society's organization and social relationships largely along lines which persist without awareness. This is illustrated in a serio-comic dispatch from London reproduced in its entirety in Figure 8.1. It shows the "unwritten law" quality of tradition.

Symbolization is a vital, defining characteristic of humanity. It refers to the importance of non-material experience, as well as to the transmission of thoughts and information without the direct presence of objects themselves. Language is the clearest expression of symbolization, and we shall deal with it in fuller detail in the next chapter. Because of Man's symbolic quality, a significant part of a culture's influ-

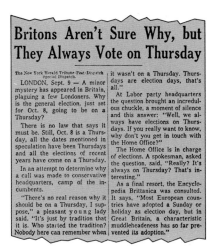

Britons Aren't Sure Why, but They Always Vote on Thursday

The New York Herald Tribune-Post-Dispatch
Special Dispatch.

LONDON, Sept. 9 — A minor mystery has appeared in Britain, plaguing a few Londoners. Why is the general election, just set for Oct. 8, going to be on a Thursday?

There is no law that says it must be. Still, Oct. 8 is a Thursday, all the dates mentioned in speculation have been Thursdays and all the elections of recent years have come on a Thursday.

In an attempt to determine why a call was made to conservative headquarters, camp of the incumbents.

"There's no real reason why it should be on a Thursday, I suppose," a pleasant young lady said. "It's just by tradition that it is. Who started the tradition? Nobody here can remember when

it wasn't on a Thursday. Thursdays are election days, that's all."

At Labor party headquarters the question brought an incredulous chuckle, a moment of silence and this answer: "Well, we always have elections on Thursdays. If you really want to know, why don't you get in touch with the Home Office?"

The Home Office is in charge of elections. A spokesman, asked the question, said, "Really? It's always on Thursday? That's interesting."

As a final resort, the Encyclopedia Brittanica was consulted. It says, "Most European countries have adopted a Sunday or holiday as election day, but in Great Britain, a characteristic muddleheadedness has so far prevented its adoption."

Figure 8.1: An example of tradition as the "unwritten law." (From the *St. Louis Post-Dispatch*, September 9, 1959, p. 1.) The British still vote on Thursday, as witness the general election of June 18, 1970, in which the Conservatives gained control of Parliament in a surprise victory.

ence rests in its psychological effects. When we speak of symbols, therefore, we include the essential substance of attitudes and values, as well as the other components of the psychological field.

Integration of a culture can neither be divorced from tradition nor from symbolization since it relies on both. All human societies can be found to have social institutions—e.g. the family, government, education, and an economy—which are interdependent. This is the heart of cultural integration. Changing one has effects upon the others. The so-called "equal rights for women" amendment proposed for the U.S. Constitution was questioned along this line with the argument that it could have unexpected society-wide effects. Hall (1959) has captured an essential preservative feature of integration in this example:

> An American these days will not normally consider the revenge of the brothers as a price for seeing a woman without her family's permission. . . . Death of the woman and revenge on the man are within the expected range of behavior in the less Europeanized parts of the Arab world. . . . What we often don't know and have difficulty accepting is that such patterns fit into larger overall patterns and that what is being guarded is not the sister's life

. . . but a centrally located institution without which the society would perish or be radically altered. This institution is the family (p. 112).

Related to integration is the concept of *functionalism* which is its close counterpart. Functionalism is ordinarily traced to Durkheim and his followers in sociology. In anthropology, Malinowski is credited with having been an early proponent of this position, beginning more than forty years ago, insofar as he stressed the interdependence of the various elements of a culture.

Broadly speaking, the functionalist position asserts that every aspect of a culture, including especially the manifest actions of members of society, fulfills a function. As Kluckhohn (1949b) and Merton (1957) have suggested, though, a distinction is needed between "manifest" and "latent" functions. An example of this distinction that Kluckhohn gives is a cowboy spending an hour to catch a horse to ride only a short distance. It takes him more time to catch the animal than it does to make the trip. As Kluckhohn notes, this act—if taken literally and superficially—seems distinctly non-functional. However, he says, while it may not have a manifest function, it fulfills more than one latent function: the cowboy escapes the ridicule to which he would be exposed if another cowboy saw him walking; he also preserves his own sense of self-respect and of the fitness of things; most importantly, the basic relation between cowboy and horse is symbolized in this pattern and thus lends support to its persistence.

In the functionalist view, therefore, even apparently non-functional elements in a culture can be imputed to have latent functions. In the instance of mechanically useless items, such as buttons on sleeves of men's jackets, there exists the latent function of preserving tradition in a symbolic sense. In short, it looks and feels "right."

EXPLICIT AND IMPLICIT CULTURE

The various definitions of culture that we have been treating also suggest that culture's effects can be partitioned into two categories. The first of these may be called the *explicit* culture which deals with the behaviors and artifacts that we associate with those visible and even striking differences between cultures.

There is, however, the more profound effect on individuals which is less visible and depends upon the *implicit* culture. This effect is essentially based in the attitudes and values which govern the behavior of the members of a society, as well as in the fundamental assumptions they accept uncritically regarding life and its meaning. As we have pointed out, culture relies upon shared meanings of a symbolic nature many of which may lie below the level of conscious awareness, for example in terms of striving for goals. Thus, Kroeber and Kluckhohn (1952) say that "one group unconsciously and habitually assumes that every chain of actions has a goal and that when this goal is reached tension will be reduced or disappear. To another group, thinking based upon this assumption is by no means automatic. They see life not primarily as a series of purposive sequences but more as made up of disparate experiences which may be satisfied in and of themselves, rather than as means to ends" (p. 157).

Culture, then, can be treated with regard to the overt behaviors that people display as well as the internal experiences which constitute part of their psychological field. These are learned from other people and also shared with them. Even given the common biological qualities of Man, vast cultural differences continue to exist with respect to the way life is led and how these primary motivations are satisfied. This now leads us appropriately to a fuller consideration of the sociopsychological aspects of culture.

The significance of culture in social psychology

Cultural patterns can be considered to be a routine way of communicating certain meanings where symbols are mutually understood. Shaking hands, for example, is one of the illustrations in our own society of an action which has symbolic meaning. Objects as well convey meanings apart from their intrinsic worth, as for example the widespread use of diamond engagement rings in our society. There are, however, other symbols which are essentially discretionary in that their purpose does not have wide significance. In matters of dress, for example, cuffless trousers are not an important issue in the same way as a topless bathing suit is for women—and once was, for men. Hair length and beards, at least for the time, represent a new wave of interest.

The ways of a culture include a wide range of behaviors which convey symbolic significance. This is made possible through the common features in the psychological fields of individuals. The culture, then, intrudes directly on the constructions that individuals place on their environment and in a sense intervenes by shaping expectations and behaviors. To understand a man's behavior, therefore, it is necessary to have an awareness of the symbols and their definitions that have become part of his psychological field through experience within the context of culture. That context is, in Plant's (1950) terms, an "envelope" within which we react. A significant feature of this process is that once symbols come to stand for things or social entities—a flag for a nation—it is possible for people to respond to them though the symbolized things are not immediately present. The venerable story of the Englishman dressing formally for dinner in a tropical outpost exemplifies the hold of culture in terms of its symbolic dictates.

Cultures also consist of important assumptions in the nature of beliefs about the world. Some of these have essentially a factual base, others are guided largely by evaluative components representing preferences. The belief that the earth is round is fundamental in most human cultures. But there may be vast differences in their beliefs about the nature of God, the way in which the economic practices of a society should be managed or not be managed, the kind of political or governmental structures that are needed to fulfill certain of the functions of the society, and the mode of upbringing that children should receive including education. All of these considerations go to make up the institutions of a culture, each of which is predicated on certain fundamental assumptions that persist in time. These are so taken for granted that it is all too easy, as with most things that are cultural, to accept them as almost God-given.

A pointed illustration of this kind of assumption arises in any discussion of the length and sequencing of education. Why should there be, for example, four years of high school followed by four years of college with high redundancy in the curriculum of the two? Educators from other countries, who follow different practices, find it hard to understand the merit in this.

All societies provide training for their young, but the differences that exist are vitally important. These grow out of cultural values and the particular needs which exist or once existed within the society. And change comes slowly, often as a consequence of competition with other cultures. In education, the spurt of interest in science subjects in the United States, beginning in the early 1960's, followed the well-publicized space achievement by the Soviet Union in the late 1950's.

The formal tea and military parade are displays which may not achieve much beyond the external, symbolic function of form. Yet, that is important in its own way. As a case in point, formal negotiations in a controversy may be seen as just that—a formality. For effective communication, especially when conducted as a public event, formal negotiations have distinct limitations; frequently, in such a setting, it is indirect communication of a less formal nature which facilitates the resolution of a conflict (Pruitt, 1969). But the formal trappings are *not* inconsequential since they represent an appropriate cultural form without which the relevant public may be troubled, because of its perceived importance.

Psychological features of culture

From a psychological standpoint, the most basic influence effect of culture is to inculcate a perspective for viewing the world. In his discussion of reference groups, Shibutani (1955) gives expression to this in these terms:

> A perspective is an ordered view of one's world—what is taken for granted about the attributes of various objects, events, and human nature. It is an order of things remembered and expected as well as things actually perceived, an organized conception of what is plausible and what is possible; it constitutes the matrix through which one perceives his environment. The fact that men have such ordered perspectives enables them to conceive of their ever changing world as relatively stable, orderly, and predictable (p. 564).

When we speak of a cultural perspective, then, we mean the shared content of the psychological field which defines and guides experience and action. In this section we will consider these as psychologically relevant effects upon value orientations, perceptual functioning, and social expectancies.

In any human society, there are values which are traditionally retained as part of implicit culture. At the individual level many of these values become incorporated as long-range, persisting motives which shape behavior. As Mumford (1951) says:

> . . . in all going cultures, Man is born into a world of established values: here every instinctual need is broadened, yet partly concealed, by a social form, as the naked body is soon covered by decorations or clothes. The production and conservation of values is one of the main concerns of human existence: all that a man does and is depends upon his taking part in this process (p. 127).

Cultural values stand, in Goldschmidt's (1959) phrase, as a "blueprint for propriety," but no more than a blue-print. There may be wide variations in the degree to which a given value is actually upheld in everyday practice. In short, some values are acted on more uniformly than others. Our society, for example, places a high value on the monogamous relationship as a uniform family pattern. From earliest experience we learn that there is one mother and one father in the family. All the influences we encounter in the society sustain the imperative quality of this as proper. Subsequently, we are oriented toward a love relationship of our own leading to monogamous marriage. As Goldschmidt (1959) puts it:

> Man must mate. But the cultured animal must select his mate according to certain rules, and the act of procreation is circumscribed by a welter of culturally established demands. We might put the matter this way: that even man's most basic animal drives are given a symbolic content and their fulfillment is caught up in the symbolism that is the culture of that particular people (p. 21).

As this example indicates, a prominent feature of values is that they are highly symbolic. The kind of behavior we evidence is both guided by and interpreted in light of values, such as virtue or honor. When we say, "I am a man of my word," we reveal a sense of appropriate behavior symbolizing such values.

Florence Kluckhohn (1953) has considered five human problems that are faced by all people, and which are expressed in the values of a culture. These provide distinctive orientations toward human behavior. They are:

> A culture's view of human nature.
> Its view of Man's relationship to nature.
> The valuation and ordering of time.
> The idealized personality type.
> The dominant modalities in Man's relationship with other men.

Each of these value problems can be seen to have three alternative orientations; for example "human nature" can be seen as good, mixed, or evil in its quality. As further developed by Kluckhohn and Strodtbeck (1961), this theory can be employed as an instrument by which to compare differential value orientations from one culture to another. They used an interview schedule for this purpose, and were able to show systematic differences between the ethnic groups in a Texas town —"Anglos," "Mexicanos," Mormons, and two Indian groups, the Zuñi and Navaho.

A more recent application of the Kluckhohn-Strodtbeck procedure was used by Nordlie (1968) to compare the values of a sample of rural Vietnamese respondents in the Mekong Delta with those of a sample of American respondents in training at the Army's Civil Affairs School, Fort Gordon. One comparison, which dealt with the content area of government and community, is shown in Figure 8.2. The differences revealed are consistent in demonstrating that: while the Americans saw man's nature as basically good, the Vietnamese respondents were evenly divided in seeing it as good, mixed, or evil; the American respondents valued dominance, and the Vietnamese respondents valued harmony, in relationships with the environment; the American respondents were predominantly goal-oriented, in the future-time sense, while the Vietnamese respondents were more situationally-oriented, in the present-time sense; the American respondents were more heavily inclined toward an achievement orientation, while the Vietnamese respondents were more inclined toward an expressive orientation; and the American respondents were distinctly more individualistic, while

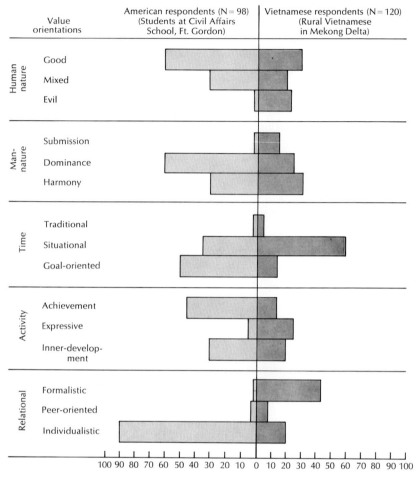

Figure 8.2: Comparison of value-orientations, obtained from American and Vietnamese respondents, regarding the content area of government and community. (From Nordlie, 1968, p. 31.)

the Vietnamese respondents tended toward a more formalistic orientation.

It would be a mistake to generalize Nordlie's findings too far, given the relatively small samples in his study. However, his data fit other observations which make them unsurprising, and consistent. Practically speaking, the consequences which follow from these value differences in connection with governmental and community development are disquieting. An American who operates with the traditional goal-orientations of his culture is in the position of imposing a view which, to say the least, is "foreign" to the Vietnamese with whom he is attempting to effect communication. Largely *un*recognized value differences can serve to block communication, inhibit co-operative efforts, and, in light of the power differentials at work, engender hostile feelings. In this connection, Hall (1959) has made the observation that Americans may too readily fall into the trap of believing that people of other cultures are merely "underdeveloped Americans."

It would be impossible for a society to retain coherence and continuity if its members did not, for the most part, share certain significant values in common. Among other benefits, this smoothes social interaction and assures individuals of social acceptance. Yet, individual differences obviously occur in the adherence to values. Furthermore, conflicts in expressed values are commonplace, especially in a complex society. If in America we place a high value on initiative and achievement, its expression, nonetheless, is often in contradiction to other prevalent values. Exponents of private enterprise, for example, are often those who would limit competition by the greater amalgamation of enterprises within an industry; higher education for all who are capable is valued, but those who have achieved it and act accordingly can be viewed with suspicion as "intellectuals"; social class distinctions are disdained, but larger and more expensive cars are sought as a conspicuous mark of social position.

Sometimes it is found that *many people privately* hold a value which they erroneously believe to be different from the predominant values of others; Schanck (1932) dubbed this "pluralistic ignorance" (see Chapter 7, p. 268). Its effect is shown in a study by Paul and Laulicht (1963) of attitudes toward defense and disarmament among a national sample of Canadian voters. They found that *personally* 70 per cent of their respondents favored disarmament even if it meant a loss of income; yet only 38 per cent of these respondents thought that *other* Canadians felt that way. In essence, then, the dominant value associated with disarmament actually existed but was not perceived to exist. This can lead to awkward conflicts within a society as was sharply seen following the publication of the first "Kinsey report" (1948) on the sexual behavior of American males. The interview data presented in the report raised doubts about the wider adherence to norms regarding sexual conduct.

In their book, *The Political Beliefs of Americans,* Free and Cantril (1967) examined "liberal" and "conservative" political values from the standpoint of ideology, operational meaning, and the identifying labels Americans attach to themselves. Their data came from two nation-wide, cross-sectional surveys of about sixteen hundred respondents each, plus some smaller supplemental surveys, all conducted for them by the Gallup Poll organization in the fall of 1964.

They report that 29 per cent of these respondents designated them-selves as "liberal," 38 per cent as "middle of the road," and 33 per cent as "conservative." But there is considerable confusion about the mean-ing of these designations, though generally, self-designated "liberals," on an index called the Operational Spectrum, tended to favor the use of governmental powers to achieve social objectives. However, in looking at the various programs individuals actually favored, in the operational sense, as against what they professed by ideology and self-labeling, it developed that the respondents were far more liberal-lean-ing than their self-identifications would suggest. Some instructive findings in this vein are shown in Figure 8.3.

Regarding this relationship, Free and Cantril (1967) comment:

> . . . the startling fact emerges that more than four out of ten self-designated "conservatives" actually qualified as liberal on the Op-erational Spectrum and only three in ten stayed in the conservative column. It thus seems apparent that most people who think of them-selves as conservative are not thinking of operational aspects of Government programs but are, as already noted, thinking of ideo-logical considerations (p. 47).

The fact that a society's values may be contradictory, or that individ-uals may give only lip service to a value, does not alter the essential point that values exist as guideposts in a cultural sense. Such discon-tinuities can still be reconciled within a general framework of the dom-inant themes of a culture. Anthropological studies frequently dwell on a culture's value-orientations as such themes. For example, the Kwa-kiutl Indians of the Northwest coast of North America were studied by Franz Boas over a period of many decades. Regarding these people, he said, "the importance of hereditary social rank, to be maintained by the

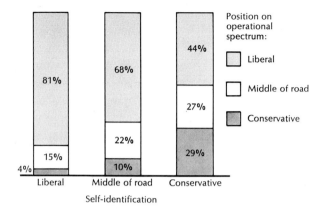

Figure 8.3: Relationship between self-identification on "Political Spectrum" and actual position on "Operational Spectrum" of "liberal" to "conservative." (Based on data from Free and Cantril, 1967, p. 48.)

display and lavish distribution, determines the behavior of the individual. It is the ambition of every person to obtain high social standing for himself, his family, or for the chief of his family. Wealth is a necessary basis for social eminence and the general tone of life is determined by these ideas" (1928, p. 152). The dominating value of status eminence, which is not unfamiliar to us in our own culture, was seen by Boas as an integrating principle among the Kwakiutl.

Ruth Benedict (1934), in her book *Patterns of Culture*, elaborated this approach in considering the dominant values of several cultures. She herself had done field work with the Zuñi Indians of the Southwest and discovered a distinct difference between them and the other Indian tribes of North America. In her terms, these other tribes were "Dionysian," in their emphasis on achieving psychological states of excess in personal experience and in ritual. The Zuñi, by contrast, tended to be "Apollonian" and to follow more restrained ways including an aversion to excess. Criticisms of Benedict's work (e.g. Barnouw, 1963, Ch. 3) mainly emphasize that the Zuñi were not all purely Apollonian and that other Indian tribes vary considerably in their Dionysian tendencies. Despite the absence of pure behavioral "types," there nonetheless appear to be central values which can be used to characterize a culture.

Apart from cultural influences as such, it is sometimes said that *all* people want a "decent standard of living." This is often merely a way of saying that humans value the satisfaction of their basic physical needs. But how very much this can vary in content is well revealed in a book by Hadley Cantril, *The Pattern of Human Concerns* (1965), in which he reports an intensive study of more than twenty-three thousand people in fourteen nations of the world ranging from those that are economically well-off countries on through those that are economically deprived. His main interest was in how people saw their own lives, and what they expressed as their own aspirations.

As part of his questionnaire survey procedure, conducted in each nation by trained native-speaking interviewers, Cantril devised what he calls the "Self-Anchoring Striving Scale" which is shown in its simple ladder form in Figure 8.4. Each respondent was shown this scale and asked to define the "top" and "bottom" in terms of *his own* assumptions, values, aspirations, fears, and worries. Then, regarding his *own* situation, he was asked three questions: (1) Where on the ladder do you feel you personally stand at the *present* time? Where on the ladder would you say you stood *five years ago?* (3) And where do you think you will be on the ladder *five years from now?* Comparable questions were also asked regarding the respondent's view of his nation's position on the ladder, though we shall not treat them here.

As Cantril plainly points out, these ratings are entirely subjective

Figure 8.4: Ladder used in "Self-Anchoring Striving Scale." Each respondend defines the "top" and "bottom" himself. (From Cantril, 1965, p. 22.)

Table 8.1: Comparison of average personal ladder ratings and shifts across time among respondents in three wealthy and three poor countries. (Adapted from Cantril, 1965, p. 204.)

COUNTRY	PAST	PRESENT	FUTURE	SHIFT
Wealthy				
United States	5.9	6.6	7.8	1.9
West Germany	4.1	5.3	6.2	2.1
Israel	4.7	5.3	6.9	2.2
Average	4.9	5.7	7.0	2.1
Poor				
Brazil	4.1	4.6	7.3	3.2
Nigeria	2.8	4.8	7.4	4.6
India	3.4	3.7	5.1	1.7
Average	3.4	4.4	6.6	3.2
Difference in Average	1.5	1.3	0.4	−1.1

and therefore a rating of 6 by one person does not indicate the same thing as a 6 given by another person. Nevertheless, consistent and significant differences were found between the average ratings given by people in different countries. For example, people in the three wealthiest nations represented in the study were found to rate themselves significantly higher on the present, the past, and the future than those from three of the poorest countries, as is shown in Table 8.1. However, this is revealed even more through the actual words of these respondents, from India and the United States as examples:

> *India*
> I should like to have a water tap and a water supply in my house. It would also be nice to have electricity. My husband's wages must be increased if our children are to get an education and our daughter is to be married. (Forty-five-year-old housewife, family income about $80 a month) (1965, p. 205-6)
> I wish for an increase in my wages because with my meager salary I cannot afford to buy decent food for my family. If the food and clothing problems were solved, then I would feel at home and be satisfied. Also if my wife were able to work the two of us could then feed the family and I am sure would have a

happy life and our worries would be over. (Thirty-year-old sweeper, monthly income around $13) (p. 206)

I hope in the future I will not get any disease. Now I am coughing. I also hope I can purchase a bicycle. I hope my children will study well and that I can provide them with an education. I also would sometime like to own a fan and maybe a radio. (Forty-year-old skilled worker earning $30 a month) (p. 206)

United States

I hope that when I retire I will have enough money to travel, not necessarily in top style. We have had a nice comfortable home life raising our children and have enjoyed it. Now I'd like to do a few different things, like traveling. (Fifty-two-year-old insurance agent) (p. 221)

I would like a reasonable enough income to maintain a house, have a new car, have a boat, and send my four children to private schools. (Thirty-four-year-old laboratory technician) (p. 222)

If I had more money I could build a home, get married, move out of the city, and take a long vacation. I would like to be able to take my bride to Europe. (Twenty-six-year-old clerk) (p. 223)

It should be evident, then, that the prevailing economic circumstances of a society, such as a nation, can affect the way in which a given value is culturally defined by its members. The difference may not be so much a matter of quality as it is one of degree, but it is there.

CULTURAL EFFECTS ON PERCEPTUAL FUNCTIONING

The influence of culture on perception has long occupied a significant place in social psychology. For the most part, it is widely recognized that the unique experiences and emphases which are culturally induced become absorbed as a vital part of the individual's psychological field.

In summarizing the effect of cultural variables on perceptual responses in humans, Tajfel (1968) maintains that these variables can be grouped into three categories. The first of these is *functional salience,* which has regard to the environmental aspects of a culture which encourage certain perceptual discriminations, for example regarding edible and acceptable foods. *Familiarity* refers to the frequency of exposure that individuals may have to some human artifacts that are unfamiliar to those living in another culture. This is illustrated by the remarkable perceptual skill that children in our society reveal in readily differentiating makes and years of automobiles, even at great distance. *Systems of communication* mainly represent language as a technique of categorization and labeling to afford ready-made interpretations of the world. We shall be treating this latter feature in more detail in the chapter which follows.

Among the most interesting research on cultural effects on perception have been the studies comparing responses of people in different cultures to the same standard stimulus, sometimes a psychological illusion or a projective device, such as the Rorschach Ink-Blot Test.

An early study of cross-cultural differences in perception was conducted by Rivers (1901, 1905). He presented two well-known perceptual illusions, the Müller-Lyer and the horizontal-vertical, to Papuans in New Guinea, to Todas in India, and to a sample of English adults and schoolchildren. These illusions are shown in Figure 8.5. In the first of these, a vertical line is placed between two pairs of inwardly pointing vertices and is perceived as shorter than a line of the same size placed between outwardly pointing vertices. In the second illusion, two lines of identical size are placed in the configuration with one horizontal and the other vertical, as in a T. Usually the vertical line is perceived as the longer. Rivers found that the English subjects tended to be relatively more susceptible to the Müller-Lyer illusion than subjects of the other cultures, and less so to the horizontal-vertical illusion.

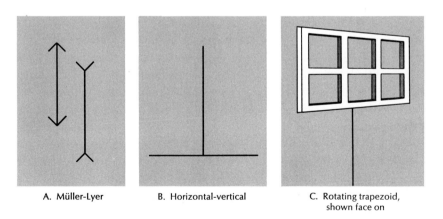

A. Müller-Lyer   B. Horizontal-vertical   C. Rotating trapezoid,
                                                        shown face on

Figure 8.5: Three perceptual illusions used in cross-cultural research.

There were differences, then, between the cultures but the nature of the difference depended upon the particular illusion.

Allport and Pettigrew (1957) undertook a study with the so-called rotating trapezoid devised by Ames (1951) (see Figure 8.5). To create this illusion, subjects are presented with a slowly rotating object which looks like a window but is proportioned like a trapezoid so that the longer edge always creates a longer image on the retina than does the shorter edge, even when the latter is closer. When viewed under optimal conditions, with one eye closed at a distance of 20 feet, the resulting perception is normally one of side-to-side movement, rather than rotation; the window seems to be swaying back and forth.

Allport and Pettigrew were interested in testing the hypothesis that familiarity with windows, and other squared-off objects which share its features, would make people more susceptible to the illusion because of the expectancies of shape they had learned. Alternatively, those living in a culture without such recurrent features should be less susceptible. They tested this hypothesis in a field study by showing the rotating trapezoid to a sample of subjects in South Africa who were Zulus in villages or in cities, and to urban South Africans of European origin. Under optimal conditions for the illusion, they did not find strikingly significant differences between the village Zulus and either urbanized Zulus or the Europeans. However, under conditions which were not optimum—such as viewing with one eye at 10 feet or with both eyes at 10 or 20 feet—they did find significant differences in the direction expected, i.e. the urban people, whether Zulus or Europeans, tended to see the illusion more frequently. One possible interpretation of these findings is that the compelling experimental condition overwhelms the effect of cultural experience which reveals itself only when the condition is less compelling. In any case, the degree of familiarity with objects of a culture appears to be a factor that does influence the individual's perception of the world.

In a series of related studies of cultural differences in geometric illusions (Segall, Campbell, and Herskovits, 1963, 1966; Campbell, 1964), subjects from more than fifteen cultures were exposed to several kinds of perceptual illusions, including the Müller-Lyer and horizontal-vertical illusions already mentioned. Among the participants were subjects from the United States and from various parts of Africa. The essential idea underlying the experiments was referred to as the "carpentered world hypothesis." This hypothesis contends that where individuals live in a squared-off world of right angles, they may be more susceptible to illusions because of the corrections they normally introduce when encountering angles in perspective. In general, the results confirm this guiding hypothesis. The Western samples, for example, showed significantly greater susceptibility to the Müller-Lyer illusion than did the people from tribal areas whose housing tends to be almost entirely rounded.

Data from anthropological field studies have also provided interesting examples of the way that cultures affect visual experience from a social standpoint. In his work with the Trobriand islanders, Malinowski (1927) reports one instance of such a pattern which can run contrary to sensory evidence. In the Trobriand culture, it is considered a social indiscretion to suggest that brothers resemble one another, though both may look like their father. Once, commenting on the likeness of two brothers, Malinowski reports that "there came such a hush over the assembly, while the brother present withdrew abruptly and the company was half-embarrassed, half-offended, at this breach of custom" (p. 92). In discussing this example, Klineberg (1954) points out the difficulty in knowing whether the Trobriand islanders actually *see* the two brothers as different, despite their obvious resemblance to one another, or whether they are merely unwilling to acknowledge such a resemblance even when they do see it. He concludes that on the basis of our knowledge "the Trobrianders failed to note any resemblance because they do not want or expect to find it" (p. 205). This conclusion is sustained as well in other cultures in terms of the influence they can exert on perception in line with the phenomenon of perceptual set.

Within the general interest in psychological effects of culture, the Rorschach Test has probably been used to a greater extent than any other single psychological measure. The test consists of ten symmetrical inkblots which are always shown in the same order to the subject. He then reports what he sees in each of the blots and the examiner records his responses. In general, the test is used as a projective measure of personality. An individual response is compared with standardized norms obtained from tens of thousands of cases to provide a view of the individual's unique psycho-dynamics. Applied as an anthropological tool in the field, however, it can determine certain of the consistencies of perception for members of the same culture.

Among the many studies of the latter kind, one by Bleuler and Bleuler (1935) found, for example, that Moroccan natives responded with a significantly greater number of "details" in the inkblots than is usually found in the norms obtained from Europeans. This could be interpreted, in a psychodynamic sense, as a sign of disorder. More appropriately, however, it reveals something of the salience of perceptual emphasis within the Moroccan culture. This is further clarified by another field investigation in which Cook (1942) found that young men in Samoa gave a very high percentage of responses which made use of the white space areas within the inkblots. Such responses are rather rare in the usual Rorschach norms. On further study, Cook found that 31 of the 50 young men reported white as their favorite color. Quite relevantly, in Samoan culture the color white is regarded as a symbol of purity.

DeVos (1961) examined Rorschach data obtained from two cultures where members lived by traditional as well as more Westernized ways. He found that while these Arab and Japanese subjects differed by grouping in the overall content of the Rorschach responses, there was a clear trend toward similarity in the responses of people in both groupings who had undergone Westernization. Thus, their convergence toward a common culture was revealed in the perceptual content of their Rorschach Test responses.

There are several obvious advantages in the use of the Rorschach Test in the field of cultural investigation. It does not require literacy; it is essentially culture-free since the blots do not represent anything in particular; and it can be used with people of different ages. There are, nevertheless, a number of difficulties associated with the administration of the test in the field. The procedure itself is cumbersome and particularly time-consuming where translation is required. Moreover, when it is used as a measure of cultural differences in personality, it is vulnerable in terms of the often unwitting bias in the selection of "typical" respondents, as well as in the interpretation of responses. These have questionable applicability to norms obtained from samples of Europeans or Americans.

From the accumulated evidence, quite beyond that part covered here, it is reasonable to conclude that perceptual functioning is influenced by culture. However, as Tajfel (1968) notes, it is not only culture as such but the broader characteristics of the physical environment which enter into the process as well. Thus, familiarity with objects, shapes, and contours cannot help but have their effect in the process of categorizing which is basic to perception.

NORMS, ROLES, AND SOCIAL EXPECTANCIES

The behavior of humans in a society follows certain organized configurations or patterns, as we have seen. These affect the experiences encountered by individuals but always within the envelope of a structured environment. Growing up within any cultural context involves exposure to examples of appropriate conduct presented recurringly from an early age. The appropriateness of some behaviors and the inappropriateness of others become incorporated in the individual's psychological field.

As we said in connection with social interaction, individuals also construe their world in ways consistent with the present situational context and in line with past experience. For the most part, this occurs through an implicit learning process that builds up "expectancies" for action, as Rotter (1954) has noted. The common expectation of regularities in conduct is the fundamental feature underlying *social norms* and *roles*.

The norms of any society can vary considerably as a consequence of different situational contexts and the meanings that they infuse into action. There are widely held forms of culturally approved behavior, however, for particular kinds of situations. Most individuals will be expected to display them. Traditionally, these fall into the broad categories of folkways and usages, conventions, and mores and taboos.

At the simplest level, *folkways* and *usages* in American society encompass such patterns of behavior as shaking hands on greeting or taking leave, or saying "hello" when answering the telephone. Violations of these norms are not punished severely, unless a special symbolic importance is attached to a given event. For example, the public refusal of a head of state of one nation to shake hands with the head of state of another nation could be a serious enough breach to create severe international repercussions. This is, however, a rare rather than a typical instance.

The norms regulating more significant aspects of social behavior are usually called *conventions*. For behavior of this kind, breaches are more severe, as is the resulting punishment. Wearing clothes in public, using silverware as opposed to one's fingers when eating, and attending to bodily functions privately are examples of conventions. Violations of these are often penalized by legal as well as social sanctions.

The most significant social norms are called *mores* and *taboos*. These are usually codified in a society's laws and religious teachings and include such important injunctions of the "Thou shalt" variety as monogamy, faithfulness to one's spouse, significance of private property, and the like. Taboos represent the "Thou shalt not" injunction, seen for example in murder and incest. Mores and taboos are of course simply counterparts of the same value. Thus, the taboo against murder is another way of asserting the positive value placed on individual human life, just as respect for private property can be viewed as a directive against outright stealing, in contrast to borrowing.

The distinctions that we have made are of a more traditional variety and do not explain the "why" of norms so much as they describe various culturally determined action. From the standpoint of social psychology, there are two interrelated points concerning these norms: they range on a rough scale regarding increasing severity of the breach from folkways to mores, and represent increasing degrees of threat to organized society and the well-being of its members.

By now it should be clear that the functioning of any society depends upon a willingness of its members to comply with certain social demands in return for having others do so. In this regard, Goldschmidt (1959) says that "Social life may be seen as a bargain in which the individual subordinates himself to customary demands and receives in turn a social environment in which to operate; whether or not it is a good bargain, it is written into the commitment to social existence" (p. 64). This has applicability as well to roles.

Roles are behaviors expected of an individual in a given social position, as we pointed out in the last chapter. They are normative in the sense that they reside in shared expectancies within a culture. Practically speaking, they are particularized norms that have to do with an individual in a specified situation rather than with everyone. At a house party, for example, it is acceptable for everyone else *but* the host and hostess to say that it is getting late and is time to go home. Their roles dictate that they should *not* evidence any sign of inhospitableness, except under special circumstances, such as illness or an early morning departure on a trip.

Members of a society usually react to some aspects of a situation as *significant aspects*. In regard to roles, therefore, people abstract those features which tend to have the most important meanings just then for them, as in the instance of "hospitality." Generally speaking, what we call role behaviors are routinized ways of transmitting such meanings. Bredemeier and Stephenson (1962) have said that "Students, for example, are supposed to be 'attentive'; women are supposed to dress 'attractively'; men are supposed to be 'considerate' of their dates" (p. 14). There is, however, a range of behavior that is covered by the terms "attentive," "attractive," or "considerate." Furthermore, it is clear that these abstract qualities can be perceived differently depending upon the other person, how much we are attracted to him or her, and the attributes that he or she is seen to possess.

Among the attributes which are significant in roles are age and sex. In any society there are cultural dictates regarding the roles associated with infants, young children, adolescents and young adults, mature adults, and old people. American society, unlike many other societies, tends to be oriented toward youth and does not generally hold those of older age in high regard merely because of their age. Most importantly for our interest here, there are roles which are only appropriate at a given age. When we say that an adult is acting "childishly" we are giving expression to one such expectancy. Age-linked roles are also bound up with sex, so much so that the term "age-sex roles" is sometimes used to describe this relationship. Little boys and girls, for example, have differential roles in regard to the kind of play in which they are expected to indulge.

As a rule, people have rather firmly fixed expectancies regarding sex roles. Illustrating this is the widespread expectancy that a nurse, and especially a secretary, should be female. Despite the fact that a high proportion of physicians in many Western societies are women, in our own society we think of this as distinctively a male role. When we speak of a "doctor" we mean a male, and females in that profession are still looked upon as an oddity—as they are in law and engineering. The best evidence indicates that women could capably fulfill these roles in greater numbers if the culture did not dictate otherwise (Klineberg, 1954, Ch. 10).

Psychologically speaking, social norms and roles are both passed along by certain shared perceptions, or common constructions of what is appropriate. It is possible, however, for one person to perceive his role in one fashion while the person with whom he interacts perceives it in another. This is dramatically observed in cross-cultural contacts where the parties involved have different expectancies for what is correct. An instance of this comes from the work of Hall (1959, 1966), who has studied the way in which time and space usage differs between cultures. He gives several instances of how American diplomats, unfamiliar with the ways of a foreign culture, misconstrue the behavior of their counterparts.

In one example concerning time, Hall (1959, pp. 17-18) tells of an American used to punctuality who becomes impatient and angry in a Latin American country when kept waiting what seemed an unconscionable time. Hall says: "The principal source of misunderstanding lay in the fact that in the country in question the five-minute-delay interval was not significant. Forty-five minutes, on the other hand, instead of being at the tail end of the waiting scale, was just barely at the beginning" (p. 18). Here we see one instance of how role interaction can be sharply affected by expectancies which are culturally induced. Another instance has regard to space. In American society we tend not to stand as close in conversation as people do in some other societies, including those of Latin America. Hall points out that we view the foreigner who seems to be getting too close, by our standards, as "pushy." A humorous consequence, with significant overtones, is revealed in Hall's report:

> I have observed an American backing up the entire length of a long corridor while a foreigner he considers pushy tries to catch up with him. This scene has been enacted thousands and thousands of times—one person trying to increase the distance in order to be at ease, while the other tries to decrease it for the same reason, neither one being aware of what was going on. We have here an example of the tremendous depth to which culture can condition behavior (pp. 160-161).

Another kind of problem produced by roles occurs when the individual operates with two sets of conflicting expectancies regarding his behavior. This is commonly called "role conflict" and results from being in two largely incompatible roles simultaneously. All of us experience this in milder forms when, for example, we first bring our best girl-friend home to dinner with our family, or meet our professor when out shopping with a friend. There is an awkwardness in such circumstances, if only momentarily, because of the combination of different expectancies. In some cases this awkwardness could be more severe, as exemplified by the case of a traffic court judge who found his wife brought before him charged with a violation. Another illustration in which role conflict occurs, but on a more persisting basis, is seen where the son or son-in-law of its president is employed in a company. The supervisor for whom he works inevitably experiences a degree of incongruence in this relationship that he would not normally encounter in the usual supervisor-subordinate relationship.

This case not only exemplifies a situation producing role conflict for the supervisor, but also reveals an instance of "status incongruence." Homans (1961) and Sampson (1963), among others, have pointed out that there usually is the expectancy of *status congruence* in interacting roles; incongruence would mean a violation of expectancy by having someone of higher status (e.g. the company president's son) in a lower status position.

As generally conceived, status congruence means a matching of the value of a person's attributes in one dimension with his position in another. For example, in supermarkets employees who check-out purchases at the cash register are perceived to have a higher status than, and to be in charge of, employees who bundle, though they might make the same wage. The more experienced employees expect to be assigned to checking because greater seniority and experience are congruent with a higher position. However, should a more experienced worker, in a busy period, be assigned to a checker with less experience, this incongruity has been found to create tension and reduce productivity (Clark, 1958).

Other kinds of background characteristics including age, sex, education, and ethnic affiliation may also enter into the perception of dimensions of status involved in this kind of attribution process. The same sort of issue underlies the once strong skepticism that a black officer could head a unit made up of white men. Notice that in these instances status is *not* earned by experience, qualifications, or actions, but instead is attributed to a person by the prior expectancies of others. Today, the "Women's Liberation Movement" is challenging many expectancies regarding proper male or female roles in society. Despite the renewed concern, there is not, as many people believe, a greater degree of participation by women in significant roles in American society, such as those in government. In 1970, in the 91st Congress, for example, there were eleven women—one Senator out of one hundred, and ten representatives out of 435. Almost a decade ago, in the 87th Congress, there were seventeen women (*The New York Times Encyclopedia Almanac*, 1970, p. 164).

Recently, a newspaper story indicated that the chairman of a draft board in a major American city was resigning after sixteen years of service because of a woman's appointment to it. He was quoted as saying that "This is a man's work with no room for a woman. . . . I don't think it would be fair to the young men who have to appear before the board. You have to be considerate and fair when you serve on a board, but you also have to be hard. . . . A boy can come in and lay his cards on the table in front of a bunch of men, and I'm not sure he could do that with a woman there." A spokesman for the Director of the Selective Service System was quoted the following day in an article indicating that 248 women were serving on draft boards across the nation at the time—July 1970. The woman whose appointment had caused the chairman's resignation challenged his position by asserting that women are not only entitled to serve on draft boards but, speaking as the mother of two sons, that "women certainly should have a voice in their sons' future." Irrespective of who has the best of the argument, these viewpoints reveal a fundamental difference in the conception of a woman's role, though they both accept the idea that a woman's contribution to the operation of a draft board might be distinctive.

In our consideration of norms and roles, we have moved back and forth between the level of culturally dictated patterns and interpersonal relations—what we called the formal and informal levels of interaction in the last chapter. This is a necessity in social psychology because a culture's influences reside in the psychological fields and related response tendencies of people. As Withey and Katz (1965) aptly observe:

> Conventional social science accepts social structure as the walls of the maze but is willing to have the psychologist study individual deviations within those walls. The social psychologist, however, is concerned with understanding the walls themselves as well as the individual deviations, because the walls of the social maze consist of the patterned behavior of people. There is no social structure

apart from the interrelated habitual actions and attitudes of people (p. 65).

Adopting this metaphor, it is also clear that the social psychologist must be concerned with how these "walls" are maintained and by what processes they are changed. It is to these issues that we will now turn our attention.

Cultural continuity and social change

Cultures have continuity despite the fact that adaptation and change within a society are possible. The forces which sustain culture have considerable potency in terms of the desirability of the familiar and congenial way of life to which individuals become accustomed. This feeling is not merely an abstraction but can run deeply within the individual's sense of being. This is illustrated by interview data obtained from Turkish villagers as part of a broader study of social change in the Middle East (Lerner, 1958). Many respondents could not conceive of any other way of life than the one they knew.

In response to the question, "If you could not live in Turkey, where would you want to live?" Lerner reports that: "The standard reply of the villagers was that they would not live, could not imagine living, anywhere else." Under persistent questioning he quotes a shepherd as replying that ". . . he would rather kill himself" (pp. 24-25). Yet, four years later that very village had undergone such transformation, with the introduction of a new highway to Ankara, electric power, and radios, that these attitudes were giving way to a broadened horizon.

There are compelling individual forces, then, which act to sustain the continuity of culture, unless significant outside factors intervene. In this vein, Weick (1969a) notes:

> People lead exciting troubled lives but they also lead mundane lives. Mundaneness is the usual; variety is the unusual. But that is an answer that wipes out some awfully important questions. Suppose we treat mundane lives as accomplishments, and ask the question, "How is it that people produce a dull, normal day?" Why assume that a mundane day is an accident, why not assume that it is engineered in quite as deliberate a way as are exciting days. Why not ask the question "How do people accomplish that complicated phenomenon of social inertia?" (pp. 995-996).

The consequences of social inertia and cultural persistence can be quite dramatic. There are still societies today living by a pattern that dates to antiquity. Goldschmidt (1959) has noted as instances that "A modern photographer can catch scenes in Egyptian villages identical to ones depicted on archeological remains several millennia ago. . . . Eskimo life appears to be at least a thousand years old, and some of its elements go back to the upper Paleolithic. The pigmies in Africa and in Southeast Asia have a fundamentally similar culture and some scholars believe that they date back to the third glaciation of the Pleistocene epic" (p. 143). He further points out that no contemporary societies could so closely approximate earlier societies if cultural continuity did not exist.

THE TRANSMISSION OF CULTURE

Culture is transmitted primarily through the social institutions of a society, such as the family or school, with which humans have their earliest experiences. The need for maintenance functions in childhood creates an especially important dependence relationship, which leads to the ready acceptance of such cultural influences, as we noted in Chapters 4 and 5.

This process is bolstered considerably by the potent device of language. The words we learn to label and categorize experience are of great significance in the transmission of culture. The symbolic quality of culture, which we have already commented upon, therefore assures that individuals will themselves carry a cultural imprint within their own psychological fields.

Experimental verification of the persistence and change of cultural norms comes from the work of Jacobs and Campbell (1961). In a laboratory setting, they established the basis for the transmission of an arbitrary tradition. The task consisted of judging the distance a light moved in the autokinetic situation, in line with Sherif's (1935) research. Groups were initially composed of one naïve subject and several of the experimenter's confederates who gave a pre-arranged set of judgments aloud before the naïve subject gave his. In subsequent trials the confederates were removed one at a time, and were each replaced by a naïve subject. When the confederates had all been removed, the same method of elimination was continued for the other group members in

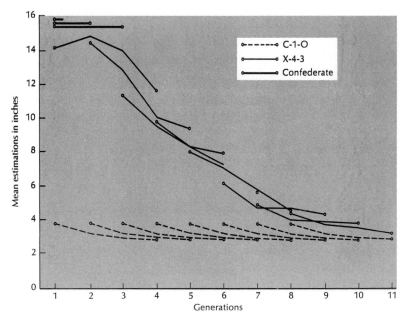

Figure 8.6: Transmission of an arbitrary perceptual norm in four-person groups (X-4-3) initially composed of a true subject and three experimenters' confederates. Control condition (C-10) involves subjects responding alone. All lines are plotted by a subject's mean responses for each of four consecutive generations. (From Jacobs and Campbell, 1961, p. 653.)

the order of their "seniority." In one control condition, subjects were alone when presented with the light and made their own independent judgments.

In Figure 8.6 results from the Jacobs and Campbell experiment are shown for an experimental group (X-4-3) made up of four people, three of whom at the outset were instructed to give an arbitrary response of 15 to 16 inches as the experimenters' confederates. For purposes of comparison, the results for the subjects in the control condition just described are also presented. In both instances, the curves show the mean individual judgments for each of four "generations" during which the subject was present. A generation was composed of thirty trials, each involving one discrete judgment by each person. This figure dramatically reveals the persistence of the "tradition" for several generations, at a level significantly different from subjects who had made judgments in solitude. The importance of this research lies in its clear demonstration that cultural transmission survives the departure of specific individuals, and also that change over time does occur in the direction of a decaying of the traditional norm.

As these experimenters themselves state, this research was not capable of capturing the richness contained within a culture. Furthermore, indoctrination into their norm came from age-mates in a brief period, rather than from adults over many years. Nonetheless, they say that "the outcome may well warn us against the assumption that a purely arbitrary cultural norm could be perpetuated indefinitely without other sources of support" (p. 657).

SOURCES OF CHANGE

A major psychological process at work in social change, which can lead to massive effects on a culture, is the perception of new alternatives. The contrast between what is and what might be—summed up in "hope"—is a powerful spur to change. Under conditions of necessity this process becomes all the more pressing, for example, when a physical resource such as water becomes scarce, or a social calamity such as war occurs. Even the sheer availability of information provides the groundwork for change. Various estimates indicate that our "information industries" are doubling their output every ten or at most fifteen years. The widely cited fact that 90 per cent of all scientists who ever lived are alive today lends further credence to these estimates.

The perception of alternatives, as we have already noted, is greatly facilitated by *cultural contact* and *technological innovation*. Their effects are illustrated dramatically by Margaret Mead's (1956) account of her return after 25 years to the island people of Manus near New Guinea. They had replaced their Stone Age culture with modern practices, a leap of literally thousands of years, largely because their territory was the site of a World War II base through which many Americans passed.

In Western civilization as well there have been many instances of cultural contact through travelers, such as the famed Marco Polo, population migrations, and wars. Today, through the mass media of communication and jet-age air travel, the possibility of such contact has been vastly increased. Supermarkets in Britain and France, *cinéma vérité* in

America, and television in Asia are only a few superficial signs of this development.

The truly big technological changes are illustrated more profoundly by the Agricultural Revolution, which Childe (1946) considers a singular landmark in human history, and by the Industrial Revolution of the last century. The Computer Revolution of this century, about which people are still glimpsing the surface, will have at least as much impact in rendering change. While industry brought people in droves to the cities for work, computer technology is likely to alter the entire work pattern of society and the cultural values associated with it.

At the beginning of this chapter, it was noted that Man is still making an adaptation to agriculture and technology. Yet, within this glacial movement of a cultural pattern, multifarious changes are occurring in society that are bound to affect that pattern. As a case in point consider the matter of farming, and its increasing mechanization. Figure 8.7 demonstrates graphically a simple fact, with more complex ramifications: there has been an almost vertical upsurge in the number of peo-

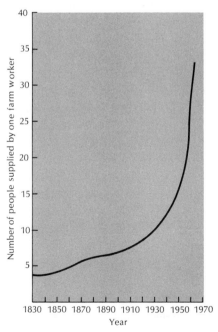

Figure 8.7: People supplied by one farm worker in the United States, 1830–1970. (From U.S. Department of Agriculture, 1966.)

ple whose needs can be supplied by a single farm worker. In 1950, that figure was fifteen; by 1970, it is estimated to be well-over double that. The other side of this trend is that the number of farm workers needed, relative to the population, is falling sharply. Near as it is to our fondest traditions, the small farm as we know it may increasingly be obliged to give way to larger, more efficient, industrialized farms, where technology is prized.

Technological change may be preceded by the awareness of a need which makes the people of a society receptive to its introduction. On the other hand, once introduced it may have striking social consequences. In this respect, Kardiner (1939) reports with Linton a study of villagers in Madagascar in the Tanala tribe. An agricultural people, they relied upon the cultivation of rice which they conducted by the "dry" method. Through contacts with their neighboring tribe, the Betsileo, they borrowed the "wet" method for cultivating rice, which on the whole is more effective agriculturally. This technological innovation had marked consequences, however, on the society of the Tanala. Among other effects noted by Kardiner and Linton were the new importance attached to land-owning, particularly in the swamps, the economic significance of slaves, and the greater power vested in a royal ruler positioned over a rigid caste system.

In a similar vein, Sharp (1952) reports on a tribe of Australian aborigines whose men had made and highly prized stone axes. With the arrival of an Anglican mission, steel axes came into plentiful supply. The important symbolic significance of an ax as a valued tool belonging especially to older men was soon undercut with profound social results. Because women and even young boys could now obtain steel axes from the mission, there was a "revolutionary confusion of sex, age, and kinship roles" with many ramifications regarding interpersonal conduct.

Paul Bohannan (1959) has studied the impact of money on the Tiz tribe living in central Nigeria. The traditional Tiz society was dominated by subsistence farmers who exchanged their produce and handicrafts as a mode of trade. In due course, there was introduced an "all-purpose" money in the form of government coins, whereas in the past only "limited purpose" money existed in the form of brass rods used to facilitate particular kinds of exchange. While trade increased considerably as part of the introduction of money, there came also rather marked changes in the character of the society and its cultural values. The Tiz had been a people disdaining great wealth or its display. This value changed drastically and along with it there came a new concept of indebtedness and concomitant shifts in kinship and status relationships as well. Bohannan pointedly says: "Money is one of the shatteringly simplifying ideas of all time, and like any other new and compelling idea, it creates its own revolution" (p. 503).

We need not look to tribal people alone for this kind of revolution, however. In American society we had a revolution which made its first major impact more than forty years ago in the widespread availability of the automobile. It, too, has contributed significant changes to our cultural patterns. In his history of the 1920's, *Only Yesterday* (1931), Frederick Lewis Allen says that the automobile

> . . . offered an almost universally available means of escaping temporarily from the supervision of parents and chaperones, or from the influence of neighborhood opinions. Boys and girls thought nothing, as the Lynds pointed out in *Middletown* [1929], of jumping into a car and driving off at a moment's notice—without asking anybody's permission—to a dance in another town 20 miles away, where they were strangers and enjoyed a freedom impossible among their neighbors. The closed car, moreover, was in effect a room protected from the weather which could be occupied at any time of the day or night and could be moved at will into a darkened by-way or a country lane (p. 70).

Other issues, not thought of much in our grandparents' and parents' day, now loom large. The automobile's relationship to Man, to the human environment, and to other cultural values which it challenges, have become matters of profound concern (Mumford, 1963). If killing on the highway, at an annual U.S. fatality rate of approximately 50,000 persons, has not had much impact, then concerns about pollution and the alteration of the landscape might.

Tom Wicker has recently commented in *The New York Times* on the enormous disparity between the automobile and train in terms of passenger flow and pollution. He says that while a highway lane can handle about 2000 passengers an hour, a railroad can carry 40,000 passengers an hour on a single track. Furthermore, since "it takes only a fourth as much thrust to move a railway car on steel rails as it does to move a rubber-tired vehicle on concrete, a modern train requires only about fifteen relatively pollution-free horsepower per passenger to perhaps ten times that for a pollution-belching auto" (December 1, 1970, p. 47).

The great premium placed on getting people places in an automobile is invoked whenever we hear controversies about the building of additional freeways through cities, and the destruction of the buildings within the neighborhoods in their path. Taking heed of this problem, Governor Francis W. Sargent of Massachusetts ordered a one-year moratorium on the construction of a major expressway near Boston on February 11, 1970, and in a forthright statement said:

> Are the roads we are building too costly—not merely in dollars, but in what they cost us in demolished homes, disrupted communities, dislocated lives, pollution of the air, damage to our environment? The answer is yes—they are too costly (*Boston Globe*, February 12, 1970, p. 1).

The automobile, after all, is a great convenience. It is one of the supreme inventions of all time, along with the airplane, radio, telephone, and television. What went wrong that some of these problems were not foreseen?

ANTICIPATING AND SHAPING THE FUTURE

Predictions about the future, even by eminent men, experts of their time, often make for humorous reading. In his fascinating book *Profiles of the Future*, Arthur C. Clarke (1965) quotes a leading astronomer, as having made the following argument, *after* the first airplanes had started to fly:

> The popular mind often pictures gigantic flying machines speeding across the Atlantic and carrying innumerable passengers in a way analogous to our modern steamships. . . . It seems safe to say that such ideas must be wholly visionary, and even if a machine could get across with one or two passengers the expense would be prohibitive to any but the capitalist who could own his own yacht (p. 3).

Another illustration in Clarke (1965) is the scientist who, in 1926, wrote as follows:

> This foolish idea of shooting at the moon is an example of the absurd length to which vicious specialization will carry scientists working in thought-tight compartments. Let us critically examine the proposal. For a projectile entirely to escape the gravitation of the earth, it needs a velocity of 7 miles a second. The thermal energy of a gramme at this speed is 15,180 calories. . . . The energy of our most violent explosive—nitro-glycerine—is less than 1500 calories per gramme. Consequently, even had the explosive nothing to carry, it has only one-tenth of the energy necessary to escape the earth . . . hence the proposition appears to be basically impossible . . . (p. 4).

The lesson from these examples is that even capable scientists may operate with the limited assumptions and intellectual resources of their time. In the framework of conventional modes of thought, we are all handicapped somewhat in making an imaginative leap to the future. Each of us carries the imprint of our own times and the "conventional wisdom," in Galbraith's phrase (1958), which holds sway.

A widespread assumption is that, in the future, the same factors operating today will operate, but with newer features. This assumes a developmental sequence, with continuity, and everything neatly in place, so that the future grows out of the past and the new substitutes for the old. This view has been called into question by C. A. Doxiadis (1968), the eminent architect and city planner, who says, "It is time to break the association in our minds between 'new' and 'right' and to clarify that 'new' has no meaning when it simply breaks with the past, but only when it makes a positive contribution to the future" (p. 29). A number of concrete instances come to mind. On balance, is the Super-Sonic Transport a contribution to the future? What about the disposable bottle?

A relatively recent effort has been under way to do more by way of predicting and intervening in the development of the future (e.g. de-Jouvenal, 1967; Heilbroner, 1961; Toffler, 1970). In September 1967 the First International Future Research Congress was held in Oslo. The basic propellant in the "futurist's" view is the sense of urgency that what is done now, or not done, affects the *alternative* futures available to us. The conventional wisdom that the future unfolds by itself is drastically out of line with the dawning awareness of the true plight of human affairs.

A research program at the Massachusetts Institute of Technology, under the direction of Dennis Meadows, is exploring the consequences on the future of various alternative actions. Computer projections are generated from the interrelationship calculated for several factors which influence the human predicament, such as population, natural resources, and capital investment. Though admittedly speculative, these projections reveal multivariate outcomes regarding pollution and the quality of life. Figure 8.8 shows one set of curves generated for a two-hundred-year span, employing actual data to date with projections based on the assumption of an immediate 20 per cent increase in capital investment to reverse the apparent decline in the "quality of life."

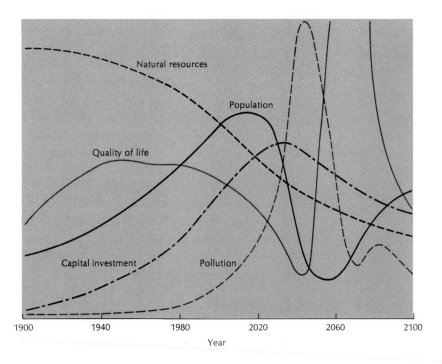

Figure 8.8: Projection of one "future" based on a computer analysis of the interrelationships among several factors governing such outcomes as the "quality of life." This projection assumes an immediate 20 per cent increase in capital investment to stem the decline in the quality of life, and indicates that it will continue to decline without a reduction in population growth, or until pollution and other factors themselves impose a curb on population. (Adapted from *The New York Times*, December 6, 1970.)

Although this factor is elusive in precise measurement terms, it is one that can be roughly gauged. Various *social indicators* have been proposed which might, in the aggregate, give a quantitative reading of shifts in quality of life. Indeed, a recent project in the Department of Health, Education, and Welfare was devoted to a probing consideration of these indicators. If efficacious, they could provide a picture of changes in the social psychological sector analogous to the "cost of living index" in the economic sector, without of course suggesting that these are totally separate. Unquestionably, economic considerations exert some influence on personal satisfaction. The point, however, is to provide a richer fund of data regarding *social psychological* correlates of change.

The usual models of change, including those involved in technical innovations, operate with a simple cause-effect linkage. Broader effects including second-order consequences, are usually left unconsidered. Speaking to this point, Bauer (1966) contends that a technical development is often judged as a response to a rather specific problem and that its implementation is seen in "purely technical" terms without regard to its wider ramifications. Bauer notes:

> Technical changes have proved historically to be particularly explosive sources of second-order social, economic, and political changes that were never envisioned. This arises largely because at the beginning technical developments tend to be viewed in a rather restricted context. They are seen as an answer to an agreed problem, and tend to be judged in terms of their adequacy in solving that problem. Probably the most dramatic example of this in modern times has been the development of potent insecticides, which were only later found to have profound effects on the ecological cycles of man and beast. Similarly, there is the instance of the innocuous substitution of detergents for soap. It was scarcely anticipated . . . that streams would be contaminated to the point of destroying their fish life (1966, p. 4).

The technological side of treating problems is bad enough, but social technology is even more potent in its unanticipated potential for disruptive reverberations. Not the least among the examples of these effects are social programs launched with great fanfare that encourage unrealistic expectations, leading to frustration, especially where they have encouraged a high degree of commitment. Wildavsky (1969) has provided this despairing comment about the expectancies sometimes raised in otherwise well-intentioned community action programs:

> A recipe for violence: Promise a lot; deliver a little. Lead people to believe they will be much better off, but let there be no dramatic improvement. Try a variety of small programs, each interesting but marginal in impact and severely underfinanced. Avoid any attempt at solution remotely comparable in size to the dimensions of the problem you are trying to solve. . . . Get some poor people involved in local decision-making, only to discover that there is not enough at stake to be worth bothering about (p. ii).

Looked at as a process involving not just a bit of tinkering here and there, shaping the future means *planning*, and with a view toward the *system* of relationships at work. Ultimately, the ability to affect change on a small or large scale, depends upon an adequate "model"—in the sense of a representation of the variables at work—in the broader system within which one operates. Selznick (1957) has said that the leader requires a "system perspective," which allows him to see the totality of the enterprise with particular reference to the achievement of values and goals. W. F. Whyte (1967), in the same vein, holds that:

> . . . many organizational problems arise because the leaders of those organizations are attempting to apply to the human problems they face an inappropriate theoretical model of organization. I also believe that most men carry in their heads an extremely limited repertoire of models. They could act with more understanding and effectiveness if they made their own models explicit and if they could become more flexible and inventive in developing and applying models to the problems they face (p. 22).

Social psychology's conceptions of structure, of norms and roles, of value hierarchies, suggest stability in varying ways. To translate those constructs to an appreciation of change processes requires a broader sense of Man's capability in exerting influence on his environment. Some of this is available through principles of group dynamics, to be considered in Chapter 13.

We are not, therefore, totally bound by our culture. Indeed, a pluralistic society affords numerous variations on the modal culture, some strikingly different from one another. Culture is an organic thing which changes and grows. We live by its dictates and are influenced by it, often in ways we barely fathom. But we can also influence it, and change it by the introduction of innovations and the alteration of tradition. Most importantly for our purposes here, culture can be studied and understood rather than uncritically accepted.

Communication is a central feature of culture. Through processes of communication, Man succeeds in influencing others and in transmitting that influence through succeeding generations. This human propensity is uniquely represented in language, found in all human cultures and the topic of the next chapter.

SUMMARY

A society's culture consists of the relationships and social arrangements which are passed on and institutionalized to handle routinely the characteristic problems of the society. These problems include survival needs as well as the requirements that arise from unique historical, geographic, and other environmental features such as natural resources, climate, and the characteristics of the neighboring societies. Teaching and protecting the young, implementing governmental forms, kinship systems, and the transmission of property exemplify major areas of life over which culture exerts considerable influence.

Man depends upon culture for a coherent outlook and approach toward life. The demands of culture are normally accepted as usual and proper. By providing social reality, the essential *psychological effect* of culture is to influence a society's members toward distinctive ways of thinking and acting.

The major features of *tradition, symbolization,* and *integration* characterize all cultures. Culture may also be partitioned into its *explicit* level, which refers to directly observable behavior and broad patterns of life, and its *implicit* level composed of the attitudes and values held by the members of a society.

The psychological effects of culture can be categorized under the headings of *value orientations, perceptual functioning,* and *social expectancies.* The values of a society are represented in individual actions, such as eating practices or monogamy, which have significant symbolic importance. Society depends upon widespread agreement on the cultural imperatives represented in values, although these may sometimes be in conflict. Anthropologists have characterized various cultures in terms of their dominant values. Values may be variously construed in different cultures, as exemplified by a desire for a "decent standard of living."

Perceptual functioning has been found to vary from culture to culture. This is indicative of the *functional salience, familiarity,* and *systems of communication* that different cultures emphasize in experience. Studies of susceptibility to *illusions,* and responses to the *Rorschach Ink-Blot Test* have dominated such cross-cultural research.

Cultural norms refer to those broad patterns of conduct which are expected in a society. In anthropological terms, these are often divided into: *folkways* and *usages, conventions,* and *mores* and *taboos.* These norms vary from those of least importance to those of greatest importance for the preservation of society. Some behaviors are significant for their symbolic *form* and not for their actual *content.*

In social psychological terms, norms and roles are in the nature of *social expectancies* which individuals share in their psychological fields. *Roles* refer especially to those particular expectancies regarding appropriate behavior for a person occupying a position in a given situation. One of these expectancies is for *status congruence,* which means a matching of the value of a person's attributes in one dimension with his position on another.

The persistence and *continuity of culture* arise from the attachment of individuals to the familiar and congenial patterns to which they have become accustomed. Such patterns are transmitted through significant social institutions such as the family and are strongly bolstered by language and other symbolic processes. Social change leading to a shift in a culture is likely to occur where new alternatives are perceived, and especially where necessity is widely recognized. *Cultural contact* and *technological innovation* considerably enhance the prospect for social change by making alternatives accessible. More than merely accepting change, increasing attention is being directed toward anticipating and shaping the future. This requires *planning* within an adequate model of the *system* of relationships at work.

SUGGESTED READINGS

From E. P. Hollander and R. G. Hunt (Eds.) *Current perspectives in social psychology.* (3rd ed.) New York: Oxford University Press, 1971.

11. George Peter Murdock: *How culture changes*
12. Milton M. Gordon: *The nature of assimilation and the theory of the melting pot*
60. Chris Argyris: *Being human and being organized*

SELECTED REFERENCES

Bredemeier, H. C., & Stephenson, R. M. *The analysis of social systems.* New York: Holt, Rinehart & Winston, 1962.

Cantril, H. *The pattern of human concerns.* New Brunswick, N. J.: Rutgers Univer. Press, 1965.

*Free, L. A., & Cantril, H. *The political beliefs of Americans.* New Brunswick, N.J.: Rutgers Univer. Press, 1967. (Paperback published by Simon and Schuster.)

*Goldschmidt, W. *Man's way.* Cleveland: World Publ. Co., 1959. (Paperback published by Holt, Rinehart, and Winston.)

*Hall, E. T. *The silent language.* Garden City, N. Y.: Doubleday, 1959.

*Heilbroner, R. *The future as history.* New York: Grove Press, Evergreen Edition, 1961.

*Kluckhohn, C. *Mirror for man.* New York: McGraw-Hill, 1949.

*Mack, R. *Transforming America: patterns of social change.* New York: Random house, 1967.

*Segall, M., Campbell, D. T., & Herskovits, M. *The influence of culture in visual perception.* New York: Bobbs-Merrill, 1966.

*Shapiro, H. L. (Ed.) *Man, culture & society.* New York: Oxford Univer. Press, 1956.

Toffler, A. *Future shock.* New York: Random House, 1970.

Williams, R. M. *American society: a sociological interpretation.* (2nd ed.) New York: Knopf, 1960.

9

Language and social communication

Language is a strikingly distinctive attribute of Man. Though animals of different species have means of communicating with one another, human relationships uniquely depend upon the subtleties of symbolic communication through words. Studies of infrahuman communication indicate that it is mainly gestural and largely predetermined by genetic factors (Scott, 1953). For example, the "bee dance" observed by von Frisch (1955) appears to be an elaborate means for signifying the location of food by patterned behavior. Humans, on the other hand, acquire spoken language and meanings associated with words through a process of learning. As Brown (1958) pointedly observes, "man does not develop language if he grows up among animals or in isolation. Language is acquired by the human being born into a linguistic community" (p. 193).

By allowing Man to deal conceptually with things in another place and time, rather than being bound to the here and now, language gives scope and dimension to life. It provides the means to have even the darkest recesses of the past opened through words across time. Indeed, the instrumentality of language is vital in the transmission of culture and in the functioning of society. Language provides a significant symbolic vehicle by which individuals cope with their environment, including the other persons with whom they are linked in social interaction. Underscoring this function, Morris (1946) says that ". . . a very widespread opinion has arisen that society . . . is dependent upon signs, and specifically upon language signs for its existence and perpetuation" (p. 205).

While language exists in all human societies, it has a highly diversi- fied character around the globe. Depending upon how one defines a unitary language, there are at least hundreds of major languages in the world, with several dozen in use in the Indian subcontinent alone. These are sufficiently different from one another so that it would be impossible for humans of different societies to communicate with one another through their mother tongues. The wider use of Man's crown- ing capacity is, therefore, severely handicapped by the diverse pattern of language over the globe. In this regard, Miller (1964) has said:

> *Every human group* that anthropologists have studied has spoken a language. The language always has a lexicon and a grammar. The lexicon is not a haphazard collection of vocalizations, but is highly organized; it always has pronouns, means for dealing with time, space, and number, words to represent true and false, the basic concepts necessary to propositional logic. The grammar has distinguishable levels of structure, some phonological some syn- tactic. . . . The syntax always specifies rules for grouping ele- ments sequentially into phrases and sentences, rules governing normal intonation, rules for transforming some types of sentences into other types (p. 34).

Language is not, however, the only means by which individuals com- municate. Messages can be transmitted through physical symbols as well as by the gestures that individuals display to one another, includ- ing especially the formal symbols contained in "sign language." Lan- guage, on the other hand, has the distinctive advantage of portability. Not only can we communicate across time and space through the written words of a language, but we can also think thoughts and antici- pate future events as a basis for action. What is more, we can be in- fluenced by language.

The social psychologist is concerned with the study of language and its acquistion especially because it has *functional* features which affect the individual's perceptions and motivations in the psychological field and it has *directive* features which influence social responses in a stim- ulus sense. In other terms, we may say that language is a tool for the individual's thoughts and also a medium of social influence. Both of these features are emphasized in this chapter. We begin, however, with some consideration of the nature of language.

The nature and basis of language

By its very nature, language is social. Carroll (1953) defines language as consisting of learned responses determined by social interaction. Sapir (1921) considers that "Language is a purely human and non-instinctive method of communicating ideas, emotions, and desires by means of a system of voluntarily produced symbols" (p. 8). Hayakawa (1964) views language as a system of agreements among human beings which allow various noises produced to systematically stand for specified happenings in their nervous system. In this sense, it "mediates" between experience and action.

Two points in particular stand out in these definitions. One of these is the consideration that language is acquired from contact with other human beings. The other is the fact that language consists of symbolized meanings which are sources of stimulation and mediators of response. Moreover, these meanings can exist in thought as well as in spoken and in written form (Osgood, 1952).

In differentiating an "authentic language" from other modes of communication, Terwilliger (1968) says that it is more than speech or communication by symbols; it must have the potentiality for dealing with things or states of affairs which are not immediately present, and for giving rise to inappropriate or "wrong" behaviors (p. 4). On these grounds, animal communication, such as the elaborate "bee dance," does not qualify. As Terwilliger puts it:

> . . . no bee was ever seen dancing about yesterday's honey, not to mention tomorrow's. . . . Their communications are never wrong, and they never communicate when there is no honey. By this criterion, they can be said *not* to have a language. Bees do communicate, however, which shows that language and communication are *not* identical. Communication is but one of the possible uses of language; and language is but one of the media through which communication may take place (p. 6, italics supplied).

From a psychological standpoint, language is at first a set of vocalized stimuli which we encounter in infancy. People peer at us and utter sounds which subsequently become associated with the quality of that experience, whether pleasant or unpleasant. The reinforcement position contends that in this fashion we then learn to relate certain sounds to the people about us and the kind of experiences they provide, such as feeding us. This process of learning occurs within a "verbal community" (Skinner, 1957). With time, it evokes responses to these stimuli which are likely to produce desired effects. Sounds then come to stand for categories of experience.

Another position, represented by Chomsky (1964, 1968), takes language to be a uniquely human capacity which grows out of a predetermined generative system. This system is the structural basis for what Chomsky considers to be a "universal grammar" underlying all languages. Lenneberg (1967) sees this as the basis for language acquisition, once the child reaches the appropriate stage of "readiness."

For the individual, language becomes a way of defining experience, with significant perceptual consequences. Words stand for things and we find it hard to conceive that it should be otherwise. If something is "cold," it has the attribute of coldness not identically conveyed by any other word. Should a child discover that in French "cold" is "froid," this may strike him initially as very strange and even silly.

Often adults appear to take seriously the "inherent" meanings of words, as though they spoke for themselves, if only repeated often enough and loudly enough. The traveler trying to make sense to a foreigner unfamiliar with his language will often repetitively pronounce his words more slowly and more loudly in the vain expectation that the foreigner should then understand and act. Imagine someone shouting at you what sounds phonetically like "sue yoke"—Turkish for "water's all gone"—and consider your own perplexity.

THEORIES OF LANGUAGE ORIGINATION

How Man came to use language continues to be an issue that is largely unresolved. As Pei (1960) indicates, this is not because linguists have been without theories, but that they are still unproven and in some instances unprovable. He says, "If there is one thing in which all linguists are fully agreed, it is that the problem of the origin of human speech is still unsolved" (p. 18).

There are several theories concerning the origin of language. Among the more common of these is the onomatopoeic theory, sometimes referred to as the "bow-wow" theory. It holds that language arose as an imitation of natural sounds. Thus, when a dog barks he makes a sound which the human speaker imitates as "bow-wow." Similarly, other words imitate sounds as in "hum," "gong," "bang," "slop," and "giggle." The difficulties with this theory are that only a small number of words within any language have this kind of onomatopoeic quality, the same supposedly natural noise is referred to differently in different languages, and such words have little to do with the abstract quality of language.

A second common theory holds that language arose from interjections, such as "oh" or "ah," that people made as a response to surprise, fear, pleasure, or pain. It is difficult, however, to see how human language could have been built up to such a variegated degree on the basis of a very few sounds of this kind, though it has been observed that animals appear to use such sounds as a simple form of communication.

A third theory proposes that there was some relationship between mouth movements and hand gestures. It has been suggested that the first regularized languages were based on a kind of sign language. At some stage, this theory contends, Man discovered that though his hands were not free, he might still communicate certain signs by means of vocalization. Eventually, the advantages of speech over gestures became apparent.

While each of these theories has some plausibility, they are all merely descriptive of an aspect of language. They do not help to understand how it might be that certain sounds came to represent persons, things, events, or concepts. Furthermore, the dispersion of different languages raises still other questions regarding the seemingly infinite variability of language.

THE EVOLUTION AND DISPERSION OF LANGUAGE

Languages persist and have the kind of continuity associated with culture, but they also may be altered through the processes of change in terms of cultural innovation. Pei (1960) gives an example of how linguistic change affects reality in the fact that the ancient Greek comic poets used the Greek letters BEH to signify a sheep's cry. While the sheep has not changed its cry, these letters have since been altered in their value so that in modern Greek they are actually pronounced as "vee" (p. 16). He says further:

> . . . all languages change in due course of time. A modern English speaker encounters some difficulty with the English of Shakespeare, far more with the English of Chaucer, and has to handle the English of King Alfred as a foreign tongue. A French speaker finds the 14th century language of François Villon a little difficult, has considerable trouble with the 12th century *Chanson de Roland,* barely recognizes the tongue of the 9th century oaths of Strasbourg, and if he goes further back has to handle the documents he finds from the Latin rather than from the French standpoint . . . (p. 21).

When language changes this is often related to cultural contact, as well as to the modeling influence of an innovator—in the past, such as a king in his court, who is imitated by his courtiers. Shakespeare influenced English by many of his unique coinages, some of which are so thoroughly commonplace today that they may strike us as clichés. Among them are these:

> "Strange bedfellows" (*The Tempest*)
> "Cold comfort" (*King John*)
> "Poor but honest" (*All's Well That Ends Well*)
> "The milk of human kindness" (*Macbeth*)
> "Not slept one wink" (*Cymbeline*)
> "In my mind's eye" (*Hamlet*)
> "Men of few words" (*Henry V*)
> "As good luck would have it" (*Merry Wives of Windsor*).

Contrary to popular belief, languages may develop in the direction of greater simplicity, in the sense of dropping more complex elements, such as gender in articles—e.g. the French *le* and *la,* or the German *der, die, das.* These have entirely disappeared from English. In modern Dutch, the neuter form is still used, but gender in articles has otherwise been eliminated.

Though it has evolved as a highly sophisticated language, English today is far less complicated in structure than many so-called "primitive tongues."

Even the most primitive tribesmen in the rain forests of the Amazon or the gibber plains of Australia have complex and luxuriant language, each the product of incomputable millennia of linguistic evolution, each endowed with its own intrinsic conventions of sound, sense, and structure (i.e., phonetics, vocabulary, and grammar) peculiar to itself and different from all others (Barnett, 1967, p. 43).

Among the most difficult languages in the world are those spoken by the very same Australian aborigines, and the Eskimos. For simple constructions, "Basic English" (Ogden, 1934) provides a core of less than 1000 words which can be used in simple noun-verb combinations with which one can say almost anything required in routine, non-technical conversation. For instance, the eighteen vital verbs in Basic English are: be, come, do, get, give, go, have, keep, let, make, may, put, say, see, seem, send, take, and will. These can be combined with prepositions to provide a quite large range of meanings as with "take up" for lift, begin, consider, "take off" for leave, remove, or ascend, and "take in" for welcome, listen, or feed on.

The upsurge of English as a widely spoken language is a comparatively recent development. Various estimates place the figure of primary speakers of English at approximately 300 million people, or about one in ten. Almost twice that number, in addition, are said to be reachable by it, in some degree. Therefore, nearly 30 per cent of the earth's population has some level of capability in the use of English, and a good part of this transformation has occurred in the last thirty years, since the time of World War II. This is reflected, for instance, in the fact that English is the language of international aviation. In addition, many English words, not just of a technical nature—such as "jet" or "missile"—have passed into other languages. Thus, contemporary terms like "supermarket," "cocktail party," "jukebox," "parking," and "teen-ager" have been absorbed into French, to the dismay of some.

In 1963, René Etiêmble, a French professor of literature, authored a best-seller entitled *Parlez-vous Franglais?* In it he estimated that many thousands of English words and technical terms had become part of everyday French during the preceding decade and, at that rate, that the French language would cease to exist in several more decades. This purist concern with the "vulgarization" of language is by no means confined to French. Some Spanish scholars, too, are among those who have been alarmed at the rapid strides English words and idioms have made, even when they are merely literal translations, as in "perrito caliente" for hot dog.

The incursions made by English as a more widely used language are neither an unmixed blessing nor an unmitigated evil. Aside from the problem of maintaining the purity of other tongues, there is no doubt that having a vehicle by which many more people can communicate— whether it be French, Chinese, Russian, or English—is of enormous utility.

The structure and form of language

All languages have three qualities which give them distinctiveness. They are: *syntax*, which is structure, in the sense of "grammar"; *semantics*, which is the meaning system; and *phonology*, the sound pattern. Rather than be separate entities, these qualities interrelate, and their relationship has been a matter of a good deal of interest. Chomsky's attention to syntactic features of language extends, for example, to the "deep structure" of sentences, quite beyond their "surface structure."

Two sentences may have the same phonology, at the surface level, but different meanings at the deep level. An illustration is provided in the sentence "Boys like sports more than girls." Phonologically, and in terms of surface structure, it is a single sentence; but, in terms of deep structure it is two. One may mean that "Boys like sports and girls like sports, but boys like sports more than girls do." The other may mean that "Boys like sports and boys like girls, but boys like sports more than they like girls." Chomsky (1957) has devised a procedure for the analysis of sentences which he calls "transformational grammar." It proceeds from the assumption that all sentences have a phrase structure, i.e. a "noun phrase" and a "verb phrase." Then, according to a precise *set of rules* his procedure involves a recasting of each part of a sentence, one at a time, as part of the analysis of meaning.

Phonology also plays tricks with meanings. The words "raise" and "raze" sound exactly the same, though they are precisely opposite in meaning; semantically, they are antonyms. Two sentences that are identical in sound, each with one of these words and everything else the same, could produce diametrically opposed meanings which would be distinguishable only by the context, or possibly by the inflection.

The "word" is the most elemental unit of language which communicates meaning. We have all been taught in grammar that it can be a "noun," a "verb," a "pronoun," or any number of other syntactic parts of speech. Yet, we do not need to know the parts of speech of words to speak a language. Indeed, what we do in the use of the language may violate the "rules" of grammar. An individual may use varying "grammars" depending on different forms and settings, such as a telephone conversation as against a letter, even to the same person (Terwilliger, 1968, pp. 214-216).

What we do learn about words and structure in our mother language may not conform to the rules in other languages. A great number of languages, for example, do without articles entirely, including Slavic tongues. In many languages no sharp distinction is made between nouns and verbs. They may be part of the same word, as in Japanese. Turkish, as is true of Latin also, is an agglutinative language in which word endings are added so that a long word by our standards may be a whole sentence. Thus, a single word is used in Turkish to ask, "Are you going?"

Many of the American Indian languages combine the noun with the verb so that the phrase "the light flashes" might be rendered with more economy as "flashing." The use of prepositions, which we have in abundance in our language, is very often handled by endings or "postpositions" in other languages. The "prepositional maze" in English is humorously illustrated by the story of the precocious child whose mother had promised to read him a book at bedtime. When she arrived in his room with the wrong one, he said, "Mama, what did you bring that book that I didn't want to be read out of up for?"

Though awkward, we have no trouble discerning the meaning of this sentence. And this of course is the essence of language—that it convey meaning. The study of meaning is called *semantics*. It encompasses both written and spoken language, though these have quite different characteristics as we shall see. As we have said, words are the major semantic units of language and they combine to create phrases, sentences, and broader statements intended to convey thoughts.

In our language words are written by letters from an alphabet. Since language is essentially an arbitrary means of symbolizing thoughts and communication, there are many alphabets, in the sense of different ways of representing things and actions. The earliest form of language, which still prevails in Chinese and Japanese, relies on pictorial-like symbols. Hieroglyphs in ancient Egypt also were used in this way—as a *semantic system*. The alphabet, on the other hand, is basically a *phonological system*, with "phonemes," that are minimal pronounceable units, fitted together.

Though we generally think of spoken language as a predecessor to written language, Brown (1958) says that it is by no means certain that speech is a more ancient form of language because the first true languages may have been these representational systems using pictures to convey commonly accepted meanings. Side by side with these, however, there may have been spoken languages where common sounds also held such meanings. Thus, the word for the actual "sun" would be uttered when speaking the picture "sun" aloud.

The alphabet which grew out of these representational systems constituted a considerable advance over them as a flexible phonological system. The origin of the word "alphabet" comes from the early Semitic letters used by the Hebrews and Phoenicians. "Aleph" originally meant ox and our modern letter *A* at one time was a drawing of the head of an ox. "Beth" meant house and the original picture for *B* represented a house. It still does; if you pass a Jewish Temple named "Beth Israel" its name means "House of Israel."

The Greeks adapted this Semitic alphabet and, in what was a comparatively short span of time as history goes, it was absorbed into what we know today as the Roman alphabet. A version of this Greek adaptation, the Cyrillic alphabet, is employed today in Bulgaria and Russia, where it was introduced with Eastern Orthodox Christianity by St. Cyril in the ninth century. He modified the Greek alphabet somewhat, with some extra letters from Hebrew, to handle Slavic sounds. These alterations lead us to find, for example, that the Greek letter rho, which looks like our capital P, has an /R/ sound, and that the modern Russian letter which looks like H is actually pronounced with our /N/ sound.

As long as there is an agreed-upon pronunciation, or phonetic, for letters or combinations of letters, they represent a method for vocalizing words and broader statements. This makes it possible to go from written to spoken language and back again. Therefore, writing involves symbols put together to form another symbol.

The written and spoken forms of language are by no means perfectly congruent, though this varies quite a bit from language to language. The smallest discernible units of speech are called *phonemes.* Thus, various combinations of letters can yield a given phoneme, just as a group of phonemes may be necessary to sound a letter. In English, for example, we employ the two letters *t* and *h* to yield the single phoneme /th/. On the other hand, the letter *x* is often pronounced as if it were "*gz*," as in *exit, exert, exhaust,* and many others.

A major trouble in learning language is the fact that letters and phonemes do not conform on a regular basis. English is full of unsounded letters as in the *k* and *gh* appearing in the word "knight." In its original Anglo-Saxon form it is believed the word was fully pronounced including the sounds /k/ and a gutteral /gh/, which has since passed out of English, but is like the modern German *Knecht.* Furthermore, the sounding of letter combinations is irregular as is seen in the three words *though, through,* and *rough,* each of which ends with a distinctive phonemic sound. Also, there is confusion because a given letter, say a vowel, may be sounded differently. Consider, for example, the pronunciation of the letter *a* in the words *father, woman,* and *nature.*

When we sometimes ask why Johnnie can't read, we might well bear in mind Brown's (1958) incisive comment that:

> There are great psychological economies in a phonetic writing such as our alphabet, economies that have caused phonetic writing to prevail over the older representational writings. However, the alphabet used for writing English has come to be a very irregular phonetic system. Some say that its irregularities are so exasperating that children ought to be taught to read English without any direct tuition in the sound values of the alphabet. Others say that this is tantamount to returning us to a hieroglyphic writing since it deprives children of the advantages that inhere in a phonetic writing (p. 17).

Despite the apparent chaos, and the obvious difficulties presented for the novitiate to English, Chomsky and Halle (1968) contend that English has considerable regularity of pronunciation, once a speaker is sufficiently exposed to it. Furthermore, in its defense, one should bear in mind that English has borrowed an amazingly large number of words from other languages over the centuries. Words of Latin root abound in English, some directly from Latin, through the Romans, and others through French, from the Normans. Many words are from Greek, including short, simple ones like *elastic* and *idiot,* as well as a wide assortment of others, such as *apostrophe, panorama,* and *symphony.* Though the etymology of many words is obscure, *tobacco, tomato, chocolate,* and *raccoon* are among those absorbed from American Indian languages. *So long* is from the Arabic *salaam* and the Hebrew form *shalom. Paradise* and *shawl* are from Persian, *cargo* and *ranch* are from Spanish, *piano* and *umbrella* from Italian, *gin* from Dutch, and *alcohol* from Arabic. And these are just a smattering of examples. Hence, the irregularities of spelling and pronunciation in English are attributable in some measure to its wealth of diverse borrowings from other languages.

Figure 9.1: The Initial Teaching Alphabet (I.T.A.) with illustrations of its use in a children's primer. (From *The New York Times,* July 19, 1964.)

In an attempt to deal with these complexities of sounded English, a device called the "Initial Teaching Alphabet" was developed some years ago by Pitman. Essentially, its 44 letters duplicate the actual phonemes in English. These are shown in Figure 9.1. Now being used in many school systems, this alphabet is said to be far easier for children to use in learning to read. Furthermore, the transition to the normal letters of the alphabet is supposedly quite smooth. Generally speaking, the reading of written language is among the most difficult tasks posed for the child.

Acquisition of language

The best estimates indicate that the English language contains anywhere from 50,000 to 100,000 words. Depending upon the criteria employed, it has been variously estimated that by the time he is four, an average child knows as many as 5000 words, in the specific sense of recognizing and acting on them, whether or not he can employ them himself. Though some authorities indicate that this is too high an estimate, it is nonetheless indicative of the massive learning process which occurs in early life. Again in terms of recognition, the average adult is said to know 35,000 words. It should be emphasized, however, that for every ten words that he can recognize, only one may be part of the functional vocabulary of the individual.

That all normal infants manage this tremendous task of acquiring language is truly phenomenal. Commenting on this process, Miller (1964) says:

> Human language must be such that a child can acquire it. He acquires it, moreover, from parents who have no idea how to explain it to him. No careful schedule of rewards for correct or punishments for incorrect utterances is necessary. It is sufficient that the child be allowed to grow up naturally in an environment where language is used. The child's achievement seems all the more remarkable when we recall the speed with which he accomplishes it and the limitations of his intelligence in other respects. It is difficult to avoid an impression that infants are little machines specially designed by nature to perform this particular learning task (p. 35).

The learning of words is only a part of the acquisition of language. Chomsky (1964, 1968) and Lenneberg (1967) are among those who consider grammar the more basic, species-specific characteristic. Grammar provides the structure within which words are arranged to create unique meanings. While we can memorize the meaning of a word, we cannot memorize the endless variety of sentences. Brown (1969) says that a sentence is comprehensible in terms of an implicit knowledge of a grammatical pattern, as follows:

> In *The New York Times* of August 3, 1969 we find the sentence "The moon and President Nixon's trip around the world dominate the headlines." That is not a sentence any of us has ever before heard or read, and so its meaning was certainly not stored in memory. However, the sentence is comprehensible to everyone who has in memory the meanings of the individual words and of the grammatical patterns in which they are arranged. . . . The meanings of sentences are created compositionally from words and patterns and the patterns are grammar (p. 5).

NATIVISTIC CONCEPTIONS

Chomsky (1964, 1968) adopts a "nativistic position" that this pattern, or structure, exists as a *universal grammar* and that all humans are born with a propensity toward it. The acquisition of a *specific grammar* is seen by him to be a function of a critical period of development in which the readiness or capacity to speak a language is "released" by appropriate stimulation from others who speak it (Chomsky, 1964).

Lenneberg (1967) asserts that language is the "manifestation of species-specific cognitive propensities." His biological orientation leads him to conclude that the basic capacity for language is a function of physical maturation, though certain environmental conditions must be present to make it possible for language to unfold. He says:

> Maturation brings cognitive processes to a state that we may call *language-readiness*. The organism now requires certain raw materials from which it can shape building blocks for its own language development. The situation is somewhat analogous to the relationship between nourishment and growth. The food that the growing individual takes in as architectural raw material must be chemically broken down and reconstituted before it may enter the synthesis that produces tissues and organs. The information on how the organs are to be structured does not come in the food but is latent in the individual's own cellular components. The raw ma-

terial for the individual's language synthesis is the language spoken by the adults surrounding the child. The presence of the raw material seems to function like a releaser for the developmental language synthesizing process (1968, p. 375).

However, in a critique of this position, Terwilliger (1968) points out that, taken literally, "readiness" would preclude the learning of a second language if the individual failed to learn it during the "critical period," say between the second and fourth years of life. There are obviously other psychological factors involved, beyond propensities and critical period conceptions alone. Nevertheless humans appear to be uniquely equipped for language.

In contrast to humans, no matter how much animals are encouraged, they manage only a few primitive words, and no recognizable grammar. This is despite the fact that some chimpanzees have made notable, and even uncanny progress in this direction. The Kelloggs (1933) raised a female chimpanzee, Gua, with their own son, Donald. She arrived at their home at the age of seven and one-half months and was treated just as was Donald, then two months older. There was no special effort made to teach Gua to talk, but she was exposed to the same environment of human speech as was Donald. Gua at first comprehended more directions than did Donald, but at nine months lagged behind him. Furthermore, she never employed more than two utterances that could be considered to have a semantic quality, and even these were actually cries characteristic of chimpanzees. One was a kind of "food bark" that meant "yes," and the other was an "oo-oo" cry that meant "no." Cathy Hayes and her husband raised a female chimpanzee, Viki, from the age of six weeks. In contrast to the Kelloggs, they made a deliberate effort to teach her to talk. In her report (1951) after three years, she indicates that Viki had learned to say "papa," "mama," and "cup," but only with imperfect articulation at best.

Recently, the Gardners (1969) have reported on their attempts to teach a chimpanzee to employ sign language as a means of "talking." They reasoned that the previous attempts to have chimpanzees use language had emphasized the articulation of speech, which requires capacities for vocalization these animals might not possess; since chimpanzees appear to have dexterity in motor performance, the Gardners saw this as an avenue by which their chimpanzee, Washoe, might communicate. They have been teaching her signs since June of

1966, when she was slightly under a year old, and in their recent report (1969) the Gardners note her progress in putting signs together in strings to convey more complex meanings. This is an exciting prospect, but all the evidence is not in, and as Brown (1970) has observed it will be an open question as to whether Washoe actually uses language until she employs the equivalent of sentences displaced in reference from her immediate context (p. 229). If, for instance, a dog needs to "go out," and he brushes his master's leg, makes head movements toward the door, and then starts off in that direction, he is not speaking a language, even if he accompanies this activity with vocalizations of a dog-like variety. Strictly speaking, he is communicating by signaling, but not within a syntactic structure, and only with reference to the immediate context.

STAGES IN LANGUAGE LEARNING

There are several stages usually seen in the child's language development. The first stage involves random vocalization with a good deal of cooing, squealing, crying, and gurgling. Several months after birth, a stage of babbling starts which is characterized by the infant's repetition of sounds in a self-stimulating way, i.e. saying the sound and then hearing it stimulates its vocalization again. The next stage, which occurs as the infant nears age one, is one of imitation of the phonetic range the child hears from others about him. The stage of true speech, seen mainly after the first birthday, involves the relatively consistent use of a given sound to mean particular things, as in "mama" and "dada."

Usually this last stage begins with terms that are used very generally first and then proceed to be particularized. For example, the child may use "dada" at first to mean a man and not just the father. As Brown (1958) indicates, the child often uses concrete terms to stand for a general category. This is not for a lack of abstracting ability but the unawareness of an abstract term such as "quadruped" for a four-legged animal, rather than the terms "dog" or "horse."

In terms of this sequence of development, Piaget (1926) offered a distinction between a child's *ego-centric* vs. *social* speech. The former is largely a function of the child's pleasure in expressing himself. Piaget contends that this is characteristic of children through the ages of six or seven. Social speech addresses others in an attempt to influence them.

It is by no means clear that this Piaget distinction is so sharp as was once thought. McCarthy (1929), for example, found that the child's ego-centric speech varied considerably across situations such that it was higher when children were playing with one another than when they were in the company of adults. Vigotsky (1939) found with infants that their so-called "ego-centric" speech was also affected by whether there were others present. He contends that even early babbling speech *is* directed toward social ends insofar as the child believes others show signs of interest and understanding. In the absence of such conditions, he reports a sharp drop-off in these infant monologues. This and other evidence appears to indicate that a very large proportion of a child's speech actually is *social* in its intent (Miller, 1951).

The growth of language facility is not only seen in learning the names of things, but also in putting these words together in utterances which convey sensible meaning. These "strings" of words constitute the beginnings of syntactic usage. Brown (1970) reports data on three children, whose speech was transcribed at various points in early childhood, once they began uttering strings which could be subjected to morphemic analysis. A *morpheme* is one or more phonemes that represent a unit of language content. A word may be more than one morpheme, e.g. "boy" is a morpheme, but "boys" or "boy*ish*" each are two morphemes because of the additional content that the endings provide.

In Figure 9.2, growth in the mean length of utterance in morphemes is shown for these three children. It serves to demonstrate how much variability exists in the rapidity with which children progress in grammatical usage. Eve advanced far more rapidly than Adam and Sarah. By the time she was two, she had reached a mean length of 3.00 morphemes, a level which they did not attain until about a year later.

Sometime during the second year of life, the child arrives at the "naming stage" where he notes and uses the words which distinguish objects and things in his environment. Up to this time the practice has usually been to depend upon pointing and special words for his satisfaction, as in "moo-moo" for milk. This illustrates the early tendency for the infant to classify objects and to use the terms needed to secure them through directive language. This process of communication can proceed, as it does between parents and their infants, by special languages which are privately understood and serve as adequately meaningful communication.

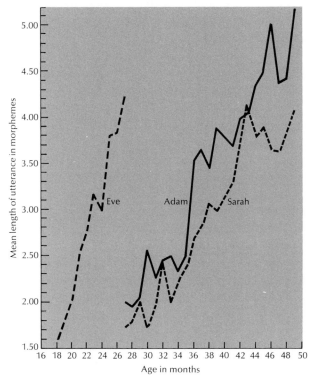

Figure 9.2: Growth in length of utterance with age for three children, Adam, Eve, and Sarah. (Adapted from Brown,1970.)

The early vocalizations of the child have been found to cover a wide range which reproduce phonemes that occur in diverse languages. Bean (1932) says, "One cannot fail to hear all the vowels and consonants, diphthongs, aspirates, sub-vocals, nasals, German umlauts and tongue trills, French throat trills and grunts, and even the Welsh 'l' " (p. 198).

During the babbling phase, the child repeats vowels and then consonants, and then combinations of these, over and over. These sounds become associated with significant happenings for the child, such as obtaining his food, having his parents play with him, being cuddled, and so forth. When the child first utters some "word" by random babbling, the favorable response of a parent who happens to be present then leads to the increased probability of that response recurring. This general phenomenon was dubbed by Thorndike (1943) the "Babble-Luck Theory" of language acquisition.

It is important to understand, however, that there are two kinds of processes at work: one is the actual use of a term and the other is its recognition. When a child responds verbally to his own needs—for example, for milk—and then uses this to stimulate others to provide him with what he requires, he directs the actions of others. On the other hand, he learns to recognize and then respond to the kind of utterances made by those around him, within a verbal community; in that case, he is obliged to act appropriately to a directive statement such as "play quietly."

In one view, indicated earlier, the building of a set of semantic categories with implications for action depends upon the reinforcement properties of the verbal community (Skinner, 1957). Essentially, the child utters some sounds and finds that they elicit positive responses from others, while other sounds are not similarly reinforced. In Mowrer's (1958) conception of learning, this pattern depends upon feelings. He says:

> Words are reproduced if and only if they are first made to *sound good* in the context of affectionate care and attention. Once words, as heard, take on positive emotional connotations, the stage is set for their reproduction, on a purely *autistic*, self-rewarding, non-communicative basis. Then, once imitated, once reproduced, words can thereafter function in the interpersonal, social modes that we call language (p. 151).

For spoken language, the child takes on formal rules in a quite literal way. Berko (1958) has studied this process by the interesting device of giving children pictures with nonsense words and having them indicate responses revealing their knowledge of plurals, past tense, and so on. One of these is shown in Figure 9.3. The text is always read to the child.

She found that 75 per cent of pre-school children, ages four and five, could give the correct ending for the plural form in the example shown in Figure 9.3. For first-graders, age six, 99 per cent could give the correct form. For past tense, she showed a picture of a man exercising. Then the text read: "This is a man who knows how to gling. He is

THIS IS A WUG.

NOW THERE IS ANOTHER ONE.

THERE ARE TWO OF THEM.

THERE ARE TWO _____.

Figure 9.3: The first of the pictures used in a study of children's knowledge of language forms, in this case the plural ending. (From Berko, 1958.)

glinging. He did the same thing yesterday. What did he do yesterday? Yesterday he _____." She found that 63 per cent of the pre-school children and 80 per cent of the first-graders could give the correct form, "glinged."

English, however, is irregular in its endings. Other answers above might have been "glung," "glunged," or "glang." Irregularities also account for the fact that the child may use a form such as "haved" or "had-ed" when using "have" in the past tense.

On the other hand, children enjoy riddles, which are often plays on words, that is, words which are phonologically the same but semantically different. Two favorites, in the circles of youngsters the author frequents, illustrate *three* uses of the word "nut." They go this way:

Q. How do you catch a squirrel?
A. By climbing a tree and acting like a nut.

Q. What's the weakest part of a car?
A. The nut at the steering wheel.

The complexity of language acquisition is also revealed in the problems of written language. The controversies concerning the alphabet, to which we have already referred, actually devolve about whether the letters of the alphabet have sufficient consistency of phonemic value for them to make their sound quality significant. It is not only, however, the problem of going from spoken to written language, or back, that proves vexacious. Another perceptual problem involved in language is revealed by the different forms that many letters of the alphabet take, whether they are in the upper case or lower case printed versions, or in their written versions. This is revealed in Figure 9.4, the point of which is to show how different a given letter might be in form, and what this implies for processes of discrimination and generalization in learning.

The letter *a*, for example, is not even vaguely the same in shape in the three forms shown, just as is the case with *b* and *r*, among other letters in the alphabet. The child, however, must learn to associate a common quality of "being an *a*" despite the differences in the perceptual configuration that is presented. Incidentally, the typical adult reaction to this example is to say that they do look alike, at least at first. The degree to which we have learned to see them as alike makes it very difficult *not* to see them in this fashion.

Figure 9.4: Three letters of the alphabet shown in each of three forms. While the forms are perceived to be alike in sharing a common stimulus property, they are actually quite different; this is seen better when they are shown as mirror images upside down, as at the right.

The written and spoken systems of language exist side by side, but as we have said, they differ in several important ways. In the first place, spoken language is not taught in the same explicit sense as is written language. We tend to reproduce involuntarily those sounds which are like the ones being made by the people around us. Furthermore, in the early learning of our first language, we do not understand enough to be tutored in its intricacies.

While written language is built upon letters and words, the spoken language is built on phonemes, morphemes, and the broader statements of a sentence. By the time we become adept in a spoken language, we no longer speak in terms of words as such, but through these broader statements. Not only does written language not follow spoken language, but we listen for particular things and fail to attend to others in talking with one another. Here is a bit of conversation reproduced in semi-phonetic fashion to illustrate the point:

> First person: "J'eet?"
> Second person: "No."
> First person: "S'koweet."

If we were to reproduce them in their written form, these sentences would be fuller and obviously intelligible to the person knowing English. Consider, however, the problem of first learning to set down these sounds in written form, given the fact that the systems of writing and of talking do not correspond. This can be seen if we think of learning

so = go = tow = dough	cow = how *not* mow
to = do = goo = through	fowl = howl *not* bowl
toes = goes *not* does	mow = sew = though = toe
does = fuzz	though = grow *not* tough
	tough = muff

laughter = after
slaughter = water
later = waiter *not* water

Table 9.1: Examples of some inconsistencies in pronunciation between written and spoken English.

to write French. When we hear the French statement "c'est," for example, we are inclined to write it as it sounds in terms of our English word "say." Within English itself there are many common incongruities of spelling and sound. Some of these are shown in Table 9.1.

As will be seen there, "so" equals "go" in pronunciation, but these do not equal "to" or "do." To get the "go" sound from "do" requires the addition of "ugh." One would think, therefore, that because of the equality of "to" and "do" that the same pronunciation would occur by adding "ugh" to "to." But, of course, that does not follow either.

The 26 letters of written English approximate only a little more than half of the sounds, or phonemes, which are required in the spoken language. Moreover, many sounds which we take for granted as being constant are not. Look at /th/, which is perhaps one of the most difficult pronunciations in English for the foreign learner. It is not simply the addition of the *t* sound plus the *h* sound, but a unique combination which is associated with the Greek "theta." Moreover, in spoken language, the /th/ yields at least two discernible patterns of "voicing," as in "thin" and "then." We are a long way, therefore, from the ideal of a high correspondence between the written and spoken forms of our language.

PROBLEMS OF IDIOMATIC USAGE

Even having overcome the difficulties of acquiring a spoken language, there are also idiomatic phrases which present problems to the new learner. Languages are full of expressions which are not supposed to be taken literally and are thoroughly inconsistent—thus "slow up" and "slow down" are identical in meaning. This quality of language is perplexing, especially to the child unequipped by past experience to understand certain associations. Consider the youngster listening to his mother talking to a friend about last evening, and a father's late arrival: "Bill got *hung up* on that case and was *all in* when he got home. He's been *burning the midnight oil* for weeks on it and I think he should *have it out* with Fred instead of being *tied up in knots* all the time."

More than the literal language, then, there are also idiomatic expressions, colloquialisms, and special figures of speech which become incorporated into written and spoken language. These often function without awareness but with considerable effect upon our thoughts. It is this feature of language that we will now consider.

Functional features of language

An essential characteristic of any language is that its words stand for categories. Since perception is fundamentally a process of categorizing experience, it is not hard to see that language should play a significant role as a source of influence on the individual's psychological field. As Strauss (1953) notes, "The social import of language development in the child is not that he learns words but that he learns group classifications for countless objects and events. . . . Implicit in the name given to the object, if it is properly learned, are directives for actions toward that object, both covert as well as overt" (p. 106).

LINGUISTIC RELATIVITY

The effect of language on thought is at the heart of the viewpoint expressed by the anthropologist Sapir (1912, 1921). It was further developed by Whorf (1956) and has since come to be called the Whorf-Sapir concept of *linguistic relativity*. This concept asserts that cultural influences affect psychological processes through language. Thus, once learned, language provides grooves for thought.

Sapir contended that since different languages employed different systems of categorization, and had different syntax, the worlds in which individuals from different societies live are distinct worlds, and not the identical world with different labels. In one of his early writings on this point (1912), he used this illustration:

> . . . a certain type of animal in the physical environment of a people does not suffice to give rise to a linguistic symbol referring to it. It is necessary that the animal be known by the members of the group in common and that they have some interest, however slight, in it before the language of the community is called upon to make reference to this particular element of the physical environment . . . (p. 228). The case may be summarized . . . by saying that to the layman every animal form that is neither human being, quadruped, fish, nor bird, is a bug or worm (p. 230).

Thus, the nature and characteristics of the physical environment are interpreted through the categories established in language. As Whorf (1956) has noted, the Eskimos have three words for snow because that distinction is important to them in coping with the physical environment. Similarly, in our society the fine use of color names—such words as "mauve," "fawn," and "chartreuse"—appears to be more common, in general, among women than men. Lindesmith and Strauss (1956) have said that the American woman is more motivated to distinguish between color words because of her interest in clothes and home decorations as important features of her environment (p. 51).

Whorf (1956) considered that these discriminations are a vital consequence of growing up within a given culture. As the sounds of a language are learned and their meanings associated, he says that the child is inclined to perceive some things and not others within the nonlinguistic world about him. In the absence of such learned discriminations, it would be difficult for a person to be aware of differences. Thus, he comments:

> . . . if a race of people had the physiological defect of being able to see only the color blue, they would hardly be able to formulate the rule that they saw only blue. The term blue would convey no meaning to them, their language would lack color terms, and their words denoting their various sensations of blue would answer to, and translate, our words "light, dark, white, black," and so on, not our word "blue" (p. 209).

Whorf also made a major point of the structure of language as a determinant of thought. His research on American Indian languages led him to conclude, for example, that the noun-verb linkage was important in viewing and interpreting events.

A good deal of research has been conducted which touches on aspects of the linguistic relativity concept. Brown and Lenneberg in summarizing their studies (1958) indicate essential support for the concept. In one of these, they found that colors were more easily differentiated from memory if a color *name* could be "coded" and stored. Other pertinent research in this vein is exemplified in studies by Brown (1957), Carroll and Casagrande (1958), Doob (1960), Flavell (1958), Johnson (1962), Lenneberg and Roberts (1956), and Maclay (1956). Viewed overall, this research work indicates that linguistic variables have an active role in such psychological processes as color discrimination and concept formation. It may be, however, that this effect is traceable to the criteria used as a basis for comparison and not merely to the words alone.

SELF-DIRECTION AND PROBLEM-SOLVING

There is also evidence to suggest that language serves the important function of *self-direction,* long since pointed out by Lorimer (1929). Our personal thoughts about what we are to do are frequently taken over from the instructions learned from others. This is seen when the child says to himself, "No. No," in response to his own actions that he has been taught are wrong, or "First this part, then the other," when building. Because a key function of thought is problem-solving, what the individual concludes also depends upon the kinds of concepts available for self-direction.

The availability of alternatives in problem-solving is conditioned by concepts which are linguistically based. While there is still some disagreement as to whether words are essential to problem-solving and self-directed action, there is no question but that they do enter into these processes. Imagine, for example, what you would most like to do on your next vacation and note how many words pop into consciousness as you "see" some panorama of activity before you.

SEMANTIC CONFUSION

One difficulty that language poses is the confusion of words with things. Though the first are merely symbolic of the latter, people act very much as if they were inseparable. This is especially true in childhood. But adults are also vulnerable to this pitfall, which can be particularly troublesome in interpersonal and inter-group relationships.

While words stand for things, they are not the things themselves. The word "table" does not resemble a table, nor does it necessarily mean a given table, unless a definite article is used. Rather, it represents a category of things that have some common set of attributes. Categories, however, tend to obliterate important variations among the units within them.

Regarding ideas about race, for example, the word "Negro" can refer to a range from a person who is black to white in appearance, who may be a physician, public official, or day laborer, who may speak any language from Oxfordian English to Zulu, who could be a follower of any number of religious practices, and so forth. Yet, as Hayakawa (1963) pointedly notes, the word "Negro" itself has considerable reality for many white people. It produces many semantic disturbances that are illogical. "It is useless to point out," he says, "that, if we in America regard as Negroes all who are part Negro, it would be just as logical to regard as white all who are part white. Many people will simply stare at you angrily and say, 'We don't *regard* part Negroes as Negroes. They *are* Negroes!' For many people, the word 'Negro' is indeed a 'thing'" (p. 19).

DENOTATION AND CONNOTATION

What a word signifies is usually referred to as its *denotative* meaning. The special and less direct sense which it conveys is referred to as its *connotative* meaning, or "emotive" meaning, as the philosopher Pierce called it. Broadly, denotative meaning is confined to the function of verbally pointing at a thing or characteristic, while the connotative meaning has to do with the subtleties of evaluation about the thing referred to—or *referent*—including plus or minus valence. Much of the connotative meaning of a word can be accounted for by the dimension of "good-bad." While the denotation of a referent may be the same, the connotation can be different. This is revealed in such word pairs as "tramp" and "vagabond," or "cheap" and "inexpensive," or "flashy" and "vivacious." The coloration of words represented in connotation is what makes languages interesting. It accounts for the assertion we some-times hear that it is impossible to directly translate the "full meaning" of a term from another language.

Even the same word may have different connotations in different circumstances for different people. Consider a word like "buddy." It conveys different qualities of meaning when used by one soldier to refer to another, when used by a father as a term of affection for his son, or when used by a beggar on the street to ask for money to buy a cup of coffee. Sometimes we are brought up sharply by the special connotation conveyed by a familiar term. On one occasion, a waitress in an English restaurant was heard to say of the manager, who was then upbraiding some members of his staff, "He's a bit of a lad," and a new connotation for the word "lad" suddenly became apparent.

Connotations are played upon in putting a better, and often deceptive cast on something. Instead of calling an item "used," it may now be referred to as "pre-owned." A garbage collector may be called a "sanitary engineer." And shares in a company which may be on the verge of bankruptcy are not just "stocks," they are "securities."

THE SEMANTIC DIFFERENTIAL

A technique for the refined measurement of semantic connotations has been developed by Osgood, Suci, and Tannenbaum (1957). It is called the *semantic differential,* and its specific purpose is to get at the meaning of a given term—e.g. "mother," "country," "politics"—by ratings of the term or concept along several scales formed by bi-polar adjectives. These usually cover three factors called the *evaluative, potency,* and *activity* dimensions. For any adjective pair a rater makes just one rating of the concept.

From data gathered in an experiment on leadership, an illustrative semantic differential profile is shown in Figure 9.5 for the rating of "self" and the "group's leader." Though an odd number of scale-points is often used in the semantic differential technique, this experiment used a six-point scale to eliminate the middle-category response alternative. In the new book by Snider and Osgood (1969), an updated consideration of this technique is presented.

The first rating was obtained before the laboratory experiment, and the second after experience with an appointed group leader who, these subjects were led to believe, wanted the majority share of the group's profits. The evaluative factor is represented in the figure by the scales "friendly-unfriendly," "cold-warm," "bright-dull," and "clean-dirty." The potency factor there is covered by "hard-soft," "strong-weak," and "old-young." The two activity scales are "fast-slow" and "passive-active." In this case, the evaluative factor gave an overall difference between the self and leader ratings that was statistically significant. The other two factors showed scale differences, but these were not as marked as those for the total evaluative factor.

Research on the semantic differential by Osgood and his associates indicates that it has high reliability (cf. Osgood, 1960), particularly

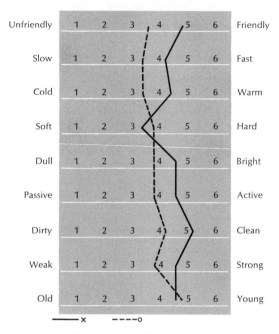

Figure 9.5: Semantic differential profiles of mean ratings of self (x) and leader (o) on nine scales for twenty subjects. (Based on data from Hollander, Julian, and Perry, 1966.)

with respect to the evaluative factor, which essentially measures valence, i.e. like-dislike. Nunnally (1959) used the semantic differential in a field survey of attitudes toward the mentally ill and found that the "neurotic man" was viewed as relatively foolish and unpredictable compared to "self." Ratings of "psychotic man" were still more sharply different.

LINGUISTIC CODING AND SOCIAL INTERACTION

Language involves encoding a message which can readily be decoded by another individual. In social interaction there is a certain economy in using terms which convey information with brevity. When a word comes into increasing usage, it may be abbreviated or replaced by a shorter word. This phenomenon, known as Zipf's Law, was pointed out by Zipf (1935) who demonstrated its effect in several languages, including English and Chinese. In twentieth-century English, we see it in the following illustrative sequences:

> automobile—car
> television—TV
> motion picture—movie
> omnibus—bus.

Linguistic coding in general tends to facilitate thought and memory, as we noted in connection with the Brown and Lenneberg study of color names (1954). Where individuals interact frequently with one another, they share mutual benefits from such coding. This can be seen especially in occupations which require repetitive reference to objects or concepts which are vital to the ongoing effort. In an electrical supply store, there are many brief terms utilized to differentiate the thousands of pieces of equipment. The same thing is true of any "lingo" that develops as part of common activity, whether in medicine, art, or traffic engineering.

In some settings, an insider's lingo is used to identify those who are accepted, as against those who are not. Using the right words or phrases is, therefore, a matter of asserting and maintaining social identity, whether in the underworld or in the military service or in a law office. In some settings, the special language is used to create impressions without revealing too much. Glittering phraseology, which can suggest but not actually say something of significance, is often prized in officialdom. Figure 9.6 shows a device humorously designed

A	B	C
0) Integrated	Management	Options
1) Total	Organizational	Flexibility
2) Systematized	Monitored	Capability
3) Parallel	Reciprocal	Mobility
4) Functional	Digital	Programming
5) Responsive	Logistical	Concept
6) Optional	Transitional	Time-Phase
7) Synchronized	Incremental	Projection
8) Compatible	Third-Generation	Hardware
9) Balanced	Policy	Contingency

Figure 9.6: An aid for "Baffle-Gab." When confronted with the need to generate an impressive phrase, think of a three-digit number and pull the corresponding words from each column. A choice of 765, for example, produces "Synchronized Transitional Concept." Because it is 10^3, this small unit has the capability of producing one thousand distinct phrases.

to be used as a generative system for phrases such as these, called "Baffle-Gab."

Linguistic coding is also a device for *gaining* social acceptance. Fischer (1958) conducted interviews with children and found that the choice of "free variants" of a linguistic form, in this case the verbalized endings "ing" and "in'," was related to the child's sex, class, personality, and formality of the conversation. These variants, which have the same denotative meaning, have symbolic value because they signify to others the relative status of the speaker. In short, they can influence the recipient's perception of the child as "one of us," and help to gain acceptance for him.

Terwilliger (1968) holds that the grammar which is taught in schools represents "correct usage" and avoidance of "mistakes," but not the usage of those with whom the child may associate in various relationships. Others have gone further to contend that there are many "grammars," each appropriate to a given grouping, and that these have a hold over people whether they be teen-agers, coal miners, slum dwellers, or the well-educated. Austin (1970), for example, says:

> What people usually mean by "grammar" is "grammar of the well-educated," and, as such, grammar here means hardly more than linguistic etiquette in which the choice of a word or a phrase is like selecting the correct fork or spoon. As a matter of fact, people of lesser education are pretty thoroughly independent and proud. Instead of wishing to emulate educated people, they are apt to look upon them with suspicion and uneasiness. Hence, they are supremely indifferent to linguistic etiquette or what we commonly call good English (pp. 45-46).

Rosenthal (1957) found that the language used by young children was also a significant determinant of sociometric position in a group. The more "popular" children were found to use language which was more active than that of those children who were low on popularity. In terms of influence effects, the form of language itself conveyed a code about the child's relative standing in the group.

THE ABSTRACTION LADDER

Words in any language may also vary in terms of their abstractness. The quality of being "abstract" arises essentially from a word's removal from a concrete referent. A word such as "table" is low in abstractness, whereas words like "freedom" or "virtue" are very high, and more difficult to define. Thus, the word "democracy" has divergent meanings in the Communist and non-Communist countries of the world.

A word which is less readily tied to concrete referents is high on the abstraction ladder while one that is low can be made concrete more readily. However, the fact that a word is low on the abstraction ladder does not mean that it is necessarily limited in connotations. The word "money," for instance, is quite concrete but may conjure up all sorts of connotations. Other examples are "fireplace," "museum," and "mink coat."

One variety of semantic confusion is often created by using words which are highly abstract without supplying relevant referents to convey intended meaning. In fact, this kind of confusion is one of the propagandist's techniques for creating impressions by labeling. In this respect, Hayakawa (1963) says that educational practices tend to foster global abstractions that need to be understood more in terms of the concrete instance or referent. He says:

> Children are taught to read and write, and the more "fluently" they talk or write, the higher the grades they get. They are trained to respond in specific ways to certain signals: "Christianity" ("a fine thing"), "the Constitution" ("a fine thing"), "Shakespeare" ("a great poet"), "Benedict Arnold" ("a traitor"), and so on. But, especially in the elementary and secondary schools, they are taught very little about how not to respond. Because Christianity, for example, is highly thought of, an organization practicing the opposite of Christian principles is likely to call itself a "Christian front"; because the Constitution is a "fine thing," it will occur to an anti-Democratic pressure group to call itself a "Committee to Uphold the Constitution" . . . (p. 24).

Language is also a potent device, then, for shaping the attitudes that people hold regarding aspects of their environment. In this respect, as well as in eliciting action, it holds significant directive features.

Directive features of language

The power of words to move people, to give impetus to their actions, is a vital feature of language. Carroll (1953) says, "it is overwhelmingly significant that every facet of a language system contributes to the way in which a community uses language in social control. Not only everyday conversation and address but also all the varieties of mass communication, such as propaganda and advertising, depend upon the precarious standards of a common language system" (pp. 112-113).

When language is used to influence others, it is said to be directive. The intent is to exercise a degree of control over their behavior. The mother says to the child, "Eat your lunch," in the hope of directing a behavioral sequence. An adjunct to such attempts is the potential in language for conveying a sense of future orientation. Thus, the mother may add the comment to the child, "And then you can have some candy." This provides the anticipation of a future reward which is far more difficult to establish without language.

THE "PROMISE" IN ADVERTISING

Hayakawa (1964) contends that virtually all directive statements have an implicit future-oriented element. By this means we transmit a sense of expectation, hope or fear, regarding consequences of presently urged action. The advertiser, wishing to influence customers, makes extensive use of such directive language. David Ogilvy, in his book *Confessions of an Advertising Man* (1963), says that the "promise" contained in an advertisement is vital. Speaking to advertisers, he says: "Your most important job is to decide what you are going to say about your product, what benefit you are going to promise. Two hundred years ago Dr. Johnson said, 'Promise, large promise is the soul of an advertisement'" (p. 116).

Evidently, Dr. Johnson followed his own advice for, in auctioning off the contents of the Anchor Brewery, Ogilvy quotes him as having said: "We are not here to sell boilers and vats, but the potentiality of growing rich beyond the dreams of avarice." Ogilvy himself recounts various examples, among them one of his own advertisements for Helena Rubenstein's hormone cream headed "How women over 35 can look younger." Note the implicit promise and the use of a directive form in the words "how" and "can." He says: "The two most powerful words you can use in a headline are FREE and NEW. . . . Other words and phrases which work wonders are HOW TO, SUDDENLY, NOW, AN-NOUNCING, INTRODUCING, IT'S HERE, JUST ARRIVED, IMPORTANT DEVELOP-

MENT, IMPROVEMENT, AMAZING, SENSATIONAL . . ." (pp. 131-132). And he then catalogues many others.

Advertisers spend literally billions of dollars each year to influence the attitudes of people toward their products. The American cigarette industry, for instance, has estimated yearly sales of about six billion dollars ($6,000,000,000), a substantial proportion of which goes into advertising. Just moving but 1 per cent of all sales to a given brand would mean a gain of $60,000,000 in additional annual revenues (Bauer, 1964, p. 322). Language is big business.

THE USE OF SEMANTIC CONFUSION

This process of cognitive biasing is quite usual as a device communicators use to influence others. As observed in Chapter 6 (p. 214), attitudes are prodded by attaching a positive symbol to something you are to approve, and a negative symbol to something you are to disapprove. In general, the intent of such labeling is deliberately to generate semantic confusion. It is often seen in two forms. One of these is the *degradation of language,* by abusing the meaning of a word or phrase. A compact car, for instance, was advertised as a "Big little beauty." A further example of the use of a compound form is seen in "genuine imitation leather."

The other rather typical device is to make an assertion which, on examination, is *semantically empty.* Usually this will take the form of claims that a product is "the biggest selling *of its kind*" or "*23% more effective* by actual clinical tests" or "lasts *twice* as long." The specific referent and the bases for comparison are usually very ambiguous or entirely absent in these cases. What is "its kind"? "More effective" than *what?* Lasts "twice as long" as what—the half-size bottle?

A way in which language can be degraded is set forth by George Orwell (1949) in his novel, *1984,* about a totalitarian state of the future. In the appendix to that work, he provides the basic ideas concerning "Newspeak," the language of thought control introduced by the ruling party of this society. Among the society's guiding slogans are: WAR IS PEACE, FREEDOM IS SLAVERY, IGNORANCE IS STRENGTH. By juxtaposing and equalizing opposites in this fashion, and limiting the availability of alternative words, an extreme form of language degradation occurs which Orwell calls "doublethink."

On the lighter side, advertisements can be charming. Sometimes they use cognitive imbalance in a delightful way, as in the ad for a famous line of raincoats showing a photograph of a duck—an actual duck—wearing a raincoat perfectly tailored to its shape. And there are other ways in which a touch of semantic confusion, leading to an "Ah, Ha" sense, can be used to gain attention. Two apt examples are the ski shop which advertises "Our business is going downhill," and the travel agency with a prominent sign reading "Please go away."

TECHNIQUES OF PROPAGANDA

All of these directive features of language are tools which can be used by propagandists, whether they are advertisers, political figures, or industrial and labor spokesmen. The term "propaganda" has come into disrepute though its original meaning conveyed the essential idea of the dissemination of information. As used today, it most often refers to the presentation of selected information to influence others for the direct benefit of the propagandist or a cause which he serves. Thus, in wartime opposing governments routinely employ propaganda to influence not only the population in enemy lands but in their own counties as well.

The techniques of propaganda has been described in various ways, but mainly they involve a highly contrived manipulation of symbols, through language, to create desired impressions. For example, in the propagandist's *message*, "facts" may be presented which are in themselves correct, but so sifted and slanted as to provide only one side of the case. This covers such techniques as the "focused truth" and "card-stacking," in which facts are selected and/or managed to yield a picture which is largely erroneous.

Deliberate cognitive biasing, discussed above, is frequently used by the propagandist in the techniques of "glittering generalities" or "transfer and testimony." In the first instance, a false conclusion may be foisted on the audience as a palatable and overly simple generalization to explain complex social phenomena, such as: "The Republican Party is the party of depression," and its counterpart, "The Democratic Party is the party of war." In transfer and testimony, the propagandist enlists a positive symbol, such as a baseball star, to endorse his breakfast cereal, thus hoping to raise the positive valence of his product and increase sales. The foundation for these attempts in "psycho-logic" is apparent (see Chapter 6, p. 216).

Finally, the propagandist can also present *himself* in ways designed to maximize positive group identity. By the "bandwagon" technique, he emphasizes that many others just like the members of the audience are with him on the "winning side," or in "buying the most popular car in America." By the technique known as "plain folks," the politician in particular may appeal to his audience as "one of the people," whether they are farmers—in which case he plays up his "roots on the farm"—or businessmen—in which case he points out that he "knows what it is to meet a payroll."

On a broader level, propaganda is necessarily practiced artfully by political leaders. This is seen especially in the development of slogans. As Pei (1968) notes, words such as "president," or "legislature," or "amendment," are relatively colorless terms. But slogans such as "New Deal," "Alliance for Progress," or "We Shall Overcome" are considerably more stimulating. Furthermore, emotional terms—those laden with strong connotations—can carry considerable impact. Some examples are "Counter-revolutionary," "John Bircher," "Liberal Eastern Establishment," "Black Power," "White Supremacy," and "Soul Brother."

Demogogic orators especially run to inflammatory language which may make little actual sense, but sways the audience by the incessant use of loaded symbols. Hitler, for example, made repeated use of such terms as "Manifest Destiny," "Master Race," and "Aryan Blood" in his speeches. Even in democracies, political figures indulge in loaded terms which are contrived to "fuzz over" meaning. Though dated by the passing from the scene of many of the names he mentions, this observation by the political writer C. L. Sulzberger (1960) still holds up well:

> France's Radical-Socialist party is neither Radical nor Socialist. Khrushchev, Tito, Nehru, and Hugh Gaitskell all employ the word "socialism" to convey contradictory ideas. And what about democracy, that precious Athenian term? It no longer has the least semantic significance. Pakistan's "controlled democracy" looks like benevolent despotism and Indonesia's "guided democracy" resembles chaos. The "popular democracies" of Eastern Europe are both unpopular and undemocratic. Each power coalition proclaims, while arming to the teeth, profound interest in peace. However, as Clausewitz remarked: "A conqueror is always a lover of peace" (p. 5).

Susceptibility to the effects of propaganda is not, however, inevitable or fixed. For one thing, as we noted more extensively in Chapter 6, a transactional view of communication considers various lines of resistance to such influence attempts. We are not therefore merely the passive receivers of propagandistic appeals, though they can do incalculable harm, especially with the highly credulous—the young, the under-educated, the inexperienced, as well as fanatics. Furthermore, as Kottman (1964) has found, the more adept individuals are in using language, the less likely they are to be influenced or misled by others' statements. With a more facile command of language, the individual evidently has a stronger attachment to the meaning of a verbal symbol and is less vulnerable to having it altered. This could be good or bad in its consequences. In either case, it encourages more precision in language usage and a greater respect for its enormous power.

As is apparent, the issues we have been considering about directive language mesh with many areas of interest in social psychology. These would include the phenomena of social interaction, leadership, conformity and attitude change, among others. Indeed, it is hard to conceive of social influence without some intervention by language.

SUMMARY

A significant defining characteristic of Man is his use of language. More than a means for transmitting information, language is an important part of culture which directly affects the individual psychologically. Its content can shape the perception and, in general, the thought and action of individuals. Language may be studied in terms of its *structure and form,* its *acquisition,* and its *functional* features including its *directive* use as an influence device.

There are several major theories about the origin of language. None of these, however, satisfactorily accounts for the abstract quality of language since they usually treat language in limited terms. Changes in language appear to follow the pattern of cultural innovation more generally. There are three basic features of a language: *syntax,* which refers essentially to grammatical structure; *semantics,* which has to do with meaning; and *phonology,* which deals with its sound patterns.

Words are structural units of language that convey symbolic representations. They "stand for" but are *not the same as* their "referents," e.g. objects, things, events, actions. The words of a language may be spoken or written. The distinction between these two *forms* of language is very important, though confusion about their relationship persists. Our alphabet, for example, is merely a set of standard symbols which can be combined together to form other symbols, i.e. written words. They also can be pronounced in various combinations, in terms of sound patterns, as a word. These basic sound patterns, the smallest units of spoken language, are called *phonemes*. They are not identical to letters. Thus, a given letter of the alphabet may be pronounced with more than a single phoneme while more than one letter may be necessary to yield a single phoneme.

The learning of language is one of the most complex tasks confronting the young child in a society, and it is accomplished at quite variable rates, as a function of individual differences in capability and experience. Basically, it necessitates learning complex associations between sounds and the objects which they denote. Later, as these sounds, or phonemes, are put together in various combinations, they come to stand for words as well as "broader statements." A sentence constitutes such a statement made up of a number of words which are constructed from phonemes. Even more complex than learning words and their associations orally is the acquisition of reading and writing. Here the child is obliged to go from a spoken form to a written form which is inconsistent with it.

A "nativistic" position, as represented by Chomsky and Lenneberg, contends that the enormously complex task of learning and using language is only accomplishable because humans are uniquely equipped for it. The acquisition of language can also be viewed as involving the reinforcement contingencies existing in what Skinner calls a "verbal community." This process is instigated by the child's early "babbling" which comes to be reinforced in terms of sounding words and relating them to objects and experiences. Words may be recognized and acted on without being part of the individual's usable vocabulary.

The most significant *psychological function* of language lies in its effect on the individual's psychological field. These functional features of language have been identified with the writings of Sapir and Whorf. Their viewpoint has been referred to as the Whorf-Sapir concept of *linguistic relativity.* In general, this position considers language as a cultural influence upon psychological processes of perception and thought. This influence comes about through the categorization of experience in terms of the culturally defined emphases embodied in language.

Another functional feature of language has to do with the distinction between the specific *referent* that is *denoted* by a word and the meaning that may also be *connoted* by it. Denotative meaning is usually considered to be confined to verbally pointing at a thing, while connotative meaning has to do with subtleties of meaning. The study of meaning is called *semantics*. Various techniques have been devised for measuring the connotative meaning of words. A prominent procedure in current use is the *semantic differential* developed by Osgood and his colleagues.

Words also represent "codes" for conveying meaning briefly. Such *linguistic codes* affect thought and problem-solving and also have a facilitating effect upon social interaction. Words may vary, too, in terms of their abstractness. The *abstraction ladder* refers to how removed a word may be from a concrete referent. The word "table" is low in abstraction; the words "freedom" or "virtue" are very high in abstraction. *Semantic confusion* is often created by using words high on the abstraction ladder without supplying concrete referents.

Language is employed in a *directive* way when the intent is to influence the attitudes and behavior of individuals. Children use it in this fashion to make their desires known to parents, and parents in turn to affect the child's actions. A widespread use of directive language is seen in advertising and political activities. This mode of social communication capitalizes on the power of language to influence others, often through semantic confusion and cognitive biasing. *Propaganda* is the name usually applied to the presentation of information for the benefit of the propagandist or his cause. It involves the manipulation of symbols regarding both the "facts" in his *message* as well as in the way he presents *himself* to the audience in terms of group identity. Resistance to propaganda depends in part on an attachment to the meaning of words.

SUGGESTED READINGS

From E. P. Hollander and R. G. Hunt (Eds.) *Current perspectives in social psychology.* (3rd ed.) New York: Oxford University Press, 1971.
Introduction to Section IV: *Language and communication*

20. Noam Chomsky: *Language and the mind*
21. Charles E. Osgood and Thomas A. Sebeok: *Communication and psycholinguistics*
22. Norman N. Markel: *The basic principles of descriptive linguistic analysis*
23. S. I. Hayakawa: *The language of social control*
24. Roger Brown: *How shall a thing be called?*
25. B. F. Skinner: *The verbal community*
26. George A. Miller: *The psycholinguists: on the new scientists of language*

SELECTED REFERENCES

*Barnett, L. *The treasure of our tongue.* New York: New American Library, Mentor Books, 1967.
*Brown, R. W. *Words and things.* Glencoe, Ill.: The Free Press, 1958.
Carroll, J. B. *The study of language.* Cambridge, Mass.: Harvard Univer. Press, 1953.
*Chomsky, N. *Syntactic structures.* The Hague: Mouton, 1964. (Paperback published by Humanities Press.)
*Hayakawa, S. I. *Language in thought and action* (2nd ed.) New York: Harcourt Brace, 1964.
*Miller, G. A. *Language and communication.* New York: McGraw-Hill, 1951.
Osgood, C. E., Suci, G. J., & Tannenbaum, P. H. *The measurement of meaning.* Urbana: Univer. of Illinois Press, 1957.
*Pei, M. *The story of language.* New York: New American Library, Mentor Books, 1960.
*Sapir, E. *Language: an introduction to the study of speech.* New York: Harvest, 1949.
*Terwilliger, R. F. *Meaning and mind: a study in the psychology of language.* New York: Oxford Univer. Press, 1968.
*Whorf, B. L. *Language, thought, and reality.* (Edited and with an introduction by J. B. Carroll.) Cambridge: MIT Press Paperback Edition 1964.

10

Personality functioning in society and culture

Personality is a way of referring to each individual's uniqueness. Just how much the culture of a society molds individual personality no one can say. However, there is widespread agreement that a person's distinguishing characteristics are inextricably bound up with the society in which he lives. This relationship is a direct outgrowth of the fact that an individual's personality develops as a function of social adjustment. The life-long necessity to balance individual needs and social requirements is vital in this process.

Regarding the interdependence of the individual and society, Kluckhohn and Murray (1948) say:

> . . . as social animals, men must adjust to a condition of interdependence with other members of their society and of groups within it, and, as cultural animals they must adjust to traditionally defined expectations. All men are born helpless into an inanimate and impersonal world which presents countless threats to survival; the human species would die out if social life were abandoned. Human adaptation to the external environment depends upon that mutual support which is social life . . . (p. 36).

In this chapter our major focus will be upon the way the individual personality is both influenced by and influences social processes. Because personality consists of manifest behaviors as well as underlying

388

psychological states, our interest will be directed not only to the typical modes of response that an individual displays to others but also to the attitudes and values which are part of his psychological field.

Some definitions of personality

The concept of personality is so broad that it is very difficult to define precisely. Indeed, there are a great many definitions of personality which have been offered, from its early origins in the Greek word *persona* or mask (G. W. Allport, 1937). One central problem concerns the development of personality and the extent to which the social environment conditions its qualities apart from organismic tendencies. Murphy (1947), for example, considers that the structure of personality arises from a complex "bio-social" process. It is not a simple matter therefore to say where these individual biological and physiological tendencies leave off and social influences begin since they are not observed in total isolation. Summing up this point, Linton (1945) asserts that "the main problem involved in the definition of personality is one of delimitation. The individual and his environment constitute a dynamic configuration all of whose parts are so closely interrelated and in such constant interaction that it is very hard to tell where to draw lines of demarcation" (p. 84).

Kluckhohn and his colleagues indicate that in some ways human beings are like all others; in some ways like some others; and in certain respects like no others (1953, p. 53). In the first category we might place certain of the basic survival needs of Man. In the second, we could point to the broad cultural similarities of people who, for example, speak the same language. In the third category, we deal with those *finely defined* differences that make for individuality. This latter element is distinctively a matter of personality which, for purposes of definition, we can consider to be the *sum total of an individual's characteristics which make him unique.*

However personality is defined, as a concept it depends upon a strong tendency to view individuals as the major locus of their own behavior. This is the essence of perceived "individuality." Krasner and Ullmann (1965) have expressed this tendency as follows: "It seems that if an observer does not know the antecedents, the behavior is attributed to the person, while if he has knowledge or control, he is inclined to consider the behavior to be superficial. We are . . . ingrained with the concept that people should be responsible for the production of their own behavior . . ." (p. 270).

Viewing personality in terms of interpersonal relations, there is a heavy element of social expectancy associated with the shaping of such relations. Once expectancies about another person's behavior become established, we come to see them as features of his personality. From this it is a short step to the assumption that these are consistent "traits," rather than modes of responding in a social setting, which includes the particular others whom he encounters there. The issue of the "consistency" of personality will be dealt with in various ways in what follows.

Levels and aspects of personality

Any definition of personality refers to an individual's distinctive characteristics, whether behavioral or in the form of psychological states. People attach significance to these individual differences, and the individual himself usually has a sense of his own identity in terms of his self-concept. One important distinction, then, concerns the external manifestations of qualities of personality and their inner workings. These can be characterized respectively as the *external* level and the *internal* level of personality. Furthermore, personality has varying aspects of permanence. It has a *dynamic* aspect, in the sense of allowing for change, as well as a *consistent* aspect, which provides continuity over time.

The external level of personality is represented by the typical behaviors of an individual and the way he affects other people in terms of what is called his "social stimulus value." Such behaviors can be "expressive" of feelings or be more in the nature of qualities of "performance." Apart from the acknowledged merit of their compositions, it is interesting, for example, to see the distinctive *expressive* characteristics of the musical notation used by three great composers, as shown in Figure 10.1 While expressive behavior of this kind can be revealing of some qualities of personality, it does not convey the full richness of psychological states which lie beneath nor reveal a great deal about

Figure 10.1: Musical notations from the works of three composers: I. Mozart; II. Bach; and III. Beethoven. (From Wolff, 1943.)

performance abilities. Using the boldly expressive notation of a Beethoven, in short, does not make a composer his peer.

The intra-psychic features of the individual—including his attitudes and values, his interests, and motivations in the psychological field—represent a set of interrelationships on the internal level. In general, it is supposed that these two levels should be in harmony with one another so that the individual behaves with an adequate "integration" between them. If someone acts in a variable way, he may be perceived as untrustworthy and devious, in terms of the attributions made about his motivation for such action. In an experiment by Gergen and Jones (1963), it was found that a person who behaved in a consistent, predictable fashion, over a variety of situations, was generally liked and trusted. A person who behaved in an inconsistent manner was reacted to in precisely the opposite way.

Personality functioning can be approached on either or both of these levels. In the first instance, observation of behavior is the primary technique employed. In the second, personality inventories, projective tests, or attitude scales may be used. However, what is obtained from one line of study may not be congruent with what is obtained from the other. For example, if a person behaves in a "dominant" fashion this may or may not accurately reveal the less apparent qualities of the person. An inference could be incorrectly drawn that he has a superior view of himself when, in fact, it could be the reverse; he might feel inferior to others and be compensating accordingly. Furthermore, two individuals may be similarly motivated or hold similar attitudes but behave quite differently, as we noted in Chapter 5. How we act is very much determined by social interaction and the situation in which it occurs.

Personality has a dynamic aspect because, among other things, humans are capable of learning and carry its effects, especially in the sense of cognitions. Social psychology also emphasizes changing demands on a person across situations, and as a consequence of new experience. When an individual encounters a dramatically new situation or identity, through marriage, advanced education, extensive travel, adversity, or other profound experience, his outlook and response tendencies may be altered. Even going from one social situation to another, as we noted in connection with the concept of role, his behavior will be altered, if only in a transitory way.

But, at the same time, personality is consistent, both at the external and the internal level. Individuals usually have characteristic modes of approaching the world, dealing with frustration, and seeking certain long-range goals in the form of values. These behaviors can be considered to derive from elements of the individual's psychological field which are less susceptible to change. In this respect, George Kelly (1963) views personality as a way of construing the world, including one's perception of self in relationship to it. Put in other terms, we may say that personality involves stable cognitive processes that generate a characteristic "style." It is in this sense that, even after a lapse of time and new experience, a person is still recognized by others as "the same old Jack."

A schematic representation of personality

As we have seen, personality is composed of external behaviors affecting others as well as internal features relating to the individual's disposition toward the world. In this section we will be making a further distinction about external behaviors, specifically in terms of those which are *typical responses* and those which are *role-related*. The internal, less visible quality of personality, can be thought of as a *psychological core*.

In Figure 10.2 these components have been schematically represented as concentric rings of wavy lines to suggest a flow, rather than a rigid partition. This diagram is useful in understanding the structure of personality, and the relationship between its components, though it is not to be taken as a literal "picture" of personality. As will be seen in the diagram, the core is the central feature of personality. It embodies the individual's psychological states, among them values and attitudes, residues of past experience, expectancies—all in all, the things we associate with the psychological field, in the usual sense of consciousness, as well as unconscious elements.

Moving outward toward increased contact with the social environment, the typical responses of the individual refer to such things as his characteristic activity level, sense of humor, and ways of responding to frustration, all of which are associated with his learned modes of adjustment. Role-related behavior is that behavior most susceptible to the

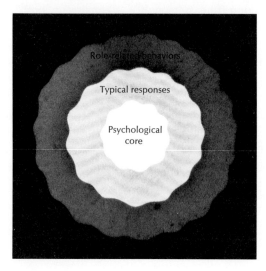

Figure 10.2: Schematic representation of personality within social environment.

demands of the particular social context in which the individual finds himself.

As already noted, there is a flow of experience through these wavy lines, such that the core of personality affects certain typical responses, these responses may in turn affect the psychological field, roles are affected by the typical behaviors the individual tends to manifest, and, indeed, the core itself is affected by roles. A major role, with a pervasive hold over one's activities, may substantially alter the psychological field, as represented here in the core.

By way of distinguishing these components further, we can now delve into them to discern their special qualities, beginning with the core.

THE PSYCHOLOGICAL CORE

The psychological core of an individual's personality contains his psychological field, and also less conscious effects of past experience. Most significantly, it holds the individual's *self-concept*—his image of what he is like. This is the centerpiece of personality functioning because, as Murphy (1947) notes, "The individual perceives himself as figure in the figure-ground pattern that is each social group" (p. 766). How the person values himself, in regard to self-esteem, has been found to be an especially significant factor in receptivity to social influence, as we shall see.

As the individual interacts with the social environment from earliest childhood, he develops a picture of what the world is like and a set of perceptions of himself. Furthermore, as was said in connection with the discussion of attitudes and values in Chapter 5, these perceptions guide behavior by providing a relatively coherent and stable approach to the environment.

A way of describing personality, then, is in terms of the individual's perceptions of self and others. This is one of the major lines of study in contemporary social psychology. Its rationale can be simply stated as follows: to the extent that we know how the individual perceives and attaches meaning to the situation in which he finds himself, successful predictions can be made about his behavior.

This approach can be characterized as *dispositional* insofar as it stresses qualities of the individual that are brought into the context of social interaction. Projective testing, for example, relies upon this characterization of personality. It is, moreover, an essential feature of psychotherapy where it is usual to have the client relate experiences, in terms of *his* perception of them.

It is well recognized that, whether consciously or unconsciously, individuals behave as they perceive and are motivated toward things. In one formulation of this, the psychoanalyst Horney (1945) contended that there are three dominant ways of approaching the social environment: some individuals have a tendency to move *toward* other people, some to move *away* from other people, and some to move *against* other people. In the sense of implying modal dispositions, this pattern of movement can be viewed as typical responses which grow out of cognitions in the psychological core, such as: people are generally pleasant to associate with, or they are generally unpleasant, or they are in one way or another "bad" and deserving of hostile treatment.

TYPICAL RESPONSES

All of us have observed that some individuals we know usually seem good-natured, others quick-tempered, or aggressive, and so on. We take this consistency largely for granted, even though it may be somewhat variable as a result of social circumstances. Sometimes we encounter a person only in one kind of situation, fulfilling a given role, and generalize excessively about the person's typical personality from just that limited observation. We say a professor is "reserved," or a comedian "light-hearted," little knowing whether this is generally true of that person or only a sign of the behavior produced by a social role.

When we first come to know someone, there is a tendency to describe his behavior and then to see it in terms of an underlying force that dictates certain patterns. The older concept of "trait" is precisely of this order. In discussing that concept critically, G. W. Allport (1966) has said: "Our initial observation of behavior is only in terms of adverbs of action: John behaves aggressively. Then an adjective creeps in: John has an aggressive disposition. Soon a heavy substantive arrives, like William James' cow on the doormat: John has a trait of aggression. The result is the fallacy of misplaced concreteness" (p. 1). Allport then considers the other extreme and points out that if we were only to describe the behavior of an individual, without some assumptions of consistency, we would wind up with an empty organism devoid of expectancies, attitudes, motives, capacities, and so on. We need to know more, therefore, about these less apparent qualities of the individual that may dispose him to characteristic behavior.

The alternative to traits is to recognize that individuals may have dispositions toward certain behaviors but that these *dispositions are actuated* as a result of the individual's perception of the situation. This would not produce complete consistency, but rather modifiability within some regularities. In this respect, Gergen (1968) observes:

> . . . a demand for thoroughgoing consistency would fly in the face of a major mode of social adaptation. It would essentially freeze the individual personality in such a way that the person would fail to meet the requisites of a changing social environment. To be continuously serious, or light-hearted, understanding, domineering, or the like, would reduce one's option for behavior. . . . And this is also to say that a prevailing need for achievement, need for positive regard, need for cognitive clarity, or any other of a host of needs or traits posited by personality theorists, will only be adaptive within a limited set of relationships. . . . It should be understood, however, that this is not to advocate a simple, chameleon-like approach to social interaction. Rather, it is to rely on the

> human capacity for rich and varied behavior, and on the fact that antithetical behavior may be enacted without losing one's feelings of honesty with self or with others (p. 307).

Viewed as an adjustive process, then, we can more readily see that the way an individual typically behaves depends upon his perception of present circumstances, based upon his past experience. If we choose to use the word "trait" we should understand that it refers to recognizable typical responses rather than some underlying force which dictates such responses. In short, *traits are typical behaviors*. From these behaviors we may infer certain things about the personality core.

ROLE-RELATED BEHAVIORS

In Chapters 7 and 8 we considered roles to be behaviors which are appropriate to the expectations of others in a given situation. Figure 10.2 indicates this feature of personality by showing role-related behavior to have the closest proximity to the social environment. In this respect, behavioral changes from one situation to another exemplify the dynamic aspect of personality.

Roles also have an interrelationship with an individual's typical behaviors and his construction of the situation in terms of his psychological core. Some roles are more lasting and more congenial to the individual's self-concept than are others. Thus, a role may be highly peripheral and short-lived, or it may be a major feature of his personal identity. Consider, for example, the person called to jury duty for the first time. The role of juror is new to him though he has some inkling about its requirements in advance. It is not, however, a dominant or persisting feature of his life. On the other hand, being in a profession, or serving as a corporation executive, has a more pervasive effect upon the whole personality of the individual because of the totality and persistence of the role itself. It will affect many of his relationships. The man who has become Chairman of the Board is continually reminded of his prestigious position by others' actions toward him in line with the power he wields. This pattern may affect the core of his personality, most notably his self-concept, but also other attitudes and values. It has another consequence, too, in the "protective" way he is defended from information that might be unpleasant to him. He is therefore liable to be cut off from knowing what others know, until some calamity arises. George Reedy (1970), who was for a time Lyndon Johnson's press secretary, has recently written about this phenomenon in connection with the protection of the occupant of the Presidency from adverse opinion.

Some roles, then, are far more central and omnipresent than others. Furthermore, a particular role into which an individual is cast may "fit" the other components of his personality, or it may not. For example, an executive may very much enjoy his high prestige and power, but perhaps dislike some other demands made upon him, such as the pressure for decisions. This problem is especially inherent in roles which can involve conflicting values. A professor, for instance, may like the intellectual give-and-take of the classroom while disliking the task of evaluating and grading students which is another feature of his role.

Though it is possible to talk about individual personality as if it were self-contained, the socially demanded relations between individuals have distinct effects on its functioning. The very conception of who we are and what we are depends upon social interaction within the framework of roles. This is seen with particular sharpness in connection with the influence of age-sex roles on behavior. One example of this influence comes from the early work of Komarovsky (1946). She found that many students in an eastern women's college reported an inconsistency between their own intellectual interests and achievements and the "feminine" role. Because a major interpersonal task of that role is to find a suitable mate, Komarovsky concluded that her women students had to indulge in concealment tactics to conform to the expectations of their dates. Two typical comments were these:

> My mother thinks that it is very nice to be smart in college but only if it doesn't take too much effort. She always tells me not to be too intellectual on dates, to be clever in a light sort of way (p. 185).
>
> On dates I always go through the "I-don't-care-anything-you-want-to-do" routine. It gets monotonous but boys fear girls who make decisions. They think such girls would make nagging wives (p. 188).

This effect may be much less potent today. But the conflict produced by a sex role is doubtless still felt by women who have the interest and capacity to go on to professional careers. Though a dubious basis for imputing too much about the motivations underlying them, the statistics on the proportion of all doctorates awarded to women show an actual decline over the last thirty years.

Such examples merely serve to point up the importance to personality functioning of the social expectancies associated with roles. However, they also suggest some features of the adjustive process which individuals undergo in fulfilling their potentialities within the framework of organized society.

Some issues in characterizing personality

An item in *The New Yorker*'s "Talk of the Town" (March 12, 1966, p. 45) neatly captures a major issue in characterizing personality. One young working girl is reported saying to another, "You should speak up to your boss more and assert yourself." The other replies, "I'm just not programmed that way."

Though its overtones are distinctly humorous, as befits the source, this item poses the question of what the "programming" of personality might mean. McDougall (1908) is remembered for putting forth a view which might have considered the young lady to have been programmed by response tendencies that were instinctive. Yet, McDougall actually recognized that there also must be a latitude for learning to respond. It was precisely in this connection that he introduced the concept of *sentiment,* which we take today to be "attitude." The most important of these sentiments, he said, was "self-regard," and added: "Insofar as they [sentiments] are associated with a strong master sentiment of self-regard . . . we are self-determined rather than impelled by our instincts" (1936, p. 140). Thus, even McDougall, who was so identified with an instinctual viewpoint, underscored the importance of processes of adjustment which gave rise to learning. He also was acknowledging the significant effect of the individual's perception of self, which has been stressed here as the self-concept (see Boden, 1965).

Returning to our young lady, the question of programming can now be viewed in terms of the influences of her past experiences on her response tendencies. Though she might be hesitant to speak back to her boss, as a result of past interactions with him or others in a similar role relationship, she might quite readily speak back to a brother or sister or parent or friend. There would be situational variations in her reactions which would suggest that this programming, if it can be called that at all, is still subject to the social context of interaction.

In the instance just given, we have been focusing on a relationship with an authority figure. This kind of relationship is a fundamental source of interaction tendencies, stemming from early childhood. Shaw and Ort (1953) present an example reported by Fisher and Hanna of a barber who had been intimidated in childhood by his father and an older brother. When anyone with an authoritative manner requested his services, he became so agitated that he was unable to wield his clippers (p. 6) Here again we are dealing *not* with an instinct but a learned response that is strongly inculcated through early experience.

THE EFFECTS OF EARLY EXPERIENCE

It is clear that personality depends on a multiplicity of social contacts and influences beginning in early life. A number of these have been treated in Chapter 5 and will be further considered in the next chapter dealing with subcultures. It will be useful here, nonetheless, to make a point again concerning early experience in personality development, and to examine it more closely.

Previously we noted that the socialization of the child has redounding consequences in later life. It is widely agreed among authorities in the area that the child's family determines in considerable degree the social influences to which he is subjected as well as the responses that are socially defined as desirable. There is also agreement that certain patterns of early experience can produce personality characteristics which persist into later life, though this effect is not considered to be the result of one crucial event.

An emphasis on early experience is founded not only on the influential views of Freud, but also on accumulated knowledge about human socialization and animal behavior. One kind of demonstration of this effect comes from experimentation on the hoarding behavior of rats deprived of food in early life (Hunt, 1941). These rats showed a significant higher rate of food hoarding than their litter mates who were not thus deprived. Other work on puppies has indicated that marked differences in development occurred among those who had been deprived of normal stimulation in their environment during the early weeks of their lives (Thompson and Melzack, 1956). Harlow in his research with infant monkeys has found profound effects on the emotional behavior in adulthood of monkeys who were deprived of affection from a mother monkey (1962).

Given the weight of evidence, therefore, it is not surprising that humans should also be seen to react in distinctive ways to early deprivation. A variety of data have been accumulated to bolster this point. Thus, a contention in the field of child psychology (e.g. Ribble, 1944, and Spitz, 1945) runs to the effect that a lack of "mothering" of the young infant may result in marked psychological damage, including depression and retardation of development. However, these effects may be readily overstated. As Orlansky (1949) observed from his review of such studies,

> In the normal range of infant experience . . . we believe that events subsequent to the first year or two of life have the power to "confirm or deny" the personality of the growing infant, to perpetuate or remake it, depending upon whether the situation of later childhood perpetuates or alters the situation in which the infant was reared (p. 35).

The subsequent development of personality, under normal circumstances, thus becomes involved in more complex relationships. Because of the range of variables, including physiological functioning, which enter into the process, a number of issues persist regarding the characterization of personality. Among these is the idea of traits as deep-seated forces, somewhat analogous to instincts. While this is not a popular position in social psychology, it is useful to consider this issue a bit further.

TRAIT AND DISPOSITIONAL CONCEPTS OF PERSONALITY FUNCTIONING

Historically, the most common way of approaching personality has been in terms of traits. In the old usage, *traits* have traditionally referred to the individual's typical behaviors which are sometimes assumed to be based in innate factors, such as instincts. As McClelland (1951) notes, "Trait psychology represents one of the earliest attempts to introduce some kind of order into the multiplicity of human responses. Its approach is simple. It consists of looking for consistencies in behavior" (p. 117).

One of the most common of the trait typologies is extroversion and introversion. Though this concept has a long history, it was popularized and is most identified with the writings of the psychoanalyst Carl Jung (see 1959). As an illustration of how these terms are used to type people consider these characterizations from Eysenck (1965):

> The typical extrovert is sociable, likes parties, has many friends, needs to have people to talk to, and does not enjoy reading or studying by himself. He craves excitement, takes chances, often sticks his neck out, acts on the spur of the moment, and is generally an impulsive individual. . . . The typical introvert, on the other hand, is a quiet, retiring sort of person, introspective, fond of books rather than people; he is reserved and distant except with intimate friends. He tends to plan ahead, "looks before he leaps," and distrusts the impulse of the moment . . . (p. 59).

One major difficulty with such characterizations of a "pure type" is that they omit a great deal of individual variation around the major types, as well as mixtures that can occur. It is possible, of course, as Eysenck has done, to develop a psychological test of extroversion-introversion and consider people to be extroverts or introverts who score high at either extreme. But this is not the same as saying that the population distributes itself naturally into these two distinct behavioral groupings, nor that people are necessarily consistent across different circumstances. The danger, of course, is that labels of this kind can be misleading, especially since they tend to disregard situational variations. Thus, in looking at the characterizations quoted above, many readers will doubtless feel that there are some things in both descriptions which seem true of oneself.

Moving to another realm, even such a characteristic as "punctuality" has been found by Dudycha (1936) to have low stability in four different situations. He checked records for students and obtained measures on their punctuality in returning library books, turning in their class assignments, returning course change cards to the registrar, and meeting appointments. He found very low intercorrelations between these independent measures, the average being .19.

Similarly, Hartshorne and May (1928) report considerable variability in the "honesty" of children viewed under varying situational circumstances. By ingenious methods they studied a large number of children in a variety of conditions in which honesty or dishonesty could be observed. For example, in one condition they returned their test papers so the children themselves could each grade his or her own. Their actual responses were known and this permitted the researchers to determine any changes made as the teacher read the correct answers aloud. While a few children were found who were consistently honest, and a few who were consistently dishonest, most varied considerably depending upon the circumstances. The results clearly established that honesty was not a stable trait but varied as a reaction to a given situation.

There are some central features of personality that do, however, appear to have stability over time. Thus, Stott (1957) studied children during a period of twelve years. Beginning in nursery school they were observed and rated on "ascendance" in spontaneous interaction. He found that this characteristic had a marked degree of stability, with only a few temporary changes from a consistent pattern. Gellert (1962), however, studied dominance behavior of pre-school children playing in pairs. She found that a change of playmate produced variability in such behavior. Children paired with the less assertive of two playmates showed greater dominance behavior. It should be borne in mind that an interpersonal characteristic such as dominance is likely to be determined by the reinforcement provided in past interaction, and therefore is not a trait in the classic sense so much as it is a learned mode of adjustment whose manifestation is subject to situational variability.

The most serious deficiency of trait typologies in understanding personality functioning is that they largely ignore the relationship between a person and his environment. They focus exclusively on responses and are excessively broad. Therefore, their application for prediction is limited, except in extreme instances. Lazarus (1963) says that the trait approach

> is most useful when the person's behavior patterns are absolutely consistent—that is, characteristic of a person regardless of circumstances. What limits the usefulness of any trait or type system is the problem of degree of trait generality. The statement that a person has the trait of submissiveness is useful for prediction only insofar as he is submissive in all or most situations. If he is submis-

sive only in certain circumstances, then we can predict his behavior accurately only if we know what those circumstances are (p. 57).

A more inclusive view of personality attends to the *dispositions* which lead to certain typical responses rather than just to the responses themselves. The concept of a disposition acknowledges the intervening influence of the individual's psychological field on his reactions to social stimuli. It is, therefore, much more given to the "cognitive style" notion in terms of the individual's perception of the world and his interaction with it. In this vein, G. W. Allport (1955) observes,

> . . . the most comprehensive units in personality are broad intentional dispositions, future-pointed. These characteristics are unique for each person, and tend to attract, guide, inhibit the more elementary units to accord with the major intentions themselves. This proposition is valid in spite of the large amount of unordered, impulsive, and conflictful behavior in every life (p. 92).

Among the dispositions which have been studied as features of personality are authoritarianism, dogmatism, Machiavellianism, achievement motivation, internal or external control, manifest anxiety, social desirability, and persuasibility. These represent various measures of personality that we will be considering later in this chapter. Each is employed in research on personality which aims at determining the processes by which individuals react differently to essentially similar stimuli. Each measure also embodies a conception of personality which contains cognitive as well as behavioral elements. Thus, while the traditional trait approach attempts to measure consistent responses, such as extroversion or introversion, dominance or submission, the dispositional approach seeks to get at the psychological components of the individual's responses to the social environment.

TRANSACTIONAL CONCEPTIONS OF PERSONALITY

The dynamic aspect of personality has been treated here largely as a process of adjustment to the social environment. But this leaves out an important process, that is, the individual's action on the social environment. The individual copes with his environment, within the range of responses available to him, in order to exert his influence or control over it. This idea is emphasized in G. W. Allport's concept of *pro-action*

(1960b). In his earlier book, *Becoming* (1955), he says, "Personality is less a finished product than a transitive process. While it has some stable features, it is at the same time continually undergoing change" (p. 19).

In these terms, Allport characterizes personality as an "open system" involving a mutual interaction or *transaction* between the person and his environment (1960a). He presents several criteria of open systems which can be paraphrased as follows: they involve an intake and output of energy or action in terms of a continuing commerce; they achieve and attempt to maintain equilibrium or balance, in the sense of homeostasis; they tend to increase in their order or structure as they become more complex in time.

Applying this scheme more concretely, we can anticipate that some individual behaviors will be internally motivated as actions on the environment rather than reactions to it. This is a phenomenon which can be ascribed to the "effectance motivation"—the motivation to be competent in dealing with the environment—on which White (1959) places great stress (see Chapter 4). Furthermore, such striving will be bound up with the individual's desire to retain a coherent and stable self-concept. Maintenance of its integrity is especially crucial to the equilibrium of personality, with particular regard to central attitudes. Thus, as Levine (1963) aptly notes, challenging a man's honesty creates a disruption of equilibrium which is far stronger than if it were his choice in neckties that was at stake (p. 45). Finally, the addition of new experiences, new motivations and social demands, requires an increasingly more elaborate organization of personality to accommodate the increased diversity of elements.

Most importantly, the transactional conception makes the individual the focus of social influence processes. For example, it recognizes that the need for identity leads to a reaching out to take hold of a group, or a cause, or a responsibility. The person is not merely a receptacle into which these social entities are poured, but an active agent transacting with them.

SELF-ESTEEM

All in all, the nub of the matter resides in McDougall's (1936) sentiment of "self-regard," or what has more recently been dubbed *self-*

esteem. This disposition may be thought of as the positive component of the self-concept. It has the greatest ramifications for social interaction and its influence effects. Later in this chapter, we consider self-esteem further in connection with persuasibility, which is a point of linkage between social influence and personality.

Though inclined to stability, the self-concept itself is still affected by the atmospherics of social situations and the other people there. We have all had the experience of becoming vaguely aware that we are not quite the person we believed we were, thus perceiving our "self" in a new light. By his notion of the "looking-glass self," Cooley (1922) accounts for the dynamics of this effect on the self-concept:

> As we see our face, figure, and dress in the glass, and are interested in them because they are ours, and pleased or otherwise with them according as they do or do not answer to what we would like them to be; so in imagination we perceive in another's mind some thought of our appearance, manners, aims, deeds, character, friends, and so on, and are variously affected by it. A self-idea of this sort seems to have three principal elements: the imagination of our appearance to the other person; the imagination of his judgment of that appearance, and some sort of self-feeling, such as pride or mortification. . . . The thing that moves us to pride or shame is not the mere mechanical reflection of ourselves, but an imputed sentiment, the imagined effect of this reflection upon another's mind. . . . We are ashamed to seem evasive in the presence of a straightforward man, cowardly in the presence of a brave one, gross in the eyes of a refined one, and so on. We always imagine, and in imagining share, the judgments of the other mind (p. 184).

In this same regard, it also tends to be true that we prefer social interactions with people who sustain self-esteem. Research studies by Harvey, Kelley, and Shapiro (1957), Howard and Berkowitz (1958), and S. Jones (1966) are among those revealing a positive linkage between perceiving a person as liking one's self and liking that person. This relationship is predictable in line with the concept of cognitive balance discussed in Chapter 7; and it fits a simple reinforcement scheme as well. However, where the individual has a negative self-concept, in the sense of low self-esteem, it is not necessarily the case that he likes those who reinforce that image, even though this would in theory be a balanced state (S. Jones, 1966).

There also appears to be a facilitation effect in terms of expressions of self-esteem. In a study by Gergen and Wishnov (1965), subjects paired with someone expressing great self-esteem were more positive in their own self-references than they had been in a set of self-ratings filled out a month before. On the other hand, the opposite tendency was evidenced for subjects paired with someone speaking in humble terms about their shortcomings. Therefore, expressed self-esteem appears to be a transient state, subject to change as a function of the other person with whom one is interacting. Studies by Gollob and Dittes (1965), Walster (1965), and Zellner (1970) are some which bear upon transient self-esteem (see p. 424 below.)

Social psychologists increasingly are concerned with the meanings and evaluations individuals attach to their own actions and reactions, as well as those of others (e.g. Bem, 1965; Kelley, 1967; pp. 133 and 195 here). In operational terms, then, personality is more than a set of behaviors or dispositions; it may better be seen as the locus for a process of striving which is shaped by self-awareness through a network of social relationships.

Approaches to the study of personality

In studying personality it is only possible at best to measure several of its features at a time. It is not surprising, then, to find that the results of such measurement provide a segmented view of the total personality. Clearly, some things about a person are more relevant than others in understanding his behavior. The first approaches took account of what was manifestly there, in terms of ratings of the individual's apparently typical behavior. Either by the ratings of others, or by self-ratings, measures were made of the person's response patterns which seemed to have consistency. Of this approach to research on personality, Gergen (1968) asserts that it

> . . . largely rests on the assumption of personal consistency. If a person fills out a questionnaire in a particular way or judges a stimulus configuration in a given manner, he may be classified as having certain personality characteristics. . . . On the assumption that the person acts consistently, and that the personality traits found in the testing situation universally characterize the person's

style of life, predictions are made and tested concerning the person's behavior under a variety of conditions (p. 299).

As we have already pointed out, this response-oriented approach has limited utility, mainly because of its failure to take account of situational variations. Nevertheless, it continues to be highly useful, and we will shortly be considering its application in areas of social psychological concern.

The trend in the contemporary study of the behavioral features of personality is exemplified by the recent research of Lorr and McNair (1965) on "interpersonal response categories." They examined various characterizations of personality and developed many categories in which observers could rate the typical behaviors of other people whom they knew well. Through the use of factor analysis, which permits the refinement of these categories, they found seven bi-polar factors which are shown (in Figure 10.3) as fourteen behaviors around a circle. Each behavior is connected by a line with its opposite number across from it in the circle. Behaviors which are close to one another around the circle are rated similarly. Those which are opposite are seen to differentiate people sharply.

Another technique for measuring overt characteristics of personality is the traditional personality inventory, such as the Bernreuter, MMPI,

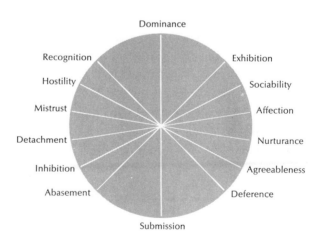

Figure 10.3: Interpersonal response categories. (Adapted from Lorr and McNair, 1965.)

or Edwards scales, which provide a profile of the individual's characteristics. This method relies on self-ratings and, as we shall be noting,
these have been found to be affected by a social desirability factor—
that is, an individual's tendency to present himself in a favorable light
—which has to be taken into account (Edwards, 1957a).

To a significant degree, the emphasis in the social psychological
study of personality has moved more and more to the measurement of
dispositions. This so-called "cognitive" approach emphasizes the stable
components of the individual's psychological field which intervene between experience and action. The techniques employed in this approach have mainly been attitude scales and projective devices. We
will now consider some of these measures of dispositions, beginning
with authoritarianism.

AUTHORITARIANISM

More than any other single development in recent years, the research
on authoritarianism has opened the way for a study of personality in
terms of dispositions that are attitudinal in nature. As was noted in
Chapter 3, the California F scale, developed more than 20 years ago,
has yielded a wide array of research on the "authoritarian personality."
Scores from this scale have been used in studies of prejudice, leadership, rigidity, adjustment, group behavior, conformity, and many other
phenomena (see Titus and Hollander, 1957; Christie and Cook, 1958).

Among the most systematic findings have been those which demonstrate that the scale is related to an individual's perceptions of others.
In one study of this, Scodel and Mussen (1953) tested the hypothesis
that ". . . authoritarians, because of their lack of insight into others
and their need to consider themselves members of the ingroup, would
perceive nonauthoritarian peers to have attitudes and personality characteristics similar to their own" (p. 184). In their experiment, 27 pairs
of subjects, each pair consisting of a high scorer and a low scorer on
the authoritarianism scale, were told to discuss such neutral topics as
radio, television, and the movies. At the conclusion of these sessions,
the subjects were given a second administration of the F Scale with
instructions to respond as they believed their discussion partners
would. As predicted by the hypothesis, the high scorers perceived their
partners as having F Scale scores similar to their own, while those with

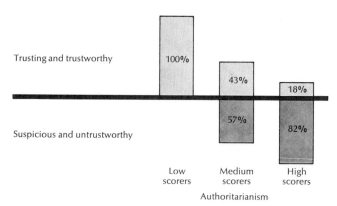

Figure 10.4: Percentages of subjects with high, medium, and low authoritarianism scores who were trusting and trustworthy or suspicious and untrustworthy with their partners. (Based on data from Deutsch, 1960).

low scores estimated their partners' scores to be significantly higher than their own, though still lower than they actually were. This study confirms a dispositional tendency for authoritarians to have the characteristic of imperceptiveness, which is supported too by the studies of Crockett and Meidinger (1956) and Rabinowitz (1956), among others.

Using a "prisoner's dilemma" situation, discussed in Chapter 7, Deutsch (1960) found significant differences between high and low scorers on the F Scale regarding their trustworthiness. In general, trusting partners and being regarded as trustworthy are highly related, as are their opposites. Figure 10.4 shows the variations Deutsch found in these pairs of responses for subjects at varying levels of authoritarianism. Clearly, a marked inclination exists for the high authoritarian subjects to be significantly more disposed to suspiciousness and untrustworthiness than the low and medium authoritarians.

In the non-social area, too, research has indicated that the authoritarian is likely to be more rigid in his perceptions. M. B. Jones (1955), for example, found with a flickering phenomenon produced by the "Necker Cube," that high scorers on the F Scale were significantly more intolerant of the fluctuation than were the low scorers who more readily acknowledged perceiving it. From this and several related findings, Jones contends that there is a basic perceptual process which underlies authoritarianism.

Some basis exists, therefore, for considering authoritarianism to be essentially perceptual, as Maslow (1943) pointed out when he characterized it as a *Weltanschauung*, or "world view." However, there is still little evidence of any direct experimental verification of a relationship between authoritarian attitudes and social behavior. It would seem that authoritarianism is therefore not a trait, in the same way as activity level, but is more a disposition toward the world. And this, of course, is the point of greatest interest here, namely that personality may be described as the individual's construction of the world which may vary as a result of different situational circumstances. This accounts for the fact that, in Fromm's (1941) original conception of authoritarianism, he described the authoritarian person as being both dominant and submissive—dominant to those whom he perceives as weaker, and submissive to those whom he perceives to be more powerful than himself. Thus, the influence of the situation, as the individual construes it, remains an important determiner of interaction patterns.

DOGMATISM

Rokeach (1954, 1960) has extended the concept of an authoritarian disposition in his work on dogmatism. Essentially, he defines dogmatism as *closed-mindedness*. The highly dogmatic individual has a set of tightly organized beliefs, usually derived from authority. A feature of dogmatism is rigidity in the psychological field, which takes the form of resistance to the acceptance of information which is contradictory to the individual's system of beliefs. An undogmatic individual would be more accepting of new experiences and information which might challenge his system.

Rokeach points out that a narrow, unsophisticated perspective leads an individual to experience threat to his closed belief system when he encounters those who are outsiders. Accordingly, he is less willing to tolerate close relationships with those who are different from himself, especially in terms of dissimilar beliefs.

The important feature distinguishing authoritarianism from dogmatism is that the dogmatic individual may be dogmatic irrespective of a particular ideology. He can be dogmatic about many things. The authoritarian, on the other hand, is usually found to be prejudiced and inclined to the political "right." In political terms, the dogmatic individual could tend either toward a "leftist" or a "rightist" viewpoint in an extreme way.

To measure dogmatism, Rokeach developed a 40-item attitude scale which was found to have a significant positive relationship with the F Scale and other measures of a similar kind (Rokeach, 1960). This scale is related to both ethnic as well as dogmatic intolerance, though it is not composed of items which refer directly to such issues.

The reliance of the dogmatic individual on authority has been experimentally verified by Vidulich and Kaiman (1961) who selected subjects on the basis of their scores at either extreme of Rokeach's Dogmatism Scale. They were then placed in an autokinetic situation where each subject privately judged the directional movement of the light for 30 trials alone and then for an additional 30 trials after a report of how another subject judged the same stimulus. Half of the subjects in each group were led to believe that this other person was a college professor and the other half that he was a high school student. They found that the individuals who were highly dogmatic agreed significantly more with the person of "high status" than with the one of "low status." Those who were low on dogmatism tended to agree more with the low rather than with the high status source. These results underscore the importance of the relationship between an individual's personality dispositions and his willingness to accept influence within a given social situation. This lends further emphasis to the necessity for jointly considering both the person's characteristics, and his immediate situation, in understanding influence processes.

Dogmatism is evidently related to other features of social interaction. Individuals who score high on dogmatism have been found to be less sensitive to the social impressions they convey to others (Haiman and Duns, 1964). This consideration has been explored further by Rosenfeld and Nauman (1969) who studied 68 freshman women, living in two comparable units in a university residence hall. The students were asked by the investigators to participate in a study of "social living" and to co-operate in four two-hour assessment sessions spaced five weeks apart. The layout and social structure of the units assured opportunities for frequent contact among the students residing there and the units thus served as the primary locus for the students' peer group ties. Among the major questionnaires administered was the Dogmatism Scale. Information was also gathered at both time periods on the interpersonal relations among members of a unit, in terms of contacts and attachments. These were analyzed with particular reference to the dogmatism of their peers.

Rosenfeld and Nauman (1969) found that peers indicated that their contacts with the dogmatic students became less satisfying over time, while their contacts with non-dogmatic students became more satisfying. Bearing in mind that the respondents did *not* know what it was, in terms of the specific dimension called "dogmatism," which put them off, it is noteworthy that the dogmatic students were increasingly evaluated negatively by their peers. On the other hand, the dogmatic students were found to have an increasingly higher rate of initiation of contact, thus suggesting that they were trying to rectify their growing isolation.

MACHIAVELLIANISM

The means by which people exert influence and control over others has proven to be a continual source of fascination. For some it is almost a preoccupation. The principles of Machiavelli, best exemplified in his classic work *The Prince* (1532), give advice on manipulating others. This characteristic has now been investigated as a personality disposition.

Christie (1962) and Christie and Geis (1968, 1970) have been engaged in studying individuals who are oriented toward such manipulation. Christie's (1962) own initial effort was largely aimed at developing a Machiavellianism attitude scale embodying items drawn from the original writings of the master, and those which were thematically consistent with them. Here are some examples:

> Never tell anyone the real reason you did something unless it is useful to do so.
> It is wise to flatter important people.
> Barnum was probably right when he said there's at least one sucker born every minute.

Other items, stated in the opposite direction were also used, so that disagreement with them would indicate Machiavellian tendencies, e.g. Honesty is the best policy in all cases.

The scale has gone through multiple refinements and revisions and now employs a Likert-type form (Mach IV) and a forced-choice form (Mach V). A considerable amount of research points to a variety of stable findings (Christie and Gies, 1968). For one thing, scores on the "Mach" scales do not correlate with those on the F Scale, which indicates that it is measuring a quite distinct aspect of personality, other than authoritarianism. Moreover, men quite routinely have higher mean scores on the Mach scales than do women drawn from the same population. In research on intended specialties, among medical students, those naming psychiatry and pediatrics as choices were highest on the scale, and those naming surgery were lowest. These and other findings suggest that people who are involved in roles demanding a good deal of interpersonal contact tend toward higher scores than those in impersonal, more distant relationships.

In a recent experiment by Epstein (1969), she had high and low scorers on the Mach scales either read a counter-attitudinal statement and then role-play arguments for that position, or simply read the statement (see Chapter 6, p. 220). Epstein's hypothesis was that "highs" would more readily adapt to role-playing against their own position and would therefore have less attitude change resulting from this treatment. Alternatively, "lows" would be more vulnerable to dissonance effects stemming from discrepant role-playing and would show greater attitude change scores. In the non-role-playing condition, in which subjects merely read counter-attitudinal material and received a participation fee, she predicted a reverse effect. Her results, in Table 10.1, yielded the predicted statistical interaction; "low" scorers on the Mach scales were more likely to show attitude change from role-playing arguments against their own views, and "high" scorers from reading the counter-attitudinal statements. One implication of these findings is that low scorers on Mach are characterized by more sincere

Table 10.1: Mean attitude change for high and low scorers on the Machiavellianism scales. (From Epstein, 1969, p. 40.)

	"HIGH" ON MACH SCALES	"LOW" ON MACH SCALES
Role-playing condition	1.50	2.85
Non-role-playing condition	2.15	1.20

involvements, and high scorers on Mach by greater detachment, in their attitudes.

ACHIEVEMENT MOTIVATION

As some of the work discussed here suggests, one defining characteristic of personality lies in motivational dispositions. Achievement motivation constitutes a widely studied exemplification of these. Its measurement has mainly been approached by presenting a subject with pictures from the Thematic Apperception Test and having him tell a story answering such questions as: What is happening? Who are the people? What has led up to this situation? What is being sought? What is wanted? What will happen? What will be done? Then, the degree of achievement imagery is assessed by content analysis.

In developing this technique of projective study, McClelland and his co-workers (1953) aroused achievement motivation experimentally in a group of subjects to determine its effect on their stories. They found that where subjects were told that their abilities or leadership were being evaluated, they wrote stories that showed far higher achievement than did subjects studied under a normal control condition. The extent of achievement imagery was a direct function of this instructional set.

A considerable amount of research evidence suggests that achievement motivation is learned early and becomes a relatively stable characteristic of individuals, given the *appropriate situational circumstances*. Thus, in a study by Atkinson and Reitman (1956) subjects with a high need for achievement only performed better on tasks involving individual initiative, not on routine group tasks. Another thing which has been found regarding achievement motivation is that it is not highly correlated with risk-taking. The high achiever takes moderate risks but avoids excessive risks.

Rotter (1966) and Feather (1967) have contended that individuals with high achievement motivation are more likely to take responsibility for outcomes, while those with low achievement motivation regard outcomes as relatively independent of their own ability and effort.

In one of a series of experiments conducted by Weiner and Kukla (1970), they divided subjects into those above the median or below the median on a measure of achievement motivation. All of the subjects

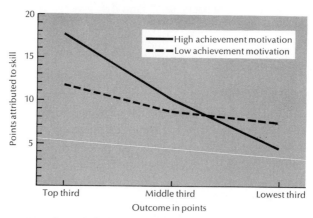

Figure 10.5: Number of skill points ascribed as a function of motive classification and task performance. (After Weiner and Kukla, 1970, p. 14.)

were then given a task to do in which on each trial they were to guess the next number in a series. The actual outcomes were determined by chance, so that in fact no ability differences were involved. Upon completion of the task, subjects were asked to estimate how many "points" of their total scores were due to "skill rather than guessing."

In Figure 10.5, the results are shown for the "high" and "low" achievement motivation groups by the outcome of their guesses. The latter has been subdivided into thirds of the distribution of scores which, it should be remembered, were due to chance. In fact, the "high" and "low" achievement motivation groups did not differ significantly in their mean scores, but, as the pattern in the figure shows, subjects who were "high" reported that they possessed relatively great skill when they succeeded, and a lack of skill when they failed. By contrast, those who were "low" on achievement motivation yielded a markedly flatter slope, with less attribution of personal characteristics in the outcome.

INTERNAL-EXTERNAL CONTROL

Related to this finding regarding achievement is the "locus of control" concept (see Chapter 7, p. 285). It is predicated on the notion that an important underlying determinant of an individual's action is the degree to which he perceives that a reward follows from his *own behavior* or is controlled by forces *outside of himself*. This conception bears a resemblance to the *re*action versus *pro*action ideas of G. W. Allport, discussed earlier. The major impetus for the current study of expectancies for internal as against external control has come from the efforts of Rotter (1966). His theory of social learning (1954) emphasized the persistence of certain "expectancies" that an individual holds, related to their reinforcement properties. Guiding this work is the view that, depending upon their experience, in terms of a history of reinforcement, individuals will differ in the degree to which they attribute the receipt of reinforcements to their own actions.

The measurement of dispositional differences among individuals in the expectancy of *internal* or *external* control began with the study by Phares (1957), a student of Rotter's who constructed a 26-item attitude scale composed of 13 items each of an external or internal kind. Subsequent refinements led to a 23-item forced-choice I-E scale with internal and external choices involved for each. Two such illustrative items, where the subject must select either the *a* or *b* alternative, are these:

> a. Many of the unhappy things in people's lives are partly due to bad luck.
> b. People's misfortunes result from the mistakes they make.

> a. In the long run people get the respect they deserve in this world.
> b. Unfortunately, an individual's worth often passes unrecognized no matter how hard he tries.

Items of this kind, from the new scale and its predecessors, have been administered to a variety of different populations for research purposes. Quite consistent differences are found, usually in the predicted direction. Thus, among other findings Rotter (1966) reports that individuals with high achievement motivation are found to be more internal in their dispositions, and that where sex differences are found, males routinely are more internal than females. He also notes that a recent study of Peace Corpsmen indicates that they are significantly more internal than the general college population from which the bulk of his data were obtained.

Experimental evidence has also accumulated which indicates differential behavior by internals versus externals. Thus, internals have been found to be more independent and resistant to influence attempts (Crowne and Liverant, 1963). Relatedly, Rotter and Mulry (1965) investigated the hypothesis that internals and externals would differ in the value placed on the same reward depending upon whether it was perceived as a matter of chance or their own skill. In this experiment, they found that individuals, who scored as internals on the I-E scale, took longer to make a decision in a matching task when that task is defined as demanding skill, than when it is defined as a matter of chance. As predicted, the opposite tendency was found with subjects who were characterized as externals; they were inclined to take more time to decide on a correct match when the task was defined as involving chance.

Following on the Rotter and Mulry research, Julian and Katz (1968) report findings from two experiments which serve to clarify these relationships. The subjects were involved in competitive tasks to earn points. Under these conditions, it was hypothesized that internals more than externals would rely on their own knowledge to yield self-determined outcomes, as against using information from their opponents. This turned out to be the case, but for both *chance* as well as *skill* conditions. Julian and Katz conclude that an important determinant of this "strategy" in this competitive situation was the enhancement of the internals' desire to predict their own outcomes, even under conditions of chance.

Ritchie and Phares (1969) recently compared internals and externals on their susceptibility to influence attempts. Using a traditional attitude change procedure, these researchers administered the IE Scale to 152 female students. They studied the 42 from the upper (external) end of the distribution, and the 42 from the lower (internal) end. Previously, these subjects had filled out an attitude questionnaire concerning economic policies and the national budget. Both groups were then asked to read an identical statement, with half of each believing that it came from a high prestige source, and the other half that it came from a low prestige source.

Because externals are said to be more sensitive to the social environment as a locus of control, Ritchie and Phares predicted that externals

Table 10.2: Mean attitude change scores for "internals" and "externals" exposed to communications from high and low prestige sources. (After Ritchie and Phares, 1969, p. 438.)

SOURCE:	INTERNALS	EXTERNALS
High prestige	6.19	8.76
Low prestige	7.24	5.33

would show greater attitude change when receiving information from a *high* prestige source than from a *low* prestige source; they also expected that this difference would be greater than that for internals exposed to these two kinds of prestige source. As shown in Table 10.2, their findings supported these predictions. While internals and externals shifted their attitudes about the same overall, the prestige of the source operated differentially on them. Externals exhibited more change than internals in the high prestige condition and less change than internals in the low-prestige condition.

The implication of these and the preceding findings is that a relationship exists between expectancies concerning source of reinforcement and an individual's responses in various circumstances. Accordingly, intellective functioning can be readily seen to be tied to a personality disposition. These results add weight to the idea that externals are not uniformly susceptible to influence, in all situations, but that they are affected more than internals by factors such as the prestige of the influence source.

MANIFEST ANXIETY

Another kind of concern in the measurement of dispositions is the degree to which the individual inclines toward emotionality in coping with the environment. This is exemplified in the concept of manifest anxiety, identified with the work of Taylor (1953, 1956). Her initial interest was in the selection of groups that would differ in "drive level" in experimental situations. She selected subjects on the basis of a self-rating personality scale using items from the MMPI (Taylor, 1953). This new scale, called the Manifest Anxiety Scale (MAS), has been validated in many studies, all of which reveal a tendency for observer ratings of anxiety to be significantly correlated with the subjects' scores on the MAS.

The importance of this work in social psychology stems mainly from the consideration that social stimuli, such as hostile interactions, can elicit varying responses from individuals as a function of their anxiety proneness (Bovard, 1959). This disposition appears to be measured by the MAS. Thus, it has been found that physiological measures, such as the Palmar-Sweat Index (PSI), are directly associated with MAS scores.

A study illustrating this line of work was conducted by Haywood and Spielberger (1966). Their aim was to investigate individual differences in physiological arousal produced by the anticipation of, and then participation in, a laboratory experiment. These investigators selected subjects who were high or low scorers on the MAS and then took a PSI measure, through a simple fingerprint applied to film, to determine the individual's basal level of arousal in the laboratory just before the experiment. Then subjects were involved in a procedure requiring the construction of sentences as part of a verbal conditioning task. After that, a second PSI print was taken. The results are shown in Figure 10.6.

As expected, the high and low groups on the MAS differed significantly in their respective PSI means. Furthermore, though both groups decreased in their physiological arousal from the first to the second

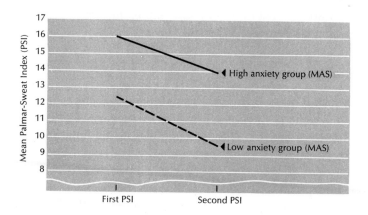

Figure 10.6: Mean levels of arousal, measured by the Palmar-Sweat Index (PSI), taken before and during an experiment, for subjects scoring high or low on the Taylor Manifest Anxiety Scale (MAS). (Based on data from Haywood and Spielberger, 1966.)

measurement of the PSI, the high MAS group continued to be significantly more aroused than those who were low on the MAS.

This experiment again points up the situation as a factor which interacts with a personality disposition in eliciting behavior. In this experiment, the anticipation of what *was to come* aroused anxiety in both groups of subjects, and this diminished once they had been in the situation for a time. Nonetheless, those entering with a disposition toward greater anxiety continued to show anxiety at a significantly higher level than those who were lower on the anxiety scale.

SOCIAL DESIRABILITY

A persisting problem in personality assessment has to do with the individual's attempt to present himself in a favorable light. This tendency has been called "social desirability" and appears to be an important feature of social relationships going beyond the personality testing situation. Edwards (1957a) developed a social desirability scale (SD) by making use of a sample of 150 items from various scales of the MMPI which were then submitted to ten judges, asked to rate them on what would be a socially desirable response for each. There was unanimous agreement on 79 items by the judges. Finally, a revised version incorporating 39 items which best discriminated between the high and low total scores on this scale became the major instrument for measuring social desirability.

It was found that this SD scale related to a number of other psychological measures. Among the major findings from one study of this measure, Allison and Hunt (1959) report that individuals scoring high on the SD scale were more likely to be affected by situational cues as to the appropriate response. Thus, aggression as a reaction to frustration varied considerably among these subjects depending upon the degree to which a norm for such expression was evident.

Crowne and Marlowe have extended the work of Edwards and developed a scale which they consider to be a measure of the need for social approval. Half of its items are culturally acceptable, but probably untrue statements, and half are true but probably undesirable statements. Using subjects selected on the basis of their scores on this scale, they have conducted a number of experiments reported in their book, *The Approval Motive* (1964). They report consistent differences in social responses by individuals who are high or low on their scale. For example, those who score high are significantly more likely to conform to the judgments of others than those who score low. It seems apparent that, given a group of attractive others whose approval is desired, individuals will attempt in varying degrees to secure their approval—or social support—as a function of personality needs. This condition is, however, founded on the interaction of the individual and particular others, and therefore appears to be affected by situational factors.

PERSUASIBILITY

The personality disposition which seems most directly implicated in the acceptance of social influence is *persuasibility*. Janis and Hovland (1959) define this factor as "any variable attribute within a population that is correlated with *consistent individual differences* in responsiveness to one or more classes of influential communications" (p. 1). The essential characteristic of a persuasible individual would be his willingness to be influenced by others across many situations.

Janis and Field (1959) developed a test of persuasibility in which subjects express their opinions on various issues before any communication is presented, then again after reading a set of communications, and finally after reading an opposing set of communications (pp. 31-32). Scores on this test are obtained by summing the number of items on which the subject changed from his own initial position in the direction advocated by either the pro or con communication.

Among the pertinent findings from some administrations of this test is the significant difference obtained between male subjects and female subjects in overall persuasibility. On the average, females are found to be more persuasible. Accordingly, Janis and Field (1959) suggest that there are at least two broad classes of dispositional factors affecting an individual's persuasibility. They say, "One class involves personality factors, while the other concerns cultural sex-typing influences which may produce more or less stereotyped differences between male and female role behavior in our society" (p. 67).

Using a similar attitude-change test with college students, Linton and Graham (1959) have reported that those who were easily persuaded tended to have a weak self-concept. Taken together with other studies, this led these investigators to the conclusion that susceptibility to influence "is related to two main areas of personality functioning: the underlying attitude toward the self and the quality of a person's reactions to the environment—his ability to cope with it and his responsiveness to its emotional and personal aspects" (p. 99).

The individual's evaluation of himself, his "self-esteem," may therefore affect his vulnerability to influence, within the framework of the resources he has available to cope with the environment. Further evidence for this comes from additional research by Janis and Field (1959) with a self-rating personality inventory that measured feelings of inadequacy and social inhibitions. Both of these were significantly correlated with high persuasibility for male high school students, though not for females.

McGuire (1968) has suggested that the relationship between self-esteem and persuasibility may be curvilinear. He contends that at least two steps are involved in being persuaded, i.e. *receiving* a message and then *yielding* to it once it is received. A given characteristic of personality, such as self-esteem, may be positively related to one of these steps and negatively related to the other. Thus, a person of higher self-esteem may attend more but be persuaded less.

While there is some basis for considering self-esteem as a persisting personality characteristic, it also appears to be vulnerable to situational variability—in terms of transient states. Experimental manipulations of self-esteem may induce a greater or lesser degree of persuasibility, in combination with other factors. This is illustrated by an experiment conducted by Gollob and Dittes (1965). Their subjects were 165 Yale freshmen who were first given an ambiguous test on which half were led to believe they had performed well ("success condition") and the other half that they had performed poorly ("failure condition"). They were asked to give their responses to three questions, read a communication, and then again indicate their attitudes to the same questions based on what they had just read.

The communication had to do with cancer research and different segments of it were constructed to test the effects of different conditions. The first condition tested the simple hypothesis of the usual inverse relationship between persuasibility and the manipulated self-esteem, by providing a clearly stated message that was not threatening. The "fear" condition was designed to create a threat by indicating that the prob-

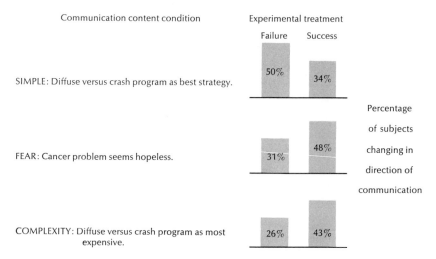

Figure 10.7: Percentage of subjects, among those given an initial set of failure or success, who changed attitudes in direction advocated by communication. (Based on data from Gollob and Dittes, 1965.)

lem of escaping cancer seems increasingly hopeless. The "complexity" condition involved an argument that was not as clearly stated. In all cases, attitudes were measured before and after on a six-point scale. It was predicted that the experimentally induced self-esteem would lead to resistance to the communication under the first condition but not for the latter two conditions. Separate questions were asked to measure their effects.

As will be seen in Figure 10.7, the results were consistent with these hypotheses. An inverse relationship between manipulated self-esteem and persuasibility was found for the simple condition. For both fear and complexity conditions the relationship was reversed. Furthermore, neither the self-rating of low self-esteem which Janis and Field (1959) found to be positively related to persuasibility in male high school students, nor a test of self-esteem developed by Dittes (1959, 1961), was significantly related to any attitude change. Gollob and Dittes conclude that a persisting disposition of self-esteem was not as important here as its experimental manipulation. In a recent experiment by Zellner (1970), she compared "persisting" self-esteem and "transient" self-esteem, produced by experimental manipulation similar to that em-

ployed by Gollob and Dittes (1965). Among other intriguing relationships, she found that *transient* self-esteem was more highly related
to persuasibility than was its *persisting* form. She interprets her findings as supporting McGuire's (1968) conceptions of receptivity as a
necessary step prior to yielding.

These experiments, taken together with other recent work, lead to
the conclusion that persuasibility is a complex outgrowth of the interaction of individual characteristics and situational requirements such
as the characteristics of the communication, the characteristics of the
communicator, and the person's sense of self-esteem in the particular
circumstances.

Some features of personality and social interaction

What primarily concerns people about the personality of others is the
way it affects them in social interaction. Most of the time, when we refer to an individual's "pleasant personality" we mean to say something
about the ease or congeniality of a relationship with that person. In
this sense, the external personality of the individual provides social
stimuli which other individuals evaluate positively or negatively, as we
indicated in connection with social interaction in Chapter 7.

Two kinds of interpersonal relationships which are affected by personality are intragroup and inter-group relationships. The first category
encompasses the effect of personality on group activity, while the second emphasizes the quality of interpersonal relationships which are
shaped by group distinctions, as in prejudice. In this section we will
consider both of these briefly as illustrations of personality's ramifications to ongoing social interaction.

GROUP PERFORMANCE

Many studies of group processes take account of the personality characteristics of the participants in the group. Indeed, one kind of research
design involves the assignment of individuals with previously assessed
personality characteristics to work with others who have the same or
different characteristics. This approach was discussed in connection
with the experiment by Scodel and Mussen (1953) who paired indi-

viduals on the basis of their authoritarianism scores. Another illustration from research where subjects are experimentally paired is the work of Smelser (1961). His procedure was first to administer a personality inventory to a large group of male undergraduates to identify those scoring very high or very low on a dominance scale. They were then assigned to participate in a co-operative problem-solving situation. In all pairs, one partner was assigned a dominant role and the other a subordinate role.

Smelser found that the most productive situation was the one in which the subject with the dominant personality had been assigned the dominant role and the one with the submissive personality was assigned to the subordinate role. As expected, the least productive situation was the one where an incongruity was established between the individual's personality score and the role requirements, that is, a reversal of the congruous pattern. In general, dominant subjects paired together performed better than did submissive subjects. Thus, the congruence of personality with the role demands within a given situation bears directly on the effective performance of individuals who depend upon one another in close interaction.

As might be expected, putting diametrically opposite "personality types" together in groups can produce distinctly negative consequences on interaction. Altman and McGinnies (1960) composed groups with equal numbers of subjects who were high or low on "ethnocentrism," as measured by the California E Scale, closely related to the F Scale discussed here previously (see p. 60). Compared to groups made up of subjects who were uniformly either high or low on this scale, these heterogeneous groups showed a lower rate of response, less cohesiveness, and less spontaneity in interaction, thus revealing substantial effects on intra-group attitudes and modes of participation.

In an elaborate experiment conducted in the Navy, Haythorn and Altman (1966) placed pairs of male volunteers together for ten days, half under a condition of social isolation, and the others not isolated from others, as a control condition. The pairs were variously composed on combinations of four personality variables, i.e. dogmatism, and the needs for achievement, affiliation, and dominance. In each pair both members were high, both were low, or there was one of each level, or one of these with mixed combinations of the rest of them.

During the ten-day period, the pairs had daily work periods in which they performed several kinds of tasks varying on such dimensions as concreteness vs. abstractness, and high vs. low co-operation. With respect to stress, and its effects on performance, it was found that isolation of the pair, as expected, enhanced subjective reports of stress. Furthermore, where both members of the pair were high on dominance, but different on achievement needs, the greatest stress was reported, and a high rate of "territoriality" was observed, in the sense of coveting one's own physical space and privacy (Altman and Haythorn, 1967). The complexity of these relationships indicates that the efficacy of homogeneity or heterogeneity of group composition depends upon a system of variables, including personality, the nature of the task and of the interpersonal situation, and the dependent measures employed, whether of performance or of attraction, as Haythorn (1968) has observed recently in his coverage of this area of research.

In several of the last studies noted, only two individuals are involved in a narrowly defined task with a high degree of specificity regarding role relationships. But what of the situation where a larger group is involved in a creative, less structured task? Some have argued that homogeneity contributes more effectively to group performance than does heterogeneity (Hemphill, 1950a). However, it seems apparent that the particular task posed for the group, as well as the variables of personality which are salient, act together to determine outcomes. Shaw (1960) has found from his studies (1959a, 1959b) that "there seems to be no systematic relation between homogeneity and group efficiency and satisfaction. Degree and direction of correlations vary with the group structure and the particular characteristic under consideration" (p. 450).

A major contribution to this line of work has come from research by Hoffman (1959). He found that groups made up of individuals with dissimilar personalities tended to produce higher quality solutions, of a creative kind, than did those made up of individuals who were most similar in personality. In a broadening of his work he and Maier (1961) conducted an experiment with four-person groups comprised of individuals who were homogeneous or heterogeneous in personality. To accomplish this they administered a standard personality inventory, the Guilford-Zimmerman Temperament Survey, and matched group members by the degree of correspondence of their profiles. Homogeneous groups were made up of individuals who had very high positive profile correlations, and heterogeneous groups were composed of people with negative or zero correlations between their profiles. Hoffman and Maier constructed 16 homogeneous and 25 heterogeneous groups on this basis, and all met weekly for case discussions, problem-solving, and role-playing.

Using various group problems, Hoffman and Maier (1961) found once again that, in general, heterogeneous groups produced a higher proportion of high quality solutions than did homogeneous groups. They also found that the satisfaction of individuals with solutions reached was highly correlated with the degree to which the individuals reported having had *influence* in determining the group solution. These authors suggest that "solutions with high quality and high acceptance can be obtained from groups in which the members have substantially different perspectives on the problem, and in which these differences are expressed and used by the group in arriving at the final decision" (p. 407).

On balance, it is not possible to say that either homogeneity or heterogeneity of personality will lead to better productivity or higher satisfaction in groups. More must be known about the task and role requirements to make this kind of prediction successful. However, a clear case can be made for the influence of the personality characteristics of group members on interactions within groups.

PREJUDICE IN PERSONALITY

Prejudice is a widespread social phenomenon which has long occupied a place in social psychological study. In recent years, increasing emphasis has been directed toward the features of personality which bolster prejudice. A good part of this has stemmed from the work on authoritarianism as a personality disposition. Typically, persons who are authoritarian are prejudiced in the sense of being negatively oriented toward groups other than their own. There are also other "functional" features of prejudice which have been revealed by research.

Because of this emphasis on the psychodynamics of prejudice, there is danger in thinking that only authoritarians or "disturbed" people are prejudiced. However, as G. W. Allport (1958) observes, many attitudes of prejudice are sustained among normal people as conformity in polite social chatter. He says:

> In the course of an evening's conversation in a gentile group it is
> not uncommon to hear the Jews blamed once or twice for some
> current evil. Everyone nods a head and goes on to the next subject.
> A group of Republicans might find the same conversational cement
> in abusing the Democratic administration, or vice versa. And a dig
> at Irish politicians is in many cities a safe adhesive to apply to a
> faltering conversation (p. 273).

Basically, then, prejudice begins as an inter-group phenomenon. It has
to do with favorable as well as unfavorable attitudes which are related
to group distinctions. The terms "in-group" and "out-group" are routinely
used to signify those groups to which we are positively attached and
those that we view from outside. Therefore, though we do not usually
think of it in this way, all of us are assigned by others to many out-
groups. While we perceive a range of individual differences within our
own in-groups, outsiders are likely to have a blanket perception, or
"stereotype," of these characteristics. Thus, although we freely talk
about a "typical Frenchman," as Americans we may be jarred by the
foreigner's stereotype of the "typical American."

For the highly prejudiced individual, this distinction takes on special
importance because of an intense motive for *social acceptance*. One
characteristic of the highly prejudiced person is the need for security
or a sense of superiority that comes from belonging to a favored in-
group and attacking members of an out-group. This phenomenon is especially seen in majority-minority group relations where, for example,
any white, no matter how inferior his status, can feel superior to any
black, no matter how well educated or economically well off.

In a related vein, the highly prejudiced individual is generally given
to mental *rigidity* and categorical thinking. Distinctions between "we"
and "they" are sharply made. Outgroup members are perceived to be
different and to hold different attitudes. This has been experimentally
verified in a study by Muraskin and Iverson (1958) who found that the
more "social distance" college students set between themselves and
other groups, the less they saw these group members as having attitudes similar to their own. Similarly, Byrne and Wong (1962) found
that prejudiced white subjects assumed that a black would have different beliefs than their own.

Psychodynamically, prejudice appears to function in unconscious,
non-rational, and impulsive ways. Therefore, it is possible for intensely

prejudiced people to maintain the appearance of composure but to operate with a great deal of *repression*. As G. W. Allport (1958) points out:

> . . . an outstanding result of studies of bigoted personalities seems to be the discovery of a sharp cleavage between conscious and unconscious layers. In a study of anti-Semitic college girls they appeared on the surface to be charming, happy, well-adjusted, and entirely normal girls . . . but probing deeper (with the aid of projective tests, interviews, case histories), these girls were found to be very different. Underneath the conventional exterior there lurked intense anxiety, much buried hatred toward parents, destructive and cruel impulses. For tolerant college students, however, the same cleavage did not exist (p. 373).

Two important unconscious elements in prejudice appear to be the mechanisms of *projection* and *rationalization*. If a person has impulses or desires that are socially disapproved, they can be projected onto disliked groups. Thus, sexual repression may readily lead to the labeling of other groups as sexy; one's own grasping tendencies may be made into others' mercenary traits; aggressive tendencies can be seen in others as warlike intentions, and so on. By this process the prejudiced individual rationalizes his prejudice by blaming it on the out-groups. Thus, some people justify prejudice and discrimination against blacks by saying that they are unintelligent and "really prefer" menial work. Others excuse anti-Semitic real estate and social club restrictions by saying that Jews are clannish and "like to stay by themselves." By such rationalizations, the *effects of prejudice are made to seem its causes*.

Since individuals vary in the degree to which they are prejudiced, a reasonable question concerns the why of these individual differences. A reasonable answer is to consider prejudice as functionally important in *bolstering the self-concept* where the individual has feelings of personal inadequacy; this was discussed in connection with Katz's functional viewpoint in Chapter 6 (p. 196). In this sense, it is an adjustive response for the individual, but one with potentially dangerous social implications.

Some have said that prejudice is merely a response to frustration. But all adjustment, in some degree, is responsive to frustration. How the individual copes with frustration is also a matter of great relevance to society. The problem with prejudice, simply stated, is that it can become such a pervasive feature of the individual's adjustment that it generates several more problems. First, a person who is highly prejudiced becomes inordinately dependent upon it for support; second, such categorical group distinctions considerably impede the effectiveness of his social relationships; third, rampant prejudice holds disabling social consequences not only to the target groups, but also in terms of the limitations it imposes on the productive energies and cooperative endeavors that any society requires to function smoothly.

By this brief discussion, we have by no means exhausted the topic of prejudice. In the next chapter more will be said about prejudice as one of the features of society associated with ethnic and sub-cultural variations. We will also be considering some of its aspects in greater detail in Chapters 12 and 13 in dealing with group processes.

The chapter to follow continues the discussion of personality, in terms of its development within various subcultures. This is appropriate to an understanding of the way that the individual's social identifications, beginning in childhood, shape dispositions and responses.

SUMMARY

Personality refers to an individual's unique characteristics. These exist on an *external* and an *internal* level. The first level consists of typical modes of response that grow out of adjustment and role-related behaviors. The second level represents the individual's underlying characteristics which comprise the psychological core. Personality can also be seen to have a *dynamic* aspect which permits change through learning, and a *consistent* aspect which provides stability.

The study of personality proceeds on both levels. Usually, it is expected that these will be consistent with one another, though this may not be the case. Two individuals who behave in a similar way may be motivated quite differently, just as dissimilar behavior may arise from a common motive. Its dynamic aspect produces changes in personality, especially through profound life experiences and also from the immediate role demands of a social situation.

Qualities of personality arise from the complex relationship between biological tendencies and social influences beginning in early life. Various kinds of evidence from animal and human research indicate that early experience has a discernible effect on personality. Thus, exposure to deprivation during the formative years has been found to be associated with subsequent behaviors and attitudes, including the individual's self-concept.

The traditional approach to personality has been oriented toward *traits*, that is, the individual's typical behaviors which are sometimes imputed to innate factors such as instincts. One example of a trait typology is extroversion-introversion. Because "pure type" traits leave out individual variations across situations, the trait approach does not have much support today. A more contemporary view of personality is concerned with the *dispositions* which lead individuals to typical responses rather than focusing on the responses alone. Dispositions are considered to function within the individual's psychological field and to intervene between experiences and responses to social stimuli.

Another approach to personality emphasizes the individual's efforts to cope with his environment. This *transactional* approach makes the individual the primary focus for understanding social influence processes in a two-directional way. In this sense, the individual not only *re*acts to the environment but also *pro*acts on it as well. At the heart of the transactional approach is a process of striving which is intimately associated with the individual's self-concept, with particular reference to *self-esteem*, the positive component of the individual's self-concept. Though it has stable characteristics, self-esteem is also subject to variability of expression, as a more situationally induced transient state.

There are various techniques for studying personality. The initial, and still widely employed technique, was concerned with measuring typical behavior, either by the ratings of others or by self-ratings. The modern trend in social psychology is inclined toward a study of personality in terms of dispositions. This is sometimes referred to as the *cognitive approach*. Among the dispositions which have been measured as features of personality are authoritarianism, dogmatism, Machiavellianism, achievement motivation, internal and external control, manifest anxiety, social desirability, and persuasibility.

A wide range of findings has been obtained which indicates a relationship between these measures and the individual's style of responding in social situations. The major thrust of this work has been to demonstrate that both the individual's dispositions and the immediate social situation in which he finds himself must be jointly considered in understanding social influence process. Experimentation employing subjects who vary on these dispositions routinely finds this interacting relationship with the situation.

In studying group processes, one kind of research design involves individuals placed in interaction with others who have been found to have the same or different characteristics of personality. A typical finding is that interaction proceeds better where there is a *high congruence* of personality characteristics with role demands, such as those for dominance and submissiveness. A good deal of research has also been done on the relationship of homogeneity or heterogeneity of group members' personalities in the efficient operation of a group. However, neither is necessarily more effective, in the sense of group productivity or satisfaction. Their effects appear to be intimately related to the kind of task and role requirements set in the situation.

Attitudes of prejudice have also been studied as a component of personality. The highly prejudiced person has been found to think in terms of *stereotypes* which oversimplify the qualities of those in his "out-groups." These attitudes persist despite the actual diversity in any human group, and the inconsistent nature of the attitudes themselves. The highly prejudiced person has been found to have an intense motive for *social acceptance* and to have several psychodynamic characteristics as well. These include *rigidity of thought, repression, projection,* and *rationalization.* Typically, those who are highly prejudiced give rationalizations which actually make the *effects* of prejudice seem the justifiable *causes* for prejudice. A major personality factor in prejudice appears to be the function it fulfills in *bolstering the self-concept* where the individual feels personally inadequate. While this may be a useful adjustive response for the individual, it has destructive implications for society at large.

SUGGESTED READINGS

From E. P. Hollander and R. G. Hunt (Eds.) *Current perspectives in social psychology.* (3rd ed.) New York: Oxford University Press, 1971.

Introduction to Section III: *Personality and society*
14. J. McVicker Hunt: *Traditional personality theory in the light of recent evidence*

16. J. Milton Yinger: *Personality, character, and the self*
19. Richard Christie and Florence Geis: *Some consequences of taking Machiavelli seriously*
62. Gordon W. Allport: *On reducing prejudice*

SELECTED REFERENCES

*Allport, G. W. *Becoming*. New Haven: Yale Univer. Press, 1955.
*Allport, G. W. *The nature of prejudice*. Garden City, N. Y.: Doubleday Anchor, 1958.
Barnouw, V. *Culture and personality*. Homewood, Ill.: Dorsey Press, 1963.
Borgatta, E., & Lambert, W. W. (Eds.) *Handbook of personality theory and research*. Chicago: Rand-McNally, 1968.
*Fromm, E. *Escape from freedom*. New York: Rinehart, 1941.
*Gergen, K., & Marlowe, D. (Eds.) *Personality and social behavior*. Reading, Mass.: Addison-Wesley, 1970.
Kaplan, B. (Ed.) *Studying personality cross-culturally*. New York: Harper & Row, 1961.
*Kelly, G. *A theory of personality: the psychology of personal constructs*. New York: W. W. Norton, Norton Library Edition, 1963.
Kluckhohn, C., Murray, H. A., & Schneider, D. *Personality in nature, society, and culture*. (2nd ed.) New York: Knopf, 1953.
*Linton, R. *The cultural background of personality*. New York: Appleton-Century, 1945.

11

Subcultural influences, personality, and individual differences

Any human society shapes the experiences of its members in a selective way. This process must necessarily affect the development of personality. As Parsons (1951) puts it, "behavior and personality are functions of the system of social relationships in which they are formed . . ." (p. 64).

While widespread social practices, especially in child-rearing, have an impact on individual personality, the idea of a society as a homogeneous unit is of course oversimplified. Any society is comprised of various social environments. Though there are dominant trends which characterize the culture of a society, sufficient diversity nonetheless exists to produce distinctive social influences. Indeed, a characteristic feature of life in modern society is the simultaneous participation of individuals in a plurality of social environments. Each of these environments or subcultures carries its own values and a view of the world.

Social psychology is concerned with the distinctive effects of various elements of a society and its culture. In this chapter we shall consider these on a general level and then move on to subcultural variations which have consequences in personality development.

Modal culture and modal personality

As we have indicated, socialization has a prominent role in the development of personality. It is clear also that the prevailing values

435

and practices of a society are significant determiners of early experience. These values and practices, including the organization of the society, constitute the *modal culture*. Kluckhohn (1953) has said that the American modal culture is characterized by such values as the emphases on individualistic achievement, future-oriented activity, and exertion of mastery over nature (see Chapter 8, p. 315).

Every society embodies major values which have wide acceptability in the practices of its members. In American society, for example, cleanliness is a major value within the modal culture. As Williams (1951) has indicated:

> A great deal of time and effort is lavished on washing hands, taking baths, preparing clean clothes, scrubbing and sweeping, collecting and disposing of trash. . . . Children are approved and otherwise rewarded for cleanly behavior, but meet frowns, censorious speech, minor deprivations, and physical chastisement for certain violations of this pattern. Although the rewards and penalties may be less obvious in later life, adults, too, face sanctions for conduct disregarding this value (p. 381).

But lest we forget, values have "survival value," though not all and not to the same degree. Cleanliness, even if easily disparaged, has vital public health as well as personal hygiene features. The recent spread of the cholera epidemic reminds us of the alternatives. Cholera, which has claimed millions of lives since 1935, when the present "pandemic" began as an epidemic in the Celebes Islands of Indonesia, is not only a painfully cruel killer, but a determined one against which even the most up-to-date vaccines offer no more than six months' immunity at best (*The New York Times*, August 16, 1970). The major protections against its spread are sanitary water for drinking and washing, and effective waste-treatment facilities.

Returning to the basic issue here, it should be understood that the concept of modal culture is essentially a statistical one. It is based on the observation that some practices and orientations are more characteristic of a people than are others. There remains a range of variation in the degree to which these practices have influence over people across the many reaches of a society.

In a highly traditional society, the posibilities for unique contacts and the accessibility of stimulation toward various modes of behavior and outlook are severely limited. Thus, the subculture of a non-urban area is likely to have a greater degree of homogeneity than that of an urban area. Commenting on this, Gardner (1963) says that the city affords wider prospects for individual choice, in these terms:

> The man who moves from a small town to a large city experiences unaccustomed freedom. He not only escapes the stultifying web of attitudes, expectations, and censorship that characterize the small town, he finds in the city more choices in every dimension—kinds of dwelling, consumer goods, entertainment, social comparisons, culture and work (p. 61).

One implication of this range of choice is the differentiation of individual characteristics that it permits. If we contend that society affects personality then, at least in some way, the richness of a society's diversity should be reflected in the variations in its members' personality. Alternatively, very simple societies, such as some primitive tribes studied by anthropologists, should have a more distinctive modal personality.

SOCIETY AND BASIC PERSONALITY TYPES

Perhaps the best known formulation of society's influence on personality is represented in the work of the psychoanalyst Abram Kardiner (1939, 1945). One of his main contentions is that every society has a typical set of child-rearing practices which express the modal culture. As a result of these practices, a particular personality structure is formed and people in the society thus become oriented in the ways dictated by the culture. He defines this "basic personality structure" as "the effective adaptive tools of the individual which are common to every individual in the society" (p. 237).

It is important to understand, as Linton (1951) who worked with Kardiner has noted, that "the concept of basic personality . . . does not correspond to the total personality of the individual . . . it represents a common denominator, a series of fundamental characteristics upon which other and more variable elements of personality content are superimposed in the case of both individuals and groups" (p. 139).

There have been several lines of criticism of this heavily deterministic viewpoint. One consideration already noted is that any society has diverse elements which constitute its subcultures. Furthermore, the concept of basic personality tends to underemphasize individual differences and to overemphasize a presumed commonality of experience. DuBois (1944) has introduced the alternative term *modal personality* to indicate better the wide range of variation within any society. She says that there may be central tendencies in the development of personality characteristics, but there are considerable variations, too, which are seen among adults in any society.

Parsons (1951) has taken issue with the schemes emphasizing personality types in a society on two grounds. First because cultures are not fully integrated in a homogeneous way; and, second, because personality represents an individual system of relationships which is not the same as those stable *inter*-individual relationships which characterize a social system (p. 69). A personality, in short, has an integrity which is not identical to a society's organization.

Thus, part of the difficulty lies in confusion regarding the very definition of personality. If typical behaviors are the focus of attention, people in a society tend to evidence many similar behaviors which are culturally defined. But these do not necessarily reflect more deep-seated commonalities in the psychological core of personality. Most observers, however, grant that there are certain mutually held attitudes and values which members of a society share in construing the world. Wallace's (1961, 1962) concept of *mazeways* of thought, discussed here in Chapter 8, is illustrative of that position. These orientations need not lead to the same behaviors, but they do serve to define what is "right" and "proper."

NATIONAL CHARACTER AND NATIONAL CHARACTERISTICS

Related to the idea of a society's modal personality is the concept of national character. As Linton (1951) says:

> The crux of the problem of national character lies in the degree to which modern civilized nations have distinctive national cultures and to what extent the culture elements shared by the various social units which compose such a nation reflect a common denominator of the personalities of the nation's members (p. 134).

Apart from everyday "stereotypes" about nations, anthropologists in particular have tried to delineate various "national characters," making use of techniques applied to the observation of primitive societies. Much of this work involves a melding of anthropological observation with Freudian interpretation. Thus, Gorer develops a major conception about American society around the theme of England as the "rejected father." Americans tend to reject authority, says Gorer (1964), because:

> In some significant ways the birth of the American republic can be compared with the mythological scene which Freud imagined for the origin of civilization. . . . The downtrodden sons combined together to kill the tyrannical father; then, overwhelmed by their crime . . . they make a compact which establishes the legal equality of the brothers, based on the common renunciation of the father's authority and privileges (p. 29).

Gorer, as well as Margaret Mead, Ruth Benedict, and Gregory Bateson, are among those who have written largely impressionistic accounts of the characteristics of people within a nation. Much of this has the air of authenticity, though it rests largely on unsubstantiated impressions. Benedict in *The Chrysanthemum and the Sword* (1946) made much of the Japanese devotion to ceremony, ritual, and position with an emphasis on the rigidity of early toilet training as a sign of a "rigid" society. But Stoetzel (1955) has raised questions concerning the accuracy of this contention. He has emphasized, too, the evident shifts in cultural values which have occurred in Japan since World War II. Apart from doubts about the validity of broad assertions concerning a nation, then, the general point is that they may be too fixed and fail to account for change.

Another point is that a factor which appears to be an explanation for one nation's conduct may be evident in other nations without the same consequences. Thus, Shaffner (1948) explained the character structure of the Germans on the basis of respect and obedience for a dominant father. But other nations also reveal such cultural patterns. Indeed, many things which are said to typify one nation are often typical of other nations or segments of them. Moreover, a single characteristic pattern can never adequately sum up the complexity of a modern nation. As Farber (1950) aptly notes, the problem in discussing national character is that the concept of a nation is essentially political-geographical. Thus, cultural patterns may vary from place to place and change from time to time. They could not, therefore, yield a singular character structure. He says:

Not only do national and cultural boundaries often fail to correspond, but we are confronted with the further difficulty of nations containing several cultures. Is it possible, for example, to make a general statement about the character structure of the people of the Soviet Union? Such a statement would have to include reference to Ukrainians, Letts, Armenians, Mongols, and a large number of other culturally diverse groups. A Canadian national character would need to include French and British Canadians, as well as, to an extent, Indians and Eskimos. . . . It becomes clear that we can not speak of a national character in multi-cultural nations, or to state it positively, that the concept offers promise only in unicultural ones (p. 308).

Klineberg (1964) has also pointed to methodological problems and argued persuasively that we would do better to substitute the concept of *national characteristics* for national character. His major contention is that we can only deal in modal trends which are found across many reaches of a nation, through various research techniques, and not with some presumed similarity that everyone in the nation must share with everyone else. In this respect, he says, for example, that the city dwellers of Paris and New York have more in common with one another, in terms of their pattern of life, than they would have with the farmers or fishermen of their respective nations (p. 133). This consideration brings us face to face again with the vital matter of diversity within a culture.

The concept of subculture

For the most part, subcultures have to do with variations in the dominant pattern of life within a society. Some of the more significant subcultures are social class, community, and ethnic identifications including race and religion. One way to look at a subculture is as a "reference group" affiliation which provides an individual with distinctive perspectives in terms of values regarding what is right, proper, decent, or possible. These may also have other ramifications in later political affiliations as well as in important life choices such as occupation.

Much of what is characterized as "deviance" in society is actually a response to the expectancies arising out of differing subcultures. As Mack (1967) observes:

Normative standards vary by social class, by ethnic group, by degree of urbanization, and by region. Is it proper to enter a store, sit down on the counter, and offer a chew of tobacco to the clerk? A group-shared expectation in a company store patronized by sharecroppers in rural Arkansas may be a violation of the norms in a Park Avenue gift shop catering to wealthy New Yorkers. Taking a hubcap from an automobile in a lower-class slum area is stealing; taking a piece of the wrought-iron picket fence (much more expensive than hubcaps) from in front of your neighbor's fraternity house at a college is only a high-spirited prank. In this case, class position determines what is or is not criminal (p. 157).

Of obvious importance in considering subcultural variations is the effect they have upon early socialization. The kinds of social interaction they engender carry considerable long-range potency in terms of the individual's values and mode of behaving represented in personality. Achievement motivation, for instance, is widely associated with the particular value-orientation emphasized by a given subculture. Some of the things about an individual, therefore, are quite intimately tied to the nature of these affiliations, even granting the shifts which can occur as a result of later social influences.

Previously we said that deprivation in early life was one example of an experience with long-range effects on personality. There is evidence from such studies as those of Berelson and his co-workers (1954), that growing up during the depression had a persistent subsequent effect upon political attitudes and voting behavior, especially for those of lower and middle class status. A poignant illustration of one kind of subcultural effect is conveyed by the observations of the anthropologist Oscar Lewis who has written on the "culture of poverty" as follows:

The people in the culture of poverty have a strong feeling of marginality, of helplessness, of dependency, of not belonging. They are like aliens in their own country, convinced that the existing institutions do not serve their interests and needs. Along with this feeling of powerlessness is the widespread feeling of inferiority, of personal unworthiness (1963, p. 17).

Lewis points out too that not all people who are poor must necessarily live in or develop a culture of poverty. He says, for example, that middle class people who have become temporarily impoverished do not automatically become members of the culture of poverty even though they may have to live in the slums for a while. The implication of this is that the shared outlooks of a subculture may not be taken on by those who have already experienced a different way of life and are still attached to it psychologically.

Just as with the culture more broadly, the quality of a subculture is transmitted through the family as a primary agent of socialization. But the family represents a focus for several different kinds of affiliations which may shape its way of life, including its upbringing practices, in a distinctive fashion. These in turn can produce effects on the psychological development of the individual in terms of personality. We will now consider a number of subcultural distinctions, beginning with social class.

Social class

In a broad way, we can think of social class as a grouping of individuals with a set of privileges, responsibilities, and powers acquired through possession of a common degree of qualities valued in a particular culture (Gittler, 1952, p. 148). In terms of our society's culture, birth or family status constitute a major determinant of class, along with such factors as education and income. Thus, social class is a way of ranking persons in the larger community across many groups. Furthermore, people are born into a class, though in varying degrees there are opportunities for movement from one class to another. Considerable psychological effects flow from class identifications. As Shils points out, "Sentiments concerning class status and the individual's identification of himself in terms of a particular class status do . . . play a very permeative role in social life" (1960, p. 768).

A study by Davis, Gardner, and Gardner (1941) in a Southern town illustrates the perspectives that class identification lends to the perception of other classes. They found a differential basis for perceiving class membership such that *upper class* individuals "think of class divisions largely in terms of time—one has a particular social position because his family has 'always had' that position. Members of the middle class interpret their position in terms of wealth and time and tend to make moral evaluations of what 'should be' . . . middle-class groups accept the time element as an important factor in the superordinate position of the 'old aristocracy'. . . . Lower-class people, on the other hand, view the whole stratification of the society as a hierarchy of wealth" (p. 72).

MEASURES OF SOCIAL CLASS

Essentially, there are two major procedures for assessing class standing. One, the *objective* method, uses indexes of income, level of education, and occupation, usually in combination. It may also involve ratings from members of a community about each other's class position. The second is the *subjective* method which defines social class by asking people where they place themselves. A problem posed in using the subjective method lies in determining what categories should be employed. If, for example, only "upper," "middle," and "lower" class alternatives are used, then the overwhelming majority of people place

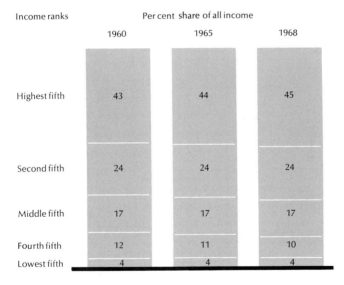

Figure 11.1: Percentage share of all income, before taxes, received by each fifth of the income distribution of family units in 1960, 1965, and 1968. A "family unit" is two or more people living in the same dwelling unit and related to each other; a single person, unrelated to the other occupants in the dwelling unit or living alone, is also considered a family unit. (Based on data reported in U.S. Bureau of the Census, *Statistical Abstract of the United States: 1970.* Washington, D.C., 1970, p. 323.)

themselves in the middle class. However, if the added alternative of "working" class is offered, about three-fifths of the respondents place themselves there (Converse, 1958).

Despite the widespread effect of class, there has tended to be a belief in the "classlessness" of American society. The objective evidence on this point, however, is very much to the contrary. The books, *The Other America* (Harrington, 1963) and *Rich Man, Poor Man* (Miller, 1965), have been among those which have awakened people to the realities. Contrary to the image of affluence projected by television, especially in its "commercials," substantial differences in income, occupation, and education prevail and sharply affect class positions in most areas of our society. Recent figures again reveal marked extremities in terms of average income and its distribution, as will be seen in Figure 11.1. The figures there for 1968 show that those in the highest fifth of income in 1968 received 45 per cent of all income. Furthermore, these same data reveal that those in the top 10 per cent on the income ladder received about 30 per cent of the income that year. Figure 11.1 also indicates that the relative shares of income for each fifth of the income distribution have remained essentially unaltered since 1960, though the average income has of course increased since that time.

SOCIAL MOBILITY

A striking feature of American society, nonetheless, is the accessibility of movement from one class to another. Commonly referred to as "social mobility," it has a high degree of influence in altering the patterns of life and the outlooks of those who experience it. As Lipset and Bendix (1959) note, "A person who moves up in the social hierarchy will tend to change his friends, join new organizations, move to a new neighborhood; perhaps he will even change his religious affiliation [and] alter his political attitudes" (p. 18).

From a psychological standpoint, it is important to recognize, however, that the prospect of social mobility cuts two ways. Its presumed availability does not insure necessarily that the members of the society will be satisfied. Expectations and hopes will be tested against reality. There is considerable evidence in the sociological literature to suggest that the rather widespread expectations for social mobility in American society can induce a sense of frustration when these are not met (e.g. Bredemeier and Toby, 1960). This is accounted for in terms of the explanatory concept of *relative deprivation,* which refers to the discrepancy between what an individual actually achieves and what he aspires to achieve (see Chapter 7, p. 291). In concrete terms, this means that a direct comparison between the material wealth of our society with another society is inappropriate to an understanding of how those in the "relatively deprived" sector of our economy may feel. To tell them that they are still better off than the majority of people on earth is essentially meaningless in terms of the standard that they see held out before them, particularly on the television screen, as noted above.

There is also a prevailing belief that the poor are free of tensions because of their lower status and lower mobility. It is the wealthier who are supposed to be subject to "executive stress" and the strains of "keeping up with the Joneses." Higher social class is in fact associated with a higher prevalence of *reported* neurosis. Yet, data on *severe* mental disorder indicate a reverse trend, especially among older persons. Hollingshead and Redlich (1958), for example, report data from a survey in New Haven of prevalence of psychotic disorders after age 55, by rate per 100,000, as follows:

Social Class	Rate
I-II (highest)	434
III	638
IV	1353
V	3161

Sharp and significant class differences in psychosis are found by these investigators beginning with ages 25-34, as will be seen in Figure 11.2. They also report that 91 per cent of the schizophrenic patients studied were in the same class as their parents (1954). Evidently, then, class standing is psychologically relevant to the adequacy of individual adjustment. Hunt (1959), however, has cautioned that social class standing also may enter into a diagnostic label, especially "schizophrenia," which is attached to a patient, thus magnifying evident class differences in prevalence. The stigmatizing effects of such labeling have been forcefully pointed out by Thomas Szasz, a professor of psychiatry, in his book *The Myth of Mental Illness* (1961). He contends that oftentimes diagnosis becomes a form of "name-calling," with damaging ef-

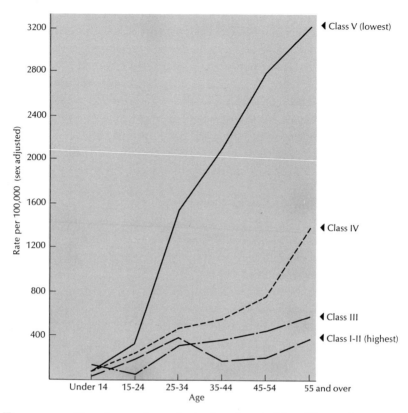

Figure 11.2: Prevalence of psychotic disorders in New Haven, by age and class. (From Hollingshead, 1958, p. 431.)

fects on an individual's freedom of choice. It falls particularly hard on the more powerless members of society who are less likely to receive psychotherapy and more likely to be placed in institutions, merely for custodial care.

EFFECTS OF SOCIAL CLASS

Several kinds of observable social relationships flow from class distinctions. Persons of similar economic or educational circumstances, for example, tend to associate together and more often than not to marry one another. Friends and playmates tend to be drawn from the same class. The occupational aspirations of young people follow class lines and, indeed, about 60 per cent of American males have been found to be in occupations about the same or no better than that of their fathers (Centers, 1949). Lipset and Bendix (1959), however, see this pattern decreasing, and a trend in the direction of upward mobility for sons.

The experiences of a child also vary within the class structure. Among other findings in this regard, Gross has pointed out that "academic achievement, level of aspiration, participation in extra-curricular activities, and the drop-out rate all tend to be positively related to social class placement of the child" (1959, p. 144). In his work on social class in America, Kahl (1953) has shown that, with IQ levels constant, at every level high school boys whose fathers are in major white-collar positions have a far higher expectation of going on to college than do those boys whose fathers fall in lower occupational categories (see Figure 11.3). This is not only a matter of economics. It also indicates the accessibility of opportunities and how these are perceived as a function of the psychological consequences of class, quite apart from intellectual capacity.

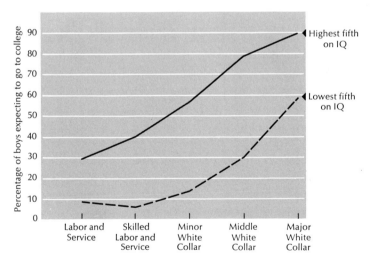

Figure 11.3: Percentage of boys who expected to go to college, among those in the highest fifth and lowest fifth on IQ, plotted by father's occupation. Total data based on 3348 second- and third-year public high school students in Boston. (Based on data from Kahl, 1953, p. 188.)

Hollingshead (1949) conducted a study of the friendship pattern of high school boys and girls in terms of their social class position. After categorizing these students into five social classes, he found that 63 per cent of all friendship ties were between members of the same social class and that another 33 per cent could be accounted for between members of two neighboring classes. Hence, boys and girls from distant classes in the social structure had very little informal relations with one another.

Perhaps the most widely studied social class phenomenon has to do with upbringing. In two papers appearing in 1948, Davis and Havighurst, and Ericson, reported research results indicating that the child-rearing practices of middle class parents were significantly different from those of lower class parents. The most important finding of this study centered about the restrictiveness of middle class mothers in the early training of the child. They were reported to be less likely to breast feed, more likely to follow a strict nursing schedule, to wean earlier and more sharply, and to begin bowel and bladder training earlier than were lower class mothers. Middle class mothers were also found to expect their children to take responsibility for themselves earlier. These results led to the inference that middle class children encountered more frustration of their impulses and that this was likely to have serious consequences in the development of their personalities. In particular, some writers voiced the view that the training of middle class children was likely to produce an orderly, conscientious, responsible, tame, but frustrated child. More recent evidence from the work of Sears, Maccoby, and Levin (1957) indicated no significant differences in infant-feeding practices between the two social classes, though they did report two major differences in the behavior of *lower class* parents: *more* severity in toilet training; and *more* restriction of aggression toward parents and peers, coupled with *more* physical punishment and deprivation of privileges. In a number of major respects, these results were in direct contradiction to the findings of the earlier work which portrayed the middle class mother as excessively rigid, restrictive, demanding, and punitive.

In summarizing the data on class factors in socialization over 25 years, Bronfenbrenner (1958) provided an historical perspective to these findings, particularly in infant-feeding and toilet training. He indicated that up to World War II there was a greater degree of permissiveness on the part of lower class mothers, but that this has since been reversed. Subsequently, middle class mothers became more permissive as a result of the widespread availability of many recommendations about child-rearing, including those embodied in Spock's influential book, *Baby and Child Care*, originally published in 1946. Bronfenbrenner concluded that there is accordingly a considerable trend toward more homogeneous child-rearing in American society, with middle class mothers becoming consistently more permissive toward the child's expressed needs and wishes and less likely to use physical punishment.

One kind of finding, however, which continues to hold important relevance to social psychology, is the high premium placed on achievement by the parents of middle class children. This kind of striving for social mobility appears to cut across other distinctions in accounting for significant values transmitted to the child in early life by the parents. Moreover, it appears to be a broadening trend which may take in more than the middle class. In England, for example, Hilde Himmelweit (1955) has found in general that middle class children tend to be more concerned about how well they do in school and to have higher educational and vocational aspirations than do working class children. However, children described as from the "working class," but who were upwardly mobile in their school and vocational aspirations, were found to have parents who adhered to middle class values more strongly than did the middle class parents in Himmelweit's study.

In another investigation with American families, Miller and Swanson (1958) have also found differences within social class. They distinguish between families that are "entrepreneurial" or "bureaucratic," based upon the father's occupational setting, and characterize the family's child-rearing practices as emphasizing respectively self-control and individual initiative *or* adjustment and getting along well. While these patterns existed within both middle and lower class families, differences between the classes were still quite evident. More importantly, it may be that both patterns represent the fundamental value of "getting ahead," though construed differently by the family in terms of its social reality. Thus, the implicit goal sought may be the same though the explicit emphases of upbringing differ.

An additional consideration is that achievement may be related to factors other than class differences, but which are correlated with those differences. Recently, for example, Kagan (1969) studied the actual interaction between mother and child in the age range one to two years. He found that middle class mothers spent more time indulging in face-to-face vocalization with their children, accompanied by smiling, and tended to be more rewarding of their child's progress than was the case with lower class mothers in comparable situations. But, it is also clear that the realities of life may have made it harder for lower class mothers to undertake face-to-face talking and play because of larger families, the not unusual necessity to work outside the home, and the relative lack of household conveniences to free their time. In sum, socio-economic factors are not just social and economic circumstances but determiners of psychological ones. Therefore, social class has to be understood as a broad category of social identity within which a variety of other "conditions of life" hold, and may act in affecting the child's personality. Among these is ethnic affiliation.

Ethnic affiliations

An "ethnic group" is comprised of people who share a subculture based on racial, religious, or national origin similarities. These may overlap and provide varying perspectives. They are most often considered separately from class, though a feature of ethnic relations in America concerns the racial distinction between blacks and whites which is related to class in that the lower segment of the class structure is still populated disproportionately by blacks. This distinction also has features of what is referred to as *caste*. In a caste system a barrier exists which sharply inhibits social mobility; while movement from one class to another may be possible, this is not so in an authentic caste system. The most pressing example of this in our society today is the caste discrimination directed against blacks, which can override social class and make it count for very little. The black professional or businessman, with income, education, and position justifying a higher class status, may still be looked upon and treated by elements in the community as inferior to any white, however low his class position. The stressful quality of such relationships and the ensuing frustration should not be hard to understand.

In a classic experiment, Clark and Clark (1947) studied the racial identifications of black children. They used white and brown dolls as objects the children were to select in answer to questions, and found that "at each age from three through seven years the majority of these children prefer the white doll and reject the brown doll" (p. 175). Fifty-nine per cent of the children selected the white doll as the "nice doll," and the same percentage of the children indicated that the brown doll "looks bad." The Clarks concluded that even at four and five these children appear to have taken on the negative attitudes toward themselves of the larger community.

Greenwald and Oppenheim (1968) reasoned that the Clarks' findings might have arisen from the necessity for the black child to choose between either a brown doll or white doll, with no intermediate choice; if the child were light-skinned, his choice could very likely reflect his

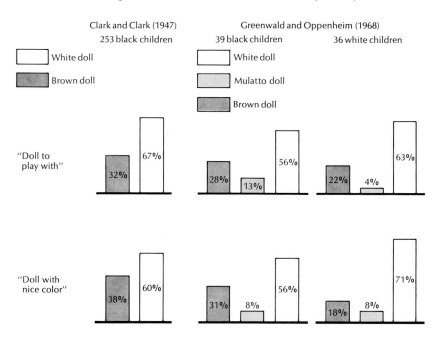

Figure 11.4: Comparison of percentage of children who chose dolls of different colors in response to the two questions indicated, in original Clark and Clark (1947) study with black children and Greenwald and Oppenheim (1968) study with black and white children. Indeterminate responses account for the difference between the total in each category and 100 per cent.

perception of the white doll as more like himself. In their study, Green-wald and Oppenheim used three dolls, a dark brown, a white, and a mulatto (in between) one. They also added a group of white children to provide a comparison with the choice patterns of the black children; it should be noted, too, that their two samples were quite small com-pared to that of the original Clark and Clark study. Moreover, the original study was conducted by black researchers and this one by whites. Nonetheless, as the results in Figure 11.4 show, there is a fair degree of correspondence for the black children between the findings of the two studies on the two critical questions, even with the intro-duction of the third doll. While Greenwald and Oppenheim report that the light-skinned black children more often than not selected the mulatto doll as looking like them, there were still a high percentage of mis-identifications among the black children, as well as among the white children, on this matching criterion.

The main element which stands out in Figure 11.4 is the relative consistency with which both the black and the white children prefer the white doll and reject the brown doll, and, in the later study, the mu-latto doll even more. This last finding may be accounted for by the grayish-brown color of the mulatto doll. But the basic findings on the other dolls appear to be stable and sobering.

There are other discriminatory policies which exist in American society as well. These are by no means unique to us, but we still enter-tain a number of significant beliefs to the contrary. The notion of the "melting pot," for example, is a widespread equalitarian value to which we pay homage. Ours is supposedly a nation in which a mixture of dif-ferent ethnic strains is greatly to be desired. Here again, the actual social pattern does not confirm the value. Thus, Gordon (1964) writes:

> Both structurally and culturally, then, the "single melting pot" vision of America has been something of an illusion—a generous and idealistic one, in one sense, since it held out the promise of a kind of psychological equality under the banner of an impartial symbol of America larger than the symbols of any of the constitu-ent groups—but one which exhibited a considerable degree of so-ciological naivete. Given the prior arrival time of the English colonists, and the cultural dominance of Anglo-Saxon institutions, the invitation extended to non-English immigrants to "melt" could only result, if thoroughly accepted, in the latter's loss of group identity, the transformation of their cultural survival into Anglo-

Saxon patterns, and the development of their descendents in the image of the Anglo-Saxon American (p. 129).

Distinctive subcultural patterns continue to be found in various ethnic groupings, for example in terms of achievement motivation. Strodtbeck (1958) reports evidence indicating a higher value for achievement among children from Jewish and Greek homes, with a lower relative value among those from Italian or Negro homes. Results for Catholics compared with Protestants were dependent upon other ethnic ties and were not consistent.

Religious identifications can serve a reference group function however. Charters and Newcomb (1958) conducted an experiment with Catholic, Protestant, and Jewish undergraduates. A questionnaire on religious beliefs was administered to all of them, but only after they had been divided so that about one-third in each religious category was assigned to either one of two control conditions or to the experimental group. Those in the latter group were told that the test would include items relevant to *their* particular faith; on the other hand, the control groups were *not* made aware of their common religious identity. The results indicated a significant response difference for the Catholic experimental group compared to the Catholic controls, in terms of more responses in line with orthodox beliefs. No significant differences were found when these subjects were compared in items irrelevant to the Catholic religion. Comparable results were not found for the Protestant and Jewish students in this experiment. The authors conclude that "the data from the Catholic groups strongly suggest that an individual's expression of attitudes is a function of the relative momentary potency of his relevant group memberships" (p. 281).

Plainly, though, individuals are not one-dimensional in reacting to the world since they have varying subcultural identities. And there are conditions of "cultural conflict" where two such identities clash. This is likely to be seen when parents are new migrants to a society and have not absorbed its culture. Their children may then learn one thing from the school and playmates and another thing at home. This effect is enhanced if the parents are from an ethnic group which is disdained by the broader community. Thus, children are caught between a desire to assimilate to the broader culture by conformity to its patterns while still being identified with their parental subculture. This mode of "minority group" treatment is quite prevalent and leads to a widening gulf between the generations. It also produces frustration because of the paradox that assimilative acts of conformity by minority group members are not necessarily rewarded by social acceptance, as Seward (1956) found in her study of culture conflict.

Nonetheless, powerful tendencies toward assimilation persist, and the acquisition of new cultural forms from the school and playmates leads the child to a weakened attachment or even open hostility to the other culture that the parents represent (e.g. Eisenstadt, 1956). This is not only a problem of minority group members. A mobile, fast-changing society has been found to create a strain on the adolescent's relationship to his parents, and this is associated with greater identification with peers (Coleman, 1961; Riley, Riley, and Moore, 1961). In the next section we will consider peers as one of a number of subcultural influences.

The peer subculture

If the family may be said to be a fundamental institution in shaping socialization, another one of considerable significance is the so-called "peer group." A great deal of attention has been directed to the peer group's influence on the child. Exemplifying this trend, Riesman, Glazer, and Denny (1950) have made a particular point of the increasing influence of the peer group, and its consequences regarding the child's "other-directedness" as against his "inner-directedness."

There is evidence, however, that the peer group is not a unitary source of influence but rather one which varies in terms of age-level and the nature of the particular group of peers involved, as well as the context and nature of their activity. Thus, there are at least three age-level distinctions that should be made in this respect.

In the first place, pre-school children appear not to be overly influenced directly by the typical attitudes or behavior of age mates (e.g. Gellert, 1961), if we mean by "influence" the alteration of behavior in the face of more than one perceived behavioral alternative. Berenda (1950) found that children of ages seven through nine were more responsive to social pressures from age mates than those from ten through thirteen. However, Hunt and Synnerdahl (1959) obtained results indicating that children of five and six are little influenced by peers in an Asch conformity situation where they are the true subjects (see Chapter 3, p. 101).

In the school years, before adolescence, the child's peer group seems to serve as a supplemental agent of socialization to the family by providing especially for play activity. In this stage children usually gravitate toward peers of the same sex. Dependence upon the parents is normally still quite high.

The adolescent peer group marks a difference in both its quality and its functions. It tends to incorporate subcultural influences at variance with the adult culture. This is often accounted for by citing the ambiguity of adolescent status in our society. Plant, for example, points to the vulnerability of adolescents to social pressures, because they have no distinctive place in society but are "in between" (1950, p. 54). This does not mean, however, that adolescents generally accept peer standards uncritically. Brittain (1963), as one example, has found that peers are more influential for some things but not for others. What appears to matter is the importance at a given time of the affiliative needs mentioned before of social identity, social reality, and social support.

Some influences may appear to be more effective on the child than others, but this is determined by the situation. Thus, in a condition of confusion those persons providing a satisfactory "social reality" may be reacted to favorably, and in circumstances of status ambiguity "social identity" may be important, as is frequently observed with adolescents.

The long-run effects of influence therefore depend upon the initial conditions under which it occurred. The fact that the family provides social support where it is much sought, as in early childhood, carries a persisting impact. The peers then become a subsequent source of influence based on these affiliative needs.

THE NATURE OF THE PEER GROUP

The peer group has been studied in many different ways with varying definitions. It has been approached first as a grouping of age mates, with no necessary considerations as to their interrelations; second, as a grouping of individuals who are familiar to each other but who do not necessarily form a natural group involving choices of other individuals, such as a classroom; third, as small natural groups in face-to-face inter-action, such as a play group. These may and indeed do overlap.

Because the definitions used involve different social relationships, apparently contradictory results are sometimes found concerning peer influence. From a socio-psychological standpoint, a peer group is best seen as a reference group of other youngsters with whom the child identifies and who have effects upon him in terms of his psychological field. While Kagan and Moss (1961) point out that "there are sub-stantial methodological difficulties in demonstrating a cause-effect re-lationship between peer attitudes and changes in a child's behav-ior . . ." (p. 469), they nonetheless suggest that "the investigations of peer group influences . . . point to the potentially important role of social power or popularity in the course of a child's development of an autonomous or a passive disposition with others" (p. 471).

THE PEER GROUP AND THE FAMILY

Numerous studies have concerned themselves with the relative weight children attach to their family as against, for example, play groups, where alternative responses are involved. Thus, Rose (1956) studying 582 high school students of both sexes found that the family was the most influential group affiliation and that this was correlated especially with fondness for parents. This seems in contrast with the finding re-ported by Rosen (1955), with a sample of Jewish adolescents in a small upper New York State city, who found that the peer group ex-erted considerable influence in whether youngsters followed forms of religious observance.

Several other findings bolster the view that experience in the family is relevant to status among peers. In this respect, Marshall (1961) has found, in a study of pre-school children, that the child's linguistic de-velopment is associated with better social acceptance by playmates. Moreover, siblings have been found to affect a child's preferences in playmates (Koch, 1957). Thus, with a single sibling of the same sex, the child shows an even stronger inclination than usual to choose play-mates of the same sex.

In line with our earlier discussion of identification with parents as part of moral development (Chapter 5, p. 159), Maccoby (1961) has studied the child's reciprocity of behavior in enforcing rules with peers. Within her study sample of sixth graders, she found this kind of interaction to be related both to the sex of the child and dependence upon the parent. In general, boys showed more inclination than girls at this age to accept rule enforcement from peers of the same sex. This was particularly so if the parents had been relatively nonpermissive about the child's earlier impulsive behavior but also warm toward the child. Therefore, says Maccoby, the child's interaction with peers is conditioned by parental relationships in that:

> . . . the child acquires a set of adult-like behavior tendencies during early childhood . . . and these tendencies find their way into overt expression during interaction with peers at a later time when peers provide the necessary stimulating conditions (p. 503).

In a broader framework, the social class position of the family may affect the child's play pattern and relationship to the peer group. In this regard, Tuma and Livson (1960) have reported that how much the adolescent accepts the rules of a group in a given situation relates to the socio-economic status of the family. Moreover, Lesser (1959) is among those finding a relationship between aggressive behavior, popularity, and the class level of the family. In particular, he has been able to demonstrate that different manifestations of aggression meet with different degrees of approval and disapproval by lower-class peers, with provoked physical aggression being relatively approved and unprovoked and indirect aggression being progressively more disapproved. It would appear, then, that modes of reacting within the peer group are interpreted in part within the context of the family's socio-economic status and its environment.

There is, however, a more general trend toward a loosening of the family's hold over the child's socialization. About this change in pattern, Pollak (1967) has commented:

> The function which truly has been taken from the family by other institutions is not education, health care, or homemaking, but the autonomy of setting its own standards. This autonomy may always have been limited . . . but against these earlier models the nineteenth century model was one of greater freedom in decision making (p. 194).

The availability of alternatives to the family, as sources of socialization, is a feature of a pluralistic society. Whether it is necessarily bad has been debated. But if the alternative source becomes the peer group, then certain kinds of emphases are to be expected. The findings of Coleman (1961), for instance, illuminate the power of the peer group in adolescence. He conducted a study in eight large high schools and found that the overriding values and behaviors there were set by the "leading crowds." With exceptions, of course, his results indicated that for boys the mark of success was athletic prowess, and for girls it was being attractive to boys. Even students who were intellectually capable of getting top grades were affected in their performance by the dominant crowd's values, despite their own parents' aspirations.

In his comparison of Soviet and American socialization practices, Bronfenbrenner (1970) concludes that the peer group has a quite different effect in the two nations. He is by no means uncritical in his assessment of the implications of the over-determined character of socialization in the Soviet Union (see Chapter 5 here, p. 176 for his comment), but he sees the American peer group's freedom to exert pressures on youngsters as a hazard to moral development. Bronfenbrenner contends that the prevailing tendency is for the American parent to say, in effect, "Latch on to your peers" (1967, p. 61).

These relationships have been given attention in a recent study (Hollander and Marcia, 1970) of two classes of fifth-graders in a suburban American public school. The major hypotheses guiding this study were that youngsters who perceived their parents to be peer-oriented in their upbringing practices would be more peer-oriented and less self-oriented or parent-oriented when faced with alternatives for action; furthermore, they would be seen by their peers on sociometric ratings as less independent and more compliant "to the other kids." Each child (30 boys and 22 girls) was interviewed with open-ended questions, and then direct questions, concerning instances where he or she wished to do something to which parents objected, and then how it was resolved, with particular reference to the peer group's part in the outcome. The interview provided the measure of parents' peer-orientation. In addition, there were questionnaires administered in the classroom subsequently to gather information on how children would respond to dilemmas involving conflicts between peer, parent, and own standards, in specific cases. Various sociometric ratings were also obtained on measures of leadership, independence, and popularity, among others. The findings confirmed the hypotheses and indicated that children whose parents gave way to the child's peers in their upbringing practices produced children who were more peer-oriented, but on the whole less popular. The most important conclusion from this study is that a peer-orientation is fostered by the complicity of parents with the peer group.

PEERS AND EXTERNAL ASPECTS OF PERSONALITY

Perhaps most relevant to a socio-psychological view of the process of interaction between the individual and the peer group is the shaping effect that the peer group may have on individual behavior. As we noted earlier, Campbell and Yarrow (1961) found, in a summer camp session with pre-adolescents, that initial evaluations by peers are very likely to shape a child's subsequent actions. Furthermore, Dornbusch, Hastorf, Richardson, Muzzy, and Vreeland (1965) have found that children tend to perceive the behaviors of other children in line with their own behavioral tendencies.

Though early peer asociations are governed by parents, this is variable. Thus, Marshall and McCandless (1957) find that pre-school children who are dependent on adults tend to have lower peer status. Girls also tend to be more emotionally dependent than boys. Subsequent work by McCandless, Bilous, and Bennett (1961) corroborates this finding with the conclusion that while it may be moderately acceptable for girls to show emotional dependency upon an adult in the pre-school situation, it is relatively unacceptable for boys. The fact that sex-typing occurs at this stage is another matter of interest. This has been further studied by Cox (1962) who observed aggressive and dependent behavior of children in a playground situation. He found that a positive attitude toward the father was associated with the establishment of competent group relationships. Boys who were reputed to be aggressive toward peers were found to reject one or both parents. Dependence was high in boys attached to their mothers.

A point of further interest is the child's acceptance by his peers. The underlying question here refers to the process by which status is achieved, in terms of the values implicit in the group's assessment. In summarizing some of the work on social acceptance, DiVesta (1961) reports that many studies indicated "a significant positive relationship between social acceptance and achievement, whether the study was conducted with grade school, secondary school, or college populations"

(p. 517). This finding accords with the work of Marshall (1958) whose results show that level of performance in 4-H clubs by boys and girls was positively correlated to their standing on a sociometric measure. Also, Mouton, Bell, and Black (1956) have reported that children having high status among their peers have greater self-confidence and appear to strive actively for recognition.

PEERS AND SELF-PERCEPTIONS

Of considerable psychological importance is the contribution made to a child's self-perception, his self-concept, by interactions with other children. The central conception of attitudes as well-springs for behavior is nowhere more important than in the core attitudes an individual acquires about himself from a significant reference group. Moreover, such acceptance by peers has been found to be associated with more positive self-oriented attitudes (Reese, 1961).

A counterpart of this is seen in the typical finding that children who are least popular among peers appear to be inaccurate in appraising their actual standing in the group. From this it is sometimes too readily inferred that they are less popular *because* they are less perceptive. Goslin (1962), for example, studied nineteen classes of seventh and eighth graders. Using a modified "social distance" scale, he identified the five most accepted and five least accepted children in each group and studied their relative accuracy in making several kinds of ratings. One of these was an estimate of how they were rated by classmates. As anticipated, those most accepted were significantly better in making accurate estimates than those who were least accepted (cf. Greer, *et al.*, 1954; Gallo and McClintock, 1962). This relationship is shown in Table 11.1.

This table makes clear what the direction of the relationship is—i.e. most accepted most accurate, and least accepted least accurate. What is not so readily apparent, however, is the inevitable bias introduced by the consideration that children—no less than adults—prefer to perceive themselves as higher in standing among their peers than they actually are, presumably to protect the self-concept. The least accepted children are accordingly most likely to seem inaccurate, on that basis, and the most accepted to appear quite accurate. Thus, a simple response bias can account for this kind of finding. What is more, a child at the low

Table 11.1: Distribution of accuracy scores in estimating ratings from class-mates, by percentage, for most and least accepted children, with 93 in each category. (Based on data from Goslin, 1962.)

LEVELS OF ACCURACY BY FIFTH OF THE DISTRIBUTION	LEAST ACCEPTED CHILDREN	MOST ACCEPTED CHILDREN
1 Highest	14%	27%
2	15%	26%
3	18%	22%
4	25%	16%
5 Lowest	28%	9%
	100%	100%

acceptance end could be quite accurate in knowing where he stands but nonetheless give a "socially desirable" response, namely that he is higher than that private estimate. It may be also that the child rejects what he considers the unfair judgment of his peers. Finally, another point in these data is that the levels of accuracy are based just upon those two categories of subjects who were high or low in acceptance, thus giving a sharper contrast by comparison of extreme groups.

The point, then, is that there is a great deal of stubtlety in how acceptance from peers affects self-perceptions. Particularly where parents encourage a greater orientation toward peer influences, selfhood becomes more closely identified with social identity as defined by peers. Alternatively, where a child acquires an orientation of resistance to such influence, his independence from them may be better maintained.

PEERS AND THE SCHOOL

The school quite obviously provides a place for many peer contacts. As a context for interaction it also has a determining influence on peer relationships, since the social structure of the classroom is often determined by scholastic performance rewarded by the teacher. Moreover, that structure embodies a good deal of competitiveness and even implied threat of exposure for deficiency, as Henry (1963, Ch. 8) has observed. It is to be expected therefore that many studies find a positive relationship between high standing in class performance and peer acceptance in school.

Williams (1958), for example, reports that more than four out of five children found to be high in total acceptance were achieving at or beyond expectancy, whereas more than three out of five children who were low in acceptance were achieving below expectancy. Also, she reports that total performance in school correlates significantly with social acceptance at a level of .43. On the other hand, with high school seniors, Ryan and Davie (1958) report that verbal aptitude grades do not correlate significantly with acceptance by peers. Popularity was measured by having each student rate the others in the senior class and this measure was found to be correlated in the high .80's with a measure of social contact with classmates. In comparing these two studies it is noteworthy that there were differences and that in one case social acceptance was measured by classroom, and in another by an entire senior class.

There is no doubt that the school encourages values associated both with school performance and family aspirations, but how this school influence is felt by the youngster clearly depends on a variety of factors. As Elkin (1960) puts it:

> Compared to the family, the rewards of the school situation—grades, promotions, permission to participate in certain activities, compliments, and leadership positions—are quite formalized. There are particular age-grade expectations with specific tasks and standards, and the child is judged by the degree to which he measures up to these expectations. Almost inevitably there are rankings and comparisons with other students . . . in disciplining and teaching the child, the school authorities may use the child's dependence on his family and peer group . . . such techniques of course are effective only if the family and peer group in some ways support the school (p. 62).

Related to this concern with the child's peer group in its relationship to the school setting is the work of Rhine (1960), who studied the effect of peer-group responses upon the attitudes of college undergraduates. Of particular importance was his finding of a characteristic dependence of these students upon the others for a kind of "social reality," much in line with the findings of researchers such as Asch (1951). This definition of the world appears to be an important function provided by groups in general, and particularly by the adolescent groups operating outside the classroom.

On the psychological side, then, the child acquires a far broader spectrum of encounters in school than the subject matter of the classes. Experiences in the classroom, playground, gymnasium, and auditorium leave their stamp upon the youngster as Jackson (1968) has observed in his studies (see p. 80 here). Moreover, even in terms of routine subject matter, the school provides the child with a "social reality" within which to view the broader world. For example, the child's conception of his nation in the scheme of human events is affected by the kind of historical and political materials he is taught. This interpretation of the world is further reinforced by the already established attitudes of parents, and by peers who are being taught similar things.

In performing its function for society, then, the school affects the child's psychological field in combination with parents and peers. While much of this may occur unintentionally, it nonetheless has significant ramifications. It is also worth noting again that the school often extends the influence of peers, particularly in establishing dimensions for social acceptance.

Society and personality: a final word

The main recurring point here is the consideration that individuals are affected by those with whom they have the closest contact. Beginning with the family, and extending outward to other subcultures, the child has distinctive social experiences. It is hard, therefore, to reconcile this range of relationships with the idea of society as a single pervasive force which stamps each of its members in the same way.

Nonetheless, there continues to be a sense in which people feel that they "know" what Frenchmen or Chinese or Scandinavians are like. If these people are Americans they may be less sure of what an "American" is like. Studies by Perlmutter (1957) and by Bruner and Perlmutter (1957) clearly demonstrate this phenomenon. American subjects in these experiments were asked to predict the characteristics of stimulus persons described by various categorical terms. Thus, a given person might be described by occupation (a businessman), by personal characteristics (intelligent), and by nationality (an Englishman). If the person was foreign, the most dominant factor in determining the subjects' predictions about him was found to be nationality. On the other hand, if the subjects were told that the person was American, this was of no relevance in their predictions; they were far more inclined to be swayed by the information regarding occupation and intelligence in making their judgments.

In explaining these findings, Pool (1965) says that typically we code the behavior of foreigners by nationality rather than by sex, age group, social class, or occupation, because we usually have less prior information on these categories. It is far easier to develop sterotypes of a people from brief encounters than from a rich stock of experience with their individual and subcultural differences. Selective exposure also has pronounced effects. As Linton (1951) says:

> . . . the picture of French personality obtained by an American who spent a year as an art student in Paris would be quite different from that of an agricultural expert who had spent a year studying French vegetable growing (p. 142).

In extending his consideration to Great Britain, Linton points to the considerable cultural variations in England, Scotland, Wales, and Northern Ireland, and adds:

> It may be urged that the cultural-social composition of Great Britain is unusually diverse, but there is little evidence for this. Other European or Oriental nations may appear more homogeneous to an American, but this is mainly due to ignorance of local conditions. Even small enclaves such as the various Scandinavian nations are keenly conscious of cultural differences within their territories . . . even China, in spite of its common written language and nationwide recruitment of the official class, presents many regional differences (p. 143).

Quite commonly, people also think in terms of a given occupational status as having a distinctive personality type. By now it should be clear that this is essentially a manifestation of role, and it is all too easy to confuse role behavior in an appropriate setting with more persisting attributes of personality. Parsons (1951) has treated this misconception in observing that:

> It is possible to categorize social groups according to status, into what as nearly as possible in social science terms it makes sense to

call uniform status—let's say urban middle-class housewives or members of the medical profession in middle-sized cities. . . . But I think no matter how fine you break down the differentiations of social status, if you are still left with a status category in which considerable numbers of people fit, you will find that those people, far from presenting a single, clear-cut pattern of personality type, will cover a widely dispersed range of different types . . . (p. 66).

The major implication of Parsons's point is that even in highly delimited groupings of people, individual differences persist. Think of the variations in personality among your classmates, for instance, and match those against the idea of the "typical college student." The core of the problem of such generalities is the use of *descriptive labels*—Frenchman, professor, housewife, college student—as if they encompassed significant elements of the person's personality. We are all subject to this tendency, however, since labeling is so much a part of language and communication. In one study, for example, it was found that college students responded to the question "Who are you?" by giving their nationality, religion, and status as students.

These "descriptive categories" convey the fabric of society, but they do not usually reveal a great deal about individual differences within a category. Nevertheless, as we have said previously, social identifications are important bases for an individual's orientations and actions. A sense of social identity can be a significant part of what we think of as individuality. We shall consider this matter further in connection with group processes in the succeeding chapters.

SUMMARY

Any society produces effects upon its individual members, particularly in the early socialization practices it employs. These practices, and the values underlying them, are part of the *modal culture*. The concepts of "basic personality" and "modal personality" are both directed at the characteristics that people in a society may share in common. Modern societies, however, provide a diversity of experience within their modal cultures.

Attempts to extend the idea of common personality characteristics to a whole nation, in terms of a "national character," have proven to be faulty on several grounds. Nations are politico-geographical units having complexity that arises from subcultural distinctions. With time and culture contacts, nations may change. Furthermore, the methodology used to study the characteristics of the people of a nation is often highly limited and impressionistic. In a modal sense, however, there may be identifiable *national characteristics* that have reference to typical attitudes and values, and culturally determined behaviors.

Subcultures are divisions of society represented in social class, community, and ethnic differences. They are important in social psychology because of their influence on the values and behaviors of individuals who are identified with them in a reference group sense.

Social class is a major subcultural variation based on the qualities valued in a society, such as family standing, income, and education. Measures of social class may use *objective* indexes of these factors or *subjective* reports by individuals of the class in which they place themselves. Objective census measures reveal substantial class differences, regarding income, for example, though some people prefer to view American society as classless.

Social mobility from one class to the next higher is often sought, though its effects are not entirely favorable. In terms of *relative deprivation,* the inability to be successfully mobile in attaining a higher level may lead to a sense of frustration. Studies of severe mental disorder indicate that psychosis is considerably more prevalent among the lowest classes, beginning with early adulthood.

Differentiation of experience by social class affects educational opportunities, occupational aspirations, and social contacts. It also has been found to be a factor in child-rearing practices, though there appears to be a growing similarity in such patterns across classes. There is still some stability in the finding that the middle class encourages in youngsters a greater value on achievement.

Ethnic distinctions based on racial, religious, and national origins also have persistent subcultural influences. The black subculture tends to represent a fusion of a *caste* distinction—which allows little prospect of "crossing" a barrier—with a mainly lower class status. Exclusionist policies also exist with regard to religious and national origin affiliations, revealing the inaccuracy of the "melting pot" concept of American society. The actual tendency lies more in the direction of encouraging assimilation toward an Anglo-Saxon mode, without necessarily guaranteeing social acceptance. Especially with parents who are recent migrants, this has the effect of causing children to break away from the family's older culture in favor of conformity to the new culture, thus widening the gulf between generations. A mobile, changing society in any case creates a strain for the adolescent in his parent vs. peer relationships.

A child's "peer group" represents a subculture which varies with age-level and activity. Very young children are not so markedly influenced by other children. By adolescence, though, peers are often a significant source of social identity, social reality, and social support, particularly because of the adolescent's ambiguous status in adult society. The family has an effect upon the peer's influences depending upon the kind of relationships involved and the attitude of the parents toward peer activities.

Social interaction with peers has a number of significant consequences in terms of the development of a child's external and internal aspects of personality, including the "self-concept." Acceptance by peers is associated with a number of performance characteristics such as high activity and school grades. The school setting thus encourages some features of peer evaluation. As an agent of society, the school also provides a locus for many values which are reinforced by the parents and by peers.

Individuals are therefore affected by a variety of subcultures. This makes the concept of a uniform influence of society upon the individual highly questionable. Though we may react to others in terms of labels arising from national, subcultural, or status differences, these categories are merely descriptive and not indicative of the range of individual differences within any one of them. It is still true, however, that social identities are important to understanding individual outlooks and actions.

SUGGESTED READINGS

From E. P. Hollander and R. G. Hunt (Eds.) *Current perspectives in social psychology.* (3rd ed.) New York: Oxford University Press, 1971.

17. Thomas Pettigrew: *Negro American personality: the role and its burdens*
63. Donald T. Campbell: *Stereotypes and the perception of group differences*
64. Oscar Lewis: *The culture of poverty*

SELECTED REFERENCES

Coleman, J. S. *The adolescent society: the social life of the teenager and its impact on education.* Glencoe, Ill.: Free Press, 1961.
*Elkin, F. *The child and society: the process of socialization.* New York: Random House, 1960.
*Gordon, M. M. *Assimilation in American life.* New York: Oxford Univer. Press, 1964.
*Gorer, G. *The American people: a study in national character.* New York: Norton Library Edition, 1964.
*Hollingshead, A. B. *Elmtown's youth.* New York: Wiley, 1949.
Kahl, J. A. *The American class structure.* New York: Holt, Rinehart & Winston, 1957.
*Liebow, E. *Tally's corner: a study of Negro streetcorner men.* Boston: Little, Brown, 1967.
*Lipset, S. M., & Bendix, R. *Social mobility in industrial society.* Berkeley: Univer. of California Press, 1959.
*Pettigrew, T. *A profile of the Negro American.* Princeton: Van Nostrand, 1964.
Sherif, M., & Sherif, C. W. (Eds.) *Problems of youth: transition to adulthood in a changing world.* Chicago: Aldine, 1965.

12

Group characteristics and functions

Groups are the most universal units of any social system. They exist primarily to carry on the necessary and significant functions in a society. In the course of our lives, all of us are caught up in many groups. The influence they exert on our individual actions and psychological states gives them a place of unparalleled importance in social psychology. Sherif and Cantril (1947) have highlighted this point in saying: "Once an individual identifies himself with a group and its collective actions, his behavior is, in a major way, determined by the direction of the group's action . . ." (p. 290).

Group processes are central to much of the research in social psychology, especially laboratory experiments. The prodigious output from this study is amply revealed in the simple quantitative fact that a recent bibliography (Raven, 1969) of published work on the small group contains 5156 entries.

This chapter, and the three which follow, all deal with various properties of groups and the processes occurring within them and between them. The last two of these four chapters treat conformity and leadership, two of the most commonly studied influence events taking place in group settings and having ramifications extending more broadly to the society at large.

Some definitions of groups

Historical controversy concerning the definition of groups goes back to the time of the "group mind" tradition at the end of the last century, and even before that (see Chapter 2). Groups may vary in size from two persons to a large political party or major organization. They may be essentially subcultures, or categories, which describe members of a society, or they may involve close face-to-face interaction directed at common goals such as one finds in the family, among playmates, or in a committee. However we define the boundaries of groups, they have the potential for an impact on their members through shared psychological states. As Newcomb (1951) puts it:

> For social psychological purposes, at least, the distinctive thing about a group is that its members share norms about something. . . . Thus an American family is composed of members who share norms concerning their everyday living arrangements, and also concerning the manner in which they behave toward one another. These distinctive features of a group—shared norms and interlocking roles—presuppose a more than transitory relationship of interaction and communication (p. 38).

Newcomb mainly refers to what we will call *functional* groups. We may define these as having members who are mutually involved in ongoing social interaction aimed at achieving a common goal. This is accomplished through their interdependent action within an organized pattern of roles and norms called group *structure*.

Two other kinds of groups, which are better called *groupings*, are *categories* and *aggregates*. As we have previously indicated, a category is made up of people who possess a common characteristic which can be used to *describe* them. An aggregate is a special category composed of individuals who share a time-space relationship, but who do not have a common goal, unless circumstances should create one. People waiting at a corner for a bus or riding in an elevator together constitute aggregates. Should an emergency arise, however, they might organize to take collective action and thus become a short-term functional group.

The term "group" will be used here almost entirely to refer to groups that are of the functional kind. It should be emphasized, however, that the groupings to which we have just referred may also have influence effects comparable in some ways to those produced by functional groups. What appears to matter especially is the degree to which the individual is motivated to be identified with a group, even if he is not strictly speaking a member. But membership is the first approximation to knowing whether a group constitutes a set of "relevant others" for an individual, and we shall consider its features now.

Kinds of group membership

Basically, there are two major ways that individuals become members of a group. The first of these is called *ascription,* the second *acquisition.* They are distinguished from one another by the quality of choice. Insofar as we are born into a family it becomes an *ascribed* group membership. Alternatively, when we join a club, it becomes a group membership we acquire. In social psychological terms, the initial basis for gaining membership is not the same. In the first case we have a low degree of choice, while in the second it is high. However, it is possible for motivations to shift. For example, workers are usually assigned to their unit, but this does not limit strong attachments and even a sense that it is "the best bunch in the department." And the reasons we become members of a group may not be the ones that eventually sustain our membership. Indeed, loyalty to an ascribed group in an organization may take precedence over other considerations, such as effectiveness. This attachment can lead to the not unusual circumstance in which members ". . . so invest in their identity as a group that they will defend an obsolescent task system from which they derive membership" (Miller and Rice, 1967, p. 42).

A TAXONOMY OF GROUP IDENTITIES

Both functional groups and descriptive categories may be entered through acquired or ascribed membership. Examples of these relationships are given in Table 12.1. In the upper right quadrant, the family and a work group illustrate functional groups that are ascribed in the sense of low choice. It is a commonplace that we cannot choose our

Table 12.1: Schematic representation of four kinds of social identifications growing out of two sources of membership in two social entities, functional groups and descriptive categories.

	Greater functionality ⟶	
Source of membership	Descriptive Categories	Functional Groups
Ascribed (assigned: low choice)	Sex Age-level	Family Work group
Acquired (joined: high choice)	Profession Magazine subscriber	Social club Civic association

⟵ Greater volition

family, and usually it is equally true that we cannot choose our co-workers, at least not within most complex organizations. On the other hand, as shown in the upper right quadrant, we may join such functional groups as a social club—where we choose our friends—or a civic association, presumably because of some commitment to its goals.

Descriptive categories are not functional groups, though they may imply functional group membership. Here, too, there is the prospect of low or high choice in terms of the individual's initiative or volition in membership. Our sex and age are dictated by forces over which we have no control. Thus, we belong to some categories, shown in the lower left quadrant, which may have a considerable effect upon us but are not of our own choosing. However, there are other categories that may describe us, which we have a greater degree of choice in determining. Typically, a profession involves a great deal of psychological investment and, on a less serious level, our decision to subscribe to a magazine usually represents a voluntary choice as well.

There are exceptions, of course, to these last assertions. For example, some people do not choose a profession but have it thrust upon them by circumstance. This is true of other identities as well. Religion and political party illustrate two descriptive categories which are most often acquired as a kind of social inheritance through the family, though they may be altered in time. Furthermore, identities such as these, including professional affiliation, may involve us in functional groups. The attorney belongs to a professional category but also may be involved in a law firm, which is a functional group.

Because of their immediate, face-to-face quality, functional groups are typically seen to be more potent in their effects than categories, but they need not be so. For instance, a broad professional identification may influence an individual considerably more than his social club, or even his family, in some critical sectors of life activity. Underlying any delineation of an individual's identifications, then, is the basic question of his motivation. This may be variously related to past experience and to the nature of rewards from his present *relationship* with groups, including the reference group sense.

PRIMARY GROUPS

Very early it was clear that some groups involve special relationships which are not characteristic of others. The family, for example, is the first point of contact the child has with society. It is a group which has highly institutionalized functions involving procreation and child-rearing. There are, therefore, a great many pervasive psychological effects which it induces in the actions, reactions, and outlooks of its members. Cooley (1909) considered that groups such as the family were *primary* groups. In the primary group, members have close personal ties with one another with an emphasis on face-to-face interaction and spontaneous interpersonal behavior. He put it this way:

> By primary groups I mean those characterized by intimate face-to-face association and co-operation. They are primary in several senses, but chiefly in that they are fundamental in forming the social nature and ideals of the individual (p. 23).

Since this kind of attachment could very well develop from other associations quite beyond the family, the qualities of primary groups have largely been absorbed within the concept of functional groups. We observe this, for instance, in connection with the child and his peers, especially in the teen years, as was noted in the preceding chapter. *Secondary* groups are by contrast more impersonal, and are characterized by contractual relations among their members. Being identified with such groups is not an end in itself but rather a means by which other ends may be achieved, such as working to earn a livelihood.

A somewhat similar distinction was made by an early sociologist, Tönnies (1887), in terms of *Gemeinschaft* and *Gesellschaft*, usually translated respectively as "community" and "society." The communal relations between people are more in keeping with the sense of social identity that goes with primary group affiiliation, while relationships based upon more formal and contractual foundations tend toward the impersonality of secondary group affiliations. As society has moved from a rural to an urban mode of life, shifts may be seen from the former to the latter pattern. A bureaucracy also exemplifies secondary relationships far more than primary ones.

In a sense, any functional group can be considered to be a primary group if it is a source of mutual attractions. Katz and Lazarsfeld (1955) provide a summary of findings, in addition to their own research, which sustains the hypothesis that "such groups actively influence and support most of an individual's opinions, attitudes, and actions" (p. 48). According to these authors, the importance of primary group ties was rediscovered after long neglect. On the significance of this, Verba (1961) says:

> The "rediscovery" of the primary group refers to the realization by researchers that systems previously thought of as purely impersonal and formal are greatly influenced by networks of informal personal relations. . . . In the first place, the researchers had not expected to find that primary relationships were important. . . . Secondly, these primary relationships were discovered in what might be called the heart of the modern industrial society . . . (p. 18).

By way of example, Verba points out that the major appeal of intense political participation may be a response to the weakened primary group attachments in the family. Thus, affiliative needs which are otherwise unsatisfied by the kind of secondary relationships existing in an industrial society may encourage ties to political groups, such as a political party, as an alternative. The motivations involved would accordingly be less political than psychological (p. 58).

COLLECTIVE EFFORTS AND SOCIAL MOVEMENTS

There are other acquired groups, mainly less well defined than organizationally based ones, which provide opportunities to express affiliation tendencies. As the point from Verba (1961) quoted above suggests, individuals may seek ties which stand as alternatives to weakened primary group affiliations. Often these are part of social movements involving collective efforts, but with highly variable rates of participaiton. Because so many aspects of social psychology are applicable to them, including various points about group processes considered elsewhere in this and the succeeding chapters, the intention here is merely to suggest a number of features which uniquely characterize collective efforts associated with social movements.

A "social movement," according to Gusfield (1968), may be defined as "socially shared demands for change in some aspect of the social order" (p. 445). For many of the people who support a cause, their own activities are of a spontaneous and short-term variety. However, these activities can provide intense group experiences and attachments which may have considerably greater persistence.

In his treatment of social movements, Toch (1965) indicates that people will often commit themselves to collective action, as part of a social movement, because it provides a sense of clarity in what is otherwise a confusing and alienating social atmosphere. Indeed, *ideology* is a powerful basis for affiliation with others, in that it provides a shared social reality that can phase into many reaches of life's problems. The "conspiracy theory" of history is a recurring example of such a pervasive ideology. From his study of movements, Toch finds that they usually center about extremes, usually of optimism or pessimism in outlook. They appear to have their appeal in uncomplicated, easily understood views that have the quality of absolute certitude.

In a strict sense, such ideological commitments by themselves do not constitute a group affiliation, but they have enormous potentialities for influence over the individual in a reference group sense. If movements are just looked at regarding what they *do*, in terms of collective efforts, then group processes become salient for study. But that may miss a large part of the point. From a psychological perspective, a movement's goal, at least initially, may be to call attention to issues which then become impressed on a wider public. Therefore, the diffuseness, or lack of continuity, in a movement does not preclude its having such an effect on many individuals. The Women's Liberation Movement, to take a very recent instance, may not turn out a great many women for a march, but its effect in homes, working places, and the halls of government, may be quite considerable.

Gusfield (1968) points out that this "mass society" conception of movements still requires organized and integrated groups that provide a platform for effective action. Not uncommonly, a shared concern—about war, human rights, pollution—can lead to a short-term commitment for intense activity, sometimes with fruitful outcomes, and sometimes without them. The differences often come down to considerations of effective group processes, which may founder on questions of *means*. These are highly relevant matters, since functionality depends upon having a good hold over the nature and process of the task, but one failing of ideology is that it often tends to leave means unclear and to place *ends* at the pinnacle of concern. People in the movement "feel good" about the values they are for, or against, even if their expressive behavior offers no organized program. Yet, the underconcern for social process inevitably produces some disillusionment. Rifts in the ranks then occur when the means come to be seen as *transforming the ends being sought*. The fractionation of many social movements, in which large numbers of individuals are psychologically invested, arises from precisely this disparity.

Proposals for action are essentially appeals for social change. Once individuals are aroused to an awareness of a problem, the necessary condition for effective social action is some kind of *invention*, not necessarily new in fact, though it may seem so in its novel context. Often, the invention may consist of establishing a new social entity, sometimes a group—as in a steering committee, or council—or a new position, such as an ombudsman. But social movements do not rely only on such inventions for their success in a pluralistic society; they also require a broadened willingness for people to act individually, as well as collectively, in behalf of the desired change. Legislation will help, but it cannot carry the total load. The recent history of the ecological movement, culminating in the first Earth Day in the spring of 1970, exemplifies this kind of wider following. Such a development frequently is accompanied by a planned information campaign, the organization of neighborhood action groups, and other kinds of collective efforts. Procedures for following through by capitalizing on the aroused sense of urgency vitally depend upon continued organization, even with the inherent lack of a well defined structure characterizing most social movements. There remains the necessity for some element of leadership to continue to direct and focus efforts. As Argyle (1967b) has observed, "Large-scale changes in society . . . consist ultimately of changes in the behaviour of a large number of individuals, and are initiated by the behaviour of a smaller number of other individuals" (p. 87).

From a social psychological perspective, an important element in social movements is the creation of social expectancies concerning what is desired and what program is advocated. Gamson (1968) notes that many social movements aimed at political leaders and public officials fail to take adequate account of the alternative sources of influence which act on them. Thus, the leadership of a collective effort aimed at change requires accurate information about the operation of persons and forces in that sphere of society, and especially where the levers of authority lie. Otherwise the collective effort may become a casualty of its own self-indulgence in public expressive behavior as a way of life.

In his analysis of "protest movements," Turner (1969) considers this issue and concludes that their effectiveness depends upon a balance between making an appeal which seems valid while avoiding an undue threat which might lead to a loss of support and counter-action. An excessive reliance on public demonstrations, especially those with displays of violence, raises the threat level to a high pitch without any compensating gain in sympathy for the appeal. The truth of the matter is that the necessary but often mundane organizing tasks of a movement do not have as much attraction as do the strident calls for taking to the barricades, and hence the latter can too easily overwhelm the former.

The nature of groups

Groups exist fundamentally to help individuals attain goals that would be unattainable otherwise. They represent an organization of effort beyond a mere aggregation of disparate individuals. As Blumer (1948) says:

> A human society is composed of diverse kinds of functional groups. To a major extent our total collective life is made up of the actions and acts of such groups. These groups are oriented in different directions because of special interests (p. 544).

It should be clear, however, that the avowed functions of a group, in terms of the interests supposedly served, may not be the same as the real functions for the members. The exclusive ladies' club which holds a charity ball seeks a goal that openly goes beyond milk for the underprivileged. The prestige value of some groups, or the fun their members get out of it, may be more real functions than those alleged publicly. Moreover, it is clear that multiple motivations may be served simultaneously by group activity. A statement deftly asserting this notion recently appeared as an anonymous clipping on a bulletin board, as follows:

> Meetings are held because men seek companionship or, at a minimum, wish to escape the tedium of solitary duties. They yearn for the prestige which accrues to the man who presides over meetings, and this leads them to convoke assemblages over which they can preside. Finally, there is the meeting which is called not because there is business to be done, but because it is necessary to create the impression that business is being done. Such meetings are more than a substitute for action. They are widely regarded as action.

In the next chapter, we shall explore these psychological relationships somewhat more, after delving now into the structure and interaction within functional groups.

GROUP STRUCTURE

Whatever motivates people to come together to achieve avowed ends in common, they take on organizational properties which create certain relationships among them. This is called *group structure,* and it in turn affects *group interaction.* In concrete terms, by a group's structure we mean that the people involved divide certain functions, establish communications links, become more sensitive to one another's expectancies regarding normative actions and attitudinal expressions, and not least take on a sense of group identity. All in all, then, group members may be said to be interdependent and to have psychological relevance to one another, which accordingly influences the interactions that occur between them.

There are a number of types of structure, as well as different elements which comprise it. One such element is embodied in the term "status," especially as it refers to the *rank* or hierarchical *position* which individuals occupy within a group. Cartwright and Zander (1968) make this observation about its relevance:

> It appears to be almost impossible to describe what happens in groups without using terms that indicate the "place" of members with respect to one another. Various words have been employed, but the most common are position, status, rank, office, role, part, clique, and subgroup. Although these do not all convey intuitively quite the same meaning, all do refer to the fact that individual members of a group can be located in relation to other members according to some criterion of placement. The prevalence of such terms in the literature on groups, moreover, suggests that such placement of individuals is important for understanding what happens in and to groups (p. 486).

Whenever several individuals come together or are brought together in a group to achieve certain ends, a structure invariably is generated. A differentiation of function occurs, and rules are laid down which become part of the normative pattern of the group. Furthermore, there is usually an associated network of communication which arises in order to have the group further its function.

Especially in formal organizations, structure often is made quite explicit by the physical arrangement of individuals, and the expectancies which go with it. Status differences are sharply etched by the assigned location and size of an executive's office, as well as by other of its features. In large offices, a man's "place" matters in the most serious of ways. This passage from *The Kingdom and the Power*, Gay Talese's (1969) engrossing book about *The New York Times*, highlights the point:

> Where one sits in *The Times'* newsroom is never a casual matter. It is a formal affair on the highest or lowest level. Young reporters of no special status are generally assigned to sit near the back of the room, close to the Sports department; and as the years go by and people die and the young reporter becomes more seasoned and not so young, he is moved up closer to the front. But he must never move on his own initiative. There was one bright reporter who, after being told that he would help cover the labor beat, cleaned out his desk near the back of the room and moved up five rows into an empty desk vacated by one of the labor reporters who had quit. The recognition of the new occupant a few days later by an assistant city editor resulted in a reappraisal of the younger re-

porter's assets, and within a day he was back at his old desk, and within a year or so he was out of the newspaper business altogether. Editors, too, must respect the system, and the story is told that one day twenty years ago an assistant managing editor, Bruce Rae, made the mistake of sitting in Edwin James's chair when the managing editor was out ill. When James heard about it, he was furious. Bruce Rae, regarded as a possible successor to James, got no further (p. 108).

Lest this example be considered a unique phenomenon of newspaper life, or one confined to employees of lesser rank, here is another instance, reported by Alan Harrington (1967), in *Life in the Crystal Palace,* his penetrating view of the operation of the executive offices of a large corporation.

I got over my impatience at the slow pace of things, but I felt it once at a lecture given to senior and junior executives. . . . We sat, without anyone suggesting it, according to rank, and I could work out the possible course of my company career, if I stayed with it, just by looking at the assemblage of heads in front of me —bald and white in the front rows, then pepper-and-salt, and gradually back where I was, the black, brown, and blond heads of hair. I thought of my own head, slowly changing through the years as I moved up a row or two . . . (p. 23).

Shortly, we shall have more to say about spatial factors in group structure and functioning. Two other key elements which go to make up structure are the *norms* of the group and its *communication pattern.* A group norm can be considered to be an expectancy regarding the appropriate behavior of members within a given facet of group activity. As was indicated before, a role can be thought of as a highly specialized norm applicable to a person occupying a given status, in the sense of position. In effect, groups are role systems. When we observe a committee in action, some of its members are more vocal than others. What they say is heeded and often reacted to positively. Others are more passive. These observed differences may be a result of higher status, dictating a more active role, as well as of personality characteristics.

Communication patterns involve the question of who communicates with whom, particularly in formal organizations where such patterns are determined in large part by authority from above. In military organizations, for example, it is necessary to "go through channels" in order to gain a hearing. This, of course, is true of most institutionalized hierarchies. Even where groups set their own communication patterns, it is still true that some people may occupy a more central place in the group's communication network than will others.

Just as with interaction in general, influence processes including the exertion of power are activated within a group's structure. Thus, power becomes a significant determinant of the relationships among members of a group. Hurwitz, Zander, and Hymovitch (1953) found that people low in power within the group structure engaged in more ego-defensive reactions. They also tended to overrate how much their superiors liked them. In a related vein, Kelley (1951) found that subjects who held insecure positions in the group structure by being low and unable to rise or high with a potential for falling, engaged in more irrelevant communication within the group, in terms of the task. Moreover, they were less satisfied with the group.

As a general rule, low status members of a group tend to better themselves with those who hold greater power in the hierarchy, as E. E. Jones (1964) has noted in his work on "ingratiation." This phenomenon has also been observed with children. Lippitt, Polansky, and Rosen (1952), for example, found that children of low power are typically inclined to engage in deferential and ingratiating behavior toward children of higher power.

INTERACTION WITHIN GROUPS

Simmel (1950) was an early sociologist concerned with the face-to-face group as a microcosm of interaction which could be studied to derive general propositions about social behavior. In his view, these "small groups" provide a prototype of society. The most noteworthy exponent of this viewpoint today is George Homans. In two books, *The Human Group* (1950) and *Social Behavior: Its Elementary Forms* (1961), he sets forth a number of factors which account for group processes. He says that we study these processes to learn something about "elementary social behavior," which occurs all about us. In a further exposition (1963) of this view, Homans contends:

Small groups are not *what* we study but *where* we often study it.
. . . If you will look at the behavior that students of small groups
actually investigate, you will find that it has the following characteristics. First, at least two men are in face-to-face contact, each
behaving toward the other in ways that reward or punish him and
therefore influence his behavior. Second, the rewards or punishments that each gets from the behavior of the other are direct and
immediate rather than indirect and deferred. And third, the behavior of the two men is determined in part by something besides
their conformity to institutional rules or roles (p. 165).

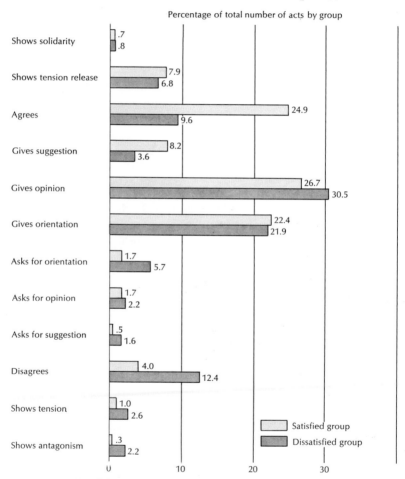

Figure 12.1: Distribution of interaction by categories within a satisfied and
a dissatisfied group. (Based on data from Bales, 1952.)

An individual's behavior in a functional group, therefore, is reinforced by such face-to-face interaction. But note that this reinforcement is reciprocal, and furthermore that it comes to be normative in the sense of commonly held expectancies. Whether these are fulfilled is a major source of satisfaction in groups. The interaction of members can be studied in terms of the Bales categories discussed in Chapter 3 (see p. 93). Figure 12.1 shows the differences in the categories of interaction for a five-person group that was satisfied with their interaction and a group that was dissatisfied. Note especially the major disparities between the groups in the categories of "agrees" and "disagrees."

The process of interaction occurs within the framework of the group's structure. Moreover, the structure itself undergoes change as a consequence of the events represented in interaction. The factor of *historicity*, insures that past interactions will have an effect upon the content of future interactions. This process may produce a change in structure. There are, of course, differences in the degree to which such alterations of structure are possible. For example, leadership, which is a structural element associated with a role of high status and influence, may be changed more readily in some situations than in others. The source of the leader's authority is of central significance in determining this outcome, and this depends upon the source of structure. Some implications of this in terms of the distinction between formal and informal groups, and the effects of spatial relations, will be considered now.

FORMAL AND INFORMAL GROUPS

In functional groups, the goal of the group—essentially, its function—sets its structure, and this structure plays a significant part in interaction. Thus, structure and interaction are tied together so that changes in one may affect the other.

The source of a group's structure may lie within the group itself or in the external system in which it is imbedded. In organizations, typically, the goals and procedures of a group are governed by factors outside of the group's direct control. A work group, for example, has functional features of a *formal* kind which are specified by regulations. There are other kinds of functional groups whose organization is

determined by the members themselves in an *informal* fashion. However, as we shall be noting further, the distinction between formal and
informal structure is probably less important than the identification
individuals have with the group.

Friendship groups are informal. They arise spontaneously out of
common interests and certain shared goals, and they are sustained by
interpersonal attraction. Research by Festinger, Schachter, and Back
(1950) and by Newcomb (1961), for example, indicates that attraction
within such groups is heavily dependent upon closeness of contact and
is then enhanced by mutual interests. Thus, the teenager will select his
friends among those who live nearby and who enjoy the same kind of
records and activities, and probably share similar problems. The major point about such groups is that they are autonomous in the sense of
determining their own activities and being relatively free of organizational constraints.

On the other hand, most of the tasks of society are fulfilled by groups
which are considerably more organized in the sense of a work orientation. Groups in organizations operate with a heavy infusion of structure
from above. They are not autonomous so much as being components
within a broader enterprise. Moreover, membership is determined for
the most part by non-voluntary factors.

Homans (1961) considers that any group constitutes a social system
that has both internal and external features. The elements in the internal system of a group are *activities, interactions,* and *sentiments.* Activities refer to movements that people do to or with non-human objects, such as typing, writing, building, driving, and so forth. By
contrast, interaction refers to things people do together, such as eating,
working co-operatively and playing games. Sentiments essentially refer
to feelings and attitudes about things or events whether human or non-
human. Homans sees these as being interrelated in such a way that if
either sentiments or activities are changed, the tone of interaction will
also change. Furthermore, this is a two-way relationship. Interaction
and positive sentiments are directly related so that, other things equal,
we tend to like those with whom we interact. These relationships,
within the internal system of a group, are intimately tied to the external
system.

Homans's essential principle of group functioning is that when several individuals form a functional group, or are formed into such a

group, an internal system of social processes comes into play. This system, including member interaction, is affected by the group's own structure which derives in part from the normative expectations in the external environment.

An example of the influence of the external system on the internal system of a group comes from research on juries by Strodtbeck, James, and Hawkins (1958). Their major interest was in the interaction process which occurred in 49 jury deliberations, with real jurors listening to a recorded trial and then discussing it. They found that, beginning with the selection of a foreman, socio-economic differentials were important determiners of internal processes. Though the jurors were meeting as equals, their status in the broader society had considerable effect. Thus, in the jurors' selection of their foreman,

> There was no instance in which mention of any socioeconomic criteria was made, but this is not to say that socioeconomic criteria were not involved . . . some foremen were selected from all strata, but the incidence was three and a half times as great among proprietors as among laborers. In addition . . . only one fifth as many women were chosen as foremen as would be expected by chance (p. 382).

A related conclusion from this study was that socio-economic status affected the rate of juror participation sharply and that, as would be expected, those who participated more were more influential in the deliberations. Furthermore, these variables were interrelated such that the first person to speak had a higher probability of being selected as a foreman, and initial speakers tended to be from higher occupational strata. They also tended to be seated at either end of the jury table— a point to be considered further in the next section.

In sum, the essential distinction between formal and informal groups therefore becomes a matter of differentiating group activities and the kinds of structures within which groups carry on their functions.

SPATIAL RELATIONS IN GROUPS

As the illustration of the *Times*' newsroom indicated (p. 479), spatial arrangements may be employed to signify structure. Research in face-to-face groups indicates that the way people are arranged, or arrange themselves, holds significance in their relationship. Terms such as "upper echelon," "inner circle," and "isolate," have been found to have physical correlates which reflect their social psychological import, though they need not correspond perfectly (Sommer, 1967). This has led to a line of relatively new research on spatial factors in groups, paralleling Hall's work (1959, 1966) on cultural determiners of spatial relations in social interaction.

Some years ago, Steinzor (1950) found in discussion groups that when one person stopped speaking, a person opposite him rather than alongside tended to speak next. Hearn (1957) pursued this finding and ascertained that this effect depended upon the degree of leadership exercised in the group: where there was minimal manifest leadership vested in one person, members of discussion groups directed more comments to those opposite; where there was a "strong leader," relatively more comments were made to those sitting in adjacent seats; where there was a greater distribution of leadership, the spatial effect was not evident. Sommer (1967), who has expanded this work in many innovative ways, attributes these results to the restraint on eye-contact with a strong leader, and the alternative provided of restricting one's gaze to those persons nearby (see Chapter 7, p. 277).

In one of his earlier studies, Sommer (1959) made observations on students in a college cafeteria that had rectangular tables. He found that persons talking to one another were most frequently seated at right angles, in an end-corner relationship, next most frequently side by side, and least frequently face to face across the table. He then conducted a simple experiment asking people to take seats and discuss a proverb. About 80 per cent of the time, he found that they selected the end-corner relationship. In subsequent research (Sommer, 1961), he studied groups of four, five, and six, and found that those designated as leaders preferred to sit in the end positions, at rectangular tables, and that other members preferred to sit in the corner position, closest to the leader. When he had the leaders sit in the corner chair, he found other members choosing to sit in the end position adjacent to the leader, or in the opposite corner. Much of Sommer's extensive research is covered in his recent book *Personal Space* (1969).

Additional confirmation of the expectancy that the leader sits at the end of the table is provided by the unique studies of juries conducted by Strodtbeck and his colleagues, mentioned on the last page. As part of the Jury Project of the University of Chicago Law School, Strodtbeck and Hook (1961) studied 69 jury deliberations carried out under standardized experimental conditions with jurors called by lot from a pool of about 300 persons. Accompanied by a bailiff, they were sent to the deliberation room where they subsequently listened to a recorded trial, deliberated on it, and returned their verdict. On entering the room, they had a choice of seats around the usual 1-5-1-5 table. Those coming in first had a wider choice of seats than those entering right after them. In this particular aspect of their project, Strodtbeck and Hook were interested in who gets to be elected foreman, from the various seating positions represented at the table. There are four of these, as shown in Figure 12.2: (1) at the ends; (2) at the corners; (3) flanks, next to the corner positions; (4) in the middle.

Once seated, the jurors' first task was to elect a foreman. Across the 69 juries in the study, it was found that the foreman was most frequently selected from one of the two persons seated at the ends of the table. Indeed, 32 foremen, almost half, were persons seated at the ends; persons in the corner positions, of which there are four, were next most frequently selected, with the other two positions vastly under-selected. Occupation was related to election as a foreman, as revealed by the results of the analysis by Strodtbeck *et al.* reported in the last section. Proprietors and managers were found to take seats in the end position about 15 per cent more frequently than by chance, and in the corner position 18 per cent less frequently, but *position effects* from socio-economic class were comparatively small.

There was a clear indication that the jurors felt that there was some intrinsic "propriety" about the foreman being at the head of the table. Strodtbeck and Hood (1961) observe:

Frequency for each seat				Positions	Frequency for positions	Mean for positions
	End					
Corner	5	17	5 Corner	2 ends	32	16.0
Flank	4		1 Flank	4 corners	22	5.5
Middle	3		2 Middle	4 flanks	10	2.5
Flank	2		3 Flank	2 middles	5	2.5
Corner	5	15	7 Corner		69	
	End					

Figure 12.2: Frequency and mean value for selection of foremen of 69 juries by position at jury table. Persons sitting at either end are overwhelmingly favored for election as foremen. (After Strodtbeck and Hook, 1961, p. 400.)

> It is even possible that a move to select someone other than a person at the end of the table would be perceived as a rejection of the persons on the ends, while the selection of a person at the end would not offend anyone because it could be presumed that being at the end was accidental (p. 401).

Other data from this study corroborated the additional point that both actual rate of participation and sociometric ratings of who was influential were related to position, with the end position always leading the others.

Group properties

In studying and differentiating groups, two levels are involved—the *group* level and the *individual* level. These terms are used to emphasize the source of primary data regarding a phenomenon. If we say that a group is productive, and we measure this by the output per unit time for the group, then we are dealing with the group level of analysis. Alternatively, if we ask the members of the group how successfully the group performed, then these responses are at the individual level. Such responses may then be summed together to provide a score or index of the group's success, as its members see it, but this is not the same as using a criterion on the group level.

Attempts to study groups in terms of their own properties, rather than as an aggregation of individual attributes, have focused on several kinds of variables. Proceeding from the broadest and most obvious group properties to the more specific and less obvious, several approaches have been followed. The first of these is the study of dimensions of groups, mainly through the *technique of factor analysis*. The other approaches in the study of groups emphasize *group size, group cohesiveness* and *group communication*.

THE FACTOR ANALYTIC APPROACH TO GROUP DIMENSIONS

A major exponent of the study of group dimensions through factor analysis is Raymond Cattell (1948, 1951). His essential contention is that a group may be described in a general way, much as one might describe an individual's personality. To achieve this Cattell proposes three sets of variables or concepts at a group level, which he calls "panels." These are *population, structure,* and *syntality.* In Cattell's system, population encompasses the psychological characteristics of group members in regard to personality and attitude-interest measures. This focus leads to a description of the attributes of individuals within the group that may bear on group productivity, some of which we considered in Chapter 10. Structure, in Cattell's terms, embodies the pattern of interaction within the group. This covers especially the kinds of relationships that exist between the individual group members as a group property.

Perhaps most important in Cattell's system is the concept of group syntality. It refers, in broadest terms, to the performance of the group as a whole (Cattell, 1948). This focus on syntality underscores Cattell's position that groups have qualities apart from those of their individual members and it has merit as one approach to understanding the broader character of groups.

When measured empirically, however, group syntality does not provide information about individual reactions, in terms of the processes occurring in a group. Thus, some things that are said to be part of syntality are an average of individual members' evaluations, and these may vary considerably. For example, two groups might have a common level of syntality, but be quite different in their internal processes of interaction, including member motivations and activities.

A wider approach to studying the dimensions of groups has been presented by Hemphill (1950a) who has set forth fifteen dimensions which can be used in distinguishing their characteristics. These dimensions represent those kinds of things at both the group and individual levels that might affect group performance. They are:

1. *Size* of the group
2. *Viscidity* or the degree to which the group functions as a unit
3. *Homogeneity* of group members with respect to socially relevant characteristics such as age, sex, and background
4. *Flexibility* of a group's activities in terms of informal procedures rather than adherence to established procedures

5. *Stability* of a group with respect to frequency of major changes over a period of time
6. *Permeability* of a group regarding ready access to membership
7. *Polarization* of a group in terms of its orientation and functioning toward a single goal
8. *Autonomy* of a group with respect to its functioning independently of other groups
9. *Intimacy* of group members in regard to mutual acquaintance and familiarity with details of one another's lives
10. *Control* or the degree to which a group regulates the behavior of individuals, while they are functioning as group members
11. *Participation* of group members in applying time and effort to the group's activities
12. *Potency* or importance of the group for its members
13. *Hedonic tone* in terms of the degree to which group membership is accompanied by a general feeling of pleasantness or unpleasantness
14. *Position* of group members with respect to an ordering of status in a hierarchy
15. *Dependence* of group members upon the group.

Hemphill and Westie (1950) have detailed the basis for measuring these dimensions. They found that individuals describing the same group, ranging from a small committee to a large university, tended to give similar ratings on the dimensions. However, Hemphill (1956) reports that depending upon the way in which a "group" is defined—in terms of descriptive categories and aggregates versus face-to-face functional groups—distinct differences in the homogeneity of ratings are found. Borgatta, Cottrell, and Meyer (1956) have surveyed this work on group dimensions, especially those studies using factor analysis, and conclude that a major need is for a more consistent use of factor names. In any event, there does seem to be a valid basis for describing group characteristics along several dimensions, and among these group size appears to be of great importance.

GROUP SIZE

As a group increases in size, certain changes are likely to occur in the relationships among members. Some of these are readily predictable on a mathematical basis. Bossard (1945), for example, pointed up the geometric increase in the possible number of relationships between group members as the number in the group increases. The formula for calculating this function is $(n^2 - n)/2$, where n equals the number of people in a group. A curve showing the sharp inclination of this function is presented in Figure 12.3. This has a bearing on member participation and satisfaction. If, for instance, a discussion group operates on the expectation that everyone will have a chance to be heard, and in turn that everyone can respond to each person's comment, then a six-person group as against a three-person group would require five times as much time if everyone is to be heard, other things being equal. Accordingly, different qualities may characterize internal group relationships as a function of group size. Carter, Haythorn, Meirowitz, and Lanzetta (1951) found quite different rates of participation within groups varying from four to eight members in size, indicating that this curve has practical significance. Yet, it is still often the case that a committee, which could have four or five members, is enlarged to twelve on the assumption that, if anything, greater size ought to be more beneficial to its operation. Obviously, other considerations, say of a "political" sort, may require representation from many constituencies, but it is purchased at a price.

Slater (1958) conducted an experiment with discussion groups each of which met four times. They ranged in size from two to seven members. He found that groups made up of five members expressed greatest satisfaction on their subsequent ratings of the group experience. When groups exceeded five members, higher rates of competitive and impulsive behavior were reported. Therefore, not only does the prospect for participation change as a consequence of group size, there also may be a corresponding change in the feeling generated by that participation. Bales, Strodtbeck, Mills, and Roseborough (1951), relatedly, have found that the larger the group the greater the disparity between the most frequent contributors to group discussion and the other members in the amount of prominence. There is a tendency toward a disproportionate share of time being taken up by a few promi-

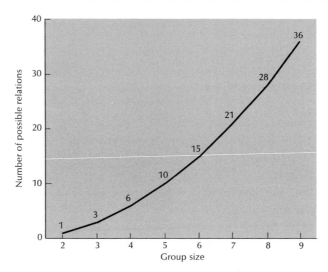

Figure 12.3: Increasing number of two-person relations illustrated for groups from two to nine in size.

nent members, and this is directly associated with member dissatisfaction.

In another vein, Bales and Borgatta (1955) have found that groups made up of an even number of members display interaction patterns on discussion tasks different from groups with an odd number of members. Most marked are the differences between groups made up of two people, *diads*, and those of two and any odd number, with two-person groups showing higher ratings on disagreement and antagonism. They explain this because two-person groups can only achieve a majority in one way, by both parties agreeing.

However, three-person groups, or *triads*, present problems too. Experimental work by Mills (1953) found that in triads a distinct tendency occurs for two members to pair against the other member. In general, the triad is considered to be unstable because of the tendency toward coalition-formation (Caplow, 1956; Vinacke and Arkoff, 1957). This varies though depending upon the members' relationship with one another. For example, research by Strodtbeck (1954) with three-person families only partially confirms Mills's findings. This may be explained as a feature of the family which requires more accommodation to maintain the integrity of the group. Strong social pressures therefore operate to reduce in family triads the split which is observed in more loosely associated groups of three in experimental situations.

Vinacke (1959) has studied triads composed of males or females involved in a bargaining game where there was one "powerful" member. As in Caplow's (1956) work, he found that the two members of "weaker power" tended to ally against the stronger, irrespective of the sex of group members. However, women were far more inclined to seek accommodation with less coalition-formation than were the men. Bond and Vinacke (1961) found that mixing sexes with a majority of men or of women essentially yielded a parallel to the all male or all female patterns already noted. The results of a further study by Uesugi and Vinacke (1963) showed that changing the content of the game to give it greater feminine interest only served to increase accommodation rather than competition among females. Thus, they contend that accommodation in triads is partly a function of culturally induced personality characteristics which appear to be more pronounced among females (p. 80).

Other studies of group size have emphasized performance and interaction processes occurring in groups of varying sizes. For example, Hemphill (1950) has studied the frequency with which "superior" leaders of larger groups (31 or more) are reported to engage in specific kinds of behavior in contrast with the "superior" leaders of smaller groups (30 or less). He reports that, in general, as the group becomes larger, demands upon the leader become greater and more numerous, and acceptance of the leader's influence becomes greater. Thus, the structure of interaction is affected by group size. This result is shown in Figure 12.4 which presents a comparison of the percentage of members in larger groups and smaller groups reporting a given leader behavior. The four behaviors shown are those that revealed the most significant differences in Hemphill's study. It should be added that "smallness" as defined in this study is quite a bit larger than the five-person group typically studied in the laboratory experiment. Had something like this criterion of small size been applied, the differences obtained might have been sharper still.

Barker and Gump (1964), in their book *Big School, Small School*, report their findings from a study of small and large high schools. Among other things, distinct differences were found in rates of participation by students, especially in extra-curricular activities, with the

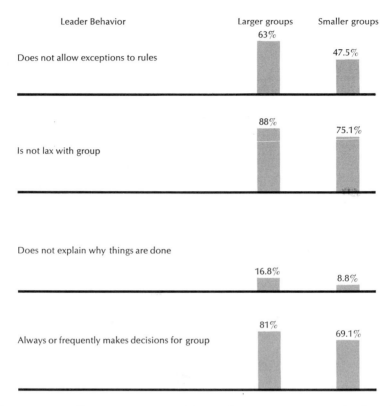

Figure 12.4: Differences in rating of four behaviors of "superior" leaders obtained from members of larger and smaller groups. (Based on data from Hemphill, 1950.)

lower rate occurring in the larger schools. Other variables may be cited, including socio-economic factors, in accounting for this finding. But for the most part there appears to be a lower availability of sheer opportunity to take on various roles in the larger schools. By contrast, there is a greater need for sharing diverse roles in schools with a smaller student body.

In summing up their coverage of the effects of group size, Thomas and Fink (1963) say that ". . . it is apparent that group size has significant effects on aspects of individual and group performance, on the nature of interaction and distribution of participation of group members . . . and on member satisfaction" (p. 383). But they also see size as a variable mediated by other variables which can enhance or di-minish its importance. One of the results of research on group size is the clear indication of the frustrations associated with largeness, espe-cially where the groups convene in face-to-face interaction. However, this need not color relationships adversely in large organizations, if members are organized into smaller work groups which provide for participation and mutual attraction. It is this latter property of co-hesiveness to which we now turn.

GROUP COHESIVENESS

Cohesiveness is a term which is used to describe a group property in the nature of solidarity or unity. Generally speaking, cohesive groups are supposed to be better co-ordinated than non-cohesive groups and have a greater sense of "we" feeling. As the term itself suggests, the members of cohesive groups are more likely to stick together, to co-op-erate, and participate in their common enterprises more fully.

While everyday observations confirm differences in the extent to which groups evidence this property, its measurement presents prob-lems. These have been handled in various ways, involving one or both levels of analysis represented by the individuals comprising a group, or the group itself. On the individual level, cohesiveness is often meas-ured by having members indicate their group's attractiveness to them. On the group level, the group's performance is usually taken as a meas-ure of cohesiveness because, practically speaking, performance is a readily observed outgrowth of activity. Yet, the performance of a group need not imply that it should necessarily be highly cohesive, though it often does (Libo, 1953). Schachter, Ellertson, McBride and Gregory (1951) are among those who have pointed out that the productivity of a group is not necessarily a direct function of the average of mem-bers' attraction to it. They indicate, for example, that a highly cohesive group could have norms encouraging low rather than high rates of productivity. This might occur in a work setting where the workers resist the standards set by management.

The research literature on cohesiveness is quite extensive and, for the most part, tends to accept a definition of cohesiveness along the line suggested by Festinger, Schachter, and Back (1950, p. 164) as the "total field of forces which act on members to remain in the group."

But as Israel (1956) notes, this definition is difficult to apply in research since it usually comes down to group attraction. An alternative definition might be the degree to which group members conform to group norms (Landecker, 1955). Hagstrom and Selvin (1965) observe, however, that this definition creates a problem of circularity because, where hypotheses about the relationship of cohesiveness and conformity are being tested, both variables would be commonly measured.

"Attraction" measures of cohesiveness remain the most typical though they can hide individual variations within the group when they are used as a simple average. This might lead to the conclusion that a group is cohesive when in fact several members inflate the average by their high ratings. Even granting this deficiency, it is acknowledged that being attracted to a group remains the most distinctive *social psychological* avenue to understanding its effects on individuals. Whether this attraction is a *unitary* variable or a combination of several factors is another matter.

Gross and Martin (1952) report that three indexes of attraction within residence groups of college women did not have uniformly high positive correlations with one another. In another study with female students in the same kind of setting, Hagstrom and Selvin (1965) found that two factors emerge from ratings of a group's attraction. One they label "sociometric cohesion," which reflects the intrinsic attraction of the group to its members, and the other "social satisfaction" which takes in the instrumental attraction of the group in terms of the activities it provides. In short, a group may be evaluated positively for the people who are its members and the values they represent, as well as for the kinds of tasks in which they engage co-operatively. Both of these effects have been verified in research. In one such study by Hollander (1964, Ch. 7), a high positive correlation was found between the perception of group members' values being similar to one's own and attraction to the group.

The broader question of how a group becomes attractive has been dealt with by Cartwright and Zander (1968). They stress that attraction arises primarily from the satisfactions a group provides through the achievement of what it is in the member's interest to have it achieve. Individual motivations are therefore of substantial importance in the emergence of a sense of group cohesiveness, as we have previously noted. The consequences of cohesiveness to group processes will be considered further in connection with group dynamics. For the moment we will look at the related phenomenon of intra-group communication.

INTRA-GROUP COMMUNICATION

An important structural property of groups is their network of communication. In the Leavitt study (1951), reported in Chapter 3, the positioning of people with regard to who could communicate to whom was found to be important to group efficiency and member satisfaction. Thus, the "wheel" was fastest, but the "circle" most satisfying (see p. 73). Leavitt interpreted his findings in line with centrality and peripherality in the group's communication network. Individuals who are more "central" are positioned to receive and send more communications and tend to be more satisfied than those who are by contrast "peripheral."

Shaw (1954) has reasoned that another factor of significance in communication networks is availability of information. In his experiment, a peripheral subject in each of the networks was given five units of information while the others were given one unit each. This considerably altered the previous results obtained by Leavitt. Shaw found that under these conditions the circle was fastest as well as the most satisfying. Furthermore, those with more information were as satisfied as those who were central. The importance of these findings is twofold. First, it indicates that it is more information, rather than merely centrality, which creates satisfaction. Second, it highlights the place of information as a group "resource" whose possession is important to the group as well as gratifying to those who can dispense it. Since a group functions in part by the flow of information, through communication, access to it increases the group's prospects for achievement. Those who provide such access are accordingly rewarded.

Being central in a communication structure is one characteristic of leadership. Typically, the leader is a group member who receives and sends more communications than others, and who thereby exerts influence on the group's activity. A person in a leadership position is, moreover, likely to have greater control over group resources, which includes information as well as his own competence in matters affecting the achievement of the group goal.

The close association between communication and leadership, as an influence process, will be considered further in Chapter 15. It is worth noting here that several experiments (e.g. Berkowitz, 1956; Medow and Zander, 1965) indicate that a person placed in a central position in a communication network evidences more assertive leader-type behavior. Furthermore, that person reports more involvement in the group's activity, and is perceived by other members to be more motivated and more responsible for the group's outcomes. Therefore, the network of intra-group communication is a property of the group's structure which has a high degree of significance to group functioning.

Communication within groups is not solely taken up with the group's task, even though laboratory experiments emphasize this feature of group functioning. In the ongoing interaction between members of a continuing group, patterns of communication may reflect normative practices about who speaks first and to whom. Seniority and tradition itself may determine such patterns, independently of any immediate task, as Parsons, Bales, and Shils (1953) observe. These are instigated through a sequence of interaction which provides reinforcement for the utterances of some members more than others, thus creating roles. As these authors put it:

> Insofar as a given person "gets on the right track" and receives positive reaction from other members, he will be reinforced in his direction of movement, and will tend to keep on talking. He will "generalize" from the premises, logical and emotional, which underlay his original successful attempt . . . and reciprocally, the other members will "generalize" from his earlier attempts, gratifying in some sense to them, to an expectation of further effective behavior on his part. The member begins to build a "specialized role" (p. 133).

Communication processes in a group therefore serve to create as well as to maintain differences in role behavior. These differences are associated with hierarchical status in the group. Such a hierarchy is shown in Figure 12.5. It is drawn from the field work of W. F. Whyte (1943) with a neighborhood gang in Boston. Doc was the leader of this group and his immediate "lieutenants" were Mike and Danny. Each member of the group had his own position in the hierarchy, indicated by the relative rank of the circles in Figure 12.5. Though their positions might remain consistent over some time, the hierarchy was not a static one. When the relationship between members changed, their positions changed.

A primary activity of this street-corner group was bowling. Doc had achieved his position of leadership partly because of his bowling skill. But the hierarchy was not built on this ability alone. Therefore it was possible for a low status member, Alec, to be a better bowler than some of those of higher status. When this happened in the presence of other group members, Alec was consistently heckled and jeered by them. Thus, communications were brought to bear to maintain the status hierarchy. Whyte reports:

> One evening I heard Alec boasting to Long John that the way he was bowling he could take on every man on the first team and lick them all. Long John dismissed the challenge with these words: "You think you could beat us, but, under pressure, you die!" [In] . . . a match held toward the end of April . . . Alec was leading by several pins . . . but then he began to miss, and, as mistake followed mistake, he stopped trying. . . . [Later] as Doc told me:

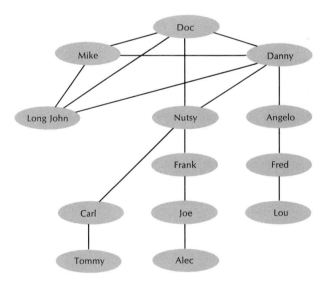

Figure 12.5: Relative positions in social organization of the Norton Street Gang. (From *Street Corner Society* by William F. Whyte by permission of The University of Chicago Press. Copyright 1943.)

"Alec isn't so aggressive these days. I steamed up at the way he was going after Long John, and I blasted him. . . . Then I talked to Long John. . . . I made him see that he should bowl better than Alec. I persuaded him that he was really the better bowler." The records of the season . . . show a very close correspondence between social position and bowling performance. . . . Bowling scores did not fall automatically into this pattern. There were certain customary ways of behaving which exerted pressure upon the individuals. Chief among these were the manner of choosing sides and the verbal attacks the members directed against one another. . . . When a follower threatened to better his position . . . the boys shouted at him that he was lucky, that he was "bowling over his head.". . . This type of verbal attack was very important in keeping the members "in their places" (pp. 19-24).

In general, then, intra-group communications follow the pattern of status in the group and thereby serve to maintain it (Klein, 1956, p. 33). But the net effect of communication is not in a static direction. Indeed, communication considerably facilitates various processes of group dynamics which we will consider in the next chapter.

SUMMARY

All human societies are organized into collective entities called groups that carry on the necessary and significant functions of the society. Individuals have affiliations with many groups, each of which has the potential for affecting the individual's actions and psychological states.

Usually, in speaking of groups, we refer to *functional groups* made up of members who have regularized social interaction aimed at the achievement of a *common goal*. Such groups require interdependent action within a pattern of organization of relationships called *structure*. Two other ways of grouping people are by *descriptive categories*, made up of people who share a common characteristic such as age level, and by *aggregates*, composed of individuals who share a time-space relationship.

People become members of functional groups and categories in two major ways—by *ascription* and by *acquisition*. An ascribed group membership refers to less voluntary or non-voluntary circumstances, such as being born into a family. An *acquired* group membership involves a greater range of choice, in the sense of joining a group. Thus, the initial motivations for membership are different, though they may change later. Both functional groups and descriptive categories may be entered through acquired or ascribed membership.

The initial psychological impact on individuals is considered to be greatest from those functional groups, including the family, called *primary groups*. Such groups provide close relationships and mutual attraction. Recent work has re-emphasized the importance of such close ties, apart from the task of groups, within work settings. Collective efforts, as part of social movements, also can provide close-knit affiliations, though often of a short-term duration. They also are inclined to be quite limited in structure.

Groups carry on their operations within a *structure*. Three features of structure are the *status differentiation* within the group, its *norms*, and its *communication pattern*. Norms and status are interrelated insofar as specialized roles are created for a person occupying a given status. In this sense, a role can be thought of as a highly specialized norm within the role system which characterizes any group.

The nature of structure affects *interaction* within groups. In functional groups, the process of interaction is determined in part by the source of structure, whether imposed or generated by the group itself. The distinction between *formal* and *informal* groups depends upon this source of structure. Organizations typically set the goals and procedures of a group which make it formal. By contrast, friendship groups are informal with a more spontaneous structure growing out of common interests and interpersonal attraction. The distinction between formal and informal groups is not always sharp since the *internal system* of any group may be affected in various ways by its *external system*.

The study of groups may be approached on two levels, the *group* level and the *individual* level; this depends on the primary data of interest in studying social phenomena. The productivity of a group exemplifies the group level of analysis, while the satisfaction of members of the group exemplifies the individual level.

Among the techniques applied to studying groups in terms of their own properties, *factor analysis* has been quite prominent. It yields several group dimensions, such as its overall performance, in terms of *syntality*, its stability, its autonomy, and its homogeneity of membership.

Group *size* is one of the more important factors in determining the functioning and psychological effects of groups. Studies of the interaction processes occurring in groups of various sizes have indicated differences between *diads*, two-person groups, and *triads*, three-person groups. Furthermore, as groups increase in size, the number of possible relationships among members accelerates sharply. The prospect for participation in groups of larger size decreases and a greater disparity is found between the frequent contributors to group discussion and the others. There are also differences in leadership within groups of larger size, and increased frustrations associated with largeness.

The *cohesiveness* of a group, in terms of its solidarity or unity, is a factor which produces and reflects the interactions within a group. The measurement of cohesiveness has largely been approached in terms of the attraction of the group to its members. On the group level, there are other measures including performance and conformity, which have been taken as signs of cohesiveness. In terms of its effect upon its members, attraction continues to be a major avenue for understanding the social psychology of group processes.

Related to cohesiveness is the *communication network* within a group. Experimental findings indicate that persons who are more central in this network tend to be more satisfied. Centrality, however, appears to be associated with an individual's accessibility to and control over the flow of information within the group. Those who are more central, and thereby control more of the group's communication resources, are found to evidence more assertive leader-type behavior. Communication also functions within a group to stabilize the status hierarchy, including the differentiation of roles.

SUGGESTED READINGS

From E. P. Hollander and R. G. Hunt (Eds.) *Current perspectives in social psychology.* (3rd ed.) New York: Oxford University Press, 1971.

SELECTED REFERENCES

Bales, R. F. *Personality and interpersonal behavior*. New York: Holt, Rinehart & Winston, 1970.

Golembiewski, R. T. *The small group*. Chicago: Univer. of Chicago Press, 1962.

Hare, A. P. *Handbook of small group research*. New York: Free Press, 1961.

Hare, A. P., Borgatta, E. F., & Bales, R. F. (Eds.) *Small groups*. New York: Knopf, 1955. (2nd ed., 1965.)

Homans, G. C. *The human group*. New York: Harcourt, Brace, 1950.

*Katz, E., & Lazarsfeld, P. F. *Personal influence*. Glencoe, Ill.: Free Press, 1955.

Klein, J. *The study of groups*. London: Routledge & Kegan Paul, 1956.

McGrath, J. E., & Altman, I. *Small group research: a synthesis and critique of the field*. New York: Holt, Rinehart & Winston, 1966.

*Mills, T. M. *The sociology of small groups*. Englewood Cliffs, N.J.: Prentice-Hall, 1967.

*Olmsted, M. S. *The small group*. New York: Random House, 1959.

Olsen, M. E. *The process of social organization*. New York: Holt, Rinehart & Winston, 1968.

*Sommer, R. *Personal space*. Englewood Cliffs, N. J.: Prentice-Hall, 1969.

*Stogdill, R. M. *Individual behavior and group achievement*. New York: Oxford Univ. Press, 1959.

*Weick, K. E. *The social psychology of organizing*. Reading, Mass.: Addison-Wesley, 1969.

13

Group dynamics and group effectiveness, inter-group and international relations

Group dynamics is often used as a general term to designate the processes which occur in groups, as well as their outcomes. In a more special usage, it refers to the tradition of experimentation on groups established by Kurt Lewin. From that impetus, group dynamics has been applied more widely though it continues to have a focus on the study of influence processes in small groups (Cartwright and Zander, 1968).

Building on the older tradition, this chapter will examine the wider scope of group dynamics with regard to social change, group effectiveness, and its important implications for those other psychological aspects of groups which extend into the areas of inter-group and international relations. As an initial point of reference, we turn to some basic processes that play a pivotal part in the inner workings of groups.

Basic processes

Lewin considered two variables to be particularly important for understanding the dynamics of a group—*group cohesiveness* and *group locomotion*. Each of these implies a process. We have already stressed the degree to which cohesiveness, seen as the sum of forces which bind individuals to a group, plays a vital role in determining the group's influence on its members. Shortly we will elaborate several points concerning its relationship to communication and conformity.

The concept of group locomotion is essentially one of movement toward a desired goal. A group is conceived to be operating in a field of forces in one region to attain a goal in another region. It is generally assumed that this locomotion is directed at the "goal region." In a political campaign, for example, the supporters of a candidate will be working toward his election and their goal is clear.

Generally speaking, the clarity of a group goal has an important enhancement effect in furthering group locomotion. In an experiment by Raven and Rietsema (1957), the group's performance was considerably faciliated by members' awareness of what goal was being sought and how it was to be achieved. Furthermore, various studies have pointed to the importance of the interdependence of group members, and their co-operation, as factors which improve locomotion (e.g. Deutsch, 1949b; Thomas, 1957). In his theory of social communication, Festinger (1950) employs locomotion as a major variable determining pressures toward conformity in a group. He postulates that such pressures will be greater to the extent that group members perceive that group movement would be facilitated by conformity.

THE INTERDEPENDENCE OF COHESIVENESS, COMMUNICATION, AND CONFORMITY

Conformity, which will be treated more fully in the next chapter, can be thought of as an individual's adherence to group expectancies. Berkowitz (1954), among others, has found conformity to be greater where a group is more cohesive. Furthermore, its probability is increased by communications from other group members directed at bringing the individual "into line." There are also reciprocal relations between these variables, as is shown in Figure 13.1. Each has an effect upon the others, and none can be considered solely an independent or a dependent variable.

Any proposition which states a functional relationship between a pair of these variables has some demonstrable validity. Greater conformity not only is positively affected by greater cohesiveness, it also tends to increase cohesiveness. When members of a group share similar

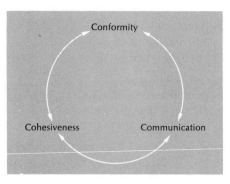

Figure 13.1: Diagrammatic representation of the reciprocal relations among cohesiveness, communication, and conformity.

attitudes and abide by normative behaviors, their cohesiveness rises (Newcomb, 1956, 1961). This is understandable with reference to the comfort and smoothness of more predictable interaction associated with greater uniformity. In the realm of ability also, Zander and Havelin (1960) have found that greater similarity strengthens group bonds. Similarly, communication is higher among members of more cohesive groups (Bales, 1950b).

Thus, when we tap into any of these three variables, we are likely to find associations with the others. An illustration of this is in the study in Westgate West by Festinger, Schachter, and Back (1950). They observed the development of group norms in this new apartment project for married veterans attending MIT. The project consisted of a number of residential courts with several buildings, each building having a number of apartments. Before coming to the project, the residents did not know each other, and they were assigned to apartments largely at random. The research found that friendship ties developed among members of this community as a result of propinquity. In Chapter 7 on social interaction, we covered a number of the obvious features of propinquity, in terms of physical contact, as a basic condition for the development of interpersonal attraction. Without contact and communication, it is of course far less likely that people can have the opportunity to develop such ties and similarity of attitude. Illustrating this, people living near the apartment mail boxes were found to know more people and have more contact with them.

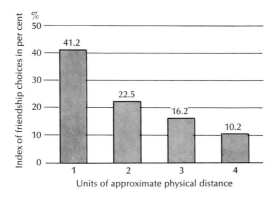

Figure 13.2: Relationship of friendship choices to physical distance on a floor of Westgate West. (Based on data from Festinger, Schachter, and Back, 1950.)

Friendship choices were also found to be based on the arrangement of apartments. On the average, the respondents gave 41 per cent of the possible number of friendship choices to people who lived very close by on their floor. As is shown in Figure 13.2, this percentage systematically dropped off as the units of distance from other residents there increased. Regarding conformity, it was found that certain prevailing norms existed with respect to the attitudes that members of a given residential court held. They had been asked how they felt about a new "tenant's council," and highly similar attitudes were found among the respondents living in the same court. Furthermore, the more the members of the court were attracted to one another, in a cohesiveness sense, the greater was the uniformity of attitude in that court on this issue and the more they communicated with one another through social interaction.

A recent study by Priest and Sawyer (1967), of a 320-man college dormitory, also reveals that the factor of physical proximity weighs heavily in the choice of friends and serves as an initial "screen" for bonds of cohesiveness. In the spring term, after more than half a year, 94 per cent of the subjects liked their roommates, but among their floor-mates that they could recognize, on the other side of the building (eight to thirteen rooms distant), they liked only 42 per cent. Distance therefore was an important determiner of liking,

. . . suggesting that even when persons on the other side of the building come to be known, they are still liked less. . . . That proximity continues to predict attraction when distances are so small indicates that more than physical space is involved. . . . Developing friendship with a person who is farther may cost more than the added seconds (pp. 640-641).

The matter of cohesiveness has vital practical implications in functional groups. During World War II, large-scale research was done on factors involved in troop morale, a major report of which is *The American Soldier* (Stouffer *et al.*, 1949). In one of a series of studies, an essential finding was that combat motivation was most related to close, primary group affiliations. One of the major reasons soldiers gave for willingness to enter battle was protection of buddies, or a desire to do what their buddies expected of them. In general, motives like this were found to be more salient to the combat soldier than were more abstract things like hatred of the enemy, political ideology, or the formal orders and disciplinary demands from above. Thus, cohesiveness implies a concern for others and a readiness to do what is expected by them.

Research with industrial work groups also indicates that cohesiveness plays a significant part in their activity. For example, Kerr and his colleagues (1951) conducted a field study in a large factory. They were investigating factors affecting absenteeism, turnover, and morale, in relationship to job efficiency and satisfaction. While it is often assumed that conversation impedes productivity, these investigators found that those groups characterized by a high degree of conversation were not lower producers. Furthermore, they had relatively low turnover, low absenteeism, and high work satisfaction. Thus, intra-group communication among employees increased the cohesiveness of their work group and actually resulted in benefits to the company, rather than the kind of loss which is often imputed to conversation on the job. This effect would of course depend upon the nature of the job to be performed, since not all tasks lend themselves to conversation. The key point, however, is that work-group cohesiveness can have a beneficial effect on the relationship of the worker to his organization. Here again, the significant determiner of this effect appears to be the cohesiveness of the group, which is nourished by communication.

EFFECTING CHANGE

The word "dynamic" usually conveys the idea of forces affecting change. And, indeed, the study of group dynamics appropriately concerns itself with the processes by which changes occur in groups. Lewin's contribution to understanding social change begins with his assertion that it has two aspects. To render change requires not only the *introduction of innovation* but also the *overcoming of resistance* represented in attachments to prevailing practices. In Lewin's terms, these practices are in a state of "quasi-stationary equilibrium" and need to be "unfrozen" before new practices at another level of equilibrium can be established. Thus, Lewin (1947) says:

> . . . it is of great practical importance that levels of quasi-stationary equilibria can be changed in either of two ways: by adding forces in the desired direction, or by diminishing opposing forces. . . . In both cases the equilibrium might change to the same new level. The secondary effect should, however, be quite different. In the first case, the process on the new level would be accompanied by a state of relatively high tension; in the second case, by a state of relatively low tension (p. 342).

Lewin is therefore quite emphatic in pointing up the importance of equilibria and the *process* by which change is brought about. In overcoming resistance to the opposing forces, Lewin considers the group as a major vehicle for bringing individuals to a more ready acceptance of new conditions and requirements. His own research on group decision-making, and the related work of Coch and French (1948), both discussed in Chapter 3 (see pp. 99 and 100), illustrates how group support can be instrumental in influencing individuals to perceive new alternatives more favorably. As a counterpoise to this emphasis, Weick (1969a) has recently contended that another question may be, "How does the human actor terminate change, retard change, take the flux out of flux?" (p. 995). In other words, how does stability work, even in the face of pressures toward change.

In an extension of Lewin's ideas about the effect of groups upon individuals in rendering change, Cartwright has set forth several principles drawn from work on group dynamics (1951). On a practical level they sum up a number of coherent points growing out of the group dynamics framework. Three of his key principles are these:

> The more attractive the group is to its members, the greater is the influence that the group can exert on its members.
>
> In attempts to change attitudes, values, or behavior, the more relevant they are to the basis of attraction to the group, the greater will be the influence that the group can exert upon them.
>
> Efforts to change individuals or some parts of the group which, if successful, would have the result of making them deviate from the norms of the group will encounter strong resistance.

Prominent among the points here is the individual identification with the group as a factor which can either increase or inhibit the prospects for change. Unless individuals share the "we" feeling associated with such identification, the functioning of the group in the face of demands for change will be impaired. In this respect, Atthowe (1961) conducted an experiment with pairs of people working together on a common task and found that the early use of the pronoun "we" was associated with more efficiency in decision-making. In those pairs where the pronoun "I" was used more frequently, especially in the earlier phases of interaction, their efficiency in adapting to the demands of the task was considerably lower. Relatedly, Fouriezos, Hutt, and Guetzkow (1950) studied the content of interaction in group meetings in terms of self-oriented versus group-oriented activity. They found that those meetings showing a high frequency of self-oriented activity were much less satisfying to group members and much less likely to produce cohesiveness.

It is reasonable to suppose from this and other research that a group composed of members with a weak sense of identity is more vulnerable to influences intended to fractionate it. Thus, Verba (1961) finds that soldiers are more likely to be affected by enemy propaganda when they no longer feel strong group identity. They are more inclined to be swayed and change their attitudes when social ties with their unit are broken. Alternatively, as Cartwright's principles above suggest, a person's attitudes will not readily change if they are anchored in a group membership of importance to the individual. Illustrating this, Kelley and Volkart (1952) conducted a field experiment with troops of boy scouts. By using a questionnaire, they were able to identify the scouts in advance who were or were not highly identified with their troop. They also obtained data on their attitudes toward scouting. Then the entire troop was presented with a speech by a guest speaker who disputed the merits of two key features of scouting—woodcraft and camping. Afterward another questionnaire was administered to determine any change in attitude on these points from those attitudes obtained originally with the earlier questionnaire. The findings were quite clear-cut. Scouts *without* a high identification with their troop showed a significantly greater shift in attitude toward agreement with the speaker than did the others.

We have been treating identification here as a factor growing out of *individual* motivations. It is not the same as cohesiveness, though it relates to it on the group level since members of a highly cohesive group are presumed to share such positive identifications. The significant point, all in all, is that change is effected through groups, but individual motivations and perceptions are necessarily implicated in the process. In the sections which follow, we will give further consideration to group effectiveness and other psychological aspects of group dynamics.

Group effectiveness

Given the great diversity of groups, and the variable nature of their membership, the idea of effectiveness as a group characteristic can be misleading. What may be effective in one group, by some criterion, may not be effective in another. Every group faces a challenge from the environment in terms of a set of goals which are to be achieved as part of the group's task. As McGrath (1964, p. 70) points out, since tasks vary in their properties, they also impose different requirements upon the group. Thus, effectiveness must always be gauged with regard to the particular group and the challenge it faces. However, there is a certain validity in considering factors yielding effectiveness, once the need for this specification of circumstances is recognized.

In formal terms, Barnard (1938) has defined effectiveness as "the accomplishment of the recognized objectives of cooperative action" (p.

55). These objectives may lie in several directions, however. Essentially, there are two ways that groups may be viewed as effective in handling their tasks. One is aimed at the success with which the group achieves its goals in terms of *performance.* Another concern relates to the *satisfaction* of the group members in the process of attaining their goals. The latter criterion has much more to do with the interactions along the way. Still another point of reference relates to the *resources* available to the group in achieving its goals. There are, then, several features to be considered in dealing with the broad issue of group effectiveness.

PERFORMANCE AND SATISFACTION

Performance is largely a matter for consideration at the group level of analysis. It is most often measured in terms of an output which may be represented, for example, in production per unit time or a team score. Alternatively, satisfaction is usually approached on the individual level. It contributes to the group phenomenon of *morale,* as a general index of the satisfaction that prevails in the group, but it stems from individual attitudes. While performance and morale may contribute to one another in a reciprocal fashion, they need not be positively related, as research often reveals (Brayfield and Crockett, 1955).

In highly competitive situations, group members will often sacrifice their own satisfactions in order for the group to win. In the case of professional baseball, we readily see by the league standings that some teams are winning many games while others are winning relatively fewer. By the simple criterion of performance, therefore, the top team in the league appears to be more effective than the bottom team. But by the criterion of member satisfaction, which is not directly revealed by the league standings, it may not necessarily be highest. Winning itself may contribute to member satisfaction, but it need not in any complete sense. Even the big league team that has just won a key game may contain players who are personally displeased with their own performance, or lack of opportunity to play, or who feel inadequately recognized for their contribution. Because of the two levels involved, it is essential to understand that peak performance by itself does not directly signify member satisfaction, nor does it reveal future outcomes in this vein.

As we observed in connection with the laboratory research on communication networks, groups may be effective in performance, though members who are peripheral, or lack information, are dissatisfied with the structure and the related processes within the group. There are implications in this in terms of the subsequent cohesiveness and stability of these groups, if they were perpetuated in time.

Attempts to discern the source of member satisfaction have usually found several variables in operation. In their survey of the research literature in this line, Heslin and Dunphy (1964) encountered three such factors which recur in findings on member satisfaction. The first of these is *status consensus*, indicating the degree of consensus concerning group structure, particularly with regard to leadership. The second relates to the members' perception of progress toward group goals, in terms of what we referred to earlier as *group locomotion*. The third refers to the perceived freedom of *participation* within the group. All of these elements relate in an interacting way to the sense the individual has of a stable environment within which he can make contributions that are rewarded. The importance of these factors will be considered further below, in connection with psychological effects.

GROUP RESOURCES: INPUTS AND OUTPUTS

Another way of viewing group effectiveness is in terms of what the group is able to achieve with its available resources. As a group goes about fulfilling its task, it has the capabilities of persons as well as features of the physical environment with which to work. Its resources are the *inputs* to its activity in dealing with the task at hand. What it does with these can be considered as its *outputs*. In some sense, a group's effectiveness is determined by how successfully it is able to muster its resources in order to secure beneficial outputs, regarding both the criteria of performance and satisfaction.

By way of illustration, consider our big league ball team again. It is low in the league standings, but it has a relatively inexperienced team without major stars. Given the resources at its disposal, it is doing rather well in terms of the output-to-input ratio represented by winning games. Looking just at the criterion of performance, while the top team in the league appears to be more effective, its ratio may not be nearly so favorable since it starts with far greater inputs, in terms of experienced players who are highly proficient. Moreover, the team low in standing, because it is playing so well with the little it has, may have comparatively high morale.

Stogdill (1959) has proposed that many otherwise contradictory findings regarding group performance and morale can be reconciled by viewing performance and member satisfaction as group outputs from the use to which group resources are put. The concept of resources helps to get away from the simple notion that good performance necessarily means great effectiveness. It also looks upon a group with reference to the characteristics of its members, their competence, and their motivation.

One of the longstanding controversies in social psychology, dating back to the work of Shaw (1932) and earlier, has had to do with the question of whether groups are more effective in problem-solving than are individuals. A newer study on this issue by Tuckman and Lorge (1962) has special relevance to the matter of resources. They had individuals solve problems initially on a separate basis, then constituted them into groups to re-solve the same problems. A set of groups was established as a control without the prior tradition of individual experience. They found that both kinds of groups in general were superior to individuals in average "quality points" for solutions. However, their data also indicated that this resulted not from the greater effectiveness of groups in solving problems so much as the greater probability of getting a good solution from a group of five rather than from any single individual. Thus, where an individual member had given a highly superior solution before, his group did better. A significant correlation of .54 was obtained between the quality point scores of the re-solving groups and of their best individuals.

As Steiner and Rajaratnam (1961) point out, the requirements of the task make a considerable difference in determining the superiority of the group as against an individual in problem-solving. For a simple task, individuals may do very adequately, but for a complex task the resources afforded by several people working together are likely to be more suitable. Therefore, the performance of a group depends upon the interrelationship of its task and the people who compose it, with particular regard to their individual qualities including competence and commitment to the group's endeavor.

THE RISKY-SHIFT PHENOMENON

One striking instance of how groups differ from, and influence, the decision processes of individuals is found in the recent work on the "risky-shift." Early work by Stoner (1961), Kogan and Wallach (1964), and Wallach and Kogan (1965) has shown that the effect of group discussion of various life problems, in the nature of dilemmas concerning money, prestige, or change of employment, is to encourage the choice of a risky alternative, riskier than the averaging of individual judgments beforehand on these same problems.

A typical dilemma question is as follows:

> Mr. A., an electrical engineer, who is married and has one child, has been working for a large electronics corporation since graduating from college five years ago. He is assured of a lifetime job with a modest, though adequate salary, and liberal pension benefits upon retirement. On the other hand, it is very unlikely that his salary will increase much before he retires. While attending a convention, Mr. A is offered a job with a small, newly founded company which has a highly uncertain future. The new job would pay more to start and would offer the possibility of a share in the ownership if the company survived the competition of the larger firms.
>
> Imagine that you are advising Mr. A. Listed below are several probabilities or odds of the new company proving financially sound. Please check the lowest probability that you could consider acceptable to make it worthwhile for Mr. A to take the new job (Kogan and Wallach, 1964, p. 256).

Subjects are asked to make their choice on a scale which has probabilities of one, three, five, seven, or nine out of ten. Thus, the riskiest decision would be one out of ten, and the opposite or most conservative decision would be nine out of ten. Usually, each subject makes judgments on twelve dilemmas, before being brought together with a group of others to decide on a unanimously acceptable level of risk for each case. Typically, on all but two or three of the dilemmas, the group's choice is riskier than were the individual judgments.

A variety of explanations have been suggested to account for the risky-shift, two of which have had the greatest prominence: *diffusion of responsibility*, initially favored by Kogan and Wallach (1964), and the *value of risk,* advanced by Brown (1965). The first is related to the earlier discussion concerning intervention as a function of the number of bystanders (Chapter 7, pp. 265-269) and it essentially contends that the riskier course is easier to take if others are implicated so that responsibility is divided. The other view is that individuals take greater risks in groups due to the "value" attached to taking risks in our culture. Individuals may start out with a degree of caution in choosing a risky alternative, lest they appear too risky, but then the group discussion may make it evident that others also value risk.

Wallach and Kogan (1965) conducted a study of three factors which might account for the diffusion of responsibility effect. These were: information about the judgment of others; achievement of consensus; and the process of group discussion. From experimental work, they concluded that neither the provision of information nor the factor of consensus adequately accounted for the results, and that *discussion* appeared to be the element producing the group's shift toward the riskier alternatives. Their more precise rationale was that the discussion afforded an opportunity for affective bonds to develop between group members. This finding was challenged, however, by the experiments of Bateson (1966) and Flanders and Thistlethwaite (1967), both of which allowed subjects to study arguments in favor of the alternatives, *without* group discussion. They concluded that the shift resulted from familiarization with the decision problems rather than discussion. But Pruitt and Teger (1967) have reported that in four separate replications of these two experiments they have not been able to reproduce these same findings: they did not find a risky-shift for *individuals* who spent as much time familiarizing themselves with these problems as did groups talking about them; however, they did find the risky-shift when subjects merely revealed their previous decisions to one another, without further discussion. This suggests that *information* may be important in creating a shift toward risk, and if so this would be in accord with the value of risk notion (Teger and Pruitt, 1967; Pruitt and Teger, 1969).

Wallach himself has been inclined more toward this interpretation of late. In a study by Wallach and Wing (1968), six of the original twelve dilemmas were administered to both male and female students who saw themselves as being more "risky," in general, than other students, at their university. Wallach and Malbi (1970) conducted another ex-

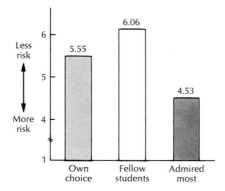

Figure 13.3: Mean level of risk chosen for self, expected to be chosen by fellow students, and admired most, in terms of odds out of ten that would be acceptable, for twelve dilemmas. The smaller the mean, the more "risky" are the odds. (Based upon data from Levinger and Schneider, 1969.)

periment comparing the effects of information and pressure toward conformity as the basis for the risky-shift, with results showing the weight of evidence favoring the informational interpretation.

Levinger and Schneider (1969) also have provided an experimental test of the "value of risk" hypothesis by asking students to respond to the twelve choice dilemmas in three ways: their own choice; what they believed their fellow students would choose; and what choice they themselves would most admire. The results are shown in Figure 13.3. These indicate that the students believed themselves to be *more* risky than the others would be and furthermore they admired a choice even more risky than their own. Accordingly, there is support for the value of risk concept, but also for the strong inference that transmission of information reduces the pluralistic ignorance occasioned by individuals *erroneously* thinking that they are more risky than others and learning that they are not. While the Levinger and Schneider study does not permit a direct test of this inference, it strengthens an informational interpretation of the process underlying the risky-shift.

Psychological effects of groups

In various ways, we have seen that groups exert influence over the psychological processes and behavior of individuals. A primary source of this influence, as we noted earlier, rests in the identification of an individual with a group. This dependency relationship is basic to an understanding of social psychology. Thus, the very quality of "groupness" has important psychological consequences. Long ago, Cooley (1909) observed:

> The result of intimate association, psychologically, is a certain fusion of individualities in a common whole. . . . Perhaps the simplest way of describing this wholeness is to say that it is a "we"; it involves the sort of sympathy and mutual identification for which "we" is the natural expression (p. 23).

Because an individual may be identified with many groups, it is necessary to seek an explanation for why some of them exert influence and others do not. In psychological terms, this is a motivational question, as was pointed out in Chapter 4. For several reasons, some groups hold more motivational valence and thereby are greater sources of identification and influence. Furthermore, the attitudes of an individual may be affected by groups to which he does not literally "belong," as in the case of "reference groups."

One way of distinguishing membership from identification has been proposed by Lambert and Lambert (1964) in terms of "membership groups" and "psychological groups." One may be a member of a group but be relatively unaffected by it, just as one may be influenced by a group and not be one of its members. These kinds of attachment may coincide, but they need not. In what follows we will be considering groups that have a psychological impact on the individual because of their value to him, in this reference group sense. The source of this value rests in several motivational bases.

MOTIVATIONAL BASES OF GROUP INFLUENCE IN GENERAL

The motivation to take part in groups is made up of two distinguishable clusters of motives. As was noted in connection with the findings of Hagstrom and Selvin (1965) regarding cohesiveness, individuals may be primarily oriented toward the *task* of the group or toward the affiliations the group provides. These clusters may be interrelated and bolster one another. In the case of task motivation, the individual is interested in joining others for the sake of the mutual goal to be achieved. They

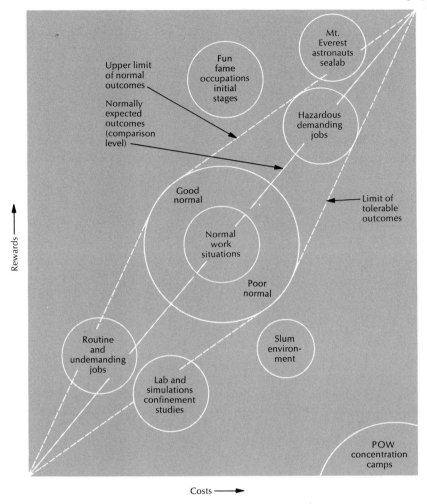

Figure 13.4: Rewards-costs matrix for various kinds of group settings. The farther to the left and above the diagonal line, the more desirable the situation for a person or group; the farther to the right and below the diagonal line, the less desirable are outcomes. (From Radloff and Helmreich, 1968, p. 123.)

depend upon one another in seeking its attainment. Whether the individual feels attachment to these others and develops attraction toward them, is of secondary importance, at least at the outset. In many sports, for example, if a person wishes to take part, it is essential that he find others with whom to play. Indeed, society is comprised of many group enterprises that individuals could not undertake on their own, and accordingly an exchange often results in which the individual gives up a degree of self-determination for the rewards associated with group activity.

Affiliation motives operate most clearly where the individual is attracted to others as a locus of social identity and social support. These, together with social reality, represent the psychological rewards achieved or sustained when the individual accepts the group as a source of influence. In line with Cartwright's principles discussed earlier, social identity, in the sense of a psychological identification with the group, appears to be the foremost motivational basis for such influence. There are, however, other rewards and costs associated with actually belonging to a group. Radloff and Helmreich (1968) have attempted to locate various groups and their settings in a rewards-cost matrix shown in Figure 13.4. Though it represents, as they put it, only an "arm chair" approximation, it does help to point up the joint operation of these factors in yielding overall satisfaction and greater identification. Radloff and Helmreich (1968) say:

> The area below the dotted line in the lower right half of the matrix is intended to define situations in which a person would not remain voluntarily, such as slum and ghetto environments and concentration and prisoner of war camps. Similarly, outcomes above and to the left of the upper dotted line are those which seldom occur because they yield normally unattainably high outcomes . . . [as in] fun and fame type occupations . . . (p. 123).

AWARENESS OF GROUP IDENTITY

A major psychological feature of groups is their function in providing individuals with social identity. By this we mean that group members become involved with one another and aware of each other as members of the same social entity. Groups, of course, may vary considerably in the degree to which they are open in their membership and therefore exclusivity very often becomes a determiner of the prestige-value of a group. We must also bear in mind that individuals have overlapping group memberships, and some of these are more important than others. Once given that importance, groups have a quality which

Goldschmidt (1959) compares to "a kind of psychological membrane which marks those within from those outside" (p. 67). This parallels the in-group and out-group distinction mentioned in Chapter 10.

Especially in groups permitting face-to-face contact, shared identities become vital aspects of an individual's approach to the world. As Durkheim put it:

> . . . it is impossible for men to live together, associating in industry without acquiring a sentiment of the whole formed by their union, without attaching themselves to that whole, preoccupying themselves with its interests, and taking account of it in their conduct. This attachment has in it something surpassing the individual (1947, p. 14).

One criticism of laboratory experimentation is that groups are often formed on an arbitrary basis without having the "real life" quality of established groups, such as a tradition (Lorge, Fox, Davitz, and Bremer, 1958). Accordingly, individuals in these groups may not be motivated to seek an identification with an assemblage of this kind. Despite this criticism, it is evident from other research findings that motivations are at work which contribute to an individual's acceptance of influence by such *ad hoc* laboratory groups. We shall consider this point further in connection with social reality.

In broader terms, identity is highly susceptible to the effects of environmental forces. Thus, a threat to a group has been found to increase its members' identification with it (e.g. Pepitone and Kleiner, 1957). In time of external strife, the people of a nation manifest a heightened sense of identity with their country and its cause. In this respect, Karl Deutsch (1954) has pointed to the overriding quality of social identity that is bound up with nationalism, because of the sense of a "common fate" which members of a nation share. Belonging, and having a place, are therefore profound sources of the psychological attachment between individuals and the social entities in their environment.

SOCIAL REALITY AND SHARED ATTITUDES

One of the demonstrably pervasive effects of groups is their effect on attitudes. An enormous amount of research has indicated that even with limited interaction, and a marginal sense of group identity at best, individuals are affected by the perceptions of others, particularly under conditions of ambiguity. For example, there is the impressive fact that in the classic laboratory experiments by Sherif (1935) and Asch (1951), referred to earlier, individuals with only limited contact were receptive to the judgments of others.

Festinger (1950) places a considerable amount of weight on "social reality" as a motivational force directing an individual toward affiliation with others and influence by them. What is perhaps less apparent is the degree to which groups as *role systems* create expectancies for individuals to hold and manifest attitudes which are in keeping with their roles. The work of Katz and Lazarsfeld (1955) on "opinion leadership" suggests, for example, a more ready acceptance of novel attitudes from those who have the status of "opinion leaders" as against those who do not.

Uppermost in any consideration of the need for social reality are the rational elements in Man's attempt to understand and cope with his environment. However, the idea of rationality should not be mistaken for logical thinking so much as an attempt to develop a coherent view of reality. Deutsch and Gerard (1955) found in their laboratory research that there are two distinguishable aspects to this process. Individuals react to *normative* as well as *informational* sources of reality. The normative source refers to what "others" do and expect. The informational source refers more to the acceptance of information from "others" as a source of knowledge. In their experiment, they found that subjects who gave only anonymous judgments were less influenced by others than those who gave judgments with which they could be identified. This private versus public dimension exemplifies the differential effect of normative influence which characterizes a good deal of the research findings on conformity. We will treat these further in the next chapter. What needs particular stress here is that identification with others leads to a greater reliance on them for "social reality," especially in terms of normative standards.

GROUP SUPPORT

While social identity provides the individual with a psychological attachment, social support sustains his activity. Groups provide all of us with the basis for carrying on activities, in terms of group tasks, but also with regard to our sense that others approve of these activities. Whether it is writing poetry, wiring a circuit, or speaking out at a political meeting, the approval of others provides a significant reinforcement function in lending support to our actions. Such support can play a vital preservative role, as we noted with regard to Durkheim's research on suicide in Chapter 2 (see p. 53).

Group support is closely tied to the motivation to take part in functional group tasks. Whenever individuals come together to achieve some function, they rely on one another for adequate performance. To the extent that individuals find the achievement of the group's goal rewarding, they will act in consonance with its achievement and be supported by the positive response of others. Uppermost in this process, from a psychological standpoint, is the individual's own investment in what the group seeks to attain. With this in mind, it is clear that a reciprocal sequence is involved; in joining groups, individuals often are attracted by the group's activity, then play a role in it which rewards them by others' approval. It is in this sense that task and affiliation motives are intertwined over time (Wyer, 1966).

A further point of interest lies in the conditions for withdrawal of group support. In an illuminating pair of experiments on this issue, Jones and deCharms (1957) found that the task-related behavior of a group member who is performing poorly is evaluated most negatively if he is perceived to be low in motivation. By contrast, if there is only a doubt raised about his basic ability to perform the task, he is not evaluated nearly so negatively by the others. Thus, disapproval from the group is conditional upon a member's perceived ability to be responsible for behavior which causes the group to fail. In the case of low motivation, the simple judgment is made that the person has not "tried enough" and therefore has "let us down." In Heider's terms (see p. 286), the person who is competent but does not try enough is perceived more as the "locus of causality" for the group's failure than the one who is incompetent but tries hard.

Group support often acts as a gauge for the individual to know how he is doing. The reactions of others thus become a source of informational influence. This process is spelled out in the discussion in Chapter 4 of the influence effects of reinforcement. In social settings, evidences of approval from others are routinely found to increase the probability of the approved response. A series of experiments conducted by

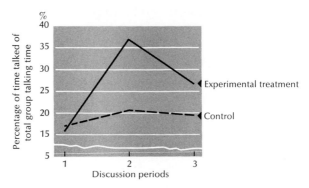

Figure 13.5: Time talked by target persons reinforced in nine experimental groups and non-reinforced in nine control groups. (Based on data from Bavelas, Hastorf, Gross, and Kite, 1965.)

Bavelas, Hastorf, Gross, and Kite (1965) has demonstrated that signs of evident approval of comments made by a previously quiet member of a discussion group increased his frequency of commenting and improved the ratings by others of his "leadership characteristics." To a significant degree, his participation in group discussion had been raised. This effect is revealed in Figure 13.5. Subjects who were "target persons" were selected from those showing a very low level of participation in the first discussion period. Then, in the experimental treatment, they were reinforced by green lights on a panel before them whenever they spoke out. The controls were matched for low initial participation and received no reinforcement. They maintained roughly the same low level while those receiving the experimental treatment spurted upward.

It would be a mistake, however, to conclude that any source of approval of any behavior will influence a person's subsequent action. The effects of group support require two conditions for their operation: first, that the individual himself be positively motivated regarding the activity; and second, that he be positively motivated toward identification with the group as a set of "relevant others," that is, people whose standards and support he desires. It is possible, of course, for a person to do something he finds personally distasteful because others whose approval he seeks are doing it. Where the choice exists, though, the typical inclination is to be associated with those who lend support to activities the individual finds satisfying. This interdependent relationship, between what the individual does and how relevant others value it, is an essential feature of the reference group concept.

Much that we have said here is applicable to features of the reference group. It should be emphasized that the affiliative motives of social identity, social reality, and social support form the psychological substructure for the reference group concept. Thus, as Kelley (1952) has observed, reference groups may be groups that can award or withhold recognition and approval to a person, as well as serve as a standard for him in making judgments.

On social psychological grounds, then, the idea of the reference group provides a useful meshing of the individual and group levels of analysis. Any group known to a person that he takes as a standard of comparison or judgment—whether it is a membership group for him or not—influences his psychological field (Shibutani, 1955). However, the fullest impact of the reference group is most likely to be felt where the individual is not only committed to its "perspectives," in Shibutani's terms, but also is in contact with members who may reward or punish his actions. In that case, the individual has a social identity, with considerable psychological investment, plus the effects of direct reactions from others to his behavior and expressions of attitudes. This feature of functional groups is especially relevant to the satisfactions they provide, as well as to their performance effectiveness, as we have seen. It also has a great bearing on intergroup relations.

Inter-group and international relations

The effects of group identity are quite readily observed in inter-group and international relations. These involve the operation of a whole range of values and attitudes, of co-operation and competition, leadership and communication, prejudice and discriminatory practices. Any circumstance which is likely to elicit a we-they distinction has elements which can drastically alter the outlook and action of group members. From the results of his UNESCO studies in India, in the aftermath of partition almost a quarter of a century ago, Gardner Murphy (1953) concluded that to be accepted in one's own group as a "good Hindu" or a "good Moslem" required expressed hostility toward the other group.

Fortunately, that situation has since become far less acute, although the relationship between India and Pakistan has at times been tense, perhaps most notably in connection with territorial claims to Kashmir.

Given the half billion people who live in India, and its expanse of many different subcultures and languages, it offers a considerable number of illustrations of inter-group relations. One more of these concerns the circumstances which followed its government's decree in 1950 that henceforth the official language of India would be Hindi, primarily spoken in the North, and that the transition from English should occur by 1965. Barnett (1967) reports that substantial dislocations were created in a sub-continent which encompasses 845 distinct languages and dialects, several dozen of which are major tongues, as was noted in Chapter 9. While he observes that the Hindu populations welcomed the change, Bengali speakers in the East and Tamil speakers in the South were among those who energetically protested the necessity to adopt a tongue as alien to them as any in the Western world. The issue was not just one of inter-group conflict alone. For over a century English had been the common tongue, even given that no more than 3 per cent of the Indian population could employ it with any degree of fluency, but these people represented the educated class occupying roles as administrators, professors, judges, legislators, and journalists. Moreover, the major newspapers in India are mainly English-language dailies, and universities had employed English as the primary language of instruction. Barnett (1967) says:

> Finally the so-called "Save Hindi" campaign was called off. The announcement, significantly, was published in English. In Parliament, Prime Minister Nehru declared that for an indefinite period English would continue as an "associate official language." While Hindi-speaking legislators listened in silence and others cheered, Nehru termed English "the major window for us to the outside world. We dare not close that window," he said. "And if we do, it will spell peril to our future" (p. 21).

THE NATURE OF INTER-GROUP RELATIONS

In general terms, *inter-group relations* refer to the character of the relationship that exists between two or more groups and their members. There are additional refinements necessary, however, to make this definition more complete. The "groups" may be functional groups, social institutions, descriptive categories that represent a "slice" of society—such as socio-economic classes—or total societies such as nations. A "relationship" may be largely a matter of perpetuating past history, or an attitude such as a stereotype. Sometimes it is neither, and in other instances it is both. Though the Battle of the Boyne was fought nearly three centuries ago, it still served as a "rallying cry" in the recent skirmishing between Catholics and Protestants in Northern Ireland, apart from other immediate irritants. This is hardly a singular case of history perpetuated, though two hundred and eighty years is a long time.

Inter-group relations can mean the active involvement of representatives of allies or of contending parties, personal relationships across groups, or institutionalized conflict in terms of outright warfare. Furthermore, as we have already observed, actual "membership" in a contending group can mean commitment to the group—or to its cause, as in a social movement—independently of formal affiliation. From a social psychological perspective, then, inter-group relations can be considered to encompass actual or implied interaction, whether collectively or individually, between persons who share distinct social identities which are particularly salient at the time.

Organized society would be unmanageable without co-operative group relationships. However, it is mainly conflict between groups which rivets our attention. Rather than being a deviant feature of life, many kinds of inter-group conflict are part of its give and take. A goodly number of conflicts are merely predictable manifestations of a concern for how resources, especially scarce ones, will be apportioned, in terms of equity and justice, and these often find their way into judicial proceedings in our courts of law. Indeed, a primary requisite in any human society is for mechanisms to regulate and manage conflict toward productive rather than destructive ends.

PROCESSES OF CONFLICT

Most popularized views of conflict among humans are permeated with the idea of aggressiveness. As was indicated earlier, however, there is at best only a limited basis for viewing aggressiveness as innate in Man. While Man certainly has the *capacity* for being aggressive, this fact has too readily led to the view that its expression is a necessity of life. What is more likely to be the case is that a good deal of aggressive behavior is *reactive* to threat, rather than a direct expression of some instinctive requirement.

Another relevant consideration in viewing aggression is that it may cover all sorts of behavior, ranging from coping with the environment in an assertive way on through hostile or destructive action. It is mainly the latter which has concerned observers of inter-group relations, particularly since it has the flavor of harming or destroying a perceived irritant or threat in the environment. Aggression of this kind, in its more violent manifestations, has been attributed to pent-up feelings of frustration among members of a group. Miller and Dollard (1941), for example, showed a relationship between the rise in the number of lynchings of blacks in the South during the 1930's and the drop in the price of cotton. They suggest that when economic conditions are bad, this results in frustration and that, accordingly, there is a tendency to show displaced aggression toward any convenient scapegoat. A similar explanation has been offered by Schuman (1939) for the rise of Hitler in Germany and the willingness of its people to follow him into World War II. There are, nevertheless, some unanswered questions in this explanation. As Klineberg (1950) points out, aggression toward blacks depends upon the time and place, including the influence of culture. He notes that white Brazilians are, on the whole, much more frustrated economically than are white Americans. Yet, he says, there was far less evident conflict there, and no lynchings of Brazilian blacks (p. 198).

In general, the approach to conflict in social psychology places little value on the views that humans are either innately aggressive or else aggressive mainly out of a sense of frustration. While conflict between groups is a widespread social phenomenon, it is not caused by a single factor. There are many different reasons for conflict which can be studied and understood. Among these are: *undeniable disputes about how valued resources should be distributed; varying definitions of a situation held in the perspectives of different groups;* and *contextual factors of an historical and institutional nature.* Therefore, the study of conflict must start with the idea of a particular system of relationships which give it impetus, even though there are regularities in the processes which may sustain it and reduce it. Indeed, from his extensive research on conflicts within communities, Coleman (1957) has said:

> The most striking fact about the development and growth of community controversies is the similarity they exhibit despite diverse underlying sources and different kinds of precipitating incidents (p. 9).

Though to a somewhat lesser degree, international conflicts leading to open warfare also appear to follow a consistent pattern of onset, as is noted here later in the section on war (p. 541).

THE IN-GROUP AND THE OUT-GROUP

The perception of differences between groups is an ubiquitous social phenomenon, which need not lead to conflict, but can be turned to productive action and social progress. Yet, the usual way of seeing an "in-group"—"out-group" distinction is in terms of conflict. In such a case, as we observed in Murphy's (1953) report of India after the time of partition, conflict makes this distinction a dominant psychological force. Its destructive overtones are furthered by the imputation of a value judgment of "goodness" versus "badness."

It is understandable, of course, that groups which are salient reference groups for individuals are usually seen by them as having virtues which others may not see. In their UNESCO study in nine countries, as an example, Buchanan and Cantril (1953) found that respondents in all of these countries agreed uniformly on one point, namely that their own nation was the most "peace-loving" among the nations they rated. When situations of conflict arise, this tendency to judge one's own group favorably takes on added potency. Then all virtue is likely to be seen in the in-group, all evil in the out-group. Each side sees itself as the instrument of higher values, up to and including divine will, as in the case of nations at war. Group loyalties and the sense of determination to overcome the evil represented by the adversary are increased. As a consequence, the prospects for reducing conflict are diminished considerably.

In his analysis of sterotypes, Campbell (1967) says that they function so that

. . . The behavior on one's own part is perceived in a different context than is comparable behavior on the part of an out-grouper. This will be particularly true of behavior directed toward the out-group. . . . This generates a set of "universal" stereotypes, of which each in-group might accuse each out-group, or some out-group or the average out-group (p. 823).

A number of parallel, but oppositely-signed descriptions from Campbell and LeVine (1961) are shown in Table 13.1.

Table 13.1: Some group characteristics as they are described in self-descriptions and in stereotypes of the out-group. (After Campbell and LeVine, 1961.)

SELF-DESCRIPTION	STEREOTYPE OF OUT-GROUP
1. We have pride, self-respect and revere the traditions of our ancestors.	They are egotistical and self-centered. They love themselves more than they love us.
2. We are loyal.	They are clannish, exclude others.
3. We are honest and trustworthy among ourselves, but we're not suckers when foreigners try their tricks.	They will cheat us if they can. They have no honesty or moral restraint when dealing with us.
4. We are brave and progressive. We stand up for our own rights, defend what is ours, and can't be pushed around or bullied.	They are aggressive and expansionistic. They want to get ahead at our expense.
5. We are peaceful, loving people, hating only our vile enemies.	They are a hostile people who hate us.
6. We are moral and clean.	They are immoral and unclean.

Bronfenbrenner (1961c) has written of his impressions, striking up conversations with people during one of his visits to the Soviet Union a decade ago, right after the "U-2 affair." He found that the Soviet citizens' picture of America, and its government, was curiously similar to the view Americans held of the Soviet Union. They were, in Bronfenbrenner's term, a "mirror image" of one another. Five of the stereotyped themes which emerged from Bronfenbrenner's analysis, as characteristics of both Soviet and American impressions, are these:

They are the aggressors.
Their government exploits and deludes the people.

> The mass of *their* people are not really sympathetic to the regime.
>
> *They* cannot be trusted.
>
> *Their* policy verges on madness.

Without in any sense arguing that there is validity to the perceptions, Bronfenbrenner claims that these perceptions nonetheless have a potential for affecting action *as if* they were quite real. He also points out that a frightening consequence of the mirror image lies in the possibility that each action from the opposing side is interpreted within the framework of the belief system. Thus, it is possible for either side to interpret concessions as signs of trickery, because of such expectancies.

Associated with the process of intensified conflict is the simplistic quality of "psycho-logic," discussed in Chapter 6. Since the evaluative dimension takes on great strength in conflict, the perceived negative qualities of the out-group make it inconsistent to believe that they may be justified in their position. This is abetted by the incendiary use of language which may portray them as "devious," "treacherous," or "aggressive," while the in-group may be characterized as "noble" in pursuing a "just cause" for the sake of "honor."

It is unlikely that in-group versus out-group distinctions can be made to vanish. However, as Gordon Allport (1958) has persuasively indicated, there is no fundamental reason why loyalty to one group must preclude loyalty to another. Identifications may be concentric such that loyalty to one's family can be accommodated within loyalty to one's community, occupation, state and nation, each at successive levels. Thus, he contends that just as identification to one's state can be readily absorbed within identification to one's nation, identification with one's nation can be accommodated within identification with the United Nations and a commitment to world order. Indeed, Guetzkow's study (1955) of members of the United Nations Secretariat indicates that loyalty to one's nation is no barrier to being a competent international civil servant. The compatibility of national and world interests is readily seen, for example, in international trade and postal agreements, weather reporting, air traffic control and public health measures, among many other day-to-day practices.

In the larger perspective, the maintenance of life on our planet urgently depends upon the extension of group loyalties beyond the tribe and the nation to the requirements of all mankind. In the perspective of a single life, when "tribalism" gets the upper hand, it makes insistent demands that frequently run counter to personal freedom. Pressures toward conformity increase and a hardening of position takes place regarding what and who is loyal. Ardrey (1966) contends that patriotism dictates a hostile response whenever a nation's "territory" is intruded upon or threatened by an adversary. The concept of "territory," however, ought to be understood more broadly to include not only physical space, but a nation's or a group's symbols. Its flag, its honor, its dignity and history, all symbolize in-group characteristics which have potent psychological significance in terms of the social identity and allegiance of individuals.

MANAGING INTER-GROUP CONFLICT

Given the reality of inter-group conflict, how is it to be managed? Practically speaking, it is achieved by a variety of social mechanisms which exist to contain and direct it toward productive ends. Of these, negotiation continues to be the most widespread. It is seen routinely in labor-management relations. Even given periodic strikes, negotiation works remarkably well in contrast with the past, when unions were attempting to establish bargaining rights with reluctant employers. Before such rights became normative, there was a great amount of turbulence on the industrial scene. To those who despair that conflicts ever can be handled in an organized way, Etzioni (1964) reminds us that until relatively recent times, in the United States,

> . . . labor organizations were viewed as conspiracies and fought with all the instruments management could marshall, including the local police, militia, armed strike-breakers, professional spies, and the like. The workers, in turn, did not refrain from resorting to dynamite and other means of sabotage nor from beating the strike-breakers (p. 244).

To be effective, negotiation requires co-operation within a set of rules. From a social psychological standpoint, these rules represent agreed-upon norms for making conflict productive rather than destructive. They set a structure for the conflict and thereby "encapsulate" it (Etzioni, 1964). However, negotiation which occurs within this structure can proceed in various ways. Oftentimes, the process of negotiation is perceived by the negotiators, the groups they represent, or by outsiders, as a zero-sum game in which there must be a "winner" and a "loser" (see Chapter 7, p. 249). This construction of the situation is not likely to encourage co-operation since it implicitly emphasizes competition (Sherif, 1958). Unless both contending parties see the necessity for accommodation, then accusations and recriminations will be the order of the day and a retreat to entrenched positions will very probably occur. To paraphrase Milburn (1961), the belief that international relationships are competitive in the sense that only one side can win means that *both sides* may very well lose.

In a study of inter-group competition, Blake and Mouton (1961b) found that a competitive, "You win, I lose" strategy caused group members to misunderstand the proposed solution of the other group. The findings are clear in indicating that inter-group problem-solving is made more difficult by the distortions created by a totally competitive strategy. They suggest that an understanding of the other party's position requires a mutual recognition of common goals to be achieved. Relatedly, Rapoport (1962) has urged that the spokesman for each side in a controversy should be required to state his adversary's position to the latter's satisfaction before responding with his own.

The effectiveness of several strategies of co-operation in negotiation has been investigated in various studies. In one of these, Solomon (1960) compared "unconditional benevolence," "conditional benevolence," and "unconditional malevolence" by P with regard to the degree of co-operation each yielded from the other person (O) in a prisoner's dilemma game. Solomon found that conditional *benevolence*, i.e. rewards for favorable actions and no reward for unfavorable ones, proved to be most effective. In another experiment, by Shure, Meeker, and Hansford (1965), it was found that a pacifist strategy employed by P in a two-person game led to exploitation by O. More recently, Deutsch, Epstein, Canavan, and Gumpert (1967) investigated the effectiveness of the strategy of "turning the other cheek" compared to strategies of "non-punitiveness" and "deterrence." In the first of these, P deals with O by attempting to elicit co-operation through an appeal to O's conscience; in the second, P rewards O for co-operation and does *not* reward him for non-co-operation; in the deterrent strategy, P *rewards* O's co-operation and *punishes* O's non-co-operation. The results of this experiment indicated that the "turning the other cheek" strategy resulted in the greatest exploitation by O, while the "deterrent" strategy yielded the lowest joint outcomes. On balance, the "non-punitive" strategy gave the highest joint outcomes and seemed to function best, because O is not punished, which might lead to a spiral of hostility; though O loses rewards for non-co-operation, this strategy allows P to show he desires to be friendly, but at the same time that he will not be exploited by O. An important feature of this study, in terms of resolving interpersonal conflict, is the distinction it points up psychologically between *non*-reward and punishment.

Appealing and useful as they are, many of the approaches to the study of negotiation and conflict management through game analysis assume too much rationality and calculation. Indeed, Deutsch (1969) calls attention to the danger that conflicts can be turned into issues of self-esteem, power, illegitimate threat or coercion, which make them all the harder to resolve (p. 1090). In this vein, Rapoport (1966), a leading figure in game analysis, comments as follows:

> Rational analysis, for all its inadequacy, is indeed the best instrument of cognition we have. But it often is at its best when it reveals to us the nature of the situation we find ourselves in, even though it may have nothing to tell us how we ought to behave in this situation. Too much depends on our choice of values, criteria, notions of what is "rational," and, last but by no means least, the sort of relationship and communication we establish with the other parties of the "game." These choices have nothing to do with the particular game we are playing. They are not *strategic* choices, i.e., choices rationalized in terms of advantages they bestow on us in a particular conflict. Rather they are choices which we make because of the way we view ourselves, and the world, including the other players. The great philosophical value of game theory is in its power to reveal its own incompleteness (p. 214).

Among the most important contributions to resolving inter-group conflict is the elaborate field experimentation by Muzafer Sherif and his co-workers (Sherif and Sherif, 1953; Sherif, Harvey, White, Hood, and Sherif, 1961) on the significance of *superordinate goals*. In two experiments in boys' summer camps, they were able to study the development of inter-group conflict among these youngsters when, at each camp, they were divided into two groups. The groups were commonly drawn from an identical sample which was highly homogeneous in terms of such factors as age, race, religion, and socio-economic status. Conflict was induced largely through intensive competitive rivalry for rewards which were limited.

In the next phase of these experiments, after a high level of conflict had been attained, the effect of factors which could reduce the conflict was carefully studied. Thus, mere contact between the groups in enjoyable activities was found to serve as an occasion for further exchanges of hostile comments. It was only when a mutual crisis was introduced— for example, an apparent breakdown in transportation carrying food for the camp—that mutual co-operation developed. Furthermore, some necessity for continuing co-operation toward the achievement of common superordinate goals had to be sustained over *time* for their effect on the reduction of inter-group hostility to be achieved (Sherif, 1962, p. 11).

REDUCING INTER-GROUP TENSION

Underlying outbreaks of inter-group conflict is the less dramatic but persistent quality of inter-group *tension*. Such tension does not require a manifest issue of pronounced conflict, a *cause célèbre*, or a dramatic incident. Whenever individuals perceive a group of others with distrust and hostility, practice discrimination, or harbor residuals of hatred, inter-group tension exists.

As was pointed out in connection with prejudice in Chapter 10, tension between groups usually takes the form of hostility toward others because of a perceived group affiliation independently of their individual characteristics. Any discriminatory practices which sharpen lines of demarcation between groups, for example on the basis of skin color or religion, serve as structural supports for prejudice. Furthermore, they prevent individuals from confronting one another on the basis of a wide range of other personal qualities they may possess, including their capacities and intelligence, mutual interests, and personality. Research on interpersonal contact as a basis for the reduction of prejudice encourages the view that once the environmental supports for prejudice are removed, tension between groups is considerably reduced. This is especially so in terms of "equal status" contacts.

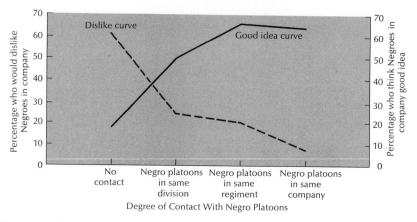

Figure 13.6: Responses of white soldiers to two questions concerning black platoons in white companies by degree of respondents' actual contact with black platoons in their own units. (Based upon data gathered in 1945 and reported in Stouffer, Suchman, DeVinney, Star and Williams, 1949.)

During World War II, before the U.S. Armed Forces were integrated by Presidential Order, some units of the army in Europe were composed of black troops who had volunteered for combat. These troops were organized into platoons, under white officers, in companies that were otherwise made up of white troops. A survey conducted by the Army's Research Branch (Information and Education Division, 1945) revealed a very high degree of satisfaction among white officers and non-commissioned officers in these companies with the performance of the black soldiers. More to the point, however, the greater the degree of contact with these soldiers the greater the degree to which white soldiers favored the idea of having companies include black platoons.

Part of the results of this survey are shown in Figure 13.6. The two questions asked were:

> Some Army divisions have companies which include Negro and white platoons. How would you feel about it if your outfit was set up something like that?

> In general, do you think it is a good idea or a poor idea to have the same company in a combat outfit include Negro platoons and white platoons?

Plainly, those who had directly experienced black troops in their companies were far more inclined to be in favor of this practice than those who did not. Those who had *not* had this encounter were overwhelmingly opposed to it. A reasonable presumption then is that a shift occurred as a result of equal status contacts, within the context of vital superordinate goals.

Comparable findings have been obtained in the realm of housing, without such evident goals but with person-to-person contact. Jahoda (1961) reports that while a majority of white Americans prefer residential segregation, that preference is reduced by *half* where white persons have had the experience of working with blacks and having them as neighbors. Deutsch and Collins (1951) studied housing projects that were integrated throughout or segregated by buildings allocated exclusively for white or for black residents. Their results indicated a far greater degree of contact of whites with blacks in the integrated housing with a corresponding decrease in prejudice among the whites toward the blacks. Here again, racial tension was highest where the two groups lived apart and where prejudice was thereby sustained through environmental support.

From this and other evidence, it is clear, therefore, that the reduction of inter-group tension can be accomplished through favorably sustained social contact, particularly where common goals are being cooperatively sought. It is equally clear that programs of information or exhortation will not in themselves effectively reduce intergroup tension without action, which also means involvement. Hyman and Sheatsley (1947) are among those finding that selective perception operates to block out information which is contrary to what a person already believes (see Chapter 6). Thus, those who are most likely to need the facts from an information campaign are often impervious to them.

A final point here concerns the widespread belief that inter-group tension and associated conflict only affect members of so-called "minority groups" in a society. They are unquestionably victimized and may suffer profoundly, up through deprivation of liberties, incarceration, and death. It is, to say the very least, unpleasant to live in a hostile environment where one's children must learn that others hate them for nothing they have done. Yet, all parties to inter-group tension, including the broader society, are adversely affected by being cut off from the resources and initiatives of individuals.

Some implications for international conflict and war

International relations are an inter-group phenomenon, but with an order of magnitude in intensity that introduces important differences. The power of the nation state is, for one thing, vastly greater than the usual "groups" about which we have spoken here. Governments have unmatched powers to conscript citizens for military service, to tax them, and to call upon them for many kinds of sacrifice. Members of a nation share in common loyalties and a feeling of mutual fate, especially regarding the potentialities for massive upheavals and destructiveness in war. Nations also stand as an embodiment of all those things that people cherish in a cultural sense of their "way of life," and this is deeply rooted in patriotism.

Virtually everything in this book is implicated somehow in understanding international relations, whether it be processes of conflict resolution, attitude change, adaptation level effects, psycho-logic, conformity, or whatever. What is less obvious perhaps it that governmental decisions regarding matters of war and peace are made by individuals, with their own assumptions, attitudes, and psychological propensities, and not by a disembodied abstraction called "the government." The UNESCO charter begins with the words: "Wars begin in the minds of men." But too little has been made of the social psychological processes in governmental actions, though some political scientists have now come to regard the "definition of the situation" as a significant element of analysis. Snyder, Bruck, and Sapin (1962), for example, have asserted that, "The key to the explanation of why the state behaves as it does lies in the way its decision makers define their situation" (p. 51).

In his book on "groupthink," Janis (1971) examines a number of badly miscalculated decisions in international affairs made by men of acknowledged experience and intellectual capability. Among these is the "Bay of Pigs invasion" of April 1961, which is at times confused with the other major Cuban event of the Kennedy years, the "missile crisis" of October 1962, which involved the Soviet Union. Janis in effect asks the question how these decision-makers could have been so grossly mistaken in their estimates of the Bay of Pigs venture. Having read all of the relevant material from the after-the-fact writings of the participants, as well as of many others, he arrives at some telling conclusions, in terms of social psychological processes, quite apart from the acknowledged limitations of intelligence information and other explanations offered. His general hypothesis is that the more amiability and *esprit de corps* among a group of policy-makers, the greater the danger of groupthink with accompanying irrational and even dehumanizing actions directed against adversaries.

Janis's main findings center about the operation of two major illusions which took hold within the group of key decision-makers, one of these their "invulnerability" and the other their "unanimity." The first has to do with a sense that what the group decides is bound to succeed, and the second that they have total consensus because no one within the group has stated a clear-cut disagreement. In the latter regard, the group's cohesiveness was strongly applied in bringing forth a uniform view in open "straw votes" which may have had the character of a conformity pressure experiment, with overtones of the "risky-shift." Coupled with these processes was the fear of disapproval for deviation in a new administration with a leader these advisors wished to support as a sign of loyalty. Finally, Janis points to the presence of "mindguards," an apt analogy to bodyguards, in the sense of those who protected the leader from injurious thoughts which might give rise to doubts. Rather than being an eccentric phenomenon, Janis concludes that "groupthink" processes characterize many other decisions, including the ones to escalate the war in Viet Nam during the Johnson administration.

Popular views to the contrary, war represents not so much "diplomacy by other means," as it does a breakdown of the normal mechanisms of diplomacy. As Karl Deutsch (1957) observes:

> Governments frequently—though not always—decide to go to war when they believe themselves to be constrained by the lack of any acceptable political alternative to war . . . but we should also ask to what extent the actual state of the attitudes of the foreign country or of inflamed domestic public opinion has itself been produced by the basic "mental set" . . . and by the further communications process through which latent attitudes of friendship or hostility are transformed into acute perceptions of a present conflict (p. 201).

Under most circumstances, the people of a nation must be "prepared" for a war. The rhetoric, both in volume and intensity, must have risen to the level where war seems justified, or at the least inevitable, usually as a result of the "intransigence" of the other side. National leaders are always careful to be seen as favoring peace themselves. Dictatorships, with their absolute control over the mass media, can organize inflammatory campaigns with wide coverage. But even in democracies the potentialities exist for rather extensive publicity to develop favoring war, or some "action." Deutsch (1957) sees this as a danger insofar as political leaders may reach a "point of no return" by allowing attitudes at home to harden too fast and too firmly.

The use of verbal "blockbusters" is especially evident when leaders feel compelled to show the tenacity with which they hold to a stand. When President Johnson said that the honor of the United States was at stake in Southeast Asia, he was not merely indulging in rhetoric, nor adopting a bargaining stance; in effect, he shifted the scope and meaning of the conflict for the American people.

In an analysis of international conflict, Fisher (1964) points out how vitally national leaders can affect outcomes by the way they *define* the conflict, especially to their own people. Generally speaking, smaller conflicts are easier to resolve than larger ones. Therefore, he says, it is usually to the advantage of the parties concerned to scale down conflicts. National leaders often have a choice in defining conflicts as larger or smaller, as is illustrated by the 1962 Cuban missile crisis. At that time, it was possible to have the United States and Soviet Union agree about the smaller issue of the placement of missiles in Cuba, when it would have been far more difficult and more dangerous to attempt to deal just then with considerations of national spheres of influence, the political complexion of Cuba, or broader issues of East-West relations. In Fisher's view, conflict is diminished when it is dealt with as a matter involving small units, of persons or issues or territory. For example, the conflict between two individuals of different races is easier to deal with in just those terms rather than as a "racial conflict." Conflict is also reduced when it is localized to the *application* of a principle, rather than being itself a *matter* of principle, which might then constitute a precedent.

Whenever groups or nations are in open conflict, the problem of limiting hostility becomes critical, as Richardson demonstrates in his *Statistics of Deadly Quarrels* (1960). The sad history of most international conflicts is that of unwanted results in war, and often in the peace which follows. On this point, Turner (1969) makes this apt observation:

> There has probably never been a war or violent revolution in which the question of what either side was fighting for did not become unclear, nor in which the issue at the close of fighting was defined in the same way as at the start of combat (p. 823).

Wars are generated by forces instigated by men, but as Turner's comment indicates, these forces come to have a life of their own. Prior to the outbreak of a war, three stages can be identified which represent an increasing loss of control over the juggernaut (Gladstone, 1959; Holsti and North, 1965). First, there occurs a period of rising tensions, including the perception that one's national goals are incompatible with those of another nation, a sense of threat, frustration and distrust. Next, a phase of avowed military preparedness, with an arms build-up, is evidenced. Then, hostile words and actions become more frequent, and it is a short step before warfare begins (Pruitt and Snyder, 1969, Part Three).

The place of armaments in preparing for or preventing wars has been argued mainly around the issue of "deterrence." Briefly, the deterrent theory holds that military preparations bolster peace by making potential aggressors wary of the costs that would be incurred were they to attack (McClintock and Hekhuis, 1961; Milburn, 1959; G. H. Snyder, 1961). Critics of the deterrent theory have argued for some time that military preparations make for war, since each side strives to achieve military superiority, rather than a balance, and therefore no end to the spiraling arms race can result other than eventual warfare, unless it is "wound down" (Fleming, 1962; Kissinger, 1957; Singer, 1962).

There is no one "right answer" regarding the efficacy of deterrence in an abstract sense, since it so readily gets confounded by issues of "who is to blame" and whether a build-up of arms is "defensive" or "offensive." That last question in fact points up a supreme illustration of perceptual distortion: one's own armaments are quite clearly defensive in nature, while the adversary's are just as clearly offensive. However, there should be no mistaking the very real sense of *threat* that both sides may feel as they see the other fellow arming to the teeth, whatever he may say about desiring peace and being concerned only over his own defense. In an analysis of a sample of cases drawn from 2000 years of history, Naroll (1969) found that, as a practical matter, ". . . leading civilized states have usually lived in danger of war and few statesmen of such societies have ever been in a position to neglect their nation's armed forces in good conscience" (p. 153). Using refined statistical techniques, Naroll finds that in the "very long run" the preparation for war appears to make war more rather than less likely, though he is cautious in calling attention to the many other contingencies involved.

Much of the social psychological research on conflict and co-operation summarized here indicates that deterrence, in the punishment sense, has only limited utility for obtaining favorable outcomes in terms of co-operation (Deutsch, 1961, 1969). It has been suggested that anything which builds trust between adversaries is more likely to make for trustworthiness. Threats of the deterrent variety are therefore only useful up to a point without the counter-balancing effects of moves toward reciprocation. Viewing the problem only in military terms, as a win-lose, zero-sum game, cannot help achieve agreements which may be beneficial to both sides.

Illustrative of such agreement was the 1963 atomic test ban treaty which had the quality of representing the achievement for its signators of superordinate goals, not the least of which was tension-reduction. A proposal for furthering this process has come from Osgood (1962) in his strategy of "graduated reciprocation in international tension-reduction" (GRIT). Just as leaders can "escalate" conflicts by their statements and their actions, Osgood proposes that they can "de-escalate" them by announcing and carrying out small conciliatory acts on a unilateral basis. Rather than be seen as a sign of weakness, such acts are likely to signalize the power and high status of a nation because they are initiated voluntarily. Furthermore, Osgood points out that initiatives can be graduated in risk so that very little is lost if they are not reciprocated initially.

Apart from its effect in reducing a hostile climate of opinion within a nation, a GRIT strategy has major merits as a possible device for establishing a better atmosphere for mutual trust between nations. While its efficacy in international relations is yet to be established, in part because of the difficulty in having a nation take the first steps as a consistent policy, GRIT has been found to work in laboratory experimentation. In one such study, Scodel (1962) found, in an experiment with a prisoner's dilemma problem, that a player who adopted a conciliatory strategy after an initial period of employing an intensely competitive strategy received significantly higher co-operation from the other player than one who had co-operated from the very outset. If nothing else, it may be that the "contrast effect" of sudden conciliation induces a more favorable psychological reaction.

In another experiment directly involving GRIT, Crow (1963) used the procedure of Inter-Nation Simulation developed by Guetzkow and his colleagues (1963) to study international relations. In this procedure, each member of a group acts as a policy-maker for a fictitious nation. Each person is given basic data on the initial strength of its nation's position. Then, over periods of time each is allowed to make policies regarding the allocation of resources, for example, to the production of consumer goods or armaments, and to enter into trade or military alliances with the other nations represented. It is possible in this procedure for the nations to go to war when the tensions increase to an extreme.

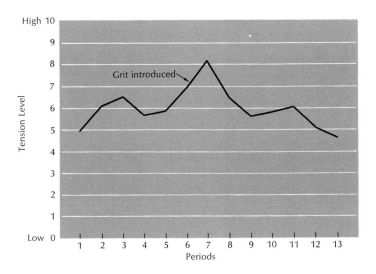

Figure 13.7: Tension level as rated by participants in Inter-Nation Simulation, run over thirteen periods, showing effect of introduction of GRIT strategy by one participant. (From Crow, 1963, p. 588.)

In Crow's research, there were five nations, two of which were very powerful. Each was represented by a policy-maker. They interacted over thirteen periods of seventy minutes each. In every period, measures of the "tension level" were taken by the ratings of the participants. As his major experimental intervention, Crow had the policy-maker of one of the powerful nations adopt a GRIT strategy at the beginning of the seventh period. As is seen in Figure 13.7, the tension level had been showing a not unusual rising tendency during the first six periods. Under such circumstances, warfare might very well be predicted. However, after a further slight rise during the seventh period when GRIT was initiated, the figure shows a marked drop-off in tension level to the lowest point, in the last period. This finding dramatizes one prospect for the creative use of techniques which may alleviate dangerous tensions in international relations.

For many, there continues to be the firmly rooted belief that war fulfills Man's "need" for aggression. The actualities appear to be otherwise, however. The drumbeat of propaganda and the inflammation of feeling against "the enemy" would not be so much a part of war-making if the aggression of men was bursting for expression. In this vein, Klineberg (1964) observes that:

> . . . every modern nation in time of war has to resort to some form of draft or conscription to satisfy the manpower needs of its armed forces. If all of us were eagerly awaiting a chance to express a latent aggression stored up for years, would coercion be necessary to build up an army? Would we not all rush to enlist instead of, in most cases, awaiting the summons? (p. 14)

Another concomitant of war is its effect on individual expression. Typically, in conflict situations, the fragile balance between personal freedom and social demands shifts against the individual. As was commented upon earlier here (p. 529), the group's insistence upon the absolute rightness of its position forces greater signs of loyalty and stifles dissent. In that circumstance, as Blake and Mouton (1962) put it:

> Disagreement, the raw material of creative thinking which can lead to the re-examination and enrichment of the position of one's group, tends to be snuffed out. Failure to go along after a certain point can arouse insidious group pressures toward conformity and, in the extreme, may even lead to the expulsion of members who resist the tide (p. 99).

Thus, the freedom to be one's self is diminished by intense social forces in inter-group and international conflict. Conformity for its own sake may then become the prevailing standard. As we shall see in the next chapter, this kind of pressure poses problems for the fulfillment of individual potentialities, as well as for the successful functioning of a group and society.

SUMMARY

Group dynamics refers generally to the processes occurring within groups, and in particular to the research tradition established by Kurt Lewin. It views groups in terms of *group locomotion,* that is, the movement of a group toward its goal. Associated with locomotion are the *interrelated variables of cohesiveness, communication, and conformity.* Each of these depends upon and affects the others.

Another approach to group dynamics concerns the forces affecting *change processes.* Bringing about change requires an alteration in the *quasi-stationary equilibrium* of prevailing practices. This involves a *process* by which sources of individual resistance are overcome through group support. In general, cohesive groups appear to exert greater influence over their members either to enhance or to impede change. Members who have a weak sense of group identification have been found to be more likely to change their attitudes in directions opposite to those of the group.

The effectiveness of a group can be considered in terms of two criteria, its *performance* and its *members' satisfaction.* These depend upon the particulars of the situation and the task confronting the group, and the satisfaction of individual members of a group is often aggregated in terms of *morale.* Studies reveal that this index of satisfaction is not necessarily tied to group performance in a one-to-one fashion.

Another aspect of group effectiveness rests in the *resources* available to a group in carrying out its functions. The outcome of this process depends upon the ratio of *inputs* from the group and its environment to the *outputs* it produces in terms of performance and satisfaction along the way. The qualities of individuals comprising a group are therefore vital to its effectiveness. There is also a tendency for group decisions to be "riskier" than those same decisions made by individuals.

The *risky-shift* appears to be a result of communication among group members indicating to the individual that he is not as risky as he had thought and that greater risk is valued.

The psychological effects of the group arise primarily from the *identifications* individuals have with it. The differential effects of various groups on individuals arise from several motivational bases. One of these is the motivation to take part in the *task*, the other is to gain from the *affiliations* that the group provides socially. The affiliation motives which appear to be most operative are those for *social identity, social reality,* and *social support.* These may be interrelated, as well as being associated with the individual's task motivation.

The identification of individuals with groups is a basic feature of life. Some of these identities are more important than others and this distinction grows out of the satisfaction of other affiliation motives. Thus, the need for social reality, in the sense of having an outlook which is corroborated by others, is one of these. The individual also requires support from others, in terms of approval of his activities. Group support provides a significant reinforcement function in shaping and giving continuity to individual actions.

The concept of *reference groups* sums up these psychological effects. Whether an individual belongs to them or not, such groups constitute "psychological groups" which provide *standards for making judgments,* in the sense of social reality, and *approval,* in the sense of group support. The reference group stands as a useful bridge between the individual and group levels of analysis. Its essential quality lies in the identification, or social identity, it provides for the individual.

Inter-group relations refer to the character of the relationship between groups, and members of them. It can encompass various kinds of actual or implied interaction where group identities are particularly salient. Though co-operative group relations are necessary to the maintenance of organized society, inter-group conflict is nevertheless a common feature of life.

The basis for *conflict* rests in the complex relationship of psychological as well as historical and institutional factors. Aggressivity in human affairs, including war, appears to be reactive rather than instinctive. It does not stem from a necessity for aggressiveness, nor solely from a response to frustration.

The distinction between an *in-group* and an *out-group* holds the potential for inter-group tension whenever a value judgment of "goodness" versus "badness" is involved. Especially where there are perceived conflicts of interest, this distinction takes on added potency. The in-group is seen as virtuous and the out-group as evil. Simplistic "psycho-logical" thinking then makes the reduction of conflict more difficult. There is no reason why group identifications must exist on an exclusive basis. They can be, and often are, accommodated within *concentric loyalties,* such as to one's family, community, state, and nation, as well as to the world.

The *management of inter-group conflict* is a vital social requirement. It is usually accomplished through *negotiation* within a set of rules, or norms, which are mutually accepted by the parties concerned. A pitfall in negotiation is that it may be perceived as a zero-sum game in which there must be a "winner" and a "loser." Given such a strategy, both parties may lose. A mutual recognition of the necessity for *co-operation* is essential for negotiation to direct conflict toward productive ends. Such recognition is facilitated by the presence of *superordinate goals* which are valued by both parties.

Inter-group tension usually takes the form of hostility and prejudice, even without a direct point of conflict. Such tension is sustained by environmental supports. When these are removed, tension is reduced by interpersonal contact on an equal status basis. But information programs designed to reduce inter-group tension are less effective than such action because they often fail to reach those for whom they are intended.

Conflicts in the realm of *international relations* offer a more intense instance of inter-group phenomena. They can be understood to have similar social psychological components, but with potent elements of shared fate and loyalties bound into patriotism. Wars take on a life of their own, often having been instigated by a failure of diplomacy and a rhetoric with related actions that achieve a flash point. International conflicts are especially vulnerable to distortions of perception and require careful definition on limited rather than more global terms if they are to be accommodated. *Tension-reduction* necessitates mechanisms for *reciprocation* of trust which go beyond a posture of deterence through arms.

The existence of inter-group or international conflict serves as a limitation on a society by cutting off the availability of individual resources. Individuals who are caught up in inter-group conflict are vulnerable to coercive pressure toward intense group conformity, and are therefore less free to exercise their independence and fulfill their potentialities.

SUGGESTED READINGS

From E. P. Hollander and R. G. Hunt (Eds.) *Current perspectives in social psychology*. (3rd ed.) New York: Oxford University Press, 1971. Introduction to Section X: *Intergroup relations*

61. Rensis Likert: *An overview of new patterns of management*
65. Ralph H. Turner: *The public perception of protest*
66. Morton Deutsch: *Some considerations relevant to national policy*

SELECTED REFERENCES

Bonner, H. *Group dynamics: principles and applications.* New York: Ronald, 1959.
Cartwright, D., & Zander, A. (Eds.) *Group dynamics: research and theory.* Evanston, Ill.: Row, Peterson, 1968. (3rd ed.)
*Gouldner, A. W. *Wildcat strike: a study in worker-management relationships.* New York: Harper Torchbooks, 1965.
Guetzkow, H., et al. *Simulation in international relations.* Englewood Cliffs, N.J.: Prentice-Hall, 1963.
Kelman, H. (Ed.) *International behavior: a socio-psychological analysis.* New York: Holt, Rinehart, & Winston, 1965.
*Klineberg, O. *The human dimension in international relations.* New York: Holt, Rinehart, & Winston, 1964.
Lippitt, R., Watson, J., & Westley, B. *The dynamics of planned change.* New York: Harcourt, Brace & World, 1958.
McNeil, E. (Ed.) *The nature of human conflict.* Englewood Cliffs, N.J.: Prentice-Hall, 1965.
*Pruitt, D. G., & Snyder, R. C. (Eds.) *Theory and research on the causes of war.* Englewood Cliffs, N.J.: Prentice-Hall, 1969.
Sherif, M., & Sherif, C. W. *Groups in harmony and tension: an integration of studies on intergroup relations.* New York: Harper, 1953.
Sherif, M., & Wilson, M. O. (Eds.) *Group relations at the crossroads.* New York: Harper, 1953.
Singer, J. D. (Ed.) *Human behavior and international politics.* Chicago: Rand-McNally, 1965.
*Stagner, R. *Psychological aspects of international relations.* Belmont, Calif.: Brooks/Cole, 1967.
*White, R. K. *No one wanted war.* Garden City, N.Y.: Doubleday Anchor, 1970.

14
Conformity and nonconformity

Conformity is a widespread social phenomenon which has attracted attention from many quarters. For the most part, social psychology's interest in conformity lies in understanding the influence effects which produce it and flow from it. This necessitates the systematic study of factors in both conforming and nonconforming behavior. In pursuing this study, judgments are not made about the absolute goodness or badness of conformity since it clearly has complex sources and ramifications. Neither conformity nor diversity is valued for its own sake. Indeed, it is well recognized that individuality of expression fulfills a significant social function, as exemplified in the generation of new ideas and innovations. Gardner (1963) for one underscores the point that stifling this feature of individuality is likely to lead to social decay because "the capacity of society for continuous renewal depends ultimately upon the individual" (p. 54).

If conformity is looked upon as adherence to social expectancies, it becomes clear that organized society would be unthinkable without it, despite the criticism alleging that we live in an "age of conformity." When used in this fashion, conformity is seen as something which undercuts individuality. This represents a legitimate concern, but it is futile to condemn any action automatically because it evidences conformity, since the world in which we live would be chaotic without predictable modes of conduct. Nevertheless, there continues to be a

549

sense of an incompatibility between conformity and individuality, and some reflection on this issue is worthwhile for clarification.

Individuality and conformity

Wilson (1964) observes that the clamor about conformity is actually the latest version of the ancient and largely fruitless dicussion of the individual versus society. A long tradition of philosophical thought surrounds this point, which is sometimes stated as freedom versus determinism. For instance, a belief in "fate" implies a primary accept- ance of external determination of the individual's actions. To speak of individual freedom, on the other hand, one must accept a view of Man as a self-determining agent of his actions. But the very formulation of this issue in an either-or form prejudges it.

There is, for example, a large question concerning what is meant by individual freedom. In the view of many, conformity inhibits freedom. But Gardner (1963), who would encourage individual expression, goes on to contend that while "the man on the street thinks of freedom as the natural state, and lack of freedom as the unnatural, artificial, con- trived state . . . freedom as we now know it has been exceedingly rare in the history of Mankind. It is a highly perishable product of civi- lization, *wholly dependent on certain habits of mind widely shared, on certain institutional arrangements widely agreed upon*" (p. 65, italics supplied). The question, then, is not an either-or matter since freedom in a practical sense relies upon social organization.

DETERMINISM

E. G. Boring (1957) considers this matter in connection with determin- ism and concludes that fredom is often employed as a negative con- cept insofar as it deals with "the absence of causes" of action or the "absence of constraints" on action. "This problem," says Boring, "is not made easier when we realize that Man's belief that he is free may itself be pre-determined. The belief in freedom could be Man's great delu- sion—nearly, if not quite, immutable" (p. 189). Yet, he emphasizes that the idea of freedom has justified itself and is one for which men fight and die. The essential point is that neither freedom as a matter of positive license nor as the negation of all constraints portrays an accurate pic- ture of the basis for individual action.

A good part of the time we want to do the things which society expects of us. Yet, a group with whom we are associated may exert influence for us to deviate from these broader expectancies, thereby setting up contradictory influences. Freedom in that case is as much the *freedom to conform* to a social norm as it is the freedom to *non-conform* to it.

The ultimate perplexity that would be introduced if everyone were constantly obliged to do as he chose—his "own thing"—is illustrated by the anecdote concerning the child in a very progressive school who asked the teacher, "Do I *have* to do what I want to do today?"

Individuals have freedom of action, but within certain prescribed standards of society. These can be confining in one sense, but they also provide distinct benefits in other ways: freedom from continuous doubt about the actions of others; relief from having to find *ad hoc* solutions every day for the patterned activities in which we take part; and positive gains available from other people in joint endeavors and as sources of rewards. Our motivation to affiliate and "go along" with others therefore provides us with the basis for group activity and the psychological rewards of social identity, social reality, and social support which can help sustain our individuality. Rather than be antithetical to one another, it is more likely the case that conformity can serve individuality.

NONCONFORMITY AND CONFORMISM

While we may not have total internal control over all of our actions, in a complex society we very often are able to react to those external controls which are more favorable to us. This is another way of saying that we may "refer" ourselves to the kinds of groups, and the norms that they set, which we find more congenial to our individual tastes. This also illuminates another feature of conformity which is often overlooked. Within the tendency to label people as "nonconformists," it is easy to disregard what is in fact their *high* conformity to some particular group. We often observe this in connection with the discussion of the nonconformity represented among so-called "hippies." Though it is true that they represent a segment of society that does not conform to certain prevailing social expectancies, they nonetheless can be observed to conform tenaciously to expectancies of their own reference groups. Thus, nonconformity to one standard may simply imply conformity to another, as we shall have occasion to point out further.

Many years ago this idea was illuminated by Thoreau's observation that the apparent nonconformer was just marching to another drummer. Cooley put it in these terms:

> There is, therefore, no definite line between conformity and non-conformity; there is simply a more or less characteristic and un-usual way of selecting and combining accessible influences . . . a just view of the matter should embrace the whole of it at once and see conformity and nonconformity as normal and complementary phases of human activity (1922, p. 302).

In the final analysis, what arouses concern is not conformity as such but over-conformity or "conformism." It is this *excessive* reliance on others as a standard for conduct and as a basis for judgments which was deplored by Riesman and his colleagues in *The Lonely Crowd* (1950) and by Whyte in *The Organization Man* (1956). The line is not sharply defined, but they contended that the individual may be so eager for the anticipated rewards associated with displays of conformism that he loses touch with his own critical faculties. And this is antithetical to the long-range interests of society itself.

Though the criticism of conformism made a case in its time, much of it may now seem dated, having been overtaken by the social ferment and change of the 1960's. The matter does not end there, however, since the issue of conformity also devolves about whose norm serves as the standard of conduct, and what value it represents. The content of conformity is highly relevant, and deserves attention. If we have merely traded the passé "gray flannel suit" of the organization man, who is now freer to wear a wider range of garb, for tenacious conformity to a "drug subculture" among his children, can we say that conformism is on the wane? If so, for whom? And from what?

Despite the serious issues which are raised by questions of this kind, it is worth reflecting for a moment on the considerable freedom for choice which is afforded in many contemporary societies. Regarding American society, for example, Mack (1967) says:

> It is perhaps a healthy sign that so many Americans worry about whether or not there is too much conformity in our society, but there is something wryly amusing about it too. The people of the United States tolerate a range of behavior in their fellow citizens that the people of most societies throughout human history would have found simply incredible.

A young man or woman in America can marry or not, as he or she wishes. Marriages are not arranged by families or by tribal elders. Marriages can be performed by civil officials or by any of a host of clergymen of different faiths.

Parents can send their child to public school or to parochial school, as they wish. Once the child has received the required minimum number of years of schooling, he can continue or not, according to his abilities, his financial situation, and his personal desires.

A person is not even required to work, if he can get along without doing so. He is certainly not assigned a place in the labor force; he is allowed to work at any job he can obtain and hold, in the city or the country, in Idaho or Georgia. He can work day or night; he can have a part-time job, or, if he wants, two jobs. He can spend most of his earnings to suit himself, and he is faced with the greatest array and variety of consumer goods ever available in human history. He is allowed to own his home if he is able to; he is not required to do so.

An American citizen can vote from a selection of candidates for office to govern him, any of whom can later be turned out of office by the citizens. He does not have to vote at all.

In substantial measure, he can do what he wants with his recreational time. Not only is he encouraged by billboards to attend the church of his choice; he is also free to choose not to attend any church at all. It is difficult for an American to realize that his ancestors were slaughtering one another only a few centuries ago for being affiliated with the "wrong" denomination of the Christian faith (pp. 162-163).

One can find fault with these points, arguing that some of the choices reflected are actually dictated by other factors, often of an economic nature. Mack (1967) himself moves on to a consideration of various "costs" of industrialization, as well as urbanization, including the multifarious problems of social inequality and of inter-group friction which are of pressing importance (see Chapters 10 and 13). Nonetheless, the potentiality for individual choice remains high, and the alternatives to having these choices must be seen in terms of the other costs their loss would surely entail.

DEVIANCY

The other side of the coin to conformism is represented by *deviancy*. As a concept, it bears a resemblance to the notion of nonconformity, but it has wider societal implications. While nonconformity has been equated at times with rather favorably toned ideas of "independence" and expressions of "individuality," "deviancy" in its popular usage often refers to anti-social behaviors up to and including criminality and law-breaking. Szasz (1961) has also applied the concept in taking the view that the label "mental illness" has become a way of stigmatizing individuals.

In an early analysis, Lemert (1951) pointed out that what is deviant is not intrinsically so but is defined by the norms of a society. The person characterized as a "deviant" may consider these norms inapplicable to himself so that, in his own eyes, he is behaving properly. Pursuing this view, Becker (1963) comments that

> . . . *social groups create deviance by making the rules whose infraction constitutes deviance,* and by applying these rules to particular people and labeling them as outsiders. From this point of view, deviance is *not* a quality of the act the person commits, but a consequence of the application by others of rules and sanctions to an "offender" (p. 9).

Given the pluralistic nature of society, various kinds of deviance are to a large degree a matter of the eye of the beholder. In a cluster of students one day, one of the boys said, "You know the guy. The one with no beard, no moustache, no sideburns—a real freak."

As was pointed out earlier, becoming a deviant in the view of the broader society may also make the individual more acceptable within his immediate circle. The adolescent who is considered a "troublemaker" by adult authority may actually be a well functioning, highly accepted member of his peer group, perhaps for displaying the same behaviors which have earned him a negative reputation elsewhere.

It would be equally in error, however, to indulge in word-magic and dismiss or overlook the intent of deviant acts. In addition, Gouldner (1968), among others, has argued that too much has been made of the underdog role of "deviants" and of the exotic subcultures which some frequent. He asserts:

> It is my impression . . . that [the] pull to the underdog is sometimes part of a titillated attraction to the underdog's exotic difference and easily takes the form of "essays on quaintness." The danger is, then, that such an identification with the underdog becomes the urban sociologist's equivalent of the anthropologist's (onetime) ro-

mantic appreciation of the noble savage. . . . Basically, it conceives of the underdog as a *victim*. In some part, this is inherent in the very conception of the processes by means of which deviance is conceived of as being generated. For the emphasis in Becker's theory is on the deviant as a product of society rather than as a rebel against it (p. 106).

The ready tendency toward glamorizing the "hip" and "beat" and "freak" side of deviancy has sometimes undercut the quite valid points made by Lemert (1951), by Tannenbaum (1951), and by Becker (1963), as representatives of a school of thought which basically renounces the practice of categorizing and stigmatizing groups in a way that is bound to be unfair to individuals.

On the matter of fairness, some kinds of deviancy, call it what you will, are quite destructive. Murder is a deviant act, and so is airpiracy. They may vary in the severity of their consequences, and they may affect some few people who are victims more than the majority of people who are not; but who can doubt that society is threatened whenever killing becomes more widespread or when freedom is impaired by the prospect of kidnapping and physical threats any time one boards an airliner. Other kinds of deviancy, as defined by some laws in some places, are nothing of the kind. Therefore, deviancy is a matter of intent, as well as of degree, and in practice the term "deviant" is wholly unsatisfactory to define a class of people.

Prejudice is also implicated in defining deviancy. Being of a different color, or size, or nationality, or class background, or school, can mark a person as different by the standards of the comparison group. Oftentimes, though not necessarily, individuals may prefer to avoid situations where they will stand out in this way and be rejected or else be obliged to work harder to gain acceptance as *individuals*. This is a facet of prejudice which those in a "majority" group can readily *mis*understand, and perceive as an unwillingness to mix, because of their own relative inexperience with the slights that go with "minority'" group status. Indeed, the "slights" themselves are often intended to be friendly utterances, but come off quite otherwise and unflatteringly, to wit:

> "There was this Negro boy in my class, and you'd be pleased at just how well he did." (*Blacks are unintel-*

*ligent, but since you're black I want you to think I don't
believe that.*)

"I don't know why people make such a fuss when
actually you Catholics are really just regular Christians
like the rest of us." (*Though Catholicism has some really
distinctive qualities, I'm willing to forgive and forget
them.*)

"That's funny. You don't seem Jewish." (*There are some
typical ways that Jewish people look, talk, and act, but
you don't fit my well developed stereotype of those.*)

The main justification for considering these elements of prejudice
under the heading of "deviancy" is that they can function, in effect,
to produce the same kind of "insider"–"outsider" distinction, quite
apart from any "deviant" behaviors. The underlying perceptual process is one of defining categories of persons by a "rule" which put some
in the acceptable category and others in the unacceptable one. Therefore, while the concept of deviancy is quite broad, and indeed rubbery
in the way it can be stretched, it has practical import in the day-to-day
functioning of society.

The nature of conformity

Conformity obviously is not a single thing, but rather a social phenomenon which can be defined in many ways. In the main, though, it refers
to a kind of uniformity of behavior which is conventionally expected in
society (Beloff, 1958). This is what was referred to above in connection
with expected standards of conduct in a society. We can call this kind
of conformity *congruence conformity*. It represents a form of response
to which an individual is likely to see no alternatives. As Asch (1959)
has pointed out, we do not usually deviate from the language and food
preferences that characterize other members of our own society. In
fact, we tend to see them as right and proper and to find them suiting
our individual taste.

A second kind of conformity has been the object of a considerable
amount of scrutiny in laboratory experimentation. This can be called
movement conformity, since it represents a shift of behavior to a socially prescribed standard, from what apparently represents an indi-

vidual's preferred tendency. This kind of influence acceptance is seen in the work of Sherif (1935) discussed in Chapter 2 (see p. 66). In that experiment individuals placed in a stimulus situation involving the autokinetic phenomenon tended to "converge" toward a group norm from their initially preferred responses. The work of Asch (1951), which was considered here in Chapter 3 (see p. 101), is also noteworthy in this regard.

A number of studies have varied the Sherif procedure, employing a range of stimuli, to study the movement of individual responses toward a group standard. In one such variant, Mausner (1953, 1954a, 1954b), Kelman (1950), and Luchins and Luchins (1961) have reinforced the subject's own accuracy to determine its effects on the degree of movement. In general, they found that reinforcing the subject for accuracy of his own response lead to a *decrease* in conformity in the direction of greater *independence* from the partner or group.

Both congruence conformity and movement conformity involve an acceptance of influence which reveals *dependence*. In the first instance, this dependence has origins in a *past* influence, such as a food preference, which encourages an individual to persist in certain modes of action; in the second, the individual responds to a *present* influence by altering his actions to fit new demands, such as a change in fashion. As Hollander and Willis (1967, p. 65) have noted, these two modes of conformity are actually negatively related. If conformity is seen, in the first sense, as *being* like others, then the person who already is conforming shows no movement while the one who has been nonconforming is credited with movement by *becoming* even a bit like others.

This last phenomenon is also related to adaptation and contrast effects, in terms of the observer's expectancies. The person who regularly lives up to a predictable pattern of friendliness or trustworthiness, let us say, comes to be taken for granted. By contrast, more notice and even favorable comment is given the "tough guy's" occasional signs of becoming more decent (see Chapter 4, p. 138).

SOURCES OF MOVEMENT CONFORMITY

Conformity has often been considered in terms of a single dimension that places perfect conformity at one end and perfect nonconformity at the other. This can be misleading in several ways, most especially because it allows only two kinds of response, as we shall be noting shortly. Sometimes, nonconformity is referred to as independence and these are equated with one another. In either case, conformity in these terms means matching a group-approved response along a undimensional scale. Though oversimplified, this conception has utility for the study of movement conformity insofar as it provides relative ease in the investigation of complex relationships. Thus, experimentation on movement conformity reveals in the first place that the more ambiguous the stimulus presented to the subject, the greater the tendency to conform to social pressure by matching the standard response. However, such behavior also appears to depend upon other properties of the situation which may cause an individual to rely upon others. Among properties found to increase the probability of movement conformity are the status, power, or competence of the others representing an influence source, and their apparent unanimity. This is not unique to the movement conformity situation alone, but has wider generalizability to the acceptance of influence.

Regarding characteristics of the individual, it is also the case that the perceived attractiveness of the group, and the general utility of conformity to achieving an individual goal, tend to encourage higher conformity. Fear or anxiety, for example, have been found to be associated with greater conformity. Walters and Karal (1960) isolated subjects and found that those who experienced greater anxiety subsequently showed greater susceptibility to influence. Relatedly, subjects identified as high on anxiety were found to conform more to the experimenter's suggestions in the Sherif autokinetic situation (Walters, Marshall, Shooter, 1960). Such findings, in line with Schachter's work on first-born children (see Chapter 5, p. 179), are usually interpreted in terms of heightened affiliation needs. Confirmation of this point has come from an experiment by Darley (1966). He found that female subjects who were made anxious in anticipation of an electric shock conformed more in an Asch situation than those who were not made anxious. Furthermore, conformity was highest if the fearful subjects believed that the others in the group were also vulnerable to the shock, thus presumably increasing the subjects' affiliation tendencies toward them. To paraphrase Schachter (1959)—misery loves company, especially equally "miserable" company.

Alternatively, there are several circumstances where individuals are less likely to be influenced to shift a response. Among these are when: they have a high degree of certainty of their own perception; they feel themselves more competent or powerful or of higher status than others; they have one or more others in the group agreeing with them against the majority judgment; they find the others an unattractive influence source, possibly unlike themselves; and, finally, they see little to be gained by conformity in terms of any important personal goals. In line with our previous consideration of persuasibility in Chapters 6 (see p. 230) and 10 (p. 422), the acceptance of influence also depends in some degree upon self-esteem, to be considered here further in connection with personality and conformity.

In general, where subjects believe that they are more accurate, they are less likely to show movement conformity in terms of convergence. In an experiment by Mausner (1954a) he had subjects judge the length of lines alone and then in pairs. The pairs were so chosen that the judgments of the two subjects when alone were quite different. Half of the subjects were told that they were right in almost all of the trials when judging alone first, while the other half were told that they were wrong on the same number of trials when judging alone. Figure 14.1 illustrates the degree of convergence which Mausner found for three pairs of subjects. In the first pair, both were reinforced; in the second, one was reinforced and the other negatively reinforced; and in the third, both were negatively reinforced. He found a significantly higher tendency for subjects who had been negatively reinforced to be influenced by their partners' judgments in the subsequent group situation.

Still other studies have looked at the degree of movement conformity created by the influence of status. For example, age differences in children (Berenda, 1950) operate so that younger children are more susceptible to the influence of older children than the reverse. Typically, greater conformity influences are found when the other person in the situation holds a higher status on some relevant dimension than does the subject. Most importantly, participants in groups that are highly cohesive are usually found to be more susceptible to movement conformity than are those subjects in groups that are less cohesive. In other terms, the group's favorable characteristics create a situation where members may be more inclined to accept its influence. This is by way of emphasizing again that dependence upon a group tends to increase with its attractiveness, as we noted in the last chapter.

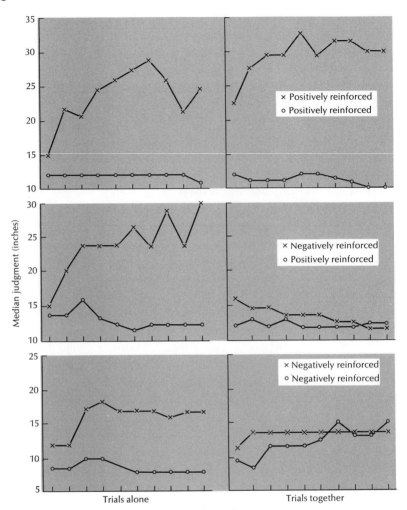

Figure 14.1: Median judgments of lengths of lines for ten trials alone and ten together for three pairs of subjects (x and o) with various combinations of prior reinforcement for accuracy. (From Mausner, 1954a.)

Back (1951) investigated this effect of cohesiveness on conformity in two-person groups where he manipulated cohesiveness in several ways. For example, some subjects were told that they were assigned to work with someone whom they would like very much because of their similarity to one another (High Cohesiveness), and others that they had a partner who did not fit their own description of someone with whom they would like to work (Low Cohesiveness). He asked these varying pairs to write a joint story about a picture which had been described to them differently. His results indicated that whatever the type of cohesiveness induced, high-cohesive groups had significantly more instances of influence attempts and resulting shifts in judgment than did low-cohesive groups.

The main thrust of this work is that there are conditions which do lead to predictably greater conformity in the sense of influence effects. As Berkowitz (1957) and Jakubczak and Walters (1959) observe, these effects appear to be explainable in terms of a heightening of dependence. Summing up this point, Blake and Mouton (1961a) say:

> . . . conformity behavior increases when it is necessary for an individual to rely more heavily on the responses of others in making his own adjustment. Attitudes are more easily shifted than are reactions to factual or logical items, probably because attitudes are more social in character. Increasing the degree of difficulty of items, reducing external cues which provide external information, and increasing the strength of command in the direction of the compliant behavior all serve to increase the effectiveness of conformity pressures in shifting a person's response (p. 11).

O'Connell (1965) has suggested that conformity operates as a phenomenon parallel to imitation. Placed in a situation with another person who is defined as capable, an individual is likely to imitate that person, especially if the setting resembles past situations in which imitation was rewarded. Accordingly, conformity to group norms in an ambiguous situation is accountable in terms of a past history of reward for imitative behavior in similar environments. O'Connell reasoned, however, that conformity may frustrate rather than reward if the setting is competitive, since reward to a successful Other implies nonreward to the Person. He conducted an experiment in which to test the hypothesis of greater conformity in co-operative environments and less in competitive ones.

Subjects were seated next to one another, so that they could readily see each other's responses in a standard psychological task involving a memory drum. For each of 120 trials, subject A made a choice as the

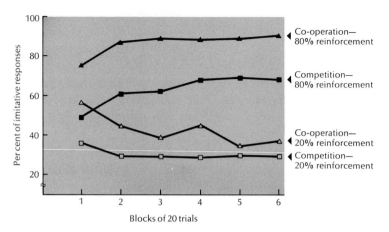

Figure 14.2: Percentage of imitative responses as a function of co-operative or competitive set and 80 per cent or 20 per cent reinforcement of the model's responses. (Based on data from O'Connell, 1965.)

"model" and then, having seen that response, B made his choice. The experimenter actually controlled feedback of which of A's choices would be confirmed as correct on any trial, in terms of a schedule of 80 per cent or 20 per cent reinforcement, i.e. 96 trials or 24 trials correct, at random. The major treatments of "co-operation" and "competition" were introduced by instructional sets, one emphasizing the facilitative effects of partnership with equal sharing of the monetary rewards, and the other of a competitive spirit and a larger share of money to the best performer.

O'Connell found that both the co-operative and competitive treatments and the percentage of reinforcement treatments yielded significant main effects. Thus, the more subjects were encouraged to co-operate, and the more the partner was said to be correct on trials, the greater the amount of conformity, in the sense of imitation of the partner's choices. These results are shown graphically in Figure 14.2. They held irrespective of the sex of the subject or partner, since males and females took part in equal numbers in same-sex pairs or different-sex pairs. This experiment indicates that the instruction to co-operate is equivalent to telling a subject to conform to his partner's decisions in this kind of social situation.

PERSONALITY AND CONFORMITY

Another line of research on conformity has tended to look at stable characteristics of the individual which may affect his acceptance of influence. The many research efforts in this vein have only revealed partial confirmation for a set of personality attributes underlying conformity. Part of the difficulty resides in the variable way in which conformity is defined operationally.

The evidence reveals only a limited tendency for individuals to conform across different situations. Thus, in a study by Vaughan (1964), he found that only 20 per cent of his subjects conformed in four different conformity situations. Alternatively, the others were affected in varying degrees by the situation in terms of the amount of movement conformity they showed. Back and Davis (1965) studied conformity in three situations and found a small though consistent trend for subjects to behave with some uniformity across them. In two situations, Samelson (1958) found that conformity was not consistently related to either the need for affiliation or the need for achievement.

Walker and Heyns have argued with some reason that, because of the reinforcements provided in the convergence situation, "groups can be made to appear as 'individualists' or 'conformists' almost at will through subtle but nevertheless effective differential reward for the two forms of behavior" (1962, p. 75). For example, by creating a situation where an individual has to make a perceptual judgment, with high stimulus ambiguity, and allegedly low status or accuracy, he is quite likely to move toward the group judgment. This response is in line with the need for social reality, but it may also serve affiliation goals of social support and social identity as well. In effect, then, characteristics of personality may not carry as much weight as the situation because they are "washed out" by strong situational factors. The diversity of findings suggests the necessity to look further at the characteristics of the situation, especially as they are defined by the subjects, in studies of conformity. These issues are illustrated by the research of Crutchfield (1955).

In a group pressure situation similar to that employed by Asch, subjects in Crutchfield's experiment observed what appeared to be the responses of others on a signal light panel before each of them. Actually, these were completely controlled by the experimenter. The tasks consisted of line comparisons as well as attitude judgments. For a sample of adult executives, Crutchfield found that conformity was higher for the line comparisons than attitudes and that total conformity correlated inversely with ratings on intellectual effectiveness, leadership, ego strength, and maturity of social relations. On a questionnaire, he also found that high conformers gave answers with "neurotic tone." No significant correlations were found, however, for conformity and scales of the MMPI, a standard measure of personality. Barron (1953) reports a similar negative finding for this measure and conformity in the Asch situation. More recent research by Barocas and Gorlow (1967), using a Crutchfield-type situation, reveals no significant relationship between conformity responses and scales from the California Personality Inventory.

Since Crutchfield's approach is a well known example of the study of personality and conformity, it is useful to be aware of several problems it poses. For one thing, even those who conformed to a high degree were aware of discrepancies between their own judgments and the group consensus. When interviewed later, some expressed doubts about their own perception, while others blamed the group's inaccuracy. Most conforming subjects, however, indicated a mixture of these reactions. Thus, conformity meant different things to them in this particular situation. Furthermore, their motivation may have been directed as much to the goal of avoiding prolongation of an unpleasant experience as to showing agreement with the group for its own sake.

A further probing in this vein is represented in the study of Moeller and Applezweig (1957). By use of a questionnaire, they selected college women with high motivation for either self-approval or social approval, or for both. Then their conformity was assessed in an Asch situation. They found that the subjects high on the need for social approval conformed significantly more to the majority than those who were high on both needs. Those who were high on self-approval conformed least and were least concerned about their nonconforming, while those high on both needs were most concerned. Thus, subjects can be aware of group pressures but not conform to them, given other sources of reward. Involvement with the group as a set of relevant others appears to be a key determinant of conformity to such pressures (Kiesler and Kiesler, 1969).

Linton and Graham (1959) have reviewed a number of studies of conformity and personality, across various situations, and conclude that patterns of personality do make a person more or less susceptible to influence. In keeping with the Moeller and Applezweig study just noted, they especially emphasize the central role of the self-concept, in terms of self-esteem, as a general factor which is inversely related to conformity. As was noted in Chapter 10 (p. 422), this position is sustained for the most part by the work of Cohen (1959) and Janis and Field (1959) among others.

In subsequent research by Costanzo (1970), a related variable of

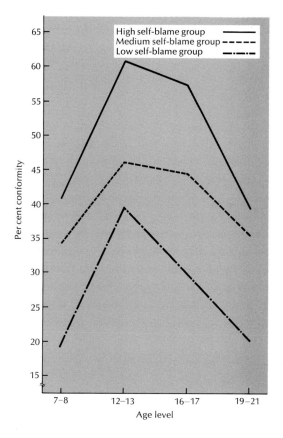

Figure 14.3: Percentage of conformity as a function of age at different levels of self-blame intensity. (From Costanzo, 1970, p. 371.)

personality, the tendency toward self-blame, was studied as a feature of conformity. He conducted an experiment in a Crutchfield situation, with male subjects who varied in age from 7 to 21. As a measure of self-blame, subjects had completed a specially designed questionnaire made up of twenty items describing situations in which an incident occurred with a friend, twelve with negative outcomes and eight with positive outcomes. For each item, the subjects indicated, in one of five categories, just how much blame or praise they attributed to themselves.

Using a line-judging task of the kind employed in the Asch experiment (see p. 101), and placing subjects with others of about the same age, Costanzo found that the rate of conformity increased by years of age from the 7-8 level to the 12-13 level, then decreased to the 16-17 level, and at the 19-21 level was back down to about the same rate as that for the 7-8 level. He also found that mean self-blame scores decreased from the 7-8 level through the subsequent levels of age. However, within each age level the results confirmed his hypothesis by yielding a significant correlation between self-blame scores and conformity. Dividing his subjects by high, medium, and low self-blame groups, he obtained the curves shown in Figure 14.3. The effects of age in raising and then diminishing conformity are clearly seen, but with self-blame producing significantly different rates of conformity.

The broadest overview of the evidence obtained with regard to personality variables and conformity is presented by Mann (1959) who surveyed 27 studies involving relationships between measures of personality and conformity. His findings are summarized in Table 14.1. As will be seen there, in some studies conformity was found to be a positive function of certain personality variables, while in others it was an uncorrelated or negative function of the same variables. For example, people who reported themselves as "better adjusted" showed a considerable tendency toward conformity. On the other hand, ratings of adjustment by *other* means, such as sociometric measures, revealed an overall result in the reverse direction; however, most studies of these relationships were ambiguous or untested statistically. Clearly, there is a dissimilarity in the operational definition of certain of these personality variables, just as there is in what is defined as conformity. As Mann notes, "Those who conform to the opinion of others describe themselves as kind, friendly, helpful, and optimistic. However, the results

PERSONALITY FACTORS AND NUMBER OF STUDIES OF EACH	NO. OF FINDINGS	% YIELDING SIG. POSITIVE RELATIONSHIP	% YIELDING SIG. NEGATIVE RELATIONSHIP	% YIELDING NEITHER
Adjustment				
Self-ratings—2	(18)	73% (13)	5% (1)	22% (4)
Sociometric ratings and personality inventories—8	(30)	7% (2)	14% (4)	79% (24)
Extroversion				
Self-ratings—2	(16)	62% (10)	6% (1)	32% (5)
Projective techniques and personality inventories—5	(10)	0% (0)	10% (1)	90% (9)
Dominance—4	(8)	0% (0)	25% (2)	75% (6)
Conservatism—6	(20)	80% (16)	0% (0)	20% (4)

Table 14.1: Percentage of significant relationships reported in a positive or negative direction for 27 studies, representing 102 findings on the relationship of various personality characteristics and conformity. (After Mann, 1959.)

employing projective and personality inventory variables do not confirm this relationship" (p. 261).

A further feature of this relationship lies in the possible confounding of variables. Mann observes that "those individuals who conform more to group opinion also tend to conform to an acceptable personality characterization in their self-descriptions" (p. 261). This is seen, too, in the operation of a tendency toward "social desirability" (Crowne and Marlowe, 1964) which is found to be associated with conformity— a point considered in Chapter 10 (see p. 421). This set of findings suggests that a disposition toward conventional responses underlies both the compliant aspects of social behavior and the tendency to give socially approved answers on paper-and-pencil personality inventories.

While Mann concludes that there is a basis for considering another variable—conservatism—as positively associated with conformity, he adds that "No single measure of the conservatism dimension emerges as an especially potent predictor of conformity in all conditions; in fact, there is a suggestion that it is important to control for a number of conditions if the relationship is to hold at all" (p. 261). In this respect, Weiner and McGinnies (1961) and Steiner and Johnson

(1963) report that authoritarians conform more only under certain conditions. Indeed, in the latter study, high scorers on the F Scale were found to conform more selectively in an Asch situation when the majority was not unanimous.

A significant consideration in this work, viewed broadly, is that complex relationships are involved, and that varying definitions of conformity may also be implicated in producing disparate findings. Goldberg and Rorer (1966) are among those who have contended, in addition, that the demonstration of a relationship between personality and conformity in one situation does not in itself establish a general pattern across different situations. An eminently reasonable position appears to be that presented by Hunt (1965), who says that personality factors are more likely to be important in their *interaction* with situational factors than in any sense of a total dominance over them.

Interpersonal effects of conformity

Studies of conformity and nonconformity have proceeded on two levels. The first treats the sources of conformity within the situation or the individual. The second concerns the *consequences* of such responses upon other persons in terms of interpersonal influence. The work on movement conformity with which we have been dealing, largely emphasizes the first approach. There is, however, a good deal of interest concerning conformity as it affects the interaction of individuals with one another (Cf., for example, Hollander, *et al.*, 1965; Savell and Healey, 1969).

To this point we have noted that research on movement conformity is defined essentially by establishing discrepancies between an individual's probable response tendencies and the behavior of other group members. When the individual alters his response to match those of the group, this is usually treated as evidence of conformity. And, as we have seen, there are a number of factors in the situation which appear to yield such behaviors. On the whole, where the individual, for one reason or another, is more dependent upon others, his conformity is likely to be greater.

A counterpart of this feature of conformity is how its public display *influences others*. Kelman (1958) has distinguished between several kinds of conformity, one of which—compliance—refers to the outward display of agreement while retaining inward disagreement (see Chapter 6, p. 209). Where an individual is forced to make a public commitment, he is usually found to be more likely to conform than would be the case otherwise. The consequences of nonconformity are amply revealed in Schachter's experiment (1951), reported in Chapter 3 (p. 103), in which the deviate was ultimately rejected as a group member by the others, especially under conditions of high cohesiveness.

Argyle (1957) did an experiment to study the effects on conformity behavior of requiring people to take a public stand. He set up 52 two-person groups, each containing one true subject and one mock subject as a partner. The true subject received standardized written messages from the partner in connection with the quality of a picture they were to judge. Half of the subjects had to make their final judgment publicly, the other half privately in an envelope. Messages from the partner were also contrived to be "accepting" in tone for some of these subjects and "rejecting" in tone for the others. Argyle found significantly more conformity to the partner's judgment occurring under public conditions, with acceptance yielding somewhat higher results than rejection for both the public and private conditions, as will be seen in Figure 14.4.

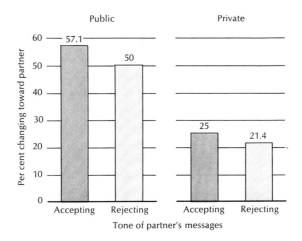

Figure 14.4: Percentage of subjects changing their opinion toward partner on final judgment under public and private conditions with differential tone in messages received from partner. (Based on data from Argyle, 1957.)

EXTERNAL AND INTERNAL ASPECTS OF CONFORMITY

An interest in external conformity has generally dominated the concern of social scientists. Indeed, as Kiesler (1969) has recently noted, internal acceptance of conformity pressures in experiments may neither be achieved by the experimental manipulations nor actually checked by post-experimental measures (p. 279). However there is far greater attention being directed now to this issue, especially in terms of the motivational elements underlying conformity (Hollander and Willis, 1967). One focus has followed the "functional" features of conformity for the individual (Katz, Sarnoff, and McClintock, 1956). In this vein, Kelman (1958, 1961) has sought to distinguish three processes of conformity represented in the acceptance of external influence, which he calls compliance, identification, and internalization. We have already noted above that compliance involves overt conformity without internal agreement. Identification means showing conformity in a satisfying role relationship where it is expected if the relationship is to be maintained. Internalization leads to both external and internal conformity because the individual finds it harmonious with his own values.

The vital element in these functional approaches to individual conformity is their attention to motivation. Inevitably, the rewards associated with conformity must be specified. Furthermore, there is a widespread assumption that external conformity reflects a motivational intent, usually to gain social approval or acceptance. Such an assumption appears unfounded as a global generalization for several reasons: first, because an individual may choose to do as others do without necessarily being dependent upon their standard in any persisting way; second, because motivation to conform may result from a desire to participate in a group task, not from seeking approval from others; and third, because in the absence of accurate perception of social demands a person could behave in line with a social standard without being motivated to do so. The converse of this last point has implications as well, i.e. if an individual apparently nonconforms, this may *not* reflect a motivational intent, but rather indicate an error of perception even in the face of a desire to conform. Thus, a psychological definition of conforming behavior would consider whether the individual *intended* to fulfill normative group expectancies as he perceived them (see Hollander and Willis, 1967).

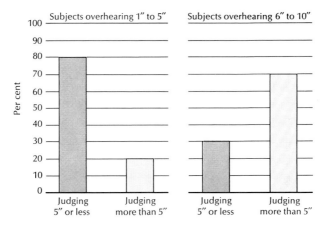

Figure 14.5: Proportions of judgments 5″ or less and greater than 5″ for subjects under two conditions of prior exposure to another's judgment. (After Hood and Sherif, 1962.)

Some light is cast on the issue of underlying change by an experiment conducted by Hood and Sherif (1962). Essentially, they were interested in determining if public compliance in the autokinetic situation was aimed at avoiding disapproval from others in the group. Accordingly, in this experiment no indication was given that the aim was to study social influence. To do this, no confrontation occurred with another subject at the time the subject made his judgment. The procedure was to have every subject first simply overhear another person making 20 judgments while apparently waiting his turn to make his own estimates. Next, the subject made his own judgments alone. One experimental group overheard judgments ranging from 1 to 5 inches and another group overheard judgments from 6 to 10 inches. As will be seen in Figure 14.5, the judgments made by those subjects when alone were significantly related to what they had overheard the other subjects saying. Subjects were later asked what degree of movement they had actually seen. It was found that these reports did not differ significantly from what they had judged in the situation.

"We may conclude," says Sherif, "that in this situation individuals 'call them as they see them' and they see them as influenced by judgments previously overheard. There is no evidence of a discrepancy between judgment and verbal report" (1961, p. 168). The generalizability of this finding is debatable, in part because of the use of an ambiguous stimulus. In the Crutchfield (1955) study, for example, noted above, he reported that, with essentially unambiguous stimuli, between 25 and 30 per cent of his subjects "freely admit on later questioning that they responded the way the group did even when they thought this not the proper answer" (p. 197). The entire issue of the accuracy of verbal reports of perception is one that has commanded a good deal of interest in psychology, and it is by no means resolved.

CONFORMITY AND SOCIAL EXCHANGE

In the world of everyday affairs, the effects of conformity can be seen in several ways. One factor of importance is the reward conformity provides in smoothing the path of interaction between individuals. This is the essential touchstone to understanding conformity in terms of reciprocity and social exchange (Homans, 1958, 1961; Thibaut and Kelley, 1959; Gouldner, 1960; Blau, 1964). These views construe conformity as a reward for others which yields positive effects from them (see Chapter 7). Jones (1964, 1965) has also called attention to the way in which conformity may be used as a technique of *ingratiation,* where a person of lower status wishes to obtain certain benefits from one of higher status in a relationship. In line with the kind of thinking represented in Goffman's work (1959), Jones sees conformity as a way of creating a favorable impression, or at least avoiding an unfavorable one. This leads, in turn to certain desired outcomes from the interaction (see Chapter 7, p. 289).

In his recent coverage of conformity as social exchange, Nord (1969) says that social approval can be obtained through conformity, and that

> . . . strong evidence was found to support the treatment of conformity as an instrumental response in positive exchanges. Conformity appears to be supplied for rewards in much the same way as other responses . . . a large number of studies have demonstrated that people conform to avoid a loss of status or approval (pp. 192-193).

An apt illustration of this phenomenon appears in John F. Kennedy's introduction to his *Profiles in Courage* (1956) in which he writes of influence pressures toward conformity in the United States Senate. He says:

> Americans want to be liked—and Senators are no exception. . . .
> We enjoy the comradeship and approval of our friends and col-
> leagues. We prefer praise to abuse, popularity to contempt. . . .
> We realize, moreover, that our influence in the club—and the ex-
> tent to which we can accomplish our objectives and those of our
> constituents—are dependent in some measure on the esteem with
> which we are regarded by other Senators. "The way to get along,"
> I was told when I entered Congress, "is to go along" (p. 3).

The thrust of this account is that conformity can be exchanged in order to gain acceptance from others, especially in terms of their support. Extending this process over time leads to the prospect that *early conformity may permit later nonconformity* to be better tolerated. This is an essential aspect of the "idiosyncrasy credit" concept to be considered now.

IDIOSYNCRASY CREDIT AND NONCONFORMITY

One feature of conformity is to reward others in social interaction, and a consequence of this reward is to alter interpersonal perceptions which may affect later interactions. The rewards given to others can lead to favorable impressions which may be thought of as an accumulation of credits that can be drawn on later to gain acceptance of the individual's subsequent actions.

Idiosyncrasy credit may therefore be considered to be the positive impressions of a person held by others, whether defined in the narrower terms of a small face-to-face group or a larger social entity such as an organization or even a total society. These credits represent *status* and have the operational property of allowing deviation, innovation, and the assertion of influence. Basically, credits *accumulate* as a result of *perceived conformity and competence*, though other factors such as seniority may also enter in (Hollander, 1958, 1964).

Perceived conformity can be looked upon as living up to the group's expectancies, which yields one input to the accumulation of status in the form of credit. This "credit balance" later permits greater latitude for nonconformity; its absence accounts for the fact that the newcomer to a group, with a minimum of credits, is more constrained to conform than an old-timer, other things being equal. *Perceived competence* has to do with the assistance the individual is seen to provide in helping the group to achieve favorable outcomes on its main task.

Associated with this concept is the view that conformity and non-conformity are not fixed to a single norm applicable to everyone, as in the traditional conception exemplified in the "J Curve." Rather, non-conforming behavior can be seen to be variously defined by the group, depending on how the actor himself is perceived. Conformity is there-fore evaluated in terms of the specific person and his credits. This fits the everyday observation that individuals of higher status have a wider latitude for nonconformity. It has also been demonstrated in experi-ments by Berkowitz and Macaulay (1961), Harvey and Consalvi (1960), Julian and Steiner (1961), Sabath (1964), and Wiggins, Dill, and Schwartz (1965). The essential result in all of these studies is that higher status members could nonconform more freely.

A key consideration in the idiosyncrasy credit model is that behavior perceived to be nonconforming for one group member may not be per-ceived as such for another. This affords the prospect that the person of rising status eventually may be subjected to new expectancies that allow his assertion of influence, which then makes it appropriate for others in the group to accept such influence. It is predictable that with a relatively high level of perceived competence a group member should have increased influence, to some maximum, over time. How-ever, if he nonconforms early to the group's norms, this should curtail his influence. Given a constant level of competence, this person's *early* nonconformity should *diminish* his effectiveness in gaining influence acceptance, and to the contrary, late evidence of nonconformity, after credits are accumulated, should produce the reverse effect. Once hav-ing attained higher status, there should be a shift in expectancies which actually makes this kind of "nonconformity" a confirming feature of status, thus enhancing influence.

To test this experimentally, Hollander (1960) engaged twelve groups of male engineering students in a task which involved fifteen trials in a seven-by-seven payoff matrix requiring a group choice of a row on each trial, in anticipation of a column "coming up" on it. Positive and negative values appeared in the cells. Of the five members in each group, one was a confederate who was always the most competent in the task, that is, in evidently figuring out the "system." All communications in the groups were carried on through microphones and headsets from the separate booths in which the subjects were placed.

Before beginning, each group agreed upon certain procedures that would prevail in their handling of the problem—such things as order of reporting choices, majority rule, and division of winnings. Since group consensus was necessary in establishing these procedures, they were in effect public statements of common expectancies. Bearing in mind the confederate's high competence, nonconformity by him was introduced experimentally at various times, e.g. in all trials, early in the trials, or late in the trials, by zones of five trials each. His actual influence was measured by the number of trials in each zone of five where his recommended solution was accepted as the group's choice.

The results showed that an increase did occur in the acceptance of the confederate's influence, over the fifteen trials, as a function of the accumulation of successive evidences of competence. However, within this broad effect, it was found that when he had nonconformed *early* this considerably diminished his ability to influence the group to accept what were in fact good solutions. On the other hand, nonconformity by him, after he *had conformed for a time,* produced significantly higher acceptance of his influence. Furthermore, the post-interaction questionnaire responses also yielded considerable consistency. For example, on the item dealing with "contribution to the group activity," 44 of the 48 subjects ranked the confederate first; on the item treating "influence over group's decisions," 45 of the 48 subjects ranked him first. Confirmation was also obtained of the acceptance of the confederate's influence apart from the task itself. In groups where he began nonconforming *after* the first zone, his nonconformity was accepted without direct challenge, and after several trials his suggestion that "maybe majority rule isn't working so well" was actually taken as the basis for shifts in the group activity such that his choice was awaited by the group and then accepted without question. Furthermore, his pattern of interrupting others was imitated, once he had established his status. The opposite effect was also noted. Where the confederate began to nonconform from the outset, his influence was diminished and he was subjected to varying degrees of censure from the others.

In a subsequent experiment (Hollander, 1961), subjects of both sexes were given a brief description of a person's competence on a task and duration of time in the group to determine the effect upon their will-

Table 14.2: Means for accorded status by experimental treatments. (From Hollander, 1961.)

TREATMENT	IN GROUP FOR SOME WHILE	NEW TO GROUP
Extremely capable performer	6.25	5.84
Capable performer	6.11	5.50
Average performer	5.06	4.50
Poor performer	2.95	2.53

ingness to accept that person in a position of authority; this was taken as a measure of accorded status. Eight descriptions were created as experimental treatments by pairing either one of the terms "been in group for some while" or "new to the group" with just one of four degrees of competence described by the terms "extremely capable performer in the group's activity," through "capable performer," to "average performer" or "poor performer." By combining these stimulus terms, it was possible to arrange a design with the four levels of task competence and two levels of time in group. Two other terms were uniformly mentioned in all treatments. These were "interested" and "generally liked." In the first phase, subjects were asked to signify on a 7-point scale how willing they would be to have this person in a position of authority. This was the measure of accorded status. The results are shown in Table 14.2. They indicate, for the first phase, that both competence and length of time in the group contributed systematically to increased accorded status.

In the second phase of the experiment, these scores for accorded status were looked at in relationship to how much the subjects would disapprove various behaviors that the same stimulus person might show in the group. Figure 14.6 shows the disapproval curves for three behaviors which yielded significant correlations with accorded status. The two innovative behaviors were less disapproved the higher the status, but alternatively, the reverse was found for a behavior involving an interpersonal act, i.e. "interrupts others." This study, therefore, demonstrates the greater latitude that a person of higher status has in such realms as innovation, but not in others.

The fact that the behavior of a person perceived to have higher

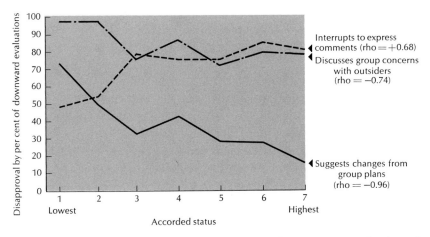

Figure 14.6: Percentage of respondents giving disapproving evaluation of stimulus person for displaying indicated behaviors, by status accorded the stimulus person. (From Hollander, 1961).

status is evaluated differently from one of lesser status provides a useful bridge for understanding the potential for innovation associated with leadership. While leaders may be initiators of change, perhaps in seemingly nonconforming ways, they may also be seen to be conformers to group norms in establishing their position initially. Further implications of idiosyncrasy credit for leadership processes will be considered in the next chapter.

Nonconformity can also be viewed with regard to the distinction between common expectancies of a group regarding its members, as well as those special expectancies associated with higher status. While there is, then, greater tolerance of nonconformity for the high status person in some ways, the results shown in Figure 14.6 reveal restrictions imposed in other ways. These particular expectancies can be thought of as role behaviors associated with a position of higher status. There are at least two reasons why these restrictions are imposed. First, because status is usually perceived to carry with it greater self-determination of behavior such that those in positions of higher status are assumed to be more responsible for their actions (Thibaut and Riecken, 1955). Second, status holds more potential for affecting important outcomes for the members of the group (Hollander, 1964, Ch. 20).

In a recent experiment, Alvarez (1968) dealt with some of these issues. He constructed simulated work organizations with nine true subjects and a confederate who was either assigned to the role of a "co-ordinator" or that of a "worker." The group task was "to generate creative ideas for greeting cards." The confederate was instructed to behave in nonconforming ways, for example, by violating the specific task instructions which had been given to the group. Initially he was to do this about 40 per cent of the time, then raise it to about 60 per cent in the second work period, and then to 80 per cent in the third and fourth periods. As the induction of "successful" or "unsuccessful" treatments, just before the second work period half the groups were told an evaluation of their work indicated it was very good, and the others that it was not of the caliber expected. Additional aspects of this elaborate experiment involved the "demotion" of coordinators and "promotion" of workers to take their place. For each work period, the subjects gave their evaluation of each other in terms of the value of the person to the group as a whole and to the subject making the rating. These evaluations served as the dependent measure of what Alvarez calls "esteem." His major findings are presented in Figure 14.7, regarding the loss of esteem

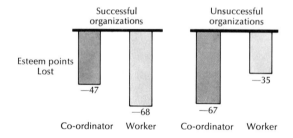

Figure 14.7: Loss of "esteem points" from first to fourth work period for the nonconforming confederate as co-ordinator or worker in "successful" and "unsuccessful" organizations. (Based upon data from Alvarez, 1968.)

from the first to the fourth work period, for the confederate functioning throughout as a coordinator or as a worker in successful or unsuccessful organizations.

Alvarez's findings lend more credence to the idiosyncrasy credit concept. They indicate that, for the same "nonconforming acts" the higher status person loses status, in the sense of esteem, at a slower rate than does the lower status one. However, this was true only in successful organizations. Where the organizations were unsuccessful, the exact opposite was true. This highlights the point that the greater responsibility and visibility typically associated with higher status means that the outcome of any given act of nonconformity will be judged in terms of the rewards produced for the group (Hollander, 1964, p. 228). With a history of past deviations which have yielded success, the high status group member's behavior is more likely to be perceived in that light, that is, as providing good outcomes to the group rather than bad outcomes. In Pepinsky's term (1961), they will be seen to be in the nature of "productive nonconformity." But the reverse holds as well. A lack of success gives these deviations a negative coloration which can rapidly drain credits. The central point here is that acts of an evidently nonconforming variety will be variously interpreted as a function of others' *perception of the actor* based on their experience with him and their attributions to him (see Chapter 7, p. 285). In sum, conformity and nonconformity are observed and evaluated with reference to past interactions and present outcomes, and they influence others' subsequent behavior toward the actor.

Group support as a basis for nonconformity

The consideration that perception of someone's higher status may alter expectancies is in line with the findings of experiments on movement conformity. However, such studies do not usually involve social interaction leading to effects from interpersonal perception. A major factor is the role of the experimenter as the one who constructs the situation and himself is an influence source. As noted earlier, Orne (1962) has pointed to the way in which "demand characteristics" of the experiment may enhance the experimenter's influence (see p. 87). Mills (1962) and Rosenthal and Rosnow (1969) have also called attention to the intended effects of the experimenter on subjects in small groups research. A further feature of conformity research in the laboratory is the extensive use of deception it entails (see Stricker, Messick, and Jackson, 1967).

In an analysis of the Asch conformity situation, Schulman (1967) indicates that three types of influence can operate there. He says:

> In the Asch situation, the subject knows the unanimous, incorrect judgments of the other members of the group before he makes his own response. Thus he may give the same answer as the others because he takes their answers as evidence about reality (informational conformity to the group). The subject gives his response publicly, hence his response may be a function of concern with the evaluation of his behavior by the group (normative conformity to the group) and/or by the experimenter (normative conformity to the experimenter) (p. 27).

With several treatments varied in terms of whether the experimenter and/or the group were perceived by the subject to be in a position to evaluate his or her responses, Schulman found that the rate of conformity was raised by informational influence for both male and female subjects. Normative influence by the group operated to increase conformity significantly for males but not for females, and experimenter influence decreased conformity significantly for males but increased it slightly for females. The latter finding, of an opposite reaction to evaluation by the male experimenter, suggests that male subjects are less willing than females to acknowledge they accept the incorrect response. However, 61 per cent of the males believed the group's responses were wrong as against 35 per cent of the females, which may account for the difference in conformity. This effect also appears to be an instance of the operation of what Rosenberg (1965) considers to be "evaluation apprehension" in experimental settings (see p. 89 and pp. 221-222).

In an experiment close to the substance of a real-life problem, Milgram (1965) provides a test of experimenter influence which also illuminates a basis for *non*conformity through group support. Briefly, as the experimenter, he instructed subjects to administer what they were previously led to believe would be a painful shock to another person. In one set of experimental conditions, two other mock subjects either agreed to administer the shock or refused to do so. He found significantly more subjects refusing to administer shock, if the other "subjects" would *not*, than actually did when instructed to do so with no others present. What is particularly striking is that he found no significant differences in willingness to give shock between subjects with two other agreeable subjects doing so or alone. These results are shown in Figure 14.8. The effect of the experimenter in influencing the behav-

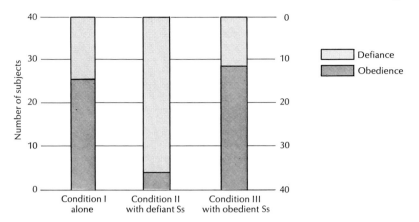

Figure 14.8: Proportion of subjects showing defiance and obedience to the experimenter's instructions under three conditions with 40 subjects in each. (Adapted from Milgram, 1965.)

ior of the subject toward an undesirable act was quite marked unless the subject had *support from others* in resisting that influence. Put in other terms, nonconformity to the experimenter was a function of conformity to others sharing an evidently common plight. Clearly, then, conformity to one standard led to nonconformity to another. The finding that others in the "group" could sustain such independence is especially significant.

Faucheux and Moscovici (1967) and Moscovici, Lage, and Naffrechoux (1969) have pointed to another feature of resistance to conformity, that is, the effect of a consistent minority. Rather than being faced only with the possibility of conforming to the group majority, the individual may adopt an alternative tack by considering how to get that majority to accept his view. Innovation of this kind is also a form of social influence, as was noted above in connection with idiosyncrasy credit.

Asch's findings (see pp. 101-102) suggest that the presence of even one nonconforming member considerably reduces the conformity of true subjects. Faucheux and Moscovici (1967) contend that this is because a minority offers another view to the subject, especially when he sees the majority as incorrect. If the minority members are consistent over time, the potentiality for their exerting influence is increased. This is, in fact, the case as the research by Moscovici *et al.* (1969) demonstrates.

In their experimental work they employed groups of six persons, two of whom were confederates. The participants were all to call out in order their perception of the color and intensity of a projected slide. For the "consistent minority treatment," on all thirty-six trials the two confederates reported that the objectively blue stimulus was "green," irrespective of their response on intensity. In another experimental variation they answered in a mixed way, that is both said green" on twenty-four random trials and "blue" on the other twelve. Compared to a control condition, without confederates, a significantly greater number of "green" responses was given by the subjects exposed to the consistent treatment. This was not the case when the confederates were inconsistent, in the mixed response treatment. Furthermore, an analysis of post-experimental reports by subjects indicated that there had been a significant "perceptual shift" toward green in the perception of the standard blue stimulus by those exposed to the consistent minority treatment. These investigators advance the provocative notion that while majorities may induce compliance of response without gaining underlying acceptance, minorities may not secure such overt compliance but nonetheless have their positions accepted. Moscovici *et al.* (1969) say:

> If this phenomenon is rare in the laboratory, it is not in political life. Thus, a political party often adopts the ideas or the vocabulary of another party or social movement. Yet citizens continue to vote for this same party, to respond to this party's slogans. For example, in France the Gaullist government in framing its own education program, adopted part of the rhetoric and the program proposed by students and workers in May 1968. Nevertheless, when a Frenchman votes for the Gaullist party he believes that he is "responding" to the same political body and in the same manner as he did in the past, although both it and its representatives have changed their opinions on very specific questions. Indeed, it is conceivable that minorities are more capable of changing the majority's code than its social response, while the majority would have more influence on the individual's verbal response than on his intellectual or perceptive code. This is an historical reality. Great innovators have succeeded in imposing their ideas, their discoveries, without necessarily receiving direct recognition for their influence (pp. 378-379).

An important question regarding nonconformity concerns the accessibility of alternatives to the individual for *resisting* influence. In this respect, Cartwright (1959) has discussed two features of power: power *over* others to influence them; and power to *resist* the imposition of influence *by* others. Both processes are implicated in conformity and nonconformity. The latter has received little attention as compared with the former, though the research studies just considered represent a distinct movement in that direction. Nonetheless, a major limitation in studying conformity has been to see it as if the individual had only one alternative to conformity. This overlooks the variability of expectancies and the different modes of nonconformity.

CONFORMITY, ANTICONFORMITY, AND INDEPENDENCE

As already noted, there are inadequacies in the usual unidimensional approaches to conformity, with conforming behavior viewed at one end of a continuum and deviations at the other. An alternative model, which departs sharply from the unidimensional tradition, has been suggested by Willis (1963) and adapted in research by Willis and Hollander (1964a; 1964b) and Hollander and Willis (1964). A major feature of this model, shown in Figure 14.9, is the provision it makes for distinguishing between two kinds of nonconforming response, i.e. independence and anticonformity. Basically, it concerns aspects of movement conformity and not congruence.

In this model two dimensions are used for the construction of an adequate representation of conformity and nonconformity. The first of these dimensions is dependence-independence; the second is conformity-anticonformity. These are at right angles to one another. They produce an isosceles triangle with points labeled conformity and anticonformity, along the net conformity dimension, and independence, at right angles to it, as shown in Figure 14.9. These points describe the three basic modes of responding to social pressures:

> *Conformity* refers to consistent movement in the direction of a social expectancy.
> *Independence* refers to a lack of consistent movement toward or away from a social expectancy.
> *Anticonformity* refers to consistent movement away from a social expectancy.

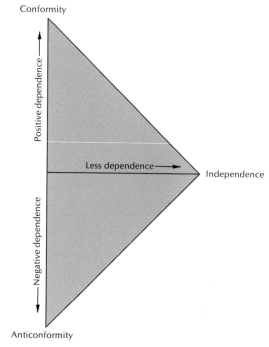

Figure 14.9: Triangular model of *conformity, independence,* and *anticonformity* responses. (From Willis, 1963.) This can be expanded to a diamond shape by extending the horizontal dimension to the left to generate *variability,* which is a mode of independence that reveals itself in a consistent change from one's own position (Willis, 1965).

It is important to note that both *conformity and anticonformity reveal dependence* upon others. In the first instance this takes the form of a positive response to their expectancies and in the second a negative response to those expectancies. Notice, therefore, that a person who nonconforms by anticonforming is still tied to a group norm as a source of influence for his actions. On the other hand, the person who responds *independently* in a situation *may or may not* behave in terms of such demands.

Thus, the person perceives relevant social expectancies but is not dependent upon them as guides to behavior. A simple example of independence would be a situation where a girl wears her hair long and prefers it that way. Suppose that other girls, as a result of new fashion dictates, start wearing their hair long so that it becomes a behavioral norm. If the girl wants to "be different" she might then cut her hair. In so doing, she would be anticonforming since she is responding in a dependent way to what others are doing, and *not* to her own preference. Independent behavior in this situation would be indicated by the girl continuing to wear her hair as before, if that is what she likes best. However, if she does keep her hair long, she might be regarded by others as a "conformist," though her intent is otherwise, i.e. to be independent.

A confusion between anticonformity and independence has been at the heart of many controversies about conformity and individuality. The anticonforming person in any circumstance can easily be taken for someone who is being "individualistic" when, in fact, he may actually be fixated on doing the *reverse* of what relevant social practices require. The difference between such negativism and independence quite obviously lies in the motivational intent, and that poses a complicated problem of interpretation. However, it is possible to create certain aspects of a situation experimentally, by giving different sets to subjects, in order to study anticonformity in contrast to independence.

As a demonstration of the variables *producing* conformity and nonconformity of both the independence and anticonforming variety, Willis and Hollander (1964a) experimentally varied the subject's own perceived competence, the perceived competence of the co-worker, the strength of the set to reaffirm initial judgments, and the reward structure. Movement in the direction predicted was found to confirm the two-dimensional triangular model as a better description of behavior than the more usual unidimensional conception.

Regarding the *effects* of these three behaviors, in another experiment these same investigators had subjects working together on a task with a co-worker who behaved in a conforming, independent, or anticonforming way, and who also was said to be more competent or less competent than the subject himself. They found that subjects reported highest perceived influence by their co-worker where he was competent in the task and behaving independently. Conformity by the co-worker, even when he was competent, led to significantly lower perceived influence. These and other findings from that study corroborate the differential effects of conformity, independence, and anticonformity in combination with competence. Therefore, though independence and anticonformity both constituted nonconformity; each evoked a distinctive pattern of reaction from subjects (Hollander and Willis, 1964).

The multi-causal nature of conformity

Many characterizations of conformity and nonconformity continue to treat these phenomena as if they satisfied a single motive. But as we have observed, this is much too narrow a conception of the diverse pressures and anticipated goals that shape behavior. For one thing, the continuity of behavior is inextricably bound up with many associations of a dependence nature, in the past and present as well as in the future. Furthermore, diverse motives may be satisfied simultaneously.

The teenager, for example, who conforms to what his peers are doing may be establishing a social identity apart from the family at the same time that he gains social support from his peers and achieves a sense of what his world is about in terms of their social reality. These affiliative needs are among various factors which may be implicated in the kind of influence relationship which leads to conformity.

A major point to be stressed, then, is the need to understand conformity and nonconformity as modes of response aimed at securing certain desired consequences for the individual, often in terms of several goals. Conformity and nonconformity both result from situational factors and individual needs which together produce a response to influence. This means that a person's evident nonconformity may represent rewards to him associated with less apparent conformity to another standard. The relationship between conformity and nonconformity is therefore complicated and not a matter of simple opposites, as we are often led to believe.

SUMMARY

Conformity is studied in social psychology in terms of its sources and effects. While some social critics are concerned about excessive conformity, the study of conformity proceeds without judgments of goodness or badness. The most widespread concern about conformity lies in the belief that it is opposite to individuality. This overlooks, however, the individual benefits gained by conforming and by knowing that others will conform.

Conformity and nonconformity are not simple phenomena that can be treated in a categorical fashion. Sometimes they refer to the degree of uniformity of expected behavior which can be called *congruence conformity,* and sometimes to a shift toward a social standard called *movement conformity.*

A broader phenomenon of nonconformity is represented by *deviancy* which, in essence, refers to a failure to adhere to one or more norms of society. Its definition greatly depends upon the "rules" a society establishes, and is often determined by the eye of the beholder. Persons labeled as "deviants" may be criminals under the law, different in their pattern of conduct, or perceived to be members of less approved groups. As in the case of prejudice, the problem with such labeling is the injustice it can do to individuals.

Movement conformity has been the basis for a great deal of laboratory experimentation which reveals a number of factors in the situation which regularly relate to such conformity, e.g. the ambiguity of the stimuli presented; a lower perceived competence or status than other group members; the presence of a unanimous majority; and the attractiveness of the group. While situational factors such as these produce a higher probability of conformity, attributes of personality are not found to be consistently related to conformity across situations.

The effects of conformity can be looked at in terms of a "social exchange" producing benefits in interaction. Thus, where an individual must make a public commitment, the probability of a conforming response is heightened. Acceptance of nonconformity is related to status in the sense of how an individual is perceived by those with whom he has ongoing interaction. Such status can be thought of as an accumulation of "idiosyncrasy credits" which represent the positive perceptions held of a person. These arise from perceived conformity and competence, among other factors, and can be used for later nonconformity and innovation as represented in leadership.

The concept of a single norm, or expectancy, applicable to everyone in a group can be modified to recognize the effects of status in producing differential expectancies for various members. Furthermore, there also exists a differential power to resist influence represented in conformity pressures. Group support appears to be one important basis for not complying with an assertion of influence. The presence of a minority opposing the majority may serve as such a counter-influence, especially where it is consistent in its position. A related point is that evident nonconformity to one social standard may reflect conformity to another less evident one.

Nonconformity can be of two distinct varieties: it may be *anticonformity*, which takes the form of high dependence upon a social expectancy as a negative basis for action, or *independence*, which represents an absence of concern for that expectancy. While anticonformity and independence may resemble one another superficially, the latter represents far greater individual initiative. *Both* conformity and anticonformity constitute responses of a heavily *dependent* nature since they are tied to a group expectancy. Several kinds of goals may be served simultaneously by these modes of nonconformity, as well as by conformity.

SUGGESTED READINGS

From E. P. Hollander and R. G. Hunt (Eds.) *Current perspectives in social psychology.* (3rd ed.) New York: Oxford University Press, 1971.

43. Howard S. Becker: *Outsiders*
44. Edwin P. Hollander and Richard H. Willis: *Some current issues in the psychology of conformity and nonconformity*
46. John W. Thibaut and Harold H. Kelley: *On norms*
47. Edward E. Jones: *Conformity as a tactic of ingratiation*

SELECTED REFERENCES

*Becker, H. S. *Outsiders: studies in the sociology of deviance.* New York: Free Press, 1963.

Berg, I. A., & Bass, B. M. (Eds.) *Conformity and deviation.* New York: Harper, 1961.

*Gardner, J. W. *Self-renewal.* New York: Harper & Row, 1963.

*Kiesler, C. A., & Kiesler, S. B. *Conformity.* Reading Mass: Addison-Wesley, 1969.

*Riesman, D., Glazer, N., & Denny, R. *The Lonely crowd: a study of the changing American character.* New Haven: Yale Univer. Press, 1950.

Sherif, M., & Sherif, C. W. *Reference groups: exploration into the conformity and deviation of adolescents.* New York: Harper & Row, 1964.

*Walker, E. L., & Heyns, R. W. *An anatomy for conformity.* Englewood Cliffs, N. J.: Prentice-Hall, 1962.

15

Leadership, supervision, and negotiation

Leadership is a process, not a person. While the leader stands out as a prominent element in the process, other elements are vitally implicated in it. The characteristics of a leader certainly bear upon the direction, nature, and effectiveness of leadership, but the prevailing view in social psychology today stresses the leadership functions to be fulfilled in the situation rather than the leader's characteristics alone.

Just as groups vary in their characteristics, so do leaders. Different circumstances may require different leader attributes for group functions to be performed. The nub of the matter is that the leader's role provides for vital group needs, and these may be performed by various persons. Any time two or more people function together to attain a mutual goal, a group structure develops. Leadership, in the sense of influence directed toward the attainment of group goals, operates within that structure, both deriving from it and also affecting it over time.

The process of leadership can therefore be considered as an influence relationship that occurs between mutually dependent group members. It can be understood with reference to the interrelation of three elements: the *leader*, with his characteristics, including motivations, perceptions, and resources relevant to the attainment of the group's goal; the *followers*, with their characteristics, including motivations, perceptions, and relevant resources; and their *situation*, involving functions to

589

be fulfilled, desired goals, and other conditions. In this chapter we will consider this interrelation and the implications it holds for group processes as well as for leader effectiveness.

The nature of leadership

Since the the two terms "leadership" and "leader" are often confused, they should be distinguished from one another at the outset. In the broadest sense, *leadership* is a process which implies the existence of a particular influence relationship between two or more persons, though it usually refers to groups of more than two. Gibb (1969) puts it this way:

> Leadership refers to that aspect of role differentiation by which all or a large number of group members make use of individual contributions which they perceive to have value in moving the group toward its goals. . . . Whenever two or more persons interact in the pursuit of a common goal, the relation of leadership and followership soon becomes evident. This relation is characterized by influence or control of one or some group members over others (p. 271).

A *leader* is a person with characteristics, including especially a given status, which allow him to exercise influence in line with the attainment of group goals. In doing so, he can be considered as someone whose role behavior constitutes a major group resource.

While the leader has been seen here mainly in regard to actual interaction in a functional group situation, the role of leader may also be fulfilled in symbolic terms, as can be observed with those noted for their great scientific or artistic achievements. Among scientists, for instance, a great figure such as an Einstein could exert considerable influence as a model or exemplar of shared values. The influence may not be as direct, but the quality of being a cherished "resource" is there and that potential could be activated. In general, wide esteem creates a "high status" which provides the basis for influence. However, status depends upon interpersonal perception. A person does not "hold" status, in some immutable sense, so much as he is "accorded" status, and this results from a process of evaluation through actual or implied interaction.

LEADERSHIP AS A TRANSACTION

The venerable view of the leader as the primary actor, one who can exercise influence over others, omits the essence of the transaction which occurs between a person in the role of leader and his followers. As Homans (1961) aptly notes, "Influence over others is purchased at the price of allowing one's self to be influenced by others" (p. 286). In this sense, the willingness of group members to accept the influence of a leader depends upon a process of exchange in which the leader gives something and gets something in return. On this feature of leader-follower interaction, Hollander and Julian (1969) assert that

> . . . the person in the role of leader who fulfills expectations and achieves group goals provides rewards for others which are reciprocated in the form of status, esteem, and heightened influence. Because leadership embodies a two-way influence relationship, recipients of influence assertions may respond by asserting influence in return, that is, by making demands on the leader. The very sustenance of the relationship depends upon some yielding to influence on both sides (p. 390).

In the transactional view, the leader is considered to be an influence agent who directs communications to his followers, to which they may react in various ways. The leader attempts to take account of the perceptual-motivational states of his followers and they, in turn, evaluate his in terms of responses to their needs. Leadership therefore cannot be meaningfully considered independently of the followers within a particular group and of the nature of the transactions involved.

Leader-follower interactions exist in many reaches of life, even in less exalted realms. Many influence events occur every day between people involved in reciprocal role relationships such as parent-child, teacher-student, husband-wife, and these have features of leadership. There is, however, a special quality associated with leadership in groups, as well as in large organizations and nations, which inevitably has compelled attention to "the leader" as the figure at center stage in the leadership process. There is a long tradition associated with the idea that the source of this process lies within the leader, and history itself is full of accounts of leaders and their acts. Some of this tradition will be reviewed now.

TRAIT AND SITUATIONAL APPROACHES: A PERSPECTIVE

Concern and controversy about leadership extend far back in philosophical thought. Typically, the leader was seen to be someone possessed of unique traits, presumably inborn. Cowley (1928) captured this theme in his contention that "The approach to the study of leadership has usually been and must always be through the study of traits" (p. 144).

The idea that leaders "are born, not made" was a keystone of the classic view. Though there unquestionably is a degree of validity in the notion of leaders as significant agents in human events, this view produced an overemphasis on the study of the traits of leaders at the expense of other factors in the situation, including followers and prevailing circumstances which shape the leader's actions. The trait approach was particularly favored as a strategy for investigating leadership among psychologically oriented investigators. Accordingly, research on the subject earlier in this century placed considerable stress on such factors as height, weight, appearance, intelligence, self-confidence, and any other variables which might be correlated positively with leadership. The broad aim was to determine what factor or factors *made* a person a leader. The results were summarized in an influential review by Stogdill (1948) and presented a very mixed picture, to say the least. The major finding was that, on the average, leaders tended to be slightly more intelligent than non-leaders. Even this finding was not, however, thoroughly stable.

Mann (1959) has since reviewed 125 studies of leadership and personality characteristics representing over seven hundred findings. These are summarized in Table 15.1. Once again, intelligence stands forth as the factor with the highest percentage of positive relationships with leadership. Mann also identifies general adjustment, extroversion, and dominance as correlates of leadership. He points out, however, that most of these studies involved a group organized around an assigned discussion task. The "superiority" of the leader, therefore, has to be viewed in that context. Gibb (1954) has summed up the matter in observing that "Followers subordinate themselves, not to an individual whom they perceive as utterly different, but to a member of their group who has superiority at this time and whom they perceive to be

Table 15.1: Percentage of significant relationships reported in a positive or negative direction for 125 studies, representing 751 findings on the relationship of various personality characteristics and leadership. (After Mann, 1959.)

PERSONALITY FACTORS AND NUMBER OF STUDIES OF EACH	NUMBER OF FINDINGS	% YIELDING SIG. POSITIVE RELATIONSHIP	% YIELDING SIG. NEGATIVE RELATIONSHIP	% YIELDING NEITHER
Intelligence—28	(196)	46% (91)	1%* (1)	53% (104)
Adjustment—22	(164)	30% (50)	2%* (2)	68% (112)
Extroversion—22	(119)	31% (37)	5% (6)	64% (76)
Dominance—12	(39)	38% (15)	15% (6)	46% (18)
Masculinity—9	(70)	16% (11)	1%* (1)	83% (58)
Conservatism—17	(62)	5% (3)	27% (17)	68% (42)
Sensitivity—15	(101)	15% (15)	1% (1)	84% (85)
* Rounded upward				

fundamentally the same as they are, and who may, at other times, be prepared to follow" (p. 915). This point suggests the necessity to see leader and follower roles as complementary, and *not* fixed but amenable to change.

The largest deficiency in the trait approach was its insistence upon looking for stable features of "leaders" across many situations. Again, this is not the same as studying "leadership" as a process. At any rate, the trait approach failed to recognize that leadership involves a network of relationships with other individuals who are engaged in a situation with a focal activity. As Gouldner (1950) viewed it:

> There is a certain degree of persistence or patterning in the activities which a group undertakes be it bowling, playing bridge, engaging in warfare, or shoplifting. These persisting or habitual group activities, among other things, set limits on the kind of individuals who become group members and, no less so, upon the kind of individuals who come to lead the group (p. 76).

The main thrust of the situational view was the attention it gave to the varying demands upon leadership imposed by the situation. These demands may grow out of the group's task or function, its structure, and other contextual features, such as external threat. As the dominant theme during and since the decade of the 1950's in research on leadership, the situational approach did *not* neglect the characteristics of the leader so much as it recognized their appropriateness to a group functioning in a given situation. It emphasized, for example, that the leader should have an acceptable level of competence on a task of importance to the group's functioning. But whether this competence displays itself in flying an airplane or in organizing an expedition for survival depends very much upon situational demands which may be fulfilled by various group members (Cartwright and Zander, 1960, pp. 494-495).

The concept of the leader as a group resource is an extension of the situational approach. It has roots in two kinds of considerations. One is the need for a functional group to operate as a system with inputs from members to produce desired outputs. The second consideration is that followers have expectancies in defining situations and responding to the leader's contributions. They do not merely passively accept influence assertions from the leader, but react to these in evaluative terms. This conception has obvious parallels to the model of persuasive communication considered in Chapter 6 (see p. 212). It means that the follower has a place as an active participant in the leadership process. As Fillmore Sanford (1950) long ago observed:

> There is some justification for regarding the follower as the most crucial factor in any leadership event. . . . Not only is it the follower who accepts or rejects leadership, but it is the follower who *perceives* both the leader and the situation and who reacts in terms of what he perceives. And what he perceives may be, to an important degree, a function of his own motivations, frames of reference, and "readinesses" (p. 4).

The situational emphasis, therefore, was more than a single "approach." It brought together a number of elements that could be studied as a counterbalance to the trait orientation of the more traditional view of leadership. But it had the deficiency of leaving out a concern with process. Typically, leaders were viewed in terms of their ability to exert influence. Studies in the mainstream of the situational emphasis gave little consideration to the followers' responses to leaders over time, including sources of rising or falling status, and the problems of leaders *maintaining* as well as *attaining* their status. Indeed, the distinction between processes governing the maintenance of leadership status as against those involved in its attainment with few exceptions were given little attention (Cohen and Bennis, 1961; Hollander, 1961a). Most of the time, therefore, the leader was viewed as someone who occupied a position in a relatively fixed sense.

In commenting on this in their recent review of research on leadership processes, Hollander and Julian (1969) say:

> . . . the two research emphases represented by the trait and situational approaches afforded a far too glib view of reality . . . neither approach ever represented its own philosophical underpinning very well, and each resulted in a caricature . . . the situational view made it appear that the leader and the situation were quite separate . . . [though] the leader, from the follower's vantage point, is an element in the situation, and one who shapes it as well . . . in exercising influence, therefore, the leader may set the stage and create expectations about what he should do and what he will do. Rather than standing apart from the leader, the situation perceived to exist may be his creation (pp. 388-389).

The importance of the leader's construction of the situation is revealed by an experiment on group problem-solving conducted by Maier and Hoffman (1965). They tested the hypothesis that disagreement in discussion could lead to hard feelings or innovation, depending upon the attitude of the discussion leader. One hundred and fifty groups of four persons each took part, all composed of middle-management executives. Each group role-played a situation in which a foreman was trying to get three employees to accept a change in work methods. The outcome of this large-scale experiment indicated that the leader's view of disagreement was crucial in the nature of the solutions achieved.

> The results clearly support the hypothesis that disagreement can either serve as a stimulant for innovation or as a source of hard feelings, depending largely on the attitude of the discussion leader. Foremen who saw some of their men as "problem employees" obtained innovative solutions least frequently; whereas those who saw some of their men only as sources of ideas obtained innovative solutions more frequently (p. 384).

The more recent developments in the study of leadership are inclined toward a greater interest in the *system* of relationships implicated in leadership, including power, authority, and social exchange.

Of particular importance is how the leader's position is attained, which is a primary consideration in legitimacy.

Characterizations of the leader

One major question in characterizing the leader rests in how he comes to be in the leader role, that is, how he achieves *legitimacy*. Much depends on the way in which that role is construed, both by the leader and the followers. As we pointed out earlier, groups may have an informal or formal structure. In the first case, the leader derives his status from others in the group who may accord or withdraw it. They are the "validators" of his position. This pattern, which depends upon group consent, can be called *emergent leadership*. By contrast, a formal structure imposes *appointed leadership* whose validators are in a position of higher authority. Mainly, this distinction is important for highlighting the sources of the leader's legitimacy, and not necessarily his style of interaction. For example, though the group is not directly involved in choosing an appointed leader, he may be perceived favorably for attributes which would make him acceptable to followers as an emergent leader as well.

THE APPOINTED LEADER AND LEGITIMACY OF OFFICE

The first and most traditional way to determine who is a leader is to find out who has been *designated* for this function. If one visits an executive, the assumption is that he is a "leader." And he is, in the sense of having the legitimacy of office, backed up by the organization. In this vein, as Janda (1960) has pointed out, leadership is a relationship in which the power-wielder, who can compel compliance up to a point, is perceived to have these rights by the recipient. But whether leaders are appointed or emergent, the expectations of followers are important.

Since appointed leaders are assigned to the group and given functions by higher authority, their activities are "pre-programmed" by those considerations. Bavelas (1960) says the question "Who is the leader?" might better be put in other terms as "What functions are to be fulfilled?" He suggests that, in the aggregate, appointed leaders are those who perform certain kinds of tasks, rather than being those with certain characteristics of personality, or styles of social interaction. Indeed, appointed leaders may primarily be decision-makers who may not require effective interpersonal relations as a dominant feature of their role.

There is a persisting idea that the appointed leader necessarily behaves in an autocratic fashion, as part of his role in the "chain of command." This idea dies hard. As Prentice (1961) ruefully notes:

> It is ironic that our basic image of "the leader" is so often that of a military commander, because—most of the time, at least—military organizations are the purest example of an unimaginative application of simple reward and punishment as motivating devices . . . . We have all heard the cry, "somebody's got to be the boss" . . . but it is dangerous to confuse the chain of command or table of organization with a method of getting things done (p. 144).

A major misconception in this traditional view is that when the leader speaks, things must happen. The exercise of power is assumed to be adequate in engaging followers in a mutual effort, but the costs in morale and resistance are likely to be great. This point will be elaborated later in connection with organizational leadership.

THE EMERGENT LEADER AND GROUP SUPPORT

In the informal group, the emergent leader occupies his status by virtue of the way he is perceived and reacted to by others in his group. He depends for his influence upon their willing support.

The emergent leader has frequently been identified by sociometric techniques considered here earlier (see p. 62 and p. 272). They provide a useful basis for determining who the members of a group perceive to be influential. In their earliest phases, sociometric studies gave a great deal of weight to popularity, which was often equated with leadership. Much of this work looked at choices among roommates or study companions. As a consequence, a general measure of liking was taken as a sign that an individual was a leader (e.g. Jennings, 1943).

More recently, it has been found that the relationship between sociometric popularity and leadership depends upon the situation, and need not be high. Simply liking a person does not mean that he would be acceptable in fulfilling a leadership role within a group. In this respect, Jennings (1947) has distinguished between attraction based upon personal liking, which she calls *psyche-tele* attraction, and *socio-tele* attraction, based upon a group standard of judgment.

It may also be that acknowledging a leader does not signify a liking for him. Bales (1955) had students involved in a group discussion task answer four sociometric questions regarding: 1) contributing best ideas; 2) guiding the discussion; 3) liking; and 4) disliking. He found that those rated at the top for "best ideas" and "guiding discussion" were near the bottom for "liking." On the other hand, the second man on these leadership functions was routinely found to be highest on liking. Bales concluded that "there must be something about high participation and specialization in the technical and executive directions which tends to provoke hostility" (p. 453). In a related work, Bales with Slater (1955) has distinguished between the "task specialist" and "socio-emotional" leadership roles; they say that both of these exist in groups. It is doubtful, however, that there is a fundamental conflict between these roles and, indeed, they may be occupied by the same person depending upon the character of the task (Marcus, 1960; and Turk, 1961). The import of Bales's work lies in the finding that participants in a group distinguish between those who contribute to a leadership function and those they like.

Leaders, in short, are not necessarily the best liked individuals in a group, nor can they always be, though they may be admired and esteemed. Corroboration for this comes also from research by Hollander and Webb (1955). In their study, they also introduced another issue in terms of "followership." For a long time the traditional sociometric approach to leadership had been based on a pyramid model with a peak of leaders at the top and a residue of non-leaders below. Non-leaders were presumed to be followers, which was one assumption tested by this research. Briefly, naval aviation cadets were asked to complete three sociometric forms upon graduation from sixteen weeks of preflight training. The first two of these forms were for "leader" and "follower," the third for friendship. On both the leader and follower forms each cadet was asked to assume that he was assigned to "a special military unit with an undisclosed mission." Then, for leadership, he was directed to nominate in order three cadets from his section whom he considered best qualified to lead this special unit and three cadets from his section whom he considered least qualified. A similar set was presented for followership with the instruction that the cadet assume that *he himself had been assigned to be the leader* of this special unit; from among the members of his section, he was instructed to nominate three cadets whom he would want as part of his unit and three whom he would not want. The friendship nomination form simply asked for the names of three friends in the section.

Hollander and Webb (1955) found that the nominations for leader and follower correlated to a high degree, r = .92. Friendship had a significantly higher relationship with followership, r = .55, than with leadership, r = .47. But apart from this, friendship nominations were *not* found to bear appreciably on the basic leadership-followership relationship. For instance, of the three friends designated by each subject, an average of more than two were not mentioned at all in the three nominations for leader made by the subjects.

These findings indicated also that the more desired followers tended to be chosen from the upper extremes of the leadership distribution; indeed, the correspondence was marked. Furthermore, the influence of friendship, often taken for leadership under the heading of "popularity," had little effect on this relationship. In a later study by Kubany (1957), comparable results were found with 87 medical school graduating seniors. A correlation of .85 was obtained between peer-nomination scores for the choices "would have for family physician" and "would turn over practice to" when away. Neither of these was as highly correlated with "friend and social associate."

INFLUENCE AND INITIATION OF STRUCTURE

Another way of identifying the leader is to consider the influence patterns of a group. One major exponent of this viewpoint, Homans (1961), considers leadership in direct influence terms:

> . . . the larger the number of other members a single member is regularly able to influence, the higher is his authority in the group. The man with highest authority we shall call the leader. By this definition authority is not just influence, for each member may have influenced every other at one time or another. Authority refers instead to differences between members in the amount of influence they exert (p. 286).

Direction of group activity is a central feature of the leadership role. Thus, leadership implies influence. As Gibb (1950) notes, group members are usually quite able to identify their peers who exert the greatest influence. Indeed, the idea of an influence hierarchy, whether explicit or implicit, is quite pervasive in human affairs (Seeman and Morris, 1950).

One pointed characterization of leadership in terms of influence is Hemphill's (1958, 1961) concept that the leader is the group member most responsible for *initiating structure*. In this view, leaders can be identified by the high degree to which they determine the group's pattern of interaction and locomotion toward its goal. The significant element here is that the leader is not simply part of the group's structure but rather is an active agent in shaping it. Hemphill also distinguishes between *attempted* leadership and *accepted* leadership. In the first instance, an individual initiates activity to influence others, and in the second, that assertion is responded to affirmatively. There is no flow of leadership, so to speak, unless both conditions are fulfilled. It is this sequence, says Hemphill, which is a basic requirement for effective leadership. As we shall be observing shortly, in connection with organizational leadership, a considerable range of research indicates initiation of structure to be a major factor in leadership across many situations.

Another way of considering the leader is to view him as the *completer* of essential group functions. This view is identified with the work of Schutz (1961) who places particular stress on the role of the leader as a resource person who insures that the group's critical functions are adequately fulfilled and maintained in harmony with one another. This idea meshes rather well with the concept of initiation of structure, especially in those circumstances where the group requires the leader's organizational efforts to move toward its goals. Accordingly, once a set of group functions can be specified, it is possible to consider that person as leader who can help to fulfill these functions by his initiative and influence.

The concept of *idiosyncrasy credit*, discussed in the last chapter, has special relevance to the leader's latitude for exerting influence, particularly in an innovative way. In operational terms, these credits provide the basis for the leader's taking actions which would be seen to be nonconforming for other members of the group. The important point, however, is that innovation in the face of situational demands is expected of the leader as a feature of his role. Inaction by the leader could therefore considerably reduce his status in the eyes of the other group members, as will be considered further below in connection with advocacy.

LEGITIMACY, POWER, AND INNOVATION

Given sufficient legitimacy, a leader can exert a good deal of influence. Often this potential is characterized as *power*, which implies a greater probability of obtaining compliance from others; at the extreme this is represented in control. Power is by no means an all-or-nothing matter, however. The unfettered use of power brings its own costs, in terms of greater resistance in the relationship of followers to the leader. Furthermore, however a leader achieves legitimacy, it is also important in maintaining it that he be seen as loyal to the group's goals and not exploitative in his motivations.

French and Raven (1959) have presented an analysis of the various bases for power. They distinguish between reward power, coercive power, referent power, expert power, and legitimate power. They view reward and coercive power as representing gains or losses for compliance or non-compliance to an authority. Referent power, in their scheme, represents an extension of reward power through a process of identification. Once such identification has been made with the agent of power, it is no longer necessary for that agent continually to monitor the behavior of the less powerful person. As the term suggests, expert power arises from conditions of specialized knowledge that has value. Finally, legitimate power is based upon the mutual acceptance of norms which requires one person to do the bidding of another within the framework, for example, of an organization (Olsen, 1968, Ch. 12).

Though power, influence, and innovation are treated at times as if they were entirely different processes, they clearly are intertwined, especially in terms of the transactions occurring in leadership. This obviously may vary considerably with the nature of the group as well as with the source of the leader's authority. It is sometimes the case, for example, that an emergent leader, within an informal group, is as powerful in directing others as one who is appointed. In a study by Carter, Haythorn, Shriver, and Lanzetta (1951) they found such an inversion of their predicted results. They had some groups working under an appointed leader and others working under a leader freely elected by the group itself. It was assumed that the former situation would lead to a greater assertion of influence by the leader. This was not the case. In general, the appointed leaders saw their position as one of co-ordination—in the sense of a distribution of responsibilities—rather than as a powerful director of the group's activities. By contrast, the elected leaders were found to be more forceful in supporting their own proposals and urging action.

There may be a question about the generalizability of this finding, given the particular nature of the groups in this situation. However, this study points up an interesting feature of leadership in terms of its legitimacy. One explanation for the finding obtained is that the appointed leader has less need to assert his authority since it is imposed from above, while the emergent or elected leader finds it necessary to establish his position in a competitive situation with other would-be leaders. In either case, there is a necessity for the leader's position to be validated in some way.

Goldman and Fraas (1965) conducted an experiment in which leaders were elected by a group vote, selected on their ability to perform the group task, or appointed by the experimenter. The task was a variant of the game "Twenty Questions," and the main dependent measure was the time and number of questions for solutions. The results showed that either an "elected" or "selected" leader was superior to the "appointed" or "no leader" (control) conditions, in terms of group performance. These investigators say that ". . . the manner in which this leader obtains his position is important . . . the significant fact is that followers will more readily accept someone who has, so to speak, proven himself (p. 88). This accords with the general point that some mechanism is required to provide legitimacy for the leader's role.

The importance of this factor is illustrated, too, in an earlier study by Raven and French (1958). In one condition they had a confederate apparently usurp a leadership position when it was not legitimately granted to him. In another condition the confederate was supposedly elected by the group. Raven and French found that attempts to exert influence in the group were much more successful in the latter condition after the leader had been invested, as they put it, with the "legitimate power of that office."

Anderson and Fiedler (1965) conducted a study with four-man discussion groups, half of which had "leaders" instructed to behave as an "officer in charge" in a supervisory way, and the other half of which were led by a "chairman" told to lead in a participatory way. In general, the participatory leaders were found to be more influential. Furthermore, the relationship between the leaders' attributes and their groups' performance was greatest under the participation condition.

The leader's willingness to deviate from group decisions was studied in a recent experiment by Hollander, Julian, and Sorrentino (1969). They gave primary attention to the leader's sense of his own legitimacy. The task selected was designed to engage interest and to permit a relatively free exchange of ideas on matters of topical concern, i.e. urban affairs. In the first phase, discussion sessions were held with no less than twelve and no more than sixteen male students. Each subject was provided with a name tag and seated in a circle with an identifying number before him. Orientation materials were then distributed, including the description of a city with many of the problems typifying those of large urban centers. Subjects were then asked to write down the problems they thought to be most important, among a host of those presented, after which they would be asked to voice their views on these. The discussion usually lasted about forty minutes, with a high level of evident involvement. At its close, the discussion leader, who had been introduced to the subjects earlier as a faculty member interested in urban affairs, indicated that they would be separated and reconstituted into three teams, each consisting of a task leader and his staff. Subjects were also told that the leaders would be separated from the others, though they could pass messages to them, mainly to determine how communication processes affect decisions about urban affairs. After subjects were placed in individual rooms, half were led to believe that they had been elected as a team leader, and the other half that they had been appointed as a team leader by the faculty member who led the discussion.

Cutting across these treatments, half of the subjects were told that they were the "top choice" for the leader's position, and the other half that they were the "third choice." The former believed that they would be leading team "A" and the latter, team "C." The design therefore had two sources of authority and two levels of strength of endorsement as bases for legitimacy. Thereafter, the main dependent measure employed was the willingness of subjects to totally reverse the top and bottom priorities that their team members had allegedly assigned to action programs for seven problem areas. For each of these areas, following three that were used as a warm-up, the leader was confronted with a "communication form" on which team members had ostensibly made their ranking of the priorities to be given the four action programs.

These forms were contrived to present leaders with precisely the reverse order of ranking for the four action programs that had been obtained previously from similar subjects in a pilot study. The leader was then to give his own ranking on the form, taking account of the team's supposed recommendation. In effect, then, leaders were being presented with a situation in which they could go along with the group, on each major problem area, or not go along in varying degrees. Thus, they were being subjected to a mode of conformity pressure. They could also write notes on the communication form, as they wished.

The most critical test of the leader's willingness to deviate from his team's choice was the measure of total reversals, i.e. where the leader made the team's choice of "one," his own "four," and the team's choice of "four," his own "one." These results are shown in Figure 15.1, in terms of the mean out of seven critical trials. As will be seen there, the

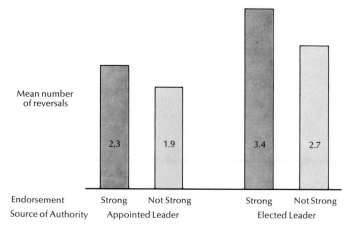

Figure 15.1: Mean number out of seven critical trials on which appointed or elected leaders, under strong or not strong endorsement, reversed team's first-rank choice. (From Hollander, Julian, and Sorrentino, 1969.)

highest reading was for elected leaders with strong endorsement (i.e. "top choice") with a mean of 3.4, indicating that on roughly half of the critical trials they totally reversed the team's priorities. While the endorsement variable was not significant in this analysis, it did reveal a significant interaction with source of authority for several of the other dependent measures. For example, a content analysis of the messages of leaders to their teams, conducted without knowledge of the treatments, indicated that a statistical interaction prevailed for the quality of showing "group-orientation," by recognition of the group's views, signs of conciliation, and accommodation. Elected leaders with strong endorsement were *lowest* on this characteristic, while appointed leaders with strong endorsement were *highest*. Evidently, then, the elected leader in this situation feels more confident of his position and is more willing to expend credits by deviation from the group's choices, and without manifest justifications. However, in situations where appointed leadership is normative, the findings might be the reverse.

Leader attributes and the situation

One of the major experimental approaches to leadership has been to study the consistency with which an individual has leadership status from one group to another. Exemplifying this approach, Bell and French (1950) had subjects participate in six discussion groups, each of which included four other men they had not met previously. Six different discussion problems were used, and at the end of each session the members of the group were asked to nominate a discussion leader for a hypothetical second meeting of the same group. They found that "varying group membership in this situation accounts for at most a relatively small portion of the variation in leadership status. Leadership status seems to be rather highly consistent despite the situational changes involved" (p. 767). However, as they point out, this result is limited since the task involved was of a particular variety, and certain characteristics of the group members were fairly homogeneous. Gibb (1950) also found comparable results but again with subjects involved in similar kinds of tasks. More recently, Cohen and Bennis (1961) found that, after systematically shifting persons in the communication networks of their groups, those identified as leaders remained fairly constant.

LEADER PERSONALITY

These findings tend to support the view that there are personality characteristics which are associated with leadership in groups of a comparable kind, in terms of the task to be performed. Whether this would be so across widely varying situations is considerably more problematic. In discussion groups, for example, the emphasis on verbal output clearly affects the pattern of leadership. Illustrative of this, Riecken (1958) among others has found that the most talkative members of a group are usually seen to be most influential in the group's solution of a problem.

In this vein, Bass (1959) has reported on a line of research with "leaderless group discussion" (LGD), in which subjects participated in the discussion of a problem without a designated leader. Leadership standing, determined by observer ratings, was found to be highly related to the category "time spent talking." Furthermore, this index was quite consistent for a person observed from one group to another.

In an early study on personality variables related to LGD behavior, Bass, McGehee, Hawkins, Young, and Gebel (1953) found a significant correlation between leadership status (a "high" LGD score) and an individual's self-ratings on ascendance and social boldness as measured by a standard personality inventory, the Guilford-Zimmerman Temperament Survey. They also found that authoritarian attitudes measured by the California F Scale correlated negatively with LGD scores. Here again, because of the standard quality of the task, situational differences were not great, though the composition of the group's membership could vary considerably.

Borgatta, Couch, and Bales (1954) also studied discussion groups across four sessions. They report that the eleven group participants who scored highest in terms of a composite of four criteria, i.e. intelligence, leadership ratings by other participants, total participation time in interaction, and popularity, were found to consistently lead groups that were more effective. In a natural setting, Beer, Buckhout, Horowitz, and Levy (1959) used sociometric ratings to compare students who had become leaders of campus organizations with non-leaders. The three attributes studied were self-acceptance, need achievement, and interpersonal skill. They found that the leaders there were rated as more confident, more willing to take responsibility, more forceful, persuasive, and diplomatic.

Interpersonal skills appear to matter more in settings in which leaders are emergent rather than appointed. McClintock (1963) identified a number of campus leaders who had held one or more responsible offices in organizations and other students who had not. Then he observed the behavior of all of these subjects in small problem-solving groups without designated leaders. He did not find those with a greater history of filling leader roles actually taking significantly more leader actions in these laboratory groups. But he did find them making significantly more friendly acts, indicating agreeableness, and displaying more concern for the group's progress. All of which is supportive of the consideration that there are *interpersonal behaviors* which, other things equal, are associated with the leader's role in many group situations.

Depending upon the structural properties of the situation, conventional personality measures may be less important than required role behaviors. Berkowitz (1956) measured the ascendance of male students with the Guilford-Zimmerman Temperament Survey and then placed high or low scorers in a central or peripheral position within a variant of the "wheel" communication network (see Chapter 3, p. 103). For three problem-solving tasks he obtained data on communications from subjects that either relayed information or were more assertive in initiating communication. In Figure 15.2 the results are presented by the proportion of informational communications out of the total given by a subject; this is a measure which reflects *lower* initiative, in leadership terms.

As expected, Berkowitz found that low ascendance subjects were more likely to give informational communications when in a peripheral position, than were high ascendance subjects, since it is more consistent with their personality. However, low ascendance subjects reacted to the central position by dropping substantially in the number of such communications, in keeping with their position; moreover, by the third task, they had dropped considerably below the high dominance subjects in that position. Berkowitz interprets this effect as "position adaptation" and concludes that the operation of a particular personality factor in leadership depends significantly upon the structural properties of the group.

Regarding this "structural effect," Rudraswamy (1964) did a study

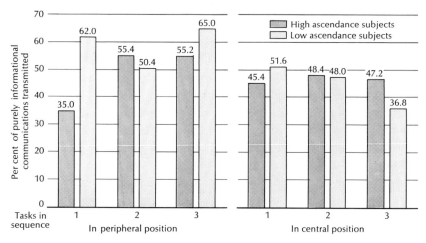

Figure 15.2: Per cent of informational communications transmitted by subjects of high and low "ascendance" assigned to peripheral and central positions in three group problem-solving tasks. (Based upon data from Berkowitz, 1956, p. 216.)

with some subjects believing they had higher status than others. He found that they not only attempted more leader acts than other group members, but even exceeded the rate for those subjects who had been given greater information about the task itself.

Group performance and satisfaction are also related to the personality of the person in a leadership position. Shaw (1959a) placed subjects who scored high or low on the California F Scale in central positions in communication networks. He found that high authoritarian leaders led groups which performed better, in terms of higher work output, under a centralized communication structure; but group members were significantly less satisfied working for the leader who was a high authoritarian. When the communication structure was decentralized, Shaw found that low authoritarian leaders led groups which performed better, as well as being better satisfied. Here again, the nature of the structure interrelated with leader personality.

RATE OF PARTICIPATION AND ACTIVITY

The participation of leaders is usually found to be at a higher rate than other group members. This is one of the major findings of the leaderless group discussion research already noted. Bolstering Riecken's (1958) findings, which showed that members who spoke most were perceived as contributing more and were more influential, Kirscht, Lodahl, and Haire (1959) found with three-person discussion groups, that those who emerged as leaders had a significantly higher rate of participation in the discussion. McGrath and Julian (1963) report similar differences in participation rate for appointed leaders in four-person negotiation groups.

Even varying the nature of the task somewhat, Carter, Haythorn, Shriver, and Lanzetta (1951) found that leaders tended to be those more likely to initiate action for solving a problem. They presented groups with four tasks in varying sequences—reasoning, mechanical, assembling, and discussion. In general, leaders were likely to participate more frequently and to stand out as more prominent in initiating action. This is in line with Hemphill's concept of initiation of structure considered above.

It should also be recalled that the activity level of an individual, in terms of leadership acts, may be varied as a result of the reinforcement provided by the other group members. This is the essential finding of the study by Pepinsky, Hemphill, and Shevitz (1958) discussed in Chapter 4 (p. 141). In that experiment, under an acceptance condition, attempts to lead were rewarded by the other group members, and under conditions of rejection such attempts were disapproved by the others. Significant differences in leader behavior were found between these two conditions, in the predicted direction. Other research by Bavelas, Hastorf, Gross, and Kite (1965) and by Zdep and Oakes (1967) lends further credence to the basic point that leader behavior can be elicited by reinforcement of a person's influence attempts.

In general, the functioning of the leader depends upon the demands of the total situation, and the rewards it provides. To be rewarded, the leader's actions should be seen as a useful resource contributing to the group's success. Banta and Nelson (1964) conducted an experiment to see the effect of reward on the rate of participation of a group member who had a valued resource. They paired 96 female college students in a situation in which the pairs were to discuss a series of problems and express opinions to reach agreement. As the external authority, the experimenter arbitrarily rewarded the pair when opinions of one of the subjects was accepted and not the other's. These may be called

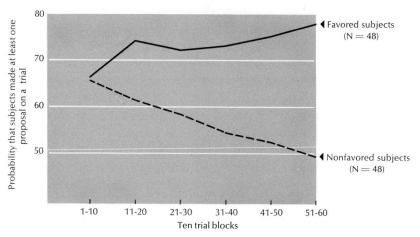

Figure 15.3: Changes in rate of participation in making opinion proposals under conditions of 100 per cent reinforcement of favored subject's proposals and zero per cent reinforcement of non-favored subject's proposals. (From Banta and Nelson, 1964, p. 496.)

the "favored" and "non-favored" subjects, respectively. In Figure 15.3 the results are shown for the average effect upon 48 subjects in each of these positions. As will be seen there, the probability of a non-favored subject expressing an opinion on a trial decreases steadily over time while the favored subjects increase beyond their initial rate of expressing an opinion. Note that these curves do not depend upon one another since it is possible for each subject to make proposals for every trial. Nevertheless, the non-favored subject clearly gives way to the one whose resources appear to be more rewarding to the group. Banta and Nelson also found that the girls who were the "favored subjects" expressed more confidence later in their personal ability and the group's joint ability.

The importance of the leader as a resource is revealed in research on leaders in various settings. Flanagan (1952), for example, conducted a study of "critical incidents" in military leadership situations. One prominent factor he found to be represented by many incidents was "Accepting responsibility for contributing to achievement of group goals." Among other factors were incidents represented by such reports as "Set example for men by remaining calm and efficient under fire."

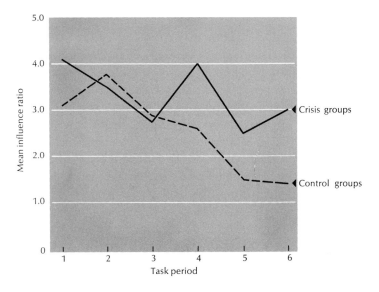

Figure 15.4: Mean influence ratios for high influencers in crisis groups and control groups by task periods. (From Hamblin, 1958, p. 330.)

A laboratory experiment on crisis conditions affecting leadership was conducted by Hamblin (1958). He studied 24 groups, twelve of whom experienced a "crisis" that took the form of changing previous rules and creating a condition of sharp ambiguity about correct procedures. The effect of this crisis was to alter drastically the prospect of being successful on a task involving a modified shuffleboard game. Leadership in both the crisis and control groups was measured by an "influence ratio" for each individual which represents the number of suggestions made by that member as against the average of other group members. A high influence ratio is associated with leadership.

Hamblin found that the leader maintained a relatively consistent influence ratio in the crisis situation. Figure 15.4 shows the mean influence ratios for the leaders of crisis and control groups. In the condition of crisis, the leaders were more likely to retain high influence across trials than for the control condition. But under crisis conditions several groups replaced their leaders if they did not have an apparent solution to the problem posed by the crisis.

The suggestion that the leader's perceptiveness has a bearing on his functional effectiveness has come from several lines of research. Chowdhry and Newcomb (1952) found that leaders were significantly better in judging the attitudes of group members than non-leaders, particularly on matters of relevance to the group. They interpreted these results to indicate that an important factor in the achievement of leadership status was the ability to assess others accurately. Earlier, Hites and Campbell (1950) had obtained equivocal findings with similar groups. In discussing this disparity, Campbell (1955) suggests that such "accuracy" may be more apparent than real. This would be so, he says, if an individual uses his own attitudes as an anchor for judging group attitudes, as is suggested by the work of Hovland and Sherif (1952). Where the leader has shaped group attitudes, his judgments of them would seem more accurate (Talland, 1954). However, there remains a body of findings supporting the view that the emergent leader, in particular, is more likely to be attuned to the needs of the group.

Bell and Hall (1954), for example, found a significant correlation between leadership standing in a leaderless group discussion situation and scores obtained on tests of empathy. Showel (1960) found that rated leadership potential in military units correlated significantly with interpersonal knowledge, even after the effect of general intelligence had been taken into account. Research by Exline (1960) indicated that such accuracy of perception was significantly affected by group cohesiveness; in his study, only in cohesive groups was the leader a more accurate judge of opinion.

A major line of work by Fiedler (1961) is based on the view that perceptiveness is a characteristic which differentiates the effective from the ineffective leader. In his work, he made initial use of a measure called "assumed similarity between opposites" (ASo). The ASo score is obtained by asking subjects to describe their most preferred co-worker by filling out a form which has approximately 20 semantic differential items, each of which consists of a personality adjective and its opposite, e.g. friendly–unfriendly, co-operative–unco-operative, etc. After he rates his most preferred co-worker, the subject follows a similar procedure for his least preferred co-worker. The score yielded by this procedure appears to measure a stable quality of interpersonal perception and has been found to be quite reliable (Fiedler, 1958). The ASo score may be interpreted to be a measure of the perceived similarity between co-workers in that a high score indicates that the subject sees these co-workers as essentially the same.

In his review of these studies, Fiedler (1958) reports a consistent relationship between this score and group productivity across a variety of task situations. Research on basketball teams, student surveying teams, and small military combat units have all shown, in general, that leaders of effective groups perceive little similarity between their most and least preferred co-workers. Fiedler does not consider these findings to be in conflict with current situational conceptions of leadership. He argues that leader effectiveness may depend upon a number of other factors such as the skill of the group members, the nature of the task, and the social context within which the group operates. Furthermore, these factors may influence to a considerable degree who is to become a leader and determine the course of his behavior once he has assumed that position.

More recently, Fiedler has modified his ASo measure in terms of a score based on the favorability of the leader's rating of his "least preferred co-worker" (LPC). It is the major component of the earlier ASo measure. A person with a *high* LPC score describes his least preferred co-worker in a relatively favorable manner. He tends to be permissive, human relations oriented, and considerate of the feelings of his men. A person with a *low* LPC score describes his least preferred co-worker in an unfavorable manner. He tends to be managing, task-controlling, and less concerned with human relations aspects of the job.

Generally, Fiedler finds (1964, 1965, 1967) support for his "contingency model" which predicts differential levels of effectiveness for combinations of situational and leader characteristics. Thus, he reports consistent evidence for a positive relationship between leader LPC and group creativity under pleasant and relaxed group conditions and a negative relationship when the group operated under an unpleasant, stressful group climate. More particularly, he also obtains significant relationships between this LPC measure and three situational factors: the quality of leader-member relations, the degree of task structure, and the leader's power. Depending upon the combination of these elements with the leader's permissiveness measured by LPC, Fiedler indicates that pronounced variations in the productivity of groups occurs. From this work we may now move to several issues regarding organizational leadership.

Organizational leadership

Organizational leadership is a large field of study in its own right, with a considerable literature on executive performance, management, and supervision. The intent here is to suggest some of its distinctive social psychological features, drawing upon points discussed earlier in this chapter.

To begin with, organizational leadership quite obviously is predicated on the formal structure imposed by authority. Except in extreme instances of power, however, such authority is not sufficient to insure loyalty and ready acceptance of influence. Work groups in all kinds of organizational settings are likely to generate informal structures which accord some authority to emergent leaders. This need not be a source of conflict with imposed authority, but smoothly functioning relationships require that this "structure" and its functions be recognized by the organizational leader for him to be fully effective.

Any organization operates in terms of two patterns of relationship. First, each person has his designated place and function within the organizational whole, represented by the imposed structure. There is also a highly important informal or emergent structure established within the groupings into which people are placed to carry out their function.

The work group, as was pointed out in Chapter 12, has a considerable effect on individual satisfactions. Likert (1956) reports that favorableness toward the work group is associated with lower absence rates, better interpersonal relationships, more favorable attitudes toward the job and company, and higher production goals. Thus, people at work find an opportunity to secure more than financial remuneration there. The work setting represents the potential for social rewards in terms of affiliations yielding recognition and participation.

SUPERVISORY STYLE

Among many possibilities, the organizational leader may be an executive decision-maker, or a sales manager, or a first-line supervisor. Whatever his position, he affects the leadership climate. A significant aspect of that climate for workers is what we have called "structure," in such particulars as these: knowing what is expected and having some feedback on how one is doing; consistent treatment in supporting the right and correcting the wrong; and, indicating changes that may affect personal welfare.

One reality to which Likert (1961) has called attention is that supervisors frequently emulate the kind of leadership style that they experience. It is often an organizational characteristic to be "employee-centered" or "job-centered" in supervision. These are not antithetical, but are more in the nature of emphases. However, this distinction is evidently meaningful in terms of morale. Likert reports in this regard that high morale groups more frequently describe their supervisor's activities by indicating his interest in the well-being of the employees through such acts as recommending promotions, transfers, pay increases, and informing men of what is happening in the company, keeping them posted on how well they are doing, and paying heed to complaints and grievances.

General supervision and close supervision have also been studied as another feature of supervisory style. Kahn and Katz (1960) report from a survey of many industrial studies that high producing units are more usually found to have general rather than close supervision. Results illustrating this finding are shown in Table 15.2 for sections of office

Table 15.2: Relation of closeness of supervision to section productivity in insurance companies. Twelve sections each are represented in the high and low categories. (Based on Table 41.5, p. 559, from Kahn and Katz in *Group Dynamics*, edited by D. C. Cartwright and A. Zander. Harper & Row, 1960.)

	CLOSE SUPERVISION	GENERAL SUPERVISION	NOT ASCERTAINED	
High producing sections	50%	42%	8%	100%
Low producing sections	92%	8%	0%	100%

workers in an insurance company. The data on supervision were obtained from the section heads themselves. As will be seen, close supervision is associated with low production. Kahn and Katz observe further that:

Close supervision often is employed as an institutional device for insuring that workers follow their job assignments correctly and assiduously. But this very practice also has negative morale and motivation implications. . . . In [a] tractor company studied, workers who perceived their foremen as supervising them less closely were better satisfied with their jobs and with the company (p. 560).

A mistaken conception which could be drawn from findings such as these is that the supervisor's function in providing a structure should be downgraded. Apart from the absolute merits of any given structure, it seems clear that it is necessary to the fulfillment of stable relationships and a sense of continuity and wholeness. In short, some supervision is essential to secure stability of expectation for the people in an organization. However, there is a balance needed in the kinds of factors which comprise organizational leadership. We will now consider some of these in greater detail.

CONSIDERATION AND INITIATING STRUCTURE

In a large-scale study of organizational leadership, Halpin and Winer (1952) analyzed a great number of ratings of leader characteristics from which they extracted several factors. In order, the two major ones were:

1. *Consideration,* representing the degree to which the leader manifests warmth in personal relationships, trust, readiness to explain actions and listen to subordinates.
2. *Initiating structure,* comprising the extent to which the leader maintains standards of performance and follows routines, makes sure his position and functions are understood, and distributes tasks.

A number of studies (e.g. Fleishman, Harris, and Burtt, 1955; Hemphill, 1955) reveal these as two dimensions of considerable weight in leader performance. Halpin (1955), for example, showed that supervisory leaders in two different roles, i.e. school administrators and command pilots on airplanes, differed on these dimensions. The administrators were more likely to show consideration than initiation of structure, and for the pilots it was the reverse.

As these results suggest, it is far too simple to say merely that these two factors are both related to leadership without specifying further some of the situational conditions which are present. Furthermore, it would be a mistake to see these factors as representing two "kinds" of leadership. As Fleishman and Peters (1961) point out, these factors may be combined in various ways together to yield various leadership practices.

An industrial study by Fleishman and Harris (1962) shows something of the complexity of the relationship between these factors in determining the rate of grievances. They separated sections into those of low, medium, or high consideration, and then further subdivided them by three levels of structure. Their results for these nine kinds of units are shown in Figure 15.5. In determining the dissatisfactions represented there, consideration appears to have a clear priority. If a foreman is low in consideration, his initiation of structure makes no discernible difference in the group's rate of grievances. On the other hand, a foreman who is characterized by high consideration can initiate high structure with only a small increase in employee dissatisfaction, though

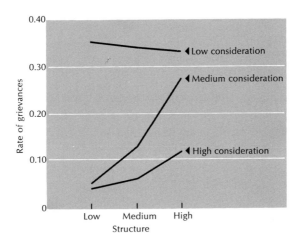

Figure 15.5: Relationship of consideration and group structure to rate of grievances. (From Fleishman and Harris, 1962.)

attention to productivity is needed to round out the picture. It is appropriate now to turn to a consideration of effective leadership.

Some features of effective leadership

While there may not be universal traits possessed by all leaders, it is possible to speak of requirements for "effective leadership." Within organizational settings, for example, various programs of selection and training are employed with precisely that end in mind. There are no absolutes in this matter, but it is quite possible to present some generalizations about effectiveness.

By and large, effective leadership may best be considered as an influence process in which the leader is able to muster willing group support to achieve certain clearly specified goals with best advantage to the individuals comprising the group. Furthermore, it is a group-oriented conception rather than one based largely on whether the leader gets what he desires for himself. An everpresent problem is that power has a great appeal for many people, including those of great charm, who may nevertheless be inadequately prepared to wield it effectively and share it with others. On this point, Cartwright and Zander (1968) have recently commented:

> It is possible for a "power grabber" to help a group achieve its goals and maintain itself. It is also possible, however, that when an individual's major motivation is the possession of power, his behavior will serve mainly his own needs without contributing to the group's locomotion or maintenance . . . (p. 311).

This conception of effective leadership can be seen to have applicability independent of the *source* of the leader's authority. The operation of a group in terms of its movement toward a goal rests on characteristics which go beyond that distinction alone.

In the preceding discussion here, a number of factors were noted which are associated with how the leader is reacted to by followers. Among these are his competence, his fulfillment of certain group expectancies for structure and action, his perceived motivation, and his adaptability to changing requirements of the situation. It should be noted that these are not fixed attributes residing in the leader himself so much as they are relevant perceptions of the leadership role and its requirements. In this respect, the role of leadership places its occupant in a highly visible position. The leader, as a high status person, is assumed to be more responsible for the actions that he displays and these actions are more likely to affect important outcomes for the members of the group. Thus, Thibaut and Riecken (1955) have demonstrated that high status is perceived to carry a greater initiative for action, and this is especially consequential where that status is bound up with the high centrality of the leadership role.

Earlier, in connection with the discussion of idiosyncrasy credit, it was observed that the leader's apparent nonconformity may be more readily tolerated by members of his group. We may now add that this probably occurs because the leader's actions are more likely to be interpreted in terms of positive outcomes. Here we observe a kind of cognitive balancing (see Chapter 7, p. 282) such that the actions of the highly regarded leader are more likely to be perceived in an equally positive way. Nonetheless, the performance of the leader is inevitably tested against a sequence of outcomes in terms of his perceived competence.

An important attribute of effective leadership, as we have stressed repeatedly, is the ability to provide a useful resource in the group's achievement of its goals. This process comes under the general heading of competence. The term does not necessarily mean some superior ability or skill on a task as such. In a highly sociable setting, for example, it may be that having a good sense of humor is what matters in terms of competence. In short, the leadership role demands functional value for the group, but this may encompass a wide variety of attributes required in the situation.

Furthermore, what may be a significant function for a group at one time may no longer be important at another. Indeed, the very act of attaining a major goal may reorient the group's activity. Accordingly, there may be redefinitions of what is required of leadership. Thus, former leadership may be deposed because of its inability to meet new demands, as Hamblin (1958) found in his study of crises, noted above. Therefore, factors which may have influenced an individual's attainment of leadership may no longer be adequate to his retention of the leadership role.

Another feature of effective leadership is to provide mechanisms for communication and participation within the group. Several ends of effective leadership are served by facilitating an exchange of information. Because groups may face new situations which require innovation, the generation of ideas or approaches is highly desirable. Furthermore, the involvement of group members in matters which affect them directly is essential if their commitment to the group's activities is to be maintained.

Effective leadership also necessarily depends upon the personality characteristics of the person in the leadership role, especially in terms of his adjustment. From his review of leadership studies, Mann (1959) concludes:

> While no single measure of adjustment can be expected to be an efficient predictor of leadership, there is strong evidence to indicate a positive relationship between an individual's adjustment and the leadership status he is likely to attain (p. 249).

One example of the importance of adjustment lies in our earlier consideration of the necessity for restraint in the use of power. In effective leadership, this is evidenced by emotional balance and predictability rather than impulsivity in the leader's actions. In most social relationships, confirmation of expectancies provides the benefit of continuity (see Watts, 1968). This is especially important, as one illustration, in terms of the distribution of rewards. Since the leader has a great deal of visibility, his actions toward others are interpreted as signifying the "goodness" or "badness" of the performance of others. Thus, by rewarding actions which are in the interest of the group and avoiding rewards for those which are not, the leader secures respect for his fairness. This is not so much a matter of gaining favor as it is a way of providing a better basis for effective leadership.

In sum, the main point of effective leadership as an influence process is that it evokes a positive response from followers, in line with the group's central activity. In the transactional view, leadership effectiveness depends upon a fair exchange with the leader securing status and exercising influence while helping the group to achieve desired outcomes. But goal attainment by itself is not a sufficient condition for effective leadership unless it is accompanied by social rewards to the individual, illustrated by recognition. A significant function of effective leadership, therefore, is to provide for meaningful social participation among the members of a group.

Finally, a pervasive quality which determines the effectiveness of leadership is its perceived identification with the group. Leaders are expected to display loyalty to the collective needs and aspirations of their group. One of the ways this shows itself, concretely, is in *advocacy*. By this we refer to the expectation that the leader will communicate his group's desires to other groups, and to higher authority, in order to facilitate goal attainment. In one study by Pelz (1952), for example, it was found with industrial workers that the ability to deal with upper echelons was rated even higher than human relations skills in evaluating their foremen. In many other settings as well, the effectiveness of leadership depends upon external dealings in the group's behalf. We will now consider this with particular reference to intergroup relations.

Advocacy and negotiation

The discussion here has sought to draw out some of the implications of influence for effective leadership. If we consider the leader as an influence agent, what he seems to be and how he stands on issues lends substance to the acceptance of his credibility as a source of influence. Indeed, competent leadership can be thought of as an analogue to credibility (see Chapter 6, p. 223).

The leader as an influence source communicates to followers not only verbally but by his actions. He increases his credibility by taking actions which make apparent his identification with things, including the group itself, valued by the followers. This is a pivotal feature of the transactional quality of leader-follower relations. For example, in a study by Kirkhart (1963) of leadership among black college students, identification with the minority group was an understandably strong element in the followers' expectations. Those black students selected by their peers for leader roles in their own group, and external groups, were found to score well above average on a questionnaire measure of black identification. Some time ago, Brown (1936) made the general observation that a highly desired quality in the leader was a sense that he shared "membership character" with followers, in terms of being "one of us." Clearly, though, the relevant dimension can be very narrow ("my kinfolk") or very wide ("my fellow human"). Advocacy and negotiation functions in leadership often involve the capacity to bridge the interests of two groups within the framework of a superordinate goal from which both benefit.

As was observed earlier, inter-group relations are often shaped by the expectations which leaders establish (see Chapter 13, p. 540). The utterances of leaders may have the effect of signifying their loyalty to group goals, but at the same time they may increase the level of conflict in inter-group relations. What is particularly important to recognize is the requirement for a balance between such manifestations of identification with one's group and the willingness to undertake co-operation with other groups when it is necessary. In such situations of inter-group negotiation, Sherif (1962) observes:

> Leaders, delegates, and representatives of the groups must remain part of the power structure of the group if their actions are to be effective. The significance of the power structure for assessing the behavior of individuals in such positions is immediately seen when their actions deviate widely from the expectations of the membership (p. 17).

The solution to this dilemma rests in the fact that leaders themselves help to establish these expectations, and are not merely their creatures. As influence agents, they are in a position to define the situation for the members of a group and to set realistic goals for potential achievement. Again, this occurs within a context of the positive perception of the leader as a trusted advocate holding high status. In the absence of such status, the leader is highly vulnerable to rejection by the group, if he appears to violate its interests. In any case, as Blake and Mouton (1961c) have found, a representative who is tied to entrenched group commitments is unable to undertake productive negotiation.

The advocacy function of leadership is therefore delicate and can produce effects in several directions. By his utterances, the leader may initially bolster his status in the group and increase a sense of morale, but also heighten the level of conflict and limit the alternatives available to him. While it is considered to be something of a canon of diplomacy that avenues be kept available to other courses of action, it is often the case that leaders do not heed the implications of this injunction in their statements.

Once the need for negotiation is granted, incendiary language damages its long-range as well as its short-range prospects. A union leader who goes into negotiations with management having told his members that "We can't accept any of their proposals," reduces the likelihood that his members will accept whatever he is able to secure from such negotiations. Furthermore, the expectations shaped by the leader's statements may have the quite unintended effect of reducing his range of influence at a later point. Much of this follows from the kind of psychological formulations which we previously noted. Thus, to publicly characterize proposals from another nation as "Just the same old devious devices," is to insure greater difficulty in the acceptance of any subsequent proposals, even when they are in fact in line with the desires and needs of the former nation.

The generation of an unalloyed hostility toward an adversary group may make it appear that any accommodation with it represents a "sell-out." The implications of this for productive negotiation must be carefully understood. As Sherif (1958) points out, it does little good to attempt discussions in an atmosphere of hostility and recrimination. It is essential to recognize that the atmosphere itself is created in great part by what leaders say and do. An example of public utterances likely to open the way for later acceptance of the outcome of negotiation, is this passage from an address by President Kennedy:

> It is a test of our national maturity to accept the fact that negotiations are not a contest spelling victory or defeat. They may succeed, they may fail. But they are likely to be successful only if both sides reach an agreement which both regard as preferable to the *status quo,* an agreement in which each side can consider that its own situation has been improved (1961).

Some pertinent research on the leader's advocacy function was recently undertaken by Julian, Hollander, and Regula (1967). In this experiment, the effects of three variables were studied: the leader's source of authority, in either election or appointment; his perceived competence at the outset of the task; and his subsequent success or failure in representing the group. The main dependent variable was the continued willingness by the group to have the leader serve as its spokesman.

The procedure was to have thirty-four, four-man discussion groups, made up of male undergraduate students, consider a case of a fellow student accused of cheating. After a short discussion the group was to send their spokesman before a "board of inquiry" which was investigating this case. The spokesman's task was to convey the attitudes and arguments of the group to the board in order to persuade it of the friend's innocence.

By a set of manipulations, it was possible to create a design with leaders who were either appointed or elected under conditions of "high" or "low" competence, and with eventual "success" or "failure." In the high competence condition the spokesman was the most frequent contributor to the discussion, and in the low competence he was the one who participated next to lowest. Source of authority was determined by either appointment by the experimenter or a mock election. After the spokesman's departure various ratings were made of his contribution, and the group awaited a report of whether he had been successful or not in his activities before the board.

The findings of this experiment indicated that the perception of the spokesman's task competence *or* his subsequent success led to greater endorsement by group members. Most striking, however, was the complex statistical interaction which prevailed between election or appointment, competence, and success or failure. In determining the favorability of members' reactions to retaining the spokesman, this pattern indicated that election created a situation of greater vulnerability for the *elected* spokesman where he was *either* seen as *not* highly competent initially or his efforts yielded an unsuccessful outcome. On the other hand, the appointed spokesman was much less vulnerable to withdrawal of support if he was either seen as highly competent initially *or* he produced a successful outcome. One implication of this experiment is that group members have a greater stake, in the sense of involvement, with someone to whom they themselves have accorded status. It is also possible, however, that the appointment of a spokesman by the experimenter might have been seen as a demand to retain the same person in that position.

From the research of Hollander, Julian, and Sorrentino (1969), noted earlier here (p. 603), we know that elected leaders, under the conditions studied, were more likely to deviate from the group's positions. Therefore, on the one hand, elected leaders may be more assertive, but on the other hand, may be more vulnerable to censure and withdrawal of support. All of which suggests, at the very least, a delicate balance.

Where a leader's credits are on the wane, he may be inclined to adopt a hardened position in negotiation. He might find it expedient to define an inter-group situation as one of greater conflict to bolster his standing with his constituents. Under conditions of implied threat to his status, the leader might also begin to espouse a cause which is attractive to his group, though it may not serve as an adequate program for action in the group's relations with the external system. This is a feature of demagoguery, insofar as the appeals are not to take up reasoned programs but to engender "in-group" vs. "out-group" feelings.

This prospect dramatizes how the leader's overconcern with retaining his own status may inhibit him from using the credits at his disposal to lead in new directions, when required. In speaking of leaders who have "vision," we mean in large measure the ability to see how present policies can yield beneficial effects in the future. Imaginative ideas are not the special province of leaders, but recognizing and using such ideas effectively is. Those who hold the reins of authority are necessarily agents of influence and of social change. Whether by accident or design what they say and do creates expectations through which the future is molded. It is not too much to hope that there will be a design, and that the vision will be one of promise.

SUMMARY

The modern view of leadership in social psychology emphasizes its variable nature. Depending upon the group, its activity and its situation, different leader attributes are called forth. Therefore, the role of leader can be filled by various group members who at the time can direct group resources toward the attainment of group goals.

The study of leadership requires attention to the *leader,* the *followers,* and the *situation* in which they interact. Their processes of interaction constitute *leadership* in the broad sense of an influence relationship in groups. A *leader* is someone whose role permits him to exercise leadership. His interaction can be seen as representing a *transaction* between himself and others in the group. By providing them with useful resources, the leader gets in return a greater degree of influence and esteem.

In the history of concern about leadership, the first and most dominant focus was upon the *traits* of the leader. Because of the irregular pattern of leader traits found across situations, this older view gave way to a focus on the demands of *situations* in which leadership occurred. This newer, situational approach stresses the various functions to be performed by those occupying a leadership role rather than stable characteristics of leaders. The situational approach also sees the follower as having an active role in leadership processes.

A major distinction in characterizing leadership is its source, specified by the terms *emergent* leadership and *appointed* leadership. The first is determined by some mode of group consent, the second by an external authority. The identification of emergent leaders is often accomplished by sociometric techniques. While the early use of this procedure left the impression that choices for leader and for friend were highly related, the stability of this relationship very much depends upon the situation. A differentiation is often found between liking certain group members and recognizing those who contribute in a leadership sense.

Leaders can also be identified as those who are highly influential in the group's operations. One way of conceiving this is with regard to *initiating structure*. In these terms, the leader is a member who contributes most to the pattern of interaction and locomotion within the group. Relatedly, the leader can be seen as the *completer* of essential group functions in that he helps the group to attain its goals by balancing off various factors in an harmonious fashion. Still another way to consider the leader's influence is to look at his potential for *innovation* through actions which would be viewed as nonconforming were others to take them. This is a function of the *idiosyncrasy credits* at his disposal, as a feature of his accorded status.

In some sense, the role of leader involves a power component which often depends on the *legitimacy* of the leader's position. Power can arise from various factors in the relationship between the leader as an agent of influence and the followers who are recipients of that influence. Thus, the basis for legitimate power in an organizational setting rests in the mutual acceptance of norms requiring one person to do the bidding of another. Power, influence, and innovation are not totally separate processes, but rather are interrelated facets of leadership.

A considerable volume of experimentation reveals that whoever emerges as a leader, from one situation to another, depends upon the nature and comparability of the tasks presented to the group. Personality attributes of the leader, such as ascendance, have been found to be consistently related to leadership emergence, especially where the tasks are largely uniform. However, the *structure of the situation* can considerably reduce the effect of personality differences. Furthermore, both the quality of group performance and member satisfactions are bound up with the relationship of the leader's personality to the requirements of the group's structure.

In many different group settings, leaders have higher rates of participation and activity. This is particularly true in discussion groups where verbal output has been found to be highly related to leadership. The rate of participation has also been shown to be affected by the rewards made available by the other participants or by the group's successes. Therefore, the resources of the leader may be variably elicited depending upon the group's needs and the rewards it accordingly provides.

Several lines of study have pointed to *perceptiveness* as a factor in leadership. The leader's functioning is facilitated by his being attuned to the other group members and the situation confronting them. The importance of perceptiveness appears to be considerably altered, however, by other conditions such as the group's cohesiveness. In any case, the leader's perceptiveness does have relevance as a feature differentiating effective from ineffective leadership.

Organizational leadership is imposed by authority. It is part of the *formal structure* which requires certain functions to be fulfilled by the appointed leader. These functions may vary from those of the first-line supervisor in a direct interpersonal relationship with many subordinates to those of an executive planner involved mainly in decision-making without much contact of that kind. Supervision is most representative of the appointed mode of leadership. Its *style* can be characterized as mainly *employee-centered* or *job-centered*. Another component of supervisory style is *general* or *close* supervision. These emphases, in various combinations, may stamp the interactions within an organization in a distinctive way.

From analyses of ratings made on supervision in organizations, two factors which are revealed to have major importance are *consideration* and *initiating structure*. The first relates to warmth in interpersonal relationships, and the second to such task elements as setting standards of performance and distributing assignments. Both are evidently involved in the supervisor's role across most situations. Consideration is important as a basic condition which engenders a greater willingness to accept the supervisor's direction without various kinds of resistance. In the absence of consideration, such resistance may reveal itself in grievances and absenteeism, in addition to lowered performance.

Essentially *effective leadership* can be viewed as an influence process in which the leader achieves willing group support in the attainment of group goals. The general features of effective leadership are not attributes of the leader so much as they are expectancies held of the role of leader and its requirements. Among those features are evidences of: *competence,* in terms of providing a contribution to the group's goals; *identification* with the group and its aspirations; provision for *communication* and *participation* by group members as a routine of group functioning; *adjustment,* with regard to stability and an awareness of the needs of others, particularly in providing rewards. Therefore, effective leadership yields an equitable transaction, not just in terms of helping the group attain its goals, but also by providing social rewards along the way such as a sense of participation and recognition.

A potent feature of leadership is in the *advocacy function* as a representative of the group in external relations with other groups or with higher authority. Advocacy is particularly critical where open conflict exists in inter-group relations. The person in this leadership position is required to show loyalty to his group's interests while opening the prospects for favorable dealings with the adversary group. Where negotiation is necessary, his statements designed to manifest loyalty to the group's position may make it harder for the group to accept the outcome of negotiation later. Thus the leader's influence may be reduced by failure to maintain the balance which shapes the group's expectations toward a position favoring reduction of tension. In inter-group dealings, co-operative strategies tend to encourage the development of mutual trust and the achievement of goals that benefit both parties.

SUGGESTED READINGS

From E. P. Hollander and R. G. Hunt (Eds.) *Current perspectives in social psychology.* (3rd ed.) New York: Oxford University Press, 1971.

Introduction to Section VIII: *Leadership, power, and change*
49. Edwin P. Hollander: *Leadership, innovation, and influence: an overview*
50. Alex Bavelas: *Leadership: man and function*
51. Fred E. Fiedler: *Styles of leadership*
52. Edwin P. Hollander and James W. Julian: *Contemporary trends in the analysis of leadership processes*
53. John R. P. French, Jr. and Bertram H. Raven: *The bases of power*
54. Marvin E. Olsen: *The process of social power*

Introduction to Section IX: *Organizational processes*
56. William G. Scott: *Organization theory: an overview and an appraisal*

SELECTED REFERENCES

Browne, C. G., & Cohn, T. S. (Eds.) *The study of leadership.* Danville, Ill.: Interstate Printers & Publishers, 1958.

Fiedler, F. E. *A theory of leadership effectiveness.* New York: McGraw-Hill, 1967.

*Gibb, C. A. (Ed.) *Leadership: selected readings.* Baltimore, Md.: Penguin Books, 1969.

Gouldner, A. W. (Ed.) *Studies in leadership.* New York: Harper, 1950.

Guetzkow, H. (Ed.) *Groups, leadership, and men.* Pittsburgh: Carnegie Press, 1951.

Haiman, F. S. *Group leadership and democratic action.* Boston: Houghton Mifflin, 1951.

Hollander, E. P. *Leaders, groups, and influence.* New York: Oxford Univer. Press, 1964.

*McGregor, D. *Leadership and motivation.* Cambridge, Mass.: MIT Press, 1966.

Petrullo, L., & Bass, B. M. (Eds.) *Leadership and interpersonal behavior.* New York: Holt, Rinehart & Winston, 1961.

Sherif, M. (Ed.) *Intergroup relations and leadership.* New York: Wiley, 1962.

Verba, S. *Small groups and political behavior: a study of leadership.* Princeton, N. J.: Princeton Univer. Press, 1961.

Bibliography

Note: Some of the common abbreviations of journal titles used here are these:

Amer. J. Sociol. = *American Journal of Sociology*
Amer. sociol. Rev. = *American Sociological Review*
Behav. Sci. = *Behavioral Science*
Hum. Relat. = *Human Relations*
J. abnorm. soc. Psychol. = *Journal of Abnormal and Social Psychology*
J. Confl. Resolut. = *Journal of Conflict Resolution*
J. exp. soc. Psychol. = *Journal of Experimental Social Psychology*
J. Pers. = *Journal of Personality*
J. Pers. soc. Psychol. = *Journal of Personality and Social Psychology*
J. soc. Issues = *Journal of Social Issues*
J. soc. Psychol. = *Journal of Social Psychology*
Psychol. Bull. = *Psychological Bulletin*
Psychol. Rev. = *Psychological Review*

Abelson, R. P., & Rosenberg, M. J. Symbolic psycho-logic: a model of attitudinal cognition. *Behav. Sci.*, 1958, 3, 1-13.

Abelson, R. P., Aronson, E., McGuire, W. J., Newcomb, T. M., Rosenberg, M. J., & Tannenbaum, P. H. (Eds.) *Theories of cognitive consistency: a source book.* Chicago: Rand McNally, 1968.

Adams, J. S. Inequity in social exchange. In L. Berkowitz (Ed.), *Advances in experimental social psychology.* Vol. 2. New York: Academic Press, 1965. Pp. 267-299.

Adorno, T. W., Frenkel-Brunswik, E., Levinson, D. J., & Sanford, R. N. *The authoritarian personality.* New York: Harper, 1950.

Allen, F. L. *Only yesterday.* New York: Harper & Bros., 1931. (Also published as a Bantam Book, New York, 1959.)

Allison, J., & Hunt, D. E. Social desirability and the expression of aggression under varying conditions of frustration. *J. consult. Psychol.,* 1959, *23,* 528-532.

Allport, F. H. The influence of the group upon association and thought. *J. exp. Psychol.,* 1920, *3,* 159-182.

Allport, F. H. *Social psychology.* Boston: Houghton Mifflin, 1924.

Allport, F. H. The J-curve hypothesis of conforming behavior. *J. soc. Psychol.,* 1934, *5,* 141-183.

Allport, F. H. *Theories of perception and the concept of structure.* New York: Wiley, 1955.

Allport, G. W. *Personality: a psychological interpretation.* New York: Holt, 1937.

Allport, G. W. *The nature of prejudice.* Reading, Mass.: Addison-Wesley, 1954. (Paperback edition by Doubleday Anchor, 1958.)

Allport, G. W. *Becoming.* New Haven: Yale Univer. Press, 1955.

Allport, G. W. The open system in personality theory. *J. abnorm. soc. Psychol.,* 1960a, *61,* 301-311.

Allport, G. W. *Personality and social encounter.* Boston: Beacon Press, 1960b.

Allport, G. W. Traits revisited. *Amer. Psychologist,* 1966, *21,* 1-10.

Allport, G. W., & Pettigrew, T. F. Cultural influence on the perception of movement: the trapezoidal illusion among Zulus. *J. abnorm. soc. Psychol.,* 1957, *55,* 104-113.

Allport, G. W., & Postman, L. J. *The psychology of rumor.* New York: Henry Holt, 1943.

Allport, G. W., Vernon, P. E., & Lindzey, G. *Study of values.* Boston: Houghton Mifflin, 1951.

Allyn, J., & Festinger, L. The effectiveness of unanticipated persuasive communication. *J. abnorm. soc. Psychol.,* 1961, *62,* 35-40.

Altman, I., & Haythorn, W. W. Interpersonal exchange in isolation. *Sociometry,* 1965, *28,* 411-426.

Altman, I., & McGinnies, E. Interpersonal perception and communication in discussion groups of varied attitudinal composition. *J. abnorm. soc. Psychol.,* 1960, *60,* 390-395.

Altrocchi, J. Dominance as a factor in interpersonal choice and perception. *J. abnorm. soc. Psychol.,* 1959, *59,* 303-307.

Alvarez, R. Informal reactions to deviance in simulated work organizations: a laboratory experiment. *Amer. sociol. Rev.,* 1968, *33,* 895-912.

Ames, A., Jr. Visual perception and the rotating trapezoid window. *Psychol. Monogr.,* 1951, *65,* No. 7.

Anderson, L. R., & Fiedler, F. E. The effect of participatory and supervisory leadership on group creativity. *J. Appl. Psychol.,* 1964, *48,* 227-236.

Ardrey, R. *African genesis.* New York: Atheneum, 1961.

Ardrey, R. *The territorial imperative.* New York: Atheneum, 1966.

Argyle, M. Social pressure in public and private situations. *J. abnorm. soc. Psychol.*, 1957, *54*, 172-175.

Argyle, M. *The psychology of interpersonal behaviour.* Baltimore: Penguin Books, 1967a.

Argyle, M. The social psychology of social change. In T. Burns & S. B. Saul (Eds.), *Social theory and economic change.* London: Tavistock Publications, 1967b. Pp. 87-101.

Argyle, M., & Dean, J. Eye-contact, distance and affiliation. *Sociometry*, 1965, *28*, 289-304.

Aronfreed, J. *Conduct and conscience.* New York: Academic Press, 1968.

Aronson, E. The psychology of insufficient justification: an analysis of some conflicting data. In S. Feldman (Ed.), *Cognitive consistency.* New York: Academic Press, 1966. Pp. 115-133.

Aronson, E. Dissonance theory: progress and problems. In R. P. Abelson *et al.* (Eds.), *Theories of cognitive consistency: a sourcebook.* Chicago: Rand McNally, 1968. Pp. 5-27.

Aronson, E. The theory of cognitive dissonance: a current perspective. In L. Berkowitz (Ed.), *Advances in experimental social psychology.* Vol. 4. New York: Academic Press, 1969. Pp. 1-34.

Aronson, E., & Linder, D. Gain and loss of esteem as determinants of interpersonal attractiveness. *J. exper. soc. Psychol.*, 1965, *1*, 156-171.

Aronson, E., Turner, J., & Carlsmith, J. M. Communicator credibility and communication discrepancy. *J. abnorm. soc. Psychol.*, 1963, *67*, 31-36.

Asch, S. E. Effects of group pressure upon the modification and distortion of judgments. In H. Guetzkow (Ed.), *Groups, leadership and men.* Pittsburgh: Carnegie Press, 1951.

Asch, S. E. *Social psychology.* New York: Prentice-Hall, 1952.

Asch, S. E. A perspective on social psychology. In S. Koch (Ed.), *Psychology: a study of a science.* Vol. 3. New York: McGraw-Hill, 1959. Pp. 363-384.

Atkinson, J. W. Motivational determinants of risk-taking behavior. *Psychol. Rev.*, 1957, *64*, 359-372.

Atkinson, J. W. *An introduction to motivation.* Princeton: Van Nostrand, 1964.

Atkinson, J. W., & Cartwright, D. Some neglected variables in contemporary conceptions of decision and performance. *Psychol. Reports*, 1964, *14*, 575-590.

Atkinson, J. W., & Reitman, W. R. Performance as a function of motive strength and expectancy of goal-attainment. *J. abnorm. soc. Psychol.*, 1956, *53*, 361-366.

Atthowe, J. M., Jr. Interpersonal decision-making: the resolution of a dyadic conflict. *J. abnorm. soc. Psychol.*, 1961, *62*, 114-119.

Austin, W. H. Grammar as a status symbol. *Quinto Lingo*, 1970, *8* (6), 45-47.

Azrin, N. H., & Lindsley, O. R. The reinforcement of cooperation between children. *J. abnorm. soc. Psychol.*, 1956, *52*, 100-102.

Bachrach, A. J., Candland, D. K., & Gibson, J. T. Group reinforcement of individual response experiments in verbal behavior. In I. A. Berg & B. M. Bass (Eds.), *Conformity and deviation.* New York: Harper, 1961. Pp. 258-285.

Back, K. W. Influence through social communication. *J. abnorm. soc. Psychol.*, 1951, *46*, 9-23.

Back, K. W., & Davis, K. E. Some personal and situational factors relevant to the consistency and prediction of conforming behavior. *Sociometry,* 1965, *28*, 227-240.

Back, K. W., Hood, T. C., & Brehm, M. L. The subject role in small group experiments. *Social Forces,* 1965, *43*, 181-187.

Bales, R. F. A set of categories for the analysis of small group interaction. *Amer. sociol. Rev.,* 1950a, *15*, 257-263.

Bales, R. F. *Interaction process analysis: a method for the study of small groups.* Reading, Mass.: Addison-Wesley, 1950b.

Bales, R. F. Some uniformities of behavior in small social systems. In G. E. Swanson, T. M. Newcomb, & E. L. Hartley (Eds.), *Readings in social psychology.* (2nd ed.) New York: Holt, 1952. Pp. 146-159.

Bales, R. F. The equilibrium problem in small groups. In A. P. Hare, E. F. Borgatta, & R. F. Bales (Eds.), *Small groups: studies in social interaction.* New York: Knopf, 1955. Pp. 424-463.

Bales, R. F. *Personality and interpersonal behavior.* New York: Holt, Rinehart & Winston, 1970.

Bales, R. F., & Borgatta, E. F. Size of group as a factor in the interaction profile. In A. P. Hare, E. F. Borgatta, & R. F. Bales (Eds.), *Small groups: studies in social interaction.* New York: Knopf, 1955. Pp. 396-413.

Bales, R. F., & Slater, P. E. Role differentiation in small decision-making groups. In T. Parsons *et al.* (Eds.), *Family, socialization, and interaction process.* Glencoe, Ill.: Free Press, 1955.

Bales, R. F., Strodtbeck, F. L., Mills, T. M., & Roseborough, M. E. Channels of communication in small groups. *Amer. sociol. Rev.,* 1951, *16*, 461-468.

Bandura, A. A case of no-trial learning. In L. Berkowitz (Ed.), *Advances in experimental social psychology.* Vol. 2. Academic Press: New York, 1965a. Pp. 1-55.

Bandura, A. Behavioral modifications through modeling procedures. In L. Krasner & L. P. Ullmann (Eds.), *Research in behavior modification.* New York: Holt, 1965b. Pp. 310-340.

Bandura, A. Influence of models' reinforcement contingencies on the acquisition of imitative responses. *J. Pers. soc. Psychol.,* 1965c, *1*, 589-595.

Bandura, A., & Walters, R. H. *Social learning and personality development.* New York: Holt, Rinehart, & Winston, 1963.

Banta, T. J., & Nelson, C. Experimental analysis of resource location in problem-solving groups. *Sociometry*, 1964, *27*, 488-501.

Barker, R. G. *Ecological psychology: concepts and methods for studying the environment of human behavior.* Stanford, Cal.: Stanford Univer. Press, 1968.

Barker, R. G., & Gump, P. V. *Big school, small school.* Stanford, Cal.: Stanford Univer. Press, 1964.

Barker, R. G., & Wright, H. F. *Midwest and its children: the psychological ecology of an American town.* Evanston, Ill.: Row, Peterson, 1954.

Barnard, C. I. *The functions of the executive.* Cambridge: Harvard Univer. Press, 1938.

Barnett, L. *The treasure of our tongue.* New York: New American Library Mentor Book, 1967.

Barnouw, V. *Culture and personality.* Homewood, Ill.: Dorsey Press, 1963.

Barocas, R., & Gorlow, R. Self-report personality measurement and conformity behavior. *J. soc. Psychol.*, 1967, *71*, 227-234.

Barron, F. Some personality correlates of independence of judgment. *J. Pers.*, 1953, *21*, 287-297.

Bass, B. M. An approach to the objective assessment of successful leadership. In B. M. Bass & I. A. Berg (Eds.), *Objective approaches to personality assessment.* New York: Van Nostrand, 1959.

Bass, B. M., McGehee, C. R., Hawkins, W. C., Young, P. C., & Gebel, A. S. Personality variables related to leaderless group discussion behavior. *J. abnorm. soc. Psychol.*, 1953, *48*, 120-128.

Bateson, N. Familiarization, group discussion, and risk taking. *J. exp. soc. Psychol.*, 1966, *2*, 119-129.

Bauer, R. A. The obstinate audience: the influence process from the point of view of social communication. *Amer. Psychologist*, 1964, *19*, 319-328.

Bauer, R. A. Detection and anticipation of impact: the nature of the task. In R. Bauer (Ed.), *Social indicators.* Cambridge, Mass.: MIT Press, 1966. Pp. 1-67.

Bavelas, A. Leadership: man and function. *Admin. Sci. Quart.*, 1960, *4*, 491-498.

Bavelas, A., Hastorf, A. H., Gross, A. E., & Kite, W. R. Experiments on the alteration of group structure. *J. exp. soc. Psychol.*, 1965, *1*, 55-70.

Bean, C. An unusual opportunity to investigate the psychology of language. *J. genet. Psychol.*, 1932, *40*, 181-202.

Becker, H. S. *Outsiders: studies in the sociology of deviance.* New York: Free Press, 1963.

Becker, H. S., Geer, B., Hughes, E. C., & Strauss, A. *Boys in white: student culture in medical school.* Chicago: Univer. of Chicago Press, 1961.

Beer, M., Buckhout, R., Horowitz, M. W., & Levy, S. Some perceived properties of the difference between leaders and non-leaders. *J. Psychol.*, 1959, *47*, 49-56.

Beez, W. V. Influence of biased psychological reports on teacher behavior and pupil performance. In M. B. Miles & W. W. Charters, Jr. (Eds.), *Learning in social settings.* Boston: Allyn & Bacon, 1970. Pp. 328-334.

Bell, G. B., & French, R. L. Consistency of individual leadership position in small groups of varying membership. *J. abnorm. soc. Psychol.,* 1950, 45, 764-767.

Bell, G. B., & Hall, H. E. The relationship between leadership and empathy. *J. abnorm. soc. Psychol.,* 1954, 49, 156-157.

Beloff, H. Two forms of social conformity: acquiescence and conventionality. *J. abnorm. soc. Psychol.,* 1958, 56, 99-103.

Bem, D. J. An experimental analysis of self-persuasion. *J. exp. soc. Psychol.,* 1965, 1, 199-218.

Bem, D. J. Self-perception: an alternative interpretation of cognitive dissonance phenomena. *Psychol. Rev.,* 1967, 74, 183-200.

Bem, D. J., & McConnell, H. K. Testing the self-perception explanation of dissonance phenomena: on the salience of premanipulation attitudes. *J. Pers. soc. Psychol.,* 1970, 14, 23-31.

Benedict, R. F. *Patterns of culture.* Boston: Houghton Mifflin, 1934. (Also published by Penguin Books, New York, 1946.)

Benedict, R. F. *The chrysanthemum and the sword: patterns of Japanese culture.* Boston: Houghton Mifflin, 1946.

Bennett, E. B. Discussion, decision, commitment and consensus in "group decision." *Hum. Relat.,* 1955, 8, 251-274.

Berelson, B. R., & Steiner, G. *Human behavior: an inventory of scientific findings.* New York: Harcourt, Brace & World, 1964.

Berelson, B. R., Lazarsfeld, P. F., & McPhee, W. N. *Voting: a study of opinion formation in a presidential campaign.* Chicago: Univer. of Chicago Press, 1954.

Berenda, R. W. *The influence of the group on the judgments of children.* New York: Kings Crown Press, 1950.

Berg, I. A., & Bass, B. M. (Eds.) *Conformity and deviation.* New York: Harper, 1961.

Berko, J. The child's learning of English morphology. *Word,* 1958, 14, 150-177.

Berkowitz, L. Group standards, cohesiveness, and productivity. *Hum. Relat.,* 1954, 7, 509-519.

Berkowitz, L. Personality and group position. *Sociometry,* 1956, 19, 210-222.

Berkowitz, L. Liking for the group and the perceived merit of the group's behavior. *J. abnorm. soc. Psychol.,* 1957, 54, 353-357.

Berkowitz, L. (Ed.) *Roots of aggression.* New York: Atherton, 1969a.

Berkowitz, L. Simple views of aggression. *American Scientist,* 1969b, 57, 372-383.

Berkowitz, L., & Connor, W. H. Success, failure, and social responsibility. *J. Pers. soc. Psychol.,* 1966, 4, 664-669.

Berkowitz, L., & Cottingham, D. R. The interest value and relevance of fear-arousing communications. *J. abnorm. soc. Psychol.,* 1960, 60, 37-43.

Berkowitz, L., & Daniels, L. R. Responsibility and dependency. *J. abnorm. soc. Psychol.*, 1963, *66*, 429-436.

Berkowitz, L., & Daniels, L. R. Affecting the salience of the social responsibility norm: effects of past help on the response to dependency relationships. *J. abnorm. soc. Psychol.*, 1964, *68*, 275-281.

Berkowitz L., & Friedman, P. Some social class differences in helping behavior. *J. Pers. soc. Psychol.*, 1967, *5*, 217-225.

Berkowitz, L., & Macaulay, J. R. Some effects of differences in status level and status stability. *Hum. Relat.*, 1961, *14*, 135-148.

Berlyne, D. E. *Conflict, arousal, and curiosity.* New York: McGraw-Hill, 1960.

Berlyne, D. E. Curiosity and explanation. *Science*, 1966, *153*, 25-33.

Berlyne, D. E. Arousal and reinforcement. In D. Levine (Ed.), *Nebraska symposium on motivation.* Lincoln: Univer. of Nebraska Press, 1967. Pp. 1-110.

Bernard, L. L. *Instinct: a study in social psychology.* New York: Holt, 1926.

Berne, E. *Games people play.* New York: Grove Press, 1964.

Bierstedt, R. An analysis of social power. *Amer. sociol. Rev.*, 1950, *15*, 730-738.

Blake, R. R., & Mouton, J. S. Conformity, resistance and conversion. In I. A. Berg & B. M. Bass (Eds.), *Conformity and deviation.* New York: Harper & Bros., 1961a. Pp. 1-37.

Blake, R. R., & Mouton, J. S. Comprehension of positions under intergroup competition. *J. Confl. Resolut.*, 1961b, *5*, 304-310.

Blake, R. R., & Mouton, J. S. Loyalty of representatives to ingroup positions during intergroup competition. *Sociometry*, 1961c, *24*, 177-184.

Blake, R. R., & Mouton, J. S. The intergroup dynamics of win-lose conflict and problem-solving collaboration in union-management relations. In M. Sherif (Ed.), *Intergroup relations and leadership.* New York: Wiley, 1962.

Blalock, H. M., & Blalock, A. B. *Methodology in social research.* New York: McGraw-Hill, 1968.

Blau, P. M. *Exchange and power in social life.* New York: Wiley, 1964.

Bleuler, M., & Bleuler, R. Rorschach Ink-blot Test and racial psychology; mental peculiarities of Morroccans. *Charact. & Pers.*, 1935, *4*, 97-114.

Blumer, H. Public opinion and public opinion polling. *Amer. sociol. Rev.*, 1948, *13*, 542-554.

Boas, F. *Anthropology in modern life.* New York: W. W. Norton, 1928.

Boden, M. McDougall revisited. *J. Pers.*, 1965, *33*, 1-19.

Bogardus, E. S. Measuring social distance. *J. appl. Sociol.*, 1925, *9*, 299-308.

Bohannan, P. The impact of money on an African subsistence economy. *J. econ. History*, 1959, *19*, 491-503.

Bond, J. R., & Vinacke, W. E. Coalitions in mixed-sex triads. *Sociometry*, 1961, *24*, 61-75.

Bonner, H. *Group dynamics.* New York: Ronald Press, 1959.

Borgatta, E. F., & Lambert, W. W. (Eds.) *Handbook of personality theory and research.* Chicago: Rand-McNally, 1968.

Borgatta, E. F., Cottrell, L. S., Jr., & Meyer, H. J. On the dimensions of group behavior. *Sociometry,* 1956, *19,* 223-240.

Borgatta, E. F., Couch, A. S., & Bales, R. F. Some findings relevant to the great man theory of leadership. *Amer. sociol. Rev.* 1954, *19,* 755-759.

Boring, E. G. When is human behavior predetermined? *Scientific Monthly,* 1957, *84,* 189-196.

Bossard, J. H. S. The law of family interaction. *Amer. J. Sociol.,* 1945, *50,* 292-294.

Bovard, E. W. The effects of social stimuli on the response to stress. *Psychol. Rev.,* 1959, *66,* 267-277.

Bowerman, C., & Day, B. A test of the theory of complementary needs as applied to couples during courtship. *Amer. sociol. Rev.,* 1956, *21,* 602-605.

Bramel, D. Dissonance, expectation, and the self. In R. P. Abelson *et al.* (Eds.), *Theories of cognitive consistency: a sourcebook.* Chicago: Rand McNally, 1968. Pp. 355-365.

Bramel, D. Interpersonal attraction, hostility, and perception. In J. Mills (Ed.), *Experimental social psychology.* New York: Macmillan, 1969. Pp. 3-120.

Brayfield, A. H., & Crockett, W. H. Employee attitudes and employee performance. *Psychol. Bull.,* 1955, *52,* 396-424.

Bredemeier, H. C., & Stephenson, R. M. *The analysis of social systems.* New York: Holt, Rinehart, & Winston, 1962.

Bredemeier, H. C., & Toby, J. *Social problems in America.* New York: Wiley, 1960.

Brehm, J. W. *A theory of psychological reactance.* New York: Academic Press, 1966.

Brehm, J. W., & Cohen, A. R. *Explorations in cognitive dissonance.* New York: Wiley, 1962.

Brehm, J. W., & Cole, A. H. Effect of a favor which reduces freedom. *J. Pers. soc. Psychol.,* 1966, *3,* 420-426.

Brickman, P. Attitudes out of context: Harvard students go home. Undergraduate Honors Thesis, Harvard University, 1964. Reported in K. Gergen, *The psychology of behavior exchange.* Reading, Mass.: Addison-Wesley, 1969. Pp. 2-5.

Brim, O. G. Socialization through the life-cycle. In O. G. Brim & S. Wheeler, *Socialization after children.* New York: Wiley, 1966. Pp. 3-49.

Brittain, C. V. Adolescent choices and parent-peer cross pressures. *Amer. sociol. Rev.,* 1963, *28,* 385-391.

Bronfenbrenner, U. Socialization and social class through time and space. In E. E. Maccoby, T. M. Newcomb, & E. L. Hartley (Eds.), *Readings in social psychology.* (3rd ed.) New York: Holt, Rinehart, & Winston, 1958. Pp. 400-424.

Bronfenbrenner, U. Some familial antecedents of responsibility and leadership in adolescents. In L. Petrullo & B. M. Bass (Eds.), *Leadership and interpersonal behavior*. New York: Holt, Rinehart, & Winston, 1961a.

Bronfenbrenner, U. The mirror image in Soviet-American relations. *J. soc. Issues*, 1961b, *17*, 45-56.

Bronfenbrenner, U. The split-level American family. *Saturday Review, 50*, October 7, 1967, 60-66.

Bronfenbrenner, U. *Two worlds of childhood*. New York: Russell Sage Foundation, 1970.

Bronfenbrenner, U., Harding, J., & Gallwey, M. The measurement of skill in social perception. In D. McClelland, A. Baldwin, U. Bronfenbrenner, & F. Strodtbeck (Eds.), *Talent and society*. Princeton, N.J.: Van Nostrand, 1958. Pp. 29-111.

Brown, J. F. *Psychology and the social order*. New York: McGraw-Hill, 1936.

Brown, R. W. Linguistic determinism and the part of speech. *J. abnorm. soc. Psychol.*, 1957, *55*, 1-5.

Brown, R. W. *Words and things*. Glencoe, Ill.: The Free Press, 1958.

Brown, R. W. *Social psychology*. New York: The Free Press, 1965.

Brown, R. W. The first sentences of child and chimpanzee. Preliminary draft. Harvard University, Department of Social Relations, 1969.

Brown, R. W. *Psycholinguistics*. New York: Free Press-Macmillan, 1970.

Brown, R. W., & Lenneberg, E. H. A study in language and cognition. *J. abnorm. soc. Psychol.*, 1954, *49*, 454-462.

Brown, R. W., & Lenneberg, E. H. Studies in linguistic relativity. In E. E. Maccoby, T. M. Newcomb, & E. L. Hartley (Eds.), *Readings in social psychology*. New York: Holt, Rinehart, & Winston, 1958.

Browne, C. G., & Cohn, T. S. (Eds.) *The study of leadership*. Danville, Ill.; Interstate Printers & Publishers, 1958.

Bruner, J. S. On perceptual readiness. *Psychol. Rev.*, 1957, *64*, 123-152.

Bruner, J. S., & Goodman, C. C. Value and need as organizing factors in perception. *J. abnorm. soc. Psychol.*, 1947, *42*, 33-44.

Bruner, J. S., & Perlmutter, H. V. Compatriot and foreigner: a study of impression formation in three countries. *J. abnorm. soc. Psychol.*, 1957, *55*, 253-260.

Buchanan, W., & Cantril, H. *How nations see each other*. Urbana, Ill.; Univer. Ill. Press, 1953.

Bucher, R. Blame and hostility in disaster. *Amer. J. Sociol.*, 1957, *62*, 467-475.

Byrne, D., & Wong, T. J. Racial prejudice, interpersonal attraction, and assumed dissimilarity of attitudes. *J. abnorm. soc. Psychol.*, 1962, *65*, 246-253.

Calvin, A. D. Social reinforcement. *J. soc. Psychol.*, 1962, *56*, 15-19.

Campbell, A., Converse, P. E., Miller, W. E., & Stokes D. E. *The American voter*. New York: Wiley, 1960.

Campbell, A., Gurin, G., & Miller, W. E. *The voter decides.* New York: Harper & Row, 1954.

Campbell, D. T. An error in some demonstrations of the superior social perceptiveness of leaders. *J. abnorm. soc. Psychol.,* 1955, *51,* 694-695.

Campbell, D. T. Conformity in psychology's theories of acquired behavioral dispositions. In I. A. Berg & B. M. Bass (Eds.), *Conformity and deviation.* New York: Harper, 1961.

Campbell, D. T. Social attitudes and other acquired behavioral dispositions. In S. Koch (Ed.), *Psychology: a study of a science.* Vol. 6. New York: McGraw-Hill, 1963. Pp. 94-172.

Campbell, D. T. Distinguishing differences of perception from failures of communication in cross-cultural studies. In F. C. S. Northrop & H. H. Livingston (Eds.), *Cross-cultural understanding: epistemology in anthropology.* New York: Harper & Row, 1964. Pp. 308-336.

Campbell, D. T. Stereotypes and the perception of group differences. *Amer. Psychologist,* 1967, *22,* 817-829.

Campbell, D. T., & LeVine, R. A. A proposal for co-operative cross-cultural research on ethnocentrism. *J. Confl. Resolut.,* 1961, *5,* 82-108.

Campbell, J. D., & Yarrow, M. R. Perceptual and behavioral correlates of social effectiveness. *Sociometry,* 1961, *24,* 1-20.

Cannon, W. B. *The wisdom of the body.* New York: Norton, 1932.

Cantril, H. The intensity of an attitude. *J. abnorm. soc. Psychol.,* 1946, *41,* 129-135.

Cantril, H. *The politics of despair.* New York: Basic Books, 1958.

Cantril, H. *The pattern of human concerns.* New Brunswick, N. J.: Rutgers Univer. Press, 1965.

Caplow, T. A theory of coalitions in the triad. *Amer. sociol. Rev.,* 1956, *21,* 489-493.

Carey, A. The Hawthorne studies: a radical criticism. *Amer. sociol. Rev.,* 1967, *32,* 403-417.

Carlsmith, J. M., Collins, B. E., & Helmreich, R. L. Studies in forced compliance: 1. The effect of pressure for compliance on attitude change produced by face-to-face role playing and anonymous essay writing. *J. Pers. soc. Psychol.,* 1966, *4,* 1-13.

Carpenter, C. R. Societies of monkeys and apes. In C. H. Southwick (Ed.), *Primate social behavior.* Princeton, N. J.: D. Van Nostrand, 1963. Pp. 24-51.

Carroll, J. B. *The study of language.* Cambridge, Mass.: Harvard Univer. Press, 1953.

Carroll, J. B., & Casagrande, J. B. The functions of language classification and behavior. In E. E. Maccoby, T. M. Newcomb, & E. L. Hartley (Eds.), *Readings in social psychology.* (3rd ed.) New York: Holt, Rinehart, & Winston, 1958. Pp. 18-31.

Carter, L. F., & Schooler, K. Value, need, and other factors in perception. *Psychol. Rev.,* 1949, *56,* 200-207.

Carter, L. F., Haythorn, W., Meirowitz, B., & Lanzetta, J. The relation of categorizations and ratings in the observation of group behavior. *Hum. Relat.*, 1951, *4*, 239-254.

Carter, L. F., Haythorn, W., Shriver, E., & Lanzetta, J. The behavior of leaders and other group members. *J. abnorm. soc. Psychol.* 1951, *46*, 589-595.

Cartwright, D. C. Achieving change in people: some applications of group dynamics theory. *Hum. Relat.*, 1951, *4*, 381-393.

Cartwright, D. C. Introduction. In D. C. Cartwright *et al.*, *Studies in social power*. Ann Arbor: Institute for Social Research, 1959.

Cartwright, D. C., & Zander, A. (Eds.) *Group dynamics: research and theory*. (2nd ed.) Evanston, Ill.: Row, Peterson, 1960.

Cartwright, D. C., & Zander, A. (Eds.) *Group dynamics: research and theory*. (3rd ed.) New York: Harper & Row, 1968.

Cattell, R. B. Concepts and methods in the measurement of group syntality. *Psychol. Rev.*, 1948, *55*, 48-63.

Cattell, R. B. New concepts for measuring leadership in terms of group syntality. *Hum. Relat.*, 1951, *4*, 161-184.

Centers, R. *The psychology of social classes*. Princeton: Princeton Univer. Press, 1949.

Chapanis, N. P., & Chapanis, A. Cognitive dissonance: five years later. *Psychol. Bull.*, 1964, *61*, 1-22.

Charters, W. W., Jr., & Newcomb, T. M. Some attitudinal effects of experimentally increased salience of a membership group. In E. Maccoby, T. M. Newcomb, & E. L. Hartley (Eds.), *Readings in social psychology*. (3rd ed.) New York: Holt, Rinehart, & Winston, 1958. Pp. 276-281.

Child, I. Socialization. In G. Lindzey (Ed.), *Handbook of social psychology*. Vol. 2. Reading, Mass.: Addison-Wesley, 1954. Pp. 655-692.

Childe, V. G. *What happened in history*. New York: Penguin Books, 1946.

Chomsky, N. *Syntactic structures*. The Hague: Mouton, 1957.

Chomsky, N. *Current issues in linguistic theory*. The Hague: Mouton, 1964.

Chomsky, N. The formal nature of language. Appendix. In E. H. Lenneberg, *Biological foundations of language*. New York: Wiley, 1967. Pp. 397-442.

Chomsky, N. *Language and mind*. New York: Harcourt, Brace & World, 1968.

Chomsky, N., & Halle, M. *The sound pattern of English*. New York: Harper & Row, 1968.

Chowdhry, K., & Newcomb, T. M. The relative abilities of leaders and non-leaders to estimate opinions of their own groups. *J. abnorm. soc. Psychol.*, 1952, *47*, 51-57.

Christie, R. Impersonal interpersonal orientations and behavior. Columbia Univer., Dept. of Social Psychology, 1962. (Mimeo.)

Christie, R., & Cook, P. A guide to published literature relating to the authoritarian personality through 1956. *J. Psychol.*, 1958, *45*, 171-199.

Christie, R., & Geis, F. Some consequences of taking Machiavelli seriously. In E. F. Borgatta & W. W. Lambert (Eds.), *Handbook of personality theory and research*. Chicago: Rand McNally, 1968. Pp. 959-973.

Christie, R., & Geis, F. *Studies in Machiavellianism*. New York: Academic Press, 1970.

Clark, J. V. A preliminary investigation on some unconscious assumptions affecting labor efficiencies in eight supermarkets. Unpublished doctoral dissertation, Graduate School of Business Admin., Harvard Univer., 1958.

Clark, K. B. *Dark ghetto*. New York: Harper & Row, 1965.

Clark, K. B., & Clark, M. P. Racial identification and preference in Negro children. In T. M. Newcomb & E. L. Hartley (Eds.), *Readings in social psychology*. New York: Holt, 1947. Pp. 169-178.

Clarke, A. C. *Profiles of the future*. New York: Bantam Editions, 1965.

Clausen, J. A. A historical and comparative view of socialization theory and research. In J. A. Clausen (Ed.), *Socialization and society*. Boston: Little, Brown, 1968a. Pp. 18-72.

Clausen, J. A. (Ed.) *Socialization and society*. Boston: Little, Brown, 1968b. Introduction, pp. 1-17.

Cline, V. B. Interpersonal perception. In B. A. Maher (Ed.), *Progress in experimental personality research*. Vol. 1. New York: Academic Press, 1964.

Coch, L., & French, J. R. P., Jr. Overcoming resistance to change. *Hum. Relat.*, 1948, *1*, 512-532.

Cofer, C. N., & Appley, M. H. *Motivation: theory and research*. New York: Wiley, 1964.

Cohen, A. M., & Bennis, W. G. Continuity of leadership in communication networks. *Hum. Relat.*, 1961, *14*, 351-367.

Cohen, A. R. Need for cognition and order of communication as determinants of opinion change. In C. I. Hovland (Ed.), *The order of presentation in persuasion*. New Haven: Yale Univer. Press, 1957. Pp. 79-97.

Cohen, A. R. Some implications of self-esteem for social influence. In C. I. Hovland & I. L. Janis (Eds.), *Personality and persuasibility*. New Haven, Conn.: Yale Univer. Press, 1959. Pp. 102-120.

Cohen, A. R. *Attitude change and social influence*. New York: Basic Books, 1964.

Cohen, A. R., Stotland, E., & Wolfe, D. M. An experimental investigation of need for cognition. *J. abnorm. soc. Pyschol.*, 1955, *51*, 291-294.

Coleman, J. S. *Community conflict*. New York: Free Press, 1957.

Coleman, J. S. *The adolescent society: the social life of the teenager and its impact on education*. New York: Free Press, 1961.

Collins, B. E. The effect of monetary inducements on the amount of attitude change induced by forced compliance. In A. Elms (Ed.), *Role-play-*

ing, reward and attitude change. Princeton: Van Nostrand, 1969.

Comte, A. *The positive philosophy of Auguste Comte.* (Translated and condensed by H. Martineau.) London: J. Chapman, 1853.

Converse, P. E. The shifting role of class in political attitudes and behavior. In E. E. Maccoby, T. M. Newcomb, & E. L. Hartley (Eds.), *Readings in social psychology.* (3rd ed.) New York: Holt, Rinehart, & Winston, 1958. Pp. 388-399.

Cook, P. H. The application of the Rorschach Test to a Samoan group. *Rorschach Research Exchange,* 1942, *6,* 52-60.

Cooley, C. H. *Human nature and the social order.* New York: Scribners, 1902. (Rev. ed., 1922.)

Cooley, C. H. *Social organization.* New York: Scribners, 1909.

Costanzo, P. R. Conformity development as a function of self-blame. *J. Pers. soc. Psychol.,* 1970, *14,* 366-374.

Cottrell, L. S. Some neglected problems in social psychology. *Amer. sociol. Rev.,* 1950, *15,* 705-712.

Cowley, W. H. Three distinctions in the study of leaders. *J. abnorm. soc. Psychol.,* 1928, *23,* 144-157.

Cox, F. N. An assessment of children's attitudes towards parent figures. *Child Development,* 1962, *33,* 821-830.

Crockett, W. H., & Meidinger, T. Authoritarianism and interpersonal perception. *J. abnorm. soc. Psychol.,* 1956, *53,* 378-380.

Cronbach, L. J. The two disciplines of scientific psychology. *Amer. Psychologist,* 1957, *12,* 671-684.

Crow, W. J. A study of strategic doctrines using the Inter-Nation Simulation. *J. Confl. Resolut.,* 1963, *7,* 580-589.

Crowne, D. P., & Liverant, S. Conformity under varying conditions of personal commitment. *J. abnorm. soc. Psychol.,* 1963, *66,* 547-555.

Crowne, D. P., & Marlowe, D. *The approval motive: studies in evaluative dependence.* New York: Wiley, 1964.

Crutchfield, R. S. Conformity and character. *Amer. Psychologist,* 1955, *10,* 191-198.

Curry, T. J., & Emerson, R. M. Balance theory: a theory of interpersonal attraction? *Sociometry,* 1970, *33,* 216-238.

Daniels, V. Communication, incentive, and structural variables in interpersonal exchange and negotiation. *J. exp. soc. Psychol.,* 1967, *3,* 47-74.

Darley, J. M. Fear and social comparison as determinants of conformity behavior. *J. Pers. soc. Psychol.,* 1966, *4,* 73-78.

Darwin, C. R. *Origin of species by means of natural selection; or, the preservation of favoured races in the struggle for life.* New York: D. Appleton & Co., 1860. (London, 1859; paperback by Mentor Books, 1958.)

Darwin, C. R. *The descent of man and selection in relation to sex.* New York: D. Appleton & Co., 1871.

Davis, A., Gardner, B., & Gardner, M. R. *Deep South: a social-anthropolog-*

ical study of caste and class. Chicago: Univer. of Chicago Press, 1941.

Davis, A., & Havighurst, R. J. Social class and color differences in child-rearing. *Amer. sociol. Rev.*, 1948, *11*, 698-710.

deCharms, R., & Moeller, G. H. Values expressed in American children's readers: 1800-1950. *J. abnorm. soc. Psychol.*, 1962, *64*, 136-142.

deCharms, R., Carpenter, V., & Cuperman, A. The "origin-pawn" variable in person perception. *Sociometry*, 1965, *28*, 241-258.

DeFleur, M. L., & Westie, F. R. Verbal attitudes and overt acts: an experiment on the salience of attitudes. *Amer. sociol. Rev.*, 1958, *23*, 667-673.

de Jouvenel, B. *The art of conjecture.* New York: Basic Books, 1967.

deSoto, C. B., & Kuethe, J. L. Subjective probabilities of interpersonal relationships. *J. abnorm. soc. Psychol.*, 1959, *59*, 290-294.

DeVos, G. Symbolic analysis in the cross-cultural study of personality. In B. Kaplan (Ed.), *Studying personality cross culturally.* Evanston, Ill.: Row, Peterson & Co., 1961. Pp. 599-634.

Dember, W. N. The new look in motivation. *Amer. Scientist*, 1965, *53*, 409-427.

Deutsch, K. W. *The political community at the international level.* Garden City, N.Y.: Doubleday, 1954.

Deutsch, K. W. Mass communications and the loss of freedom in national decision-making. *J. Confl. Resolut.*, 1957, *1*, 200-211.

Deutsch, Martin. Happenings on the way back to the forum. *Harvard Educat. Rev.*, 1969, *39*, 523-557.

Deutsch, Martin, and associates. *The disadvantaged child.* New York: Basic Books, 1967.

Deutsch, M. A theory of cooperation and competition. *Hum. Relat.*, 1949a, *2*, 129-152.

Deutsch, M. An experimental study of the effects of cooperation and competition upon group process. *Hum. Relat.*, 1949b, *2*, 199-231.

Deutsch, M. Trust and suspicion. *J. Confl. Resolut.*, 1958, *2*, 265-279.

Deutsch, M. Trust, trustworthiness, and the F scale. *J. abnorm. soc. Psychol.*, 1960, *61*, 138-140.

Deutsch, M. A psychological basis for peace. In Q. Wright, W. M. Evan, and M. Deutsch (Eds.), *Preventing World War III: some proposals.* New York: Simon & Schuster, 1962. Pp. 369-392.

Deutsch, M. Socially relevant science: reflections on some studies of interpersonal conflict. *Amer. Psychologist*, 1969, *24*, 1076-1092.

Deutsch, M., & Collins, M. E. *Interracial housing: a psychological evaluation of a social experiment.* Minneapolis: Univer. Minnesota Press, 1951.

Deutsch, M., & Gerard, H. B. A study of normative and informational social influence upon individual judgment. *J. abnorm. soc. Psychol.*, 1955, *51*, 629-636.

Deutsch, M., & Krauss, R. M. The effect of threat on interpersonal bargaining. *J. abnorm. soc. Psychol.*, 1960, *61*, 181-189.

Deutsch, M., & Krauss, R. M. Studies of interpersonal bargaining. *J. Confl. Resolut.* 1962, *6*, 52-76.

Deutsch, M., & Krauss, R. M. *Theories in social psychology.* New York: Basic Books, 1965.

Deutsch, M., & Solomon, L. Reactions to evaluations by others as influenced by self evaluations. *Sociometry*, 1959, *22*, 93-112.

Deutsch, M. Epstein, Y., Canavan, D., & Gumpert, P. Strategies of inducing cooperation: an experimental study. *J. Confl. Resolut.*, 1967, *11*, 345-360.

Dittes, J. E. Effect of changes in self-esteem upon impulsiveness and deliberation in making judgments. *J. abnorm. soc. Psychol.*, 1959, *58*, 348-356.

Dittes, J. E. Impulsive closure as a reaction to failure-induced threat. *J. abnorm. soc. Psychol.*, 1961, *63*, 562-569.

DiVesta, F. J. Meaningful learning: motivational, personality, interpersonal, and social variables; peer relationships. *Rev. educat. Res.*, 1961, *31*, 511-521.

Doob, L. W. The effect of codability upon the afferent and efferent functioning of language. *J. soc. Psychol.*, 1960, *52*, 3-15.

Dornbusch, S. M., Hastorf, A. H., Richardson, S. A., Muzzy, R. E., & Vreeland R. S. The perceiver and the perceived: their relative influence on the categories of interpersonal cognition. *J. Pers. soc. Psychol.*, 1965, *1*, 434-440.

Doxiadis, C. A. *Architecture in transition.* New York: Oxford Univer. Press, 1968.

DuBois, C. *The people of Alor: a social psychological study of an East Indian island.* Minneapolis: Univer. of Minnesota Press, 1944.

Dudycha, G. J. An objective study of punctuality in relation to personality and development. *Archives of Psychology*, 1936, No. 204.

Dunn, L. C., & Dobzhansky, T. *Heredity, race and society.* New York: New American Library, 1946. (Rev. ed., 1952.)

Durkheim, E. *De la division du travail social.* Paris: Alcan, 1893. (Trans. *The division of labor in society.* Glencoe, Ill.: Free Press, 1947.)

Durkheim, E. *Le suicide; étude de sociologie.* Paris: Alcan, 1897. (Trans. *Suicide, a study in sociology.*)

Edwards, A. L. *The social desirability variable in personality assessment and research.* New York: Dryden, 1957a.

Edwards, A. L. *Techniques of attitude scale construction.* New York: Appleton-Century-Crofts, 1957b.

Eisenstadt, S. N. *From generation to generation.* Glencoe, Ill.: Free Press, 1956.

Elkin, F. *The child and society: the process of socialization.* New York: Random House, 1960.

Elms, A. C. Influence of fantasy ability on attitude change through role playing. *J. Pers. soc. Psychol.*, 1966, *4*, 36-43.

Epstein, G. F. Machiavelli and the devil's advocate. *J. Pers. soc. Psychol.*, 1969, *11*, 38-41.

Ericson, M. Child rearing and social status. *Amer. J. Sociol.*, 1948, *52*, 190-192.

Etiemble, R. *Parlez-vous Franglais?* Paris: Gallimard, 1963.

Etzioni, A. On self-encapsulating conflicts. *J. Confl. Resolut.*, 1964, *8*, 242-255.

Exline, R. V. Interrelation among two dimensions of sociometric status, group congeniality, and accuracy of social perception. *Sociometry*, 1960, *23*, 85-101.

Eysenck, H. J. *Fact and fiction in psychology.* Baltimore, Md.: Penguin Books, 1965.

Farber, M. L. The problem of national character: a methodological analysis. *J. Psychol.*, 1950, *30*, 307-316.

Faucheux, C., & Moscovici, S. Le style de comportement d'une minorité et son influence sur les réponses d'une majorité. *Bulletin du Centre d'Études et Recherches Psychologiques* (Paris), 1967, *16* (October-December), 337-360.

Feather, N. T. The relationship of persistence at a task to expectation of success and achievement related motives. *J. abnorm. soc. Psychol.*, 1961, *63*, 552-561.

Feather, N. T. Valence of outcome and expectation of success in relation to task difficulty and perceived locus of control. *J. Pers. soc. Psychol.*, 1967, *7*, 372-386.

Festinger, L. Informal social communication. *Psychol. Rev.*, 1950, *57*, 271-282.

Festinger, L. A theory of social comparison processes. *Hum. Relat.*, 1954, *7*, 117-140.

Festinger, L. *A theory of cognitive dissonance.* Evanston, Ill.: Row, Peterson, 1957.

Festinger, L. The psychological effects of insufficient rewards. *Amer. Psychologist*, 1961, *16*, 1-11.

Festinger, L. Behavioral support for opinion change. *Publ. Opin. Quart.*, 1964a, *28*, 404-417.

Festinger, L., with the collaboration of Vernon Allen and others. *Conflict, decision, and dissonance.* Stanford: Stanford Univer. Press, 1964b.

Festinger, L., & Carlsmith, J. Cognitive consequences of forced compliance. *J. abnorm. soc. Psychol.*, 1959, *58*, 203-210.

Festinger, L., & Katz, D. (Eds.) *Research methods in the behavioral sciences.* New York: Dryden, 1953.

Festinger, L., & Maccoby, N. On resistance to persuasive communications. *J. abnorm. soc. Psychol.*, 1964, *68*, 359-366.

Festinger, L., Schachter, S., & Back, K. *Social presures in informal groups: a study of a housing project.* New York: Harper, 1950.

Fiedler, F. E. *Leader attitudes and group effectiveness.* Urbana, Ill.: Univer. of Ill. Press, 1958.

Fiedler, F. E. Leadership and leadership effectiveness traits. In L. Petrullo & B. M. Bass (Eds.), *Leadership and interpersonal behavior*. New York: Holt, Rinehart, & Winston, 1961.

Fiedler, F. E. A contingency model of leadership effectiveness. In L. Berkowitz (Ed.), *Advances in experimental social psychology*. Vol. 1. New York: Academic Press, 1964.

Fiedler, F. E. The contingency model: a theory of leadership effectiveness. In H. Proshansky & B. Seidenberg (Eds.), *Basic studies in social psychology*. New York: Holt, Rinehart, & Winston, 1965.

Fiedler, F. E. *A theory of leadership effectiveness*. New York: McGraw-Hill, 1967.

Fischer, J. L. Social influences on the choice of a linguistic variant. *Word*, 1958, *14*, 47-56.

Fisher, R. Fractionating conflict. In R. Fisher (Ed.), *International conflict and behavioral science: the Craigville papers*. New York: Basic Books, 1964.

Flanagan, J. C. (Ed.) *Leaders reaction test*. Pittsburgh: Amer. Inst. for Research, 1952.

Flanders, J. P. A review of research on imitative behavior. *Psychol. Bull.*, 1968, *69*, 316-337.

Flanders, J. P. and Thistlethwaite, D. L. Effects of familiarization and group discussion upon risk taking. *J. Pers. soc. Psychol.*, 1967, *5*, 91-97.

Flavell, J. H. A test of the Whorfian theory. *Psychol. Rep.*, 1958, *4*, 455-462.

Fleishman, E. A., & Harris, E. F. Patterns of leadership behavior related to employee grievances and turnover. *Personnel Psychol.*, 1962, *15*, 43-56.

Fleishman, E. A., & Peters, D. R. Interpersonal values, leadership attitudes, and managerial success. *Personnel Psychol.*, 1962, *15*, 127-143.

Fleishman, E. A., Harris, E. F., & Burtt, H. E. *Leadership and supervision in industry*. Columbus, Ohio: Bureau of Educat. Res., Ohio State Univer., 1955.

Fleming, D. F. *Does deterrence deter?* Philadelphia: American Friends Service Committee, 1962.

Fouriezos, N. T., Hutt, M. L., & Guetzkow, H. Measurement of self-oriented needs in discussion groups. *J. abnorm. soc. Psychol.*, 1950, *45*, 682-690.

Fox, R. Chinese have bigger brains than whites—are they superior? *The New York Times Magazine*, June 30, 1968, p. 13.

Free, L. A., & Cantril, H. *The political beliefs of Americans*. New Brunswick, N.J.: Rutgers Univer. Press, 1967.

Freedman, J. L. Involvement, discrepancy, and change. *J. abnorm. soc. Psychol.*, 1964, *69*, 290-295.

Freedman, J. L. Long-term behavioral effects of cognitive dissonance. *J. exp. soc. Psychol.*, 1965, *1*, 145-155.

Freedman, J. L., & Sears, D. O. Warning, distraction, and resistance to influence. *J. Pers. soc. Psychol.*, 1965, *1*, 262-266.

French, J. R. P., Jr., & Raven, B. H. The bases of social power. In D. Cartwright (Ed.), *Studies in social power*. Ann Arbor, Mich.: Univer. of Michigan Press, 1959. Pp. 118-149.

Freud, S. *Beyond the pleasure principle*. New York: Bantam Classics, 1949. (Originally published in German, 1920).

Freud, S. *Group psychology and the analysis of the ego*. New York: Bantam Books, 1960. (Originally published in German, 1921.)

Freud, S. *Civilization and its discontents*. New York: Norton, 1961. (Originally published in German and English, 1930.)

Fromm, E. *Escape from freedom*. New York: Rinehart, 1941.

Fromm, E. Psychoanalytic characterology and its application to the understanding of culture. In S. S. Sargent & M. W. Smith (Eds.), *Culture and personality*. New York: Viking Fund, 1949.

Fromm, E. *The sane society*. New York: Holt, Rinehart, & Winston, 1955.

Galbraith, J. K. *The affluent society*. Boston: Houghton Mifflin, 1958.

Gallo, P. S., & McClintock, C. G. Behavioral, attitudinal and perceptual differences between leaders and non-leaders in situations of group support and non-support. *J. soc. Psychol.*, 1962, *56*, 121-133.

Galton, F. *Hereditary genius: an inquiry into its laws and consequences*. London: Macmillan, 1869. (Also published in paperback by Meridian Books, 1962).

Gamson, W. A. *Power and discontent*. Homewood, Ill.: Dorsey Press, 1968.

Gardner, J. W. *Excellence*. New York: Harper & Row, 1961.

Gardner, J. W. *Self-renewal*. New York: Harper & Row, 1963.

Gardner, R. A., & Gardner, B. T. Teaching sign language to a chimpanzee. *Science*, 1969, *165*, 664-672.

Gellert, E. Stability and fluctuation in the power relationships of young children. *J. abnorm. soc. Psychol.*, 1961, *62*, 8-15.

Gellert, E. The effect of changes in group composition on the dominant behaviour of young children. *Brit. J. soc. clin. Psychol.*, 1962, *1*, 168-181.

Gergen, K. J. Personal consistency and the presentation of self. In C. Gordon & K. J. Gergen (Eds.), *The self in social interaction*. Vol. 1. New York: Wiley, 1968. Pp. 299-308.

Gergen, K. J., & Jones, E. E. Mental illness, predictability, and affective consequences as stimulus factors in person perception. *J. abnorm. soc. Psychol.*, 1963, *67*, 95-104.

Gergen, K. J., & Marlowe, D. (Eds.) *Personality and social behavior*. Reading, Mass.: Addison-Wesley, 1970.

Gergen, K. J., & Wishnov, B. Others' self-evaluations and interaction anticipation as determinants of self-presentation. *J. Pers. soc. Psychol.*, 1965, *2*, 348-358.

Gibb, C. A. The sociometry of leadership in temporary groups. *Sociometry*, 1950, *13*, 226-243.

Gibb, C. A. Leadership. In G. Lindzey (Ed.), *Handbook of social psychology*. Vol. II. Reading, Mass.: Addison-Wesley, 1954.

Gibb, C. A. Leadership. In G. Lindzey & E. Aronson (Eds.), *The handbook of social psychology.* (2nd ed.) Vol. 4, Reading, Mass.: Addison-Wesley, 1968. Pp. 205-282.

Gibb, C. A. (Ed.) *Leadership: selected readings.* Baltimore, Md.: Penguin Books, 1969.

Gibson, J. J. *The senses considered as perceptual systems.* Boston: Houghton Mifflin, 1966.

Gittler, J. B. *Social dynamics.* New York: McGraw-Hill, 1952.

Gladstone, A. I. The conception of the enemy. *J. Confl. Resolut.,* 1959, *3,* 132-137.

Goffman, E. *The presentation of self in everyday life.* Garden City, N.Y.: Doubleday Anchor, 1959.

Goffman, E. *Asylums.* Garden City, N.Y.: Doubleday Anchor, 1961.

Goldberg, L. R., & Rorer, L. G. Use of two different response modes and repeated testings to predict social conformity. *J. abnorm. soc. Psychol.,* 1966, *3,* 28-37.

Goldman, M., & Fraas, L. A. The effects of leader selection on group performance. *Sociometry,* 1965, *28,* 82-88.

Goldschmidt, W. *Man's way.* Cleveland: World Publ. Co., 1959.

Golembiewski, R. T. *The small group.* Chicago: Univer. of Chicago Press, 1962.

Gollob, H. F., & Dittes, J. E. Effects of manipulated self-esteem on persuasibility depending on threat and complexity of communication. *J. Pers. soc. Psychol.,* 1965, *2,* 195-201.

Goranson, R. E., & Berkowitz, L. Reciprocity and responsibility reactions to prior help. *J. Pers. soc. Psychol.,* 1966, *3,* 227-232.

Gordon, C., & Gergen, K. J. (Eds.) *The self in social interaction.* Vol. 1. New York: Wiley, 1968.

Gordon, M. M. *Assimilation in American life.* New York: Oxford Univer. Press, 1964.

Gorer, G. *The American people: a study in national character.* New York: W. W. Norton, 1948. (Rev. ed., Norton Library Paperback, 1964.)

Goslin, D. A. Accuracy of self perception and social acceptance. *Sociometry,* 1962, *25,* 283-296.

Gottheil, E. Changes in social perceptions contingent upon competing or cooperating. *Sociometry,* 1955, *18,* 132-137.

Gouldner, A. W. (Ed.) *Studies in leadership.* New York: Harper, 1950.

Gouldner, A. W. *Wildcat strike.* Yellow Springs, Ohio: Antioch Press, 1954. (Available as Harper Torch Book, New York, 1965.)

Gouldner, A. W. The norm of reciprocity: a preliminary statement. *Amer. sociol. Rev.,* 1960, *25,* 161-179.

Gouldner, A. W. The sociologist as partisan: sociology and the welfare state. *Amer. Sociologist,* 1968, *3,* 103-116.

Greenstein, F. I. *Personality and politics.* Chicago: Markham, 1969.

Greenwald, H. J., & Oppenheim, D. B. Reported magnitude of self-misidentification among Negro children—artifact? *J. Pers. soc. Psychol.*, 1968, 8, 49-52.

Greer, F. L., Galanter, E. H., & Nordlie, P. G. Interpersonal knowledge and individual and group effectiveness. *J. abnorm. soc. Psychol.*, 1954, 49, 411-414.

Gross, N. The sociology of education. In R. K. Merton *et al.* (Eds.), *Sociology today: problems and prospects.* New York: Basic Books, 1959. Pp. 128-152.

Gross, N., & Martin, W. E. On group cohesiveness. *Amer. J. Sociol.*, 1952, 57, 546-554.

Grossack, M. M. Some effects of cooperation and competition upon small group behavior. *J. abnorm. soc. Psychol.*, 1954, 49, 341-348.

Group for the Advancement of Psychiatry. *Psychiatric aspects of the prevention of nuclear war.* New York: Committee on Social Issues, 1964. Rep. #57.

Guetzkow, H. (Ed.) *Groups, leadership and men.* Pittsburgh: Carnegie Press, 1951.

Guetzkow, H. *Multiple loyalties.* Princeton: Princeton Univer. Press, 1955.

Guetzkow, H., Alger, C. F., Brody, R. A., Noel, R. C., & Snyder, R. C. *Simulation in international relations.* Englewood Cliffs, N.J.: Prentice-Hall, 1963.

Gusfield, J. R. The study of social movements. In D. S. Sills (Ed.), *International encyclopedia of the social sciences.* Vol. 14. New York: Crowell Collier and Macmillan, 1968. Pp. 445-452.

Guttman, L. The basis for scalogram analysis. In S. A. Stouffer, L. Guttman, E. A. Suchman, P. F. Lazarsfeld, S. A. Star, & J. A. Gardner (Eds.), *Measurement and prediction.* Princeton, N.J.: Princeton Univer. Press, 1950. Pp. 60-90.

Haaland, G. A., & Venkatesan, M. Resistance to persuasive communications: an examination of the distraction hypotheses. *J. Pers. soc. Psychol.*, 1968, 9, 167-170.

Haas, H., Fink, H., & Hartfelder, G. Das placebo-problem. *Fortschrifte der Arzneimittelforchung*, 1959, 1, 279-454. Verlag, Basel, Switzerland. A translation of selected parts appeared in the *Psychopharmacology Service Center Bulletin*, 1963, 8, 1-65.

Hagstrom, W. O., & Selvin, H. C. Two dimensions of cohesiveness in small groups. *Sociometry*, 1965, 28, 30-43.

Haiman, F. S. *Group leadership and democratic action.* Boston: Houghton Mifflin, 1951.

Haiman, F. S., & Duns, D. F. Validation in communication behavior of attitude scale measures of dogmatism. *J. soc. Psychol.*, 1964, 64, 287-297.

Hall, C. S., & Lindzey, G. The relevance of Freudian psychology and related viewpoints for the social sciences. In G. Lindzey & E. Aronson (Eds.), *The handbook of social psychology.* (2nd ed.) Reading, Mass.: Addison-Wesley, 1968. Pp. 245-319.

Hall, E. T. *The silent language*. Garden City, N.Y.: Doubleday, 1959.

Hall, E. T. *The hidden dimension*. Garden City, N.Y.: Doubleday, 1966. (Doubleday Anchor edition, 1969.)

Hallowell, A. I. Temporal orientation in Western civilization and in preliterate society. *Amer. Anthropologist*, 1937, *39*, 647-670.

Halpin, A. W. The leader behavior and leadership ideology of educational administrators and aircraft commanders. *Harvard Educat. Rev.*, 1955, *25*, 18-32.

Halpin, A. W., & Winer, B. J. *The leadership behavior of the airplane commander*. Columbus: Ohio State Univer. Research Foundation, 1952.

Hamblin, R. L. Leadership and crises. *Sociometry*, 1958, *21*, 322-335.

Hammond, L. K., & Goldman, M. Competition and non-competition and its relationship to individual and group productivity. *Sociometry*, 1961, *24*, 46-60.

Hare, A. P. *Handbook of small group research*. New York: Free Press, 1961.

Hare, A. P., Borgatta, E. F., & Bales R. F. (Eds.) *Small groups*. New York: Alfred A. Knopf, 1955. (Rev. ed., 1965.)

Harlow H. F. The heterosexual affectional system in monkeys. *Amer. Psychologist*, 1962, *17*, 1-9.

Harrington, A. *Life in the crystal palace*. New York: Avon Books, 1967.

Harrington, M. *The other America*. Baltimore, Md.: Penguin Books, 1963.

Harrison, A. A. Response competition, frequency, exploratory behavior, and liking. *J. Pers. soc. Psychol.*, 1968, *9*, 363-368.

Harrison, A. A. Exposure and popularity. *J. Pers.*, 1969, *37*, 359-377.

Hartshorne, H., & May, M. A. *Studies in deceit*. New York: Macmillan, 1928.

Harvard Crimson, Feb. 6, 1970, p. 2.

Harvey, O. J., & Consalvi, C. Status and conformity to pressures in informal groups. *J. abnorm. soc. Psychol.*, 1960, *60*, 182-187.

Harvey, O. J., Kelley, H. H., & Shapiro, M. M. Reactions to unfavorable evaluations of the self made by other persons. *J. Pers.*, 1957, *25*, 398-411.

Hastorf, A. H., & Cantril, H. They saw a game. *J. abnorm. soc. Psychol.*, 1954, *49*, 129-134.

Hayakawa, S. I. *Symbol, status, and personality*. New York: Harcourt Brace & World, 1963.

Hayakawa, S. I. *Language in thought and action*. (2nd ed.) New York: Harcourt Brace & World, 1964.

Hayes, C. *The ape in our house*. New York: Harper, 1951.

Haythorn, W. W. The composition of groups: a review of the literature. *Acta Psychologica*, 1968, *28*, 97-128.

Haythorn, W. W., & Altman, I. Personality factors in isolated environments. In M. Appley & R. Trumbull (Eds.), *Psychological stress*. New York: Appleton-Century-Crofts, 1966. Pp. 363-386.

Haywood, H. C., & Spielberger, C. D. Palmar sweating as a function of individual differences in manifest anxiety. *J. Pers. soc. Psychol.*, 1966, *3*, 103-105.

Hearn, G. Leadership and the spatial factor in small groups. *J. abnorm. soc. Psychol.*, 1957, *54*, 269-272.

Heider, F. Social perception and phenomenal causality. *Psychol. Rev.*, 1944, *51*, 358-374.

Heider, F. Attitudes and cognitive organization. *J. Psychol.*, 1946, *21*, 107-112.

Heider, F. *The psychology of interpersonal relations.* New York: Wiley, 1958.

Heilbroner, R. L. *The future as history.* New York: Grove Press, Evergreen Edition, 1961.

Heilbroner, R. L. *The worldly philosophers.* (Rev. ed.) New York: Simon & Schuster, 1961.

Helson, H. Adaptation-level as a basis for a quantitative theory of frames of reference. *Psychol. Rev.*, 1948, *55*, 297-313.

Helson, H. Adaptation level theory. In S. Koch (Ed.), *Psychology: a study of a science.* Vol. 1. *Sensory, perceptual, and physiological formulations.* New York: McGraw-Hill, 1959. Pp. 565-621.

Hemphill, J. K. Relations between the size of the group and the behavior of "superior" leaders. *J. soc. Psychol.*, 1950, *32*, 11-22.

Hemphill, J. K. Leadership behavior associated with the administrative reputation of college departments. *J. educ. Psychol.*, 1955, *46*, 385-401.

Hemphill, J. K. *Group dimensions: a manual for their measurement.* Columbus: Ohio State Univer., Ohio Studies in Personnel, Monogr. #87, Bureau of Business Research, 1956.

Hemphill, J. K. Administration as problem-solving. In A. W. Halpin (Ed.), *Administrative theory in education.* Chicago: Midwest Administration Center, 1958.

Hemphill, J. K. Why people attempt to lead. In L. Petrullo & B. M. Bass (Eds.), *Leadership and interpersonal behavior.* New York: Holt, Rinehart, & Winston, 1961.

Hemphill, J. K., & Westie, C. M. The measurement of group dimensions. *J. Psychol.*, 1950, *29*, 325-342.

Henry, J. *Culture against man.* New York: Random House, 1963.

Heslin, R., & Dunphy, D. Three dimensions of member satisfaction in small groups. *Hum. Relat.*, 1964, *17*, 99-112.

Heslin, R., & Rotton, J. Incentive or dissonance effects of reinforcement for counterattitudinal advocacy. *Proceedings of the 77th annual convention, APA*, 1969, *4*, 311-312.

Himmelweit, H. T. Socio-economic background and personality. *Int. soc. Sci. Bull.*, 1955, *7*, 29-35.

Hites, R. W., & Campbell, D. T. A test of the ability of fraternity leaders to estimate group opinion. *J. soc. Psychol.*, 1950, *32*, 95-100.

Hitt, W. D. Two models of man. *Amer. Psychologist*, 1969, *24*, 651-658.

Hobbes, T. *Leviathan.* London: Andrew Crooke, 1651.

Hoffman, L. R. Homogeneity of member personality and its effect on group problem-solving. *J. abnorm. soc. Psychol.*, 1959, *58*, 27-32.

Hoffman, L. R., & Maier, N. R. F. Quality and acceptance of problem solutions by members of homogeneous and heterogeneous groups. *J. abnorm. soc. Psychol.*, 1961, *62*, 401-407.

Hollander, E. P. Conformity, status, and idiosyncrasy credit. *Psychol. Rev.*, 1958, *65*, 117-127.

Hollander, E. P. Competence and conformity in the acceptance of influence. *J. abnorm. soc. Psychol.*, 1960a, *61*, 361-365.

Hollander, E. P. Reconsidering the issue of conformity in personality. In H. P. David and J. C. Brengelmann (Eds.), *Perspectives in personality research*. New York: Springer, 1960b. Pp. 210-225.

Hollander, E. P. Emergent leadership and social influence. In L. Petrullo & B. M. Bass (Eds.), *Leadership and interpersonal behavior*. New York: Holt, Rinehart, & Winston, 1961a. Pp. 30-47.

Hollander, E. P. Some effects of perceived status on responses to innovative behavior. *J. abnorm. soc. Psychol.*, 1961b, *63*, 247-250.

Hollander, E. P. *Leaders, groups and influence*. New York: Oxford Univer. Press, 1964.

Hollander, E. P., & Hunt, R. G. (Eds.) *Current perspectives in social psychology*. (3rd ed.) New York: Oxford Univer. Press, 1971.

Hollander, E. P., & Julian, J. W. Leadership. In E. F. Borgatta & W. W. Lambert (Eds.), *Handbook of personality theory and research*. Chicago: Rand McNally, 1968. Pp. 890-899.

Hollander, E. P., & Julian, J. W. Contemporary trends in the analysis of leadership processes. *Psychol. Bull.*, 1969, *71*, 387-397.

Hollander, E. P., & Marcia, J. E. Parental determinants of peer-orientation and self-orientation among preadolescents. *Dev. Psychol.*, 1970, *2*, 292-302.

Hollander, E. P., & Webb, W. B. Leadership, followership, and friendship: an analysis of peer nominations. *J. abnorm. soc. Psychol.*, 1955, *50*, 163-167.

Hollander, E. P., & Willis, R. H. Conformity, independence and anticonformity as determiners of perceived influence and attraction. In E. P. Hollander, *Leaders, groups, and influence*. New York: Oxford Univer. Press, 1964. Ch. 19.

Hollander, E. P., & Willis, R. H. Some current issues in the psychology of conformity and nonconformity. *Psychol. Bull.*, 1967, *68*, 62-76.

Hollander, E. P., Julian, J. W., & Haaland, G. A. Conformity process and prior group support. *J. Pers. soc. Psychol.*, 1965, *2*, 852-858.

Hollander, E. P., Julian, J. W., & Perry, F. A. Leader style, competence, and source of authority as determinants of actual and perceived influence. *Technical Report 5, ONR Contract 4679*. Buffalo: State Univer. of N.Y., September 1966. Also reported in Hollander, E. P., & Julian, J. W. Studies in leader legitimacy, influence, and innovation. In L. Berkowitz (Ed.), *Advances in experimental social psychology*. Vol. 5. New York: Academic Press, 1970. Pp. 33-69.

Hollander, E. P., Julian, J. W., & Sorrentino, R. M. The leader's sense of legit-

imacy as a source of his constructive deviation. *Technical Report 12, ONR Contract 4679.* Buffalo: State Univer. of N.Y., July 1969. Also reported in Hollander, E. P., & Julian, J. W. Studies in leader legitimacy, influence, and innovation. In L. Berkowitz (Ed.), *Advances in experimental social psychology.* Vol. 5. New York: Academic Press, 1970. Pp. 33-69.

Hollingshead, A. B. *Elmtown's youth.* New York: Wiley, 1949.

Hollingshead, A. B. Factors associated with prevalence of mental illness. In E. E. Maccoby, T. M. Newcomb, & E. L. Hartley (Eds.), *Readings in social psychology.* (3rd ed.) New York: Holt, Rinehart, & Winston, 1958. Pp. 425-436.

Hollingshead, A. B., & Redlich, F. C. Schizophrenia and social structure. *Amer. J. Psychiat.,* 1954, *110,* 695-701.

Hollingshead, A. B., & Redlich, F. C. *Social class and mental illness.* New York: Wiley, 1958.

Holmes, J. G., & Strickland, L. H. Choice freedom and confirmation of incentive expectancy as determinants of attitude change. *J. Pers. soc. Psychol.,* 1970, 14, 39-45.

Holsti, O. R., & North, R. C. The history of human conflict. In E. B. McNeil (Ed.), *The nature of human conflict.* Englewood Cliffs, N.J.: Prentice-Hall, 1965. Pp. 155-171.

Homans, G. C. Group factors in worker productivity. In Committee on work in industry of the National Research Council. *Fatigue of workers: its relation to industrial production.* New York: Reinhold, 1941. (Republished in H. Proshansky & B. Seidenberg (Eds.), *Basic studies in social psychology.* New York: Holt, Rinehart & Winston 1965.)

Homans, G. C. *The human group.* New York: Harcourt Brace, 1950.

Homans, G. C. The cash posters. *Amer. sociol. Rev.,* 1954, *19,* 724-733.

Homans, G. C. Social behavior as exchange. *Amer. J. Sociol.,* 1958, *63,* 597-606.

Homans, G. C. *Social behavior: its elementary forms.* New York: Harcourt Brace, 1961.

Homans, G. C. Small groups. In B. Berelson (Ed.), *The behavioral sciences today.* New York: Basic Books, 1963. Pp. 165-175.

Homans, G. C. Fundamental social processes. In N. Smelser (Ed.), *Sociology.* New York: Wiley, 1967a. Pp. 27-78.

Homans, G. C. *The nature of social science.* New York: Harcourt, Brace & World, 1967b.

Hood, W. R., & Sherif, M. Verbal report and judgment of an unstructured stimulus. *J. Psychol.,* 1962, *54,* 121-130.

Horney, K. *Our inner conflicts.* New York: Norton, 1945.

Hovland, C. I. (Ed.) *The order of presentation in persuasion.* New Haven: Yale Univer. Press, 1957.

Hovland, C. I. Reconciling conflicting results derived from experimental and survey studies of attitude change. *Amer. Psychologist,* 1959, *14,* 8-17.

Hovland, C. I., & Janis, I. L. (Eds.) *Personality and persuasibility.* New Haven: Yale Univer. Press, 1959.

Hovland, C. I., Lumsdaine, A. A., & Sheffield, F. D. *Experiments on mass communication,* New Jersey: Princeton Univer. Press, 1949.

Hovland, C. I., & Rosenberg, M. J. (Eds.) *Attitude organization and change.* New Haven: Yale Univer. Press, 1960.

Hovland, C. I., & Sherif, M. Judgmental phenomena and scales of attitude measurement: item displacement in Thurstone scales. *J. abnorm. soc. Psychol.,* 1952, 47, 822-832.

Hovland, C. I., & Weiss, W. The influence of source credibility on communication effectiveness. *Publ. Opin. Quart.,* 1951, 15, 635-650.

Hovland, C. I., Campbell, E. H., & Brock, T. The effects of "commitment" on opinion change following communication. In C. I. Hovland (Ed.), *The order of presentation in persuasion.* New Haven: Yale Univer. Press, 1957. Pp. 23-32.

Hovland, C. I., Harvey, O. J., & Sherif, M. Assimilation and contrast effects in reactions to communication and attitude change. *J. abnorm. soc. Psychol.,* 1957, 55, 244-252.

Hovland, C. I., Janis, I. L., & Kelley, H. H. *Communication and persuasion.* New Haven: Yale Univer. Press, 1953.

Howard, R. C., & Berkowitz, L. Reactions to the evaluations of one's performance. *J. Pers.,* 1958, 26, 494-507.

Hunt, J. McV. The effect of infant feeding frustration upon adult hoarding in the albino rat. *J. abnorm. soc. Psychol.,* 1941, 36, 338-360.

Hunt, J. McV. Traditional personality theory in the light of recent evidence. *Amer. Scientist,* 1965, 53, 80-96.

Hunt, J. McV. Has compensatory education failed? Has it been attempted? *Harvard Educat. Rev.* 1969, 39, 278-301.

Hunt, R. G. Socio-cultural factors in mental disorder. *Behav. Sci.,* 1959, 4, 96-107.

Hunt, R. G., & Synnerdahl, V. Social influences among kindergarten children: an experimental note. *Sociol. & soc. Res.,* 1959, 43, 171-174.

Hurwitz, J. I., Zander, A. F., & Hymovitch, B. Some effects of power on the relations among group members. In D. Cartwright & A. F. Zander (Eds.), *Group dynamics: research and theory.* Evanston, Ill.: Row, Peterson, 1953. Pp. 488-492.

Hyman, H. H. *Interviewing in social research.* Chicago: Univer. of Chicago Press, 1954.

Hyman, H. H. *Survey design and analysis.* Glencoe, Ill.: Free Press, 1955.

Hyman, H. H. *Political socialization: a study in the psychology of political behavior.* Glencoe, Ill.: Free Press, 1959.

Hyman, H. H., & Sheatsley, P. B. Why information campaigns fail. *Pub. Opin. Quart.,* 1947, 11, 412-423.

Hyman, H. H., & Singer, E. Introduction. *Readings in reference group theory and research.* New York: Free Press, 1968. Pp. 3-21.

Ichheiser, G. Misunderstandings in human relations: a study in false social perceptions. *Amer. J. Sociol.*, 1949, *55*, 1-70.

Insko, C. A. *Theories of attitude change.* New York: Appleton-Century-Crofts, 1967.

Israel, J. *Self-evaluation and rejection in groups.* Stockholm: Almqvist & Wiksell, 1956.

Jackson, P. W. *Life in classrooms.* New York: Holt, Rinehart & Winston, 1968.

Jacobs, H. A. To count a crowd. *Columbia Journalism Review*, 1967, *6*, 37-40.

Jacobs, R. C., & Campbell, D. T. The perpetuation of an arbitrary tradition through several generations of a laboratory microculture. *J. abnorm. soc. Psychol.*, 1961, *62*, 649-658.

Jaeger, G., & Selznick, P. A normative theory of culture. *Amer. sociol. Rev.*, 1964, *29*, 653-669.

Jahoda, M. Race relations and mental health. In UNESCO, *Race and Science.* New York: Columbia Univ. Press, 1961.

Jakubczak, L. F., & Walters, R. H. Suggestibility as dependency behavior. *J. abnorm. soc. Psychol.*, 1959, *59*, 102-107.

Janda, K. F. Towards the explication of the concept of leadership in terms of the concept of power. *Hum. Relat.*, 1960, *13*, 345-363.

Janis, I. L. Psychological effects of warnings. In C. W. Baker and D. W. Chapman (Eds.), *Man and society in disaster.* New York: Basic Books, 1962.

Janis, I. L. Effects of fear arousal on attitude change: recent developments in theory and experimental research. In L. Berkowitz (Ed.), *Advances in experimental social psychology.* Vol. 3. New York: Academic Press, 1967. Pp. 166-224.

Janis, I. L. *Victims of groupthink: a psychological study of foreign policy decisions and fiascos.* New York: Harcourt Brace Jovanovich, 1971. In press.

Janis, I. L., & Feshbach, S. Effects of fear-arousing communications. *J. abnorm. soc. Psychol.*, 1953, *48*, 78-92.

Janis, I. L., & Field, P. B. Sex differences and personality factors related to persuasibility. In C. I. Hovland & I. L. Janis (Eds.), *Personality and persuasibility.* New Haven: Yale Univer. Press, 1959. Pp. 55-68.

Janis, I. L., & Gilmore, J. B. The influence of incentive conditions on the success of role playing in modifying attitudes. *J. Pers. soc. Psychol.* 1965, *1*, 17-27.

Janis, I. L., & Hovland, C. I. An overview of persuasibility research. In C. I. Hovland & I. L. Janis (Eds.), *Personality and persuasibility.* New Haven: Yale Univer. Press, 1959. Pp. 1-26.

Janis, I. L., & Mann, L. Effectiveness of emotional role-playing in modifying smoking habits and attitudes. *J. exp. Res. in Pers.*, 1965, *1*, 84-90.

Janis, I. L., & Terwilliger, R. An experimental study of psychological resistance to fear-arousing communications. *J. abnorm. soc. Psychol.*, 1962, *65*, 403-410.

Janowitz, M., & Little, R. *Sociology and the military establishment.* (Rev. ed.) New York: Russell Sage Foundation, 1965.

Jenkins, W. O., & Stanley, J. C. Partial reinforcement: a review and critique. *Psychol. Bull.*, 1950, *47*, 193-234.

Jenness, A. The role of discussion in changing opinions regarding a matter of fact. *J. abnorm. soc. Psychol.*, 1932, *27*, 279-296.

Jennings, H. H. *Leadership and isolation.* New York: Longmans Green, 1943. (2nd ed., 1950.)

Jennings, H. H. Sociometry of leadership. *Sociometry Monogr.*, 1947, *14*, 12-24.

Jensen, A. R. How much can we boost IQ and scholastic achievement? *Harvard Educat. Rev.*, 1969, *39*, 1-123.

Johnson, R. C. Linguistic structure as related to concept formation and to concept content. *Psychol. Bull.*, 1962, *59*, 468-476.

Jones, E. E. *Ingratiation.* New York: Appleton-Century-Crofts, 1964.

Jones, E. E. Conformity as a tactic of ingratiation. *Science*, 1965, *149*, 144-150.

Jones, E. E., & Daugherty, B. N. Political orientation and the perceptual effects of an anticipated interaction. *J. abnorm. soc. Psychol.*, 1959, *59*, 340-349.

Jones, E. E., & deCharms, R. Changes in social perception as a function of the personal relevance of behavior. *Sociometry*, 1957, *20*, 75-85.

Jones, E. E., & Davis, K. E. From acts to dispositions. In L. Berkowitz (Ed.), *Advances in experimental social psychology.* Vol. 2. New York: Academic Press, 1965. Pp. 219-266.

Jones, E. E., & Harris, V. A. The attribution of attitudes. *J. exp. soc. Psychol.*, 1967, *3*, 1-24.

Jones, M. B. Authoritarianism and intolerance of fluctuation. *J. abnorm. soc. Psychol.*, 1955, *50*, 125-126.

Jones, R. A. Volunteering to help: the effects of choice, dependence, and anticipated dependence. *J. Pers. soc. Psychol.*, 1970, *14*, 121-129.

Jones, S. C. Some determinants of interpersonal evaluating behavior. *J. Pers. soc. Psychol.*, 1966, *3*, 397-403.

Jordan, N. Behavioral forces that are a function of attitudes and of cognitive organization. *Hum. Relat.*, 1953, *6*, 273-287.

Julian, J. W. The study of competition. In W. E. Vinacke (Ed.), *Readings in general psychology.* New York: American Book Co., 1968. Pp. 289-297.

Julian, J. W., & Katz, S. B. Internal versus external control and the value of reinforcement. *J. Pers. soc. Psychol.*, 1968, *8*, 89-94.

Julian, J. W., & Perry, F. A. Cooperation contrasted with intra-group and inter-group competition. *Sociometry*, 1967, *3*, 79-90.

Julian, J. W., & Steiner, I. D. Perceived acceptance as a determinant of conformity behavior. *J. soc. Psychol.*, 1961, *55*, 191-198.

Julian, J. W., Hollander, E. P., & Regula, C. R. Endorsement of the group

spokesman as a function of his source of authority, competence, and success. *J. Pers. soc. Psychol.*, 1969, *11*, 42-49.

Julian, J. W., Regula, C. R., & Hollander, E. P. Effects of prior agreement from others on task confidence and conformity. *J. Pers. soc. Psychol.*, 1968, *9*, 171-178.

Julian, J. W., Ryckman, R. M., & Hollander, E. P. Effects of prior group support on conformity: an extension. *J. soc. Psychol.*, 1969, *77*, 189-196.

Jung, C. G. *The basic writings of C. G. Jung.* V. de Laszlo (Ed.) New York: Random House, 1959.

Kagan, J. The concept of identification. *Psychol. Rev.*, 1958, *65*, 296-305.

Kagan, J. Impulsive and reflective children: significance of conceptual tempo. In J. D. Krumboltz (Ed.), *Learning and the educational process.* Chicago: Rand-McNally, 1965a.

Kagan, J. Individual differences in the resolution of response uncertainty. *J. Pers. soc. Psychol.*, 1965b, *2*, 154-160.

Kagan, J. Body build and conceptual impulsivity in children. *J. Pers.*, 1966a, *34*, 118-128.

Kagan, J. Reflection-impulsivity: the generality and dynamics of conceptual tempo. *J. abnorm. soc. Psychol.*, 1966b, *71*, 17-24.

Kagan, J. Inadequate evidence and illogical conclusions. *Harvard Educat. Rev.*, 1969, *39*, 274-277.

Kagan, J., & Kogan, N. Individual variation on cognitive processes. In P. H. Mussen (Ed.), *Carmichael's Manual of Child Psychology.* (3rd ed.) New York: Wiley, 1969.

Kagan, J., & Moss, H. A. Personality and social development: family and peer influences. *Rev. of educat. Res.*, 1961, *31*, 463-474.

Kahl, J. A. Educational and occupational aspirations of "common man" boys. *Harvard Educat. Rev.*, 1953, *23*, 186-203.

Kahl, J. A. *The American class structure.* New York: Holt, Rinehart & Winston, 1957.

Kahn, R., & Katz, D. Leadership practices in relation to productivity and morale. In D. Cartwright & A. Zander (Eds.), *Group dynamics: research and theory.* Evanston, Ill.: Row Peterson, 1960. Pp. 554-570.

Kaplan, B. (Ed.) *Studying personality cross-culturally.* New York: Harper & Row, 1961.

Kardiner, A. *The individual and his society.* New York: Columbia Univer. Press, 1939.

Kardiner, A., with the collaboration of R. Linton, C. DuBois, & J. West. *The psychological frontiers of society.* New York: Columbia Univer. Press, 1945.

Kardiner, A., & Preble, E. *They studied man.* New York: New American Library, Mentor Book, 1963.

Katona, G. *The powerful consumer.* New York: McGraw-Hill, 1960.

Katona, G. *Mass consumption society.* New York: McGraw-Hill, 1964.

Katz, D. The functional approach to the study of attitudes. *Publ. opin. Quart.*, 1960, *24*, 163-204.

Katz, D., & Stotland, E. A preliminary statement to a theory of attitude structure and change. In S. Koch (Ed.), *Psychology: a study of a science.* Vol. 3. New York: McGraw-Hill, 1959. Pp. 423-475.

Katz, D., Sarnoff, I., & McClintock, C. G. Ego-defense and attitude change. *Hum. Relat.*, 1956, *9*, 27-45.

Katz, E., & Lazarsfeld, P. F. *Personal influence.* Glencoe, Ill.: Free Press, 1955.

Kelley, H. H. The warm-cold variable in first impressions of persons. *J. Pers.*, 1950, *18*, 431-439.

Kelley, H. H. Communication in experimentally created hierarchies. *Hum. Relat.*, 1951, *4*, 39-56.

Kelley, H. H. Attitudes and judgments as influenced by reference groups: two functions of reference groups. In G. Swanson, T. M. Newcomb, & E. L. Hartley (Eds.), *Readings in social psychology.* (2nd ed.) New York: Holt, 1952. Pp. 410-420.

Kelley, H. H. Salience of membership and resistance to change of group-anchored attitudes. *Hum. Relat.*, 1955, *8*, 275-290.

Kelley, H. H. Experimental studies of threats in interpersonal negotiations. *J. Confl. Resolut.*, 1965, *9*, 79-105.

Kelley, H. H. Attribution theory in social psychology. In D. Levine (Ed.), *Nebraska symposium on motivation.* Lincoln: University of Nebraska Press, 1967. Pp. 192-238.

Kelley, H. H., & Volkart, E. H. The resistance to change of group-anchored attitudes. *Amer. sociol. Rev.*, 1952, *17*, 453-465.

Kelley, H. H., Condry, J. C., Dahlke, A. E., & Hill, A. H. Collective behavior in a simulated panic situation. *J. exp. soc. Psychol.*, 1965, *1*, 20-54.

Kellogg, W. N., & Kellogg, L. A. *The ape and the child.* New York: McGraw-Hill, 1933.

Kelly, E. L. Consistency of the adult personality. *Amer. Psychologist*, 1955, *10*, 659-681.

Kelly, G. *A theory of personality: the psychology of personal constructs.* New York: W. W. Norton, Norton Library Edition, 1963.

Kelman, H. C. Effects of success and failure on "suggestibility" in the autokinetic situation. *J. abnorm. soc. Psychol.*, 1950, *45*, 267-285.

Kelman, H. C. Compliance, identification, and internalization: three processes of opinion chance. *J. Confl. Resolut.*, 1958, *2*, 51-60.

Kelman, H. C. Processes of opinion change. *Publ. Opin. Quart.*, 1961, *25*, 57-78.

Kelman, H. C. (Ed.) *International behavior: a socio-psychological analysis.* New York: Holt, Rinehart & Winston, 1965.

Kelman, H. C. Human use of human subjects: the problem of deception in social psychological experiments. *Psychol. Bull.*, 1967, *67*, 1-11.

Kennedy, J. F. *Profiles in courage.* New York: Harper, 1956.

Kennedy, J. F. Address at the University of Washington, November 16, 1961.

Kerckhoff, A. C., & Back, K. W. *The June bug: a study of hysterical contagion.* New York: Appleton-Century-Crofts, 1968.

Kerckhoff, A. C., & Davis, K. E. Value consensus and need complimentarity in mate selection. *Amer. sociol. Rev.,* 1962, *27,* 295-303.

Kerr, W. A., Koppelmeier, G., & Sullivan, J. J. Absenteeism, turnover, and morale in a metals fabrication factory. *Occup. Psychology,* 1951, *25,* 50-55.

Kiesler, C. A. The nature of conformity and group pressure. In J. Mills (Ed.), *Experimental social psychology.* New York: Macmillan, 1969. Pp. 235-306.

Kiesler, C. A., & Kiesler, S. B. *Conformity.* Reading, Mass.: Addison-Wesley, 1969.

Kinsey, A. C., Pomeroy, W. B., & Martin, C. E. *Sexual behavior in the human male.* Philadelphia: W. B. Saunders & Co., 1948.

Kirkhart, R. O. Minority group identification and group leadership. *J. soc. Psychol.,* 1963, *59,* 111-117.

Kirscht, J. P., Lodahl, T. M., & Haire, M. Some factors in the selection of leaders by members of small groups. *J. abnorm. soc. Psychol.,* 1959, *58,* 406-408.

Kissinger, H. A. *Nuclear weapons and foreign policy.* New York: Harper and Row, 1957.

Klapper, J. T. *The effects of mass communication.* Glencoe, Ill.: Free Press, 1960.

Klein, J. *The study of groups.* London: Routledge & Kegan Paul, 1956.

Klineberg, O. *Tensions affecting international understanding.* New York: Social Science Research Council, Bulletin 62, 1950.

Klineberg, O. *Social psychology.* (Rev. ed.) New York: Holt, 1954.

Klineberg, O. *The human dimension in international relations.* New York: Holt, Rinehart, & Winston, 1964.

Kluckhohn, C. *Mirror for Man.* New York: McGraw-Hill, 1949a. (Also available in paperback from McGraw-Hill.)

Kluckhohn, C. The limitations of adaptation and adjustment as concepts for understanding cultural behavior. In J. Romano (Ed.), *Adaptation.* Ithaca: Cornell Univer. Press, 1949b. Pp. 99-113.

Kluckhohn, C., & Murray, H. A. (Eds.) *Personality in nature, society, and culture.* New York: Knopf, 1948.

Kluckhohn, C., Murray, H. A., & Schneider, D. M. *Personality in nature, society, and culture.* (2nd ed.) New York: Knopf, 1953.

Kluckhohn, F. R. Dominant and variant value orientations. In C. Kluckhohn, H. A. Murray, & D. M. Schneider (Eds.), *Personality in nature, society, and culture.* New York: Knopf, 1953.

Kluckhohn, F. R., & Strodtbeck, F. L. *Variations in value orientations.* Evanston, Ill.: Row, Peterson, 1961.

Knox, R. E., & Inkster, J. A. Postdecision dissonance at post time. *J. Pers. soc. Psychol.*, 1968, 8, 319-323.

Koch, H. L. The relation in young children between characteristics of their playmates and certain attributes of their siblings. *Child Development*, 1957, 28, 175-202.

Kogan, N., & Wallach, M. A. *Risk taking: a study in cognition and personality.* New York: Holt, Rinehart, & Winston, 1964.

Kohlberg, L. Development of moral character and ideology. In M. L. Hoffman & L. W. Hoffman (Eds.), *Review of child development research.* Vol. 1. New York: Russell Sage Foundation, 1964.

Kohlberg, L. Moral and religious education and the public schools: a developmental view. In T. Sizer (Ed.), *Religion and public education.* Boston: Houghton Mifflin, 1967.

Kohlberg, L. *Stages in the development of moral thought and action.* New York: Holt, Rinehart, & Winston, 1969.

Komarovsky, M. Cultural contradictions and sex roles. *Amer. J. Sociol.*, 1946, 52, 184-189.

Kottman, E. J. Language internalization and intentional orientation. *Etc.*, 1964, 21, 456-466.

Krasner, L. Studies of the conditioning of verbal behavior. *Psychol. Bull.*, 1958, 55, 148-170.

Krasner, L., & Ullmann, L. P. *Research in behavior modification: new developments and implications.* New York: Holt, Rinehart, & Winston, 1965.

Krech, D., & Crutchfield, R. S. *Theory and problems of social psychology.* New York: McGraw-Hill, 1948.

Kroeber, A. L., & Kluckholm, C. Culture, a critical review of concepts and definitions. *Papers of the Peabody Museum of American Archaeology and Ethnology*, 47 (1). Cambridge, Mass.: Harvard Univer., 1952, 1-223.

Kroeber, A. L., & Parsons, T. The concepts of culture and of social system. *Amer. sociol. Rev.*, 1958, 23, 582-583.

Kubany, A. J. Evaluation of medical student clinical performance: a criterion study. *Dissert. Abstr.*, 1957, 17, 1119-1120.

Kutner, B., Wilkins, C., & Yarrow, P. R. Verbal attitudes and overt behavior involving racial prejudice. *J. abnorm. soc. Psychol.*, 1952, 47, 649-652.

Laing, R. D. *The divided self: a study of sanity and madness.* Chicago: Quadrangle Books, 1960.

Lambert, W. W., & Lambert, W. E. *Social psychology.* Englewood Cliffs, N.J.: Prentice-Hall, 1964.

Lambert, W. W., Solomon, R. L., & Watson, P. D. Reinforcement and extinction as factors in size estimation. *J. exp. Psychol.*, 1949, 39, 637-641.

Lana, R. E. *Assumptions of social psychology.* New York: Appleton-Century-Crofts, 1969.

Landecker, W. S. Types of integration and their measurement. In P. F.

Lazarsfeld & M. Rosenberg (Eds.), *The language of social research.* Glencoe, Ill.: The Free Press, 1955. Pp. 19-27.

Lane, R. E. *Political thinking and consciousness.* Chicago: Markham, 1969.

LaPiere, R. T. Attitudes versus actions. *Social Forces,* 1934, *13,* 230-237.

Latané, B., & Darley, J. M. Group inhibition of bystander intervention in emergencies. *J. Pers. soc. Psychol.,* 1968, *10,* 215-221.

Latané, B., & Darley, J. M. Bystander "apathy." *Amer. Scientist,* 1969, *57,* 244-268.

Latané, B., & Rodin, J. A lady in distress: inhibiting effects of friends and strangers on bystander intervention. *J. exp. soc. Psychol.,* 1969, *5,* 189-202.

Lazarsfeld, P. F., & Rosenberg, M. (Eds.) *The language of social research.* Glencoe, Ill.: Free Press, 1955.

Lazarsfeld, P. F., Berelson, B., & Gaudet, H. *The people's choice.* (2nd ed.) New York: Columbia Univer. Press, 1948.

Lazarus, R. S. *Personality and adjustment.* Englewood Cliffs, N.J.: Prentice-Hall, 1963.

Lazarus, R. S. *Psychological stress and the coping process.* New York: Mc-Graw-Hill, 1966.

Leavitt, H. J. Some effects of certain communication patterns on group performance. *J. abnorm. soc. Psychol.,* 1951, *46,* 38-50.

LeBon, G. *The crowd: a study of the popular mind.* (2nd ed.) London: T. F. Unwin, 1897.

Lee, R. B., & DeVore, I. Problems in the study of hunters and gatherers. In R. B. Lee & I. DeVore (Eds.), *Man the hunter.* Chicago: Aldine, 1968. Pp. 3-12.

Leiderman, P. H., & Shapiro, D. (Eds.) *Psycho-biological approaches to social behavior.* Stanford: Stanford Univer. Press, 1964.

Lemert, E. M. *Social pathology.* New York: McGraw-Hill, 1951.

Lenneberg, E. H. *Biological foundations of language.* New York: Wiley, 1967.

Lenneberg, E. H., & Roberts, J. M. The language of experience: a study in methodology. *Int. J. Amer. Linguistics,* 1956, *22,* Memoir No. 13.

Lependorf, S. The effects of incentive value and expectancy on dissonance resulting from attitude-discrepant behavior and disconfirmation of expectancy. Unpublished doctoral dissertation, State Univer. of New York at Buffalo, 1964.

Lerner, D. *The passing of traditional society.* Glencoe, Ill.: Free Press, 1958.

Lesser, G. S. Relationships between various forms of aggression and popularity among lower-class children. *J. educ. Psychol.,* 1959, *50,* 20-25.

Leventhal, H., & Niles, P. A field experiment on fear-arousal with data on the validity of questionnaire measures. *J. Pers.,* 1964, *32,* 459-479.

Leventhal, H., & Niles, P. Persistence of influence for varying durations of exposure to threat stimuli. *Psychol. Rep.* 1965, *16,* 223-233.

Leventhal, H., Singer, R. P., and Jones, S. The effects of fear and specificity

of recommendation upon attitudes and behavior. *J. Pers. soc. Psychol.*, 1965, 2, 20-29.

Levine, L. S. *Personal and social development: the psychology of effective behavior.* New York: Holt, Rinehart, & Winston, 1963.

Levine, R., Chein, I., & Murphy, G. The relation of the intensity of a need to the amount of perceptual distortion. *J. Psychol.*, 1942, 13, 283-293.

Levinger, G. Note on need complimentarity in marriage. *Psychol. Bull.*, 1964, 61, 153-157.

Levinger, G., & Schneider, D. J. Test of the "risk is a value" hypothesis. *J. Pers. soc. Psychol.*, 1969, 11, 165-169.

Levinger, G., Senn, D. J., & Jorgensen, B. W. Progress toward permanence in courtship: a test of the Kerckhoff-Davis hypotheses. *Sociometry*, 1970. In press.

Lewin, K. *Principles of topological psychology.* New York: McGraw-Hill, 1936.

Lewin, K. Group decision and social change. In T. M. Newcomb & E. L. Hartley (Eds.), *Readings in social psychology.* New York: Holt, 1947. Pp 330-344.

Lewin, K., Lippitt, R., & White, R. K. Patterns of aggressive behavior in experimentally created "social climates." *J. soc. Psychol.*, 1939, 10, 271-299.

Lewis, O. The culture of poverty. *Trans-action*, 1963, 1, 17-19.

Libo, L. M. *Measuring group cohesiveness.* Ann Arbor: Univer. of Michigan, Research Center for Group Dynamics, Institute for Social Research, 1953.

Liebow, E. *Tally's corner: a study of Negro streetcorner men.* Boston: Little, Brown, 1967.

Likert, R. A technique for the measurement of attitudes. *Archives of Psychol.*, 1932, No. 4.

Likert, R. Motivation and productivity. *Mgmt. Rec.*, 1956, 18, 128-131.

Likert, R. *New patterns of management.* New York: McGraw-Hill, 1961.

Linder, D. E., Cooper, J., & Jones, E. E. Decision freedom as a determinant of the role of incentive magnitude in attitude change. *J. Pers. soc. Psychol.*, 1967, 6, 245-254.

Lindesmith, A. R., & Strauss, A. L. *Social psychology.* (2nd ed.) New York: Dryden Press, 1956.

Lindzey, G. (Ed.) *Handbook of social psychology.* Reading, Mass.: Addison-Wesley, 1954.

Lindzey, G., & Aronson, E. (Eds.) *The handbook of social psychology.* (2nd ed.) Cambridge, Mass.: Addison-Wesley, 1968.

Lindzey, G., & Borgatta, E. F. Sociometric measurement. In G. Lindzey (Ed.), *The handbook of social psychology.* Reading, Mass.: Addison-Wesley, 1954. Pp. 405-448.

Linn, L. S. Verbal attitudes and overt behavior: a study of racial discrimination. *Social Forces*, 1965, *43*, 353-364.

Linton, H., & Graham, E. Personality correlates of persuasibility. In C. I. Hovland & I. L. Janis (Eds.), *Personality and persuasibility.* New Haven: Yale Univer. Press, 1959. Pp. 69-101.

Linton, R. *The cultural background of personality.* New York: Appleton-Century-Crofts, 1945. (Also published as a paperback by Appleton-Century-Crofts.)

Linton, R. A concept of national character. In A. H. Stanton & S. E. Perry (Eds.), *Personality in political crisis.* Glencoe, Ill.: Free Press, 1951. Pp. 133-150.

Lippitt, R., & White, R. K. An experimental study of leadership and group life. In T. M. Newcomb & E. L. Hartley (Eds.), *Readings in social psychology.* New York: Holt, 1947.

Lippitt, R., Polansky, N., & Rosen, S. The dynamics of power. *Hum. Relat.,* 1952, *5*, 37-64.

Lippitt, R., Watson, J., & Westley, B. *The dynamics of planned change.* New York: Harcourt, Brace & World, 1958.

Lippmann, W. *Public opinion.* New York: Harcourt, Brace, 1922.

Lipset, S. M. *Political man.* Garden City, N.Y.: Doubleday, 1960.

Lipset, S. M., & Bendix, R. *Social mobility in industrial society.* Berkeley: Univer. of Calif. Press, 1959.

Loomis, J. L. Communication, the development of trust and cooperative behavior. *Hum. Relat.,* 1959, *12*, 305-315.

Lorenz, K. Z. *On aggression.* New York: Harcourt, Brace, & World, 1966.

Lorenz, K. Z. Interview. *The New York Times Magazine,* July 5, 1970. Pp. 4ff.

Lorge, I., Fox, D., Davitz, J., & Bremer, M. A survey of studies contrasting the quality of group performance and individual performance, 1920-1957. *Psychol. Bull.,* 1958, *55*, 337-372.

Lorimer, F. *The growth of reason.* New York: Harcourt, Brace, 1929.

Lorr, M., & McNair, D. M. Expansion of the interpersonal behavior circle. *J. Pers. soc. Psychol.,* 1965, *2*, 823-830.

Luchins, A. S., & Luchins, E. H. On conformity with judgments of a majority or an authority. *J. soc. Psychol.,* 1961, *53*, 303-316.

Lundberg G. A., & Stule, M. Social attraction patterns in a village. *Sociometry,* 1938, *1*, 375-419.

Lynd, R. S., & Lynd, H. M. *Middletown: a study in contemporary American culture.* New York: Harcourt, Brace, 1929.

McCandless, B. R., Bilous, C., & Bennett, H. Peer popularity and dependence on adults in preschool-age socialization. *Child Development,* 1961, *32*, 511-518.

McCarthy, D. A comparison of children's language in different situations. *J. genet. Psychol.,* 1929, *36*, 583-591.

McClelland, D. C. *Personality.* New York: Dryden, 1951.

McClelland, D. C. The use of measures of human motivation in the study of society. In J. W. Atkinson (Ed.), *Motives in fantasy, action, and society*. Princeton: Van Nostrand, 1958. Pp. 518-552.

McClelland, D. C. *The achieving society*. Princeton: Van Nostrand, 1961.

McClelland, D. C., Atkinson, J. W., Clark, R. A., & Lowell, E. L. *The achievement motive*. New York: Appleton-Century-Crofts, 1953.

McClintock, C. G. Group support and the behavior of leaders and non-leaders. *J. abnorm. soc. Psychol.*, 1963, *67*, 105-113.

McClintock, C. G., & Hekhuis, D. J. European community deterrence: its organization, utility, and political feasibility. *J. Confl. Resolut.*, 1961, *5*, 230-253.

McDougall, W. *An introduction to social psychology*. London: Methuen, 1908. (23rd ed., 1936.)

McDougall, W. *The group mind*. New York: G. P. Putnam's Sons, 1920. (Rev. ed., 1928.)

McGrath, J. E. *Social psychology: a brief introduction*. New York: Holt, Rinehart & Winston, 1964.

McGrath, J. E., & Julian, J. W. Interaction process and task outcome in experimentally-created negotiation groups. *J. psychol. Studies*, 1963, *14*, 117-138.

McGrath, J. E., & Altman, I. *Small group research: a critique and synthesis of the field*. New York: Holt, Rinehart & Winston, 1966.

McGregor, D. *Leadership and motivation*. Cambridge, Mass.: MIT Press, 1966.

McGuire, W. J. Order of presentation as a factor in "conditioning" persuasiveness. In C. I. Hovland (Ed.), *The order of presentation in persuasion*. New Haven: Yale Univer. Press, 1957. Pp. 98-114.

McGuire, W. J. Inducing resistance to persuasion. In L. Berkowitz (Ed.), *Advances in experimental social psychology*. Vol. 1. New York: Academic Press, 1964. Pp. 191-229.

McGuire, W. J. Attitudes and opinions. In P. R. Farnsworth (Ed.), *Annual review of psychology*. Vol. 17. Palo Alto, Calif.: Annual Reviews, 1966. Pp. 475-514.

McGuire, W. J. Personality and susceptibility to social influence. In E. Borgatta and W. Lambert (Eds.), *Handbook of personality theory and research*. Chicago: Rand McNally, 1967. Pp. 1130-1187.

McGuire, W. J. *Immunization against persuasion*. New Haven: Yale Univer. Press, 1968.

McGuire, W. J., & Millman, S. Anticipatory belief lowering following forewarning of a persuasive attack. *J. Pers. soc. Psychol.*, 1965, *2*, 471-479.

McGuire, W. J., & Papageorgis, D. Effectiveness of pre-warning in developing resistance to persuasion. *Publ. Opin. Quart.*, 1962, *26*, 24-34.

McNeil, E. (Ed.) *The nature of human conflict*. Englewood Cliffs, N.J.: Prentice-Hall, 1965.

Maccoby, E. The taking of adult roles in middle childhood. *J. abnorm. soc. Psychol.*, 1961, *63*, 493-503.

Maccoby, E. The development of moral values and behavior in childhood. In J. A. Clausen *et al.*, *Socialization and society*. Boston: Little, Brown, 1968. Pp. 227-269.

Maclay, H. S. Language and nonlinguistic behavior: an experimental investigation. *Dissert. Abstr.*, 1956, *16*, 1039.

Mack, R. *Transforming America: patterns of social change.* New York: Random House, 1967.

Maddi, S. R. Affective tone during environmental regularity and change. *J. abnorm. soc. Psychol.*, 1961, *62*, 338-345.

Maddi, S. R. Meaning, novelty, and affect: comments on Zajonc's paper. *J. Pers. soc. Psychol., Monograph Supplement*, 1968, *9*, 28-29.

Maier, N. R., & Hoffman, L. R. Acceptance and quality of solutions as related to leader's attitudes toward disagreement in group problem solving. *J. appl. Beh. Sci.*, 1965, *1*, 373-386.

Malinowski, B. *Sex and repression in savage society.* New York: Harcourt, Brace, 1927.

Mandelbaum, D. G. *Soldier groups and Negro soldiers.* Berkeley: Univer. of Calif. Press, 1952.

Mann, L. The effects of emotional role playing on smoking attitudes and behavior. *J. exp. soc. Psychol.*, 1967, *3*, 334-348.

Mann, L., & Abeles, R. P. Evaluation of presidential candidates as a function of time and stage of voting decision. *J. Psychol.*, 1970, *74*, 167-173.

Mann, L., & Janis, I. L. A follow-up study on the long-range effects of emotional role playing. *J. Pers. soc. Psychol.*, 1968, *8*, 339-342.

Mann, L., & Taylor, K. F. Queue counting: the effect of motives upon estimates of numbers in waiting lines. *J. Pers. soc. Psychol.*, 1969, *12*, 95-103.

Mann, R. D. A review of the relationships between personality and performance in small groups. *Psychol. Bull.*, 1959, *56*, 241-270.

Marcus, P. M. Expressive and instrumental groups: toward a theory of group structure. *Amer. J. Sociol.*, 1960, *66*, 54-59.

Marrow, A. J. *The practical theorist: the life and work of Kurt Lewin.* New York: Basic Books, 1969.

Marshall, H. R. Prediction of social acceptance in community youth groups. *Child Development*, 1958, *29*, 173-184.

Marshall, H. R. Relations between home experiences and children's use of language in play interactions with peers. *Psychol. Monogr.*, 1961, *75*, No. 5 (Whole No. 509).

Marshall, H. R., & McCandless, B. R. Relationships between dependence on adults and social acceptance by peers. *Child Development*, 1957, *28*, 413-419.

Marshall, S. L. A. *Men against fire.* Washington, D.C.: Combat Forces Press, 1951.

Masling, J. Role-related behavior of the subject and psychologist and its effects upon psychological data. In D. Levine (Ed.), *Nebraska symposium on motivation.* Lincoln: Univer. of Nebraska Press, 1966. Pp. 67-103.

Maslow, A. H. The authoritarian character structure. *J. soc. Psychol.,* 1943, *18,* 401-411.

Maslow, A. H. *Motivation and personality.* New York: Harper, 1954. (Revised ed., 1970.)

Mausner, B. Studies in social interaction: III. Effect of variation in one partner's prestige on the interaction of observer pairs. *J. appl. Psychol.,* 1953, *37,* 391-393.

Mausner, B. The effect of prior reinforcement on the interaction of observer pairs. *J. abnorm. soc. Psychol.,* 1954a, *49,* 65-68.

Mausner, B. The effect of one partner's success in a relevant task on the interaction of observer pairs. *J. abnorm. soc. Psychol.,* 1954b, *49,* 557-560.

Mead, G. H. *Mind, self and society.* (C. M. Morris, Ed.) Chicago: Univer. of Chicago Press, 1934.

Mead, M. *Male and female.* New York: William Morrow & Co., 1949. (Also available as Penguin Paperback.)

Mead, M. *New lives for old.* New York: William Morrow & Co., 1956. (Also available as a Mentor Book, New York, 1961.)

Meade, R. D. An experimental study of leadership in India. *J. Soc. Psychol.,* 1967, *72,* 35-43.

Medow, H., & Zander, A. Aspirations for the group chosen by central and peripheral members. *J. Pers. soc. Psychol.,* 1965, *1,* 224-228.

Merton, R. K. The self-fulfilling prophecy. *Antioch Review,* 1948, *8,* 193-210. Also in R. K. Merton, *Social theory and social structure.* New York: Free Press, 1957. Pp. 421-436.

Merton, R. K. *Social theory and social structure.* Glencoe, Ill.: Free Press, 1957.

Milburn, T. W. What constitutes effective deterrence? *J. Confl. Resolut.,* 1959, *3,* 138-145.

Milburn, T. The concept of deterrence. *J. soc. Issues,* 1961, *17,* 3-11.

Milgram, S. Liberating effects of group pressure. *J. Pers. soc. Psychol.,* 1965, *1,* 127-134.

Milgram, S., & Toch, H. Collective behavior: crowds and social movements. In G. Lindzey, & E. Aronson (Eds.), *The handbook of social psychology.* (2nd ed.) Vol. 4. Reading, Mass.: Addison-Wesley, 1968. Pp. 507-610.

Milgram, S., Bickman, L., Berkowitz, L. Note on the drawing power of crowds of different size. *J. Pers. soc. Psychol.,* 1969, *13,* 79-82.

Miller, D., & Swanson, G. E. *The changing American parent.* New York: Wiley, 1958.

Miller, E. J., & Rice, A. K. *Systems of organization.* London: Tavistock Publications, 1967.

Miller, G. A. *Language and communication.* New York: McGraw-Hill, 1951.

Miller, G. A. The psycholinguists. *Encounter,* 1964, *23,* 29-37.

Miller, H. P. *Rich man, poor man.* New York: Signet Books, 1965.

Miller, L. K., & Hamblin, R. L. Interdependence, differential rewarding, and productivity. *Amer. sociol. Rev.,* 1963, *28,* 768-778.

Miller, N., & Campbell, D. T. Recency and primacy in persuasion as a function of the timing of speeches and measurements. *J. abnorm. soc. Psychol.,* 1959, *59,* 1-9.

Miller, N. E., & Dollard, J. *Social learning and imitation.* New Haven: Yale Univer. Press, 1941.

Miller, R. E., Murphy, J. V., & Mirsky, I. A. Modification of social dominance in a group of monkeys by inter-animal conditioning. *J. comp. physiol. Psychol.,* 1955, *48,* 392-396.

Millman, S. The relationship between anxiety, learning and opinion change. Unpublished doctoral dissertation. Columbia Univer., 1965.

Mills, J. Opinion change as a function of the communicator's desire to influence and liking for the audience. *J. exp. soc. Psychol.,* 1966, *2,* 152-159.

Mills, J., & Aronson, E. Opinion change as a function of the communicator's attractiveness and desire to influence. *J. Pers. soc. Psychol.,* 1965, *1,* 173-177.

Mills, T. M. Power relations in three person groups. *Amer. sociol. Rev.,* 1953, *18,* 351-357.

Mills, T. M. A sleeper variable in small groups research: the experimenter. *Pacific Sociological Review,* 1962, *5,* 21-28.

Mills, T. M. *The sociology of small groups.* Englewood Cliffs, N.J.: Prentice-Hall, 1967.

Minard, R. D. Race relationships in the Pocahontas coal field. *J. soc. Issues,* 1952, *8,* 29-44.

Mintz, A. Non-adaptive group behavior. *J. abnorm. soc. Psychol.,* 1951, *46,* 150-159.

Moede, W. *Experimentelle Massenpsychologie.* Leipzig: S. Hirzel, 1920.

Moeller, G., & Applezweig, M. H. A motivational factor in conformity. *J. abnorm. soc. Psychol.,* 1957, *55,* 114-120.

Montagu, A. *The biosocial nature of man.* New York: Grove Press, 1956.

Montagu, A. *Human heredity.* New York: Mentor Books, 1960.

Montagu, A. (Ed.) *Man and aggression.* New York: Oxford Univ. Press, 1968.

Moreno, J. L. *Who shall survive?* Washington: Nervous and Mental Disease Publishing Co., 1934.

Moreno, J. L. Foundations of sociometry, an introduction. *Sociometry,* 1941, *4,* 15-38.

Moreno, J. L. *Who shall survive?* (Rev. ed.) Beacon, N.Y.: Beacon House, 1953.

Moreno, J. L. (Ed.) *The sociometry reader.* Glencoe, Ill.: The Free Press, 1960.

Morgan, C. T. *Introduction to psychology.* (2nd ed.) New York: McGraw-Hill, 1961.

Morris, C. *Signs, language, and behavior.* New York: Prentice-Hall, 1946.

Morris, C. *Varieties of human value.* Chicago: Univer. of Chicago Press, 1956.

Morris, D. *The naked ape.* New York: McGraw-Hill, 1968.

Moscovici, S., Lage, E., & Naffrechoux, M. Influence of a consistent minority on the responses of a majority in a color perception task. *Sociometry,* 1969, *32,* 365-380.

Mouton, J. S., Bell, R. L., & Blake, R. R. Role playing skill and sociometric peer status. *Group Psychotherapy,* 1956, *9,* 7-17.

Mowrer, O. H. *Learning theory and personality dynamics.* New York: Ronald, 1950.

Mowrer, O. H. Hearing and speaking: an analysis of language learning. *J. Speech & Hear. Disorders,* 1958, *23,* 143-152.

Mowrer, O. H. *Learning theory and behavior.* New York: Wiley, 1960.

Mumford, L. *The conduct of life.* New York: Harcourt, Brace, & World, 1951.

Mumford, L. *The highway and the city.* New York: Harcourt, Brace & World, 1963.

Münsterberg, H. *Psychology, general and applied.* New York: D. Appleton & Co., 1914.

Muraskin, J., & Iverson, M. A. Social expectancy as a function of judging social distance. *J. soc. Psychol.,* 1958, *48,* 11-14.

Murphy, G. *Personality: a biosocial approach to origins and structure.* New York: Harper, 1947.

Murphy, G. *Historical introduction to modern psychology.* (Rev. ed.) New York: Harcourt, Brace and Company, 1949.

Murphy, G. *In the minds of men.* New York: Basic Books, 1953.

Naroll, R. Deterrence in history. In D. G. Pruitt & R. C. Snyder (Eds.), *Theory and research on the causes of war.* Englewood Cliffs, N.J.: Prentice-Hall, 1969. Pp. 150-164.

Newcomb, T. M. *Personality and social change.* New York: Dryden, 1943.

Newcomb, T. M. *Social psychology.* New York: Holt, Rinehart, & Winston, 1950.

Newcomb, T. M. Social psychological theory: integrating individual and social approaches. In J. Rohrer & M. Sherif (Eds.), *Social psychology at the crossroads.* New York: Harper & Row, 1951. Pp. 31-49.

Newcomb, T. M. An approach to the study of communicative acts. *Psychol. Rev.,* 1953, *60,* 393-404.

Newcomb, T. M. The prediction of interpersonal attraction. *Amer. Psychologist,* 1956, *11,* 575-586.

Newcomb, T. M. Individual systems of orientation. In S. Koch (Ed.), *Psychology: a study of a science.* Vol. 3. New York: McGraw-Hill, 1959.

Newcomb, T. M. *The acquaintance process.* New York: Holt, Rinehart, & Winston, 1961.

Newcomb, T. M. Persistence and regression of changed attitudes: long-range studies. *J. soc. Issues*, 1963, *19*, 3-14.

Newman, H. H., Freeman, F. N., & Holzinger, K. J. *Twins: a study of heredity and environment*. Chicago: Univer. of Chicago Press, 1937.

Niles, P. The relationship of susceptibility and anxiety to acceptance of fear-arousing communications. Unpublished doctoral dissertation, Yale Univer., 1964.

Nord, W. R. Social exchange theory: an integrative approach to social conformity. *Psychol. Bull.*, 1969, *71*, 174-208.

Nordlie, P. G. The role of values in psychological operations. In HSR Conference on psychological operations and communications with foreign nationals, *Research Report 68/9-CR*. McLean, Va.: Human Sciences Research, Inc., 20 June 1968. Pp. 26-37.

Nunnally, J. C. *Tests and measurements*. New York: McGraw-Hill, 1959.

Nuttin, J. M., Jr. Attitude change after rewarded dissonant and consonant "forced compliance." *Int. J. Psychol.*, 1966, *1*, 39-57.

O'Connell, E. J. The effect of cooperative and competitive set on the learning of imitation and nonimitation. *J. exp. soc. Psychol.*, 1965, *1*, 172-183.

Ogden, C. K. *The system of Basic English*. New York: Harcourt, Brace, 1934.

Ogilvy, D. *Confessions of an advertising man*. New York: Dell, 1963.

Olmsted, M. S. *The small group*. New York: Random House, 1959.

Olsen, M. E. *The process of social organization*. New York: Holt, Rinehart & Winston, 1968.

Orlansky, H. Infant care and personality. *Psychol. Bull.*, 1949, *46*, 1-48.

Orne, M. T. On the social psychology of the psychological experiment: with particular reference to demand characteristics and their implications. *Amer. Psychologist*, 1962, *17*, 776-783.

Orwell, G. *1984*. New York: Harcourt, Brace & Co., 1949. (Also available as a Signet Book, New York, 1950.)

Osgood, C. E. The nature and measurement of meaning. *Psychol. Bull.*, 1952, *49*, 197-237.

Osgood, C. E. Cognitive dynamics in the conduct of human affairs. *Publ. Opin. Quart.*, 1960, *24*, 341-365.

Osgood, C. E. *An alternative to war or surrender*. Urbana: Univer. Illinois Press, 1962.

Osgood, C. E., & Tannenbaum, P. H. The principle of congruity in the prediction of attitude change. *Psychol. Rev.*, 1955, *62*, 42-55.

Osgood, C. E., Suci, G. J., & Tannenbaum, P. H. *The measurement of meaning*. Urbana: Univer. of Illinois Press, 1957.

Osgood, C. E., Ware, E. E., & Morris, C. Analysis of the connotative meanings of a variety of human values as expressed by American college students. *J. abnorm. soc. Psychol.*, 1961, *62*, 62-73.

Papageorgis, D., & McGuire, W. J. The generality of immunity to persuasion produced by pre-exposure to weakened counterarguments. *J. abnorm. soc. Psychol.,* 1961, *62,* 475-481.

Parsons, T. *The social system.* Glencoe, Ill.: Free Press, 1951.

Parsons, T. Personality and social structure. In A. H. Stanton & S. E. Perry (Eds.), *Personality and political crisis.* Glencoe, Ill.: The Free Press, 1951. Pp. 61-80.

Parsons, T., Bales, R. F., & Shils, E. A. (Eds.) *Working papers in the theory of action.* Glencoe, Ill.: Free Press, 1953.

Patchen, M. A conceptual framework and some empirical data regarding comparison of social rewards. *Sociometry,* 1961, *24,* 136-156.

Paul, J., & Laulicht, J. *In your opinion: leaders' and voters' attitudes on defence and disarmament.* Vol. 1. Clarkson, Ontario: Canadian Peace Research Institute, 1963.

Pei, M. *The story of language.* New York: New American Library, Mentor Books, 1960.

Pei, M. *Words in sheep's clothing.* New York: Hawthorn, 1969.

Pei, M. *How to learn languages and what languages to learn.* New York: Harper & Row, 1966.

Pelz, D. C. Influence: a key to effective leadership in the first-line supervisor. *Personnel,* 1952, *29,* 209-217.

Pepinsky, P. N. Social exceptions that prove the rule. In I. A. Berg & B. M. Bass (Eds.), *Conformity and deviation.* New York: Harper & Bros., 1961. Pp. 424-434.

Pepinsky, P. N., Hemphill, J. K., & Shevitz, R. N. Attempts to lead, group productivity, and morale under conditions of acceptance and rejection. *J. abnorm. soc. Psychol.,* 1958, *57,* 47-54.

Pepitone, A. Attributions of causality, social attitudes, and cognitive matching processes. In R. Tagiuri & L. Petrullo (Eds.), *Person perception and interpersonal behavior.* Stanford, Calif.: Stanford Univer. Press, 1958. Pp. 258-276.

Pepitone, A., & Kleiner, R. The effects of threat and frustration on group cohesiveness. *J. abnorm. soc. Psychol.,* 1957, *54,* 192-199.

Perlmutter, H. V. Stereotypes about Americans and Europeans who make specific statements. *Psychol. Rep.,* 1957, *3,* 131-137.

Petrullo, L., & Bass, B. M. (Eds.) *Leadership and interpersonal behavior.* New York: Holt, Rinehart & Winston, 1961.

Pettigrew, T. *A profile of the Negro American.* Princeton: Van Nostrand, 1964.

Phares, E. J. Expectancy changes in skill and chance situations. *J. abnorm. soc. Psychol.,* 1957, *54,* 339-342.

Piaget, J. *The language and thought of the child.* London: Kegan Paul, Trench, Trubner & Co., 1926.

Piaget, J. *The psychology of intelligence.* London: Routledge, Kegan Paul, 1947.

Piaget, J. *The moral judgment of the child.* Glencoe, Ill.: Free Press, 1948. (Originally published in 1932 by Harcourt Brace.)

Pilisuk, M., & Skolnick, P. Inducing trust: a test of the Osgood proposal. *J. Pers. soc. Psychol.*, 1968, 8, 121-133.

Plant, J. S. *The envelope: a study of the impact of the world upon the child.* New York: Commonwealth Fund, 1950.

Pollak, O. The outlook for the American family. *J. Marriage and the Family*, 1967, 29, 193-206.

Pool, I. Effects of cross-national contact on national and international images. In H. C. Kelman (Ed.), *International behavior: a socio-psychological analysis.* New York: Holt, Rinehart, & Winston, 1965. Pp. 106-129.

Prentice, W. C. H. Understanding leadership. *Harvard Bus. Rev.*, 1961, 39, 143-148, 151.

Price, K. O., Harburg, E., & Newcomb, T. M. Psychological balance in situations of negative interpersonal attitudes. *J. Pers. soc. Psychol.*, 1966, 3, 265-270.

Priest, R. F., & Sawyer, J. Proximity and peership: bases of balance in interpersonal attraction. *Amer. J. Sociol.*, 1967, 72, 633-649.

Proshansky, H., & Seidenberg, B. (Eds.) *Basic studies in social psychology.* New York: Holt, Rinehart & Winston, 1965.

Pruitt, D. G. Reward structure and cooperation: the decomposed prisoner's dilemma game. *J. Pers. soc. Psychol.*, 1967, 7, 21-27.

Pruitt, D. G. Indirect communication in the search for agreement in negotiation. Working paper No. 1. Center for International Conflict Studies, State Univer. of N.Y. at Buffalo, Oct. 15, 1969.

Pruitt, D. G., & Snyder, R. C. (Eds.) *Theory and research on the causes of war.* Englewood Cliffs, N.J.: Prentice-Hall, 1969.

Pruitt, D. G., & Teger, A. I. Is there a shift toward risk in group discussion? If so, is it a group phenomenon? If so, what causes it? Paper presented to the American Psychological Association in 1967.

Rabinowitz, W. A note on the social perceptions of authoritarians and nonauthoritarians. *J. abnorm. soc. Psychol.*, 1956, 53, 384-386.

Radke, M. J., & Klisurich, D. Experiments in changing food habits. *J. Amer. Dietetics Assn.*, 1947, 23, 403-409.

Radloff, R., & Helmreich, R. *Groups under stress: psychological research in SEALAB II.* New York: Appleton-Century-Crofts, 1968.

Rapoport, A. Rules for debate. In Q. Wright, W. M. Evan, & M. Deutsch (Eds.), *Preventing World War III: some proposals.* New York: Simon & Schuster, 1962. Pp. 246-262.

Rapoport, A. *Two-person game theory.* Ann Arbor: Univ. of Michigan Press, 1966.

Rapoport, A., & Chammah, A. M. *Prisoner's dilemma: a study in conflict and cooperation.* Ann Arbor: Univ. of Michigan Press, 1965.

Raven, B. H. (Ed.) A bibliography of publications relating to the small group. (4th ed.) *Supplement to Technical Report No. 24, ONR Contract 233 (54).* Univer. of California at Los Angeles, July, 1969.

Raven, B. H., & Eachus, H. T. Cooperation and competition in means-interdependent triads. *J. abnorm. soc. Psychol.*, 1963, *67*, 307-316.

Raven, B. H., & French, J. R. P. Group support, legitimate power, and social influence. *J. Pers.*, 1958, *26*, 400-409.

Raven, B. H., & Rietsema, J. The effects of varied clarity of group goal and group path upon the individual and his relation to his group. *Hum. Relat.*, 1957, *10*, 29-45.

Reedy, G. E. *The twilight of the presidency.* New York: World New American Library, 1970.

Reese, H. W. Relationships between self-acceptance and sociometric choices. *J. abnorm. soc. Psychol.*, 1961, *62*, 472-474.

Rest, J. Developmental hierarchy in preference and comprehension of moral judgment. Unpublished doctoral dissertation, Univer. of Chicago, 1968.

Rest, J., Turiel, E., & Kohlberg, L. Level of moral development as a determinant of preference and comprehension of moral judgments. *J. Pers.*, 1969, *37*, 225-252.

Rhine, R. J. The effect of peer group influence upon concept-attitude development and change. *J. soc. Psychol.*, 1960, *51*, 173-179.

Ribble, M. A. Infantile experience in relation to personality development. In J. McV. Hunt (Ed.), *Personality and the behavior disorders.* Vol. 2. New York: Ronald Press, 1944. Ch. 20.

Richardson, L. F. *Statistics of deadly quarrels.* Pittsburgh: Boxwood Press, 1960.

Riecken, H. W. The effect of talkativeness on ability to influence group solutions to problems. *Sociometry*, 1958, *21*, 309-321.

Riesman, D., Glazier, N., & Denny, R. *The lonely crowd: a study of the changing American character.* New Haven: Yale Univer. Press, 1950.

Riley, Matilda W., Riley, J. W., Jr., & Moore, M. E. Adolescent values and the Riesman typology. In S. M. Lipset & L. Lowenthal (Eds.), *Culture and social character.* New York: Free Press, 1961. Pp. 370-386.

Ritchie, E., & Phares, E. J. Attitude change as a function of internal-external control and communicator status. *J. Pers.*, 1969, *37*, 429-443.

Rivers, W. H. R. Vision. In A. C. Haddon (Ed.), *Reports of the Cambridge anthropological expedition to the Torres Straits.* Vol. 2. Cambridge: Cambridge Univer. Press, 1901.

Rivers, W. H. R. Observations on the senses of the Todas. *Brit. J. Psychol.*, 1905, *1*, 321-396.

Rodrigues, A. The biasing effect of agreement in balanced and imbalanced triads. *J. Pers.*, 1968, *36*, 138-153.

Rohrer, J., & Sherif, M. (Eds.) *Social psychology at the crossroads.* New York: Harper-Row, 1951.

Rokeach, M. The nature and meaning of dogmatism. *Psychol. Rev.*, 1954, *61*, 194-205.

Rokeach, M. *The open and closed mind.* New York: Basic Books, 1960.

Rokeach, M. The organization and modification of beliefs. *Centennial Rev.*, 1963, *7*, 375-395.

Rokeach, M. *Beliefs, attitudes, and values.* San Francisco: Jossey-Bass, 1968.

Rokeach, M., & Rothman, G. The principle of belief congruence and the congruity principle as models of cognitive interaction. *Psychol. Rev.*, 1965, *72*, 128-142.

Rose, A. M. Reference groups of high school youth. *Child Development*, 1956, *27*, 351-363.

Rosen, B. C. Conflicting group membership: a study of parent-peer group cross-pressures. *Amer. sociol. Rev.*, 1955, *20*, 155-161.

Rosenberg, M. J. Cognitive structure and attitudinal affect. *J. abnorm. soc. Psychol.*, 1956, *53*, 367-372.

Rosenberg, M. J. A structural theory of attitude dynamics. *Publ. Opin. Quart.*, 1960a, *24*, 319-340.

Rosenberg, M. J. An analysis of affective-cognitive consistency. In C. I. Hovland & M. J. Rosenberg (Eds.), *Attitude organization and change.* New Haven: Yale Univer. Press, 1960b. Pp. 15-64.

Rosenberg, M. J. Cognitive reorganization in response to the hypnotic reversal of attitudinal affect. *J. Pers.*, 1960c, *28*, 39-63.

Rosenberg, M. J. When dissonance fails: on eliminating evaluation apprehension from attitude measurement. *J. Pers. soc. Psychol.*, 1965, *1*, 28-42.

Rosenberg, M. J., & Abelson, R. P. An analysis of cognitive balancing. In C. I. Hovland & M. J. Rosenberg (Eds.), *Attitude organization and change.* New Haven: Yale Univer. Press, 1960. Pp. 112-163.

Rosenfeld, H. M., & Nauman, D. Effects of dogmatism on the development of informal relationships among women. *J. Pers.*, 1969, *37*, 497-511.

Rosenthal, F. Some relationships between sociometric position and language structure of young children. *J. educ. Psychol.*, 1957, *48*, 483-497.

Rosenthal, R. On the social psychology of the psychological experiment. *Amer. Scientist*, 1963, *51*, 268-283.

Rosenthal, R. Interpersonal expectations: effects of the experimenter's hypothesis. In R. Rosenthal & R. Rosnow (Eds.), *Artifact in behavioral research.* New York: Academic Press, 1969.

Rosenthal, R., & Jacobson, L. *Pygmalion in the classroom.* New York: Holt, Rinehart, & Winston, 1968.

Rosenthal, R., & Rosnow, R. (Eds.) *Artifact in behavioral research.* New York: Academic Press, 1969.

Rosow, I. Issues in the concept of need complementarity. *Sociometry*, 1957, *20*, 216-253.

Ross, E. A. *Social psychology.* New York: Macmillan, 1908.

Rotter, J. B. *Social learning and clinical psychology.* Englewood Cliffs, N.J.: Prentice-Hall, 1954.

Rotter, J. B. Generalized expectancies for internal vs. external control of reinforcement. *Psychol. Monogr.*, 1966, *80*, 1-28.

Rotter, J. B., & Mulry, R. C. Internal versus external control of reinforcement and decision time. *J. Pers. soc. Psychol.*, 1965, 2, 598-604.

Rubin, Z. Measurement of romantic love. *J. Pers. soc. Psychology.* In press, 1970.

Rubin, Z., & Zajonc, R. B. Structural bias and generalization in the learning of social structures. *J. Pers.*, 1969, 37, 310-324.

Rudraswamy, V. An investigation of the relationship between perceptions of status and leadership attempts. *J. Indian Academy of appl. Psychol.*, 1964, 1, 12-19.

Ryan, F. J., & Davie, J. S. Social acceptance, academic achievement, and academic aptitude among high school students. *J. educ. Res.*, 1958, 52, 101-106.

Sabath, G. The effect of disruption and individual status on person perception and group attraction. *J. soc. Psychol.*, 1964, 64, 119-130.

Samelson, F. The relation of achievement and affiliation motives to conforming behavior in two conditions of conflict with a majority. In J. W. Atkinson (Ed.), *Motives in fantasy, action and society.* New York: Van Nostrand, 1958. Pp. 421-433.

Sampson, E. E. Status congruence and cognitive consistency. *Sociometry*, 1963, 26, 146-162.

Sanford, F. H. *Authoritarianism and leadership.* Philadelphia: Institute for Research in Human Relations, 1950.

Sapir, E. Language and environment. *Amer. Anthropologist*, 1912, 14, 226-242.

Sapir, E. *Language: an introduction to the study of speech.* New York: Harcourt, Brace & Co., 1921. (Also available in a paperback as a Harvest Book, New York, 1949.)

Sargent, F. W. Televised speech reported in the *Boston Globe*, Feb. 12, 1970, p. 1.

Sargent, S. S. Emotional stereotypes in the *Chicago Tribune. Sociometry*. 1939, 2, 69-75.

Savell, J. M., & Healey, G. W. Private and public conformity after being agreed and disagreed with. *Sociometry*, 1969, 32, 315-329.

Schachter, S. Deviation, rejection, and communication. *J. abnorm. soc. Psychol.*, 1951, 46, 190-207.

Schachter, S. *The psychology of affiliation.* Calif.: Stanford Univer. Press, 1959.

Schachter, S. The interaction of cognitive and physiological determinants of emotional state. In P. H. Leiderman & D. Shapiro (Eds.), *Psychobiological approaches to social behavior.* Stanford: Stanford University Press, 1964. Pp. 138-173. Also in L. Berkowitz (Ed.), *Advances in experimental social psychology.* Vol. 1. New York: Academic Press, 1964. Pp. 49-80.

Schachter, S., & Singer, J. Cognitive, social and physiological determinants of emotional state. *Psychol. Rev.*, 1962, 69, 379-399.

Schachter, S., & Wheeler, L. Epinephrine, chlorpromazine, and amusement. *J. abnorm. soc. Psychol.*, 1962, *65*, 121-128.

Schachter, S., Ellertson, N., McBride, D., & Gregory, D. An experimental study of cohesiveness and productivity. *Hum. Relat.*, 1951, *4*, 229-238.

Schaffner, B. *Fatherland.* New York: Columbia Univer. Press, 1948.

Schanck, R. L. A study of a community and its groups and institutions conceived of as behaviors of individuals. *Psychol. Monogr.*, 1932, *43*, No. 2.

Scheff, T. J. A theory of social coordination: application to mixed-motive games. *Sociometry*, 1967, *30*, 215-234.

Schulman, G. I. Asch conformity studies: conformity to the experimenter and/or to the group? *Sociometry*, 1967, *30*, 26-40.

Schuman, F. L. *The nazi dictatorship.* (2nd ed.) New York: Knopf, 1939.

Schutz, W. C. The interpersonal underworld. *Harvard Business Rev.*, 1958, *36*, 123-135.

Schutz, W. C. The ego, FIRO theory and the leader as completer. In L. Petrullo & B. M. Bass (Eds.), *Leadership and interpersonal behavior.* New York: Holt, Rinehart, & Winston, 1961. Pp. 48-65.

Scodel, A. Induced collaboration in some non-zero-sum games. *J. Confl. Resolut.*, 1962, *6*, 335-340.

Scodel, A., & Mussen, P. Social perception of authoritarians and nonauthoritarians. *J. abnorm. soc. Psychol.*, 1953, *48*, 181-184.

Scott, J. P. Implications of infra-human social behavior for problems of human relations. In M. Sherif & M. O. Wilson (Eds.), *Group relations at the crossroads.* New York: Harper & Bros., 1953.

Sears, R. R. A theoretical framework for personality and social behavior. *Amer. Psychologist*, 1951a, *6*, 476-482.

Sears, R. R. Effects of frustration and anxiety on fantasy aggression. *Amer. J. Orthopsychiat.*, 1951b, *21*, 498-505.

Sears, R. R. The 1958 summer research project on identification. *J. nursery Educat.*, 1960, *16*, (2).

Sears, R. R., Maccoby, E., & Levin, H. *Patterns of child-rearing.* Evanston, Ill.: Row, Peterson, 1957.

Secord, P. F., & Backman, C. W. Personality theory and the problem of stability and change in individual behavior: an interpersonal approach. *Psychol. Rev.*, 1961, *68*, 21-33.

Seeman, M., & Morris, R. T. *A status factor approach to leadership.* Columbus: Ohio State Univer. Research Foundation, 1950.

Segall, M. H., Campbell, D. T., & Herskovits, M. J. Cultural differences in the perception of geometrical illusions. *Science*, 1963, *139*, 769-771.

Segall, M. H., Campbell, D. T., & Herskovits, M. J. *The influence of culture in visual perception.* New York: Bobbs Merrill, 1966.

Selltiz, C., Jahoda, M., Deutsch, M., & Cook, S. W. *Research methods in social relations.* (Rev. ed.) New York: Holt, Rinehart, & Winston, 1959.

Selznick, P. *Leadership in administration.* Evanston: Row, Peterson, 1957.

Seward, G. *Psychotherapy and culture conflict.* New York: Ronald, 1956.

Shapiro, D., & Crider, A. Psychophysiological approaches in social psychology. In G. Lindzey & E. Aronson (Eds.), *The handbook of social psychology.* (2nd ed.) Vol. 3. Reading, Mass.: Addison-Wesley, 1969. Pp. 1-49.

Shapiro, H. L. (Ed.) *Man, culture & society.* New York: Oxford Univer. Press, 1956.

Sharp, L. Steel axes for stone-age Australians. *Human Organization,* 1952, *11,* 17-22.

Shartle, C. L., & Stogdill, R. M. *Studies in naval leadership.* Columbus: Ohio State Univer. Research Foundation, 1952.

Shaw, F. J., & Ort, R. S. *Personal adjustment in the American culture.* New York: Harper, 1953.

Shaw, Marjorie E. Comparison of individuals and small groups in the rational solution of complex problems. *Amer. J. Psychol.,* 1932, *44,* 491-504.

Shaw, Marvin E. Some effects of unequal distribution of information upon group performance in various communication nets. *J. abnorm. soc. Psychol.,* 1954, *49,* 547-553.

Shaw, Marvin E. Some motivational factors in cooperation and competition. *J. Pers.,* 1958, *26,* 155-169.

Shaw, Marvin E. Acceptance of authority, group structure and the effectiveness of small groups. *J. Pers.,* 1959a, *27,* 196-210.

Shaw, Marvin E. Some effects of individually prominent behavior upon group effectiveness and member satisfaction. *J. abnorm. soc. Psychol.,* 1959b, *59,* 382-386.

Shaw, Marvin E. A note concerning homogeneity of membership and group problem solving. *J. abnorm. soc. Psychol.,* 1960, *60,* 448-450.

Shaw, Marvin E., & Costanzo, P. R. *Theories of social psychology.* New York: McGraw-Hill, 1970.

Shaw, Marvin E., & Wright, J. M. *Scales for the measurement of attitudes.* New York: McGraw-Hill, 1967.

Sherif, C. W., Sherif, M., & Nebergall, R. E. *Attitude and attitude change: the social judgment-involvement approach.* Philadelphia: Saunders, 1965.

Sherif, M. A study of some social factors in perception. *Arch. Psychol.,* 1935, *27,* No. 187.

Sherif, M. *The psychology of social norms.* New York: Harper, 1936.

Sherif, M. Superordinate goals in the reduction of intergroup conflict. *Amer. J. Sociol.,* 1958, *63,* 349-358.

Sherif, M. Conformity-deviation, norms, and group relations. In I. A. Berg & B. M. Bass (Eds.), *Conformity and deviation.* New York: Harper, 1961. Pp. 159-198.

Sherif, M. (Ed.) *Intergroup relations and leadership.* New York: Wiley, 1962.

Sherif, M., & Cantril, H. *The psychology of ego-involvements.* New York: Wiley, 1947.

Sherif, M., & Hovland, C. I. *Social judgment.* New Haven: Yale Univer. Press, 1961 .

Sherif, M., & Sherif, C. W. *Groups in harmony and tension: an integration of studies on intergroup relations.* New York: Harper, 1953.

Sherif, M., & Sherif, C. W. *Reference groups: exploration into the conformity and deviation of adolescents.* New York: Harper & Row, 1964.

Sherif, M., & Sherif, C. W. (Eds.) *Problems of youth: transition to adulthood in a changing world.* Chicago: Aldine, 1965.

Sherif, M., & Wilson, M. O. (Eds.) *Group relations at the crossroads.* New York: Harper, 1953.

Sherif, M., Harvey, O. J., White, B. J., Hood, W. R., & Sherif, C. W. *Intergroup conflict and cooperation: the Robbers Cave experiment.* Norman, Oklahoma: Univer. of Oklahoma Book Exchange, 1961.

Shibutani, T. Reference groups as perspectives. *Amer. J. Sociol.,* 1955, *60,* 562-570.

Shils, E. A. Class. In *Encyclopedia Britannica, 5,* 1960. Pp. 766-768.

Showel, M. Interpersonal knowledge and rated leader potential. *J. abnorm. soc. Psychol.,* 1960, *61,* 87-92.

Shrauger, S., & Altrocchi, J. The personality of the perceiver as a factor in person perception. *Psychol. Bull.,* 1964, *62,* 289-308.

Shure, G. H., Meeker, R. J., & Hansford, E. A. The effectiveness of pacifist strategies in bargaining games. *J. Confl. Resolut.,* 1965, *9,* 106-117.

Silverman, I., Shulman, A. D., & Wiesenthal, D. L. Effects of deceiving and debriefing psychological subjects on performance in later experiments. *J. Pers. soc. Psychol.,* 1970, *14,* 203-212.

Simmel, G. *The sociology of Georg Simmel.* (Trans. and edited by K. H. Wolff.) Glencoe, Ill.: Free Press, 1950.

Singer, J. D. *Deterrence, arms control, and disarmament.* Columbus, Ohio: Ohio State Univer. Press, 1962.

Singer, J. D. (Ed.) *Human behavior and international politics.* Chicago: Rand-McNally, 1965.

Skinner, B. F. *Verbal behavior.* New York: Appleton-Century-Crofts, 1957.

Slater, P. E. Contrasting correlates of group size. *Sociometry,* 1958, *21,* 129-139.

Smelser, W. T. Dominance as a factor in achievement and perception in cooperative problem solving interactions. *J. abnorm. soc. Psychol.,* 1961, *62,* 535-542.

Smith, M. B., Bruner, J. S., & White, R. W. *Opinions and personality.* New York: Wiley, 1956.

Snider, J. G., & Osgood, C. E. (Eds.) *Semantic differential technique: a sourcebook.* Chicago: Aldine, 1969.

Snyder, G. H. *Deterrence and defense.* Princeton, N.J.: Princeton Univer. Press, 1961.

Snyder, R. C., Bruck, H. W., & Sapin, B. *Foreign policy decision-making: an approach to the study of international politics.* New York: Free Press, 1962.

Solomon, L. The influence of some types of power relationships and game strategies upon the development of interpersonal trust. *J. abnorm. soc. Psychol.*, 1960, *61*, 223-230.

Sommer, R. Studies in personal space. *Sociometry*, 1959, *22*, 247-260.

Sommer, R. Leadership and group geography. *Sociometry*, 1961, *24*, 99-110.

Sommer, R. Small group ecology. *Psychol. Bull.*, 1967, *67*, 145-152.

Sommer, R. *Personal space.* Englewood Cliffs, N.J.: Prentice-Hall, 1969.

Spector, A. J. Expectations, fulfillment, and morale. *J. abnorm. soc. Psychol.*, 1956, *52*, 51-56.

Spitz, R. Hospitalism: an inquiry into the genesis of psychiatric conditions in early childhood. *Psychoanalytic Study of the Child*, 1945, *1*, 53-74.

Spock, B. *The common sense book of baby and child care.* New York: Duell, Sloan, & Pearce, 1946.

Stagner, R. *Psychological aspects of international relations.* Belmont, Calif.: Brooks/Cole, 1967.

Staub, E. Effects of variation in permissibility of movement on children helping another child in distress. *Proceedings of the 77th annual convention, APA*, 1969, *4*, 385-386.

Staub, E. A child in distress: the influence of age and number of witnesses on children's attempts to help. *J. Pers. soc. Psychol.*, 1970, *14*, 130-140.

Steiner, I. D. Interpersonal behavior as influenced by accuracy of social perception. *Psychol. Rev.*, 1955, *62*, 268-274.

Steiner, I. D., & Fishbein, M. (Eds.) *Current studies in social psychology.* New York: Holt, Rinehart & Winston, 1965.

Steiner, I. D., & Johnson, H. H. Authoritarianism and conformity. *Sociometry*, 1963, *26*, 21-34.

Steiner, I. D., & Rajaratnam, N. A model for the comparison of individual and group performance scores. *Behav. Sci.*, 1961, *6*, 142-147.

Steinzor, B. The spatial factor in face to face discussion groups. *J. abnorm. soc. Psychol.*, 1950, *45*, 552-555.

Stoetzel, J. *Without the chrysanthemum and the sword.* London: Heinemann, 1955.

Stogdill, R. M. Personal factors associated with leadership. *J. Psychol.*, 1948, *25*, 35-71.

Stogdill, R. M. Leadership, membership and organization. *Psychol. Bull.*, 1950, *47*, 1-14.

Stogdill, R. M. *Individual behavior and group achievement.* New York: Oxford Univer. Press, 1959.

Stoner, J. A. F. A comparison of individual and group decisions involving risk. Unpublished masters thesis. School of Industrial Management, Massachusetts Institute of Technology, 1961.

Storr, A. *Human aggression*. New York: Atheneum, 1968.

Stotland, E. *The psychology of hope*. San Francisco: Jossey-Bass, 1969.

Stott, L. H. Persisting effects of early family experiences upon personality development. *Merrill-Palmer School Quarterly* (Detroit), 1957, 3, No. 3.

Stouffer, S. A., Suchman, E. A., DeVinney, L. C., Star, S. A., & Williams, R. M., Jr. *The American soldier: adjustment during army life*. Vol. 1. Princeton, N.J.: Princeton Univer. Press, 1949.

Strauss, A. L. Concepts, communication, and groups. In M. Sherif & M. O. Wilson (Eds.), *Group relations at the crossroads*. New York: Harper & Bros., 1953.

Strauss, A. L. *George Herbert Mead on social psychology*. Chicago: Univ. of Chicago Press, 1964.

Stricker, L. J., Messick, S., & Jackson, D. N. Suspicion of deception: implications for conformity research. *J. Pers. soc. Psychol.*, 1967, 5, 379-389.

Strodtbeck, F. L. Husband-wife interaction over revealed differences. *Amer. sociol. Rev.*, 1951, 16, 468-473.

Strodtbeck, F. L. The family as a three-person group. *Amer. sociol. Rev.*, 1954, 19, 23-29.

Strodtbeck, F. L. Family interaction, values, and achievement. In D. C. McClelland, A. L. Baldwin, U. Bronfenbrenner, & F. L. Strodtbeck (Eds.), *Talent and society*. Princeton, N.J.: Van Nostrand, 1958. Pp. 135-194.

Strodtbeck, F. L., & Hook, L. H. The social dimensions of a twelve-man jury table. *Sociometry*, 1961, 24, 397-415.

Strodtbeck, F. L., James, R. M., & Hawkins, C. Social status in jury deliberations. In E. E. Maccoby, T. M. Newcomb, & E. L. Hartley (Eds.), *Readings in social psychology*. (3rd ed.) New York: Holt, 1958. Pp. 379-388.

Suchman, E. A. The intensity component in attitude and opinion research. In S. A. Stouffer, L. Guttman, E. A. Suchman, P. F. Lazarsfeld, S. A. Star, & J. A. Gardner (Eds.), *Measurement and prediction*. New Jersey: Princeton Univer. Press, 1949.

Sulzberger, C. L. "Sound and fury signifying nothing?" In the *St. Louis Post Dispatch*, March 15, 1960, Section B, page 5.

Sumner, W. G., & Keller, A. G. *The science of society*. Vol. 1. New Haven: Yale Univer. Press, 1927.

Szasz, T. *The myth of mental illness*. New York: Paul B. Hoeber, 1961.

Tagiuri, R. Relational analysis: an extension of sociometric method with emphasis upon social perception. *Sociometry*, 1952, 15, 91-104.

Tagiuri, R. Introduction to R. Tagiuri & L. Petrullo (Eds.), *Person perception and interpersonal behavior*. Stanford, Calif.: Stanford Univer. Press, 1958. Pp. ix-xvii.

Tajfel, H. Value and the perceptual judgment of magnitude. *Psychol. Rev.*, 1957, 64, 192-204.

Tajfel, H. Social and cultural factors in perception. In G. Lindzey & E. Aronson (Eds.), *The handbook of social psychology.* (2nd ed.) Vol. 3. Reading, Mass.: Addison-Wesley, 1968. Pp. 315-394.

Talese, G. *The kingdom and the power.* New York: World New American Library, 1969.

Talland, G. A. The assessment of group opinion by leaders and their influence on its formation. *J. abnorm. soc. Psychol.,* 1954, *49,* 431-434.

Tannenbaum, F. *Crime and the community.* New York: McGraw-Hill, 1951.

Tannenbaum, P. H. The congruity principle revisited: studies in the reduction, induction, and generalization of persuasion. In L. Berkowitz (Ed.), *Advances in experimental social psychology.* Vol. 3. New York: Academic Press, 1967. Pp. 271-320.

Tannenbaum, P. H., Macaulay, J. R., & Norris, E. L. The principle of congruity and reduction of persuasion. *J. Pers. soc. Psychol.,* 1966, *3,* 233-238.

Tarde, G. *The laws of imitation.* (Trans. from 2nd French edition by E. C. Parsons.) New York: Holt, 1903.

Taylor, J. A. A personality scale of manifest anxiety. *J. abnorm. soc. Psychol.,* 1953, *48,* 285-290.

Taylor, J. A. Drive theory and manifest anxiety. *Psychol. Bull.,* 1956, *53,* 303-320.

Teger, A. I., & Pruitt, D. G. Components of group risk taking. *J. exp. soc. Psychol.,* 1967, *3,* 189-205.

Teilhard de Chardin, P. *The phenomenon of man.* New York: Harper & Row, 1961.

Terhune, K. W. Motives, situation, and interpersonal conflict within prisoner's dilemma. *J. Pers. soc. Psychol.,* Monograph Supplement, 1968, Vol. 8, No. 3.

Terman, L. M. *The measurement of intelligence.* Boston: Houghton Mifflin, 1916.

Terwilliger, R. F. *Meaning and mind.* New York: Oxford Univer. Press, 1968.

Thibaut, J. W., & Riecken, H. W. Some determinants and consequences of the perception of social causality. *J. Pers.,* 1955, *24,* 113-133.

Thibaut, J. W., & Kelley, H. H. *The social psychology of groups.* New York: Wiley, 1959.

Thomas, E. J. Effects of facilitative role interdependence on group functioning. *Hum. Relat.,* 1957, *10,* 347-366.

Thomas, E. J., & Fink, C. F. Effects of group size. *Psychol. Bull.,* 1963, *60,* 371-384.

Thomas, W. I., & Znaniecki, F. *The Polish peasant in Europe and America.* 5 vols. Boston: Badger, 1918-1920.

Thompson, W. R., & Melzack, R. Early environment. *Scientific Amer.,* Jan. 1956, 38-42.

Thorndike, E. L. *Man and his works*. Cambridge, Mass.: Harvard Univer. Press, 1943.

Thrasher, F. M. *The gang*. Chicago: Univer. of Chicago Press, 1927. (Republished in abridged paperback edition, 1963.)

Thurstone, L. L., & Chave, E. J. *The measurement of attitudes*. Chicago: Univer. of Chicago Press, 1929.

Titmuss, R. M. *Problems of social policy*. London, England: His Majesty's Stationery Office and Longmans, Green, 1950.

Titus, H. E., & Hollander, E. P. The California F scale in psychological research: 1950-1955. *Psychol. Bull.*, 1957, *54*, 47-65.

Toch, H. *The social psychology of social movements*. Indianapolis, Ind.: Bobbs-Merrill, 1965.

Toffler, A. *Future shock*. New York: Random House, 1970.

Tönnies, F. *Gemeinschaft und Gesellschaft. Abhandlung des Communismus und des Socialismus als empirische Culturformen*. Leipzig: Fues Verlag, 1887.

Trans-action. Roundup of current research, 1966, 3 (5), 3.

Triandis, H. C. Cultural influences upon cognitive processes. In L. Berkowitz (Ed.), *Advances in experimental social psychology*. Vol. 1. New York: Academic Press, 1964.

Triandis, H. C., Vassiliou, V., & Nassiakou, M. Three cross-cultural studies of subjective culture. *J. Pers. soc. Psychol.*, Monograph Supplement, 1968, 8.

Triplett, N. The dynamogenic factors in pacemaking and competition. *Amer. J. Psychol.*, 1897, *9*, 507-533.

Tuckman, J., & Lorge, I. Individual ability as a determinant of group superiority. *Hum. Relat.*, 1962, *15*, 45-51.

Tuma, E., & Livson, N. Family socioeconomic status and adolescent attitudes toward authority. *Child Development*, 1960, *31*, 387-399.

Turk, H. Instrumental and expressive ratings reconsidered. *Sociometry*, 1961, *24*, 76-81.

Turner, R. H. The public perception of protest. *Amer. sociol. Rev.*, 1969, *34*, 815-831.

Tylor, E. B. *Primitive culture. Researches in the development of mythology, philosophy, religion, language, art, and custom*. Vol. 1. New York: Henry Holt, 1877.

Uesugi, T. K., & Vinacke, W. E. Strategy in a feminine game. *Sociometry*, 1963, *26*, 75-88.

UNESCO. *Human rights, comments and interpretations; a symposium edited by UNESCO, with an introduction by J. Maritain*. London: Wingate, 1950.

UNESCO. *The race concept; results of an inquiry*. Paris: 1952.

United States Bureau of the Census. *Statistical abstract of the United States*. Washington, D.C.: Govt. Printing Office, 1970.

United States Department of Agriculture, *Agricultural handbook No. 300*, 1966.

Upshaw, H. S. The effect of variable perspectives on judgments of opinion statements for Thurstone scales: equal-appearing intervals. *J. Pers. soc. Psychol.*, 1965, *2*, 60-69.

Vaughan, G. M. The trans-situational aspect of conformity behavior. *J. Pers.*, 1964, *32*, 335-354.

Vaughan, G. M., & Mangan, G. L. Conformity to group pressure in relation to the value of the task material. *J. abnorm. soc. Psychol.*, 1963, *66*, 179-183.

Verba, S. *Small groups and political behavior: a study of leadership*. Princeton, N.J.: Princeton Univer. Press, 1961.

Verplanck, W. S. The control of the content of conversation: reinforcement of statements of opinion. *J. abnorm. soc. Psychol.*, 1955, *51*, 668-676.

Vidulich, R. N., & Kaiman, I. P. The effects of information source status and dogmatism upon conformity behavior. *J. abnorm. soc. Psychol.*, 1961, *63*, 639-642.

Vigotsky, L. S. Thought and speech. *Psychiatry*, 1939, *2*, 29-54.

Vinacke, W. E. Sex roles in a three-person game. *Sociometry*, 1959, *22*, 343-360.

Vinacke, W. E. Variables in experimental games: toward a field theory. *Psychol. Bull.*, 1969, *71*, 293-318.

Vinacke, W. E., & Arkoff, A. An experimental study of coalitions in the triad. *Amer. sociol. Rev.*, 1957, *22*, 406-414.

von Frisch, K. *The dancing bees*. New York: Harcourt, Brace, 1955.

Vroom, V. H. *Work and motivation*. New York: Wiley, 1964.

Walker, E. L., & Heyns, R. W. *An anatomy for conformity*. Englewood Cliffs, N.J.: Prentice-Hall, 1962.

Wallace, A. F. C. *Culture and personality*. New York: Random House, 1961.

Wallace, A. F. C. The new culture and personality. In T. Gladwin & W. C. Sturtevant (Eds.), *Anthropology and human behavior*. Washington: Anthropological Society of Washington, 1962. Pp. 1-12.

Wallach, M. A., & Kogan, N. Aspects of judgment and decision making: interrelationships and changes with age. *Behav. Sci.*, 1961, *6*, 23-26.

Wallach, M. A., & Wing, C. W., Jr. Is risk a value? *J. Pers. soc. Psychol.*, 1968, *9*, 101-106.

Wallach, M. A., & Malbi, J. Information versus conformity in the effects of group discussion on risk taking. *J. Pers. soc. Psychol.*, 1970, *14*, 149-156.

Walster, E. The effect of self-esteem on romantic liking. *J. exp. soc. Psychol.*, 1965, *1*, 184-197.

Walster, E. Assignment of responsibility for an accident. *J. Pers. soc. Psychol.*, 1966, *3*, 73-79.

Walster, E., & Festinger, L. The effectiveness of "overheard" persuasive communications. *J. abnorm. soc. Psychol.*, 1962, *65*, 395-402.

Walters, R. H., & Karol, P. Social deprivation and verbal behavior. *J. Pers.*, 1960, *28*, 89-107 .

Walters, R. H., Marshall, W. S., & Shooter, J. R. Anxiety, isolation, and susceptibility to social influence. *J. Pers.*, 1960, *28*, 518-529.

Waly, P., & Cook, S. W. Effect of attitude on judgments of plausibility. *J. Pers. soc. Psychol.*, 1965, *2*, 745-749.

Watson, G. Do groups think more effectively than individuals? *J. abnorm. soc. Psychol.*, 1928, *23*, 328-336.

Watson, Jeanne. A formal analysis of sociable interaction. *Sociometry*, 1958, *21*, 269-281.

Watson, J. B. *Psychology from the standpoint of a behaviorist*. Philadelphia: Lippincott, 1919.

Watson, J. B. *Behaviorism*. New York: W. W. Norton, 1925.

Watts, W. A. Predictability and pleasure: reactions to the disconfirmation of expectancies. In R. P. Abelson *et al.* (Eds.), *Theories of cognitive consistency: a sourcebook*. Chicago: Rand-McNally, 1968. Pp. 469-478.

Webb, E. J., Campbell, D. T., Schwartz, R. D., & Sechrest, L. *Unobtrusive measures: nonreactive research in the social sciences*. Chicago: Rand McNally, 1966.

Weber, M. *The theory of social and economic organization*. (Trans. & ed. by T. Parsons & A. M. Henderson.) New York: Oxford Univer. Press, 1947.

Weick, K. E. Social psychology in an era of social change. *Amer. Psychologist*, 1969a, *24*, 990-998.

Weick, K. E. *The social psychology of organizing*. Reading, Mass.: Addison-Wesley, 1969b.

Weiner, B., & Kukla, A. An attributional analysis of achievement motivation. *J. Pers. soc. Psychol.*, 1970, *15*, 1-20.

Weiner, H., & McGinnies, E. Authoritarianism, conformity, and confidence in a perceptual judgment situation. *J. soc. Psychol.*, 1961, *55*, 77-84.

Weinstein, E. A., & Deutschberger, P. Tasks, bargains, and identities in social interaction. *Soc. Forces*, 1964, *42*, 451-456.

Weisbrod, R. M. Looking behavior in a discussion group. Unpublished paper, Cornell Univer., 1965. Cited by Argyle, M., & Kendon, A. The experimental analysis of social performance. In L. Berkowitz (Ed.), *Advances in experimental social psychology*. Vol. 3. New York: Academic Press, 1967. Pp. 74-98.

Weiss, W. Opinion congruence with a negative source on one issue as a factor influencing agreement on another issue. *J. abnorm. soc. Psychol.*, 1957, *54*, 180-186.

White, R. K. *Nobody wanted war*. (Rev. ed.) Garden City, N.Y.: Doubleday Anchor, 1970.

White, R. W. Motivation reconsidered: the concept of competence. *Psychol. Rev.*, 1959, *66*, 297-334.

Whorf, B. L. *Language, thought, and reality.* (Edited by, and with an introduction by J. B. Carroll.) Cambridge, Mass.: Technology Press, 1956. (Also available in an MIT Press Paperback Edition, 1964.)

Whyte, W. F. *Street corner society.* Ill.: Univer. Chicago Press, 1943.

Whyte, W. F. Models for building and changing social organizations. *Human Organization,* 1967, *26,* 22-31.

Whyte, W. H. *The organization man.* New York: Simon & Schuster, 1956.

Wiggins, J. A., Dill, F., & Schwartz, R. D. On "status-liability." *Sociometry,* 1965, *28,* 197-209.

Wildavsky A. Prefatory note. In D. P. Moynihan, *Maximum feasible misunderstanding.* New York: Free Press, 1969. P. ii.

Williams, Meta F. Acceptance and performance among gifted elementary-school children. *Educ. Res. Bull.,* 1958, *37,* 216-220, 224.

Williams, R. M. *American society: a sociological interpretation.* New York: Knopf, 1951. (2nd ed., 1960.)

Willis, R. H. Two dimensions of conformity-nonconformity. *Sociometry,* 1963, *26,* 499-513.

Willis, R. H. Conformity, independence, and anti-conformity. *Hum. Relat.,* 1965, *18,* 373-388.

Willis, R. H., & Hollander, E. P. An experimental study of three response modes in social influence situations. *J. abnorm. soc. Psychol.,* 1964a, *69,* 150-156.

Willis, R. H., & Hollander, E. P. Supplementary note: modes of responding in social influence situations. *J. abnorm. soc. Psychol.,* 1964b, *69,* 157.

Wilson, E. Conformity revisited. *Trans-action,* 1964, *2,* 28-32.

Winch, R. F. The theory of complementary needs in mate selection: final results on the test of the general hypothesis. *Amer. sociol. Rev.,* 1955, *20,* 551-555.

Winch, R. F. *Mate-selection: a study of complementary needs.* New York: Harper and Row, 1958.

Winch, R. F., Ktsanes, T., & Ktsanes, V. The theory of complementary needs in mate selection: an analytic and descriptive study. *Amer. sociol. Rev.,* 1954, *19,* 214-249.

Winch, R. F., Ktsanes, T., & Ktsanes, V. Empirical elaboration of the theory of complementary needs in mate selection. *J. abnorm. soc. Psychol.,* 1955, *51,* 508-514.

Withey, S. B., & Katz, D. The social psychology of human conflict. In E. McNeil (Ed.), *The nature of human conflict.* Englewood Cliffs, N.J.: Prentice-Hall, 1965. Pp. 64-90.

Wolff, W. *The expression of personality: experimental depth psychology.* New York: Harper & Bros., 1943.

Worchel, S., & Brehm, J. W. Effects of threats to attitudinal freedom as a function of agreement with the communicator. *J. Pers. soc. Psychol.,* 1970, *14,* 18-22.

Wright, P. H. Personality and interpersonal attraction: basic assumptions. *J. indiv. Psychol.*, 1965, *21*, 127-136.

Wundt, W. Elements of folk psychology. Vols. 1-3. New York: Macmillan, 1916. (Originally published in German as *Völkerpsychologie*, in ten volumes, 1910-1920.)

Wyer, R. S. Effects of incentive to perform well, group attraction, and group acceptance on conformity in a judgmental task. *J. Pers. soc. Psychol.*, 1966, *4*, 21-26.

Zajonc, R. B. Social facilitation. *Science*, 1965, *149*, 269-274.

Zajonc, R. B. Attitudinal effects of mere exposure. *J. Pers. soc. Psychol.*, Monograph Supplement, 1968, 9, No. 2.

Zajonc, R. B. Cognitive theories in social psychology. In G. Lindzey & E. Aronson (Eds.), *Handbook of social psychology*. Vol. 1. New York: Addison-Wesley, 1968. Pp. 320-411.

Zander, A., & Havelin, A. Social comparison and interpersonal attraction. *Hum. Relat.*, 1960, *13*, 21-32.

Zdep, S. M., & Oakes, W. I. Reinforcement of leadership behavior in group discussion. *J. exp. soc. Psychol.*, 1967, 3, 310-320.

Zellner, M. Self-esteem, reception, and influenceability. *J. Pers. soc. Psychol.* 1970, *15*, 87-93.

Zimbardo, P. Involvement and communication discrepancy. *J. abnorm. soc. Psychol.*, 1960, *60*, 86-94.

Zipf, G. K. *The psycho-biology of language*. Boston: Houghton Mifflin, 1935.

Znaniecki, F. *Social relations and social roles*. San Francisco: Chandler, 1965.

Name Index

Subject Index

Achievement motivation, 135-36, 415-16
  in American society, 317, 436; by ethnic grouping, 453; in middle class, 449-50
  assessed by content analysis, 109-10
  and economic development, 109-10
  techniques for measuring, 415-16
Adaptation level, 138, 146
  and adjustment, 138; effects of new experience from, 138
  as process of judgment, 138
  in social exchange, 296-97
Adjustment, 114-46 (see also Learning; Motivational processes; Perceptual processes)
  and adaptation level, 138
  capacities for irritability, response, and learning in, 120-22; implicit and explicit learning differentiated, 121
  definition of, 115-16
  human capacity for, 25, 114-15
  learning-to-like through exposure, 139-40
  mechanisms of response in, 117-18
  and personality development, 566-67
  and psychological reactance, 119-20
  as response to internalized frustration and conflict, 117-19
  as response to social influence, 116-17; conformity in, 566

Affiliation motivation
  as feature of social influence, 20
  group influence from, 496, 520-21, 558
  ideological commitment as, 475
  social identity, social support, social reality, defined, 21, 161, 190
Aggression (see also Inter-group relations)
  direct vs. displaced, 118-19
  in Freudian psychology, 47
  frustration-aggression hypothesis, 119
  as instinctual, 40-43
  in inter-group conflict, 527-37
  and war, 40-41
Altruistic behavior, 173-77, 265-69
Attitude, 18, 147-86 (see also Attitude change; Attitude measurement; Value)
  acquisition of, through socialization, 148-80; identification with parents, 162-66; new reference groups in, 182-85; schematic model of, 160
  and action, 150, 199; situational hurdles to, 206-9
  as attributions, 194-96; correspondent inference theory of, 195
  authoritarian, 409-11; California F Scale in measurement of, 61, 107-8, 180, 409-10